A HISTORY
OF THE
ROMAN WORLD
753–146 BC

H. H. SCULLARD, FBA, FSA

A HISTORY
OF THE
ROMAN WORLD
753–146 BC

METHUEN & CO. LTD
LONDON AND NEW YORK

First published 28 *March* 1935
Second edition, revised, 1951
Third edition 1961
First published as a University Paperback 1969
Reprinted four times
Fourth edition 1980
Published by Methuen & Co. Ltd
11 New Fetter Lane, London EC4P 4EE
Published in the USA by
Methuen & Co. Ltd
in association with Methuen, Inc.
733 *Third Avenue, New York, NY* 10017
© 1980 *H.H. Scullard*
Printed in the United States of America

British Library Cataloguing in Publication Data

Scullard, Howard Hayes
A history of the Roman world,
753 to 146 BC. -4th ed.
1. Rom—History
I. Title
937'.02   DG231   80–40033

ISBN 0-416-71480-3
ISBN 0-416-71490-0 Pbk

CONTENTS

Part III Rome and the Mediterranean   241

Part IV Roman life and culture 339

MAPS

PREFACE TO FIRST EDITION

In this volume I have attempted to provide an up-to-date account of the Roman world from earliest times until the Age of the Great Conquests. Political history naturally takes the first place, and while military history of necessity forms a considerable part of the story, I have tried to emphasize the economic and social life of the times, as well as the achievement of the Roman people in the fields of literature, art and religion. The reliability of any history of Rome depends to a considerable extent upon the reliability of the sources. Where the narrative of authoritative ancient historians survives, the margin of error naturally must be limited, but for the history of Rome before the fourth century such a source is lacking, and only legend and tradition fill the gap. The work of modern archaeologists has illumined many dark places, but unfortunately experts do not always agree among themselves. In this present work, in which at times considerations of space may have led to dogmatic statements where dogmatism is neither justified nor desirable, I have adopted a fairly conservative attitude towards the early history of Rome, but at the same time I hope that I have given sufficient indication of the nature of the problems involved and of the reasons of my divergence from those critics whose method is more iconoclastic. Finally, I am very conscious that history means 'enquiry', not certainty.

I acknowledge with gratitude the great debt that I owe to the *Cambridge Ancient History*, and to the *Storia dei Romani* of Professor G. De Sanctis ; he would, indeed, be foolish who sought to avoid incurring such a debt. More particularly I would mention my indebtedness to the work of Mr Hugh Last and Professor F. E. Adcock on the early history of Rome, to Sir H. Stuart Jones on matters constitutional, to Professor Tenney Frank on matters economic, to J. Kromayer and G. Veith on military history, and to M. Holleaux on Rome's eastern contacts. I have to record with gratitude the general advice and the numerous helpful suggestions which I have received from Dr M. Cary : only he who has had the privilege of submitting his work to Dr Cary can realize the nature of my obligations. I am also grateful to him for allowing me to see the proofs of his forthcoming *History of Rome* during the final revision of my work. Finally, it is a pleasure to express my thanks to my friend, Mr J. M. K. [Sir John] Hawton, for his kindness in reading through the whole of my book in typescript and for his helpful criticism.

H. H. S.

October 1934

PREFACE TO SECOND EDITION

In this second edition I have attempted not only to remove some of the errors and slips of the first, but also to bring this book up to date in the light of the work accomplished in this field of Roman history during the past fifteen years. While retaining the original compass, I have rewritten sentences, paragraphs and even pages where this seemed necessary and have also added a brief summary of references to the ancient sources.

H. H. S.

September 1951

PREFACE TO THIRD EDITION

In this third edition the pagination of the second edition has been retained for most of the main text, and I have made those changes which seemed both possible within these limits and necessary in the light of recent work in this field. As our knowledge of early Italy and early Rome has progressed, I have added a new appendix on this topic, as well as making additions and adjustments to many of the others. The bibliography also has naturally been brought up to date. I have thus tried to make this work serviceable for another period of years, without at the same time radically altering its structure.

H. H. S.

November 1960

PREFACE TO FOURTH EDITION

Since the third edition of this book was published eighteen years ago, a great amount of research has been done on this period of history, not least on its earliest phases and on the cultural environment in which the Romans emerged into the light of history. Fascinating material has accumulated, such as the Etruscan-Phoenician inscriptions from Pyrgi; the inscription which Sostratus, a Greek trader from Aegina, set up at Gravisca, the port of Etruscan Tarquinii, the thirteen massive Latin altars, some fifty archaic statues and probably the hero-shrine of Aeneas at Lavinium; the rich tombs and chariot-burials of the early Latin settlement at Decima. New excavation and the reappraisal of older evidence have taken place at numerous Etruscan and Italian sites. Archaeological discovery and reassessment of the literary sources have advanced together, sometimes hand in hand, at other times in conflict in areas where controversy is inevitable. Major contributions have been made by such scholars as Professors A. Alföldi, E. Gjerstad, J. Heurgon, A. Momigliano, R. M. Ogilvie and M. Pallottino. I have naturally tried to take account of their main viewpoints, although space has allowed only brief assessments of the extremely complicated issues involved.

I am very grateful therefore to Messrs Methuen for having generously allowed me freedom in revising this book. In addition to general revision throughout, I have largely rewritten the first two chapters. In the interests of economy and further revision the footnotes as such have been replaced by a large and extended body of notes at the end; these also incorporate the material that appeared in appendices in earlier editions, apart from a discussion of the sources, which now forms a separate chapter. The bibliography has of course been revised, and I have added a further map (a plan of early Rome). Thus I have tried to bring this book up to date, without at the same time abandoning too much of its original structure, and so I hope it may be found to be of use for a further period of time.

My grateful thanks are also due to Dr Tim Cornell who not only cheerfully shared in the burdensome task of proof-reading but also saved me from error on a number of points thanks to his great knowledge of early Rome and the Latins.

H. H. S.

July 1978

INTRODUCTION

The two crowning achievements wrought by the Roman people during the period covered by this volume were the unification of Italy and the founding of an overseas empire. The Greeks had revealed aspects of the spirit of man before undreamt of; the Romans could only gaze up at many of the peaks that their predecessors had scaled and show their admiration by a humble imitation and by passing on the legacy to later generations. But in one sphere the Greeks of the city-state, despite their genius, had failed: their rejection of permanent co-operation among themselves at length proved fatal, and noble strivings after independence often degenerated into petty bickering and quarrels. But the peculiar genius of the Roman people, their predilection for law and order, and their powers of organization and administration, unlocked the doors at which the Greeks had hammered in vain: a city-state proved itself able to weld the various peoples of a country into a nation and to govern an empire.

In the first half of the nineteenth century Prince Metternich declared that Italy was 'only a geographical expression'; the succeeding century has witnessed the growth of a united nation. The Austrian Chancellor's dictum could be applied with truth to Italy during the early days of the Roman Republic, while by the middle of the third century BC the whole country was united within the framework of a confederacy, designed by Rome, which was strong enough to withstand the disruptive influence of foreign invaders, whether Pyrrhus' professional soldiers, drilled in the latest methods of Hellenistic warfare, or Hannibal's untiring military genius. If the final unification of Italy was not achieved till the first century BC, she was at any rate welded by the genius of Rome into a confederation, the like of which the Greek world had never seen.

When Rome had transformed Italy into a world power, she came, partly by design, but more by accident, into contact with the Mediterranean world, with Carthage in the west and the Hellenistic monarchies in the east. Her struggle with Carthage was a life-and-death tussle, and modern western civilization owes much, if not everything, to her ultimate victory. In the east the older monarchies collapsed like a house of cards at Rome's touch. 'The surprising nature of these events is sufficient to challenge and stimulate the attention of everyone, old or young . . . events for which the past affords no precedent.' So thought a contemporary Greek historian, Polybius, who was himself interned in Italy for sixteen years. What Alexander the Great might have achieved, had he lived, what, indeed, he even hoped to achieve, must remain shrouded in doubt. It was reserved for Rome to realize an ecumenical ideal, to introduce a unity into world history, and to embrace western civilization within one political system.

'Can anyone be so indifferent or idle as not to care to know by what means and under what kind of polity almost the whole inhabited world was conquered and brought under the dominion of a single city of Rome, and that too within a period of not quite fifty-three years?' So wrote Polybius. To the Greeks the cause of the advance of the Romans was their moral qualities and their excellent constitution. To these we may add the advantages derived from their geographical conditions, their superior manpower and war-craft. As the Marquis d'Azeglio in 1839 prophesied that the new railways would 'stitch the boot of Italy', so ancient Italy was knit together by the roads and nodal colonies which Roman statesmen planned and Roman engineers constructed. But however many contributory causes there might be to this or that particular line of advance, all Rome's conduct was marked by empirical methods and by a spirit of adaptation and receptivity: she was willing to learn from friend and foe alike. Guided by practical problems, not by cut-and-dried theories, the Romans adapted their constitution and methods to meet present difficulties. During the period covered by this volume their success was unbounded, but before the end a change is perceptible. Foreign influences began to undermine the moral qualities and the ancestral discipline of the Roman people, lust for power at times superseded desire for law and order, foreign conquest appeared to many as a source of profit, the institutions of a city-state were strained to the breaking-point in an attempt to govern a far-flung Empire, the revolutionary era ushered in by the Gracchi was approaching and the fabric of the Republic began to totter.

PART I

ROME AND ITALY

I

THE LAND
AND ITS PEOPLES

1. THE LAND[1]

The history of a people is determined in the long run by their moral and intellectual qualities, by their character and initiative, but geographical environment has a profound influence upon racial characteristics. History is governed, if not determined, by geography, and the physical formation of a country lies at the root of the history of its early settlement. As from before the dawn of history until the Norman Conquest the flat south and east coastlines of England tempted wave after wave of sea-going adventurers to fling themselves on the rich lowlands and to drive the older inhabitants ever further into the mountains of the north and west, so the early history of Italy is essentially that of 'Italy and her invaders': Illyrians from across the Adriatic claimed a foothold on her eastern shores, Greek colonists established thriving settlements around her southern and south-western coasts, her north-western seaboard fell to Etruscans who were probably invaders from the eastern Mediterranean, and waves of other peoples surmounted the icebound barrier of the Alps and poured down into the rich plains of Lombardy, forcing the dwellers there ever further southwards down into the peninsula.

The development of any nation is conditioned by one or both of two factors: its land and its access to the sea. It was Rome's achievement to build up a mighty empire which rested on both land and sea power, but it was from Mother Earth that she received her early nourishment and training. And the rigour of that training was due not a little to the mountainous character of the land. The great northern plain between the

Alps and Apennines was long regarded as part of Gaul (Gallia Cisalpina) and was not incorporated into the administrative system of Italy until the end of the Roman Republic. It is cut off from peninsular Italy by the barrier of the Apennines, which here run almost east and west to meet the western Alps. Turning southwards the Apennines then run down the length of Italy; in fact, they virtually are Italy, for at least three-quarters of the land is hill country. These mountains are not very inhospitable, but naturally they retarded the growth of unity among their inhabitants. In the northern sector they form a narrow and almost continuous chain, but after reaching the Adriatic they are broken up into a series of parallel ridges of rugged limestone, divided by narrow gorges and towering in places to nearly 10,000 feet. The southern highlands are less steep, and gradually marl and limestone give place to the granite of the wild forest-clad promontory of Bruttium. The main central chain lies nearer to the Adriatic coast than to the western shore; it approaches the sea so closely that in places there is scarcely room for a road until it expands into the windswept moorland plateau of Apulia. Apart from the cornland of the Aufidus valley the Adriatic coast has little fertile land and few harbours; it faces the wild shores of Dalmatia and Illyria, and is accessible by land only from the northern non-Italian plain of the Po: add to this, that the north and east winds render it draughty and cold, and it will be seen that Nature planned that Italy should turn her back on the eastern coast and face westwards. There the aspect is different. South of the irregular mountains of Etruria, which are marked off by the Arno and Tiber, the central highlands approach the western coast in the Volscian hills, but north and south they leave room for the two plains of Latium and Campania. Here the genial climate and the fertile land, enriched by volcanic ash, watered by generous streams, and fanned by the moist south-west winds, attracted many invaders. And it was in the Latin plain, to be described below (p. 36), in the centre of Italy that one city developed the sense of unity which created a nation.

Since the mountains dominate the land, and few parts of Italy lie more than seventy miles from the coast which stretches for two thousand miles, it might well be thought that the inhabitants would have developed into a seafaring people who aspired to rule the waves. But Italy lacked what Britain possessed: harbours and rivers to receive what the sea might bring. On the west coast the sea was shallow, and flat-bottomed vessels could be beached with ease, but there were few harbours. Tarentum and those in the bay of Naples were early seized by the Greeks. Many of the rivers were mountain torrents which in winter rushed headlong to the sea and in summer left their beds stony and dry. The larger rivers swept down such masses of silt that a port at their mouths would need constant attention: the Tiber, for instance, kept many an emperor employed in planning fresh harbour and dredging works at Ostia, the port of Rome. Such rivers did not favour shipping; Virgil tells how Father Tiber himself had to stay his course before Aeneas' ship could sail up to the site of Rome. It was laborious to tow barges upstream and no help was received from tidal estuaries, for the Mediterranean is virtually tideless. Thus the attractions of foreign trade were less than those of the soil and the peoples of Italy remained for many centuries essentially agricultural and continental.

But though the nature of the coast and the fertility of the plains might turn the thoughts of the inhabitants landwards, they were soon to find that they were part of a larger world. The Mediterranean united as well as sundered. Its climate, common to the lands whose shores it washed, helped to produce a feeling of unity in social and political life. The trader from Tyre doubtless felt much more at home in the rich kingdom of Tartessus in Spain than when sailing through the mists and gales of the Atlantic to the Tin Islands of the north and 'perfidious Albion'. In this Mediterranean world Italy occupied the central position. The Alps formed a protective shield when Rome began to look around the Mediterranean, since they were comparatively easy to defend; at the same time they were a sufficient barrier to force Italy to make contact with the Mediterranean rather than with northern Europe. Yet had they been an impassable barrier Italy would have fared ill, as only by attracting peoples and trade over the Alpine passes did she equip herself to become the peer, and later the ruler, of the other Mediterranean peoples. As she faced west and lay back-to-back with Greece, it was with Sicily, Carthage, and Spain that she first came into contact. When once she had been united by Rome, her very safety depended on controlling Sicily at her toe. This involved conflict with Carthage who dominated the western Mediterranean. With Carthage conquered, Italy cut the Mediterranean in half; the west at once fell into her hands and the east soon followed. It was largely to her dominant central position that she owed this rise to power, after which she could call the Mediterranean *mare nostrum*.

Nature had prepared the stage, but it was the peculiar genius of the Roman people that enabled Italy to play the role of a world power.

2. EARLY MAN[2]

Throughout the dim ages when early man was painfully struggling up the first steps of civilized life, the centre of interest in Europe constantly fluctuated with the appearance of new peoples and with man's discovery of new metals or of fresh skill in handling them, until there gradually evolved two contrasting civilizations of the western and eastern Mediterranean. As the ice of the last great glacial period advanced, and mammoth and cave-bear wrested the lordship of creation from elephant, rhinoceros and hippopotamus, so the primitive hunters of the Old Stone Age appeared upon the stage which nature was setting for them in western Europe. But later a more revolutionary change came about. Palaeolithic man had taken the world much as he found it, but with climatic changes there appeared in the west new peoples who tried to alter the world to suit their needs. These newcomers of the Neolithic Age began to cultivate the earth, and to domesticate animals ; they invented the sickle, millstone and hammer-axe, and they discovered the art of making pottery, hand-made with impressed decoration. These early farming communities continued for centuries. Man's next great stride forward was when he discovered that by heating certain stones he obtained a substance which he could model or mould into a more efficient tool than stone. He thus initiated the Copper or Chalcolithic Age, which in turn was gradually merged into the Bronze Age when he found out that an admixture of tin with copper produced in bronze much harder and more serviceable tools. Metallurgy flourished much earlier in the east than in the west, and culminated there in the splendid Bronze Age civilization of Crete and the eastern Mediterranean.

Meanwhile the west had witnessed some remarkable developments. During the fourth millennium BC, if not earlier, Neolithic peoples had spread westwards from Anatolia to the Danube basin and to the lands along the northern shores of the Mediterranean as far as the Iberian peninsula. During the second half of this millennium skills and ideas from the more advanced civilizations of the Near East were radiating ever westwards, diffused by traders, settlers and individuals. The use of larger megalithic graves spread to Malta, Sicily, Sardinia, Spain and France, and thence to Brittany and England. Somewhat later in some of these graves in the west bell-shaped vases have been found. These were made by the so-called Bell Beaker folk, a warlike brachycephalic people who helped to spread metal implements (copper not bronze) and to open up trade routes in Europe. They comprised two main groups, one in central Europe, the other (by the late third millennium BC) in the Iberian peninsula, whose mineral wealth had already attracted prospectors and settlers from the Aegean world. Many authorities believe the peninsula to have been the original home of the Bell Beaker people. Around 2000 BC warriors from the Caspian area began to spread the use of the stone battle-axe in Europe (e.g. in Greece); they used the horse, and they decorated their pottery with horizontal cord-impressions; these Corded Ware people were probably speakers of an Indo-European tongue. They led the way to the full flowering of the European Bronze Age of the fifteenth century. Meanwhile another group of people in the middle Danube area, who also had contacts with the east, made extensive use of bronze, improved agricultural methods and cremated their dead, whose ashes they buried in urns in large cemeteries. This Urnfield culture spread widely north of the Alps from c. 1250 BC into the Rhineland, and eventually into southern France (before 700) and into part of Spain; it also affected Italy. At this time the east also was suffering great changes: the collapse of the Hittite empire in Asia Minor, the sack of Troy and the downfall of Mycenaean power in Greece, the attacks of the Peoples of the Sea on Egypt and the Philistine invasion of Palestine. The impulse for some of these upheavals may have stemmed ultimately from the movements of the Indo-European peoples of the Urnfield culture. The use of iron, which became common soon after 1000 BC, confirmed the superiority of the north, and the more westerly parts of Europe became a barbarian region, culturally less developed than the neighbouring classical civilization which, though having many ties with transalpine Europe, yet increasingly differed from it.

Thus the limelight, which reveals fascinating glimpses of man's early progress, plays first on the lands of the western and eastern Mediterranean: Italy, the central peninsula, long remained obscure. Traces of the Palaeolithic Age (starting some 200,000 years ago) have been found in the cave-dwellings of Liguria, in the foothills of the Apennines, and in the neighbourhood of Rome. Descendants of this age of hunters and food-gatherers may have survived, but they do not appear to have influenced the development of their successors in any significant way. The first important settlement in Italy was due to the appearance of men who practised the arts of polishing stone implements and making pottery (c. 5000 BC). These Neolithic folk were of Mediterranean stock and short in stature. They came from overseas and brought precious seed-corn with them. At first they may have lived in caves, but gradually many settled in villages. Some certainly came from across the Adriatic, since their remains are found in northern Apulia on the Tavoliere, a plain around Foggia. Here aerial photography first revealed extensive settlements: their villages were surrounded by ditches, within which huts were grouped in smaller compounds, each in turn enclosed within its own ditch; the largest village embraced an area of some 500 by 800 yards and included a hundred smaller compounds.

The inhabitants of such villages, although still given to hunting, were a pastoral people who cultivated their land and had domesticated the goat, sheep, pig, ox, ass and dog. They buried their dead in contracted positions. Their stone implements display a variety of styles, and they even obtained obsidian, a hard glass-like material, from the island of Lipari off the northern coast of Sicily. Their pottery, not yet the product of the potter's wheel, was plain with simple impressed decoration, but it improved artistically with the passage of centuries. By inventing a needle with an eyelet they were able to sew clothes.

Although more settled than their nomadic predecessors, these Neolithic farmers might move on to other virgin areas if their population became too large or the soil around their villages became exhausted. Thus they spread out in southern and eastern Italy, while from about 3500 BC increasing desiccation of the Tavoliere led to expansion in the north and west, including a settlement at Sasso di Furbara north of Rome. Further north still, other groups had emerged from early Neolithic times, both in Liguria and in the northern Italian plain on either side of the eastern stretches of the Po. The latter group may have come partly from lands east of the Adriatic and partly from the south up the Italian coast of the Adriatic. Subsequently, external influences increased, deriving from the Neolithic cultures of western Europe in France, Spain and North Africa; thus the skills of spinning and weaving perhaps first reached Italy. A late Neolithic settlement at Lagozza di Besnate near Varese is typical of many villages built alongside the Italian Lakes of Maggiore and Garda, constructed on piles at the edges of the lakes (*palafitte*). At the same time others grew up by the swampy rivers of the Po valley.[3]

3. THE COPPER AND BRONZE AGES[4]

Under the impulse of 'warrior' immigrants from central Europe Italy began to move into the Copper Age. Three main centres are known. In the north a typical site is found at Remedello near Brescia, and later, as the Bronze Age advanced, a fairly uniform culture, called Polada from a village on Lake Garda, spread over much of north Italy (*c.* 1800–1450 BC). Further south remains from the Copper Age are found in two areas, at Rinaldone in Tuscany and at Gaudo near Paestum not far from Salerno. The older Neolithic population of course lived on in part, affected in varying degree by the fresh influences, while the new metal was too scarce to replace stone for most of the tools and implements of everyday life : flint daggers and stone battle-axes continued to be used, and supplies of obsidian were still needed from Lipari. In the north some Bell-Beaker influences are found (including burials as well as beakers), while in the Italian peninsula itself the discovery in 1971 of some beakers near Viterbo (at Fosso Conicchio) shows some degree of penetration.[5] To what extent these central and more southerly settlements were affected by Aegean influences also remains somewhat uncertain.

With man's ability to turn copper into bronze we reach Bronze Age Italy, which divides into two distinct cultural areas, one in the north, the other along the Apennines. In the north, as we have seen, a steady development occurred around the Lakes and in the Po valley from Neolithic times onwards, but in the middle or later Bronze Age a new phase developed with settlements which archaeologists have named Terremare from the 'black earth' (terra mara) which modern farmers have used as a fertilizer for its rich nitrogenous content. These settlements were thought to have been regular in type, with huts raised on wooden platforms on pile foundations and divided into regular blocks by parallel streets ; outside lay cemeteries where the ashes of the dead were buried in urns, incineration being the distinctive mark of this culture. In fact the similarity of the supposed regular construction to the layout of later Roman camps and towns led some archaeologists to suppose that these people were both the architects of the Bronze Age in Italy and the ancestors of the Romans, some of them having migrated southwards through Etruria to the site of Rome. It is, however, now clear that they did not arrive from the Danube area until the mid-fifteenth century, some three hundred years after the earliest Bronze Age settlements, and that they did not expand towards Rome. In fact their villages are confined to the modern provinces of Modena, Reggio Emilia, Parma and Piacenza. They were often surrounded by an earthen bank, wooden palisade and a ditch which would protect them against enemies and flooding, and the huts were built on raised terraces or piles. Climatic deterioration towards the end of the second millennium BC may have promoted increased building on piles and may possibly have contributed to the ultimate abandonment of the settlements. Thus these Terramaricoli were not ancestors of the Romans ; they might perhaps in some sense be regarded as 'cousins' of the Palafitticoli of the Lakes, but they were probably fresh immigrants from the central Danube area.

They were in the main agriculturalists and stock farmers, though many continued to hunt boars, deer and bears, and perhaps to fish. Fowl and duck now joined the farmyard, and the horse was widely used for draught purposes. Remains of flax, beans, lentils and two kinds of wheat, together with wild fruits such as hazel nuts, pears and apples have been found in their settlements. They worked in wood, bone and horn as well as bronze, and carried on textile and ceramic industries : their pottery was distinctive but varied. The discovery of many razors and combs suggests an interest in their personal appearance, while the comparative absence of weapons points to a fairly peaceful existence. Two aspects of their culture that were significant for the future were their cremation cemeteries and the fact that in all probability they spoke an Indo-European language. Further, as they kept up a connection with the Danube area, which had probably been their original homeland, they formed a communication channel by which the more northerly Bronze Age culture spread southwards; they thus became an important link in the trade routes of Europe. But they were manufacturers as well as importers and their products ultimately began to move southwards into Apennine Italy, which was poor in metals.

The other main area of Bronze Age settlement was the Apennine culture, which reached its full development $c.$ 1500 BC and was far less advanced than the northern settlements, though more central to peninsular Italy. The people consisted of descendants of the Neolithic and Copper Age population, intermixed with some 'warriors' who may have come in small groups from overseas (from the Aegean world) and landed either in Apulia or on the west coast, and who probably spoke an Indo-European language. They show relatively few traces of settled agricultural life, but comprised a scattered population of herdsmen who moved between semi-permanent winter settlements on low ground (often mere caves by watercourses) to summer pastures high up in the Apennines. Such seasonal transhumance of flocks has continued into modern times. By the twelfth century they had become somewhat more settled and practised some agriculture, perhaps influenced by the more settled Terramara and Urnfield peoples of the north. Their semi-nomadic way of life would have helped to spread their language, which may well have been the ancestor of the later Umbro-Sabellian dialects spoken by the Samnites. Unlike the northern Bronze Age folk, they buried their dead, and they lacked the northerners' technological skill in metal work : their domestic sites have produced very little bronze. Their dark burnished pottery, which was quite attractive and varied in shape, has been found widely : at the future site of Rome, in south-east Emilia, through Etruria, Latium, Campania, Apulia and in Lipari. Some scholars have seen in this culture the primary continuing factor in the composition of the Italic people from Lipari to the Po.[6]

In the late Bronze Age the two groups, the Terramaricoli and the Apennine folk, began to move closer together. The former may well have sought the copper of Etruria to supplement their supplies from north of the Alps. At any rate, whether or not they brought copper with them, some of the Apennine people had settled in open villages near the Adriatic and the mouth of the Po by the eleventh century. The northerners in turn worked the metal and began to send their products not only to Etruria but also down the Adriatic coast as far south as the neighbourhood of Tarentum where (at Scoglio del Tonno) an Apennine settlement had been trading with the Mycenaean Greeks until the collapse of their empire (see below). Thus in the final phase of the Bronze Age, from c. 1150 BC, a more uniform culture began to spread throughout all Italy and the two main groups drew closer together, as may be seen, for instance, at a settlement at Pianello inland from Ancona. Above all, from c. 1000 BC cremation and urnfields appeared in many areas where previously inhumation had prevailed, though in many central and southern parts the old Apennine culture and inhumation persisted well into the Iron Age. But before turning to this obscure transitional period we must glance at two other aspects of the Italian Bronze Age.

The extent to which merchant adventurers fared forth into western waters from Minoan Crete is uncertain, though some have left their traces in Sicily and Lipari, while the tradition that an expedition was launched against Sicily to avenge the death of Minos reflects some interest in the west. However the Mycenaean Greeks took stronger action. Their presence in Sicily and Lipari has been detected even before 1400 BC; not only did individual traders subsequently press on into southern Italy as well, but some even established a permanent trading post near Tarentum where they continued to operate until their own world collapsed in the twelfth century. From Tarentum they could extend their trade over the heel of Italy, up the Adriatic coast, and to Sicily and Lipari. Thus Mycenaean pottery has been found around Syracuse, at Mylae in north-east Sicily, at Lipari, at the island of Ischia off Naples, and most surprisingly five pieces, dating to c. 1250 BC, at Luni in Etruria. This last item strengthens the likelihood that one of the principal objectives of Mycenaean trade was the bronze of Etruria. If, though it is far from certain, the name 'Metapa' found on a Linear B tablet at Pylos represents the later Greek city of Metapontum in southern Italy then this area may even have come under some control by Nestor's kingdom of Pylos in the Peloponnese. At all events, Mycenaean trade in the west was consider-able, and some trade between Greece and Italy apparently continued on a smaller scale even after the collapse of the Mycenaean empire and the abandonment of the settlement at Tarentum in the twelfth to eleventh century.[7]

Lipari and the other volcanic Aeolian Islands, lying some twenty-five miles north-east of Sicily, owed their early significance to the native obsidian which was exploited even in Neolithic times, while Greek pottery, imported during the Bronze Age, has provided valuable dating material. In about 1250 BC the Middle Bronze Age villages on the citadel of Lipari and on other islands were destroyed and succeeded by a culture which belonged to the Apennine group. This conquest has been linked by some scholars to the story, told by Diodorus, that Liparus, the son of the king of the Ausonians in central-southern Italy, seized Lipari and established a city there; consequently this new cultural phase has been called Ausonian. But since the remains of the new settlement appear to have more links with the Adriatic side of Italy than with Campania and the south, others would associate Diodorus' Ausonians with the slightly later Final Bronze Age period, when in the islands (and at Milazzo in north-east Sicily) we find a fusion of Terremare and Apennine elements such as occurs on the mainland at Pianello, with cremation predominating, as in the Urnfields of Italy. This phase (Ausonian II) must have been due to fresh invaders from the peninsula and continued at least into the ninth century; later it faded out, for when the Greeks arrived to establish a colony at Lipari in 580 BC they found a population of only five hundred. Thus Ausonian culture led on to the Early Iron Age and the Villanovans, while the material from Lipari has some close parallels with the early Bronze Age remains from the Palatine and Forum at Rome.[8]

4. THE EARLY IRON AGE VILLANOVANS[9]

The main Early Iron Age population of Italy has been named Villanovan, after a typical site discovered in 1853 at Villanova near Bologna, and it had reached its peak by the mid-eighth century BC. However, both the process and the dating of the merging of the Bronze into the Villanovan period remain obscure in detail, and archaeologists bridge this interval of some four hundred years in different ways: some would date the beginning of the Iron Age back to 1000, others place the transition about 900, while others again bring it down to about 800 by postulating Sub-Apennine and Proto-Villanovan periods to fill the gap. One main factor is the date of the appearance in Italy of the Urnfields which as we have seen spread widely north of the Alps from the mid-thirteenth century onwards, while some similar influences may have reached Italy from Illyria across the Adriatic.[10] At any rate there was a gradual increase in the uniformity of culture in Italy which began to spread from the mid-twelfth century, as we have seen (p. 11). Its early manifestations occur at Pianello and at Timmari in Apulia in the south, and cremation cemeteries appear throughout the peninsula. But while aspects of their pottery and metalwork link them strongly to the Central European Urnfields, some of their products foreshadow those of the later Villanovans; hence this period (c. 1100–900 perhaps) has been called Proto-Villanovan. Greater skill in metallurgy was acquired, particularly in the making of sheet-bronze for buckets, helmets and greaves, while pottery developed, as did the use of *fibulae*. Although some archaeologists date the beginning of the Early Iron Age at 900 BC, there was no dramatic change overnight, and the new metal came into use only very gradually. The later Villanovans fully exploited the rich iron deposits of Tuscany, and iron was employed for many everyday implements; nevertheless, bronze continued in constant use, particularly in decorative work. There remains one final question to which archaeologists can offer no certain and agreed answer: who were the essential antecedents of the Villanovans or, more crudely, who were the Villanovans? One view is that they came by sea from the Balkan area, some sailing up the Adriatic to the Po valley, others coming round the foot of Italy to the west coast and Etruria; some scholars would say that they developed from the Terramara people, others that they represent a local evolution of the Apennine culture, whilst others again stress the Central European connections. It is certainly not improbable that a fresh group of northerners came down into Italy and thus helped to transform the existing cultures in the Proto-Villanovan period into the fully-fledged culture of the Iron-Age Villanovans. If so, it would not have been a matter of mass movements (as it was with the Dorians who were invading Greece at about this time), but rather of gradual penetration, so that the resultant culture did not represent a monolithic ethnic unit.

Villanovans, or at any rate Villanovan culture, spread down the east coast of Italy as far as Rimini, but reached no further than this because of the survivors of the inhuming Apennine culture, which persisted into the Iron Age and was subjected in Picenum to the immigration of 'warrior' Illyrians from across the Adriatic. As a result, the Villanovans were forced into Tuscany and Latium, west of a line from Rimini to Rome. Archaeologists distinguish two main groups: the northern Villanovans around Bologna, who flourished from c. 800 to 400 BC, and the southern Villanovans of Tuscany and northern Latium, who settled as far south as the Alban Hills and at Rome, where they occupied the Palatine and used the Forum as a cemetery. In the north an outlying settlement was established at Fermo in the Marche near the Adriatic, but in the south expansion from Latium was more extensive and reached as far as the district around Salerno. All these Villanovans shared a common culture and practised cremation: they placed the ashes of the dead in an urn which they put into a round hole in the ground, sometimes enclosed by stones, and with it were laid ornaments, such as brooches, bracelets and razors, though not many weapons. But there were naturally some local differences: the northerners covered their biconical cinerary urns with inverted pottery bowls, while some Villanovans in Etruria used helmets (metal, or pottery copies) for this purpose; in other parts of Etruria and in Latium and the south, urns modelled like huts replaced the northern type of ossuary.

The largest settlement of the northern group was at Bologna, which held a strategic position astride the early trade routes. In return for the copper, and later the iron, that came from Tuscany, it exported manufactured metalwork as well as agricultural products: by the eighth century it had become 'the Birmingham of early Italy'. Commerce increased, chiefly by land, though there was some shipping trade. Artistic skill and prosperity advanced hand in hand, while the womenfolk seem to have made increasing claims for personal adornments. Villages began to cluster together, forming larger communities which, although not yet to be regarded as towns (except possibly at Bologna), gave increased economic strength. The *gens* may now have begun to replace the family as the more important social unit. The arts of peace were cultivated; swords and spears have not been found in the tombs in such numbers as to suggest widespread warlike activity, although this may have increased somewhat later in the sixth century. No 'warrior class' apparently existed; at most there was a citizen militia. For long these Villanovans remained comparatively free from the orientalizing and Greek influences which were spreading among the southern group in Tuscany, but even when these increased in the later sixth century the northerners did not respond by developing into 'Etruscans' like the southerners. Indeed, when in about 500 BC the Etruscans advanced northwards over the Apennines to found Felsina on the site of modern Bologna, very near the existing Villanovan settlement, the two peoples remained curiously aloof from one another. The reason why the northern Villanovans were not transmuted into 'Etruscans' while the southerners in Tuscany were so changed is closely bound up with the question of Etruscan origins, which is discussed below. However, soon afterwards Villanovan culture declined and in the early fourth century the area fell to invading Celts.

The southern Villanovans in early times shared essentials of culture with the northerners: agriculture was the basis of life for the village communities, while the developing metal industry led to greater economic growth. The huts in which they lived can be reconstructed from their clay replica cinerary urns, and the foundations of three huts have been found on the Palatine at Rome (see pp. 43f.). They were roughly rectangular in shape and cut into the tufa rock; the disposition of the post-holes indicates the arrangement of the wooden superstructure, which had walls of wattle and daub. Remains of charcoal and ash attest a hearth inside the hut, while fragments of cooking-stands, smoke-blackened household utensils and charred animal bones reveal the nature of family meals and life of the early Romans. Clusters of such huts formed village settlements, and recent excavations at Veii in Etruria, some twelve miles north of Rome, show how several such villages built around a strong-point on a hill later fused into a unified town settlement.[11] This seems to show a greater instinct in the Villanovans for social development than was previously realized. Other changes occurred: while they retained their practice of putting their cremation urns at the bottom of a pit (*pozzo*), from about 750 BC inhumation began to appear beside cremation, the bodies being placed in trenches (*a fossa*). The objects in the graves became finer and included more imports, including Greek vases, now that the Greeks were beginning to establish colonies in southern Italy. In the seventh century inhumation became normal in Tuscany and the dead were placed in chamber-tombs cut into the rock. The grave-goods became even richer; Greek and Oriental imports including gold and silver work increased, as did the use of iron. This orientalizing phase in art was seen first in the settlements near the coast, and spread inland only very slowly. Villanovan culture was being transformed: villages were growing into wealthy cities and men were beginning to use the Etruscan language. Whether this was due merely to the influx of new cultural influences or to the arrival of the Etruscans from overseas is discussed below (pp. 25f.). It is very remarkable that whereas the northern Villanovans retained their own culture until they died out, those of the southern group who lived north of the Tiber became Etruscan.

South of the Tiber the Villanovan settlements fall into two groups: one in Latium, the other around Salerno. The former, which is now sometimes distinguished as 'Latial', is found at Rome, on the Alban Hills and elsewhere. A substratum of Apennine culture was overlaid by incoming

Villanovans, who in turn were later reinforced by some representatives of the Fossa culture; these developments are discussed below (p. 37). Evidence for the still more southerly group has come to light only in recent years with the discovery of a series of Villanovan cemeteries: at Sala Consilana in the Valle di Diano (about a thousand graves), at Capodifiume near Paestum, at Pontecagnano south-east of Salerno and at Capua in two cemeteries of the eighth to seventh centuries. Although these settlements were gradually infiltrated by other elements and finally absorbed by the native population, their extent is surprising.[12]

Beside the Villanovans two other main kindred groups who cremated their dead can be distinguished in North Italy from about 900 BC. onwards: the Golasecca culture and the Atestine, the former around Lake Maggiore, in Piedmont and Lombardy, and around Lake Como, where regional differences occur; the latter around Este (ancient Ateste) in Venetia. The Golaseccans, unlike the Atestines and Villanovans of Bologna, had a warrior class, as is clear from the chariots and weapons found in the graves of some of their chieftains. In the fifth century trade increased with the Etruscan and Greek areas; Celtic penetration followed and then final absorption by Rome. While the Golaseccans may originally have entered Italy from over the Alps, the Atestines probably came from Illyria under the impulse of the movement of peoples which led to the Dorian invasion of Greece. Although they show fewer traces of a sharp distinction between rich and poor than do the Golaseccans, their metal work almost rivals that of the northern Villanovans. Their pictorially decorated bronze buckets (*situlae*) provide splendid scenes of everyday life, involving ploughmen, huntsmen, soldiers, charioteers, boxers and banqueters.[13] Their language, which was written in an alphabet derived from the Etruscan, was Indo-European and closely related to Latin, as is shown by inscriptions which are found on offerings to Reitia, a goddess of healing. In the fourth century their culture became so Celticized that Polybius described the second-century Veneti as practically indistinguishable from the Celts except in language. Although they had by then come under Roman control, their language and customs survived into Christian times.

There is still some doubt about the Ligurians, whom the classical writers placed in a wide area from southern France to the western part of the plain of the Po valley; archaeology has supplied no clear evidence for a single culture over such a great stretch of country after the Neolithic Age. Probably Neolithic man was pressed back into the mountains by invaders who spoke an Indo-European tongue, since this was the language in Liguria in classical times. From the beginning of the Iron Age, Urnfield elements are strong, and some settlements on the coast run parallel to the culture of Golasecca, Bologna and Este. These coastal people enjoyed a fairly rich culture, thanks to trade, while those who lived in the mountains (possibly descendants of the Neolithic people) remained wild and backward even into Roman times.

Contrasted with these cremating peoples are various groups of Iron Age cultures in which inhumation was practised. (*a*) The Picenes of the Adriatic coast and Umbria (roughly the present-day region of the Marche). Recent excavations at Ancona illustrate their domestic life and supplement our knowledge derived from the famous cemeteries at Novilara near Pesaro. The Picenes were probably invaders from Illyria who mingled with the indigenous population; their language, as recorded later, was Indo-European and akin to Illyrian. They were a warrior race; their cemeteries contain an extraordinary number of weapons, and *stelae* of the sixth century depict their ships in battle, presumably protecting their trade in the Adriatic. By 500 BC this trade included the importing of many Greek works from Apulia and Tarentum and also of amber. A seventh-century rich woman's grave at Novilara illustrates their wealth. (*b*) The Fossa Grave culture of Campania and Calabria, named from its trench graves, which first appeared during the final stages of the Late Bronze Age. One such trench-grave cemetery of the tenth or ninth century was found at Cumae, at the foot of a hill. On this hill was an important settlement which traded as far north as Etruria and as far south as Calabria and Sicily; it imported Greek pottery probably of the ninth century, and also shows traces of Villanovan influence. Other Fossa culture settlements are known on the offshore islands of Ischia (Pithecusae) and Vivara, where they succeeded to Apennine villages. However, about the mid-eighth century, as we shall see (p. 22), the settlements at both Cumae and Ischia were superseded by the arrival of Greek colonists. The Fossa sites in Calabria are closely linked to others in Sicily: this accords with the Greek tradition, preserved by Hellanicus in the fifth century, that when Greek colonists reached eastern Sicily in the late eighth century they encountered a people named the Siculi who had recently come to Sicily from southern Italy. (*c*) The peoples of Apulia in the heel of Italy, who were later known to the Romans as Daunians, Peucetians and Messapians. Since Greek legend attributed an Illyrian origin to Daunus, Iapyx and Peucetius, and since Illyrian tribal and place names recur in Messapia, these tribes were probably of Illyrian origin. After the founding of Taras and other Greek colonies in south

Italy they increasingly came under the influence of this superior culture, but continued to produce distinctive pottery: Daunian ware (*c.* 600–450) was fanciful and even grotesque.

5. THE ITALIC PEOPLES

Such in brief is the picture drawn by the archaeologist. But there are other strands of evidence, both literary and linguistic. The names of the various peoples which are recorded in written history are almost numerous enough to give the racial map of pre-Roman Italy the appearance of a mosaic, while remains of numerous dialects and varying alphabets exist. These three strands of evidence, however, cannot always be woven into as neat a pattern as might be desired. For instance, the pre-Etruscan inhabitants of Etruria were called Ombrikoi, but it must not necessarily be assumed that they spoke the dialect known as Umbrian or that they are to be equated with the southern Villanovans of the archaeologists. Archaeology sometimes supplements linguistics by providing inscriptions, but not, unfortunately, for the beginning of the Iron Age, when the peoples of Italy were illiterate and therefore left no inscriptions. What languages they spoke can only be inferred by arguing backwards from the later known tongues of Italy.

Within the widespread variety of Indo-European languages philologists used to distinguish an Italic-Celtic group, and concluded that the ancestors of the Italic peoples and of the Celts of historical times had once lived together in immediate contact for a long period, but this view is now regarded as improbable. In any case the Celts did not try to press into Italy until the fifth century, while the Italic dialects, wherever they originated, had been spoken in Italy for many centuries before that. Here two main groups of Italic speakers appeared, differing in dialect and fortune, but alike in temperament, social organization, and religious outlook: the Latins and the Umbro-Sabellians (the term 'Italic dialects' is strictly applied only to the latter, but it is convenient to include the kindred Latin and indeed all Indo-European languages of the peninsula).[14] The Latins were a relatively small group who were gradually driven into the coastal plain of Latium to the east and south of the Tiber and were hemmed around by other peoples; they remained essentially a lowland race, soon outstripping their kinsmen in the less fertile hills thanks to their geographical position which favoured the growth of city life and common action. One branch, the Falisci, thrust themselves like a wedge into southern Etruria. To the south and east of Latium proper was a group of tribes, the Marsi, Aequi and Hernici, who used the Latinian tongue, although the Marsi and Aequi probably originally spoke dialects of the Osco-Umbrian group. Further south the indigenous population of Campania, the Ausones (or Aurunci), seem to have used, before the spread of Latin, a dialect similar to that of the Volsci (Osco-Umbrian group?); they also appear originally to have been called Opici or Osci, before they were overwhelmed in the mid-fifth century by the Sabellian highlanders of Samnium and Lucania (see pp. 108f.) whose language in turn (confusingly) became known as Oscan.

The Umbro-Sabellian speaking peoples, who lived east of the Latins, occupied the mountains and evolved a lower type of political organization. Separated by valleys and hills, they only united in face of common danger, and had no towns comparable with the cities of the plains, which were organized into federal leagues for self-protection. But the various tribes were at least united by a common tongue, Safine or Osco-Umbrian, which divided them sharply from the Latins: thus Oscan *pod* contrasts with Latin *quod* (cf. the Brythonic Celts who used *p* where the Goidelic used *q*) and whereas the Latin for fire was *ignis* Umbrian used *pur* (cf. the Greek for fire). From this speech derivative dialects are known, Volscian and Umbrian, the latter being represented by the Iguvine Tables, the liturgy of a sacred brotherhood.[15] The names of these tribes usually had the suffix *-ni* (thus Vestini, Sabini, Marrucini, Paeligni, Frentani, Safineis) (as the Samnites called themselves), Hirpini and Lucani). This is in contrast with the older and rarer suffix *-ci* or *-tes* (as in Osci). The process of domination is seen in the transformation of the Marruci and Ardeates into the Marrucini and Ardeatini. From their mountain fastnesses the Samnites and Lucani later descended to harass and supplant the cities of Campania and the toe of Italy. Naturally the distribution of these peoples and dialects was not accomplished in a short period, but it was accelerated by a custom called the Sacred Spring (*ver sacrum*), by which all living creatures born in a given year were vowed to a deity; all the boys and girls thus dedicated were obliged, when grown up, to leave their homes and seek fresh territory.[16]

How these various peoples were related to the Bronze Age Villanovan folk is uncertain: there is no unbroken bridge between the prehistoric and historical peoples, no firm interlocking between the archaeological and linguistic evidence. While it is generally agreed that the Italic dialects originated from a common source, which most would find more immediately in the Danube area, it is less clear how they reached Italy, whether by land or sea (though Venetic in the north and Messapic in the south were almost certainly brought by Illyrians from across the Adriatic). Their arrival may have involved the immigration of large numbers of people; or they may have spread mainly through the infiltration of small numbers. If they were the result of mass movements, the individual dialects may have arisen either before or after their speakers arrived in Italy. Such speculations have evoked varied answers. According to what was for long the generally accepted view, two waves of Indo-European speakers crossed the Alps into Italy; first the cremators who settled west of a line from Rimini to just south of Rome, and secondly the inhumers who settled east of this line. But since the inhuming Italici have left no traces in north Italy, this half of the theory must be abandoned (we will return to the other part below). Rather, the Osco-Sabellian dialects will have emerged in the old Bronze Age Apennine culture with the infiltration of a relatively small number of speakers, since there is no need to presuppose a mass immigration, from whatever precise direction they came.

The settlers west of the Rimini-Rome line, namely Terramaricoli, Villanovans and Latins, came probably from the north and spoke Indo-European. The view that the Urnfield culture reached Etruria by sea from the east rather than by land from the north is far less acceptable. Another theory is that the Villanovans did not come from anywhere but were autochthonous, and that their culture was a native growth, based on Apennine culture which absorbed Urnfield elements brought (perhaps by land and sea) by immigrants in such small numbers as to make no basic ethnic change; in that case the Indo-European dialects could have reached Italy in successive waves from across the Adriatic, as has been suggested.[17] However, the idea of a northern origin still seems tenable, and 'Villanovan' is best used to denote a common culture rather than to suggest a somewhat rigid and unified racial and linguistic block.

6. GREEKS, PHOENICIANS AND CELTS

In the merging of prehistory into history two other peoples played a major part in the mingling of the races in early Italy: Etruscans and Greeks. The contribution of the Phoenicians and Celts was more indirect and less significant, though of considerable importance in the wider setting of the western Mediterranean which Rome was later to dominate. The Etruscans, early Rome's greatest rivals in Italy, are discussed in the next and following sections.

In the Bronze Age, Mycenaean Greeks, as we have seen (p. 11), traded with southern Italy and Sicily and even appear to have maintained a permanent post at Tarentum. With the fall of Mycenaean civilization in the twelfth century this link was naturally almost severed, though perhaps not completely since some tenuous Greek influence appears to have lingered on in some of the smaller settlements near Tarentum.[18] But any large-scale trade was suspended for centuries, and before it was resumed the Phoenicians were extending their exploration of the western Mediterranean.

While Greece was in turmoil during its Dark Ages, groups of Phoenician merchants and colonists from Tyre, Sidon and other coastal towns of Palestine and Syria were adventuring in the western Mediterranean. The conditions of their native land had ever focused their attention on the sea rather than on the soil as a means of livelihood, while their expanding population had been harassed by the Philistines and by pressure from the Hebrews of the desert. Exploration and the establishing of small trading-posts must have preceded the founding of large settlements, but the dating of both is uncertain: several were founded traditionally as early as *c.* 1100 BC, but there is no archaeological evidence for Phoenician settlements in the west before the eighth century. However, the Phoenicians gradually established themselves at Utica, Carthage and other sites in North Africa, at Gades on the Atlantic coast of Spain, where they soon encountered the kingdom of Tartessus in Andalusia, rich in silver, and also on the Spanish Mediterranean coast at Malaca and Sexi. They also ventured into the Atlantic through the Pillars of Hercules (Gibraltar) with settlements not only at Gades but also on the Moroccan coast at Lixus; from these they sailed down the African coast four hundred miles to the little island of Mogador, while northwards they tapped the tin route to Brittany and Cornwall.[19] But as Phoenicia from the seventh century was gradually oppressed by the great Oriental powers, the new settlement at Carthage took the lead in the west and continued the colonizing movement as well as establishing friendly relations with the Etruscans (see pp. 158ff.).

It is just possible that the Phoenician made some small settlements (as opposed to temporary landings for trade and barter) on the coast of Italy but if so, no remains of them have yet been found. However, Phoenician influences on the development of art during the orientalizing phase in Etruria and Latium were considerable: the princely tombs at Caere and Praeneste (p. 39f.) contain precious objects which were either imports from Phoenicia or inspired by Phoenician artists. They recall the silver mixing-bowl described by Homer: 'Sidonians, well skilled in handiwork, had wrought it, and men of the Phoenicians brought it over the misty deep'. An attempt has been made to show that the sanctuary of the Ara Maxima of Hercules in the Cattle Market (Forum Boarium) at Rome was preceded by a temple of the Phoenician god Melqart (= Hercules) dedicated by Phoenician merchants, but this is extremely doubtful; the presupposition of an early Tyrian settlement in this Forum is even more dubious.[20] The Phoenicians, however, did give Rome one priceless gift, the alphabet. The legacy was mediated through the Greeks who took over this flexible instrument and adapted it to the needs of an Indo-European language. They then naturally took it with them to their colonies in Italy, whence both Etruscans and Romans received it. Thus it was that Italy became literate and written history eventually became possible.

The precise order in which Phoenicians and Greeks began to establish themselves in the west is still hotly debated by modern scholars, but there is no question as to their relative importance in Italy. From the second half of the eighth and during the seventh and sixth centuries the Greeks of the Aegean area established a series of colonies on the coast of Sicily, and others in western and southern Italy from the Bay of Naples round to Taranto, so that this latter area became known as Magna Graecia. The earliest and most northerly colony was settled in about 760 BC by Eretrians and Chalcidians from Euboea on the island of Pithecusae (Ischia) just north of the Bay of Naples. The fact that the settlers pressed so far north up the coast when there was good agricultural land available in the south suggests that their motive (unlike that of many later Greek colonists) was not purely agricultural: they wanted to trade with the mainland and obtain copper and iron from Etruria and Elba.[21] Soon afterwards some of these colonists crossed over to the mainland and established themselves at Cumae and, supplanting the older Fossa culture settlement (p. 17), became a thriving community, whence both economic and cultural influences radiated outwards in Italy. The claim of Cumae to be the place from which the Greek alphabet spread to Etruria and Rome is illustrated by an inscription on a cup found at Pithecusae, written in the Chalcidian alphabet, which proclaimed that anyone who drank from it would be inflamed by Aphrodite and alleged that the cup was superior to that of Nestor, while another inscription in the same form of lettering on an early seventh-century vase from Cumae states, 'I am the vessel of Tataei; may anyone who steals me be struck blind'. It is significant that the owner of the first cup knew about Nestor's cup in the *Iliad* (further, a scene on a locally made geometric vase showing a shipwreck could perhaps refer to Odysseus): the Greeks were bringing to Italy not only their alphabet but also the Homeric poems. In consequence, whereas at first the wanderings of Odysseus after the fall of Troy were located in the east in the regions of the Black Sea (Pontus), places mentioned in the *Odyssey* were later located in the west: Scylla and Charybdis were identified with the Straits of Messina, the home of Aeolus with Lipari, the rocks of the Sirens with some rocks off Positano; an entrance to the underworld was placed at Cumae, and the sorceress Circe was commemorated by the headland named Circeii in Latium. Cumae also became the home of a sibyl, the prophetess of Apollo, whose oracles were thought to contain the destinies of Rome.[22]

Another recent discovery which shows how Greek cultural influences began to penetrate into central Italy is a Greek sanctuary of *c.* 580 BC which was found, together with large quantities of Greek pottery, in the Etruscan town of Gravisca, the port of Tarquinii. This suggests a settlement of resident Greeks; early in the fifth century it was taken over and enlarged by the Etruscans. Among many inscriptions, which include dedications to Hera, Aphrodite and Demeter, is a sixth-century dedication to Apollo in the alphabet and dialect of Aegina: 'I belong to Aeginetan Apollo; Sostratus son of . . . had me made'. This Sostratus is almost certainly the Aeginetan Sostratus, son of Laodamus, of whom Herodotus spoke: of all the Greek traders known to the historian he brought back the greatest wealth 'and none could rival him'. He prospered even more than Colaeus the Samian master-mariner, who was the first Greek to reach Tartessus. It has often wrongly been assumed that Sostratus also made his profit from Tartessus, but Herodotus does not say this; the immensely rich source that Sostratus tapped now appears to have been Etruria.[23] In fact, by this date Greek pottery had begun to flood central Italy; long before this another Greek trader, Demaratus, a noble of Corinth, migrated to Etruria when his native city fell into the hands of a tyrant (*c.* 655 BC). He took with him his workmen, potters and painters, and settled at Tarquinii where he married an Etruscan noblewoman: their son later moved to Rome, where he gained the throne and reigned as Tarquinius the elder. Sceptical historians have been all too ready to dismiss Demaratus as a legendary figure (though recent evidence from Gravisca may now give them some reason to pause). However, even if Demaratus himself was fictitious, his story reflects the historical developments of the years between 750 and 500 BC, when Italy became one of the chief markets for the Greek export trade. Numerous traders arrived on the shores of Etruria, where they were perhaps allowed greater freedom of movement inland in the seventh than in the sixth century.

Others sailed from Tarentum up the Adriatic coast to Hadria (near the Po estuary) and advanced inland as far as the Apennines.[24]

The further spread of Greek colonization belongs to the history of the Greek rather than of the Roman world, but we may note some stages. Control of the Straits of Messina, which formed a sea link with Greece, was vital to trade and expansion, so some settlers from Cumae and Chalcis colonized Zancle-Messene (modern Messina) and these in turn, reinforced by some Messenians from the Peloponnese, founded Rhegium across the Strait on the toe of Italy. Sybaris was colonized by Achaeans traditionally in 721, to be followed by Locri, Croton, Metapontum, Caulonia and others; Taras (Tarentum) was also occupied (this district had enjoyed links with Mycenaean Greece centuries before). Sybaris, whose growing wealth gained her a reputation for luxury, was cut off from the Straits by the rival Chalcidians, so she established a land route across the toe of Italy, with colonies at Laos and Scidros and subsequently at the much more important Poseidonia (Paestum). She could thus act as a middle-man and send to the Tyrrhenian Sea and Etruria the woollens, carpets and other valuable goods of Miletus which her Chalcidian trading rivals excluded from the Straits. All these Greek cities shared in a marvellous flowering of architecture, town-planning, art, sculpture, the plastic arts, coinage, literature, science and philosophy, as is apparent, for example, in the temples of Paestum, the terracottas of Locri, the bronzes of Tarentum, the philosophers of Elia, the Pythagoreans at Croton. In some ways they remained a group of closed communities, cut off from the rest of Italy, often quarrelling among themselves or suffering civil war within a city. Thus they lacked the power or the will to try to extend the area of their dominance, and their bickerings would not have encouraged other Italic peoples to imitate their more advanced institutions. However, through commerce and other contacts many aspects of their culture began to reach central Italy; thus Greek religious ideas and deities spread outwards, so that Apollo, Heracles, and Castor and Polydeukes became known in Latium and Rome and were 'Italicized', together with many of the figures of Greek mythology; while Etruscan art, though maintaining its own flavour, owed an infinite debt to the Greeks.

The Celts did not play an important role in Rome's history until the beginning of the fourth century when they sacked the city, but since they formed an influential part of the early western European 'barbarian' scene, they require brief mention here. As we have seen, by 1000 BC bearers of the Urnfield culture had spread widely across central Europe, from the Upper Danube to the Rhine, the Rhône, the Seine and the Low

Countries. Their identification with the Celts is maintained by some, and qualified by other, scholars; probably this culture (as at Hallstatt, a typical site in Austria) resulted from gradual infiltrations rather than from a massive invasion. In France it increasingly became marked by the practice of inhumation in mounds; from c. 650 BC chieftains, laid on a wagon with its wheels beside it and accompanied by iron spears and swords, were buried in wooden chambers under great tumuli: iron, inhumation and wagon-burial reinforced older Urnfield practices. Whether the impetus came from foreign settlers or only from foreign influences remains uncertain, but from these wagon-buriers developed the people we call the Celts. From c. 550 they began to import Greek pottery: imports into France came from the Greek city of Massilia (Marseilles) and along the Rhône and Saône valleys. The most famous tomb is at Vix in Burgundy where a princess was buried on a wagon surrounded by Greek and Etruscan ornaments, including the famous bronze *crater* nearly five and a half feet high. Gradually this Celtic culture merged into that of La Tène (a typical site near Lake Neuchâtel) which imported fewer Greek and more Etruscan goods. Further contacts between Celt and Etruscan and the advance of some Celtic tribes over the Alps into the northern plain of Italy are discussed below.[25]

7. THE ETRUSCANS[26]

The people that we call Etruscans were named Tyrsenoi or Tyrrhenoi by the Greeks, Etrusci or Tusci by the Romans, and Rasenna by themselves. They were known to the early Greek poet Hesiod c. 700 BC, and archaeology shows that by then a splendid culture was beginning to flower in Etruria. How did this come about? Were the creators of this civilization native Italians or were they immigrants, like the Greeks further south in Italy? In the mid-fifth century BC Herodotus told how during a famine a Lydian king sent his son Tyrsenus with half the population to seek a new home among the Ombriki. All other ancient writers, beguiled perhaps by the charm and authority of the Father of History, accepted the Lydian origin of the Etruscans, except for Dionysius of Halicarnassus who, living in the time of the emperor Augustus, referred to the shadowy Pelasgians who changed their name to Tyrrhenes and were autochthonous in Italy. The controversy has been carried on ever since, with various degrees of passion and interest, but little general agreement. Mommsen dismissed the question as on a par with that of the name of Hecuba's mother: 'neither capable of being known, nor worth the knowing'. Others feel strongly that Herodotus can not be dismissed out of hand, and that the value of Etruscan culture and the importance of its role in Italian history, including its great influence on Rome, demand full investigation. Latterly, less emphasis has been laid on origin, and more placed on the formation of the Etruscans on Italian soil and analysis of the contrasting elements in Italy and from overseas which combined to create the culture.[27]

The supporters of the theory of autochthonous origin rely on archaeological evidence, which indicates that most Etruscan towns developed on precisely the same sites as former Villanovan settlements. At Veii, for instance, some twelve miles north of Rome, the early Villanovan settlements appear to represent small independent villages, each with its own cemetery, but all grouped on or around the rocky tufa plateau on which the later Etruscan city was built. The types of tombs in Etruscan cemeteries seem to develop in an uninterrupted series, as does the style of their contents. At Tarquinii, for instance, Villanovan cremation burials in urns (*a pozzo*) were first supplemented and then superseded by inhumation in trenches (*a fossa*); as the richness of the contents increased and inhumation became the usual practice, chamber-tombs were cut in the rock; tomb-painting, sculpture and ceramics flourished, and impor-ted Greek and oriental objects became more common. Thus, it is argued, Etruscan civilization had arrived without the intervention of any obvious major break : Villanovans had become Etruscans. The Etruscans spoke a non-Indo-European language, and the Villanovans must therefore presumably have done likewise. If so, since there was no obvious influx of a new population, this language presumably derived from a much earlier Bronze (or even Neolithic) Age stratum going back to before the spread of Indo-European tongues from *c.* 2000 BC.

Scholars who follow the Asiatic flag of Herodotus rather than the Italian flag of Dionysius point out that to transmute small villages into strong cities presupposes technical skills and administrative abilities of a much higher order than that shown by the Villanovans. True, the cemeteries do not indicate any startling break, but the method of dis-posing of the dead does change, and this is an area of custom in which the feelings of primitive peoples run strong and tend to be conservative. Certainly few scholars today would argue for a mass immigration into Etruria from overseas in one great influx, but if groups of newcomers who practised a different form of burial only gradually asserted themselves in the land they occupied, then any change in burial habits would naturally be somewhat slow. Further, similarities between certain tombs in Etruria and Asia Minor have been found, and Etruscan culture has many aspects which seem more oriental than Italic: the luxury of the Etruscans, their love of feasting, music and dancing, and many of their religious practices such as hepatoscopy have eastern parallels. Then there is the startling fact that an inscription on a warrior's tombstone is in a language which has connections both with Etruscan and with the tongues of Asia Minor. This was found on the island of Lemnos in the Aegean, where, according to the historian Thucydides, the pre-Greek population was Tyrrhenian. It *could* be argued that native Italian Etruscans sent out a colony to Lemnos during the early days of Greek colonization, or alternatively that a very old Mediterranean language managed to survive just in these two points amid a sea of Indo-European speakers, but it is much more tempting to see in Lemnos a staging-post in an Etruscan migration from Asia Minor where some of the travellers stayed behind.

Although skulls and bones have been examined by anthropologists, and blood-groups studied by medical biologists, no clear answer has emerged, and the leading Etruscologist, M. Pallottino, has concentrated rather on the historical reality of the Etruscan nation in Italy, considering it more valuable to discuss the origin of the ethnic, linguistic, political and cultural elements that contributed to the process of ethnic formation that took place on the soil of Etruria itself, than to continue to speculate about provenance. One thing however is clear: whether with or without the introduction of incomers from the Eastern Mediterranean, the varied elements were fused together during the orientalizing phase in the early seventh century. The basic population of Etruria remained of Villanovan origin; it adopted new ideas of burial and social organization and imported more and more Greek and oriental wares (including some artists and craftsmen) which were gradually imitated by local artists. But some enquirers will still remember Herodotus and continue to speculate whether these changes were only the upsurge of native talent under eastern cultural influences, or were so fundamental as to justify belief in the impact of foreign occupation. The opening up of the countryside and the transformation of villages into cultured cities may well have required the influx of a relatively small number of men with administrative skills and the power to organize large labour forces.

If on balance we may accept an oriental element in the Etruscan nation, a view to which the Etruscans themselves officially subscribed at the beginning of the Roman Empire (Tacitus, *Annals*, iv, 55), we can imagine how they came in small bands and settled in strong positions near the coast whence they dominated the surrounding districts, much as the Norsemen descended upon the coasts of Scotland. This movement may even represent the final spasm of disturbances in the eastern Mediterranean that went back to the results of the collapse of the Mycenaean and Hittite empires and sent various groups of Peoples of the Sea roving around from the beginning of the twelfth century in search of plunder and new homes. The Etruscans cannot have arrived in Italy before about 800 BC (Herodotus put their migration before the fall of Troy, late thirteenth century), though some might have arrived in Lemnos earlier. The magnet that drew them to Etruria will have been its mineral wealth. They were presumably groups of warriors, with few womenfolk, who brought their experience in war, administration and the arts of city life, together with their language. Their numbers may not have been large and their arrival may have continued over many years. In Etruria they found a Villanovan population which lived in villages, spoke an Indo-European tongue and cremated its dead. Superior powers of organization enabled the invaders to impose themselves as a conquering aristocracy; they intermarried with the Villanovans, their language and burial habits gradually gained the ascendancy, and they organized the subjugated Villanovans to clear the forests, drain the land, and build cities. By exploiting the copper and iron of the country they were enabled to build up an overseas trade which brought them many of the luxurious artistic products of the East. Thus by the beginning of the seventh century an Etruscan nation was born on Italian soil; the bulk of its people were Iron Age Villanovans whose latent abilities and tastes had been gradually sharpened by pressure from men who shared some of the qualities which later enabled the Normans to subdue the Saxons in England. However, the warning should be sounded once again that many scholars still prefer a theory of 'continuous creation' within Etruria itself.[28]

8. ETRUSCAN CULTURE

Etruria was enclosed by the rivers Arno and Tiber and by the lower slopes of the Apennines, but differed considerably in the north and south. In the north were fertile alluvial valleys, plains and rolling hills of limestone and sandstone, where such cities as Clusium, Cortona, Perusia and Faesulae grew up and lived on through to modern times thanks to the attractiveness of their sites. Southern Etruria, on the other hand, where the earliest Etruscan cities developed, was a volcanic zone, whose tufa rock had weathered into peaks and plateaux, separated by deep valleys and gullies, while much of the wild landscape was covered by forest and macchia ; here cities such as Tarquinii, Vulci, Caere and Veii are found on hills which rise where rivers or streams meet to offer protective arms. Though the Villanovans had begun to penetrate into this formidable barrier, emergent Etruscan engineering skills and the organization of labour promoted further land-reclamation, drainage, forestry and road-building. But even so, groups of settlers found themselves cut off from each other by physical barriers which hindered communications. So, like the early Greek city-states, they found intercommunication and therefore political co-operation difficult. Ancient writers might speak of an Etruscan nation, but in fact it was an aggregation of largely independent city-states. The basis of life was naturally agriculture, supplemented by hunting and fishing, but the copper and iron of the country were quickly exploited. Mineral wealth also provided building stone for cities as well as raw materials for export in exchange for foreign goods ; at the same time the land was sufficiently fertile to support a large population. Only technical and administrative skills were needed to produce a rich civilization.

The Etruscans laid out their cities in accordance with religious practices prescribed in ritual books ; each city must be enclosed within a sacred boundary (*pomerium*) in order to ward off unseen dangers from outside. Temples had to be correctly planned and orientated, and this may have led to some symmetry in the layout of other public buildings, but the rough and hilly nature of many sites must have precluded the exact use of a careful grid system such as the Etruscans used later when founding cities on more level ground, as at Marzabotto near Bologna *c*. 500 BC (p. 35). This desire for symmetry may have influenced the later grid system, based on the axial crossing of two main streets (the *cardo* and *decumanus*) which the Romans used in their camps and colonies, although the Etruscan practice was rather closer to the system of alternating wider and narrower divisions which many Greek cities in the west used from *c*. 500 BC. For long years most of the Etruscan cities relied on the strength of their natural position, but when from *c*. 400 BC the power of Rome on their southern horizon began to seem threatening, they built walls of dressed stones. An Etruscan temple, squarer than Greek ones, had a wide frontage ; the front half had a colonnaded portico, while the back comprised either three shrines (*cellae*) for three deities or one *cella* with two flanking wings. The main framework, which rested on stone foundations, was made of wood covered with gay multi-coloured terracotta ornamentation. Small private houses were usually rectangular, of mud-brick, laced with timber, and built on stone or pebble foundations; larger houses had upper storeys, with flat or gabled roofs. The mansions (*domus*) of the rich aristocracy were in internal appearance like some of the elegantly decorated stone chamber-tombs and were the predecessors of the *atrium* (central courtyard) type of house which the Romans later used.[29] These large tombs were laid out in rows, with streets running between them, forming 'cities of the dead' (*necropoleis*); there are examples at Caere and Orvieto. A few cities, however, in northern and inland Etruria retained the practice of cremation. The contents of the larger tombs, themselves often shaped like houses, reveal the luxury and artistic tastes of the Etruscan nobles. Some of the pottery in these tombs was native *bucchero* ware (a black polished clay, sometimes brilliant and elegant), but they also contained vast quantities of imported Greek vases, of every type from 'geometric' to Attic, together with local copies: one tomb alone in Caere contained 150 excellent early Greek vases, and large numbers found at Vulci from the early nineteenth century onwards have enriched the museums of Europe. The metal work of bronze and gold was mostly of native workmanship, but of high quality. Bronze toilet-cases and mirrors with incised decorations show strong Greek influence, but the exquisite gold filigree work was less dependent on foreign models. This jewellery and metal-work was widely exported, even to Celtic lands. Two larger bronze masterpieces survive in the Capitoline wolf in Rome and the Chimera of Arezzo. Sculpture in stone was limited by the quality of the local stone (the marble quarries of Luni were not exploited until Roman times), but the Etruscans excelled in sculptured terracotta, which was brightly painted and widely used to decorate the wooden superstructure of temples and even for life-size statues, of which the Apollo of Veii survives as the work of a master. The gaily coloured wall-paintings in the tombs, especially those at Tarquinii, show great *joie de vivre*, but also some grim figures of demons in the underworld. Scenes of banqueting, dancing and music, horse-racing, athletics, wrestling, hunting and fishing, all throw a vivid light on Etruscan life, as well as reflecting Greek painting of the archaic school, of which nothing survives in Greece itself. However, here, as in the rest of Etruscan art, the main inspiration is Greek and oriental, but infused with an individual character all its own.[30]

Of the Etruscans Livy wrote: 'no people was ever more devoted to religious observances'. They believed that their religion had been revealed to them in early days by seers. This teaching, the *Etrusca disciplina*, was enshrined in a number of books of ritual, and it prescribed in minute detail how the will of the gods was to be ascertained and followed: life was dominated by fate, and the Etruscans had only ten *saecula* of existence granted to them. *Libri fulgurales* interpreted the significance of thunder and lightning, while *libri haruspicini* instructed professional *haruspices* in the art of divination based on the inspection of the livers of sacrificed animals (hepatoscopy): a model bronze liver survives which is divided into forty-four areas, marked with the names of gods and orientated to the Etruscan heaven, showing the place occupied by each deity. The Romans later often appealed to Etruscan *haruspices* to interpret omens which they themselves failed to understand. Other books dealt with the founding of cities, consecrating temples, matters concerning war and peace, and most aspects of public and private life. The names, though not always the precise functions, of many Etruscan deities are known, and they were soon assimilated to Greek deities: thus Tin (Zeus/Jupiter), Uni (Hera/Juno), Menvra (Athene/Minerva), Fufluns (Dionysus/Bacchus), Sethlans (Hephaestus). Etruscan religion, at least in its later phases, became gloomy and cruel, unlike most Greek and Italic cults: tomb-paintings depict the torments of the departed inflicted by demons in the underworld. To appease these demons the Etruscans appear to have offered human sacrifices. The Romans were much influenced by many aspects of Etruscan religion; their gladiatorial contests probably derived from the Etruscan practice of dispatching their victims by making them kill each other in duels.[31]

The Etruscan language, which was non-Indo-European, bequeathed a few words to Latin, but in the main had remarkably little influence on it. However, both Etruscans and Romans took their alphabets from the Phoenicians via the Greeks, and if the Romans did not derive their version direct from Cumae, then the Etruscans must have acted as intermediaries. Etruscan survives in a large number of inscriptions, over 10,000 altogether, but nearly all are very short and usually late (third century BC or after). Most are epitaphs, giving the names of the deceased and of his father and mother, together with his age and any magistracy he held. Three longer inscriptions dealing with religious or legal matters survive, and two religious dedications, with a third in Punic, have recently been found at Pyrgi, the port of Caere. The language still defies complete and detailed decipherment, but the general meaning of most inscriptions can be ascertained, not least by the so-called bilingual method, which for instance, finds parallels in the religious and legal formulae of the Etruscans and those of the Latins and Umbrians which can be read with accuracy.[32]

The Etruscans had a considerable body of religious literature, but the extent of their secular literature is uncertain since whatever existed has all perished. However, even as late as the early Roman Empire much material about the Etruscans still survived, some at least almost certainly in Etruscan, sufficient in fact to enable the emperor Claudius to write twenty books of Etruscan history, *Tyrrhenika*; some of this material presumably came direct from Etruscan historical sources. Varro actually refers to *Tuscae Historiae*. Further, painted scenes in a tomb at Vulci depict historical episodes showing Etruscan warriors from different cities in combat with Roman warriors, among them Mastarna, who according to Etruscan sources was a king at Rome (p. 53); these scenes presuppose a historical tradition, since the painting was done *c*. 340–310 BC, some two hundred years after the episodes depicted. A lively interest in local history is also shown by a number of *elogia*, written in Latin and set up in Tarquinii: one celebrates Velthur Spurinna, who was *praetor* twice; during one magistracy he kept his army at home, in the other he led it across the sea to Sicily. These inscriptions were put up in the first century of the Roman Empire, which indicates the long survival of family traditions either in written histories, national or local, or less probably in oral or epigraphic sources. Thus quite a considerable body of Etruscan history seems to have existed, but unfortunately we can only speculate about its detailed nature and the ways in which the Etruscans wrote history. One other aspect, however, is important: a common literature provides a powerful element in the formation of any nation (the possession of the Homeric poems created a strong sentimental link between the scattered communities of early Greeks). Since it is generally agreed that Etruscan culture was not the product of a single racially pure ethnic unit, the possession of a religious and historical literature must have been a potent factor in creating an Etruscan 'nation'.[33]

In early days each Etruscan city was ruled by a king (*lucumo*), who was surrounded with great pomp. He wore a robe of purple and a golden crown, sat on an ivory seat, and was escorted by servants who carried an axe in a bundle of rods (*fasces*), symbols of his power to execute or scourge. Many of these trappings of office were later adopted by Roman Republican magistrates after Etruscan kings had occupied the throne at Rome. During the sixth and fifth centuries nobles began to challenge the power of the kings, some of whom tried to bolster up their waning authority by reorganizing the city's political institutions in order to give the middle class more military and political influence to counterbalance the nobility, as occurred in Rome (see p. 55). However, gradually the kings were overthrown, and although thereafter some military adventurers may have gone on the warpath in an attempt to gain personal ascendancy, they were soon reduced to the level of their fellow nobles, and from then on the cities were administered by local aristocracies, who held such magistracies as those of *zilath, maru* or *purthne*, offices which appear normally to have been annual but whose detailed functions escape us.[34]

The chief of these autonomous city-states formed a League of Twelve Cities and annually sent representatives to celebrate common cult and games at a federal sanctuary, Fanum Voltumnae near Volsinii, Voltumna being the chief god. The strength of these federal ties varied: the cities clearly developed some feelings for national unity and did on occasion act as a League, but local loyalties often proved stronger. Thus the Etruscans failed to establish an integrated political structure, inspired by unity of purpose, and this failure was later to prove fatal to them when they came into conflict with Rome, which in contrast had built up a strong confederacy.[35]

The Greek and Roman sources, which are seldom favourable to the Etruscans and are often hostile and slanderous, give a general impression that Etruscan society was sharply divided between a powerful and rich aristocracy and an immense body of clients, serfs and slaves, but such a gap may have been lessened in the sixth century when the Etruscans adopted the Greek military formation of a closely-knit battle-line of heavily armed infantry (hoplites). The citizen body was formed by a gentilitian system into clans or families, with strong feeling for the family and the place of the mother, although older views of Etruscan society as matriarchal have been abandoned. Little unfortunately is known in detail about the status or conditions of the serfs and slaves who worked the land for their overlords.[36]

9. THE ETRUSCAN EMPIRE

If Cato exaggerated when he wrote that 'almost the whole of Italy belonged to the Etruscans', he at least emphasized the existence of a large Etruscan empire. After the rapid development of Etruscan from Villanovan culture in Etruria itself, it soon spread much further afield, and with it an uncertain measure of political control or dominance, both to the south and north.[37] Some Etruscans advanced over the Tiber into Latium and occupied Rome and other centres (p. 39). Others moved

further southwards, advancing by land or sea, into Campania, where
some Villanovan settlements had already emerged (p. 16). Here they
established themselves at Capua (perhaps *c.* 650 BC), calling their settlement Volturnum; Etruscan inscriptions have been found at Pompeii,
Nola and elsewhere. They thus came face to face with Cumae and other
Greek colonies, while at the same time Greek penetration into western
waters was threatening the spread of Etruscan control. On the other
hand, the Greek cities of southern Italy had provided the Etruscans with
new markets for their metals and metalwork, and a widespread trade had
been built up especially in Greek pottery (p. 23). But events took a fresh
turn when the Phocaeans of Asia Minor in *c.* 600 BC founded Massilia
(Marseilles), which in turn sent out colonies along the coast of southern
Gaul and north-eastern Spain. The first people to react sharply to this new
challenge were the Carthaginians, who tried to keep the Phocaeans out of
this western areas, but they were defeated in a naval battle which
Thucydides recorded (i, 13, 6). When the Phocaeans moved closer to the
shores of Etruria itself by settling at Alalia on the east coast of Corsica
the Etruscans joined Carthage against the intruders; a naval battle off
Alalia in 535 BC resulted in a 'Cadmean victory' for the Phocaeans, who
ultimately settled at Elea, the home of the Eleatic philosophers. The
majority of the captured crews were taken to Agylla (Caere) where they
were stoned to death.[38] This reference to one Etruscan city, Caere, is a
reminder that very often when action by 'the Etruscans' is mentioned in
the sources, we do not know in detail how many or precisely which cities
shared in such action: indeed many of the colonial efforts may have been
made by individual cities only. However, the battle of Alalia allowed the
Carthaginians to control Sardinia, and the Etruscans Corsica, and either
after or before the battle these two peoples entered into a formal alliance,
since it is into this period that a treaty between Carthage and Etruria,
which Aristotle mentions but does not date, best fits; again, who signed
for the Etruscans, whether the League or individual interested cities,
remains unknown.[39]

Encouraged by these events, the Etruscans tried to strengthen their
control in Campania by attacking Greek Cumae in 524 BC, but they were
defeated by land by the Cumaeans under the leadership of Aristodemus.
Before very long Etruscan influence began to weaken in Latium also and
they lost control of Rome when Tarquinius was driven out. The other
Latin cities were encouraged to seek freedom from the Etruscans and
while resisting Etruscan counter-attacks they appealed to Cumae, which
sent a force by sea under Aristodemus. He routed the Etruscans under

Arruns, the son of Lars Porsenna of Clusium, at Aricia *c.* 506 BC. Aristodemus used his success to become tyrant at Cumae, and the victorious Latins could now cut the land communications between Etruria and Campania. Some years later, in 474, Cumae, either threatened again by the Etruscans or else herself taking the initiative against them, appealed to Hiero king of Syracuse, who had recently, at the battle of Himera, smashed a Carthaginian attempt to occupy eastern Sicily. At a naval battle off Cumae the Greek allies broke Etruscan sea-power: the Greeks regained the freedom of the seas around Naples, and the Etruscan cities in Campania were now isolated by sea as well as by land.[40] Thus the southern part of the Etruscan empire collapsed, but in fact the victors did not enjoy independence in Campania for long, since Sabellian tribes began to descend from the mountains, and by 420 both Etruscan Capua and Greek Cumae had succumbed to their assault (p. 109)

The second main line of expansion was northwards over the Apennines; it originated from the cities of the interior of Etruria and began near the end of the sixth century, a considerable time after the start of the southern expansion, and in fact when the Etruscans' grip there was weakening. The chief colony was founded alongside the old Villanovan settlement at Bologna and was named Felsina; it soon became a prosperous city of farmers, industrialists and traders, and imported large numbers of Greek vases. These came more immediately from Spina at the head of the Adriatic, which became the chief port for Greek goods, especially Athenian vases: it was originally a Greek settlement in which the Etruscans secured a strong foothold. The third important base in the north was the Etruscan settlement at Marzabotto (probably called by them Misa or Misna), some seventeen miles south of Felsina, in a key position to control the valley leading southwards over the Apennines to Etruria itself. Its interest lies not least in the facts that it was an entirely new foundation (*c.* 500 BC) on virgin soil, and has not been built over since: it thus provides an outstanding example of a late Etruscan city and its street-planning. The extent of Etruscan settlement beyond the area of these three cities is uncertain, since archaeological evidence is lacking for widespread settlement in the northern plain (especially north of the Po), and the tradition that the Etruscans established a League of Twelve Cities here, as in Etruria (and allegedly in Campania), is doubtful. Etruscan trade, but only limited settlement, therefore seems to have spread northwards, where before very long it encountered opposition from Celtic tribes who were tempted to cross the Alps and try to occupy the northern plain of Italy. They may have started on a small scale earlier in the fifth century, but by the end of it they were sweeping all before them. The final attacks fell on Marzabotto and Felsina. The latter was overwhelmed *c.* 350; burial stones depict the horsemen of Felsina struggling against naked Gallic warriors. Thus Etruscan power north of the Apennines was gradually pushed back and then smashed; the northern plain fell to the Celts and became known to the Romans as Cisalpine Gaul. Soon it would be the turn of Rome itself to face a Gallic incursion (p. 103).[41]

Thus in pre-Roman Italy there flourished an empire which corresponded in extent roughly with the Napoleonic kingdom of Italy, created probably rather by the haphazard needs and initiative of individual cities than by concerted action of the Etruscan League which was bound together more by cultural and religious than political ties. But it might have resulted in the spread of a common culture, if not in the creation of a single state, from the Alps to the Strait of Messina – had not a sudden collapse occurred, so that this achievement was reserved for the genius of Rome.

10. EARLY LATIUM

Latium was for long years inimical to man. The coastal plain, a late creation in geological time, was subject to flooding, while the Ciminian and Alban Hills displayed volcanic activity as late as 1000 BC; more than fifty craters can be found within twenty-five miles of Rome. When finally the volcanoes had died down and had covered the area with an ash rich in phosphates and potash, cultivation of the soil still remained impracticable until the jungle growth had formed a surface soil containing nitrogenous matter. This was soon provided by the forests which spread rapidly over the hills and gave Latium a different appearance and climate from today, when the wheat is harvested in June and the Roman Campagna is bare and parched in the summer months; then harvest-time was in July. As late as the third century BC Theophrastus wrote that Latium was well-watered: the plain bore laurel, myrtle and beech trees, the hills fir and pine, while oaks flourished on the Circeian promontory. This difference of moisture in ancient and modern times is probably due to the later deforestation of the hills behind Latium, rather than to a supposed rainy age in classical times. Thus a rich soil, provided by volcanic ash and vegetation, and a moist subsoil, provided by the forest reservoirs, rendered Latium habitable, and men settled south of the Tiber on that semicircle of hills, the dominating positions of which were later controlled by the towns of Tibur, Praeneste and Aricia.[42]

Man did not appear in Latium until relatively late, and then in small and scattered settlements. Traces of Palaeolithic occupation are rare: they include some remains of Neanderthal man near Rome, and a cave near Tivoli used for several millennia by Upper Palaeolithic people. Continuing volcanic activity may have made Latium unattractive during the Chalcolithic and Bronze Ages: traces of 'Apennine' material are only sporadic although they do reveal a settlement on the site of Rome itself (p. 43). However, despite a few traces of evidence at Lavinium and near Ardea, any continuing links with the Iron Age are as yet slender: the population explosion in the early Iron Age suggests new settlers from outside. This new culture, now known as 'Latial' rather than 'southern Villanovan', spread to Rome, the Alban Hills and southwards to Terracina. As we have seen (p. 16) it closely resembled the Villanovan culture of Etruria, though cinerary urns shaped like the huts of the inhabitants were used (as in southern Etruria, in contrast with the biconical urns of northern Etruria). This new people imposed itself on any 'Apennine' stratum that survived, but it was soon reinforced by representatives of the inhuming Fossa culture from the south (p. 17). This new mixture marks the beginning of the Iron Age in Latium, which some archaeologists place as early as 1000 BC, others as late as 800; perhaps 900 may be nearer the mark. It lasted for a considerable time, but it began to change when the Etruscans expanded southwards.[43]

Cemeteries of these Latin villages have been found in Rome (these are discussed in the next chapter) and on the western and southern slopes of the isolated Alban Hills which rise up from the plain some thirteen miles south of Rome and whose extinct craters formed the lakes of Albano and Nemi. Other Latins settled at Ardea, Antium, Satricum and other centres, large and small. Although Rome was traditionally founded as a colony of Alba Longa, archaeological evidence does not support the primacy of Alba. An important site, discovered in 1972, lay at Castel di Decima, some ten miles south of Rome, which is almost certainly ancient Politorium which the Roman king Ancus Marcius is said to have conquered. Of the 115 Fossa tombs excavated, the earliest is c. 740–20, most belong to the first half of the seventh century, and none is later than c. 600; this accords well with the traditional capture by Ancus. Many of the tombs are rich; four contained chariots, and in one of these (c. 700) a richly adorned woman was buried. Another recent identification is Ficana on Monte Cugno between Rome and Ostia, whose tombs suggest a settlement similar to that at Decima; here there is also some Bronze Age material. Other sites where excavation is throwing new light on Latin settlements are at La Rustica (= Caenina?) north-east of Rome, and at Osteria dell 'Osa to the east of Rome, not very far from Gabii, where the remains in the cemetery (the majority inhumations) run from the ninth to the seventh centuries.[44] Thus our knowledge of early Latium is rapidly expanding, and Latial culture is now divided into three groups, Boschetto, Alba and Campagna, in accordance with local variations – though these need not be detailed here since resemblances far exceed minor differences.

The lack of material wealth and of harbours meant that the early Latins did not advance quite so quickly as the Northern Villanovans, but they began to enter into the wider life of Italy from about 700 BC. At first perhaps given to war and plunder and for long remaining semi-nomadic herdsmen, they gradually became essentially agriculturalists, growing wheat, millet and, later, barley; the vine was probably not cultivated until the Etruscan period, and the olive was a later arrival, but the fig was grown in early times. Pigs, sheep and oxen and perhaps goats were raised; the horse came later. Timber was a valuable source of wealth. The population soon grew large, as shown by the smallness of individual land-holdings (2 *iugera* or $1\frac{1}{3}$ acres) and also by the extensive drainage works, tunnels and dams which were constructed partly for irrigation, but mainly to prevent the rainwater sweeping the precious soil down the hillsides: volcanic rock is easily dried up and washed away. Some of the larger works like those below Velitrae, or the *emissarium* of the Alban Lake, may be inspired by somewhat later Etruscan example, but they testify to the value set on preserving the fertile soil. While they were busy clearing the forests and cultivating the ground, many of the Latins settled in villages, congregating on hills to find protection against man and beast and to escape the unhealthiness of the plain. Here they lived, as Varro says, 'in huts and cabins and knew not the meaning of a wall or gate'. The appearance of their huts is shown by their cinerary urns, while the process by which separate settlements coalesced into one large village is illustrated by the growth of early Rome (p. 45). Each village (*vicus*), which may have been strengthened by a wooden palisade, had a *pagus*, the extended area in which its inhabitants carried on their pastoral or agricultural work, but sometimes various *vici* might hold a *pagus* in common and thus become linked in cantons. The *vici* were probably organized on the basis of clans (*gentes*), but the strongest social unit was the *familia* or household in which the *pater-familias* or eldest living male held almost absolute control. Surviving lists of Latin *populi* suggest some forty or fifty early villages, while the Prisci Latini ('Original Latins') are given as thirty.[45]

The fact that all these small settlements shared a common language must have helped to develop a sense of unity. This was also fostered by common religious practices and led on to some common action in other fields. The Latins, who used to gather for a spring festival at the very ancient shrine of Jupiter Latiaris on Monte Cavo, the summit of the Alban Hills, formed a League which was probably fairly extensive; but although the leadership passed from Alba to Rome, the League probably remained of chiefly religious significance and did not provide a framework through which Rome could exercise political hegemony in Latium. Other gropings after unity are found in the common cults of Venus at Lavinium and of Diana near Tusculum, at shrines common to all the Latins at Ardea and Lavinium, and more especially the cult of Diana at Aricia at the source of Aqua Ferentina. While some historians try to explain some of these leagues as the various stages in the growth of one single Latin League, more probably several co-existed. Of these the Arician federation attained considerable importance in the sixth century. The primitive state of these early cults is illustrated by the worship of Diana at Nemi, where the golden bough grew; amid the forests lurked the *rex nemorensis*, 'the priest who slew the slayer, and shall himself be slain.' But it is the political potentialities of these federations that are important in the history of Italy.[46]

With the coming of the Etruscans Latium entered upon a new phase (c. 650), but although it was subjected to Etruscan cultural influences it remained essentially Latin, since the Latin language survived almost untouched. The Etruscans encouraged agriculture, large drainage works, industry and commerce, and they promoted synoecisms. Thus Latium was swept into a wider world. Further, Greek ideas were reaching it from the south, and it is not always easy to determine whether any particular gift, above all that of the alphabet, came direct from the south or was mediated through the Etruscans. Nor can we establish the extent of direct Etruscan political influence, except at Rome which was governed by Etruscan kings during the sixth century (pp. 53ff.). But though evidence for direct rule is lacking in other Latin cities, the general promotion of city life by the Etruscans need not be questioned. Latin Praeneste, which may have formed a key point in the Etruscan advance southwards since it commands the route to the Liris valley, was clearly subjected to Etruscan influences. Its two famous tombs, the Bernardini and Barberini, contain princely gold and bronze objects which resemble those of a similar Etruscan tomb at Caere of *c*. 650, yet a gold fibula which may have come from one of them bears an inscription written in Latin ('Manios made me for Numasios'). Until very recently these tombs were often regarded as the resting-places of Etruscan nobles, but since the richness of the tombs of other Latin cities such as Decima has now been revealed, the finds at Praeneste may reflect a wider social-economic background existing throughout Latium rather than providing evidence for the direct intrusion of Etruscan princes. At the same time the genuineness of the Latin inscription on the fibula has been seriously questioned. The names of some Latin cities, as Tusculum, Velitrae, and Tarracina, seem to link them with the Etruscans, but how far Etruscan political domination extended is uncertain. However, the earliest treaty between Rome and Carthage of *c*. 509 BC (p. 160) suggests that the Etruscan rulers of Rome may have exercised some control over Ardea, Antium, Circeii, Tarracina and perhaps Lavinium.[47]

A striking witness to Latium's wider contacts is provided by the emergence of a new architectural form, the temple. At Rome, Satricum, Velitrae, Lavinium and other towns temples arose, whose gaily coloured terracotta decorations closely resemble those in Etruria and also many in Campania. Latium was becoming part of a common culture, based on Etruscan and Greek ideas. Many of the latter came via the Etruscans, but a recent discovery has emphasized the direct channel with the Greek cities of the south. A series of thirteen massive archaic stone altars was found at Lavinium (Pratica di Mare) about sixteen miles south of Rome. One altar had a bronze tablet inscribed in archaic Latin with a dedication to Castor and Pollux. This strengthens the likelihood that the cult of the Dioscuri reached Latium from the south rather than from Etruria.[48] In addition to the altars Lavinium has recently produced another startling find (unpublished at the time of writing). Some fifty terracotta statues and other objects belonging to a sanctuary have been discovered. They appear to have been buried (for safety?) perhaps in the second century BC. The earliest date to the sixth century, but the majority to the fifth and fourth. The chief piece is a slightly larger than life-size statue of Minerva in battle. When this find has been properly assessed it will throw much light on the importance of early Lavinium and on the attraction of Latium to artists from Greek southern Italy. Etruscan influence lies behind the development of larger settlements: by 500 BC the original fifty or so communities had been reduced by a process of absorption to some ten or twelve, of which the largest, such as Praeneste, Tibur and Tusculum, dealt for a considerable time with Rome on equal terms. Thus Etruscan influence on Latium in the seventh and sixth centuries left permanent marks, but it was sporadic and did not undermine the basic nature of the native culture. The future of Latium lay not with Etruria but with one of its own cities, Rome.

II

REGAL ROME

1. THE FOUNDATION OF ROME: ARCHAEOLOGICAL EVIDENCE

About fifteen miles from its mouth the River Tiber winds through a group of hills which rise from the Latin plain. Here was the natural meeting-place of the Etruscans, Latins and Sabellians, and the objective of any ambitious people. Far enough from the sea to protect its inhabitants from the danger of piracy, the settlement which spread over these hills lay on the chief river of central Italy. It commanded both the Tiber valley, which gave access to Etruria and the central highlands, and a ford which lay south of an island in the Tiber; any traffic from north to south or from the eastern hills to the sea would pass through it. It was thus a natural centre and a point of distribution.[1] The hills themselves were well wooded, fairly precipitous and defensible; some were isolated, others formed spurs of a surrounding plateau. Though the ground between them was marshy and subject to flooding by the Tiber, the hills afforded some protection against disease, as well as against man and beast. Some, though not all, of the potential natural advantages of the future site of Rome must have been obvious to the earliest settlers.

The chief hills of ancient Rome, except the Janiculum, all lay on the east bank of the Tiber. From a plateau there projected westwards towards the river (in order, from north to south) the Quirinal, Viminal, three spurs of the Esquiline called Cispius, Fagutal and Oppius, and the Caelius; between the Caelius and the river lay the Aventine. Within this semicircle were two nearly isolated hills, the Capitoline and Palatine, the former between the Quirinal and Tiber island, the latter connected by a ridge in the east, called the Velia, with the Oppius. The Palatine was spacious and had steep cliffs on three sides, which overlooked the moat-like marshes that later were converted into the Forum, Velabrum and Circus Maximus; on the fourth side its isthmus, the Velia, ensured communication with the interior, and this was the hill nearest to the ford below the island. It is here that ancient tradition places the first settlement of the Latins. The isolation of some of the hills was increased by the streams which flowed in gullies between the Quirinal, the Viminal, the Cispius and the Oppius; these joined the main stream that flowed through what was later the Roman Forum to reach the Tiber.

Whatever geographical, commercial or military advantages of the site contributed to the future growth of Rome, in origin it was probably merely a shepherds' village or group of villages lying midway between the plain and the hill country. Sporadic finds of flint implements, stone axes and a copper dagger, which were discovered in the 1870s, show that much of the Esquiline was inhabited at the end of the Neolithic period and at the beginning of the Chalcolithic, but the continuity or duration of this early settlement is uncertain. Then quite recently some Bronze Age 'Apennine' pottery was found in the Forum Boarium: it came from a soil filling made when a very early temple there had been rebuilt after a fire in 213 BC. This indicates that the settlement from which the earth had originally been taken lay nearby, probably on the Capitoline, Palatine or Aventine; it should be dated around 1500 BC, but continuity of habitation until the Iron Age settlements arrived cannot yet be confidently asserted.[8]

Early in the eighth century Iron Age village settlements began to appear on the hilltops of the Palatine, Esquiline, Quirinal and probably the Caelian. These shepherds and farmers lived in wattle-and-daub huts and disposed of their dead on the slopes and valleys between the hilltops. The village on the Palatine was well placed: the hill commanded the Tiber and was easily defensible, but was also comparatively spacious and reasonably accessible from the landward side. It claimed to be the earliest settlement, founded by Romulus himself, whose Hut (*casa Romuli*) was preserved in historical times. In fact there were two heights on the Palatine, the Germalus and the Palatine itself; a cremation-grave has been found between them under the so-called House of Livia, so probably at first two separate communities existed, divided by a cemetery. That on the Germalus was probably slightly the older, since here lay the Hut of Romulus, and it is here that the foundations of three huts cut in the tufa rock were discovered in 1948. They are roughly rectangular (some 13½ × 11¾ feet), with drainage channels around. The disposition of the post-holes, together with the appearance of surviving clay hut-urns, enables the wooden superstructure to be reconstructed. A central wooden pillar held a ridge-piece, from which a gabled roof descended to, and extended beyond, the upright sides of the hut. In front of the door was a small porch or extension of the roof. The roof and walls consisted of wattle and daub (branches and thatch laid on a coating of dry clay). Clusters of such huts thus formed the earliest villages of Rome. The settlers on the Esquiline hill, however, buried their dead *a fossa*, while on the Quirinal the earliest tombs are *a pozzo* cremations—which are followed by *a fossa* inhumations. A main burial-ground lay at the foot of the Palatine on the site of the later Forum: here again both cremation and inhumation burials have been found, but with cremation dominant in the earliest tombs. These cremations are almost certainly the burials of the Palatine village (the alternative of a Velian village is less likely), and the inhumations those of the occupants of other hills; they extend from the eighth to the early sixth century. No traces of early settlement have yet come to light on the Capitol, despite its dominant position, a steep and narrow bluff; it may have served as an *oppidum* or temporary refuge rather than attracting a permanent settlement. Although their pottery showed some individual characteristics, the inhabitants of these villages shared a common Latial culture, those on the Palatine being closer to the Villanovans of the Alban Hills, while finds on the Esquiline have their parallels at Tibur and in southern Latium. The Esquiline graves from about 700 BC, however, contain many weapons; this points to the intrusion either of a wave of Fossa culture people or of the Sabines whom later Romans believed to have formed a substantial element in the early population. (p. 51). Thus the earliest settlers may have been joined by others from the area of the central Apennines; the Anio valley afforded easy access to the basin of the Tiber.

As the population increased in the seventh century the villagers began to spread down the hillsides and finally built some huts on the top of earlier tombs in the Forum valley. These seem to have been destroyed by flooding, but after more successful attempts were made to drain the Forum brook, by works which pre-dated the later Cloaca Maxima, settlement was renewed after *c.* 625, and two or three decades later was extended to the Velabrum valley and site of the Forum Boarium. By this time the various villages were merging, but it is too early to think in terms of an urbanized unit. Such unity was achieved in various stages.

The earliest phase, when each village was an independent community, is reflected in two later festivals. During the Lupercalia the Luperci used to run round the Palatine in a ceremony of purification: this suggests an originally isolated settlement there. Further, the procession that annually visited the twenty-four shrines of the Argei proceeded later not around the continuous circuit of the whole city but in four separate circuits around four areas; this reflects conditions when Rome had reached a stage of development where it was known as the City of the Four Regions (see below), but it seems also to point to an even earlier time when each of these four areas was an independent unit and had its own chapels (which in fact, so far as their positions have been identified, were on top of hills and not in the valleys, i.e. they were grouped according to the hills rather than as common sacred places).[3] The first move to unity is reflected in the festival of the Septimontium, which probably means of seven hills (*septem montes*) rather than, as more recently suggested, palisaded hills (*saepti montes*). The hills involved were not the later Seven Hills of Rome, but the original components of three groups, namely the Palatine (comprising the Germalus, Palatinus and Velia), the Esquiline (i.e. the Oppius, Cispius and Fagutal) and the Caelius: the Quirinal and Viminal were excluded, and the frontier between the two communities was the Forum brook.[4] Provision had to be made for peaceful passage across this sacred running water, and so inaugurated bridges, Jani, were built at places where tracks reached the brook: the Ianus Summus, Medius and Imus (the last in the Velabrum).[5] Thus even if the Septimontium was little more than a grouping of villages for religious worship, it paved the way for wider co-operation. We do not know where the initiative for this movement arose, but the tradition of the priority of the Palatine may point in that direction.

The next stage was the union of the enlarged Palatine community with its neighbours on the Quirinal. This too was reflected in the organization of the Luperci, who were divided into two groups which appear to represent the Palatine and the Quirinal, as also were the Salii, two colleges of dancing warrior priests made up of the Salii Palatini and the Salii Collini (= of the Quirinal); the antiquity of the Salii is confirmed by their Bronze Age type of armour. This new 'twin city' was organized into four regions, namely Palatine, Caelius, Esquiline and Quirinal, which as we have seen are indicated in the ritual of the Argei. This area, which excluded the Capitoline and Aventine, corresponded roughly both with the four 'urban' tribes or city wards of the later Republican period and also with the district within the *pomerium*, a ritual furrow made by a yoked bull and cow to mark off the area of an augurally constituted city, as among the

Etruscans. This spiritual boundary was not necessarily strengthened at this time by a surrounding defensive rampart, and the separate villages may have had no fortifications other than their own steep hillsides, although these may have been reinforced with wooden palisades; there may possibly have been some earth walls across the Oppius, Cispius and Quirinal.

While the isolation of the villages was breaking down during the seventh century, domestic industry was being complemented by more professional craftsmen who began to peddle their wares beyond the confines of Rome itself. The distribution of wealth was widening, as shown by a warrior's chariot and armour of *c.* 650 BC found in a *fossa* tomb on the Esquiline. External influences also increased: from *c.* 625 BC Etruscan *bucchero* and metalwork from Veii and Caere begin to appear, together with Etruscan imitations of Greek proto-Corinthian and Corinthian pottery, and before long some of the inhabitants were beginning to leave their huts for houses with tiled roofs. The archaeological evidence agrees in a remarkable manner with the Roman literary tradition that the first Etruscan king, Tarquinius Priscus, gained the throne of Rome in 616 BC: this is the very time when the material remains show Rome entering the ambit of Etruscan civilization and the scattered villages becoming an Etruscan *urbs*. The literary traditions about early Rome must now be considered.

2. THE FOUNDATION OF ROME: THE LEGENDS

Legends about the foundation of Rome, and variants of them, abound in Greek and Roman writers. A brief account of what became the standard story, as given for instance by Livy at the beginning of the Roman Empire, runs something like this: when King Latinus ruled over the aborigines in Laurentum, some Trojans arrived under the leadership of Aeneas after the fall of their city. Aeneas married Lavinia, the daughter of Latinus, and after the King's death he ruled over the Trojans and aborigines, now called Latins. After founding a city, Lavinium, in honour of his wife, Aeneas died and was succeeded by his son Ascanius, known to the Romans as Iulus, who founded Alba Longa. After him twelve kings reigned in Alba, until a prince Amulius wrongfully seized the throne in place of his elder brother Numitor, whose daughter, Rhea Silvia, he forced to become a Vestal Virgin. But she bore to Mars the twins Romulus and Remus, who were miraculously saved from the death by drowning which Amulius had planned; they were washed up under a fig-tree, Ruminalis, near the Palatine where they were suckled by a wolf and nurtured by the shepherd Faustulus. Later they slew Amulius and set Numitor in his place and set forth to found a city on the spot where they had been saved. But while Romulus wished to build on the Palatine, Remus preferred the Aventine. The omens favoured the choice of Romulus, but Remus in scorn leapt over his brother's rising wall and was slain by him. Thus on 21 April, 753 BC, tradition records, Rome was founded even if it was not built in a day.

Such a story resulted from the intermingling of two traditions which in some respects were mutually exclusive: Roman accounts which attributed the founding of Rome to Romulus, and Greek accounts which made Aeneas the chief character.[6] Greek writers frequently invented stories about the adventures of various heroes, not least Odysseus, who after the fall of Troy sailed off to the west and founded cities, and as early as the fifth century at least two historians, Hellanicus and Damastes of Sigeum, had attributed the founding of Rome to Aeneas. Further, the story of Aeneas' flight from Troy reached Etruria by the sixth century: at least seventeen vase paintings (525–470 BC) found there depict the scene, and nearly as many show Aeneas in battle.[7] The possible early popularity of Aeneas in Etruria is reinforced by votive statuettes of Aeneas carrying his father Anchises in flight from Troy found at Veii: they have usually been dated to the sixth century, although some scholars now argue that they are not earlier than the fall of Veii at the beginning of the fourth century. Complications, however, would arise when Greek writers who regarded Aeneas as Rome's founder came across the Roman tradition of Romulus and Remus: one way out was to make them sons or grandsons of Aeneas. But a further difficulty arose when soon after 300 BC the historian Timaeus brought the date of the foundation of Rome down to 814 BC (in order to synchronize it with that of Carthage), i.e. 370 years later than the reported date of the fall of Troy, which was fixed at 1184 BC by the scholar Eratosthenes in the second half of the third century. Further, Latin tradition knew only seven kings at Rome before the establishment of the Republic in 510 BC. Thus if a reasonable reign was allowed to each king, the foundation of Rome could not have been earlier than the middle of the eighth century. So an ingenious solution was found: to fill the gap the Romans invented thirteen kings at Alba Longa, interpolating them between Aeneas and Romulus. Thus this line of Alban kings made possible a reconciliation between Romulus and a Latin origin, and Aeneas and a Trojan origin of Rome.

Variations of the chief legends proliferated: between twenty-five and thirty distinct versions can be derived from Greek writers, all differing from the later official Roman account as given, for instance, by the annalist Fabius Pictor. These ramifications cannot be pursued here in any detail, yet some consideration must be given to the stories of Romulus and Remus, and of Aeneas, since both had a profound effect on later Roman sentiment. The legend of Romulus and Remus, which seems an essential part of Rome's story, has been assessed in varied ways : to some it appears to be a very old native myth, while others regard it as a comparatively late literary invention, partly because it is not mentioned by Greek writers before the third century. It had, however, clearly developed by the end of the fourth century; in 296 BC two aediles, the Ogulnii, set up a statue of the she-wolf and the two children at Rome, and some thirty years later the wolf and twins were depicted on early Roman coins (p. 354). It is, however, improbable that the much earlier statue of the Capitoline wolf (c. 500 BC) was connected with Romulus and Remus; the figures of the twins were added in Renaissance times. Neither has an Etruscan *stele* in the Bologna museum which depicts a wolf suckling a child anything to do with Rome (though it does testify to the spread of such legends).

The names of the twins have caused difficulty: whereas the Romans called them Romulus and Remus, Greek writers gave Romulus and Romus. One line of argument is to believe that the Greeks invented Romus as the eponymous founder of Rome and that when the Romans, who called their founder Romulus, heard of Romus, they combined the two as twins, changing the name Romus to Remus. A more complicated explanation suggests that Romulus was only the Latin form of the Greek Romus and that the later Greeks, not realizing this, thought that they had to deal with two men and so invented the twins; when this version reached Rome, the Romans accepted it, only changing Romus to Remus. Other theories, such as that Remus was a later invention designed to account for the collegiate magistracy, need not be pursued here. On the contrary, it is not unreasonable to accept an old Roman origin, since both words are authentic Roman names : in historical times both a *gens* Romilia and a *gens* Remmia existed. And since the archaeological evidence suggests the merging of two communities at an early stage in Rome's development (p. 45), the tradition might well have derived from the existence of two early village chiefs. This would then be developed by later writers in the light of the numerous folk legends about twins and their miraculous upbringings.

Aeneas was regarded as the founder of Rome only by some Greek authors, and by no Roman writers except Sallust. The Romans, therefore, may have based the idea of their Trojan descent on Aeneas as the ancestor of the Latins rather than as the founder of their city. His story may have reached Rome from southern Etruria and Veii where he was popular at least in the fourth if not the sixth century, as shown by the statuettes, but this need not have involved the belief that he was the founder of Rome. He was, in fact, more closely linked with Lavinium which he had founded. Here the historian Timaeus learned from the inhabitants that among holy objects kept in the city was a Trojan earthenware jar which presumably contained the Penates which Aeneas had brought from Troy; these were the gods of the store cupboard (*penes*), which later were identified with Castor and Pollux. The tradition that the Trojan Penates came to Rome from Lavinium is strengthened by the discovery there of the inscription to the Dioscuri (p. 40). Further, there is said to have been a cult of Aeneas Indiges, i.e. Aeneas the divine ancestor, near Lavinium. If *LARE AINEIA D(ONUM)* is the correct reading of a fourth-century inscription found nearby, this would be additional confirmation, but unfortunately both *AINEIA* and therefore a connexion with Aeneas are uncertain. But in contrast to Lavinium there was no public cult of Aeneas at Rome itself. Further, Dionysius of Halicarnassus says that the Latins erected a hero-shrine (Heroon) to Aeneas. Again a recent archaeological discovery may or may not provide direct confirmation. A small fourth-century shrine at Lavinium had been built within the circle of an earlier seventh-century tomb, suggesting that a famous person was venerated there, but slight caution is required since it does not correspond completely with Dionysius' description of Aeneas' shrine. However that may be, close links existed between Rome and Lavinium from very early days and continued into historical times; after 338 BC all Rome's major magistrates had to go to Lavinium each year to sacrifice to the Penates and Vesta at the beginning and end of their periods of office.[8]

Varied views were also held about the precise date of the foundation of the city. The poet Ennius appears to have gone back beyond Timaeus' date of 814 BC to about 900, while at the end of the third century the annalists Fabius Pictor and Cincius Alimentus advanced it respectively to 748 and 728. Cato and Polybius followed Fabius, but a century later 753 BC, proposed by the scholar Varro, became the official date. Soon afterwards under Augustus the legends received their greatest literary enshrinement in Livy's History and Virgil's *Aeneid*. Although Timaeus and Naevius mentioned Aeneas' visit to Carthage *en route* for Italy, the story of Aeneas and Dido was Virgil's great contribution.

3. THE EARLY KINGS

The existence of kings in early Rome can only be questioned by a baseless scepticism. Their presence is attested by the analogy of the political development of other Indo-European peoples, by the institution of the interregnum, by the existence of the *rex sacrorum* and of the Regia, and by the word *regei* on the inscription found in the Forum beneath the Lapis Niger near the traditional tomb of Romulus. The attempt to dismiss them as gods is discredited, since no cult of kings existed and there is no sure indication of their divine origin either in their names or legends. Equally unsuccessful has been the attempt to regard the seven kings as personifications of the seven hills. On the other hand much of the Roman tradition about them is obviously false, and even their personal existence is open to question. After Romulus, it is said, there reigned Titus Tatius, Numa Pompilius, Tullus Hostilius, Ancus Marcius, Tarquinius Priscus, Servius Tullius, and Tarquinius Superbus. This canonical list was fixed by the fifth century; as these names differ from those of the great men of that century, they can scarcely have been invented in order to link later heroes with the kings of old; bearers of their gentile names only appear later in Republican history. Though a very long reign would have to be allotted to each king to fill the time between the traditional founding of Rome and of the Republic (753 and 510), yet it is not impossible that they represent the last seven kings of Rome. Indeed, the monarchy of Rome, contrasted with the leadership of a village, can hardly have existed earlier than the establishment of Rome of the Four Regions in the seventh century; this is confirmed by the central position of the palace (Regia) at the foot of the Velia.[9]

Romulus and Titus Tatius must remain as legendary as the stories told about them. Romulus is said to have increased the number of his people by two methods: he established an asylum or sanctuary on the Capitol where all outlaws could take refuge, and he planned the famous rape of the Sabine women. By holding a splendid festival in honour of Consus, the god of the granary or storehouse, he attracted to Rome many Sabines and other neighbours; his men then seized the women for themselves. Titus Tatius, king of the Sabine town of Cures, replied by leading the Sabines against Rome, and captured the Capitol through the treachery of Tarpeia (coveting what they carried on their left arms, she betrayed the citadel, only to receive as her reward the crushing weight of their shields instead of the gold armlets which she had intended). In the battle that followed, the Sabine women intervened so that peace was made and the

Romans and Sabines became one people, Romulus ruling on the Palatine, Tatius on the Capitoline. Until the death of Tatius the two kings used to take counsel with the elders and people in the valley of the Forum where they had fought; thereafter Romulus ruled alone until he was translated to heaven in a chariot by Mars.

Such legends have little historical basis, but they create many problems. The dual monarchy of Romulus and Tatius may be an attempt to explain the origin of the collegiate magistracy of the Roman Republic. The story of the asylum, which was a right used in Greek cities, might have been invented to reflect Rome's later generosity in extending her citizenship, or else to explain the origin of a 'holy' spot on the Capitol, for instance a place struck by lightning. Some historians would dismiss the rape of the Sabine women either as an attempt to find an historical explanation for certain features of Roman marriage customs or for some other reason. Others believe that the tradition of a Sabine settlement on some of the hills of Rome and its union with a Palatine settlement, together with all the related legends, should be completely rejected. But there was a Sabine element in Rome which seems to have been very early: not only was there a small infusion of Sabine words into the vocabulary of the Romans, but the latter also received a few specifically Sabine deities among their state cults. One of these was the mysterious Quirinus who was identified by the Romans with both Mars and the deified Romulus; the word may be connected with the Quirinal and also the Quirites, a name by which the Romans sometimes called themselves. Since the archaeological evidence points to the appearance of an inhuming people who occupied the Quirinal and Esquiline in early times, it seems reasonable to equate this new element with the people the Romans knew as Sabines. The word Tatius is more probably the latinized form of a Sabine rather than of an Etruscan name, but he is such a shadowy figure even in the legend that he must surely be consigned to limbo, and his name explained as designed to account for the 'Romulean' tribe Tities and the priesthood of *sodales Titii*. But nevertheless his legend may reflect a general historical truth.[10]

The figures of the next three kings stride dimly through the mists of legend: mighty priests, warriors and law-givers – but men? Naturally many institutions and deeds were wrongly attached to these heroic figures, but when they have been stripped of all their trappings by modern critics there still remains the possibility, or even the probability, that they were in some form historical persons.

Numa Pompilius was said to have been a Sabine who settled on the

Quirinal. Though the name Numa may be Etruscan, Pompilius is Sabine, the Roman form being Quinctilius, and he bears witness in all probability to the existence of those people who buried their dead on the outer hills of Rome. Moving later to a new home near the Forum, he built a palace (the Regia) and reigned in peace for forty-three years. He is the priest-king who according to Roman tradition organized the religious life of the community by establishing regular cults and priests (*flamines, pontifices*, Salii and the Vestal Virgins) and by reforming the calendar: he correlated the lunar and solar year by introducing a twelve-month in place of the 'Romulean' ten-month year. All this cannot be taken quite at its face value, since some of the changes may have been earlier, some later. Thus the Salian priests had armour of the Bronze Age type which points to an earlier institution, while the reform of the calendar seems more likely to have been the work of the later Etruscan kings. However, as few would deny the existence of Moses, though not attributing all the Mosaic legislation to the lawgiver, so some of the religious organization that took place during the regal period at Rome may well have been the work of one man who was strong enough to impose reform on the people. Thus Numa Pompilius may well have had a more material existence than his legendary counsellor, the nymph Egeria.

To the peaceful Numa succeeded the warrior Tullus Hostilius, who reigned traditionally for thirty-two years (673–642), repulsed an Alban invasion, destroyed Alba itself and transferred its population to Rome. Although there is no archaeological evidence for a catastrophic sacking of Alba in the mid-seventh century, the Iron Age settlement there gradually disappeared at about this time, and thus may have provided a basis for the story of Hostilius' action. Further, the name of the Alban Mettius Fufetius, who succeeded the dead king as commander, may be historical (Mettius is the Latin form of an Oscan magistrate called *meddix*). Tullus Hostilius has one monument in favour of his existence, the Curia Hostilia, where the Senate met; as the Hostilii did not reach the consulship or become prominent until the second century, long after the establishment of the Curia and the enrolment of Tullus in the regal canon, there is here some ground for the king to stand on.

Like Hostilius, his predecessor, Ancus Marcius belonged to a family whose later members did not reach the consulship until long after his name had been incorporated in the list of kings: the Marcii first gained the consulship in 357 BC, and they were plebeians. Thus there are two good reasons to suggest the historical reality of Ancus. He was the king wise in peace and strong in war, and although some of his exploits were invented to please the later Marcian family, he may be credited with extending Roman influence to Ostia at the mouth of the Tiber. He did not found a colony there, as asserted by tradition, but he probably gained control of the salt-pans south of the river, in rivalry with the Etruscans who held those on the north bank as well as controlling the crossing of the Tiber at Fidenae above Rome. This salt could be traded with the tribes of the interior to the east, but as it first had to be brought over the Tiber, the tradition that Ancus built the first bridge at Rome is reasonable : the fact that this Pons Sublicius was made entirely of wood (*sublica* means a 'pile') indicates its antiquity, and its construction may be linked with the *pontifices*, whose name means 'bridge-builders'. Though Ancus probably did not incorporate the Janiculum hill into Rome, as tradition tells, he may well have established a bridge-head on it to protect the salt route and his new bridge. Finally it was during his reign that Tarquinius came to Rome.

4. THE SIXTH-CENTURY KINGS

The three last kings, L. Tarquinius Priscus (616–579 BC), Servius Tullius (578–535) and L. Tarquinius Superbus (534–510), form a strong contrast to their Latin or Sabine predecessors. They emerge a little further from the twilight of legend: there can be no reasonable doubt concerning the historicity of at least two of them, and they represent a period during which Rome was either continuously or intermittently under the domination of Etruria. However much patriotic Roman tradition tries to disguise the fact, this domination was political as well as cultural; at least one Etruscan king reigned in Rome, even if an Etruscan dynasty did not establish itself. But despite the cultural influence of Etruria, Rome remained essentially a Latin city even when under direct political control. So far from being overwhelmed, she was soon able to shake off the foreign yoke and with it the monarchy.

The connection of the Tarquins with Rome is attested by Etruscan, as well as by Roman tradition. A wall painting from the François tomb at Vulci, dating from the fourth century or a little later, depicts the rescue by Macstrna (Mastarna) and Aule Vipinas (Aulus Vibenna) of Caile Vipinas (Caelius Vibenna) who had been captured by Cneve Tarchu Rumach (Cn. Tarquinius Romanus); and the killing of Tarchu himself by Marce Camitlnas. The assumption that these men were historical rather than fictitious characters is strengthened by the welcome discovery of a *bucchero* vase which was dedicated by a certain Aulus Vibenna at Veii in the mid-sixth century, whether or not this man was the same as Mastarna's friend. Attempts have been made to discredit the elder Tarquin as the double of Superbus, since many details of their careers are similar; but then though many of the deeds of Elijah are also attributed to Elisha, it is not thought necessary for that reason to roll the two prophets into one. Since the first Roman annalists to record this period lived some three hundred or more years after it, and the fuller historians, Livy and Dionysius of Halicarnassus, lived half a millennium after the fall of the Roman monarchy, it is not surprising that uncertainties may have arisen as to which of two similarly named men certain actions should be ascribed. (The fact that both also traditionally shared the name Lucius need not invalidate the evidence of the Vulci painting, since the name may be due to confusion with the Etruscan title *lucumo*.)

But if Tarquinius Priscus is to be retained because arguments against his existence are not strong, it must be admitted that little can be attributed to him with any certainty. If his end was violent, as depicted in the Vulci fresco or told in Roman tradition, which assigned his death to men suborned by the sons of Ancus Marcius, his beginnings were peaceful enough: coming from Caere or Tarquinii, he is said to have driven to Rome in a cart (Henry Tudor's later triumphal entry into London in a coach of a type used by women instead of riding on a war-horse, caused the citizens great astonishment). This tradition, even if exaggerating his peaceful entry, suggests that the Etruscan element was at first small. With a few well-chosen armed retainers he may have seized a city already surrounded by his kinsfolk and have retained his position by the beneficent influence of Etruscan culture. He was traditionally the son of Demaratus who had emigrated from Corinth to Etruria, and no doubt followed his father's interest by promoting the pottery industry (p. 23). He is said to have added a hundred members to the Senate, who were called *minores gentes*; this tradition, together with the occurrence of several Etruscan family names among the titles of the tribes established by his successor Servius (e.g. Papiria, Voltinia), suggests that Tarquin encouraged many Etruscan families to settle in Rome, where they would strengthen his power. Among other innovations attributed to him were the construction of the Cloaca Maxima to drain the Forum Valley, and the establishment of the Roman Games. Since both drainage works and games were typically Etruscan interests, he should not be denied these achievements, even though this first Cloaca was only an open drain.[11]

Servius Tullius, traditionally Tarquin's son-in-law, secured the throne through the boldness of his wife Tanaquil. One line of tradition represents him as a Latin, another as an Etruscan whose name was Mastarna. As 'Macstrna' rescued Caeles Vibenna during the mêlée in which Tarchu was killed, according to the tradition depicted on the Vulci tomb, he might well have become Tarquin's successor, as the antiquarian emperor Claudius later believed. Yet the great veneration in which Servius was held by later Romans suggests a Latin origin rather than an equation with the Etruscan Mastarna, while his historicity is supported by his Latin name which was later used only by plebeians: a fictitious king would have been given a patrician name. But even if a Latin king was thus sandwiched in between two Etruscan Tarquins, Etruscan influence nevertheless continued in Rome throughout his reign, and he perhaps even encouraged the fusion of the two cultures.[12]

Servius' reign was remarkable for many reforms, though some are falsely assigned to him. Some authorities would even rob him of his Etruscan wife, Tarquin's daughter, arguing that she was invented to illustrate the hereditary nature of the monarchy; however, the importance of women in Etruscan society advises caution. Servius' major reform was to institute new military units and property classes and thus to create a timocratic constitution. Details of this are discussed below (pp. 71ff.): it strengthened the monarchy against the nobles by advancing the middle class who supplied the legionary hoplites for the army, and it enfranchised many men whom increasing trade and industry had attracted to Etruscan Rome. He protected the city by constructing earthworks over the eastern hills, though probably not the continuous stone wall which was named after him (p. 58). He also asserted Rome's political leadership in Latium, perhaps at the expense of Aricia, an older centre of the Latin League, by establishing on the Aventine hill (a plebeian quarter of Rome) a cult of Diana, as a common federal sanctuary to which some neighbouring Latin towns had agreed.[13]

Finally, the younger Tarquin, the son or more probably the grandson of Priscus, was instigated by his ambitious wife, Tullia, Servius' own daughter, to murder Servius. He then usurped the throne, set aside the Ordinances of good king Servius and oppressed his people; he was represented in the literary tradition as a Greek tyrant dressed up in Roman regalia, but neither his historical existence as the last king of Rome nor his Etruscan nationality should be questioned. Further, his achievements were not all bad: his buildings in Rome included the temple of Jupiter Capitolinus and the Cloaca Maxima (pp. 56, 58) which would provide employment for many at Rome besides any artists or workmen that he summoned from Etruria, while he extended Roman influence in

Latium and made a treaty with Gabii (p. 61). The story of his son Sextus
and the rape of Lucretia may have little historical value, but it should not
be denied that Tarquinius Superbus was deposed by a revolution that
established the Republic. Though the Roman festival of the Regifugium
has no connection with the ejection of Tarquinius, yet the hatred which
he engendered is demonstrated by the fact that the word *rex* continued to
stink in the nostrils of the Romans until the end of the Republic. The
story of his fall will find its place in the account of Rome's relations with
her neighbours (pp. 74 ff.).

5. ETRUSCAN ROME

Whatever impetus the Etruscans may have given to the unification of the
villages, they certainly provided the architectural and engineering skills
that created the new buildings that made Rome into a city. The ground of
the later Forum had to be prepared for a civic centre by drainage, which
was traditionally carried out by both the Tarquins; there is some evidence
for such work in *c.* 620 and *c.* 570 BC (though the cappellaccio work in the
Cloaca Maxima dates to after 350). A pebble floor was then laid over the
older graves and the huts, which were replaced with houses of sun-baked
brick with tiled roofs early in the sixth century. The main street, the Via
Sacra, followed the course of the controlled stream: it ran between the
Regia and the temple of Vesta and so on towards the Capitol, while the
Vicus Tuscus diverged from the Forum to the Cattle Market (Forum
Boarium). Around this Vicus, in which stood a statue of the Etruscan god
Vortumnus, lived Etruscan craftsmen and traders.

On the north side of the Via Sacra the early huts were replaced by a
complex building, the Regia. This was described as having a double
character, being both the house (*domus*) of a *rex* (the king or possibly the
priestly *rex sacrorum*? Later it became the seat of the Pontifex Maximus)
and also a *fanum*, a sacred area containing the *sacraria* of Mars and Ops
Consiva, together with an altar. Recent excavations have revealed
something of the history of the Regia buildings, but their precise
functions remain uncertain. The first buildings belong to the period of
590–570 and were decorated with bright terracottas and reliefs of
animals and a Minotaur; a second phase, around 540, was marked by
rebuilding and the use of terracottas showing Etrusco-Ionian influence.
These earlier buildings were replaced *c.* 500 BC with a new Regia.
Although the arrangement of the earlier sixth-century buildings has
suggested to some that they were the dwelling of the *rex sacrorum*, the

traditional view that the Regia was in fact the home of the king, at any rate in his capacity as head of Roman religion, may well be true. The word *rex* scratched on a *bucchero* cup of the seventh century, found during earlier excavations in the Regia, is significant and (like the *regei* on the cippus under the Lapis Niger in the Forum) may well refer to king rather than to priest.[14]

On the opposite side of the Via Sacra was the temple of Vesta which is dated *c.* 575–550 BC by the Greek pottery found in its votive deposits. At the north-west corner of the Forum was the Comitium, the later assembly-place of the Roman people which may have been used as such when its first pavement was laid; but below this was a gravel surface of *c.* 575 BC. Terracottas similar to those of the Regia suggest a building here corresponding to the first phase of the Regia. Nearby, under a black stone (the Lapis Niger) are the remains of a shrine (*sacellum*), with a later altar flanked by two lions which was held to be the tomb of Romulus; an *aedicula*, dedicated to a primitive but unknown deity, dates to *c.* 575 BC. This Lapis Niger complex, rather than a site near the north corner of the Forum, may represent the sanctuary of Volcanus, an altar in an enclosed area which formed a platform from which the king could address his people.[15]

This great outburst of building in the sixth century is matched by similar developments in the neighbouring Forum Boarium, as excavations around the church of Sant' Ombono have revealed. A primitive altar was superseded by a temple that was erected *c.* 575 BC on a moulded podium; its terracottas resemble those of the first phase of the Regia and of the Comitium. In the third quarter of the sixth century it was reconstructed on a large new podium, with many new architectural features, together with statues of Athene and Heracles. Whether or not this archaic temple was dedicated to either Fortuna or Mater Matuta, it lay below two temples which were dedicated to these two deities, and which were built about the beginning of the fifth century. They were attributed to Servius Tullius, who may well therefore have been responsible at least for the rebuilding of the archaic temple, since its date accords with the traditional period of his reign. The site has yielded much Greek pottery from *c.* 575–450; the terracotta plaques depicting horses and charioteers are especially pleasing.[16]

The Tarquins extended the city to include the Capitoline hill where on the south side they built a great temple to Jupiter Optimus Maximus, making it the religious centre of the city. Traces of other early buildings have been found, together with a *bucchero* bowl inscribed with one of the three Etruscan inscriptions so far discovered in Rome.[17] Jupiter's temple was the crowning architectural glory of Etruscan Rome; vowed by Priscus, it was almost finished by Superbus and dedicated in the first year of the Republic. Only parts of its massive stone foundations and fragments of its terracotta antefixes and tiles still survive. It contained three *cellae*: for Jupiter, flanked by Juno and Minerva. An Etruscan master-sculptor, Vulca, was summoned from Veii to make the terracotta cult-statue of Jupiter. The temple was 180 feet wide, 210 feet long and 65 feet high, with three rows of six columns, eight feet in diameter, forming a *pronaos* in front of the *cellae*. Its gaily-coloured painted terracotta, which covered the wooden superstructure, its figured friezes and the towering figure of Jupiter in a four-horse chariot (*quadriga*) over the pediment provided an impressive yet cheerful sight.

If the artistic influence of Etruscan statues and temples on the early Romans was great, the religious impact was no less. The vaguer spirits which men hitherto had worshipped were now conceived in the form of men and women, who were honoured with temples in place of rustic altars; Jupiter, the Greatest and Best, became the state-god of the whole community. Further, this new cult was linked with the elaboration of a simple Latin ceremony, the triumph. The king led a victory procession to the temple and sacrificed on the Capitol to the god whom he had represented in the procession.[18] He then descended to the Circus Maximus in the valley between the Palatine and Aventine, where the Roman Games were held in the god's honour. These Games were ascribed to Romulus, but since the Etruscans were devoted to horse-racing they were no doubt elaborated, if not first instituted, by the Tarquins, who built wooden stands for the spectators.[19]

This expanding city needed protection, which Servius provided. It is generally agreed that the existing 'Servian' Wall belongs in the main to the fourth century; some pieces made of cappellaccio tufa may possibly represent sixth-century defence walls of some of the separate hills, but there is no evidence for a complete girdle of walls. However, Servius is to be credited with an earthwork (*agger*), more than 25 feet high and with a parallel ditch, which ran across the Quirinal, Viminal and Esquiline, blocking the heads of the valleys leading into Rome and similar to the earthworks which still survive at neighbouring Ardea and which are roughly contemporary.[20]

Thus under Etruscan rule Rome became a centralized city with a unified government, and with public buildings worthy to be set alongside those in Etruria itself; indeed, the Capitoline temple may have even outshone anything there. Something of the spirit of public life is reflected in the gaily coloured decorations and in the scenes shown on the friezes : banqueting, horsemen, chariots and men walking in procession, chariot races, strange feline beasts and minotaurs. The quantity of imported Greek pottery shows how far the cultural level of the upper classes had advanced beyond that of their predecessors who were living in huts not long before. The sixth century saw a spectacular change in Roman public life.

Under Etruscan rule Rome remained basically an agricultural community (p. 341), enriched now by the vine and viticulture,[21] but at the same time she received an immense stimulus to develop industry and commerce. The growth of town life created many fresh needs, and the technical skill of the Etruscans in metal and clay set an example for many Roman craftsmen to follow. The labour guilds which are attributed to the regal period are quite credible : bronzesmiths, potters, goldsmiths, dyers, carpenters, leather-workers, tanners and flute-players. The various pieces of terracotta revetments of the sixth century found in many parts of the city testify to the growth of a pottery industry. In bronze work the Capitoline Wolf is unique : if made by an Etruscan artist, it at least set a very high standard for native Romans to admire and imitate. It is difficult to distinguish the contribution of immigrant Etruscan artists from what is due to native Romans. No less important than any actual industry at Rome is the fact that the Etruscans extended Rome's horizon beyond the limits of a parochial state. Etruscan Rome almost certainly had a formal treaty agreement with the great trading nation of the western Mediterranean, Carthage, since the first treaty between Rome and Carthage made at the beginning of the Republic (p. 160) was probably the renewal of an earlier agreement. The Pyrgi inscriptions (p. 31) demonstrate the close contacts between Carthage and Etruscan Caere : the Tarquins of Rome will not have wished to lag behind the city from which they themselves perhaps derived (p. 54). The site of Rome offered many commercial advantages : it lay at the point where sea commerce stopped and river traffic began, it commanded the old salt route (Via Salaria) from the Tiber mouth to central Italy, while the Pons Sublicius led into the heart of the city and probably carried a large part of the growing trade between Etruria and Campania. With the development of Roman trade may be linked the beginning of a new settlement on the Aventine hill, alongside which the first river wharves were built, and the institution of a fair at the sanctuary of Diana (p. 55) where merchants from other Latin towns could meet traders from overseas.

The scale of Roman imports is shown by the quantity of Greek pottery found on the site of the city. Fragments of at least 306 vases of the period 575–500 BC (and only 26 before that date) survive, and 203 of these belong to 530–500, while no less than 253 are Attic. Thus in the latter sixth century the upper classes in Rome were not behind other Etruscan cities in their appreciation of Attic pottery.[22] Imports, of course, had to be paid for (coined money did not yet exist: cattle, or lumps of copper (*aes rude*) weighed in the balance, served as currency). What Rome had to offer was salt from the pans at the Tiber mouth, timber from the upper valleys of the Tiber and Anio, perhaps some slaves acquired as prisoners of war, and possibly some products of her industry.

Rome's debt to the Etruscans in other spheres will be mentioned in due place. However, we may note here that besides founding temples under Etruscan influence, the Romans derived anthropomorphic conceptions of deity and learnt to elaborate the practice of augury from Etruria. Politically, it was under the Etruscan kings that Rome gained a centralized government, while the trappings and insignia of the magistrates came from the same source: the lictor's axe and rods (*fasces*), the curule chair, the purple toga, the ivory rod and the golden wreath. But despite all these great changes which completely transformed Rome in the sixth century, Rome was never in any real sense an Etruscan city; she merely had to endure the domination of a small number of powerful families and receive into her midst a number of Etruscan workers. Apart from some eighth-century tombs on the Esquiline, the nearest Etruscan burial yet found lies four miles from the Forum on the Colle di S. Agata near Monte Mario. The Romans borrowed much, but they remained essentially Latin, in race, language, institutions, and religion. But their relations with the Latins were gradually altered, for the Etruscans had reorientated the city. Previously it had been a northern outpost of the Latins against Etruria; it became a southern outpost of Etruria against the Latins. The spear-head was turned from north to south.

Between the early Iron Age and the end of the regal period Rome's relations with her Latin neighbours varied considerably. According to the earliest indications her territory stretched about five miles around the city, but by the end of the sixth century it had increased to about seven times this size, as a result of almost continuous struggles which arose, often from cattle-lifting, despite the fact that Roman fetial law (p. 66) forbade wars of aggression. When a village was destroyed its land was acquired by Rome; the conquered people were often taken to Rome, though sometimes they may have been forcibly transported to a less defensible position near their captured hill town, a regular practice in the third century. Small settlements often gained security by yielding (*deditio*) before attack and the population might become the *clientes* of the king or some noble house. Thus Rome began her career of conquest with a policy of incorporation.

A few incidents stand out from a long series of raids and counter-raids. Towards the Tiber mouth Rome's expansion was early, as shown by the tradition that Ancus Marcius won the salt-pans near the site of Ostia (p. 53),[23] and that he also captured Ficana nearby; as we have seen (p. 37), recent archaeological evidence shows the importance of the sites of Ficana and Decima (Politorium) but the very latest evidence (1980) suggests that the latter survived after the traditional date of Ancus. North of the Tiber little could be done in face of the power of the Etruscan city of Veii, though the last three kings may have won some temporary successes; this is not contradicted by the existence of an Etruscan regime at Rome, because Etruscan cities often fell out with each other. To the north-east Fidenae blocked the advance of the Romans, who gained little permanent control further than some ten miles beyond the Anio. They did not join with the Faliscan peoples around Mt Soracte, who were akin to them.[24]

In the Alban Hills the Roman advance was early and successful. The tradition that Alba Longa was captured and destroyed by King Tullus is strengthened by the disappearance of Alba from history and by the fact that Aricia before long headed a Latin League, although the epic fight of the three brothers on each side, the Horatii and Curiatii, may be dismissed as legendary. Some of the defeated Albans were perhaps settled at the lower-lying Bovillae. South of the Anio the elder Tarquin took Collatia, but Tibur retained its independence. Between Tibur and the Alban Hills lay Gabii and Tusculum. With the former Tarquinius Superbus made a treaty, which was written on the ox-hide covering of a shield and was said to have been preserved until the time of Augustus in a temple on the Quirinal; there is no strong reason to suppose that it was a forgery.[25] Good relations were also probably established with Tusculum, whether or not the story that Tarquin's daughter married the chief citizen of Tusculum, Octavius Mamilius, is true (the *turris Mamilia* at Rome was very ancient and shows that the Mamilii were linked to Rome in the regal period). The extent of Rome's influence further south in Latium remains uncertain. She probably came into conflict with some of the members of the Arician League, one of which was Pometia. This town, north of the Pomptine Marshes, is said to have been captured by Tarquinius and to have yielded spoils worth forty talents of silver which were devoted to building the Capitoline temple (a record of such a dedication might well have survived into later times). Rome's control of Pometia gave her a base against pressure from the Volscians beyond. Circeii, much further south, is said to have been colonized by Tarquin; this cannot be accepted, but since Circeii is among the towns named in the first treaty between Rome and Carthage (as noted below) as 'subject to the Romans', Tarquin seems to have gained some control there.

Absorption of tribal villages by conquest was at first easy, but when many of these villages grew into politically self-conscious townships, opposition to Rome would stiffen. Rome reacted by developing a new form of incorporation, as illustrated by her relations with Gabii which entered into the Roman state by treaty (see above). The extent of this system during the regal period is uncertain, but in the treaty with Carthage, which Polybius assigns to 508 (p. 160), Rome spoke for the cities of the Latin coast who were 'subject' to her (i.e. Ardea, Antium, Circeii, Tarracina and probably Lavinium) and for those who were not. The former were probably *socii*, who recognized Rome's military leadership in individual treaties, as that of Gabii. Rome's claim to speak for those Latins 'such as were not subject' suggest that she was acting as spokesman for a league of which she was a prominent member. As has been said (p. 39), among several incipient leagues the Arician League at Lucus Ferentinae had gradually overshadowed the rest. Doubtless Rome sought to win control of these groups: thus Servius Tullius tried to centralize, rival or supplant the cult of the Arician League by building the temple to Diana on the Aventine (see p. 55). The advantages of membership of such leagues were obvious. Between all the Latins there existed a general isopolity which would probably receive greater definition among fellow-members of the league. To be able to buy and sell, to hold property or to contract a lawful marriage in another village or town (privileges later crystallized as *iura commercii et conubii*) was a great benefit. Thus under the Tarquins Latium became more united under the lead of Rome, from both the political and social points of view.

6. NOBLES, COMMONS AND THE PRIESTHOOD

The basis of Roman society was not the individual but the family, at whose head the father (*paterfamilias*) wielded autocratic power (*patria potestas*: see p. 359). When he died, his sons in turn became heads of their own households, so that the *familiae* increased. Gradually relationship would be forgotten, but various families found themselves linked by the use of a common name; thus a new social body was formed, the house or clan (*gens*), which played a vital part in Rome's growth.²⁶

Each man had a name (*nomen*) denoting his *gens*, of which there were according to Varro about a thousand, a personal name (*praenomen*), of which only thirty are known to us and about fifteen were in common use, and a surname (*cognomen*) which marked the family or group of families within the *gens*, e.g. Publius (*praenomen*) Cornelius (*nomen*) Scipio (*cognomen*). In early times the *gens* had common religious observances (*sacra*) and possessed a common place of burial, but probably it did not hold land in common. The fact that Romulus is said to have distributed conquered land *viritim* shows that the Romans themselves regarded private ownership as primitive; yet at one time there may have been some restriction on conveying or mortgaging land.²⁷ Closely attached to the *gens* or family, and enjoying some of the privileges, though not full members, were the dependants (*clientes*) who stood in a filial relationship to their patrons (*patroni*). Their origin is clear: in a primitive state the man who lacked the protection of his family could not safeguard his life or property without the legal assistance of a 'patron' – for instance, the manumitted slave, the son who broke away from his family, the stranger whom trade had attracted, or even the poor citizen who had fallen under the domination of the nobles. The patron granted protection and land for occupation; in return the client, like a medieval vassal, was expected to render certain services, such as help in ransoming his patron if captured in war, or in dowering his daughter. They were bound together by moral and religious sanctions, which are apparent in the use of the word *fides*, while he 'who weaves a net of guile about his client' is placed by Virgil on a level with the man who strikes his father.

Roman society was sharply divided into two classes, patricians and plebeians, or nobles and commons, and the early history of the Republic consists largely in the struggle of the plebeians to attain complete equality with the patricians. But the origin of the two orders is shrouded in mystery. Livy and Cicero thought that the distinction was political: Romulus selected a hundred senators whom he named *patres* and whose descendants were called patricians; the rest of the population was plebeian. Various modern theories have been advanced to explain the origin of the plebeians. One school saw in them a distinct racial element, representing a conquered people, like the English after the Norman conquest. But great divergence was displayed in determining who the conquered were: the original population subdued by Indo-European invaders or by Etruscans; or the inhabitants of conquered cities transported to Rome; or the Sabines conquered by northern invaders coming immediately from the Alban hills; or the original Latin settlers conquered by the Sabine tribes. Such views are now out of favour. Thus although there was a definite Sabine element in the state and although some believe in a Sabine conquest of Rome, ancient tradition neither identifies this element with the patricians, nor supports the view that the Roman state originated by conquest; any differences between the orders in ritual or in ceremony (e.g. marriage and burial) are due to divergences in rank and wealth, not in race. A second school, that of Mommsen, maintained that the patricians were the original settlers, the plebeians their clients and dependants. It is not, however, now generally admitted that the original settlement consisted entirely of patricians, nor is the struggle of the plebs to be conceived as the effort of a depressed non-citizen class of clients to win independence. Further, it is difficult to see how the struggle began if the plebs were originally bound by ties of loyalty and interest to their patrician patrons, for it is unlikely that they ever sank to serfdom; nor is it probable that so large a part of the population would have arisen in this way.[28]

A more satisfactory explanation is that class differences and the caste system arose from economic conditions. A *plebs urbana* would gradually be formed by the humble traders who were attracted to the city and by clients who lost their patrons; and later, when the nobles became more exclusive, even by more wealthy merchants. At the same time a *plebs rustica* arose from the farmers ruined by war or other causes. Land varied in productivity; the soil of the central plains might be washed away or deteriorate under continual cultivation, so that some farmers would gain at the expense of their fellows whom they could exploit more and more as their capital increased. A caste system of the successful and the failures grew up and hardened under the Etruscan rule; no such distinct cleavage between the orders is noticeable in other Latin cities which were not subjected to the Etruscans for so long. Yet the plebeians probably did not in early times sink to the condition of serfs, bound to the soil, for the oligarchical tendencies of the aristocracy were checked by the Etruscans who made the plebs class-conscious.[29]

It can no longer be maintained that the citizen body of early Rome was composed solely from the patrician clans. The plebs were citizens, and their struggle against the nobles was not for admission to citizenship but for certain privileges from which they were excluded. Like the patricians, they were organized in *gentes*, some of which even bore the same names as patrician *gentes*. And since the *gentes* had no official position in the state, the aristocracy could not easily have objected to the organization of successful plebeian families into *gentes*, constituted for the practice of common cults and the exercise of rights of succession, nor even to them attaching clients to themselves. The point at which the citizen body definitely hardened into these two sharply divided orders must probably be set later than is often supposed: while doubtless a distinction between oligarchy and the masses was always a feature of Rome's political existence, the emergence of a patriciate as such may belong only to the later regal period and the early fifth century. In fact, the patricians probably made a final attempt to increase their exclusiveness when in 450 the decemviral legislation forbade intermarriage with plebeians, probably for the first time.[30]

The origin and meaning of the division of the patrician *gentes* into *maiores* and *minores* are uncertain. Traditionally Tarquinius Priscus added to the *patres* a hundred members *minorum gentium*, who perhaps were either less successful patricians or else a highly successful body of plebeians who were admitted into the patriciate while it was still hardening into a caste. When Alba fell, its chief families were added to the *patres* by Tullus Hostilius, while even after the fall of the monarchy the Sabine *gens* of the Claudii is said to have migrated to Rome and to have been co-opted into the patrician body by the Senate. Nevertheless the aristocracy increasingly tried to assert its supremacy, alike in political, social and religious life. The political aspect will be dealt with in the next section; suffice it to say that they alone in practice formed the Senate and held any offices which existed under the monarchy. Socially they maintained their exclusiveness by avoiding intermarriage with the plebs. They practised a form of marriage, named *confarreatio* after the cakes of spelt (*far*) offered to Jupiter, at which the Pontifex Maximus and *flamen Dialis* officiated. The plebs used two forms of marriage, both legally valid: *coemptio*, originally marriage by purchase, and *usus*. This avoidance of intermarriage was one cause of the decline of the patricians: of the seventy *gentes* represented in the early Republic only twenty-four are found among the higher magistrates between 366 and 179 BC. This gradual extinction, which was hastened by the heavy toll which war levied on the nobles, incidentally favoured the rise of the plebs, whose ranks would be swelled by the clients of patrician families which died out.

The third factor in the caste system was the patrician control of the religious institutions of the state (see Chapter XVIII). The two great priestly colleges of pontiffs and augurs were in the hands of the *patres*. At the head of the pontiffs was the Pontifex Maximus who controlled the priesthoods of the flamens, Salii and Vesta. The pontiffs who were traditionally established by Numa were the guardians of the *ius divinum* and had charge of the Roman calendar. By determining what was *fas* or *nefas* they elaborated the earliest criminal code and the procedure in private law; by declaring what days were lucky (*fasti*) or unlucky (*nefasti*) and by their interpretation of prodigies they obtained considerable influence over public business. Hardly less political power was wielded by the College of the Augurs, which Romulus is said to have established. All state business needed *auspicia*, signs duly observed which showed the favour of heaven. Although the king, and in Republican times the magistrates, 'had the auspices' and were responsible, the augurs interpreted the signs vouchsafed by the gods and thus gained considerable political power.

Finally, another guild of priests, the *fetiales*, played an important role in Rome's international relations. They were established by one of the early kings to perform a ritual for which he himself had been responsible: the declaration of war and the swearing of treaties. When complaints of any act of aggression by their neighbours reached the Senate, the fetial board investigated the matter and, if necessary, sent one or more of their number to seek redress with the formula (*rerum repetitio*): 'If I unjustly or impiously demand that the aforesaid offenders be surrendered, then permit me not to return to my country.' If restitution was not made during a thirty-days' interval while the Roman citizens were mustering for war and a standard was flying on the citadel, the *fetiales* returned and called on the gods to witness that they had been wronged and that their cause was just (*testatio deorum*). The Senate then decided on war, which was confirmed by the people, a messenger was sent to hurl a magical charred spear into the enemy's territory, and a 'just' war was thus proclaimed (*indictio belli*). This procedure demonstrates that the normal relationship between Rome and her neighbours was that of peace, not war, and that Roman custom did not recognize an aggressive spirit or territorial covetousness as legitimate causes for war: a custom which arose less perhaps from moral scruples than from an inherent desire for law and order and from a clear recognition of the value of peace. As fetial priests existed in other Latin towns and even among the Samnites, they helped to build up a primitive, but generally accepted code.[31]

Such then were some of the privileges which the patricians reserved for themselves. The plebeians were citizens and had a vote in the meeting known as the Comitia Curiata (*ius suffragii*); if in theory they could sit on the Council of the *patres* or hold any magisterial office (*ius honoris*), in practice they would seldom succeed. Of the private rights of trade and marriage (*iura commercii et conubii*) they exercised the former, which included the right to hold property, but if they possessed the latter they were seldom able to avail themselves of it. In addition, they were excluded from knowledge of the law and from the conduct of the state's relations with its gods. Large numbers of them were bound by the ties of personal *clientela* to individual patrician *patroni*, whose interests they were obliged to foster, while those who lacked a patron's protection may well have been in an even worse position.

7. POLITICAL ORGANIZATION

In primitive times the Roman people was divided into three tribes (*tribus*), the Ramnes, Tities and Luceres, about which very little is known. They probably do not represent three original settlements of Romans, Sabines and Etruscans and may even comprise groupings that existed before Rome in any sense became a city. Some scholars believe that their names are Etruscan, and that consequently their origin is much later, but the names could be later Etruscanized forms of earlier Latin words. Unlike the Greek phylae, they had, as far as we know, no political significance.[32] Rather, the earliest group of importance is the *curia*, ten of which were said to form each tribe.

The establishment of thirty *curiae* is attributed to Romulus. A *curia* meant both a 'gathering of people' (*co-viria*, i.e. a section of the Roman people included in the three tribes) and a place where they met, on the north-east corner of the slopes of the Palatine. The names, of which eight survive, are based on gentile or place names, such as Acculeia or Veliensis. The *curiae* were perhaps formed on the basis of kinship rather than of locality, because each was composed of a number of *gentes* (so that membership of a *gens* determined to which *curia* a man belonged), while the number of *gentes* in each *curia* probably varied, as did the size of the clans. The *curiae* correspond to the Attic *phratriae* and are found among other Latin peoples beside the Romans. The members banded themselves together for mutual protection, and developed three aspects, religious, military and political. Each *curia* may have had its own territory, and like any early association, each had its own cult and *sacra* presided over by its *curio*; further, groups of *curiae* held communal agricultural festivals such as the Fordicidia (when pregnant cows were sacrificed) and the Fornacalia (a feast of ovens), partly separately in each *curia*, and partly together, when they were presided over by a *curio maximus*. They paid special devotion to Juno Quiritis. Although not part of the organization of the army, each *curia* nevertheless was the unit from which a hundred infantrymen (*centuria*) were raised. Three centuries of cavalry were also raised, but perhaps directly from the tribes, since they had the tribal names of Titienses, Ramnes and Luceres (which they retained when their number was doubled to six, traditionally by Tullus Hostilius : Romulus' three centuries of *celeres* became the *sex suffragia*). As the state became more powerful than the individual families of which it was composed, the *curiae* gradually assumed the aspect of a corporate political body, the Comitia Curiata. In very early days its will was probably expressed by shouting, but at some point a system of group voting was evolved, a fundamental Roman device : within each *curia* a majority vote of all its members decided the vote of the *curia*, which counted as one unit in the vote of the whole Comitia. It included all the citizens, not the patricians alone (if in fact such a clear-cut division yet existed), but its powers and duties were limited by the executive power of the king and the consultative rights of the Senate. In practice, the method of voting was less democratic than it appears, for in each *curia* the well-organized noble clans and their dependents outweighed the scattered votes of the plebs ; a majority of groups, not necessarily an absolute majority of individuals, decided each question. The Comitia Curiata met to witness certain private acts, such as adoption and the execution of the early form of will. It conferred authority (*imperium*) on the king, but had little choice as to the ruler himself, who had been nominated by an *interrex* and ratified by the Senate. It met to hear the king's decrees, as there was no other way of publishing them, and it might be called upon to express consent to the declaration of war. Thus the power of the people found little effective expression.[33]

A Council of Elders (*senatus*) was formed by certain leading members of patrician *gentes*, but not by the heads of all of them ; it was rather a body of advisers selected by the king from the ruling families. Its numbers varied ; Romulus is said to have chosen one hundred ; with Tatius he doubled the number by admitting representatives of the *minores gentes*. Livy attributes this action to Tarquinius Priscus who, according to Dionysius, raised the total to three hundred, which remained the normal number till the day of Sulla ; but these figures are doubtless too large for the early period and are suppositions on the part of later writers. Once appointed, the senators held office for life, and vacancies were filled by the king who added to the list (*conscribere*); thus the Senate had the double title of Patres (et) Conscripti.[34] Its powers were at first consultative rather than deliberative.

Custom demanded that the king should summon and consult the *patres*, but he could reject their advice (*senatus consultum*). At the king's death, the one occasion when they could meet unsummoned, they appointed an *interrex* or viceroy, or several in succession, to nominate a king. The existence of *interreges* thus upheld the continuity of *imperium*, and there was no 'demise of the Crown'. The candidate chosen by the *interrex* had then to be sanctioned by the *patrum auctoritas*. As the Senate lived on while kings came and went, it became the repository of ancestral custom and of the traditional knowledge of divine and human law, by which the *pax deorum* could be maintained; it conferred on the king himself, and later on the consuls, the authority to perform the *auspicia* to determine the will of heaven. It thus came to gain a unique authority in the state, though in the regal period it was of little political account.

All administrative and executive power (*imperium*) was vested in the king or in those to whom he delegated it. The kingship was elective, not hereditary; though the king may have nominated or suggested his successor, who might coincide with the choice of the *interrex*, he had apparently no right to do this. However simple the outward style of the earlier Latin kings may or may not have been, the authority of the later Etruscan kings was reflected in their trappings of office. On formal occasions they sat, arrayed in purple, on an ivory chair (*sella curulis*, so called because it was set on a chariot, *currus*) and were attended by lictors carrying the *fasces* which grimly exhibited their *imperium* (p. 32). After successful campaigns they led their army in triumphal procession through the city streets. At this ceremony, which may originally have involved a ritual purification of the soldiers and city, the Etruscan kings wore the purple and gold clothing of Jupiter, and had their faces painted with vermilion like that of the god's terracotta statue in the Capitoline temple. As the triumphator stood in his four-horsed chariot, his escorting army shouted '*io, triumphe*' (while a servant in the chariot kept repeating: 'Remember that you are mortal').[35] Once elected, the king held office for life and was supreme as general, priest and judge. Perhaps his primary function had been to rule and guide (*regere*) the people in war. To this end he could impose a war tax (*tributum*), and he exercised power of life and death over his troops. As priest he was responsible for maintaining the *pax deorum* and for the performance of religious rites, auspices and festivals. He could delegate any of his functions to subordinates: he could leave a *praefectus urbi* in charge of the city when he rode forth to war, and he nominated pontiffs, augurs or flamens to share his religious duties.

One of his chief duties as priest was fixing the calendar of the year.

Numa as we have seen (p. 52) was credited with the creation of a new twelve-month calendar to replace the older ten-month one (March to December) which in turn had traditionally been the work of Romulus. This reform, however, although almost certainly belonging to the regal period, was more probably the work of one of the Etruscan kings. The new calendar helped to correlate the lunar with the solar year, but had to be adjusted at suitable intervals by the insertion of an intercalary month of 22 or 23 days (a refinement which was perhaps added or elaborated in 450 BC). The king was responsible personally for reporting to his people, on the calends (the first day of the month), after a minor priest had announced to him the appearance of the new moon. King and priest then sacrificed to Juno, while the *regina*, the king's wife, sacrificed to her in the Regia. He then summoned the people (cf. *calare*, to call) and an announcement was made about how many days would elapse until the nones (either the fifth or seventh day). This notice was required in order to give the country people time to gather on the nones to hear the king himself announce which days of the month would be *fasti*, which *nefasti*, that is, days on which public business, such as the summoning of an assembly or the dispensation of justice, might or might not be transacted.[36]

As judge the king wielded wide powers, especially in cases of treason and homicide, although we cannot trace in detail the relationship of public to private law. A number of *leges regiae* were ascribed to the regal period.[37] To some extent the king's jurisdiction was limited by the authority of the *paterfamilias* over his household and by the power of the *gentes*, so that his ability to intervene in disputes between private citizens was restricted. On the other hand, he was responsible for the security of the state, so he delegated capital cases to specially appointed officials: *duoviri perduellionis*, who dealt with cases of treason (*perduellio*), and *quaestores* (later *quaestores parricidii*) to investigate murder (the precise meaning of *parricidium* is uncertain: later it was applied to the murder of a father).[38] The punishments suggest great antiquity: hanging on a tree sacred to the infernal gods for *perduellio*, and sewing in a sack and casting into the Tiber for *parricidium*. Whether any possibility of appeal to the people (*provocatio*) existed in the regal period is uncertain. Cicero (*de rep.*, i, 54) said that it did: this he said on the authority of the records of the pontiffs and the augural books of his own day. If he was right, any revision of a capital sentence by the Comitia Curiata must surely have depended on the king's pleasure rather than on any law. In general, the king's control of criminal justice seems to have been effective; at any rate the blood-feud, which bedevilled so many early states, as for instance Athens, was absent from early Rome.

The extent of the king's authority depended upon his relation to the Senate. Many have judged that this had a contractual basis: the leaders of the *gentes* chose a leader for war and religious matters, while retaining for themselves in the Senate considerable power. Others have insisted on the absoluteness of the king's authority. The truth may lie perhaps somewhere between these extremes, which in a sense correspond to the two successive stages which Roman historians later saw in the development of the monarchy: the early Latin-Sabine kings respected the *gentes*, while the later Etruscan rulers were more aggressive and lawless.

Servius Tullius is credited with a reform, military in origin and political in development, which had far-reaching consequences. In order to meet the growing military needs of the day it was considered necessary to take a census of the people and to reclassify them on the basis of wealth and age in a new structure that would supersede the old 'Romulean' tribes and gentile *curiae*. A chief reason for the complexity of the reform was the desirability of incorporating into the citizen body all the immigrants whom trade had attracted to Rome in order to make them liable for military service, but this could scarcely be effected through the existing conservative *curiae*, which were based on kinship. So a system of new tribes was devised, which was based on a census of all free residents and in which domicile was the title to citizenship. From this change there developed a new political assembly, which gradually ousted the older Comitia Curiata. The ancient accounts of this reform record many details which were elaborated only after years of development: consequently many scholars would date the reform to the fifth or even the beginning of the fourth century. But although it scarcely sprang complete from the head of Servius, its essence probably goes back to the regal period. It will therefore be described at this point, though it must be remembered that its principles rather than its details belong to this age.

For the sake of simplicity it will be convenient to consider the military aspects first: this will involve tracing the growth of the Roman army. The earliest army comprised some 3,000 infantry, each of the three Romulean tribes providing 1,000 men commanded by a *tribunus militum*, and each of the corps being divided into ten units (*centuriae*) which corresponded to the ten *curiae* of each tribe (p. 67). In addition, three squadrons of 100 horsemen (*equites* or *celeres*), each under a *tribunus celerum*, were raised, directly from the tribes. Armed probably with a long body-shield and throwing-spear, the early Roman soldier fought in a somewhat rough-

and-ready fashion, like the armies of other city-states in their earlier 'heroic' stages of growth. The nobles (whether patricians alone is uncertain) provided the cavalry, whose role in battle is also obscure: possibly the *equites* may primarily have formed the king's bodyguard and not have played a major part in battle tactics.[39] But radical changes in methods of warfare had been taking place in Greece in the early seventh century and had spread to Etruria certainly by the time of Servius Tullius. These consisted in the adoption of a new battle-line of heavily-armed soldiers (hoplites) who were suitably equipped: the full panoply comprised helmet, breastplate, greaves, shield, sword and spear. To meet Rome's expanding military, economic and social needs Servius Tullius instituted a major reform of the army: he doubled the number of men, levied them on the basis of wealth, of new tribes (see below) in place of the old three, and of centuries in place of the old thousands. The new levy (*legio*) now consisted of 6,000 infantry, organized into sixty centuries ; the men were armed with a sword and a round shield (*clipeus*) fastened to the forearm (one such bronze *clipeus* has been found in a tomb of *c*. 600 BC on the Esquiline).[40] The cavalry was also increased, either to six centuries (*sex suffragia*) or possibly in two stages, first (by Tarquinius Priscus ?) to six and then by Servius to eighteen ; these consisted of sixty *turmae*, each of thirty *equites*, corresponding to the sixty centuries of the legion.[41] The new battle-line of sixty centuries of hoplites was the *classis*, with all the rest named *infra classem* ; or possibly, even at the time of its establishment by Servius a division into five *classes* had already been made, and the battle-line was formed by members of the top three *classes*. In other words, some scholars would see two stages of development here (first a single undifferentiated *classis*, then a fivefold subdivision), others only one (five *classes* from the beginning of the reform).[42] The next stage of development, which falls after the regal period (either when the Republic was established or later) was the division of this organization into two legions, each of 3,000 legionaries, each commanded by a consul.

The basis of the Servian reform was a registration of property, primarily in land, and a classification of the population in accordance with their scheduled wealth for military purposes. In order to accomplish the registration, the three Romulean tribes were superseded by the creation of four *urban* tribes in Rome and sixteen *rustic* tribes in the *ager Romanus*.[43] The Roman people, beside being registered in these tribes, was then divided into five *classes* differentiated by their equipment. According to the traditional scheme each member of the first class provided for himself a full panoply, the second class lacked a bronze corslet, the other classes had less, the fifth nothing but slings and stones. This classification was based on a registration of property; the ratings ranged from 100,000 *asses* of the first class to 11,000 of the fifth. These figures represent the attempt of a later generation to interpret the early ratings in terms of a bronze currency which had not yet been introduced; but the proportions of the five ratings $(20:15:10:5:2\frac{1}{2}:$ or 2) may represent an original apportionment in land, the minimum being a plot of two *iugera*. More important was the subdivision of these five classes into centuries or companies; in each class half the centuries were made up of elder (*seniores*; men from 47 to 60) and half of younger men (*iuniores*; from 17 to 46). The centuries in each class were unequal in number, as the state naturally drew more heavily upon the well-equipped richer men than on the poorly-equipped masses. Thus the first class contained 80 centuries; the second, third and fourth 20 each; the fifth 30. This makes a total of 170 centuries of combatant infantry, half senior, half junior. Below this there were 5 (or 6) centuries of unarmed men, whose property was too little to justify enrolment in the fifth class. They were registered by 'heads' (*capitecensi*) and served the state not by giving their money in taxes or their life-blood in war, but in such capacities as armourers, smiths, trumpeters, etc. They, or one century of them, were the *proletarii*. At the other extreme was the cavalry (*equites*), which consisted of 18 centuries: 6 already established and 12 more added. These were raised by the leading men who could keep their own warhorses, and they took precedence over the five classes.

This new organization based on 193 centuries was designed for military needs. The centuries formed the basis for recruiting, and the junior centuries of the first three classes probably formed the infantry of the line. But from it there developed a political body called the Comitia Centuriata, or the assembly-by-centuries. Its military origin is clear: it was summoned by blast of trumpets, it met in the Field of Mars outside the city, and during its meetings red flags which were struck on the enemy's approach flew on the Arx and the Janiculum. It was the 'nation in arms'. But as the census embraced the whole free population a century would contain more men than were actually called up to serve as a military century. Within the meeting of the centuries a system of group voting prevailed as in the Comitia Curiata. Each century recorded a vote which had been determined by a majority vote of its members. The centuries voted in order of precedence, first those of the equites, then the five classes in succession and finally the last five centuries of supernumeraries. As the centuries of the cavalry and the first class numbered 98 (18 and 80) they obtained a clear majority in the total of 193 centuries if they voted solid. That is, the rich, though numerically inferior, could outvote the poor by means of an actual majority of group votes; this was by no means unfair, as it was they who had to bear the chief burden of fighting and financing the wars. The system was thus timocratic, somewhat similar to that established by Solon at Athens in 590 (of which the Romans may not have been unaware).

How soon the centuries began to function as a political assembly remains controversial. It must have been before the mid-fifth century, since the mention in the Twelve Tables of a *comitiatus maximus* almost certainly refers to the Comitia Centuriata (though some still apply it to the Curiata). It is reasonable, therefore, to place its beginning not later than the establishment of the Republic, and, if so, it does not strain credulity to date it where Roman tradition dated it (although its structure at that time may have been simpler than the quintuple class division). If, then, it met in the regal period, it presumably voted on proposals of the king concerning peace and war and approved the choice of commanders created by him, but it will have lacked the right to initiate business.[44]

Thus Servius may be credited with setting in motion far-reaching reforms: he skilfully created new tribes in order to incorporate an enlarged citizen body (as Cleisthenes did at Athens); he was thus enabled to increase the size of the army and modernize its method of fighting; this involved a new grading of wealth which gave rise to a timocratic assembly. However, by enlarging the army he strengthened not only Rome but also his own power, since the backbone of the army was formed by the middle class. The nobles, who relied on the support of their *gentes*, will have been resentful, and the process by which they were beginning to form a separate class, the patriciate, by claiming more religious, social and political privileges, was probably slowed down. After Servius had been murdered by his daughter Tullia his successor Tarquinius Superbus is said to have maintained his rule for another quarter of a century; but nevertheless the days of the monarchy at Rome, as in other Etruscan cities, were numbered.

8. THE FALL OF THE MONARCHY

The fall of Tarquinius Superbus at Rome, the collapse of Etruscan power in Latium, the history of Lars Porsenna, the gradual decline of Etruscan influence at Rome, and the establishment of a Republican constitution all form part of an interrelated story, which can scarcely be reconstructed in any detail today. Legend tells that the rape of Lucretia, wife of Tarquinius

Collatinus, by Sextus, son of Superbus, provoked L. Iunius Brutus and a band of nobles to encompass the fall of Superbus by inciting the people and army of Rome to revolt. While Sextus fled to Gabii, where he was killed, his father and two brothers found refuge in Caere.[45] At Rome the monarchy was abolished and two annually-elected magistrates took the helm. One of these, Brutus, subsequently slew his own sons who had joined a conspiracy to bring back the house of Tarquin, and then met his death in an indecisive battle at Silva Arsia against the forces of Etruscan Tarquinii and Veii which the exiled Tarquins had summoned to their aid. Lars Porsenna of Clusium then rallied the Etruscans in Tarquin's cause and marched on Rome, which he would have captured had not Horatius (and two companions who had Etruscan names) held the bridge over the Tiber; later he called off the siege of the city, impressed by the bravery of the Romans shown in the exploits of Mucius Scaevola and Cloelia.[46]

This heroic tradition, however, was designed to veil the fact that Porsenna at one time succeeded in capturing Rome, as Tacitus and other later Roman writers knew. One difficulty in the story, namely that Clusium was beyond Rome's political horizon, is surmounted by a modern theory which sees in Porsenna a chieftain of Veii (an alternative ancient tradition derived him from Volsinii).[47] However, it is unlikely that he was in league with the Tarquins, who despite his success were not restored to Rome; rather it is likely that it was he who helped to overthrow them. In any case his stay in Rome was brief. Other Latin cities, encouraged by Rome's example to seek freedom from the Etruscans, sought help from Aristodemus of Cumae, who had checked the Etruscan advance into Campania many years before (pp. 34f.); at Aricia their combined forces defeated the army, led by Porsenna's son Arruns, which he sent against them (c. 506). Whether Porsenna, after his success at Rome, was attempting to push further south, or whether Aristodemus and the Latins were mounting a counter-attack, is not certain, but at any rate Rome had no part in the battle since she was in Etruscan hands. The immediate result of the battle was that the victorious Latins could now cut the land communications between Etruria and Campania, while Aristodemus strengthened his rule at Cumae. The record of these events provides important support for the essential reliability of the Roman tradition. Fortunately Dionysius of Halicarnassus described these operations at some length (vii, 5–6), and his account was based on a local history of Cumae or at any rate on a source quite separate from the Roman annalistic tradition. Thus the chronology of the fall of the monarchy at Rome is confirmed in general terms by an independent Greek tradition, a fact which many critics of the early Roman tradition have tended to overlook.[48]

Tarquinius Superbus then found refuge with his son-in-law, Mamilius Octavius of Tusculum, who had persuaded the Latins, according to Roman tradition, to take up arms on behalf of the exiled king and to engage the Romans at the battle of Lake Regillus. Tarquin was probably not in fact the cause of the battle : the Latins, who had successfully co-operated at Aricia, were organized in a league from which Rome was excluded, and two rival groups clashed (p. 92). Soon afterwards, in 495, Tarquin is said to have died at Cumae where Aristodemus had granted him a final refuge. Thus although the story of Superbus was decked out by the Roman annalists with a mass of fictitious details, some of which were borrowed from Greek stories of wicked despots, there is no need to doubt that he made himself odious by tyrannical conduct and that his fall in 510/09 was brought about by a conspiracy of nobles; with this bloodless revolution the monarchy was replaced in Rome by a republic, the whole series of events forming one episode in the collapse of Etruscan dominion in Italy. However, the expulsion of an Etruscan ruler did not mean the abrupt end of Etruscan influence in Rome : the revolution was political rather than cultural, and there was no wholesale expulsion of Etruscans who had settled in Rome. In fact some magistrates with Etruscan names were even elected to office in the course of the next few years, Etruscan art flourished in the city for another half-century, and Greek pottery continued to be imported though on a declining scale, and new temples were still built (p. 82). Thus the fall of Tarquin was followed by a few decades which may be called sub-Etruscan, marked by the activities of men like Porsenna. Nor was Rome's condition unique : times were disturbed, and in other Etruscan cities control was passing from kings to ambitious nobles, who with bands of their clients strove for power. The story of how the clan of the Fabii and their clients fought against Veii at the Cremera (p. 98) in *c*. 475 illustrates the way in which individual groups could still operate.

The traditional account of the end of the monarchy admittedly provokes many serious problems, but the solutions proposed by various modern writers who abandon the main outline are varied and often mutually contradictory, so that many still feel that what the later Romans themselves believed about these events may be nearer to the truth. An account of some recent theories is therefore given in the notes rather than here.[49]

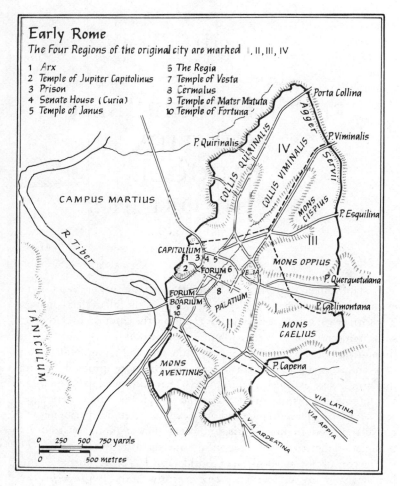

Early Rome

The Four Regions of the original city are marked I, II, III, IV

1 Arx
2 Temple of Jupiter Capitolinus
3 Prison
4 Senate House (Curia)
5 Temple of Janus
6 The Regia
7 Temple of Vesta
8 Cermalus
9 Temple of Mater Matuta
10 Temple of Fortuna

CAMPUS MARTIUS

R. Tiber

IANICULUM

Porta Collina

P. Quirinalis

P. Viminalis

Agger

COLLIS QUIRINALIS

COLLIS VIMINALIS

Servii

IV

MONS CISPIUS

P. Esquilina

CAPITOLIUM

1 3 4 5
2
FORUM 6
7
VE 1A

III

MONS OPPIUS

P. Querquetulana

FORUM
BOARIUM
9
10

8

PALATIUM

I

P. Caelimontana

II

MONS CAELIUS

MONS AVENTINUS

P. Capena

VIA LATINA

VIA APPIA

VIA ARDEATINA

0   250   500   750 yards

0   500 metres

MAP I

III

THE NEW REPUBLIC
AND THE
STRUGGLE
OF THE ORDERS

1. THE REPUBLICAN GOVERNMENT

The establishment of the Roman Republic was due either to revolution or evolution; it was either the effect or the cause of the fall of the monarchy. The former view is that presented by tradition, the latter is a hypothesis of some modern scholars. We may here accept the traditional view that after the sudden fall of Tarquinius Superbus the monarchy was abolished and two annual magistrates named consuls (or more probably at first 'praetors') were established in its place.[1] They continued to be appointed throughout the history of the Republic except when they were superseded once by a Decemvirate and on occasions by 'military tribunes with consular power'. In times of crisis, however, they might be constrained to nominate a dictator, who temporarily overshadowed them.[2]

The consuls (or 'praetors') had considerably less power than the kings, but they were invested with supreme executive authority (*imperium*) and were the executive head of the state. They possessed full military *imperium*, which included powers of life and death in the military sphere. They exercised supreme criminal and civil jurisdiction and could 'coerce' private citizens even in peace-time. But 'at home' (*domi*) within the *pomerium* their criminal jurisdiction was checked by the right of every citizen to appeal (*provocare*) to the people against a capital sentence: a right which the Romans believed to have been coeval with the Republic (Lex Valeria).[3] With their subordinate officers they were responsible for the financial and general administration of the state. This supreme executive authority, which was a basic constitutional conception, was conferred by the Comitia Curiata on those candidates who had been designated by the previous consuls and chosen by the Comitia Centuriata. It was only vested in the consuls and praetors (i.e. the original 'praetors' and the judicial praetors established later) or in those who took their place: the dictator, his master of horse and the *interrex*. Later magistrates, e.g. censors and aediles, who took over some of the consuls' duties, did not obtain *imperium*.[4]

The great power of the consuls was limited in the religious sphere, where they had not the same prestige as the kings, by the *rex sacrorum* and the Pontifex Maximus. The former was the direct successor of the kings and was provided with an official house in the Forum, the Regia, but it was the Pontifex Maximus who soon became the more influential: he gained control of the calendar, nominated the Flamines and the Vestal Virgins and generally wielded great authority. In fact the nobles may well have created this office, which was held for life, in order to prevent the priesthoods, which they themselves held, from being controlled by the successor of the king, the *rex sacrorum*.[5]

The two main brakes which prevented the consuls driving the state chariot wherever they wished were the time-limit of their office and the principle of mutual control. They had to abdicate at the end of a year; continuity of government rested in the Senate, not in the magistrates. Secondly, the principle of collegiality, i.e. of investing the two consuls with equal and co-ordinate authority, enabled the one to check and nullify the acts of his colleague by right of veto (*intercessio*), for 'no' always overcame 'yes'. Further, the consul was hampered by the theoretical sovereignty of the people, and by custom, *mos maiorum*; for instance, he was forced by weight of public opinion (at some point) to allow the right of appeal and, like the king, he consulted the Senate from moral, not legal, obligations. The main body of the patricians, who formed the economic and military, though not the numerical, basis of the state, was sufficient to check any consul's aspirations to tyranny;[6] and later the consul's own power became more limited, while the Roman people found in the tribune a protector against both the patricians and any magistrate who aspired to unconstitutional power.

Beside the consuls were the *quaestores parricidii*, or investigators of murder, whose origin is obscure (p. 70). In historical times the quaestors were responsible for public finance under consular supervision. Probably they had been temporary assistants to whom the king had delegated authority and they were still appointed to help the consuls in criminal jurisdiction and finance. Possibly they were nominated by the consuls themselves until 447 BC, when the office was filled by popular election in the Comitia Tributa. One of their legal duties may have been to pronounce on the consul's behalf sentences against which an appeal might be lodged, in order that the consular *imperium* should not be technically infringed.

In addition to the regular magistrates was the extraordinary office of dictator which superseded the others in time of internal or external danger. Appointed by the consuls for six months, the dictator had absolute power even within the city. Unlike the king or consuls who had twelve lictors, he had twenty-four. His original title may have been *magister populi*, and he himself nominated an assistant, *magister equitum*. The origin of the office is obscure. It probably does not represent a temporary reversion to monarchy, or the survival of a king with much-reduced powers, or of an auxiliary regal office. As dictators are found in other Latin towns and at the head of the Latin League, possibly Rome borrowed the conception from her kinsmen or even from the Etruscan *zilath*. If so, this would explain why Roman dictators were also appointed to celebrate the games and festivals, for the Latin dictator had religious duties. There is reason to doubt the historicity of many dictatorships recorded in the fifth century, but tradition may be correct in naming T. Larcius the first dictator *c.* 500 BC. The antiquity of the office is shown in the customs whereby the dictator was nominated at dead of night and was forbidden to mount a horse.[7]

Thus the Romans had provided an executive by creating a regular magistracy together with an extraordinary emergency one. This executive was expected by custom to rely largely on the Council of Elders and in practice it did. After the monarchy the ranks of the Senate were increased by the consuls, but the manner is uncertain; the numbers perhaps reached three hundred. But control remained essentially patrician and exclusively aristocratic. A few exceptional plebeians may have crept in, though no plebeian senator is recorded before 401 BC; but in any case certain privileges were reserved for the patrician members. Though the Senate was a deliberative body which discussed and need not vote on business, it had the right to veto all acts of the assembly which were invalid without senatorial ratification. Its advice need not be taken by the consuls and it was not as powerful as it became later when consular authority was weakened, but through its permanency it attained considerable prestige. Few consuls would flout its wishes, especially as they themselves were senators. Finally, of the two Assemblies of the People the Comitia Centuriata gained increasing political influence and took over many of the functions of the Comitia Curiata, which sank into the background only to emerge to confer *imperium* on the magistrates.

2. LAND AND DEBT

The political history of the two hundred years which followed the fall of the monarchy is mainly that of the struggle of the social orders, as the plebeians sought protection from, and then equality with, the patricians. The kings may have tried to temper the power of the nobles by giving consideration to the people, but in the Republic the plebeians had no protection against the consuls, and their political disabilities were numerous. Most, if not all, magistrates, priests and judges were patricians. But when the losses in the numerous wars with the Etruscans, Aequi and Volsci (see Chap. IV) fell mainly on the patricians, they were soon forced to realize the military value of the rapidly increasing plebeians. At the same time the plebeians, who risked their lives in Rome's defence, became conscious of their rights and found a means by which to extort them. Their method was a general strike (*secessio*); they threatened to withdraw from Rome when their military services were most needed. Tradition records five such secessions between 494 and 287 BC; not all of them are historical and many of the details are false, but this was certainly the method adopted.

This struggle between the orders was political and social, but it was also economic; the influence of this aspect has been very differently estimated. As our records of the struggle were composed after the agrarian troubles of Gracchan days, many have supposed that the economic element has been greatly exaggerated in order to provide precedents for later agrarian legislation, and that the party fights are modelled on the political upheavals of Sulla's day. Undoubtedly the influence of later history has falsified much of the traditional account, but the basic elements may still be sound. In so far as the concessions won by the plebs were political, we may suppose that the richer plebeians worked to that end. But as economic legislation also resulted, it cannot be denied that economic distress was a real cause of the trouble; whether directly or only because the leaders of the movement were clever enough to use it as a handle for their own political ends, is another question. Probably the urban plebs wanted protection and political recognition and privilege, while the country plebs clamoured for more land and greater freedom. The whole history of the struggle is closely interrelated with Rome's wars with her neighbours which are recounted in the next chapter.

The new Republic presumably wished to maintain Rome's earlier trade relations, and indeed made a treaty with Carthage which probably merely renewed an earlier agreement of regal times (p. 59). Nevertheless, her commerce and industry suffered a gradual decline. Greek pottery was still imported, but on a smaller scale than in the sixth century, until a dramatic change took place in the mid-century: fifty-three red-figure vases imported from Athens have been found at Rome which date from the years 500–450 BC, whereas only two occur from the years 450–420, and the trade did not begin to revive until *c.* 400.[8] During the early part of the fifth century Rome's commerce was matched by much building activity in the city: temples to Saturn in 496, to Mercury (the god of commerce) in 495, to Ceres, Liber and Libera on the Aventine in 495 (to secure their favour for the corn supply), to the Dioscuri in the Forum in 484, and to Dius Fidius in 466. Thus Greek artists and Roman workmen were kept busy; but then the activity died down: economic difficulties were obviously increasing, while Etruscan cultural influences were waning (as we have seen, a few men with Etruscan names occasionally even held the consulship until 487, but only a small number appear between 461 and 448). Rome was clearly reverting to a simpler state and greater dependence on what was always her main interest, agriculture.

With the decline of industry in the city, some of the workers who remained, being landless, may have sunk into some kind of dependence. But the plight of the farmers formed the main grievance. This arose from shortage of land. A strip of two *iugera* ($1\frac{1}{3}$ acres), which formed a minimum *heredium* in early Rome, was hardly sufficient to support a family, and its soil might soon be overworked and become less productive. It could be supplemented by grazing animals on commons, while the *ager publicus* could be rented from the state by individual tenants. But this was of little use to the peasant who lacked capital. The situation was aggravated by the harsh laws of debt, for a peasant would soon fall into debt when his crops failed through a series of bad seasons or when he returned from military service to find his farm ruined through mishandling or enemy raids during his absence. Whether or not he had to pay high rates of interest the nature of the contract which he formed soon reduced him to serfdom.[9] As the development of full private property was slow, probably at this period a peasant could not alienate his land outside his family, or mortgage it. At Solonian Athens land was not entailed within the family, but farms were expropriated and later restored to the debtors; at Rome we hear of no such process. As a man could not offer his land as security, he must perforce offer his person. He might anticipate events by becoming a client; if he failed to achieve this status he had to enter into a formal contract (*nexum*) which pledged personal service as security, so that the peasant became a serf until he worked off his debt. Defaulters (*addicti*) could be sold into slavery or even put to death by their creditors (at any rate in theory).[10] Though extreme cases may have been rare, it can easily be understood that the plight of the debtor was wretched. His misery and that of the town-dweller was often increased by actual shortage of food, due in part to the ravages of war. So severe were these famines in the fifth century that the government had to interfere and to import foreign corn into the home market, for instance from Cumae (492) and Sicily (488).[11] In 440 or 439 a famine was so acute that the plebs appointed L. Minucius to deal with the corn supply; when he failed, a rich plebeian, named Spurius Maelius, appeared as a *deus ex machina*, distributed corn to the people and was thereafter killed by C. Servilius Ahala for aspiring to a tyranny. Whatever the truth about Maelius may be, attempts to undermine the historicity of Minucius have failed, and there is good reason to suppose that Rome on occasion suffered from famine in the fifth and fourth centuries, as well as outbreaks of severe epidemics.[12]

The wretchedness of their economic position induced the peasants to raise the cry that land from the *ager publicus* should be distributed to individuals. Though the amount of public land at this period was small, and though such a cry was typical of Gracchan times, there is no cause to doubt this. The leader of the movement, the consul Sp. Cassius, who proposed to distribute public land, was killed for aiming at kingship (486). Many details of his story are false, and he himself bears a suspicious resemblance to Gracchus, but he may well be an historical figure who voiced the grievances of the peasants and pricked the conscience of the patricians.[13] For thirty years after his death we hear of continued but unsuccessful agitation to renew his proposal. In 456 on the proposal of L. Icilius the public land on the Aventine was distributed to provide dwellings for the plebs. This would relieve the unemployed proletariat in the city (if such existed), but it hardly affected the distress of the peasantry, which was ameliorated rather by the foundation of colonies, or outposts of Roman citizens; these served both as garrisons in newly-conquered territory and as outlets for surplus population. The conquered land would doubtless have been exploited by the patricians, so that its employment for colonies was a useful concession by the nobles, though the earlier colonies were not so numerous as tradition alleges, and many were of Latin foundation.

3. A STATE WITHIN THE STATE

Livy speaks of '*duas civitates ex una factas*' as a result of the agitation of the plebs; it would be more accurate to say that the plebs succeeded in forming a state within the state by setting up their own organizations to resist the oppressive government of the patricians. They established plebeian assemblies and officers, and forced their rivals to recognize these. Such an attempt might well have led to a bloody revolution, but tolerance and patience averted this calamity; the Romans preferred to adapt their institutions to existing needs rather than to risk disaster by trying to pour new wine into old bottles. The prelude to the bloodless revolution was the First Secession of 494 BC, when the plebs on returning from a campaign refused to enter Rome and withdrew to the Mons Sacer (the 'Mount of Curses' rather than the 'Sacred Mount'). Menenius Agrippa at last persuaded them to return, showing by a parable of the 'Belly and the Limbs' that they were a vital part of the state. A *lex sacrata* confirmed the terms of a compact, which guaranteed some economic relief to the peasants and the establishment of two plebeian tribunes as their champions. This tradition is doubtful and many historians would jettison the whole account as designed to explain the early existence of the tribunes. Others would suppose that there is a kernel of truth in the story and that early in the fifth century the plebs did secede to the Aventine, possibly in 471 when, as will be seen, the patricians officially recognized the tribunes.[14] In any case the two orders did not enter a formal contract in 494; at the most the plebs swore an oath to slay anyone who destroyed their tribunes: that is, a section of the people declared its rights and that the infringement of these would justify a revolution.

The comparative facility with which the plebs established their own assembly and officers was due to the recent 'Servian' organization of the whole people into tribes. Whatever the chief object of this reform may have been, it produced a result which its promoters can hardly have foreseen. The plebs may already have been accustomed to hold meetings to discuss their common needs; in such gatherings, which were perhaps summoned by *curiae*, the urban plebs and the clients of patrician families would predominate. Whether or no such early meetings existed, it is certain that a plebeian gathering was now organized on the new tribal and territorial basis so that the small farmers and proprietors got the upper hand, or at least a fair representation. This new Concilium Plebis Tributum had at first no constitutional position, but the patricians were gradually forced to take note of it, until in 471 a law (*lex Publilia*) gave the plebs the right to meet and elect their officers by tribes: the Concilium Plebis and the tribunes were officially recognized.[15]

So convenient was the arrangement by tribes, compared with the more cumbersome centuriate organization, that later (perhaps in 447 when the quaestorship was thrown open to popular election) it was imitated by the creation of a new assembly of the whole people meeting by tribes to simplify the conduct of business in matters of minor importance. This assembly was called the Comitia Tributa Populi and is quite distinct from the Concilium Plebis; assemblies of the whole people (*populus*) were called Comitia, meetings of the plebs alone, Concilia.[16] The functions of election, jurisdiction and legislation of the tribes remained distinct from those of the centuries.

The powers of the Concilium Plebis were strictly limited. It elected tribunes and aediles, but the Comitia Centuriata continued to elect all magistrates who had *imperium*; the Comitia Tributa, if in existence, was not yet an electing body. In jurisdiction the Concilium Plebis was not a high court of justice in capital cases tried on appeal, as legend asserts; this duty was reserved to the Comitia Centuriata. It may, however, have tried cases relating to the infliction of fines on magistrates who in any way violated the rights of the plebs; such cases came later before the Comitia Tributa. Legislation was reserved for the Comitia Centuriata, but the Concilium Plebis passed its own resolutions (*plebiscita*) which bound the plebs only; if confirmed by the centuries they became laws (*leges*). The attempt to make these resolutions binding on the whole community without other sanction forms a large factor in the subsequent history of the struggle. In other respects these meetings by tribes resembled the Comitia Centuriata. The initiative lay with the presiding officer, the tribune, and the meeting could only answer his question (*rogatio*) by voting on the group vote system. There was no debate; if discussion was necessary, it took place at a preliminary *contio*. But the plebs had won a great victory in establishing their Concilium and still more in forcing through the recognition of their officers.

The origin of the *tribuni plebis* is obscure. They were not created by the secession of 494, but are to be explained by the growth of the tribal system. Doubtless there were tribal leaders who took the initiative in administrative matters relating to the tribes; these were gradually transformed by force of circumstances into annually elected magistrates who championed the plebs. Alternatively they may have originated from landed gentry who were outside the patrician circle, held minor commands as *tribuni militum*, and voiced the grievances of the plebeians. Their power was not legal, but sacrosanct: the plebs swore that he who did violence to a tribune should be an outlaw, *sacer Iovi*. Similarly, the number of the tribunes is obscure; originally two, they were increased to perhaps four in 471 BC and to ten probably before 449 BC. Their powers were negative over the whole people, and positive over the plebs. Most important was their right to help a plebeian against the arbitrary exercise of a magistrate's *imperium* (*ius auxilii*); for this purpose the house of the inviolable tribune remained open night and day and he was forbidden to leave the city. He could enforce his will by his right to constrain even a magistrate (*coercitio*). There gradually developed a power to veto (*intercessio*) or annul any official act, so that the tribune could check the whole state machinery. On the positive side he acquired the right to consult the plebs and convene its meetings (*ius agendi cum plebe*) and thus became a plebeian magistrate. Yet he was not technically a magistrate as he had no *imperium* and his authority did not extend beyond the city. Though he checked the magistrates and represented a kind of extension of the principle of collegiality to the plebs, he too was subject to the restraint of his colleagues.[17]

In one further respect the plebs modelled their institutions on those of the city: the tribunes were given two assistants, called aediles, who stood in the same relation to them as the quaestors to the consuls. They kept the archives of the plebs (doubtless documents relating to tribal adminis-tration) in the temple of Ceres on the Aventine Mount, and after 449 BC copies of senatorial decrees were deposited with them. They had other functions, such as seizing the victims of the tribunes' *coercitio*, and later they took an important share in municipal administration.

The tribune's sacrosanctity secured his person from danger, but he lacked the trappings of office. The consul wore a robe bordered with purple (*toga praetexta*) or of full royal red when in command of an army; twelve lictors attended him with their bundles of rods (*fasces*) which, beyond the city walls, contained an axe; he had an official seat (*sella curulis*) which later gave its name to the curule offices. All this outward show of dignity the tribunes lacked, but their power grew at the expense of the consuls'. Many were the clashes between the two authorities, as can be surmised from the early story of Coriolanus, the type of proud noble who tried to spurn the tribunes' power. But the good sense of the Roman people, shown in the timely concessions of the patricians, who counten-anced the creation of plebeian assemblies and officers, averted an open revolution.

4. THE DECEMVIRS AND LAW

Having gained protection against the magistrates, the plebs next demanded that the law should be published so that the patricians might no longer be able to interpret unwritten custom as they willed. Tradition relates that the agitation started with the tribune C. Terentilius Harsa, who in 462 proposed to set up a commission of five men with consular power to write down the laws (less probably their purpose was to limit the consular *imperium*). The patricians resisted the proposal and a regular struggle between the orders continued until a compromise was reached in 454, when three commissioners were sent to Greece to study foreign legal systems. On their return it was decided to suspend the regular constitution and the magistrates, consuls and tribunes alike, and to set up as the executive government in 451 a Commission of Ten who were unhampered by the right of appeal. These decemvirs, all of whom were patricians, acted with vigour and justice and issued a code inscribed on Ten Tables, which was duly sanctioned by the Comitia Centuriata. In 450 a similar commission was established to complete their work; apart from its leader, Appius Claudius, its members were all different from those of the first commission, and some were plebeians. These commissioners added two more tables of what Cicero dubs 'unjust laws' to the existing ten and began to rule oppressively, refusing to resign. During a reign of terror when most of his colleagues were absent on military service Appius Claudius, in particular, played the tyrant. Two acts of violence heralded their fall: a brave warrior and tribune, Sicinius Dentatus, was murdered, and the maiden Verginia was slain by her own father to save her from the clutches of Appius. The plebs thereupon seceded, the decemvirs abdicated, and negotiations resulted in the restoration of constitutional government. Ten tribunes and an *interrex* were appointed, and L. Valerius Potitus and M. Horatius Barbatus were elected consuls for 449.

Few details of the account are above suspicion, but the outline is certain and is supported by the Fasti and by the fragments of the code which, though revised by later Roman jurists, still survive. Many details about Terentilius are merely later inductions, but the rarity of his name and the consensus of sources regarding the importance of his work may establish him as the pioneer in the movement to obtain a written code. The supposed visit to Greece is more doubtful, since the object was to publish existing law, not to make new laws. The story of Dentatus, a plebeian hero who was the object of patrician treachery, may have been incorporated into the more famous legend of the tyranny of the decemvirs. The poetical legend of Verginia bears some similarity to that of Lucretia, who caused the fall of another tyrant. The oppression of the second decemvirs may have been overemphasized; the necessarily somewhat harsh conditions of a primitive code may have given rise later to the view that the lawmakers were themselves harsh: were not Draco's laws said to be written in blood? Or, since the names of the second decemvirs are somewhat suspect, this second group might have been invented merely because the commission lasted more than one year. Further, the secession of the plebs is difficult to explain if five of the decemvirs were really plebeian. It has been suggested that Appius Claudius sought to abolish the 'state within the state' by allowing the plebeians a share in the supreme magistracy as well as equal laws. But as certain concessions were won by the plebs in the following year, possibly these resulted from a secession that had aimed at restoring the tribunes and the regular government when once the immediate object of the publication of the law had been attained.[18]

The Twelve Tables contained the 'whole body of Roman law' and formed 'the fountainhead of all law, public and private'.[19] Schoolboys in Cicero's day still learnt their sentences by heart. In some respects they were the Ten Commandments of the Romans. Like many early codes, such as Hammurabi's, they were a medley of primitive survivals and more progressive ideas. But they affirmed the equality of all free men in the eyes of the law and so they survived as a sound basis for society, while Hammurabi's code, which, though superior in some respects, recognized a regal power superior to law, collapsed with the civilization of Babylon. In the main the Twelve Tables are the codification of customary law, now made statute law; but in the process they were simplified and brought up to date. Though not directly modelled on Solon's code, they show the influence of Greek law, which came perhaps from contact with Greek colonies: hence the story of the Roman embassy to Greece. As the form in which they survive shows traces of further modernization by later Roman jurists, clearly they were regarded not merely as of antiquarian interest, but as a continuing living source of law.

It is not possible here to discuss the contents of the Tables or their relative antiquity, though some may be enumerated to illustrate the wide scope of the legislation. In private law a slight weakening of the *patria potestas* is noticeable in a greater recognition of a wife's rights (pp. 358ff.). But intermarriage between members of the two orders was forbidden in one of the two supplementary Tables. Since hitherto it is likely that custom rather than law had discouraged intermarriage, this measure looks like a somewhat desperate bid by the patricians to create an even stricter caste system at a time when they saw other privileges threatened. Other rules facilitated the emancipation of sons and of slaves, granted freedom of testamentary disposition, regulated inheritance, debt, usury, contracts and conveyances e.g. : 'If a man enters into a personal obligation or makes a purchase, as the tongue has spoken, so shall it be.'); the rights of association were defined, assemblies by night were forbidden as leading to treason, while guilds were permitted. Amid much that was progressive in civil law, such as a clear conception of contract and liberal testamentary laws, the executive machinery of criminal law was lacking, apart from the *quaestores parricidii*. For instance, a plaintiff received little help in carrying out a judgment which was given in his favour, and the *lex talionis* survived: 'If one breaks another's limb and fails to compound with him, let limb be given for limb'; a burglar at night could be killed on the spot. Hanging was the penalty for the destruction of standing corn; this represents an old religious survival. But while the rules of procedure for all civil actions were published, yet the set forms of words in which pleadings were to be conducted (*actiones*) remained the secret of the patrician pontiffs. The plebs had won a great victory, but they had even so to press close on the heels of their retreating foe.

5. THE WEAKENING OF PATRICIAN CONTROL

Tradition records that the legislation brought forward by Valerius and Horatius, the consuls who in 449 BC replaced the decemvirs, was a landmark in the history of the orders : the right of appeal was restored, *plebiscita* were given the force of law, and the sacrosanctity of the tribunes was reaffirmed. But, although modern writers have been busy removing the ancient landmarks, it is nonetheless possible to retain the view that by a secession in 449 the plebs forced the patricians to recognize in law the rights of the tribunes, which hitherto they had been forced to recognize only by custom. This was a great victory. Further, although it is improbable that the decrees of the people were really given the force of law, the plebs may have asserted their right to issue laws, just as previously they had asserted the rights of their tribunes; but the patricians were not yet ready to yield to this fresh plebeian attack.[20] Thus the plebs had finally established their state within the state and had obtained a clear exposition of the law. It remained for them to claim greater social equality and for their leaders to storm the stronghold of the patrician magistracies. During this siege the two opposing forces were gradually welded into one.

In 445 a tribune named Canuleius launched an attack on both the social and political fronts. He forced through a law repealing the statute of the Twelve Tables which prohibited intermarriage between the two classes ;

it was decreed that children should be enrolled in the *gens* of their father, whatever form of marriage had been contracted by the parents. Though the patrician rite of *confarreatio* was left untouched, the inclusion of sons of plebeian women in patrician *gentes* undermined the religious claim of the patricians that their clans alone were acceptable to the divine powers. Canuleius' colleagues then proposed that the consulship should be opened to the plebeians. To parry this thrust the Senate virtually abolished the office by decreeing that 'military tribunes with consular power' should be appointed in place of consuls; these officials, who at first numbered three, might be patricians or plebeians. Probably one of the military tribunes first elected in 445 was a plebeian, but plebeian representation was very slight before 400.[21] The device was a compromise: the appointment of a larger number of high officials may have answered the military needs of the day, but a real political concession had been wrested from the patricians.

At the same time the patricians, seeing their monopoly of office threatened, strove to retain some control by dividing the functions of the chief magistracy. Hitherto the consuls had been responsible for maintaining the *census* or roll of citizens; it was now decided to appoint special censors. It has been suggested that the 'Servian' reforms belong to this date and that censors were created to deal with the new classification of the citizens. Although the origin of this reform is found in the regal period, it is not improbable that the system of classes and centuries was extended at this date. Thus the establishment of the censorship allowed the consuls or military tribunes more freedom from civil affairs, and the patricians to cling to their prerogatives: for whether or not the censorship was closed to plebeians by law, no plebeian held the office for nearly a century (351). There were two censors, appointed first in 443; ten years later their period of office was fixed at eighteen months. It is uncertain how often they were appointed in the early days, but later they took office every five years, when they solemnly purified the people by a *lustrum* ('cleansing'), a ceremony at which a pig, a sheep and a bull were led in a three-fold procession and then sacrificed while a sacred fire was rekindled. At first the censors' duties were to register all citizens and their property and to assign them to the due tribes and centuries. They also made up a list of those liable to cavalry service (the equites), and later were empowered by a Lex Ovinia (before 312) to revise the list of the Senate. Gradually they acquired a general oversight over public morals and became responsible for leasing state contracts, as an Office of Works. These various wide powers soon endowed the censors, who lacked *imperium*, with an authority and dignity that raised their office to one of the most honourable in the state: it came to be regarded as the climax of a successful public career.[22]

The necessity to delegate business had resulted in the creation of the quaestors (p. 79). In 421 their number was raised to four and the office was opened to plebeians, and in 409 three out of the four quaestors were plebeians. Their functions were largely financial and they did not receive *imperium*, so that the patricians perhaps regarded this concession as small. But it was the thin end of the wedge. Later the quaestorship became the first step in an official career and gave the right to a seat on the Senate.

Thus during the fifth century the plebeians had wrested many concessions from the patricians. In civil law the two orders were equal. Socially, the right of intermarriage was affirmed despite patrician tactics. Politically, the plebeian institutions were recognized, although they did not yet form part of the constitution; the power of the tribunes increased. The patricians were still entrenched behind their religious privileges and maintained their leadership in the Senate and assemblies. Towards the end of the century the plebeians slackened in their demands, partly because there was less unity of purpose among the rich and poor members of their order; partly because the energy of many of their leaders was distracted by the foreign wars against the Aequi, Volsci and Etruscans. When the Gauls sacked Rome in 390, therefore, a fair unanimity had been established in domestic affairs. But the distress of the aftermath fanned the embers once more into a fierce blaze, which finally destroyed the patrician monopoly of government.

IV

THE ROMAN
REPUBLIC
AND ITS
NEIGHBOURS

1. THE TRIPLE ALLIANCE

When the Etruscan power in Latium collapsed after the Latin *revanche* and the battle of Aricia, the Latins naturally came into conflict with Rome, the most southerly outpost of Etruria. Yet clearly it was to their mutual advantage that ties of blood should prevail and that Rome should once again become the spearhead of the Latins, thrust into the Etruscan flank. Amid the dim mists of legends which envelop this period two facts emerge clearly: that a war was fought between Rome and the Latins, and that it ended in an alliance.[1]

The earliest treaty between Rome and Carthage shows clearly that Republican Rome claimed to uphold the hegemony in Latium which her kings had exercised. The Latins, however, refused to tolerate this and organized themselves into a league from which Rome was excluded. The identification and development of the early federations of Latins, as has been seen (p. 39), is an obscure subject. One federation met at the *nemus Aricinum*; a list of members, preserved by Cato who perhaps saw the inscription which he records, shows us that it once was led by a dictator Laevius (or Baebius) Egerius of Tusculum and included Tusculum, Aricia, Lanuvium, Lavinium, Cora, Tibur, Pometia and Ardea, an area of some 600 square miles. It quite probably should be identified with a league which met at Aqua Ferentina, in which Aricia played a leading part in the time of Tarquinius Superbus (Livy, i, 50). However that may be, the Latins probably gathered *ad caput Ferentinae* to agree their plans for war against Rome. The allied forces then met the Romans at the battle of

Lake Regillus (probably Pantano Secco) near Tusculum (499 or 496). Although tradition enlivens the fray with the presence of the Great Twin Brethren and other romantic episodes, the battle itself remains an historical fact, though it was hardly a glorious Roman victory.[2]

As a result a treaty was concluded by Spurius Cassius in 493 between Rome and thirty Latin cities as two independent powers. Rome formally resigned any claim to hegemony in Latium and recognized her position as an equal of the Latins. The Latins were willing to conclude an agreement, not because of any fictitious military disaster, but the Volsci and Aurunci were pressing hard upon them and had perhaps recently destroyed two Latin cities, Cora and Pometia. It was essential that the Latins should present a united front against their foes. The terms of this treaty, the *foedus Cassianum*, were that perpetual peace should be established between Rome and the Latins; they should render mutual aid in war and have equal shares of the booty; possibly the military command should be held in alternate years by Rome and the League; further, there should be a community of private rights between citizens of Rome and any Latin city. This last clause is of fundamental importance as it lays down the principle by which Rome ultimately united Italy. The Cassian treaty, of which a bronze copy survived in the Roman Forum till Sulla's day, remains a landmark in the early history of Rome.[3]

Soon after the Latin alliance Rome concluded a similar treaty with the Hernici of the Trerus valley, who formed a league under the leadership of Anagnia.[4] The traditional details of the alliance are uncertain; it is unlikely that the Hernici obtained the treaty by surrendering some of their territory to Rome, while its similarity to the *foedus Cassianum* explains why it also was attributed to Spurius Cassius. But its object is clear: the Hernici were saved from being crushed between the Aequi and Volsci, and the Romans by an early application of the principle of *divide et impera* won a buffer state between their enemies.

This triple alliance of the Romans, Latins and Hernici resulted from a pressing danger. At the beginning of the fifth century the Sabellian tribes of the central Apennines became restless, possibly under the first stirrings of Celtic pressure from the north. Following their tribal emblems, the wolf, bull or boar, the bands of the Sacred Spring were ever advancing to settle in new territories and coveting the fertile lowlands where they saw good winter pasturage for their herds. Their strongest thrust was in southern Italy, but they also pressed hard upon the inhabitants of the mountains that encircle Latium. These in turn presented a grave danger to the Latins. The external history of Rome during the fifth century is the story of how she and her allies had to fight for their very existence against this foreign pressure. For Rome was ringed around by foes. In the north were the Etruscans; in the north-east between the Tiber and Anio were the Sabines from around Reate; in the east among the mountains between the Anio and Trerus lay the Aequi; and in the south between the Aequi and the sea on the bastion of Monti Lepini were the Volsci. In the nick of time Rome patched up her quarrel with the Latins by a timely self-effacement and then drove a wedge between two of her enemies by the Hernican alliance.

THE SABINES, AEQUI AND VOLSCI

The Sabines caused much of this general unrest among the hill tribes, but it is uncertain how far they came into direct contact with Rome. A modern theory suggests that their influence was catastrophic: not only did they, rather than the Latins, drive the Etruscans from Latium, but they actually captured Rome in the first half of the fifth century and were not checked until a Roman victory in 449. The evidence for this view rests on the undoubtedly great influence which the Sabines exercised over Rome and on Livy's account of how Appius Herdonius with a Sabine army suddenly occupied the Capitol in 460. This story is rather improbable and the whole theory scarcely squares with the facts ;[5] these point to gradual Sabine infiltration rather than to a definite conquest, which is indicated neither by the general tradition nor by the Fasti. The Sabines had mingled with the Romans from the days when the inhuming Sabines of the Quirinal and Esquiline joined with the cremating peoples of the Palatine, and Titus Tatius was a Sabine. In 504 Attius Clausus had migrated with all his clan to Rome, where he was admitted to the patriciate ; his people received Roman citizenship and settled beyond the Anio; his Roman name was Claudius and from him sprang the famous Claudian *gens*.[6] It is more probable that other Sabines settled in and were absorbed by Rome in a similar manner, than that the Sabines conquered Rome, which did not become a Sabine, any more than an Etruscan, city; the Latin-speaking people were not unduly influenced by contact with the Sabine dialect. Further, tradition relates that Rome fought on the Sabine front for the first half of the fifth century, and it has even been suggested that she annexed Sabine territory. During the fifth century Rome occupied some of the territory between the Anio and Tiber and created the tribe of Clustumina; no doubt many skirmishes occurred, but the details of the wars recorded are mainly late inventions. After 449 nothing is said of the relations of Rome and the Sabines for the next hundred and fifty years; perhaps they were friendly, as the need to transfer sheep from summer to winter pasturage and the trade in salt would link the mountain tribes with the Roman Campagna. It was rather on the southern and northern fronts that Rome had to face serious dangers.

The Volsci, who belonged to the Osco-Sabellian group of people, dwelt during the regal period in the upper Lris valley to the west of the Fucine Lake. But the pressure of the tribes of central Italy forced them westwards to the hills between the Trerus and the coast, while the collapse of the Etruscan power in Latium tempted them still further towards the rich farms and cities of the plains below. They captured Pometia and Ardea, to judge from the legend of the maiden of Ardea; their power reached southwards to Antium and perhaps to Anxur. The most north-westerly point of their advance was Velitrae, which they either founded or captured. The origin of some of the cities in this district is uncertain; Signia, which commanded the Trerus valley, and Velitrae and Norba, which guarded the fertile plain below the Alban hills, are said to be Roman colonies founded in 495, 494 and 492. More probably they were Latin colonies, composed of men from Latin cities and Rome and established as outposts by the League, themselves full members of the League.[7] Some of them succumbed to the Volscian advance, but such hill towns as Cora, Norba and Signia towered up like rocks above the tide of the warfare which surged to and fro for long years. The traditional details of these wars are scarcely trustworthy. One episode is the story of Coriolanus. It contains three acts: the hero captures Corioli; he opposes the distribution of corn to the starving plebs and withdraws from Rome to Volscian Antium; at the head of the Volscian army he storms up to the gates of Rome in 491 and is only turned aside by his mother's prayers. Whether he was the eponymous founder of Corioli or its captor, a Roman or a Volscian, is uncertain. Possibly the story was designed to explain away a Volscian raid across the Campagna as the work of an exiled Roman; if so, the incident may be historical. Though the Volscian conquests under Coriolanus were more limited than tradition records, the Volsci may really have seized Labici and Pedum in a northern assault from Velitrae along the eastern frontiers of Tusculum; the object of this brilliant stroke will have been to cut off the Hernici from the Latins and to open up their own communications with the Aequi.[8]

Meanwhile the Aequi were battering on the eastern front of the Latins. These highlanders, whose ethnic connections are uncertain, descended from their poor and inaccessible country which stretched north-west from the Fucine Lake. Crossing the Anio one branch came down to the district around Tibur, another pressed on the Hernici, while between them a third reached the heart of Latium through the Algidus gap. Praeneste, which lay on their route, must have succumbed or allowed them free passage, while at Pedum and Labici they joined hands with their Volscian allies; it was perhaps as a result of this co-operation that Tusculum fell. The Latins, however, with the aid of the Hernici, soon snatched Tusculum out of the Aequian-Volscian pincers (484). For the next twenty years frontier struggles continued and the Aequi maintained their ground though the Latins and Hernici successfully barred the gate to the Campagna. It was on these two members of the Triple Alliance that the brunt of the fighting fell, but in 458 a Roman consul, L. Minucius, was trapped in the valley below the Mons Algidus and only five horsemen broke through to bring the news to Rome. This disaster is the prelude to the appearance of Cincinnatus, the heroic counterpart of Coriolanus in the Volscian wars. Called from the plough to assume the dictatorship, Cincinnatus soon turned the tables on the Aequi, defeated them in the same valley and then, laying aside his office, gladly returned to his farming. Many stories which were told about this pattern of early Roman manhood are naturally to be rejected, particularly those relating to such political actions as his clash with the tribunate; but it is not necessary to consign him to the realm of legend since folk-memory may have preserved some record of him. His campaign, though idealized, was typical of the long years of border warfare.

Thus for many years Rome held her own against the Aequi and Volsci with difficulty, while a large part of the burden fell on her Latin allies. But in the second half of the fifth century her army became stronger and she moved gradually to the offensive. In 444 a treaty was made with Ardea where possibly a Latin colony was sent, as a base from which to win back the Latin coast (442).[9] The decisive battle was fought against the Aequi in 431 when A. Postumius Tubertus defeated them on the Algidus. This victory, though resembling that of Cincinnatus, can scarcely be questioned. The unusual fact that it is attributed to a definite day, 19 June, speaks in its favour, while the success of the subsequent Roman offensive can only be explained by postulating such a victory. The scales were turning, Latium was freed and the Romans began to recover the lost Latin cities. In 418 Labici, which commanded the Algidus gap, received a Roman garrison. In 393 the northern thrust of the Aequi was thwarted by their ejection from the district of Tibur. The Volsci fared similarly. They were turned from Ferentinum by the Hernici in 431, and notwithstanding certain reverses, the Romans advanced steadily. Anxur was reduced in 406; Velitrae received a garrison in 404; a colony was sent to Circeii, the Gibraltar of the Latin coast, in 393; and Satricum submitted at least for the moment. Though the peace which the Volscians obtained in 396 may be an annalistic fiction, it represents correctly their exhausted condition. A century of warfare by the Triple Alliance had won back the ground lost at the beginning of the century. Though the Aequi and Volsci are called 'the implacable and daily foes of the Romans', these wars were not large-scale operations. Often in the spring each side sallied forth to burn his opponent's crops and perhaps to catch him unawares; the campaigning season was passed in raid and counter-raid and then operations were suspended till the next year. But it was in these somewhat petty struggles that Rome learnt the art of war and disciplined her sons to fight. The success which attended this gradual advance is shown by the fact that when the Gauls attacked Rome the Aequi and Volsci were not in a position to profit by Rome's weakness, but remained quiet among their hills.

3. THE DUEL WITH VEII

While Rome had co-operated with her allies on the eastern and southern fronts, she was left to face the northern menace by herself. This was centred in the city of her old rival, Etruscan Veii, some twelve miles away on the west bank of the Tiber. Veii was perched on a precipitous hill, surrounded by ravines on all sides but one; its territory was larger and more fertile, its position stronger and more healthy than that of Rome. Ancient writers tell of the wealth of this '*urbs opulentissima Etrusci nominis*' (Livy, v, 22), traces of which have been found in its necropolis and in the beauty of its temples and their statues. But Rome stood in the path of its expansion and commanded its two routes down to the Tiber, one by the Cremera valley, the other by the old Via Veientana. There was a third approach to Veii, via Caere to the coast; but Caere, though Etruscan, was hostile to Veii and friendly to Rome. A conflict between Rome and Veii was thus probable and would involve Fidenae, which lay on the east of the Tiber commanding the Cremera valley leading to Veii. The nature of the struggle was dictated by the twofold attempt of the Veientanes to keep a foothold east of the Tiber by holding Fidenae (and Eretum, a little further north), and to preserve their authority west of the Tiber, where at times they pushed down to the Janiculum Hill and the sea.

The rivalry of the two cities was ancient, arising from the attempts of each to control the salt pans at the Tiber mouth, where a small body of Roman salt workers may have settled in very early times (p. 53). If the suggestion is correct that the Porsenna to whom Rome surrendered was a king of Veii (p. 75), we then have another incident in the contest. Border raids may have long continued, but a real war is first recorded in 483–474. Tradition tells that M. Fabius and Cn. Manlius avenged a previous defeat by a victory over the Veientanes in 480. The next year, however, the Veientanes occupied the Janiculum; as a counter-thrust the Fabian *gens* fortified a camp on the Cremera, which cut Veii's communications with Fidenae. With a great variety of detail the story is told that the whole Fabian *gens* except one youth was annihilated on the Cremera in 479.[10] Thereafter the Veientanes threatened Rome itself, but as the Etruscan power weakened, their pressure slackened and a Forty Years' Peace was made with Rome in 474.

Much of the account is false, for instance the supposed siege of Rome may be a reduplication of Porsenna's siege, but it is unreasonable to reject the whole incident of the disaster on the Cremera. The record of a defeat, its connection with a particular family and its definite localization are not likely to have been invented, especially as a keen appreciation of the underlying strategy is shown. The three hundred Fabii presumably represent a few Fabii together with a number of their clients. The connection with one clan may be explained by supposing that the Fabii either had property in the area or had come to an agreement with the state to extend their territory in that direction (Diodorus recounts an ordinary battle between Romans and Veientanes on the Cremera, where the losses fell most heavily upon the Fabii). In any case the one incident of these wars which in essence can be accepted with certainty is that the Romans tried to cut the communications of Veii and Fidenae and were defeated on the Cremera. Fidenae may have been captured by Rome soon after 500, but probably it was frequently taken and retaken during the century. A formal peace may not have been established, but this tradition represents the true condition of affairs : for the following forty years nothing is heard of Veii. The Etruscan power was waning. After their collapse in Latium the Etruscans were defeated off Cumae by Hiero of Syracuse whose fleet soon harassed the shores of Etruria. Veii was an outlying part of Etruria and received only feeble support from her neighbour Caere. Thus she was quite ready to lapse into a period of obscure peace with continued control of the right bank of the Tiber, especially as Rome had behind her the full weight of the Latin League.

Rome's next step forward was to win permanent possession of

Fidenae : confused accounts of this struggle have survived. With the help of Veii Fidenae revolted; four Roman ambassadors were murdered; Cornelius Cossus won the *spolia opima* by killing Tolumnius, prince of Veii; finally Q. Servilius Fidenas captured Fidenae by driving a tunnel beneath it in 435. Fidenae again revolted in 426 and was regained in 425; the incidents of this war are so closely parallel to those of the first, that one must be a 'doublet' of the other. Two actual memorials of the struggle survived in later times : the breastplate of Lars Tolumnius, which Cossus had dedicated to Jupiter, and of which the Emperor Augustus read the inscription; and statues of the murdered Roman envoys, which stood on the Rostra till Sulla's time. Unless Augustus was guilty of a voluntary or involuntary mistake, the evidence conclusively attests the historicity of the second war and its dates as 428–425.[11] Which side took the initiative is uncertain : whether Veii made one last attempt to recover her control of the left bank of the Tiber, or Rome determined to thrust her foes beyond the river. Probably their recent victory over the Aequi on the Algidus encouraged the Romans to break down Veii's outposts. Thirty years later they carried the war to their enemy's gates.

At the end of the fifth century Rome and Veii grappled in a mortal struggle and after a long siege Veii fell in 396 In this contest Veii received little help from Etruria. A federal council of the Etruscans is said to have met, but it did little and abandoned Veii to its fate; the excuse that the Gauls were becoming a pressing danger is sometimes put forward, but more probably lack of national sentiment explains Veii's isolation. Even the neighbouring Caere refused help and maintained a benevolent neutrality towards Rome. Tarquinii indeed is said to have raided Roman territory in 397, but it was elsewhere that Veii found substantial support. Two cities, Capena near Mt Soracte, and Falerii further up the Tiber valley, which were racially Latin but politically Etruscan, anticipated Rome's northern advance and rallied to Veii's cause in 402; Falerii had also helped Fidenae earlier. Traditionally the Romans besieged Veii for ten years with varying fortunes until in 396 M. Furius Camillus was appointed dictator; with his appearance a series of strange portents and stratagems enliven the narrative. When it was reported by the Delphic oracle that Veii would not fall until the waters of the Alban Lake, which had risen abnormally high, had been drained, the Romans at once set about draining the Lake. Camillus then drove a tunnel under Veii and the Roman sappers heard the King of Veii, who was sacrificing to Juno in the temple above their heads, say that whoever should offer the sacrifice would have the victory; breaking through, the Romans offered the sacrifice and thus Veii fell. But Camillus, who was accused of keeping back part of the spoil, withdrew from Rome in exile. Much of the story is to be rejected, but the traditional date of Veii's fall is probably roughly right. The ten years' siege, though suspiciously like the ten years' siege of Troy, may be correct. A very important innovation was made during the war in the introduction of pay for the yeoman soldiers ; this marks the first stage in the transformation of a citizen militia into a professional army. Its connection with the siege of Veii lends probability to the length of the siege and suggests that this was the first time that the army, which was used to short summer campaigns, had to keep the field the whole year round. The critical tunnelling under Veii, a stratagem which is also attributed to the attack on Fidenae in 435, is improbable in view of the city's precipitous position ; it may have been suggested by local drainage systems or by the draining of the Alban Lake, if this was roughly contemporary. A memorial of the war survived into later times : Camillus had vowed a tithe of the booty to Delphi, so that a golden bowl was sent there and placed in the Treasury of the Massiliotes.[12]

The capture of Veii, which was facilitated by Rome's possession of Fidenae as an operational base, marks an important stage in Rome's external advance. The captured land was annexed and soon afterwards was formed into four new rustic tribes. This not only made Rome the largest city in Latium, but also increased her military strength since the Roman army was recruited from men who held property ; further, it gave great impetus to the democratic movement, as much of the land was made available for the plebs. Rome quickly came to terms with Veii's allies, Capena and Falerii (395 and 394). These towns were not taken over, since Capena was not at first included in one of the new tribes and Falerii survived to challenge Rome later.[13] The Romans secured their northern frontier by advancing further and reaching some agreement with Sutrium and Nepete, which Livy describes as the very gateway of Etruria : *'velut claustra inde portaeque'*. Latin colonies were soon settled at these two towns, though the exact dates are uncertain; Sutrium was perhaps colonized after the fall of Veii and Nepete some ten years later. Rome thus shared her conquest with her allies to whom she allotted the northern towns ; she herself kept the *ager Veiens* which marched with the *ager Romanus*. Her northern horizon now reached the Ciminian Hills, and Etruria lay open to attack.[14]

The century had been one of territorial conquest for both Rome and the Latins, but it also witnessed a gradual change in their relations. In the early decades conquered territory had been used for Latin colonies, such

as Signia and Norba; these became full members of the Latin League and
comprised citizens from any of the League cities or Rome. But the
Romans and Hernici soon became discontented, since all the benefits fell
to the League alone, and many of their citizens would hesitate to sacrifice
rights at Rome or Anagnia merely to become members of a Latin colony.
So they began to claim some of the conquered district for themselves; for
instance, Rome earmarked some land near the Algidus, and the Hernici
kept Ferentinum. But these acquisitions of Rome, even including the
Veientane territory, were easily eclipsed by the later conquests of the
League when it obtained Circeii, Velitrae, Antium, Satricum and Anxur,
in addition to Sutrium and Nepete, which had been ceded to, if not
colonized by, the Latins before the Gallic invasion. In extent the Latin
League had won more than Rome, perhaps a third as much again; but it
was at a grave disadvantage. Whereas the Roman territory was a compact
mass, the Latin possessions were scattered and often separated by Roman
property. In these circumstances the Latins found common action
difficult, so that a profound change came over the League. Rome almost
unconsciously assumed the leadership. A city in distress would turn more
readily to the united and ready forces of Rome than to the disunited
Latins; and the Romans would often call on the Latins to supply their
contingents without waiting to summon a federal council. Gradually the
arrangement for an alternating military command and the meetings at the
Ferentine Spring fell into disuse. The initiative passed to Rome and the
equal alliance collapsed. The Latin League was further weakened by some
of the new colonies; in some a large proportion of the settlers might be
Roman citizens, mindful of their origin, others included Volscian states
which were forced into the League and would hardly live at peace with
their neighbours. Rome, on the other hand, increased in strength when
any Latins migrated thither and sought citizenship. In short, by a century
of hard defensive fighting Rome had nearly doubled her own territory
and had extended her horizon to the Ciminian Hills in the north and
Anxur in the south; she dominated, if she did not yet lead, the Latin
League; the moment was ripe for the Latins to make one last bid for
independence. But suddenly the storm-clouds swept down past the
Ciminian Hills and there burst upon Rome the tempest of the Gallic
invasion.[15]

4. THE GALLIC CATASTROPHE

During the fourth century marauding bands of Celts, migrating from their
great empire in central Europe, spread terror throughout the peninsulae

of southern Europe (p. 25). Various tribes began to pour into Italy. The Insubres entered by the Ticinus valley and defeated the Etruscans near Melpum (Roman Mediolanum and modern Milan), which they captured and settled. Other tribes followed: the Cenomani, Boii, Lingones and Senones. Gradually some advanced over the Po and a few over the Apennines. But they met with a stout resistance from the Etruscans. Naturally the country dwellers submitted easily and the ancient Ligurians, if any survived, were pushed back into the mountains or else were assimilated. But the towns were not so swiftly won. Felsina, for instance, resisted till about 350 and the funeral *stelae* of the citizens, which depict battle scenes against the Gauls, show the rigour of the struggle. The Etruscan town at Marzabotto also bears witness: the foundations of its buildings are covered with a thick layer of ashes; skeletons and weapons are scattered over its soil. The Veneti succeeded in beating off the attack and retained their independence, but most of the valley of the Po down to the Adriatic shore had succumbed before the end of the fourth century; to the Romans the district became known as Cisalpine Gaul.

These restless Celtic hordes had attained a high level of culture in some respects, but in others they were mere savages. Given to drunkenness, human sacrifices and head-hunting, fickle, adventurous and brave, they rushed naked into battle on foot, on horseback or in chariots; their iron weapons, long swords, high stature, streaming hair and weird cries terrified the disciplined armies of the south when first they appeared. But their staying power and sense of unity were short-lived, as they scattered to plunder or to enjoy their spoil. They were warriors and stock-breeders, impatient of the discipline of agriculture, but with ready adaptability some gradually settled down and became good farmers. In North Italy they eagerly adopted the products of the superior Etruscan civilization and began to till the land, until Cisalpine Gaul became a land of peasants. But some tribes remained on the warpath and in 390 a horde of Senones led by Brennus crossed the Apennines in search of plunder rather than of land and appeared at the gates of Clusium. Etruria was in truth waning. Disunited at home, deprived of Latium and Campania, hard pressed by Rome in the south and now battered by the Gauls in the north, she was at her last gasp. Yet it was Rome that bore the full blast of the storm which threatened to wreck the patient building of a hundred years.

Clusium is said to have appealed for help to the Romans, who despatched envoys to negotiate. These men, however, abandoned their position of strict neutrality and fought shoulder to shoulder with the men of Clusium: one of them even killed a Gallic chief. Thus Rome drew on herself the vengeance of the Gauls. This improbable account seems to have been designed to explain the subsequent defeat of the Romans as divine punishment for the crime of their ambassadors; the appeal made by the barbarians to the *ius gentium* is ridiculously anachronistic. Nor is it likely that Clusium would appeal to Rome; more probably Diodorus is correct in saying that the Romans heard of the invasion and sent a force to Clusium to reconnoitre. In any case the Gauls abandoned their attack on Clusium and swept like a mountain torrent towards Rome which lay only eighty miles away. Their numbers reached some 30,000. The Romans had only two legions, which inclusive of the cavalry and light-armed troops might number 10,000 men. Even if they were not abandoned by their allies to face the peril alone, as is recorded, they would hardly muster more than 15,000 men; but it was perhaps the greatest army that Rome had yet put into the field. Then dawned that day which ever stood in black letters in the annals of Rome's history. In the narrow Tiber valley to the north of Fidenae at the eleventh milestone from Rome flowed the little stream of the Allia. Here on the left bank of the Tiber the Romans took up their position. Their left wing was covered by the river, their main force was on the level plain, their right wing of reserves rested on the lower slopes of the Crustuminian mountains. The Gauls swiftly turned the Roman flank by routing the force on the hills and drove the main army back to the Tiber. Here some escaped across the river to Veii, but large numbers were cut to pieces; some of those on the hills may have fled to Rome. Three days later the Gauls arrived at Rome. The priests and the Vestal Virgins had fled to Caere. There was no resistance except in the citadel on the Capitol; the rest of the unresisting city was plundered and burnt.[16]

At this point legend steps in and relates how the Gauls found the senators who were too old to fight sitting on their ivory seats like gods upon their thrones, awaiting their fate in quiet dignity. Then the survivors at Veii begged Camillus to return from exile at Ardea and to save his country. Pontius Cominius swam the Tiber and reached the Capitol, whence he brought word that the Senate and People of Rome had chosen Camillus dictator. But the Gauls had marked the track of Pontius and would have taken the Capitol by surprise, had not the sacred geese aroused M. Manlius, surnamed Capitolinus, in the nick of time. After a siege of seven months the defenders were forced by famine to offer the Gauls a thousand pounds of gold to withdraw. But even as the gold was being weighed Camillus and his men appeared and drove the Gauls out of the city. This last incident is plainly designed to retrieve Roman honour. The story of Camillus' exile was perhaps invented to save the conqueror of Veii from blame for the catastrophe and in order that he might be able to rally the survivors outside Rome; doubtless he played a leading part in the story of Rome's recovery. All that results is that the Romans on the Capitol held out and at length bought off the Gauls, who had attained their object of plundering Rome; it is not likely that they had come to settle, and their departure was hastened by their sufferings from fever and by the fact that their own territory in Cisalpine Gaul was being threatened by the Veneti. The departing guests may even have been speeded on their way by a force of survivors, refugees from Rome and Latin volunteers, who mustered at Veii; but it was the Gauls' own decision to retire.[17]

Rome suffered serious internal damage, especially as most of the houses were made of wood; traces of the work of the destructive fire have been found on the Palatine. But the later Romans tended to overestimate the loss, partly from a desire to explain the paucity of early historical documents; in fact the Gauls from superstitious awe may have left untouched some of the temples, where official documents were kept. Soon the city arose fresher and stronger from among her ashes, but the damage to her prestige took longer to heal. Rome's power in central Italy collapsed, as it had in 509 when the Etruscan dynasty fell; the work of the fifth century had to be repeated in the first half of the fourth. Yet there was another side to the picture; common fear of the Gauls strengthened the idea of unity among the Italians. Finally, it was largely owing to Roman courage in defeat and resolution in rebuilding a barrier against the north that France and not Italy became the home of the Celts.

5. THE RECOVERY OF ROME

The city was destroyed; its internal stability was shaken; there was no army of defence; the alliance with the Latins and Hernici had collapsed; the Gauls might return. But in these dark days the spirit of the Roman people did not waver. Wise leadership and the patriotism of the citizen body saved Rome. The internal struggle of the orders reached fever pitch in 367, but concessions were granted just in time to avoid disaster. So Rome set her shoulder to the gruelling task of reconstruction at home and abroad; that she accomplished so much is due largely to the wise direction of Camillus. The main work was to rebuild and protect the city. As earthworks had proved useless against the Gallic attack, a solid stone wall some twelve feet thick and twenty-four feet high, backed by the earlier *agger* which was now raised to the same height, was constructed around the whole city, including the Aventine, a distance of $5\frac{1}{2}$ miles; traces of this so-called Servian wall still survive. It was perhaps not begun till 378 and was constructed of large blocks of tufa from the Grotta Oscura near Veii; the masons' marks suggest that Rome, like any contemporary Greek city, imported a special building staff of Greek contractors, though the labour may have been supplied by the Roman army.[18] The modernization of the army and the adaptation of the constitution to meet the pressing demands of the plebs, whose military services were more vital than ever, will be discussed later. How Rome addressed herself to her external problems is now the question.

Once again the Romans were forced to fight on many fronts and to face the hostility of Etruscans, Hernici, Aequi, Volsci and Gauls; and although there was no general revolt of the Latins as in 496 or 340, individual cities were restless and discontented. The traditional account of these wars is accepted in outline by some modern historians, but by others it is completely rejected: for instance, the verdict of K. J. Beloch is that 'in the thirty years after the Gallic catastrophe Rome had not to wage any great wars'.[19] The tradition is confused and confusing: great battles are won with little or no apparent result; cities are taken and retaken with monotonous regularity; the indefatigable Camillus is here, there and everywhere; vanquished foes reappear in full force the year after their defeat and even Livy begins to wonder whence the Volscians derived their inexhaustible supply: 'unde totiens victis Volscis suffecerint milites' (vi, 12, 2). The chronology is confused; many incidents are obviously duplicated and some are mere inventions dictated by national or family pride. But if due allowance is made for the unevenness of the annalistic tradition, and for the fact that many of these wars were merely glorified border raids, it may be conceded that the main lines of Rome's recovery are clearly defined. With this warning in mind the traditional account may be briefly followed.

The Etruscans, who were the first to take advantage of Rome's weakness by attacking Sutrium and Nepete in 389, were quickly beaten back by Camillus (Livy (vi, 3, 9) wrongly recounts similar events in 386). It was at this time that the territory of Veii was annexed and formed into the four new tribes and now, if not earlier, Sutrium and Nepete received their Latin colonists. Rome's willingness to share these two outposts against Etruria with her Latin allies is the measure of her weakness and her wisdom. For the next thirty years Etruria gave little trouble.[20] Of the

Latin towns Tibur severed relations with Rome, though it did not break into open war until 360. Praeneste, which had probably remained outside the League, and Velitrae were ready to join hands with the Volsci. Tusculum, which was surrounded by Roman territory, showed slight hesitation in 381; but when the Romans approached it and found everything quiet they granted it peace and soon afterwards full Roman citizenship. Aricia, Ardea, Lavinium and Lanuvium remained loyal, as did some Latin cities in Volscian territory: Cora, Norba and Signia, together with Setia, which received a colony in 382. It is recorded that the Latins in alliance with the Volsci were defeated in 386 and 385 and again in 377 after they had captured Satricum; thereafter they remained quiet. The Hernici, who joined in the disturbances of 386, shared in the defeat and remained inactive for twenty-three years. The neighbouring Aequi had already been vanquished at Bola in 388. It was the Volsci who gave most trouble. They were led by the men of Antium and Satricum and supported by Velitrae; but these western towns were separated from the eastern ones of the Liris valley by the colonies at Circeii and Setia. The war ended with the destruction of Satricum and the forced re-entry of Antium and Velitrae into the League, but the details are doubtful. It is said that the Volsci who advanced to Lanuvium were defeated by Camillus at Marcion (or Maecium) in 389 and at Satricum in 386, and by A. Cornelius Cossus in 385, when a colony was planted at Satricum. Further Roman victories are recorded in 381 and 377; in the course of the war, which was not completed till 338, Satricum was said to have been captured no less than four times and Velitrae was repeatedly besieged.[21]

During the decade following 377 Rome enjoyed comparative peace abroad, but suffered at home from the disturbances which led up to the Licinian reforms; the annalists had sufficient domestic news without having to elaborate the border fighting. At the end of the 360s foreign affairs again predominate. With their internal difficulties now alleviated the Romans turned to the Hernici. After a defeat in 362 they captured Ferentinum in 361; three years later the Hernici asked for peace and were readmitted to alliance with Rome, but on less favourable terms than before. The Latin cities of Velitrae, Tibur and Praeneste were also restless and even employed Gauls as mercenaries against Rome; these were defeated near the Colline Gate in 360. By 358 Rome had reasserted her authority over the Latins, who had to renew the old treaty of Spurius Cassius, probably on less favourable terms. Naturally they were no longer allowed to appoint a commander in turn; the new League was under the nominal control of two annual praetors who were subordinate to the

Roman consuls in the federal army. The defaulting cities were forced to re-enter the League; Velitrae, Antium, Tibur, Nomentum, Pedum, Privernum and Praeneste had all toed the line by 354. Antium was deprived of part of its territory, which was not incorporated into the League but was annexed by Rome and formed into two new tribes (the Pomptina and Poplilia; 358) as the Veientane territory had been. This raised the total number of tribes to twenty-seven.

The renewal of the Latin League appeared as a threat to Etruria. In 359 the men of Tarquinii took up arms, and they were aided two years later by Falerii. In 353 Caere joined Tarquinii, but was quickly defeated by Rome and was accorded a hundred years' truce. Tarquinii and Falerii were brought to heel in 351 and were granted a forty years' truce. Eight years later Falerii exchanged the truce for a permanent alliance with Rome. The details of these Etruscan wars are uncertain but the result is important. For forty years Rome was free from danger on her northern front while she was busy asserting her authority in central Italy. Rome's treatment of Caere is controversial. At some time Caere received *civitas sine suffragio*, which meant that it shared the private privileges and obligations of Roman citizenship (*commercium, conubium* and *militia*). It was later regarded as the first *municipium* to receive this privilege, which was granted as a reward for protecting the Vestal Virgins during the Gallic invasion of 390. Another tradition, which suggests that this treatment was regarded as a punishment (for some unspecified revolt in the third century?), reflects conditions of a later period when *civitas sine suffragio* was considered an inferior form of citizenship. If this latter tradition be accepted, Caere probably received a contract of *hospitium* with Rome in 390, a treaty of alliance for 100 years in 353, and *civitas sine suffragio* perhaps between 353 and 338 or not until *c.* 274.[22]

For thirty years after the sack of Rome the Gauls, according to Polybius, refrained from further attack; when they returned Rome was safe behind her new-built walls. Livy, however, recounts various battles against the Gauls in 367, 361 and 360; in one of these T. Manlius Torquatus fought a duel with a gigantic Gaul and robbed him of his torque or collar. Doubtless the Gauls who had penetrated as far south as Apulia occasionally raided Latium, but the traditional Roman victories in the field may be questioned.[23] In 332–331 when the Celtic advance on the Danube was checked by Alexander the Great, the Romans concluded a thirty years' treaty with the Senones. The Gallic effort was slackening. They could not capture walled towns and began to question their ability to repeat the performance of Allia. For fifty or more years they had been a serious menace, but they had presented no real hindrance to Rome's revival. Indeed, by weakening Etruria, by forcing on Rome the role of Italian martyr, and by making the Italic tribes more conscious of their ethnic unity and their indebtedness to Rome, the Gauls hastened the recovery of the city they had laid low. After a number of transitory raids and one or two major episodes they withdrew beyond the Apennines, but they left behind an uncomfortable memory from which the Romans never quite shook themselves free.

6. ROME'S WIDENING HORIZON

At one moment it appeared possible that the growing power of Rome might have been ground to insignificance by the upper and nether millstones of Etruria and Magna Graecia, but in the end the central power expanded at the expense of the extremities. The decline of Etruria, caused by internal dissension and weakness and by the pressure of other nations, had been gradual. After the loss of Rome and Latium southern Etruria had echoed to the tramp of Roman armies. Carthage, Etruria's ally, had so weakened under the Greek attack in Sicily that the Sicilian Greeks became strong enough to help Cumae to break the Etruscan sea power in 474. The Etruscan hold on Campania was finally lost at the end of the fifth century when the Sabellian tribes swept down from the mountains over the Campanian plain, overwhelming Etruscan and Greek alike. Finally, the Etruscans had lost control of the region of the Po under the assault of the Gauls; by 350 their stronghold Felsina succumbed, and some fifteen years later the Adriatic shore submitted. At the same time Hellenism in southern Italy was weakening. As ever, the Greek cities were frequently torn by party strife; even if united internally they often quarrelled with their neighbours, whether for racial, political, constitutional, or economic reasons. But a more potent cause was the threat from the inland peoples, a danger to which Greek coastal colonies were always exposed. In southern Italy they had easily reached a *modus vivendi* with the early inhabitants, but the balance was upset by the arrival of the Sabellian tribes.

The steady southward movement of the Sabellian peoples has already been mentioned. Caused by overpopulation and pressure from the north and expedited by the custom of the Sacred Spring, it led to a new grouping of the powers, by which the Etruscan and Greek colonies lost their primacy. The Sabellian mountain-dwellers, shouldered off by the Etruscans and the warlike Picenes, had pressed further southwards, thus

incidentally forcing the Aequi and Volsci down into the Latin plains
where they had been checked by the Latins. The Sabellians themselves
had gradually reached the hills and valleys above the Campanian plain and
were soon tempted down by its fertility. The invaders quickly swept over
the plain; Capua succumbed c. 423 and Cumae in 421. Neapolis served as a
refuge for the fleeing Greeks, but virtually the whole of Campania from
Cumae to Salerno became Sabellian. Yet the superior Greek and Etruscan
civilization of the earlier inhabitants soon conquered the hardy mountain-
dwellers who adapted their mode of life to their new surroundings. These
Campanians, now in possession of the richest land in Italy which
produced three garden crops a year, soon settled down to city life and
grew very wealthy. Their chief city, Capua, became the second city of
Italy and the head of a league, which did not, however, include all the
Oscan towns of Campania. The attractiveness and ease of their life led to a
certain deterioration of character, so that later they readily became a spoil
to their mountain kinsmen, especially as foreign tyrants were constantly
draining their military resources by hiring mercenaries from them.[24]

South of Campania another band of Sabellians, known as the
Lucanians, settling in what is practically the instep of the foot of Italy,
absorbed the earlier population. Here the Greek cities were hard pressed
by Dionysius of Syracuse, who, having defeated the Carthaginians in
Sicily, tried to carve out in South Italy a continental addition to his
Sicilian empire (405–367). To this end he entered into a league with the
Lucanians and recruited Gallic mercenaries. The allied Greek cities were
defeated by the Lucanians in 390 and at Elleporus in 389 by Dionysius
himself, who captured Rhegium, raided the Etruscan coast, reoccupied
Elba and pressed up the Adriatic coast, founding colonies at Ancona and
Adria. Hellenic Italy was saved from the Syracusan danger on the death of
Dionysius' son, but it had not learnt its lesson. Cities continued to
quarrel, though Tarentum attained some eminence under the wise rule of
Archytas. This weakness elicited further attacks from the Italians in the
second half of the fourth century. The aggressions of a league of the
Bruttians in the toe of Italy forced the Greeks to appeal to the mother
country, whence King Archidamus of Sparta and later Alexander of
Epirus came to champion the cause of western Hellenism, just as
Timoleon had come from Corinth to save the Sicilian Greeks. It was
during these disturbed days following the break up of Dionysius' empire
that some Greek privateers raided the coast of Latium.[25]

The Sabellians who settled in central Italy were known to the Romans
as Samnites. They formed a loose league, which did not include outlying

tribes as the Lucanians, the Oscans of Campania, the Paeligni, Marsi, Marrucini or Vestini. They were highland farmers and crofters, who lived in villages rather than towns, and though some larger landowners probably existed, differences in wealth were not great. Each valley or plateau comprised a *pagus* with an elective leader (*meddix*), whose functions were largely limited to leadership in war and a summary jurisdiction. These *pagi* were loosely grouped together in cantonal associations (Caraceni, Pentri, Hirpini, and Caudini), and each of these *populi* formed a *touto*, led by a *meddix tuticus*. These in turn were grouped in a wider league with a central meeting-place at Bovianum Vetus, where cantonal chiefs would gather in emergencies to appoint a federal commander-in-chief and where a federal council, and possibly an assembly, also met. But the lack of a really strong central administration made it difficult for the Samnites to sustain a long war. Though they could easily be roused to heroic vigour and had a passionate sense of unity in defence of their land, they tended to scatter quickly when on the hunt for booty. In 354 they made an alliance with the Romans, and the interests which both peoples had in the middle Liris valley were probably defined to their mutual satisfaction. However, a more potent factor in driving them to co-operate was probably common fear of the Gauls, and when this fear became less urgent the preoccupation of Rome with the Latins and of the Samnites with southern Italy rendered the alliance still useful. In the same year Rome had made a truce with Praeneste; perhaps she feared a coalition of Latins and Samnites. But beside bringing the Romans and Samnites into contact for the first time, the Samnite alliance created a barrier in central Italy against the southward advance of the Gauls and the northward spread of Greek civilization.[26]

In another direction also Rome's horizon widened. In 348 she made a treaty with Carthage, which revised the old agreement reached at the beginning of the Republic. The fact that the Romans allowed Carthage to stiffen up the conditions shows that their real interests were still confined to Italy and that their commercial ambitions were very humble. The treaty asserted Rome's claim to speak for the cities of the Latian coast as far south as Tarracina (Anxur). Antium and the Volsci naturally disliked this and trouble followed; in 346 M. Valerius Corvus captured Satricum and celebrated a triumph over the Antiates, Volscians and men of Satricum.[27] This discontent quickly communicated itself to the Latins who decided to make one supreme bid for freedom. But before the Latin revolt broke out, the Campanians, who by defending the Sidicini had drawn a Samnite attack on themselves, are said to have appealed to Rome for help against the Samnites; the Romans responded and waged the First Samnite War in 343–341 against their former allies. The military details of this war are very confused and improbable, and Diodorus knew of no such war before the great Samnite War of 327. Further, it is very unlikely that the Romans would risk breaking with their Samnite allies on the very eve of a Latin revolt. Many believe, therefore, that the war was invented to justify Rome's later dealings with Campania. The evidence is not conclusive, but it must be admitted that the whole narrative of these years becomes clearer if the war is rejected. In any case the Romans renewed their alliance with the Samnites in 341 and disclaimed any responsibility for the Sidicini, the very people on whose behalf their war with Samnium is said to have been fought.[28]

7. THE END OF THE LATIN LEAGUE

The Latins determined to profit by Rome's domestic troubles (p. 118). In 343 they launched an attack against the Paeligni in an attempt to cut the communications between Rome and Samnium. When two years later these two states renewed their alliance the Sidicini, feeling themselves threatened by the Samnites, appealed successfully to the Latins for protection. Thus the Latins and Sidicini, together with the Campanians, ranged themselves against Rome and Samnium.[29] The storm broke when the Latins demanded from the Romans independence or equality; the request that Livy puts into their mouths – full Roman citizenship and a half share in the government – is clearly an anticipation of the claims made by the Latins two hundred and fifty years later on the eve of the Social War. Their demand was refused, and the Latins mustered for their war of independence. In 340, while one consul protected Rome, T. Manlius led a force through the territory of the Paeligni, joined the Samnites and marched with his allied forces down the Liris. At Trifanum near Suessa he met the Latin allied forces in a great battle. The Campanian horsemen, who might have outflanked the Romans, were sadly ineffective, and the Latin resistance was broken. The Romans quickly made peace with the Campanians, and two years later all resistance was stamped out: in 339 Q. Publilius Philo celebrated a triumph over the Latins and in 338 L. Furius Camillus defeated the northern Latin towns of Pedum and Tibur, while C. Maenius overcame the southern Latins and Volscians in a battle near Antium, which was taken. The various Latin cities submitted and their independence was ended (338).[30]

The Latin League, which had survived numerous changes, was now dissolved. Many of the cities and colonies were deprived of their rights of *commercium* and *conubium* with each other and of all common political activity. Although religious gatherings on the Alban Mount were permitted to continue, the meetings at the Caput Ferentinae were forbidden and the League was politically dead. If the Romans had followed this destructive policy alone, they would merely have driven the Latin opposition underground, stored up trouble for the future, and weakened themselves for their future struggles against the Etruscans, Gauls and Samnites by forfeiting the military support of their old allies. Instead they created a confederacy. They bound the conquered Latins to themselves by ties of common interest, and by a wise liberality they stimulated the patriotism of the Latins for a state of which they became members. Not all were to be fully privileged members from the beginning; complete citizenship was a prize which the Romans held out as an attainable ideal of practical value. Rome became the mother of Italy, training her children by carefully graded stages up to the privilege of full family life. This was an immense stride forward in Rome's history and indeed in the history of mankind. The conquered people were not to be dragged along at Rome's chariot wheels as slaves; they were asked to share in the privileges and responsibilities of their conqueror. Rome thus grounded her hegemony of Italy on moral principles, however much they may have been dictated by self-interest. The moral justification of the Roman conquest of Italy is that when Pyrrhus and Hannibal came to deliver the Italian peoples from the yoke of Rome, they failed because the Italian confederacy preferred to remain loyal to Rome's leadership.

The elaborate scheme of enfranchisement which Rome evolved was not the work of a moment, but its main lines were laid down by the settlement of 338. First, some of the nearest Latin towns (Lanuvium, Aricia, Nomentum and Pedum, together with Tusculum if it had not already been incorporated in 381) were granted full Roman citizenship and retained their municipal governments. Rome thus counterbalanced the ravages of war by increasing the number of her full citizens; within a generation a Tusculan noble reached the Roman consulship (322). In 332 two new tribes were formed in Latium, named Maecia and Scaptia. Secondly, some towns (*municipia*) accepted *civitas sine suffragio*, which at this time was not regarded as an inferior brand of Roman citizenship, but was an alliance whereby Rome and the *municipium* exchanged social rights (*conubium* and *commercium*). These *municipia* remained separate *respublicae* with full local autonomy except that they surrendered an independent foreign policy, provided Rome with troops (their *munus*), and were liable to visits by Roman judicial prefects. Their status thus resembled that of *ius Latii*, while their citizens could obtain full Roman citizenship by settling in Rome itself; gradually, however, the balance of power was tipped further in Rome's interest and the character of the *municipia* declined. The first towns to accept *civitas sine suffragio* were not Latin, but Campanian or Volscian: Fundi, Formiae, Capua, Suessula and Cumae; and Acerrae in 332. The aristocracy of Capua is said to have received full, as opposed to half-, citizenship, but this is improbable, although they perhaps received some economic privileges. Thirdly, the other Latin cities and colonies retained their old status. Officially they remained on the same footing as Rome, being allies (*socii Latini nominis*), bound by an 'alliance on terms of equality' (*foedus aequum*) But in view of the disparity of strength between themselves and Rome, they would in practice have to fight on Rome's behalf rather than on their own. And they were limited by being bound to Rome and not to each other. They were forbidden *commercium* and *conubium*, at least temporarily, with one another, but retained these rights with Roman citizens; as about half Latium consisted of Roman citizens the limitation was not drastic. The underlying principle of 'divide and rule' was a keystone of Roman policy. The cities of this class were the Latin colonies, Signia, Norba, Ardea, Circeii, Sutrium, Nepete and Setia. Tibur and Praeneste were deprived of some of their territory, but, like Cora and Gabii, retained their alliances with Rome. Fourthly, Antium received special treatment. It occupied an important position and had practised piracy for some time. After destroying its fleet the Romans allowed the Antiates to retain possession of their city, but a small Roman colony was sent to occupy a part of their territory. These settlers retained their Roman citizenship and had local home rule, like the *municipia*, but instead of serving in the Roman army they guarded the seaport. Only nine Roman citizen-colonies of this sort were founded before the First Punic War, since the type of Latin colony was preferred. Velitrae received somewhat similar treatment: the rebels were driven into exile and their lands were distributed to Roman settlers who kept their citizenship.

Such in brief was the organization by which Rome built up a federation in Italy. The allies supplied troops to fight alongside the Romans in their common interests, but it was the Roman citizens who paid the taxes to support citizen and allied troops alike. The allies of Athens, who soon contributed money in place of naval help, came to feel that they were paying tribute to a mistress. Rome avoided levying tribute; she fought her battles side by side with her allies who thus felt the reality of their alliance.

It was this policy of generating mutual interest and sentiment that won for Rome the hegemony of Italy and the power to unify its peoples into a nation. (See also Chapter VI, 7.)

V

THE UNION OF
THE ORDERS
AND THE
CONSTITUTION

1. ECONOMIC DISTRESS

The Gallic invasion brought in its train a period of extreme distress. Amid this confusion the demands of the plebeians became more insistent until in 367 the Licinian Rogations won for them a considerable political victory which went far to unite the orders. Economic depression formed the background to much of the discontent. This centred around conditions of land tenure and the harsh laws of debt; it was aggravated by actual shortage of food. It has already been seen how pressing were these problems in the early days of the Republic (pp. 82f.). During the fifth century, and especially in its last decades, Rome's conquests in Italy had increased the amount of *ager publicus*. If the plebs had been refused a fair share of Roman territory earlier, it would obviously be fatal to refuse their demands when this territory had been so greatly increased partly as a result of their efforts. So although some land may have been sold by the state to those who could afford to buy, some was distributed in plots to individual citizens as their absolute property (*assignatio*) The tribunes were not yet powerful enough to propose such measures, which were moved by magistrates and voted by the Comitia Centuriata with the Senate's approval. Part of the land taken from Veii was distributed in this way in 393 in allotments of perhaps 4 *iugera* each (Diodorus, xiv, 102, 4; Livy v, 30, 8, gives 7 *iugera*). Patricians could apply for such land, but would probably sell or lease their portions; the poorer citizens were the chief gainers. By such grants of land the Romans secured the proximity and the interest of responsible self-supporting property owners who would rally to defend the state in hours of need. There were other means of relief for those who lacked land: they could share in the founding of colonies where they received allotments, and it is estimated that some 50,000 people may have gone to colonies between 450 and 290 BC. Or land could be obtained by squatting (*occupatio*) on state property with the right of *possessio*. Nominally a rent was paid, but most of such land fell into the hands of the richer farmers who could afford to develop it and who in practice seldom paid their dues.

In these circumstances it is not surprising that the legislation of this period should include some agrarian enactments. Such are found in the Licinian Rogations of 367 by which the amount of public land held by any individual was limited. Since the form of the law, as preserved, is similar to that enacted by Tiberius Gracchus in 133 BC, many historians reject the economic clauses of the Licinio-Sextian legislation as anticipations of later conditions. This radical criticism seems unjustified. Some details, for instance, that the limit was set at 500 *iugera* (300 acres), may be due to Gracchan influences, but a clause which limited the tenancies of public land may be accepted.[1] This measure, however, did not solve the land problem, which was rather met by the rapid advance of Rome in Italy, by the increasing number of colonies, by fresh distributions of land and perhaps by the slow growth of industry.

The second main grievance arose from the harsh laws of debt. The story of how the patrician M. Manlius Capitolinus, who had saved the Capitol from the Gauls, gave up his property to redeem debtors from slavery and was killed for aiming at a tyranny, may deserve little credence, but it does reflect the serious economic situation. As Solon at Athens proclaimed a *Seisachtheia*, so the tribunes Licinius and Sextius in their Rogation of 367 decreed that interest already paid should be deducted from the original loan, and the balance, if any, should be repaid within three years. Modern attempts to discredit this measure are not very convincing; it was a temporary expedient which treated the symptoms rather than the disease.[2]

Attempts at relief consisted either in limiting the rate of interest or in bankruptcy laws, neither of which was very successful. No experiment was tried on the lines of allowing the debtor to compound with his creditor for a sum rather less than the full amount. In 357 M. Duilius and L. Menenius, two tribunes, fixed the rate of interest at one-twelfth ($8\frac{1}{3}$ per cent); if such a law had been contained in the Twelve Tables it was now re-enacted (p. 88). In 352 a Commission of Five was set up by the consuls as a state bank. They had powers to make advances from the state to debtors in difficulties, to take over mortgages on adequate security, or to settle them by allowing bankruptcy proceedings. Five years later the legal rate of interest was reduced by half, and another three years' moratorium was declared; as the state had taken over many mortgages, the Treasury would have to stand the loss in such cases. In 342 a tribune, L. Genucius, carried a measure to forbid loans and usury; Livy appears a little doubtful about this law, but it may well have been another temporary expedient which soon fell into disuse. Foreign conquests and increased colonization offered some relief in the following years, but in 326 (Livy, viii, 28) or 313 (Varro, L. L., vii, 105) the question of enslavement for debt was once more faced and finally settled. It was scarcely possible to amend the law relating to *nexum* laid down by the Twelve Tables, but it could be rendered harmless. The *Lex Poetelia* stands out like an ancient Magna Charta. 'In that year', wrote Livy, 'the liberty of the Roman plebs had, as it were, a new beginning; for men ceased to be imprisoned for debt.' The details are obscure, but apparently it was decreed that judgement must be obtained before execution was carried out; and Pais may be correct in supposing that loans were to be made on the security of the property, and not of the person of the borrower. 'The bonds of the citizens were released and thereafter binding for debts ceased,' wrote Cicero.[3] A landmark had been set up, but the financial and agricultural problems still awaited a permanent solution.

2. VICTORIES OF THE PLEBEIANS

Since plebeians had been elected consular tribunes, it would be illogical to exclude them from the consulship if it should be re-established. Yet the plebeian demand for this privilege resulted in the most famous constitutional struggle in Roman history: the ten years' agitation which produced the Licinian laws. In 376 two tribunes, C. Licinius and L. Sextius, proposed that the consulship should be restored and that one consul should be a plebeian; their economic proposals have already been mentioned. Their eight colleagues blocked the measure. For ten years, it is said, Licinius and Sextius were re-elected to office while the struggle raged. According to Livy no patrician magistrates were elected for five years, though Diodorus reduces the period of ἀναρχία to one year. Camillus twice was elected dictator. In 368 the patrician resistance began to weaken: the number of commissioners who regulated various religious ceremonies (*sacris faciundis*) was raised from two to ten, of whom five were to be plebeians. At one point the poorer plebeians were willing to drop the law about the consulship, if only the economic measures were passed: but the plebeian leaders stiffened their backs, until finally in 367 all the measures were passed and became law; L. Sextius himself was elected as first plebeian consul for 366. Many details of this struggle are suspicious, but the passage of the bill in 367 should not be questioned.[4]

The patricians tried to minimize their loss by depriving the consuls (or *praetores consules*) of some of their duties. The ordinary civil jurisdiction of the city was handed over in 366 to a regular magistrate with *imperium*, inferior to that of the consuls; he was named, like them, praetor, but was never called consul, while the consuls themselves retained this part of their title and dropped the additional *praetores*. This praetor probably was to be patrician, but by 337 the plebeians won admission to the magistracy. In 367 two curule aediles were elected from the patricians, but in the following year it was arranged that this office should alternate annually between the two orders. And thus, notwithstanding attempted patrician evasions, a settlement had been reached. The wealthy plebeians had secured access to the consulship: the other magistracies would be attained in course of time. The Licinian Laws decided the struggle of the orders in every real sense. The final compromise may have been brought about partly through the intervention of the aged Camillus, 'the second founder of Rome', who died two years later, but not before he is said to have vowed a temple to Concord (Concordia Ordinum) to commemorate the equalization of the orders.[5]

When once the principle of equality of office had been established, the plebeians soon reached all the magistracies; a plebeian was dictator in 356 and censor in 351. But the number of plebeian families which held the consulship was small: the Genucii and Licinii were the chief representatives before 361, the Poetelii, Popillii, Plautii and Marcii in the following few years. Sometimes there were apparently no suitable plebeian candidates, or else they were shouldered out by their rivals, since on six or seven occasions between 355 – 343 two patrician consuls were elected.[6] In consequence some legislation was carried in 342, resulting from a mutiny of the army in Campania and from the initiative of a tribune, backed perhaps by a secession. A *lex sacrata militaris* forbade the degradation of a military tribune and the forcible discharge of a soldier, thus checking the power of the consul on active service. L. Genucius is said to have passed laws (1) prohibiting the taking of interest, (2) forbidding the holding of the same office twice within ten years, and (3) declaring that both consuls might legally be plebeians. Of these measures the first is reasonable; the second, if genuine, was certainly not observed;

the third is possible as a theoretical ruling; it was not till 172 BC that two plebeians held the consulship together, yet it is unlikely that two patricians did so after 342.

More important than these Leges Genuciae were the Leges Publiliae of 339. The consul Q. Publilius Philo, who later had a distinguished career, becoming the first plebeian praetor in 337 and the first consul to have his magistracy extended by a *prorogatio imperii* in 326 (p. 132), was named dictator by his colleague in 339. In the Comitia Centuriata he carried three laws in favour of the plebeians; two of them strengthened the popular sovereignty. These concessions were obtained perhaps because of the severity of the Latin revolt which emphasized the value of the Roman people on the field of battle. The measures were: (1) That one of the censors must be a plebeian; this ended the patrician monopoly of an office which had been created partly to evade the consequences of admitting the plebeians to the consulship. (2) That the sanction of the *patres* must be given beforehand to all laws proposed by a magistrate in the Comitia Centuriata. Before this enactment the only exclusive rights left to the patricians were the occupancy of a few priesthoods, the appointment of an *interrex*, and the *patrum auctoritas* by which they decided on the form of a law. By this last privilege they could block a law passed in the Comitia Centuriata on the ground of its faulty form; but by Philo's enactment faults could be corrected before submission to the Comitia and so the power of the *patres* was weakened. Yet as a magistrate proposing a law now had to discuss it before the Senate, the influence of that body as a whole increased over the magistrates, as it decreased over the people. The *patres*, however, had been robbed of a useful political weapon. (3) That *plebiscita* should be binding on the whole *populus*. This was a reassertion of one of the clauses of the Valerio-Horatian laws of 449, if the latter are considered genuine. It is not, however, probable that *plebiscita* were recognized as having the force of laws (*leges*) without some limiting clause until 287.[7] But the Publilian legislation was another landmark in the history of the orders, and during the fifty years which followed the Gallic invasion the equalization of the orders had been almost completed.

3. SOCIAL AND POLITICAL ADJUSTMENTS

Before reaching calmer waters the ship of state encountered further squalls, arising partly from a radical social readjustment which had begun with the Licinian-Sextian legislation. These laws had in practice abolished the outstanding political differences between the orders, and the patricians were forced to hand over the helm to a new nobility, composed partly of themselves and partly of plebeians. But while this exclusive body absorbed many of the older plebeians, there grew up in the place of the latter a new populace in Rome with fresh demands. The old contrast between patricians and plebeians gave place to a coalition of the moderates of both parties, while at one extremity there remained a small right wing of patricians, at the other an urban proletariat.

The creation of this new patricio-plebeian nobility was caused by the decline of the patricians, whose *gentes* were steadily decreasing in number, and by the increasing political influence and numbers of the plebeians, which were due to the large annexations of territory, the extension of Roman citizenship in Italy, the attraction of the capital and the value of the plebeians in war. Their leaders gradually fused with the more moderate patricians and formed a new caste during the second half of the fourth and the beginning of the third centuries. Outstanding figures were the patrician P. Valerius Publicola and Q. Fabius Rullianus, and the plebeian Q. Publilius Philo, P. Decius Mus and his son, C. Marcius Rutilus and M'. Curius Dentatus. The number of plebeian families to attain to the consulship varied at different times: when the office was first opened to them it was monopolized by a few; during the decade after 340 eight new *gentes* were admitted to the charmed circle, but then the numbers lessened until the last decade of the century when more *novi homines* were successful. It is uncertain to what extent families from Latin and Campanian cities shared this privilege of office: Tusculum gave Rome the Fulvii and Ti. Coruncanius and indeed more consular families than any other municipality.[8] Many Latins doubtless settled in Rome, where they enjoyed the rights of *commercium* and intermarriage and where by residence they could claim full citizenship. But a large number of them probably belonged to the poorer classes and had little prospect of or desire for office, and many, being landless, would be enrolled in one of the four urban tribes where their voting power was restricted since the constituency was larger than those of the rustic tribes.

In contrast to the new nobility was the steadily increasing urban population, which included these poorer Latins and indeed all the humbler artisans that were attracted to the capital. Many half-citizens (*cives sine suffragio*) and strangers would take up residence in Rome, as economic conditions and the growth of small industries increased the importance of the city. A large part of this urban populace consisted of freedmen. The manumission of slaves was becoming common, especially as many were prisoners of war who were often as civilized as their masters. As early as 357 a government tax of 5 per cent was levied on manumission and, although a freedman (*libertus*) could not officially be enfranchised, his sons (*libertini*) could, and the *liberti* were doubtless often able to circumvent the law. As most of the *libertini* would be engaged in industry rather than in possession of land, they too would be included in the four urban tribes; possession of land, which was not a necessary qualification for registration on the citizen-roll and the tribes, probably alone entitled a man to registration in a rustic tribe.

The first attempt to improve the position of this urban population was made by Appius Claudius, one of the outstanding personalities of early Rome, at a time when the Romans needed to mobilize their resources against the Samnites and Etruscans. The censorship of Appius in 312 was memorable for his public works and political independence. He improved the water supply by building the first of the Roman aqueducts, which brought water from the Sabine Hills to the increasing population of the city, and he constructed one of the great military roads, with which Rome secured her hold on Italy, the Via Appia between Rome and Capua. (He later built a temple to Bellona, the goddess of war, in the Campus Martius, where the Senate often met, especially to receive victorious generals and foreign ambassadors.) Though a patrician, he attempted to win over the landless urban population by distributing these *humiles* throughout all the tribes (i.e. rustic as well as urban), and by allowing each man to register his property where he chose. This reform gave the landless (but not necessarily poor) population an advantage over the landholders of the rustic tribes, who might not always be able to leave their farms and come to Rome in sufficient numbers to assert their will in public business, whereas previously they had easily been able to outvote the four urban tribes. Appius' measure won him the support of the proletariat and the extreme patricians at the expense of the new nobility. He is said to have given further offence to the nobility in revising the list of the Senate, a right which recently had been transferred to the censors from the consuls by a *lex Ovinia*. He admitted the sons of freedmen to the Senate, but they were promptly rejected by the consuls of the next year, if they were in fact ever admitted. But now that the curule magistracies were open to them and they had a voice in the assemblies they might reach the Senate through a magistracy: for instance, Cn. Flavius, aedile in 304, was the son of a freedman. The reform of Appius provoked considerable opposition and it was repealed by the censors of 304, Q. Fabius Maximus Rullianus and P. Decius Mus, leaders of the new nobility.[9] The proletarians and *libertini* were again confined to the four urban tribes, and landed property came back into its own. Appius' career, which seems more typical of a Cleisthenes or Pericles than an early Roman statesman, was checked for the moment, though he crossed swords with the new nobility more than once in the first decade of the next century.

Cn. Flavius, a magistrate's clerk (*scriba*) and the son of a freedman, who was elected aedile in 304, published a legal handbook of phrases and forms of procedure (*legis actiones*) and posted up in the Forum a calendar of the *dies fasti* and *nefasti*, showing the court days. The traditional account presents many difficulties, since *inter alia* the calendar already had been included in the Twelve Tables. According to Pliny, Flavius was acting with the help of Appius; but Pomponius relates that Flavius stole the book of *legis actiones* from Appius, who had composed it, and presented it to the people who promptly elected him tribune, senator and curule aedile. Though the law was common to both orders, magistrates could often block proceedings on technical grounds, through their more intimate, if not exclusive, knowledge of the precise and intricate phraseology. Perhaps by publishing for the first time, or more probably by making widely known these forms of procedure, the *ius civile Flavianum* marks a real step in the equalization of the orders.

In the year 300 the struggle of the orders entered its penultimate phase. The consul M. Valerius Maximus passed a law which defined and confirmed the right of appeal to the people against a capital sentence; the judicial and coercive powers of the magistrates in the city were checked. At the same time two tribunes, Cn. and Q. Ogulnius, despite the opposition of Appius Claudius, carried a law to enlarge the priestly colleges and throw them open to plebeians. The number of pontiffs was raised from five (probably) to nine by the inclusion of four plebeians; and the four patrician augurs received five plebeian colleagues. Thus the plebeians won a majority in the lesser of the colleges, and later even in the college of pontiffs, where they were assigned another post some time between 292 and 218. Thus the plebs had won their way into the very heart of the camp of the patricians, who retained the monopoly only of the offices of *interrex, rex sacrorum* and *flamen*. Some time after 293 a Lex Maenia extended the clause of the Publilian law of 339 which decreed that the sanction of the *patres* must be given beforehand to legislative enactments; such preliminary sanction was now made necessary in elections, so that the privileges of the patrician members of the Senate were reduced to pure formality.

About 287, at the end of the Samnite wars, the final scene of the drama was enacted. Unfortunately our knowledge of it is small in comparison with its importance. Troubles arising from debt provoked the last secession of the plebs, who withdrew over the Tiber to the Janiculum. A plebeian, Q. Hortensius, was appointed dictator and carried a law that the resolutions of the plebeian assembly (*plebiscita*) should have the force of law and be binding on the whole community. Thus the right first claimed by Valerius and Horatius more than a hundred and fifty years earlier was at last conceded. The Lex Hortensia has been called the final triumph of democracy at Rome. The people were sovereign. At the time when the Romans were completing the unification of Italy, the struggle of the orders was ended.

4. THE MAGISTRATES AND SENATE

The Republican constitution was now unified. The plebs had constructed a state of their own within the patrician state, and without a revolution the two had been fused into one. There was naturally much overlapping of function: for instance, there were four assemblies, the aedileship was duplicated and the tribunes of the plebs did not fit easily into the magisterial picture, but thanks to the Roman genius for adaptation, tempered by traditionalism, the constitution was co-ordinated. When setting up new institutions the Romans preferred to modify rather than to abolish the old, which had religious as well as secular sanctions; practices which were at first adopted for emergencies were then tacitly assumed to be authoritative. Guided less by political theory than by the need to overcome everyday difficulties, the Romans had built an edifice which could always be modified; it was not a cast-iron structure like some of the written constitutions of the Greeks that could only be changed by revolution. Previous enactments could be repealed by subsequent legislation, as they can in England in contrast with the United States of America, where certain fundamental rules cannot be abrogated. (There were, however, certain restrictions, e.g. the Twelve Tables established that laws should lay down general principles, by forbidding a law to be passed against an individual: *privilegia ne irroganto*. Forbidden *privilegia* would cover an English Act of Attainder, as that by which Henry VIII disposed of Thomas Cromwell.) The Roman constitution endured because it was internally flexible and adapted the substance while retaining the form. This flexibility can be traced, for example, in the fundamental changes in the nature of the tribunate or quaestorship or in the growth of the power of the Senate with its theoretical inability to legislate. 'The reason for the superiority of the constitution of our city to that of other states', Cato is reported to have said (Cicero, *de rep.* ii, 1, 2), 'is that the latter almost always had their laws and institutions from one legislator. But our Republic was not made by the genius of one man, but of many, nor in the life of one, but through many centuries and generations.' Polybius writes (vi, 10, 13) in the same strain that the Romans did not achieve their constitution 'by mere thinking, but after many struggles and difficulties, always choosing the best course after actual experience of misfortune'.

There had been three main tendencies at work in the early Republic: the struggle for political equalization, the devolution of power among an increasing number of magistrates, and the extension of the power of the Senate. Amid the constant clash of interests three great organs of the state had been evolved: the magistrates, the Senate and the assemblies. That they worked in harmony was a triumph of compromise and common sense. We must next consider them separately. At the fall of the monarchy the king's power had passed mainly to the two consuls (or praetors) who had been forced to share it in the course of time with an increasing number of magistrates. These had been created partly in a vain attempt by the patricians to retain a monoploy of government, partly because the growing needs of an expanding state necessitated the sharing of responsibility. The most characteristic feature of the magistracy is perhaps that it was simply an *honos*: no salary was paid to an official. This determined its nature, for only the well-to-do propertied classes could attain to it. The plebeians might win the right of entry into the patrician preserves, but only their richer representatives could go in. In theory the magistrates were elected by the whole citizen body, but this electorate was so scattered that the elections were often easily manipulated in favour of a given class; as early as 358 a tribune, C. Poetelius, tried to regulate electioneering propaganda outside Rome (Livy, vii, 15, 12). Thus there had grown up the new nobility of rich landowners who handed down from generation to generation the tradition of office within their own families, and it became more difficult for a *novus homo* who belonged to a family outside the governing circle to win his way to a magistracy. Hence a steady level of efficiency was maintained, but few men of outstanding genius were produced. The early Roman magistrates seem types rather than individuals.

A remarkable feature of the magistracy is the fewness of the offices. Each year there were two consuls, primarily for military affairs, one praetor for jurisdiction, two quaestors for the Treasury and two to accompany the consuls, two curule and two plebeian aediles for policing the city; there were ten plebeian tribunes who at first tended to hinder rather than assist the work of government but who were later worked into the scheme; there were *decemviri stlitibus iudicandis*, later at any rate judges in suits which involved liberty and citizenship; at intervals two censors were appointed to revise the list of citizens and of senators, to supervise public behaviour and to let out state contracts; finally, in an emergency a dictator might be appointed. Thus the higher administrative magistrates, excluding the tribunes, numbered only eleven or at the most fourteen. They were assisted sometimes by a board of technical advisers of senatorial rank (*consilium*), and by numerous subordinates, such as lictors, clerks (*scribae*), messengers (*viatores*) and heralds (*praecones*). Later other appointments were made: the four prefects (*quattuorviri*) to whom the praetors delegated the administration of justice in Campania in 318; the police officers, *triumviri capitales*, appointed about 290, who exercised a summary jurisdiction over petty offenders; and the *duoviri navales* chosen by popular election in 311. But a more important method of dealing with the paucity of magistrates than that of allowing them to delegate authority or of establishing minor magistracies was the *prorogatio imperii* whereby a consul or praetor after his year of office was allowed to act *pro consule* or *pro praetore*. First established in 326 to meet specific military needs, this practical device later became a normal part of constitutional procedure, and from such small beginnings there grew the basis of the military commands that eventually undermined the Republic.

Of the magistrates the consuls, who acted as presidents at home and generals abroad, retained their primacy, but their wings had been clipped. The establishment of consular tribunes had damaged the prestige of the consulship, the creation of other magistracies had robbed it of many of its functions, the extraordinary appointment of proconsuls in effect widened the basis of the office, dictators were appointed frequently, and the growing power of the Senate encroached on the consular field of action. But nevertheless the consuls' powers remained very great, especially as the theatres of war increased. The comparative frequency of the appointment of dictators was due to the exigencies of the great wars of 366–265, but many were nominated for special non-military purposes, such as for holding the elections in the absence of the consuls (*comitiorum habendorum causa*) or for religious purposes. Like the military dictators, these special dictators were required to resign their office when their business was ended. This new use of the dictatorship was one cause of its decline; further, a dictator's sentence was made subject to *provocatio* within the city, perhaps by the Lex Valeria of 300.

The new magistracy created in 366, the praetorship, proved very useful. By custom the praetor relieved the consuls of their civil jurisdiction; as their colleague, though vested with lesser *imperium*, he took their place in Rome when they were absent, summoning and presiding over the Senate, calling an assembly, or if necessary himself commanding an army. But it was his judicial duties that came to be the peculiar mark of his office. Enough has already been said in connection with Appius Claudius to demonstrate the increasing power of the censors, especially when the *lectio senatus* came within their competence. In 339 it was enacted that one censor must be a plebeian; and no act was more symbolic of the real union of the orders than the ceremonial cleansing of the state (*lustrum*) by a plebeian censor in 280. The two sets of aediles, curule and plebeian, were soon harmonized; they were responsible mainly for municipal administration, such as the safety of roads and buildings, public order, market regulations, weights and measures, the water and corn supply, and arrangements for public festivals, but they also had judicial authority to prosecute for offences against the community such as usury and the occupation of public land. The quaestors, whose numbers were raised to four in 421, and to eight in about 267, remained chiefly financial officials, but those who served on a consul's military staff not only administered his financial affairs but also could themselves undertake military duties. Finally, the tribunes of the plebs, though not strictly magistrates of the Roman people, were gradually recognized as such; by a wise compromise the patricians worked these plebeian officers into the constitution. At first the tribune was the revolutionary officer under whose aegis and leadership the plebeians had won political equality, but after the middle of the fourth century he became less of a class leader and more of a representative of the rights of the individual against the claims of the state. He could act as public prosecutor against any magistrate for political offences except the dictator (as was done in 423, 420, 362 and 291; in the last case in the interests of the Senate), and he could pass laws through the Concilium Plebis. Gradually he acquired the right to speak in and finally (in 216) to convoke the Senate, which soon realized the value of the tribune's veto as a means of controlling the other magistrates as well as his fellow tribunes; and there would be few years when the Senate was unable to win the support of at least one of the ten tribunes.

While magistrates came and went the Senate remained. The need of a permanent governing body which could make quick decisions in times of crisis led to an immense increase in its powers. Theoretically it could not legislate, but its resolutions (*senatus consulta*) were generally obeyed, and it came to wield a predominating moral guidance in the state. After the fifth century more plebeians won entry, and the rise of the new nobility strengthened its authority at a time when patrician prestige was weakening. Originally its numbers had been filled by the kings and then by the consuls at will, but tradition gradually restricted the consuls' choice to ex-magistrates. When the duty of revising the list was transferred from the consuls to the censors by the Ovinian law they were instructed to give preference to ex-magistrates. As members retained their seats for life, the Senate might justly be considered a representative council, embodying all the experience of past and present. The sovereign people who claimed ultimate authority were more ready to acquiesce in its rule, since it was they who elected the magistrates and thus they were indirectly responsible for the composition of the Senate. It tended, however, to remain conservative, since the higher magistrates were elected by the Comitia Centuriata where wealth predominated. Its great reverence for custom, *mos maiorum*, together with its numbers, tended to stereotype its policy in a safe and mediocre mould; but if it lacked brilliance it guided the state safely through many troublous seas and its collective wisdom often checked the extravagant or dangerous whims of the sovereign people.

The people, with their more cumbrous assemblies, were willing for the most part to acquiesce in the growth of the Senate's power: still more were the magistrates over whom it soon exercised almost absolute control. It became customary for the consul to refer every matter of importance to the Senate, and he was morally bound to follow its advice when formally expressed in a *senatus consultum*. The average official would not dare to challenge the authority of a body composed of ex-magistrates, on which he himself would sit for the rest of his career; if he was bold enough to withstand this moral pressure, he could generally be checked by a tribune. Thus the magistrates became the executive of a senatorial administration which claimed by right of custom alone to direct the policy of the state in all its important branches, especially in finance and foreign affairs. Only the actual declaration of war and concluding of peace were left to the people, and even then the preliminary diplomatic negotiations had been conducted by the Senate, which was able to give the people a strong lead. Finally, the dignity rather than the actual power of the Senate has found its classic expression in the report of Pyrrhus' ambassador, Cineas, that the Senate was an assembly of kings.

5. THE ASSEMBLIES AND PEOPLE

In practice the Roman people were willing to allow the Senate and magistrates to conduct a large part of the business of the state, but in theory they claimed to represent the ultimate source of authority. During the century that followed the Gallic invasion they expressed this authority through the legislative, judicial and electoral activity of their assemblies, the Curiata, Centuriata and Tributa, and of the purely plebeian Concilium Plebis: but they could only take action on matters submitted to them by the presiding magistrate. The tendency was, however, in the direction of real democracy; but it was checked by the skill with which the nobles manipulated the tribunate and religion and by the rapid expansion of Roman arms which distracted attention from domestic affairs and increased the control of the Senate. But in theory the Comitia were sovereign.

In conformity with their custom and conservatism the Romans allowed the various Comitia to exist side by side; none was abolished, although their functions were more clearly differentiated as time passed. The Comitia Curiata continued to assent to private acts like adoption and bequests, but its chief function remained its right formally to confer *imperium* on consuls and praetors. This, however, became such a formality that thirty lictors and three augurs could form a quorum of the *curiae*. The three other assemblies, Centuriata, Tributa, and Concilium Plebis, all had the right to legislate by the year 287; before this date the Concilium Plebis only claimed the right without possessing it by law. The Comitia Tributa gradually superseded the Comitia Centuriata in many spheres; although it is not always easy to determine through which body a given bill was passed, the tribal assemblies, especially the Concilium Plebis, were becoming the main legislative organs, partly because the thirty-five tribes were easier to handle than 193 centuries, and partly because when the presiding officers, who were the regular magistrates, included an increasing number of plebeians, these would tend to lay their proposals before the newer assembly. So the influence of wealth and age, which prevailed in the Comitia Centuriata, gave place to the predominance of the smaller country landowners who formed the backbone of the tribes, in which every man, rich and poor alike, had an equal vote. Indeed, it may have been the growing importance of the middle classes to the state that led to the shift from the centuries to the tribes; and later the Comitia Centuriata itself was reformed to bring it more into line with the Tributa and to give greater weight to the small landowner (p. 187). But while most legislation was carried through the tribal assemblies, the Centuriata still legislated regarding the declaration of war, the signing of peace, and conferring plenary power on the censor. The electoral functions of the assemblies remained divided: the Centuriata elected consuls, praetors and censors, the Tributa curule aediles and quaestors, the Concilium Plebis tribunes and plebeian aediles. Jurisdiction likewise was divided. The Comitia Centuriata remained the court of appeal in capital cases, while the Tributa heard cases on appeal when the punishment was only a fine; it is possible that trials still took place before the separate Concilium Plebis.

In all branches of government the Roman people was supreme, but in all the Senate overshadowed them: 'senatus populusque Romanus' was not an idle phrase. The people, or more precisely all adult male citizens, comprised the electorate, but in practice their choice of candidates was limited to those who could fulfil the duties of office. In legislation they had ultimate authority, but the resolutions of the Senate had in effect the same validity as their laws; and in time the Senate and praetors took over much of the detailed legislation from the assemblies. Further, the senators often invited tribunes to discuss a measure with them, before presenting it to the tribes. Judicial affairs also gradually passed into the hands of the praetors and Senate, though the assemblies did not allow interference in certain cases, as has been seen. The executive was elected directly by the people, but it was to the Senate rather that the magistrates showed deference. Finally, the administration was in practice transferred by the people to the Senate which acted as a Cabinet in place of the unwieldy assemblies; and the people only elected the Senate in an indirect manner. Thus at the very time when the Lex Hortensia proclaimed the sovereign right of the Roman people and Rome was approaching a democracy, the pendulum swung back in favour of a more oligarchical form of government. This was partly due to the draining off to the colonies of many poorer citizens with the consequent increase in the influence of the remaining landholding nobility, and partly to the complication of business which forced the Senate and magistrates to take the initiative. Further, the average Roman was not much interested in politics. Elections generally meant merely a change in the executive magistrates, not in the policy of the state: the legislative assemblies and the Senate, which determined Rome's policy, remained the same. As long as the government protected his interests the small farmer cared little about the form of that government. Some of the nobility might be inspired by abstract Greek theories of government, a tribune might be a progressive democrat or the tool of the conservatives, but while his daily life ran smoothly the average farmer or town worker worried less about who governed him than about the efficiency and justice of that government. Thus at the very moment that the theoretical powers of the Roman people were emphasized and a real democracy was within their grasp, they in fact succumbed more and more to the control of the senatorial oligarchy.

VI

ROME'S CONQUEST AND ORGANIZATION OF ITALY

1. ROME AND CAMPANIA

Whether or not Rome had already crossed swords with her Samnite allies, the days when such a conflict would blaze up were fast approaching. Though distracted by the presence of Alexander of Epirus in southern Italy, the Samnites coveted the fertile plain of Campania and would not be held at bay for ever; and the Latin revolt had already drawn the Romans into the vortex of Campanian politics. Rome had granted half-citizenship to several cities there: Fundi, Formiae, Capua, Suessula and Cumae. The Sidicini were still unpunished for their participation in the Latin war: those around Teanum were attacked in 336 and granted alliance with Rome, while Cales was stormed and received a Latin colony (334). This outpost, which commanded the valley between Latium and Campania, protected the Campanian plain from the Sidicini and formed a buffer state between the Samnites on the east and the Roman possessions on the west. Despite the recent Latin revolt Rome wisely continued her policy of founding Latin colonies, in which all her allies were allowed to share; Cales received 2,500 colonists and was granted the right of coinage. In 332 Acerrae was granted the Roman *civitas sine suffragio*, and soon afterwards Rome entered into alliance with Fabrateria and Frusino, which lay in and above the Trerus valley not far from the Samnite frontier (*c.* 330). In 329 Privernum was taken and the anti-Roman leaders were banished; it was granted *civitas sine suffragio*, part of its territory was confiscated and was later formed into a Roman tribe, the Oufentina (318). In the same year Tarracina, which commanded the coast road, received a

Roman colony, and in 328 a Latin colony was settled at Fregellae to block the north-western entrance to the fertile plain of the middle Liris. Thus the Romans gradually extended the bounds of their new confederacy and created a barrier against the north-west frontier of the Samnites.

In 326 the Romans strengthened their influence in Campania by winning the alliance of Neapolis, the Greek commercial centre of mid-Italy. The detailed account of how this came about is largely apocryphal, but the cause was political dissension within the city. The 'Old Citizens' (the Palaeopolitai, perhaps the refugees from Cumae; p. 109) with the help of Nola introduced a Samnite garrison into the town, or at any rate entered into friendly relations with the Samnites. Capua appealed on behalf of the Neapolitans to Rome. Q. Publilius Philo was sent to besiege the town in 327 and as the siege continued he was kept in his command for the next year as proconsul. Neapolis ultimately got rid of the Samnite garrison; the pro-Roman Greeks surrendered the town to the Romans and were doubtless glad to put their commercial activity under Roman protection against Samnite raids. An alliance was granted to Neapolis on favourable terms, by which the city was freed from the obligation of military service in return for patrolling and guarding the harbour.[1] About this time Nuceria also entered into alliance with Rome.

Not only had the Romans thus acquired an alliance which the Samnites had desired to preserve for themselves, not only had they gained control of all Campania except Nola, but they followed up this success by capturing Rufrium and Allifae on the Samnite frontier. War was at hand. The actual cause of the outbreak is uncertain and unimportant. Samnite expansion and Rome's desire for order on her frontiers led to the inevitable clash, which was hastened by the recent extension of these frontiers by colonization and alliance. Rome is said to have found allies on the other flank of Samnium in the Apulians who, after long struggles with Tarentum, realized that their interests lay with the Greeks against the Oscan invaders. If such an alliance was in fact made, the Romans would have found it difficult to join hands with their new allies, since they could not pass Oscan Nola and the Lucanians without violating their neutrality. In any case, Apulia played little part in the beginning of the Second Samnite War.[2]

2. THE GREAT SAMNITE WAR

Mommsen's fervid nationalism led him to declare that 'history cannot but do the noble people [the Samnites] the justice of acknowledging that they understood and performed their duty', that is, they fought for Italian liberty. In the same strain Livy made a Samnite spokesman declare : 'Let us settle the question whether Samnite or Roman is to govern Italy.' But probably neither side was conscious of what fate held in the balance. War developed from some petty frontier dispute and its result was still hidden in the womb of time. Rome was conscious, or soon became conscious, of the immediate difficulty rather than of the ultimate meaning of the task that lay ahead. The mountain warriors of Samnium might be defeated by the Roman phalanx and the Campanian cavalry on the plains, but once they had to be tackled amid the broken ground of their mountainous terrain, fighting for their homeland in small organized bands, they would present the Roman legionaries with a stiffer problem, though one not insuperable to a nation so adaptable as Rome. It was probably to meet these needs, rather than those that had arisen just after the Gallic sack of the city, that the Romans decided to make their army more flexible by introducing manipular tactics in place of the stiffer phalanx : these reforms are discussed below in the context of the history of the army (pp. 343ff.).

The military history of the early years of the Second Samnite War, which broke out in 326, is very obscure, as the details given by Livy are unreliable. While one legion covered Latium or Campania a second could take the initiative. In 325 D. Junius Brutus in a turning movement through the central Apennines won a victory over the Vestini ; the other small Sabellian tribes, the Marsi, Paeligni, and Marrucini, were presumably friendly to Rome. The dictator of 324 L. Papirius Cursor, is credited with a victory at the unknown Imbrivium. The Romans scarcely penetrated into Apulia, as tradition maintains, though a Samnite attack on Fregellae is plausible. Little is known of these years of guerrilla warfare, during which the Romans were learning more plant tactics. In 321 they determined on more vigorous action. The two consuls, T. Veturius and Sp. Postumius, marshalled both consular armies at Calatia in Campania and advanced in what was probably an attempt to defeat the Caudini in Samnium itself. Alternatively, they may have been tricked into believing that the Samnite army under Gavius Pontius was in Apulia, and thrust forward in the hope of cutting it off from its base and winning a decisive victory on the Apulian plains. Whatever their intentions, they advanced into the valley of the Caudine Forks, where they found the way blocked by the Samnites. On trying to withdraw they discovered that the entrance to the defile was also held by the enemy. After vain attempts to cut their way through the encircling ring the consuls surrendered to avoid starvation. Pontius dictated terms : the Romans were to withdraw their garrisons from territory which the Samnites regarded as their own ; they were not to reopen the war ; six hundred Roman knights were to be given as hostages ; and the Roman army was to pass under a 'yoke' of spears.[3]

Roman annalists tried to palliate the disgrace by making the Senate repudiate the agreement, and by crediting the Roman legions with a series of fictitious victories. In fact, however, the peace was observed; the Romans surrendered Fregellae and refrained from hostilities against the Samnites.[4] Yet the blow to Rome's prestige made some of the subject communities restless. Hostages were exacted from Canusium and Teanum in Apulia, and Roman prefects were sent to steady Capua and Cumae in 318. Two new tribes were formed in land which was still lying idle ; the territory confiscated from Privernum became the home of the Oufentina tribe, and the district north of Capua of the Falerna.

By 316 both sides were ready for war again. The Romans had quietened much of the discontent and were now able to put four legions into the field each year; the Samnites were looking askance at Rome's increasing influence in Apulia. War restarted when the Romans seized Satricum-on-Liris; in 315 they sent L. Papirius Cursor to capture Luceria, where he established a Latin colony (in 314). But the Samnites, who were now strengthened by the adhesion of the league of Nuceria, advanced past Sora to the Liris valley and the coast where they defeated a hastily levied army of Roman reserves at Lautulae, near Tarracina (315). They perhaps even forced their way into the Latin plain and raided Ardea.[5] Rome was in grave danger, her prestige was shaken, the Aurunci and Capua revolted, the Campanian cities began to waver, but the Latins remained loyal. The Samnites had reached the high-water mark of their success and could not shake the solidarity of the Roman confederacy: Lautulae, no less than Hannibal's successes later, tested and proved the wisdom of Rome's treatment of her allies. In the next year, with characteristic doggedness and untiring energy, the Romans gathered strength to launch an offensive and won a great victory over the Samnites, probably at Tarracina.

It remained to reassert their leadership. Capua and the Aurunci were speedily brought to heel; Fregellae and Sora were recaptured and the latter was severely punished (313 or 312) ; Nola and Calatia were defeated and made allies. Latin colonies were sent to Suessa Aurunca and Pontia to watch the coast road, to Saticula to cover the Campanian frontier, and to Interamna to guard the middle Liris valley. The construction of the 'Queen of Roads', the Via Appia, through the Volscian and Campanian

coast land was commenced. In 311 the Romans, persuaded perhaps by
their new Greek allies at Naples, turned their thoughts to the sea ; a small
Naval Board, *duoviri navales*, was set up, perhaps to reorganize the fleet
captured from Antium in 338. The following year a small squadron,
doubtless manned largely by Greeks, was sent to effect a landing at
Pompeii and to attack the district of Nuceria, but the move was not a
success. The days of an effective Roman fleet were not yet come, though
the ships may have afforded some protection to the colony at Ostia. Thus
by 312 Rome had recovered from the disasters of Caudium and Lautulae,
had strengthened her hold on Campania and her influence in Apulia, and
had begun to hem in Samnium with a narrowing ring of allies and fortress
colonies. Her recovery was due not a little to her superior numbers and to
her wisdom in adapting her equipment, tactics and strategy to meet her
foe (pp. 346ff.).

The Etruscans had long remained quiet and had taken no share in the
Roman-Samnite struggle, partly perhaps because remembering how the
restless Samnites had overthrown their empire in Campania they did not
desire to see them become their southern neighbours in place of the more
civilized Romans ; and partly because towns like Sutrium, Nepete, Caere,
Tarquinii and Falerii were on friendly terms with Rome and would check
any hostile feeling on the part of their northern kinsmen, who, in the days
of their decadence, were preoccupied with the Gauls. But when this
danger decreased and when they saw that Rome's star was rising, they
were more ready to interfere to restore the balance. Further, Rome's forty
years' truce with Tarquinii was now expiring. In 311, therefore, the
Etruscans threw in their lot with Samnium and advanced against
Sutrium. But in 310 the Roman consul Q. Fabius Rullianus in a bold
counter-stroke forced his way through the dread Ciminian Hills into
central Etruria, where he is credited with a victory. The Romans made
treaties with Cortona, Perusia and Arretium; Volsinii was taken, and in
308 the alliance with Tarquinii was renewed for another forty years and
alliances were made with the Umbrian towns of Camerinum and
Ocriculum.[6]

Meantime the Samnite war dragged on. In 312 the Romans captured
Peltuinum in the country of the Marrucini, and attacked Samnium from
northern Apulia, where they only succeeded in capturing Allifae. No
sooner had Q. Fabius induced Nuceria to return to her alliance with
Rome than he had to hasten north to the country of the Marsi, which the
Samnites invaded in 308. Just when Rome might have been expected to
undertake a more vigorous offensive the Hernici revolted: Sora,

Arpinum, Frusino, Anagnia, and Calatia all went over to the Samnites, though Aletrium, Ferentinum and Verulae remained inactive. In 306 Q. Marcius stormed Anagnia, which received *civitas sine suffragio*, while the inactive towns were made Roman allies; Frusino surrendered. In 305 the Aequi and Paeligni supported the uncrushed Hernici, and the Samnites broke into the *ager Falernus*. They were repulsed, and after a severe struggle a relieving Samnite army was defeated, probably near Bovianum;[7] the capture of Arpinum, Sora and Cerfennia ended the resistance of the Hernici and Paeligni. In 304 the Aequi were defeated by P. Sempronius, and the Samnites at long last accepted the *foedus antiquum*. Alliances were made with the Marsi, Paeligni, Marrucini, and Frentani, and two years later with the Vestini. *Civitas sine suffragio* was granted to Arpinum and Trebula. A Latin colony was settled at Sora, and two strong ones on Aequian territory at Alba Fucens (303 or 300) and at Carsioli (302 or 298). The territory confiscated from the Aequi was distributed to Roman citizens. Two new tribes were formed in 299, the Aniensis from Aequian territory south of Carsioli and the Teretina in the Trerus valley from land taken from Frusino.

Thus after twenty years of stiff fighting the Samnites still retained their independence but had been thrust back into their own country. Rome's gains were solid rather than spectacular. She had won some frontier towns, for example, Saticula, Arpinum, Sora and Luceria; she had allied herself with the hill folk of the Abruzzi in central Italy and with the people of northern Apulia; the treaties with Nola and Nuceria completed her hold on Campania; and her fortresses along the Liris and at Luceria were real accessions to her strength. She had thus become the first state in Italy, and, as such, a Mediterranean power.[8] Consequently, when the Carthaginians wished to avert the risk that Agathocles of Syracuse, who was contesting their control of western Sicily, might appeal to Italy for help, the two republics may well have entered into a closer political agreement which excluded the Romans from interfering in Sicily and the Carthaginians in Italy (306).[9] Though Rome was not yet ready to measure her strength against Carthage or against the kingdoms of Macedon, Egypt and Syria which at this very time were being carved out of Alexander's empire, yet her territory exceeded not only that of each of the surviving leagues of Italy, but also that of the Syracusan empire of Agathocles.

3. ROME'S TRIUMPHANT ADVANCE

The consolidation of Rome's confederacy was rudely interrupted by a Gallic invasion which tempted the Samnites and some of the Etruscans to try conclusions with the Romans once again. New hordes of Celts had crossed the Alps and were unsettling their kinsmen in Cisalpine Gaul. One band swept down through Etruria and even invaded Roman territory in 299, but the main body was fighting the Veneti. The Romans hastily tried to block their southern advance by forming an alliance with the Picentes and capturing Umbrian Nequinum where they founded a Latin colony named Narnia. While Rome was thus preoccupied the Samnites made a final bid for freedom and invaded Lucania. One of the consuls of 298, L. Cornelus Scipio Barbatus, captured Taurasia and Cisauna in south-west Samnium, drove back the Samnites, and exacted hostages from the Lucanians. Meantime his colleague, Cn. Fulvius, attacked northern Samnium where he captured Aufidena, though probably not Bovianum.[10] But while the consuls Q. Fabius Rullianus and P. Decius Mus continued the campaign in Samnium during the next two years and captured Murgantia and Romulea in the east, the Samnites, under the leadership of Gellius Egnatius, conceived the bold plan of co-operating with the northern enemies of Rome in a combined attack. In 296, while the storm was gathering, the Samnites raided the Falernian plain, perhaps to distract attention from the north, but they were driven back by Volumnius, and two maritime colonies of Roman citizens were planted at Minturnae and Sinuessa on the Appian Way; Volumnius himself was recalled to support his colleague Appius Claudius in southern Etruria. The next year the Romans hurried their full force through Umbria to prevent the Samnites joining forces with the Gauls. They were too late and their advance guard was defeated near Camerinum. The situation was very grave. It remained to face the allied forces of Samnites, Gauls, and perhaps some Umbrians. A great battle was fought at Sentinum, where the heroic sacrifice of the veteran Decius Mus, the skill of Fabius, and the steadiness of the Roman legions broke the forces of the coalition.[11] The disaster of Allia was avenged and the fate of central Italy was sealed. The surviving Gauls and Samnites scattered to their homes, while Fabius marched back through Etruria. The next year the Romans ended the unrest in Etruria by granting a peace for forty years to Volsinii, Perusia and Arretium; as they still had to deal with the Samnites, they were ready to be lenient in Etruria.

But although the coalition was broken and its designer, Gellius Egnatius, lay on the field of Sentinum, the Samnites were far from crushed and succeeded in defeating L. Postumius near Luceria in 294. The Romans were hampered by the visitation of a plague, but in 293 they again took the offensive. The geographical details of the campaign are obscure, but it appears that Sp. Carvilius captured Amiternum to check some Sabine restlessness, while his colleague L. Papirius won a great victory at Aquilonia (Lacedogna) on the Apulian frontier and thus completed the work begun at Sentinum. In the following year a truce was reached with Falerii which had revolted; in 291 L. Postumius stormed Venusia, which controlled the main route from Campania to Apulia, and a large Latin colony was settled there. The Samnites were at last exhausted and peace was re-established in 290. The terms are not preserved, but Rome's booty was great and the Samnites were mulcted of territory, so that henceforth the Upper and Middle Volturnus replaced the Liris as the dividing line between Rome and Samnium. Although the Samnite League apparently was allowed to continue in existence, the Samnites were no longer friends but 'allies', subject to Rome's demands for troops and obedience in foreign policy. In this same year, 290, M'. Curius Dentatus marched through the territory of the Sabines who were still independent, though doubtless they had become largely Romanized. The whole population was granted *civitas sine suffragio* and enrolled in the Roman state; not long afterwards it received full franchise. A few square miles of the territory of the Praetuttii, an offshoot of the Sabines, was annexed; a Latin colony was established at Hadria to guard the coast road along the Adriatic.

After a few years of peace the Gauls again gave trouble. The Senones crossed the Apennines and besieged Etruscan Arretium which remained faithful to its alliance with Rome. Caecilius Metellus tried to relieve Arretium and met his death in a battle which cost the Romans some 13,000 men (284). This grave disaster encouraged Etruscan Vulci and Volsinii to revolt, while some Samnites and Lucanians in the south followed suit. But though the Romans had to face danger from several directions, their enemies could not unite to form another coalition. After the Senones had murdered some Roman ambassadors, M'. Curius Dentatus marched into the *ager Gallicus* and drove them out with merciless vigour.[12] Their land was annexed and a Roman colony was settled at Sena on the Adriatic. In 283 the Boii took up the cudgels laid down by their kinsmen and joined the Etruscan cities in their revolt. On their southward march they were defeated by Cornelius Dolabella at Lake Vadimo, only fifty miles from Rome. The next year a similar attempt ended in a similar disaster near Populonia; after this the Boii remained quiet for fifty years. Volsinii and Vulci held out till 280 when they were defeated, deprived of part of their territory and enrolled as Rome's allies. It is possible that the Etruscan towns of Tarquinii, Rusellae, Vetulonia,

Populonia, and Volaterrae had participated in the revolt and were now coerced into alliance with Rome. But no sooner were the Gauls defeated and the Etruscans pacified than the Romans were forced to turn to southern Italy where the Samnites and Lucanians were restless, where Thurii appealed for Rome's help and where in 280 the Greek adventurer, Pyrrhus, King of Epirus, had landed.

4. THE GREEKS OF SOUTHERN ITALY

The sun of Hellenism was slowly sinking in the west. The Greek cities in southern Italy had long suffered at the hands of the Sabellic Lucanians and Bruttians, who were receiving the final thrust of that pressure of peoples which began beyond the Alps. Unwilling, as always, to co-operate voluntarily, and not forced into a semblance of unity by the strong hand of a tyrant, many Italiote cities had succumbed to the natives. The southernmost cities, of which Tarentum was the strongest thanks to its trade with the neighbouring hinterland and with Greece, had maintained their ground by hiring professional soldiers from Greece. Archidamus of Sparta had been called in and involuntarily did Rome the service of distracting the attention of the Samnites during the Latin revolt before he fell fighting in 338. Soon afterwards, with the help of Alexander the Molossian, King of Epirus and brother-in-law of Alexander the Great, the Tarentines tried to establish a claim to the downlands of Apulia. It was perhaps at this time that they made a treaty with Rome, by which Roman warships were not to sail east of the Lacinian promontory, near Croton; the Romans were not yet particularly interested in Apulia or the south.[13] Alexander's ambitions, which soon outran the desires of his Tarentine employers, were quenched by his death in 330. Rome's alliance with Naples in 327 must have attracted the notice of the southern Greeks, while her operations in Apulia during the Second Samnite War, especially the founding of a colony at Luceria, irritated the Tarentines, who were probably forced to resign their claims to northern Apulia. Renewed attacks by the Lucanians induced the Tarentines to call in Cleonymus of Sparta in 303; his personal ambitions soon caused his dismissal after a defeat by the barbarians, who were probably not supported by the Romans as tradition relates. The intervention of Agathocles of Syracuse temporarily checked the Bruttians (c. 298–295), but more significant was the founding of a Latin colony at Venusia in 291.[14] The smaller Greek cities began to look for help from the Romans, who though allied to the Lucanians had overthrown the Samnites, rather than from Tarentum or from Agathocles, whose early brilliance had declined and whose empire collapsed at his death in 289.

About 285 Thurii appealed to the Romans for help against the Lucanians. Some aid was apparently given, in return for which a Roman tribune was honoured with a golden crown. In 282 Thurii again appealed and the Romans sent C. Fabricius with a consular army to drive back the Lucanians and to garrison Thurii. Rhegium, Locri and perhaps Croton also availed themselves of Rome's protection. Rome was thus suddenly forced to define her policy towards southern Italy. After due deliberation she decided to intervene rather than to abandon the Greek cities to the onslaughts of her Lucanian allies; this decision was due perhaps to the influence of the younger plebeian leaders whose power was increased by the recent political victory of the plebs in 287.[15] But although it was becoming increasingly evident that the Senate must now think in terms of Italy as a whole and extend the range of its policy, it is equally true that the Romans liked quiet neighbours. Alexander of Epirus had advanced as far as Paestum and Agathocles had caused considerable trouble; Rome would be glad to end the need for these foreign *condottieri*. Also the infant Roman fleet might find Thurii a useful station now that Rome had established colonies on the Adriatic. Finally, as the Lucanians had become restless when the Gauls attacked Rome's northern frontier, the Romans would welcome the opportunity of punishing them. Thus all considerations forced Rome to undertake the cause of Thurii.

The Tarentines, who had done little to justify their hegemony among the Italiotes, replied by attacking ten Roman ships which appeared off their harbour; they sank four, captured another and scattered the rest. They followed up this unprovoked attack by marching to Thurii, driving out the Roman garrison and sacking the town. Roman envoys, who demanded very moderate reparations, were insulted. War was forced on the Romans; the consul L. Aemilius Barbula was sent to attack Tarentum if it still refused to make redress (281). The Tarentines, who had already summoned the help of Pyrrhus, King of Epirus, were on the point of capitulating when the King's envoy, Cineas, arrived and turned the scales in favour of war. The cause of this remarkable outburst is perhaps found in the party politics of Tarentum. It is true that by sailing east of the Lacinian promontory the Romans had broken their formal treaty; but as this was old and had been made with King Alexander it might well be considered to have been abrogated. The Roman fleet may have been innocently cruising round on a tour of inspection or on its way to the new Adriatic colonies, but more probably it had come to offer moral if not physical support to the pro-Roman oligarchs in Tarentum. The Tarentine democrats may thus have had good cause to distrust its presence and resorted to violence in the expectation of help from Pyrrhus. Rome's quarrel with Tarentum would have soon been over and have had little significance, had not Pyrrhus answered the appeal.

5. THE ITALIAN ADVENTURE OF PYRRHUS

Pyrrhus, the chivalrous king of Epirus, was quite ready to turn his back on the troubled waters of Hellenistic politics and to seek fresh adventures in the west at the call of Tarentum. Being the son-in-law of Agathocles and also a relative of Alexander the Great, this Hellenistic prince may well have dreamed of building up an empire in the west. Courageous and ambitious, a skilful soldier and an inspiring leader, he could count on the help of the Samnites, Lucanians, Bruttians, and Messapians together with the Greek cities of Tarentum, Metapontum and Heraclea, in a crusade against Rome. And perhaps he might even hope to shake the Italian confederacy, especially as Rome was distracted on her northern front, where the Gauls had only recently been defeated and some Etruscan cities were still resisting. Beguiled by his ambitions, he landed at Tarentum with a force of 25,000 professional soldiers and twenty elephants (280). Profiting by the experience of his predecessor Alexander the Molossian, he demanded that the Tarentines should hand over their citadel and give him complete control for the duration of the war; in return he promised to remain in Italy no longer than was necessary. He utilized his new powers to force the Tarentines to transfer their attention from the theatres and gymnasium to the parade ground.[16]

The Romans hastened to the attack, perhaps without full realization of the gravity of the situation. In the early summer of 280 one consul was busy beating out the smouldering resistance in Etruria, while his colleague, Valerius Laevinus, marched south to meet Pyrrhus in battle near Heraclea. The opposing forces were about numerically equal, but the citizen militia of Rome and her allies were face to face with a first-class professional Hellenistic army. The Roman legion met the Macedonian phalanx for the first time. The tactics employed by Pyrrhus were essentially similar to those of Alexander and Hannibal. He sought to hold or wear down the Roman infantry with the serried ranks of his phalanx, which presented to the short swords of the legionaries a hedge of projecting spearheads, almost as impenetrable as a barbed-wire entanglement; at the same time his elephants and cavalry not only prevented his line from being outflanked but also broke the enemy's wings and turned their flanks instead. So it fell out at Heraclea. The Romans were terrified by their first encounter in battle with elephants, which untrained horses will not face. Their cavalry was driven back, and leaving 7,000 men on the field they fled to Venusia, where Aemilius, a consul of the previous year, was still stationed. But Pyrrhus, whose resources were far more limited than those of his foe, lost 4,000 men in this 'Pyrrhic' victory, though his cause was strengthened by the support of the Lucanians and Samnites and by the adhesion of Croton and Locri; Rhegium would have followed suit, but for the energy of the officer commanding the garrison troops.

Pyrrhus followed up his victory by a dash towards Rome, not hoping to storm the city, but perhaps anticipating like Hannibal later that the allies of Rome would rally to his cause; he may also have wished to join forces with the Etruscans. But he was disappointed. Capua and Naples shut their gates against him; Laevinus and Aemilius hung on his heels; the Latins gave no sign of disaffection; and the two legions in Etruria, having finished their task, were recalled to block his advance. When forty miles from Rome he turned back to Tarentum, while his army retired to winter quarters in Campania. In the autumn he received a Roman embassy under Fabricius, who had come to negotiate for the return of prisoners. Having received proof of the solidarity of Rome's confederacy Pyrrhus was ready to treat and sent Cineas back to Rome with Fabricius, together with some of the prisoners on parole. He offered to restore all prisoners and to end the war, if the Romans would make peace with Tarentum, grant autonomy to the Greeks, and return all territory conquered from the Lucanians and Samnites. These terms would have severely limited the spread of Roman interests in the south and have created a Tarentine domination there. The offer was accompanied by lavish presents to the leading senators who, unaccustomed to the ways of Hellenistic diplomacy, rejected the gifts as bribes. A party in Rome favoured peace, but it was soon silenced by the oratory of the blind old censor, Appius Claudius, who rebuked the Senate for discussing terms while a victorious enemy was still on Italian soil. Pyrrhus must again try the hazard of war.[17]

Having failed in Campania, Pyrrhus threatened the Roman strong-holds of Luceria and Venusia in Apulia and perhaps hoped to press up the Adriatic coast and detach the northern Samnites. His forces, now strengthened by contingents of Samnites and Lucanians, were about equal to the two consular armies, which were concentrated near Venusia in 279 to check his advance. He met the Romans in a second pitched battle not far from Asculum on rough ground which enabled the legionaries to resist his phalanx for a whole day. The next morning Pyrrhus drew up his troops on more level ground where the phalanx forced back the Roman line, which was rolled up by an elephant charge. The Romans avoided complete disaster by regaining their camp, and though they had lost one consul and 6,000 men Pyrrhus left 3,500 men on the field. He was, however, prevented from following up this victory by news from Greece and Sicily which made him eager to conclude peace in Italy.

A Celtic invasion of Macedonia offered Pyrrhus the opportunity of playing the role of champion of Greece with the chance of gaining the Macedonian throne, while the Syracusans sent envoys begging him to save them from the Carthaginians who were within an ace of winning the whole of Sicily. Unable to serve the cause of Hellenism in two countries at once, Pyrrhus chose the Sicilian venture and tried to rid himself of his Italian commitments by reaching terms with Fabricius who, as consul for 278, had led his troops into Campania ; perhaps Pyrrhus claimed no more than immunity for Tarentum. Carthage, however, was alive to the desirability of keeping Pyrrhus engaged in Italy and sent Mago with 120 warships to remind Rome of their old alliance and to offer help against Pyrrhus. When the Romans abruptly declined this aid, Mago sailed off to visit Pyrrhus ; he perhaps promised to arrange peace between Rome and the king, so that the latter would be free to return to Greece, while he threatened to wreck negotiations with Rome if Pyrrhus persisted in crossing to Sicily. His offer was rejected, and Mago returned to Rome, where he obtained an agreement which kept Rome from making peace. No defensive alliance was struck, but it was arranged that if they made an agreement against Pyrrhus, it should be with the stipulation that it should be lawful to render mutual aid in whichever country Pyrrhus attacked, i.e. a temporary suspension of the restrictions imposed by a treaty of 306 (p. 136). Whichever party might need help, Carthage was to provide ships for transport or war, and to aid Rome by sea, though she was not obliged to land troops against her will. Rome thus gained money to finance the war and a fleet to blockade Tarentum, while if Pyrrhus crossed to Sicily she was not obliged to help Carthage there. His object achieved, Mago sailed off to Syracuse, leaving *en route* five hundred Roman soldiers to strengthen the garrison at Rhegium. Pyrrhus meanwhile had retired to Tarentum where he left half his troops to defend his allies ; with the rest he set sail for Sicily in the autumn of 278.[18]

During Pyrrhus' absence the Romans gradually forced the Samnites,

Lucanians and Bruttians into submission; whether they were equally successful against the Italiote Greeks is more doubtful. It is recorded that Fabricius won over Heraclea in 278, that Locri revolted and Croton was captured in 277, and that the Campanian garrison of Rhegium seized Croton for themselves. After a meteoric career in Sicily, Pyrrhus decided to return to Italy; if he failed to win a great victory, which alone could restore his fortunes, he would proceed to Greece. On crossing from Sicily late in 276 he was defeated by the Punic fleet in an engagement which must have confirmed his decision to leave the west.[19] He then recaptured Locri and Croton (if it is admitted that he had ever lost them). After pillaging the temple treasure of Persephone at Locri, to the superstitious horror of the Greeks, he reached Tarentum. In 275 he marched northwards with his diminished forces on a brilliantly-conceived campaign, which ended in an inglorious rearguard action. One of the consuls, Manius Curius, was near Malventum (the future Beneventum), the other was posted in Lucania. Anticipating the junction of the two armies Pyrrhus hastily struck at Curius, but failed to reach his objective in a night surprise. The Romans repelled his attack in open battle and captured several of his elephants.[20] Before he was caught between the two Roman armies Pyrrhus withdrew to Tarentum. There he left some troops to encourage the Italiote allies whom he had failed; with the rest of his army he set sail for Greece. In the following year he withdrew his force, except for a garrison, from Tarentum, and two years later he was killed in street-fighting at Argos by a tile thrown by a woman from a house-top. His Sicilian campaign had prevented the island from becoming a Carthaginian province, while his whirlwind career in Italy had even more far-reaching effects. It sealed the fate of the Italiote Greeks, it demonstrated the rock-like solidarity of the Roman confederacy, against which Pyrrhus had flung his professional soldiers in vain, and it showed the whole Hellenistic world that the unknown barbarians of central Italy were in fact a great military and imperial state, with which Ptolemy II of Egypt now established diplomatic relations and *amicitia* (273).

6. THE END OF PRE-ROMAN ITALY

The fate of Magna Graecia was decided when Pyrrhus left Italy and sealed when it was known the king would never return. Rome merely had to put the finishing touches to the work of pacifying and organizing Italy. In the south the Lucanians were defeated, but received no severer punishment than the settlement of a Latin colony at Paestum (273); the Bruttians were deprived of half their forest-land though they retained some autonomy; Velia, Heraclea, Thurii and Metapontum became allies of Rome in 272, if not earlier; Croton and Locri were brought back to the Roman fold;[21] the Epirote garrison of Tarentum surrendered at the approach of a consular army (272); the garrison of Campanian mercenaries in Rhegium, who had mutinied and seized the town like the Mamertines in Messina across the Straits, was stormed by Cornelius Blasio, and 300 survivors were executed in Rome (270);[22] finally Apulia and Messapia were brought into alliance (267–266), the Sallentini in the heel of Italy were defeated, and land was confiscated from Brundisium which received a Latin colony some years later (244); by their possession of Rhegium and Brundisium the Romans held the keys to both the Tyrrhenian and Adriatic seas.

The exact status of these Greek cities which came into alliance with Rome is uncertain; perhaps they were generously treated as 'equals' and were granted protection without return, for unlike the other members of the Italian confederacy they did not have to supply troops. Shortly afterwards, however, they provided a quota of ships, which at first formed a transport service rather than a fighting force. These *socii navales* retained full autonomy, apart from Tarentum, which though granted the status of a *socius navalis* was punished for its part in the recent war by having to offer hostages and to receive a Roman legion in its citadel. This was Rome's first standing garrison, designed to watch over southern Italy and to shut the door against any other Greek *condottieri*.

The Romans also settled accounts with their old enemies and rivals in central and northern Italy. A brief revolt by the Samnite Caraceni in 269 led to severe consequences. The Samnite League was dissolved and the tribal states were broken up into fragments. In fact thereafter they were seldom referred to under the general name of Samnites (which was often applied only to the Pentri); each community was named after its own town. They became isolated states, separate 'allies' of Rome. Further, they had to cede much territory to Rome and held less than half of what they had occupied at the beginning of the Samnite Wars. On some of this land two Latin colonies were planted as watchdogs: at Malventum (now renamed Beneventum) against the Hirpini in 268 and at Aesernia against the Pentri in 263. Further, a group of Picentes, who also had revolted, were punished by transportation to an area on the western borders of Samnium (*ager Picentinus*), thus confining the Samnites still further. In Etruria a Latin colony was settled at Cosa on land ceded by Vulci (273). In 265 an incident at Volsinii demonstrated the internal unrest in Etruria.

Commerce had declined, the mines were becoming exhausted and expansion was prevented by Rome, so that the nobles became less wealthy and their retainers less necessary. (Arretium, however, retained a position in the industrial world by producing pottery in place of metal work.) The serfs of Volsinii turned against their masters who appealed to Rome for help. The Romans stormed the city and established the aristocracy in a new town on Lake Bolsena; the serfs perhaps were enslaved (264).[23] In Umbria, which had never attained to a real unity, some of the Senones may have lingered at Sarsina until the town was taken by Rome in 268. At the same time the northern frontier was strengthened by sending a Latin colony to Ariminum in the *ager Gallicus*, where the Apennines reach the Adriatic coast (268).[24] In the same year the Sabines were granted full franchise in place of half-citizenship. Finally, the warlike Picentes, who had become Roman allies in 299, revolted in 269 as we have seen, and were quelled the next year. Some were transported to the hills behind Salernum and Paestum; only Asculum retained a treaty of alliance, while the rest of Picenum was incorporated into the Roman state with half-franchise. Their future behaviour was watched over by a Latin colony at Firmum (264). The neighbouring Greek city of Ancona retained its alliance with Rome. Thus the whole of peninsular Italy was brought into the Roman confederacy. An epoch was ended and the history of Roman Italy begins.

7. THE ROMAN CONFEDERACY

From Ariminum and Pisa to Rhegium and Brundisium, the whole of Italy was now bound together in the Roman federation. The main lines of policy which wrought this crowning achievement of the early Republic have already been described (Chapter IV, 7), but it is well to consider the completed organization which endured nearly two hundred years until all the inhabitants of Italy received full franchise after the Social War. The two guiding principles of Roman policy were incorporation and alliance. Peoples covered by the former principle became in some sense citizens of Rome; communities grouped in alliance remained in theory independent states, whose members were politically allies (*socii*) and legally aliens (*peregrini*). But both classes alike were subject to military service under the Roman government.

First then the citizens, who fall into two clearly-defined classes: full citizens and half-citizens. The full citizens constituted three groups, two originating direct from Rome, the third formed by incorporation: (*a*)

Those who lived in Rome itself or who had been granted individually (*viritim*) allotments of 3–7 *iugera* of public land annexed during the conquest of Italy. All these were enrolled in the four urban or thirty-one rustic tribes. (*b*) The Roman colonies, which comprised about three hundred Roman citizens and their families and were founded on *ager publicus*. The colonists formed a garrison, not least to protect the coast against hit- and-run raids, and this duty excused them military service in the Roman army. At first they constituted a strong contrast to the older inhabitants who were generally made half-citizens; but they gradually mingled. In early days they must have been subject to some local military authority and control, but its precise nature is uncertain, while the civil competence of magistrates must have been small. Later, however, when after 183 BC the size of new colonies was increased (p. 321), municipal authority was vested in praetors or *duoviri*. The early citizen colonies were all on the coast (Ostia; Antium 338; Tarracina 329; Minturnae and Sinuessa, 296; Sena Gallica *c*. 290; and Castrum Novum Etrurii, 264); and they were few in number, because the colonists found it difficult in practice to exercise their rights as Roman citizens, so that Romans preferred to share in Latin colonies which formed autonomous states. (*c*) Communities incorporated into the Roman state: *oppida civium Romanorum*, as Tusculum and cities like Lanuvium, Aricia and Nomentum, which were incorporated when the Latin League was dissolved. Called municipalities, in imitation of the proper municipalities of half-citizens, they retained their local magistrates,[25] who had, however, limited judicial and financial power. Their proximity to Rome involved supervision by the Roman praetors, while they were not allowed to mint money. But they exercised full political rights in Rome and were registered in the tribes. Occasionally a new tribe would be established to include newly incorporated communities (e.g. the tribes Quirina and Velina for Sabines and Picentes in 241), but generally these were enrolled in neighbouring tribes and new ones were formed only for Roman citizens who received viritane allotments. Finally, another group may be mentioned, namely centres in country districts, Conciliabula and Fora, formed by Roman citizens, originating from Rome. They had incomplete self-government and in time were often transformed into municipalities.

Secondly there were the incorporated *cives sine suffragio*, who enjoyed only the private rights of *provocatio, commercium* and *conubium*; they could not vote in the Roman assemblies or stand for office and were not enrolled in the thirty-five tribes. The earliest *municipia* had been willing allies with full local autonomy (p. 112), but gradually the status of *municeps* came to be regarded as an inferior limited franchise which was given to conquered peoples (e.g. Sabines and Picentes) before they were considered ripe for full citizenship. Thus their conditions varied considerably. Some were allowed no local government (e.g. Anagnia, which was taken in 306, and Capua after 211); but the majority were allowed to keep their magistrates, local municipal councils and popular assemblies. Roman law was encouraged but perhaps was not enforced. Jurisdiction was divided between the local magistrates and the Roman praetor, who exercised it in Rome itself or else locally through deputies (*praefecti*); it is uncertain whether such prefects or circuit judges were sent to all municipalities. The local magistrates had fairly extensive powers and their variety was maintained (e.g. meddix at Cumae, dictator at Caere, aedile at Fundi); the local authorities were not adapted to the Roman model as quickly as those of the allies. Local languages persisted and local cults survived, though under supervision by the Roman pontiffs. With certain exceptions, the municipalities were not allowed to mint money, but they enjoyed the civil rights of *conubium* and *commercium* with other Roman citizens. By this training in citizenship they were gradually raised to the privileges of full citizenship, which the Sabines, for instance, received in 268; by about 150 they had disappeared as a class. Thus full or half-citizenship was granted to a large part of central Italy from Latium to Picenum, from sea to sea, including the south of Etruria and the north of Campania.

The rest of Italy was associated with Rome by alliance, and consisted of treaty states (*civitates foederatae*), whose inhabitants were aliens and allies (*peregrini* and *socii*) and not Roman citizens. Each city or state was bound to Rome by a separate treaty, but while many had only the *ius peregrinum*, others formed a special class of allies with peculiar privileges called the *ius Latinum*. These allied Latins, who represent the creation of a new Latium after the destruction of the old Latin League, fall into three classes: (*a*) a few original federal colonies of the Latin League, namely, Signia, Norba, Ardea, Circeii, Nepete, Sutrium and Setia; (*b*) Latin colonies founded after the Latin War between 338 and 268 and formed partly by Roman colonists who surrendered their citizenship; (*c*) Latin colonies planted after 268 with restricted *ius migrandi* (see note 24 above), such as Firmum, Aesernia or Brundisium. All these Latin colonies had complete internal government. They were bound to Rome, not to one another, but this early mutual segregation must gradually have broken down. With Rome they had rights of *conubium* and *commercium*, and any of their citizens on migrating to Rome could obtain Roman citizenship, although after 266 he had to leave a son behind in the colony; further, a Latin visiting

Rome could vote in an especially allotted tribe. Though Latin colonies had to raise and pay their quota of troops, they did this on their own authority. The number of colonists, which varied in different colonies, was large, varying from 2,500 to 6,000. It was these fortresses, linked closely with the road system, that held Italy together. They guarded southern Etruria and the Adriatic coast and formed an iron ring around the Samnites.

The remainder of Rome's allies (*civitates liberae*) were bound to her by treaties, which contained varying conditions; many were bilateral (*foedera aequa*) but some were unilateral. Like the Latin colonies, these allies had to supply military or naval contingents, which were kept distinct from the citizen troops. The number to be supplied by each state was fixed, but normally it would not be necessary to call up the whole contingent.[26] The majority of the allies were free from direct Roman supervision, although Tarentum had to maintain a Roman garrison. They had full independence in civil and ordinary internal affairs, though they tended to adapt their institutions to the Roman model and to refer their disputes to Roman arbitration. Some may have had the right to coin money, but apart from purely local coinage, they soon ceased to use this right. Their citizens were probably limited in the exercise of the rights of *commercium* and *conubium* both with Roman citizens and with other allies. In this respect their status may have varied individually in accordance with their previous history: voluntary alliance and alliance imposed by conquest would produce different privileges. Indeed, the units with which the Romans made treaties varied. Their policy was to choose the smallest existing group, either the city as in Etruria and Magna Graecia, or the tribe as among the hills of central Italy. Where an ethnic group, such as the Samnites, appeared dangerous, it was cut down to the minimum by separate alliances with the outlying members; further, it was watched by Latin colonies. Rome ever followed the policy of 'divide and rule', and when she had made her divisions she tended to treat each section according to its degree of civilization. Etruria, which was alien alike in language and religion, was not assimilated till after the Social War, while the more cognate Sabines were soon welcomed into Roman citizenship. But 'divide and rule' is only a half-truth. By this policy Rome had won the hegemony of Italy; she retained her position only because she welded the divisions into a higher unity.

Such, in brief, was the Roman confederation, ranging from Roman colonies and municipalities of full citizens through municipalities of half-citizens to the allies of the Latin name and other allies of varying privilege. The claims that Rome made on Italy were small compared with the advantages she bestowed, but she did demand some surrender of independent sovereignty and the offering of men and money. Those who received the Roman franchise merely merged their interests with a wider loyalty; of the allies some officially retained their independence, though others surrendered all individual foreign policy. In fact, however, as Rome was so much more powerful than her separate allies, her will was paramount, and she even interfered on occasion with the internal affairs of cities. The main burden imposed by Rome was military service. Both citizens and allies had to supply troops; the former provided a little under half the total force. The allied troops were kept distinct from the Roman citizens, but came under Roman command.

As in military service, so in taxation the citizens and allies were organized separately. All Roman citizens had to pay a direct capital tax according to their capacity; at first this was levied on real property alone, but after 312 the whole personal estate of the taxpayer was included. This tax (*tributum*), however, was not permanent. It was only levied for military purposes in time of need, and taxpayers might later be reimbursed by the Treasury if it could afford it. The allies, on the other hand, were free from all direct taxation, although any who had settled on Roman state land naturally paid a regular rent (*vectigal*). Finally, citizens and allies alike were subject to a tariff in the form of customs duties (*portoria*).

But Rome's gifts to Italy easily outweighed her impositions. The greatest of these was the *pax Romana*. Peace was substituted for war as the normal condition. Foreign invaders, except only Hannibal, were held at arm's length, the coasts were protected by a line of Roman colonies, neighbouring cities could no longer fly at each other's throats, and party strife within each city was quelled. Rome, who had won her hegemony at the point of the sword, now assumed the roles of judge and policeman. By skilfully grading the status of the various members of the body politic, she avoided the risk that the Italians might develop a sense of unity among themselves as a subject people under the heel of a common mistress. Instead she trained them all to look to her away from one another, and thus she obtained law and order throughout the peninsula as well as the loyal co-operation of its peoples. Rome was the head of a confederacy, not primarily a dominating military power. The *pax Romana* also fostered the growth of economic life. Except under the Etruscans and among the Greek towns of the south, commerce had been somewhat restricted. Now, protected by Roman law, it could spread throughout

Italy along the Roman roads which began to link up the peninsula. The Viae Appia, Latina, Salaria, Flaminia, Clodia and Aurelia were the real arteries of the economic life of Italy, which was further united when Roman coinage began to oust local currencies. Other public works beside roads, such as bridges, aqueducts and drains benefited Italy. The roads also helped to diffuse Roman culture. The Romans did not impose their civilization on Italy, but just as they themselves succumbed to Greek cultural influences from southern Italy, so their own civilization now penetrated slowly throughout Italy. Local languages, customs and cults gradually gave place to a common culture based on the Latin tongue and Roman law, and very slowly but surely the various races of Italy became a nation.

The creation of a confederacy which gave the whole of Italy some kind of political, economic and social unity was a landmark in the political history of the ancient world. It was not an enlarged commonwealth like Sparta with her *perioikoi*, nor a confederation of separate sovereign states such as the Panhellenic League of Corinth founded by Philip II and upheld by Alexander; it was not a federal state of the type created by a king, as Thessaly, or a league that grew out of a cantonal commune, as the Aetolian League, or a league of cities, as the Achaean; nor was it the imperial rule of a city-state over subject communities, as the Athenian land-empire of Pericles. It was a new creation which blended many of these principles into a unique confederacy. By about 260 BC it extended for some 52,000 square miles, of which about 10,000 consisted of Roman territory; of the remaining 42,000 square miles of allied territory the Latins occupied nearly 5,000. It thus exceeded the empires of Macedonia, Carthage and the Ptolemies; it was inferior in size only to the Seleucid kingdom. The adult male Roman citizens numbered 292,000 in 264 BC. The allies, excluding the southern Greeks and Bruttians, could supply 375,000 regular troops in 225 BC; perhaps this figure should be doubled to represent the total number of adult male allies. That is, the Roman and allied adult males numbered over one million, although not all would be fit for active military service. The Roman citizens and their families numbered nearly one million, the allies double that figure; perhaps nearly a quarter of the allies enjoyed Latin rights. This total of some three million was small compared to the thirty million of the Seleucids, the ten millions of the Ptolemies, the five millions of the Carthaginian empire; it approximated to the population of Macedonia.[27] But though the numbers were small, the military experience and the moral qualities of the old Roman character easily counter-balanced the hordes of Syria. Rome had

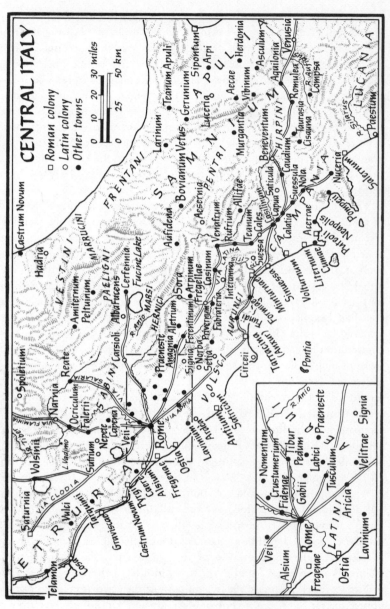

MAP II

become a world power, and when once the Carthaginian Empire had been broken there was no other military power in the whole Mediterranean basin that could meet her on equal terms.

PART II

ROME AND CARTHAGE

VII

THE FIRST
STRUGGLE

1. THE CARTHAGINIAN EMPIRE

Of the settlements which, as we have seen (p. 21), the Phoenicians planted in the central and western Mediterranean, the most important was the New City, Carthage (Qart Chadascht), which the Tyrians are said to have founded about 814 BC.[1] The Tyrian princess, Elissa, it is said, fleeing from King Pygmalion with a few faithful followers, reached Africa, where the tribes granted her as much land as she could cover with a cowhide (*byrsa*). By ingeniously cutting this into narrow strips she surrounded enough ground to form the citadel of her new city, the Byrsa of Carthage. Later writers wove around the story of Elissa a mass of myth and legend, until the saga received its final shape at the hands of the magician Virgil who moulded from it an undying drama of love and death. Elissa, now named Dido, welcomes to her new city the Trojan hero Aeneas. At heaven's bidding he forsakes his new love to fulfil his destiny of founding Rome, while deserted Dido stabs herself on her funeral pyre, and her cry goes up to heaven: '*Exoriare aliquis nostris ex ossibus ultor.*' The drama of the struggle of Rome and Carthage has come to birth.

The native tribes of North Africa, with whom the Phoenician settlers came into contact, had formed no extensive political union although they were all of similar stock, being the predecessors of the modern Berbers and racially distinct from the negroes of the south. Those who later became subjects of Carthage were known to the Greeks as Libyans, the rest as nomads or Numidians. Among these primitive and semi-nomadic peoples Carthage soon became the dominating power, thanks to her superior civilization and to her magnificent geographical position. Situated on a peninsula which afforded room for expansion and protection from the natives, the city lay sheltered in the heart of a bay. Her hinterland was fertile and her prominent position in the mid-Mediterranean allowed her to trade with east and west and to control trans-Mediterranean shipping.

In her early days Carthage maintained a link with her mother city of Tyre, but from the seventh century the Phoenicians of the home country were smitten by the great oriental monarchies, one after another: Assyria, Babylon, Egypt and Persia. Consequently the Phoenicians of the west were left to their own devices: to preserve their independence, their scattered energies must be united. Carthage stepped into the breach, and from the sixth century she became mistress of an empire which gradually extended far beyond the confines of North Africa.

The centre of this empire was the hinterland which Carthage took into her possession, stretching from Hippo Regius in the west, inland to Theveste and thence to Thenae on the east coast; it was guarded by a frontier called the Phoenician Trenches. The inhabitants served in the army of their mistress and supplied her with a quota of their produce. Under Carthaginian protection agriculture prospered and the population increased. In addition, the inhabitants of the African colonies of Phoenicia and Carthage, which stretched from beyond the Straits of Gibraltar to the three great towns in Tripoli called Emporia, became the loyal allies of Carthage. Known as Libyphoenicians, they supplied contingents in wartime and in some cases at any rate paid tribute. The individual towns were allied with Carthage on varying conditions, much as the Italian cities were with Rome. Including the territory of these Libyphoenician cities, Carthage controlled an area of about 28,000 square miles and a population of three to four million. Further, the Numidian tribes beyond often found it expedient to seek her friendship and thus formed a great potential source of power.

But the ambition and commercial aims of Carthage were not limited to Africa. For many a year she was not strong enough to aid the early Phoenician traders in Sicily, who had been driven to the west end of the island by the advancing tide of Greek colonists, but in about 580 BC she was drawn into the troubled waters, until despite the efforts of Malchus and his successors her advance in Sicily was checked by the battle of Himera, which saved Greek civilization in the west from being overwhelmed (480). The vicissitudes of the struggle between Carthage and the Greeks in Sicily, which recommenced about 400 BC after a period of economic recession and continued till the days of the first Punic War, belong to the history of the Greek rather than of the Roman world.

Carthage was more successful in Spain. In the late seventh and early sixth centuries the empire of Tartessus was flourishing, freer now from Phoenician influence. Its King, Arganthonius, the 'Silver Man', encouraged friendly relations with the Greeks who were now penetrating the western seas. As early as 620 BC Colaeus, a mariner from Samos, was blown by an easterly gale to Tartessus (p. 23), and the Phocaeans founded two colonies in Spain at Maenace and Hemeroscopium to open up the Tartessian market. This was little to the taste of the traders of Carthage, and the clash of interests ultimately culminated in the sea battle of Alalia, when the combined Carthaginian and Etruscan fleets broke the Phocaean thalassocracy in the west (p. 34). As a result Carthage made settlements in Sardinia, leaving Corsica to her allies, and then, as a stepping-stone to Spain, she occupied the island of Ebusus which the Phoenicians had already visited. Finally, by destroying Tartessus and Maenace, she entered into the heritage of the Tartessian Empire, although she could not drive the Greeks from northern Spain beyond Cape Palos (near Cartagena).[2] In southern Spain Carthage gained an almost inexhaustible source of natural wealth and of manpower, as well as control over the Atlantic trade of her predecessors. Merchants now sailed forth from Gades instead of from Tartessus; Himilco was sent to explore the tin routes of the north, while Hanno voyaged down the west coast of Africa to bring back gold and ivory. But the Carthaginians were careful not to share this new prize; they jealously barred the gates of the Atlantic and closed the western Mediterranean to foreign shipping.

Carthage had thus won an overseas empire which she selfishly exploited. The old Phoenician colonies abroad assumed much the same relation to her as the Libyphoenician towns in Africa. In Sardinia and southern Spain some of the natives were reduced to subjection; the rest were exploited commercially and supplied mercenary troops. In Sicily the Carthaginians had to tread more warily, to avoid driving the whole island into the arms of her enemy Syracuse. The Punic province in the west gradually embraced some native and Greek cities, but these retained their internal autonomy and paid a tithe on their produce instead of supplying troops. Further, Carthage had to keep an open market in her Sicilian province. On the whole the condition of her subjects, though tolerable, was far inferior to that of most of the allies of Rome, who had infused her federation with a feeling of loyalty and imposed no tribute. The subjects of Carthage had no real bond, although common interests might sustain their loyalty for a time. Like the members of the naval confederacies of Athens they became increasingly dependent on their mistress without sharing in the advantage which the Greeks had enjoyed of all entering into relation with their leader at approximately the same time.

During this period of external expansion Carthage first came into contact with Rome. The intermediaries were her Etruscan allies, whose ports in Italy had long been open to Phoenician merchants. The product of such trade is seen in the rich seventh-century tombs at Caere and Praeneste: silver and gilded bowls, painted ostrich eggs, and ivory plaques like those made for Solomon's temple by Tyrian artists. When the Etruscan dynasty was driven from Rome, Carthage struck a treaty with the new Republic. A copy of this treaty, engraved on brass, was preserved in the Treasury at Rome and was known to the historian Polybius. It was obviously the work of Carthage, as all the restrictions imposed were in her favour; only Rome's lack of commercial interests can explain why she accepted it. The Romans agreed not to sail west of a point, the Fair Promontory, close to Carthage itself, unless driven by stress of weather or fear of enemies; men trading in Libya or Sardinia were to strike no bargain save in the presence of a herald or town clerk; any Romans coming to the Carthaginian province in Sicily should enjoy all rights enjoyed by others. Thus Carthage was already enforcing the policy of a *mare clausum*: Numidia, Morocco, and the Straits of Gibraltar were closed: conditions of trade in Libya and Sardinia were restricted, though Carthage was not yet strong enough to claim a monopoly there or to close western Sicily. Further, it is assumed that the ports over which Rome had any control were to remain open. In return for these substantial advantages Carthage merely pledged herself to abstain from injuring certain towns in Latium. When this treaty was renewed, probably in 348, Rome allowed Carthage to stiffen up the conditions very considerably. By the new agreement Roman traders were excluded from Sardinia and Libya and from the western Mediterranean from the Gulf of Tunis to Mastia (Cartagena) in Spain; Carthaginian Sicily and Carthage itself alone remained open. Thus the new Republic willingly sacrificed any commercial interests which Rome may have had under the Etruscan regime; for many a long year her thoughts turned landwards while her future rival was transforming the western Mediterranean into a Carthaginian lake.[3]

2. CARTHAGE

The felicity of the Carthaginian Empire depended largely on the unusual stability of her constitution, which attracted the interest of Greek political thinkers such as Aristotle (*Politics*, ii, 1). The Phoenicians of the west probably did not model their new cities on the monarchical pattern of the mother country: to have set up new kings (*melakim*) would have smacked of disloyalty. Instead, at the head of the state we find two annually appointed judges or Suffetes (Shophetim; cf. the judges of early Israel) whom the Greeks and Romans probably misnamed βασιλεῖς and *reges*. In original function these magistrates were judges rather than generals: the early aims of Carthage were commercial, not military. The real conduct of state affairs rested with a Council of (perhaps) Thirty, which included the Suffetes, and with a Senate of Three Hundred, of which the Thirty were a subcommittee. Matters carefully prepared by these bodies, or questions on which the higher powers could not agree, might be brought before a popular assembly of citizens; but where agreement was reached, the assembly would not usually be consulted. In the assembly, however, there was great freedom of speech, and it was the people who, with certain restrictions, elected the Suffetes, the members of both councils, and the generals. Common commercial and economic interests helped to preserve the balance of power between the governing class and the people. Stability was further increased by vesting judicial power, not in the people, but in a Council of One Hundred and Four, chosen from the larger Senate. This court of judges, which was first established to check the tyrannical tendencies of the house of Mago, supervised the administration of the magistrates. Yet as these judges were elected, not by the people, but by a group of magistrates whom Aristotle called Pentarchies or Boards of Five, the state gradually succumbed to the domination of a close and corrupt oligarchy of judges and pentarchs, until the day when Hannibal cleansed the administration.

The effective government was thus in the hands of an oligarchy of nobles. But it is uncertain how far they formed an aristocracy of birth or of wealth, how far they closed their ranks against other aspirants to office, and how far their interests were commercial or agricultural. The original settlers may have formed an aristocracy of birth, but being merchants and manufacturers they would gradually become an aristocracy of wealth. This in turn may have been somewhat exclusive: the leaders of the nation known to history came from surprisingly few families, and their names, repeated constantly in the same and different generations, form a very small proportion of the names known from Punic inscriptions. But it can scarcely be doubted that the ranks of the nobles were often increased from the aspiring *nouveaux riches*; indeed, the great house of Barca, which appeared in the mid-third century, seems to have been a new family.

Many of these nobles continued to derive their wealth from commerce and industry, but others, in answer to the needs of the growing population for food, gradually turned to agriculture and became landowners. Big estates were cultivated with cheap slave labour, and the success achieved by the landed gentry in scientific farming may be gauged by the fact that after the fall of Carthage the Roman Senate had Mago's thirty-two books on agriculture translated into Latin for the benefit of Roman colonists. It has been suggested that from the fourth century the nobility became so immersed in their estates that they left the profits of commerce to others; and that politically their interests were represented by the Suffetes and the Senate of Three Hundred, those of the commercial aristocracy by the Hundred and Four and the pentarchs. Such a rigid cleavage, however, is not very probable, though at times a clash of interest may have occurred between the landowners and merchants. And it is not necessary to suppose that all who turned to agriculture automatically lost their interest in trade.[4]

To support her empire Carthage needed money, men and ships. The first she derived from tribute and customs dues, but our evidence is insufficient to allow a reliable estimate of the amount.[5] Her army, originally formed of citizens, did not suffice for her great wars abroad, so that she began to conscript her subjects – Africans, Sardinians and Iberians – and to employ mercenaries. By the third century her citizens no longer served in her armies, except as officers, or in wars fought in Africa itself. This development had many obvious advantages for a people whose interests lay in commerce rather than in war, but it brought its peculiar dangers. Outstanding generals might aspire to military dictatorship, particularly when after the First Punic War armies of mercenaries became a permanent feature; but the oligarchical institutions of the city were devised to check the too-successful general, while crucifixion was the punishment for failure. Further, when the subject Africans found themselves serving no longer with citizens but merely with allies, mercenaries, or other subjects, they acquired a dangerous estimate of their own importance; the Numidians also realized their own value when Carthage made increasing use of their cavalry. The army was thus always a potential source of danger. Although often a motley crew with little or no national feeling, when disciplined and organized by a general of genius it developed into a first-class fighting machine.

The navy also was maintained from the tribute of the subjects, who were relieved of the duty of self-protection. The skill of the seamen and navigators of Carthage was well known and the maintenance of a large fleet offered a good excuse for exacting tribute. But it is unlikely that she normally found it necessary to keep her whole navy afloat in order to safeguard her commerce and to protect or threaten her subjects. Many vessels would be laid up in the great arsenals and dockyards at Carthage, and the crews called up only in time of need. The praise accorded to the Punic navy by patriotic Roman writers arose partly from sincere admiration, but partly from a desire to exaggerate the achievements of their own victorious fellow-countrymen.

The civilization of Carthage has left little mark on world history, and our knowledge of it derives mainly from biased Greek and Roman writers and from the results of recent archaeological investigation. But when every allowance has been made the resultant picture is not attractive. Carthage tapped the caravan routes of Egypt and Africa, her merchants sailed to Britain and Senegal, and she became one of the richest states of the world, but she was rather a carrier than a productive state; and curiously, she did not issue coins until early in the fourth century and at first only to pay her troops in Sicily rather than for commercial reasons. Her industry aimed at mass-production and cheapness rather than beauty. Her art was unoriginal and owed much to Egypt and Greece. Her nobles might acquire a taste for Greek art, but this was met by importing foreign artists and works of art or by the imitation of Greek models. Even the equipment of the tombs, which in early days were richly adorned, became increasingly cheaper. We hear of Carthaginian books and libraries, but there is no evidence to suggest that she was gifted with any real literary inspiration. The Punic language, however, which belongs to the North Semitic group and is akin to Hebrew, was more virile, as is shown by its persistence and by the numerous inscriptions which have come to light. Carthaginian religion and cult were cruel, gloomy and licentious. The Canaanitish deities, Ba'al Hammon, Tanit, Melkart, Eshmun and Astarte inspired in their worshippers a fanatical devotion, which did not shrink from self-immolation or human sacrifice. Contact with the civilized world may have mitigated the barbarity to an extent, but the fires of the sacrifice called Moloch continued to receive their tribute of infants from noble families at hours of crisis in the city's history.[6]

Carthage thus gave the world little of value. Even the spirit of the great house of Barca came rather to destroy than to build. To the end the Carthaginian remained Oriental and was only superficially tinged with Greek culture; and he was not popular in the western world. 'Bearded Orientals in loose robes, covered with gaudy trinkets, often with great rings of gold hanging from their nostrils, dripping with perfumes, cringing and salaaming, the Carthaginians inspired disgust as much by their personal appearance as by their sensual appetites, their treacherous cruelty, their blood-stained religion. To the end they remained hucksters, intent on personal gain, careless or incapable of winning the goodwill of their subjects.'[7] They may have been thus conceived by some Greeks and Romans, but it is well to recall that a Carthaginian named Hasdrubal and renamed Cleitomachus became head of the Academy at Athens in 129, and to balance the picture with the words of Cicero: 'Carthage would not have held an empire for six hundred years had it not been governed with wisdom and statecraft.' (*de rep.*, i, frg. 3.)

3. THE CAUSES OF THE WAR

The early treaties between Rome and Carthage were treaties of friendship and for trade, formed to limit their spheres of influence. But in 306 the two Republics may have formed a closer political agreement which debarred the Carthaginians from interfering in Italy, and the Romans in Sicily (p. 136). Carthage again negotiated with Rome in 279; no defensive alliance was struck, but an emergency measure was designed, chiefly to keep Pyrrhus in Italy (p. 143). During the war Carthage neither received nor asked for help, not wishing to bring Romans into Sicily; Rome also kept to herself.

In 272 a puzzling incident occurred. When the Romans were besieging Tarentum, which was still held by Pyrrhus' lieutenant Milo, a Carthaginian fleet suddenly appeared in the harbour, but quickly sailed off again. Had it come in reply to an appeal from Milo or on its own initiative; to help the Romans or to capture Tarentum? Later Roman writers accused Carthage of having tried to seize Tarentum, alleging that the action was a breach of treaty rights; but the Carthaginians had not tried to land. Indeed, far from acting contrary to the agreements, the Punic admiral may have sailed up in accordance with Mago's treaty to see whether he could help the Romans. It is perhaps most likely that the Carthaginians were reconnoitring on the offchance of turning the situation to their advantage, but when this seemed impossible they sailed away, while the home government disavowed the admiral's action and Rome accepted the apology, as recorded by Orosius. But whether Rome suspected treachery or merely rebuffed a friendly gesture, the result would hardly improve relations between the two Republics.[8]

When Pyrrhus left the shores of Sicily he is reported to have remarked: 'What a cockpit we are now leaving for Carthaginian and Roman to fight in.' The recent history of the island justified this prophecy. The Punic expansion had been checked during the reign of Agathocles as King of Syracuse (304–289), but after his death the Carthaginians again advanced their standards, until driven back by Pyrrhus. When he retired to Italy they defeated the Syracusan fleet, recovered their lost possessions and captured the Greek cities of central Sicily. Thus by 275 Syracuse's influence was confined to eastern Sicily, and even there she met with rivals. Certain of Agathocles' discharged Italian mercenaries on their return home had treacherously seized the town of Messana (c. 288). Styling themselves Mamertines, after the Sabellian war god Mamers, they settled there and proceeded to plunder the surrounding districts, Carthaginian and Greek alike. Defeated but not exterminated by Pyrrhus, they were later defeated by the Syracusans under Hiero who now, if not earlier, assumed the title of king (265–264) and then undertook the siege of Messana. At this point the Carthaginians intervened, refusing to look on while Syracuse won control of the Sicilian straits by capturing Messana. Their admiral threw a Punic garrison into the town with the consent of the Mamertines, and Hiero was obliged to return to Syracuse, disregarding the complimentary exhortations of the poet Theocritus to continue fighting. But the Mamertines did not wish to keep their new garrison indefinitely: some advocated reaching an agreement with Carthage by which their autonomy would be respected, others preferred to seek alliance with a less alien people, the Romans. The latter party prevailed and Rome was suddenly faced with a request for alliance and help. What was she to do?

Rome and Carthage were thus brought abruptly face to face. By ejecting from Rhegium the Campanians who had tried to play at pirates like the Mamertines in Sicily the Romans had won control of the Straits (270). But now a Carthaginian garrison at Messana faced them from the opposite shore: it barred their access to Sicily, and constituted a *point d'appui* from which, following the example set by Dionysius and Agathocles, the Carthaginians could sail against the towns of the Italian coast, once they had taken eastern Sicily. There could be no doubt that they would extend to Sicily the monopoly which they exercised throughout the western Mediterranean. That might not be of direct concern to the Romans, who were little interested in foreign trade, but it would be a severe blow to their allies in southern Italy. And there was the further danger that if Rome neglected her new Greek allies, they might turn to Carthage for protection in a desperate effort to preserve their Sicilian trade. It did indeed seem that Rome would have to listen to the appeal of the Mamertines, even though this might involve crossing swords with Carthage and possibly a deadly duel.

But the swords which the Mamertines virtually thrust into the rivals' hands could scarcely have been kept permanently sheathed. Rome and Carthage had little in common. Different in race, culture and religion, with divergent moral and material interests, they would gravitate towards conflict when once the minor states between them had been eliminated or assimilated. In the Hellenistic east a common culture held the three great monarchies in a precarious balance of powers. When Rome had absorbed something of that culture, she adapted her policy in order to try to maintain the balance. But in the west rivalry would lead to war: compromise was difficult, if not impossible.

The immediate question before the Roman Senate was the appeal of the Mamertines, not war with Carthage, though the more far-sighted must have seen that this would probably follow the granting of the request. When the Senate failed to reach a decision the question was referred (by Appius Claudius?) to the people, who voted to send help to the Mamertines. Polybius, who here follows Fabius Pictor and thus gives at least a pro-Roman account, if not a tendentious justification, explains that the Senate hesitated, in spite of a full recognition of the danger of the advance of Carthage, because it felt unable to ally itself to a robber-state, especially as it had recently executed the brigands at Rhegium. But the weight of this moralistic argument has been questioned, since the seizure of Messana by the Mamertines had occurred twenty-five years earlier and the new state was now standing on its own feet and had been recognized by Carthage and several Greek cities; it was presumably autonomous and therefore Rome would not break her fetial law by granting alliance. Further, the parallel with Rhegium is weak, for there Rome interfered on behalf of her own allies, whereas she had had no dealings with Messana. But even if conscientious scruples were among the motives of the Senate's hesitation, others also must be found in the fear of war with a great sea power, and in the aversion of the conservative element in the Senate to an expansionist policy which increased the power of the people and of the popular leaders whom a new war might bring into prominence. A further reason was probably that Roman interference in Sicily would involve a definite breach of the treaty of 306. The popular leaders who wanted war might argue that the Carthaginians had themselves annulled this agreement by their action at Tarentum, and by their general attitude which was, according to Polybius (i, 7), one motive that had stimulated Rhegium to ask Rome for protection (c. 280). But the Senate perhaps hesitated to disregard formal obligations.[9]

The people had accepted the Mamertine alliance because of the advantages which their leaders said would attend it. These suggested benefits would not be land, tribute, or even booty, but the checking of the advance of Carthage and the increase of allies with the consequent decrease of effort by the citizen army. The personal advantages to the popular leaders from success in war was an aspect which they would hardly emphasize, but of which such families as the Otacilii of Beneventum and the Campanian Atilii would be fully conscious. But the main motive which led Rome to accept the alliance of the Mamertines was to secure an outpost which was necessary to the safety of Italy. The two rivals may both have rushed to secure this key position, but their motives were different; defensive imperialism dominated Rome's policy, an exploiting commercial imperialism actuated Carthage.

4. ROME'S NAVAL OFFENSIVE

In 264 the consul Appius Claudius Caudex was sent with two legions to announce Rome's acceptance of Messana's request for alliance and to garrison the town. His advance guard under his relative C. Claudius forced the Straits with little opposition: after a slight skirmish the Carthaginian admiral merely returned some ships, which he had captured, with the threat that he would not let the Romans so much as wash their hands in the sea. The attitude of the Punic commander in Messana was equally cautious. On the arrival of C. Claudius and under pressure from the Mamertines he evacuated the citadel, only to be crucified later for his lack of initiative and *pour encourager les autres*. The scrupulous behaviour of these Punic generals who, wishing to avoid any openly hostile acts, refused either to contest the passage of the Straits or to hold Messana, contrasts strongly with the decisive vigour of the Roman leaders.

The Roman occupation of Messana stung the Carthaginian government to action. War had not yet been formally declared, but the time was ripe. Further, Hiero of Syracuse was willing to forget the age-long hostility of Carthage to the Sicilian Greeks and to co-operate with the erstwhile enemy. This unnatural alliance was brought about mainly because both parties saw their common interests threatened by the rising power of Rome. Punic troops were sent to Sicily under Hanno, son of Hannibal, who garrisoned Agrigentum and encamped at Messana. Hiero also arrived there and camped further south of the town, while the Punic fleet anchored to the north. Seeing Messana thus blockaded, Appius Claudius succeeded in transporting his troops across the Straits by night. Then, or possibly before crossing to Sicily, he sent an embassy to the Carthaginians and Hiero, ordering them to raise the siege of a town which was allied to Rome. On their refusal he formally declared war and the First Punic War had officially started.[10]

Claudius acted quickly. Taking advantage of the distance between the two enemy camps, he assailed first Hiero's and then Hanno's. The result of these engagements is not certain; both sides according to their own historians claimed them as victories. But Hiero, who was displeased with his allies for allowing the Romans to cross to Sicily so easily, fell back on Syracuse soon afterwards (or perhaps not until the following year). Hanno also withdrew to garrison and protect the Carthaginian cities in Sicily.[11] The next year both consuls, M'. Valerius and M'. Otacilius, were sent to Sicily with about 40,000 men. Though the retreat of Hiero and Hanno freed Messana, Rome must advance further in Sicily, not to conquer the island, but to force her enemies to recognize her Messanian alliance. When Valerius marched southwards many towns around Aetna submitted to him, yet he could have had little hope of taking Syracuse itself without control of the sea. Hiero, however, who could look for little support from his allies after abandoning them at Messana, began to make friendly overtures, to which the Romans readily responded. He was granted an alliance (renewed in 248) and the control of some thirty miles of territory around Syracuse in return for an indemnity of 100 talents (Diodorus' reference to an annual tribute of 25 talents may be due only to a misunderstanding of a first instalment of the indemnity); he remained Rome's loyal ally till his death in 215. His most immediate service was to help the Romans with supplies.

In March 262, Valerius celebrated a triumph over the Carthaginians and Hiero, and decorated a wall of the Curia Hostilia with a painting of his success. The Senate proposed to send out only two legions this year, but learning that the Carthaginians were recruiting in Spain, Liguria and Gaul, they despatched instead both consuls. These won the support of Segesta in the Punic province in Sicily, and advanced against the Carthaginian headquarters at the Greek city of Agrigentum, which lay on a hill whose steep sides made attack possible only from the south. Here they pitched two camps, joined by a double line of trenches, and besieged the city for five months. Before starvation forced the Punic commander Hannibal to capitulate, strong reinforcements arrived under Hanno who, ensconced on a neighbouring hill, cut off the Roman supplies, which the loyal Hiero supplemented with great difficulty. After two months Hanno gave battle in a desperate attempt to relieve the city. Though he was defeated, the Roman losses were so heavy that Hannibal and his garrison were enabled to escape from the doomed city. The next day Agrigentum was sacked and its inhabitants were sold into slavery; an act of clemency, which might have won over the Sicilians, would have proved a better investment for the future than this barbarity. As the fall of Agrigentum did not bring Carthage to her knees and the consuls of 261 achieved little in Sicily, the Senate realized that peace could only be attained by conquering the whole island and driving out the Carthaginians. This could never be done while the Punic fleet threatened the seaboard towns of Sicily and even ravaged the coast of Italy. So Rome had to face the task of challenging the naval supremacy of her enemy.

The success with which the land-lubbers of Rome created a navy and defeated the Queen of the western Mediterranean naturally led later ages to embellish with legendary adornments what was undeniably a magnificent achievement. It was said that having no fleet of their own the Romans took a wrecked Punic vessel as a model and built 120 ships within sixty days from the hewing of the timber; meanwhile crews were taught to row on great wooden stages erected on land. The speed of this achievement has often been regarded with some scepticism, but the recent discovery of a Punic warship off Marsala shows methods of prefabrication and mass-production which the Romans may well have imitated. Although since 311 BC *duoviri navales* had commanded a squadron of 20 ships (for example, in 282, a *duovir* with 10 ships had been attacked by the Tarentines), such squadrons were probably only fitted out when required and were then laid up; thus Appius Claudius had to cross to Sicily in ships from allied Italian towns, because there was no Roman squadron ready equipped. Further, after the Pyrrhic War various southern Italian towns were perhaps liable by treaty to furnish ships, but these would not number more than 25 vessels all told. When Rome determined to challenge Carthage at sea, she built 20 triremes and 100 quinqueremes. The former represented the old type of duumviral squadron, the latter were built on a new model like the Punic vessels. More difficult than the construction was the manning of the new fleet. Many men could be drawn from the *socii navales* of the seafaring towns of southern Italy; but others would have to be trained to handle an oar instead of a plough, men who had no experience of the sea. To counteract their lack of skill the Romans determined to turn sea battles into land battles by avoiding the manoeuvring and ramming tactics of the enemy, and by adopting boarding tactics. This was achieved by the use of some kind of device which Polybius describes as a complicated boarding-bridge, known to the soldiers colloquially as a 'crow' (*corvus*) because its 'beak' was an iron spike which grappled the enemy's deck. Thus the Romans intended to thwart their enemy's superior naval skill, while they made doubly sure by outbuilding the Carthaginians. In all they probably raised 160 vessels, while the enemy had only 130 at sea. Rome was then ready to contest the sea, and when every allowance has been made for patriotic exaggeration in the traditional account, the plain fact is a magnificent tribute to her adaptability and resolve.[12]

While the new fleet was mustering at Messana the commander Cn. Cornelius Scipio sailed off with seventeen vessels to negotiate for the surrender of Lipara, but he was surprised and captured by a Punic squadron; this exploit gained for him the suitable cognomen, Asina. Thereupon the other consul of 260, C. Duilius, took over the command and relieved Segesta, which was besieged by Hamilcar, Hanno's successor. But Duilius had greater claim to fame. Encountering the Punic fleet off Mylae near the north-east corner of Sicily he overcame the enemy's tactical skill by grappling their vessels with his 'crows', so that his men soon swept the decks clear. With their superior numbers (perhaps 140 against 130) the Romans accounted for some 50 vessels, including the admiral's flagship. Thus Rome in her first venture on the sea defeated a nation whose seafaring traditions were centuries old. Well might Duilius celebrate the first naval triumph in Rome and be honoured by the erection in the Forum of a column ornamented with the bronze rams of the vessels he had captured.[13]

The Punic fleet had been defeated, but not destroyed; and Rome did not attempt to blockade by sea the Carthaginian strongholds of Panormus or Lilybaeum, still less to attack her enemy in Africa. Instead, one consul of 259, L. Cornelius Scipio, led an expedition against Sardinia and Corsica. This could have little effect on the main issues of the war, but it trained the Romans in the idea of sending expeditionary forces abroad and reduced the possibility of Punic or piratical raids on the Italian coast. Scipio captured Aleria in Corsica and won the island, but he failed to take the Punic fortress of Olbia in northern Sardinia. The appearance of Hannibal with reinforcements terminated his activity, but the next year his successor, C. Sulpicius, defeated the enemy's fleet off Sulci in Rome's second naval victory.

Meanwhile Hamilcar had made good progress against the one consular army operating in Sicily. After a successful engagement near Thermae he advanced as far as Enna and Camarina and fortified Drepana. To make good these losses the Romans prolonged Aquillius' command as proconsul through the winter and sent out another consular army to join him in 258. Together the Roman generals advanced towards Panormus, where Hamilcar declined battle, and then by capturing Camarina and Enna they confined the enemy once more to the western end of the island. In 257 all effort in Sardinia was abandoned and little was achieved in Sicily, except that the consul. C. Atilius Regulus, after raiding Melita (Malta) fell in with the Punic fleet off Tyndaris and sank 18 vessels (Rome's third naval victory).

5. ROME'S OFFENSIVE IN AFRICA

Only two ways seemed open to Rome to terminate the struggle : to take the offensive more actively against the Punic province in Sicily, or to strike at Africa. As the former plan offered no prospect of a speedy conclusion, the latter was adopted. Rome braced herself for the effort. The fleet was raised to 250 battleships and 80 transport ships, while perhaps 100,000 men were required for the crews. The Carthaginian navy was also increased, to a figure perhaps a little less than the Roman. In the summer of 256 the Roman fleet, under the command of L. Manlius Vulso and M. Atilius Regulus, sailed round the eastern coast of Sicily and encountered the enemy off Cape Ecnomus. The Romans advanced in four squadrons on a narrow front, the Carthaginians sailed in order of battle in one long line abreast with the intention of outflanking their enemy. But the Roman first two squadrons, led by the two flagships, broke through the Punic centre and thanks to the *corvus* were soon victorious. Meanwhile the Roman third squadron had been forced inshore by the Carthaginian left wing, while the fourth Roman squadron was faring badly at the hands of the Carthaginian right. But part of the victorious Roman squadron returned in time to save their fourth line by driving off the Carthaginian right wing, and then the combined victorious squadrons converged against the enemy's left wing near the shore; here they captured 50 vessels, having sunk 30 others. The Roman losses were only 24. It was a great victory, the fourth that Rome had won at sea; the passage to Africa was now secure.[14]

After refitting their ships the Romans sailed to Africa and disembarked at Clupea (Aspis) on Cape Bon, the promontory to the east of Carthage, as

Agathocles had done before. Here they were in good communication with Sicily, and could threaten Carthage from the rear, while cutting her off from many of her rich subject cities. After capturing Clupea and ravaging the district, unopposed by Carthage, the Roman generals reported their success to the Senate, who recalled one consul with the fleet and left Regulus with a small squadron and two legions. This force, which was inadequate to attack Carthage, could have maintained the Roman position and have seriously embarrassed Carthage if Regulus had supplemented it by winning the support of the Numidian princes who were ready to revolt; Agathocles had already shown what a small army could achieve. But Regulus was no Agathocles; though brave and confident, he lacked the Greek's ability.

When the Carthaginians realized that the Romans intended to continue the campaign, they raised forces and recalled others from Sicily. Then, advancing against Regulus who was besieging Adys (Uthina), they suffered defeat on hilly ground which crippled their cavalry and elephants. Regulus could now advance to Tunis, where he confidently encamped for the winter. Thinking that the Carthaginians were hard pressed, especially as the Numidians were restive, he offered terms of peace (possibly after overtures from Carthage), but these were far too severe to be accepted. Apart from his folly in trying to negotiate on unreasonable terms, it is unlikely that a peace could have been arranged, for Rome would probably have insisted on the complete evacuation of Sicily, while Carthage, though ready to make concessions in order to rid herself of the African war, could hardly have sacrificed the western end of the island.

In the spring of 255 the Carthaginians were again ready to try conclusions, for during the winter their army had been drilled and trained on Greek lines by a Spartan mercenary officer named Xanthippus. Before Regulus had bestirred himself Xanthippus led out the Punic army; instead of waiting for reinforcements from Italy Regulus advanced and gave battle in a plain on ground chosen by the enemy. Xanthippus formed his main troops into a phalanx with a hundred elephants in front and the cavalry on the wings. In vain the Romans strengthened their centre; they were only trampled to death more easily. The battle was decided by the Punic cavalry who outflanked and surrounded the Romans; a small division on the Roman left routed the Punic mercenaries, but retreated with heavy losses after the general defeat. Regulus and 500 others were captured; only 2,000 Romans escaped to Clupea. The African expedition had failed.[15]

Meanwhile the Romans had prepared a fleet, intending to blockade Carthage by sea while Regulus attacked by land. This scheme was now wrecked, but nevertheless the fleet of about 210 vessels, commanded by the two consuls, sailed to Africa to face the Punic navy and to rescue the survivors at Clupea. Off the Hermaean Promontory they met and defeated the fleet of perhaps 200 ships with which the Carthaginians, encouraged by their victory over Regulus, were contesting the right of way. After capturing many vessels by jamming them against the shore, and having won the fifth naval victory of the war, the consuls rescued the survivors at Clupea and sailed for home. But fresh tragedy awaited them. In taking to the sea the Romans had minimized their inexperience by adopting grappling tactics, but they could not compensate for their admirals' lack of skill and experience in navigation. Natural forces, rather than the Punic fleet, threatened them. On returning from Africa they encountered a terrific storm between Camarina and Cape Pachynus, and only 80 vessels survived.[16] However, the two consuls were voted triumphs for their previous victory and a *columna rostrata* was erected to commemorate it.

6. STALEMATE AND CHECKMATE

Rome did not despair or slacken her efforts. In the winter of 255–254 taxes were raised to build a new fleet. By the spring she had at least 220 ships and could be confident that Carthage was not in a position to challenge her at sea. As further activity in Africa was impracticable, four legions were sent to storm western Sicily. Cn. Cornelius Scipio, who had regained his freedom and reputation, led an attack by land and sea on the Punic base at Panormus (Palermo), which was divided into two settlements. The Old City lay between two streams which ran into the harbour (the modern Cala) and was thus strongly protected. The Romans first stormed and captured the New City with the help of Greek engineers and then turned to the Old City, which capitulated. Thirteen thousand citizens who could not raise the requisite ransom were sold into slavery. Other towns, such as Tyndaris and Solus, were soon captured. Little resistance had been offered by the Carthaginians because they were busy suppressing a rising of Numidians in Africa, and because since the recall of Hamilcar they had not enough forces in Sicily to offer battle. Their general, Carthalo, made one counter-attack by storming Agrigentum; but fearing that he was not strong enough to hold it, he burnt the city to the ground. The Carthaginians now only held a few towns in Sicily:

Drepana, Lilybaeum, Selinus, Heraclea Minoa, and the isolated Thermae, together with the Lipari and Aegates Islands.

After a vain attempt upon Lilybaeum the consuls of 253 raided Tripolis, an unwise dispersal of effort; they got into difficulties on the shallows of the Syrtes. In returning to Italy the fleet encountered a storm off Cape Palinurus and suffered considerable damage (150 ships lost, according to Polybius). This fresh disaster caused some discouragement at Rome : clearly the fleet, which had achieved such unexpected success in war, could not face the elements. The Carthaginians too were tired; they had to deal with the Numidians, and though their communications with Sicily were now safer and they sent over an army and many elephants under Hasdrubal (probably in 253 or even 251 rather than 255–254), they made no attempt to regain their lost ground. The next two years passed uneventfully, except that in 252 the Romans captured Thermae and the Lipari Islands.

This lull in hostilities was followed by a period of renewed effort lasting for two years (250–249). The Romans built 50 new ships which they intended to send under the two consuls of 250 BC against Lilybaeum, while Caecilius Metellus advanced against the town by land from Panormus. But before they moved Hasdrubal took the offensive by marching against Panormus and ravaging the surrounding plain, the Conca d'Oro. Metellus lay low and thus enticed the enemy over the Oreto up to the trenches which he had dug near the city wall. Here the Punic elephants were met with a shower of weapons and stampeded back on their own lines. A sally on Hasdrubal's flank completed the confusion, and his army was nearly destroyed. His dreaded elephants were all captured, while he himself fled to Lilybaeum, whence he was recalled to face death at Carthage.[17]

After this victory the Romans could blockade Lilybaeum by land and sea. The city, which was strongly fortified, lay on a promontory; its harbour, facing northwards, was small but difficult of access. Within the city were the expatriated inhabitants of Selinus, and a garrison of 10,000 mercenaries. The consuls of 250 BC advanced with (probably) 120 ships and four legions and laid siege to the town, cutting it off from the mainland by a wall and trench which connected their two camps. By sea Hannibal ran the blockade and landed reinforcements; he then sailed out again in safety to join the main Punic fleet under Adherbal at Drepana. Thanks to the occasional success of another blockade-runner, Hannibal the Rhodian, to the loyalty of the garrison, and to a successful attempt to burn the Roman siege works, Lilybaeum withstood the blockade; the

Roman supplies were threatened by Punic cavalry from Drepana and only Rome's determination and the loyal help of Hiero secured the continuance of the siege. Lilybaeum did not fall till eight years later.

P. Claudius Pulcher, consul of 249, realizing the inefficiency of the naval blockade at Lilybaeum, resolved to attack the Punic fleet which was stationed at Drepana, some sixteen miles to the north. Trusting in his superior numbers and in the fact that Adherbal was as yet unaware that the Roman losses of the previous year had been made up by the arrival of 10,000 *socii navales*, Claudius hoped to surprise the enemy with success. But his tactical skill did not support his strategic plan. Drepana was situated on a sharp spit of land, with the harbour on the south side protected by the islet of Colombaia. Hither Claudius sailed with 123 vessels. But while his leading ships were entering the harbour, Adherbal succeeded in manning his fleet (about 100 vessels), and by sailing round the island he fell on the flank of the Roman line. Claudius quickly ordered a retreat, which led to much confusion, and when the enemy attacked he was driven inshore with the loss of 93 vessels, though a large part of the crews swam to land and ultimately reached Lilybaeum. This was the first and only defeat which Rome suffered at sea during the war. Claudius was recalled and condemned to pay a heavy fine. The pious attributed his defeat to his insistence on fighting when the omens were unfavourable: learning that the sacred chickens would not eat, it is said, he contemptuously dropped them overboard, remarking 'Well, let them drink'. But his plan was not ill-conceived, had his naval skill been greater; while the fact that he probably knew that Adherbal was about to receive a reinforcement of 70 ships explains his haste and his impatience with the chickens.

The other consul, L. Junius Pullus, meanwhile was preparing to bring supplies to the troops at Lilybaeum. He sailed from Syracuse with 800 transport ships escorted by 120 warships in two divisions, but fell in with a Punic fleet of 100 vessels commanded by Carthalo, who after attacking the 30 surviving Roman ships at Lilybaeum now came to intercept the reinforcements. Without fighting, Carthalo skilfully forced ashore each of the Roman detachments in turn, one near Phintias (Licata), the other near Camarina; then, anticipating a storm, he doubled Cape Pachynus and left the Roman ships exposed to the fury of the tempest on a lee shore. The entire fleet was wrecked and Rome was left without a navy; some 20 ships alone survived of the 240 with which she had started the year. It was now impossible to continue the blockade of Lilybaeum by sea, but, nothing daunted, Junius, who had escaped with two ships, landed there and marched to Drepana, behind which rises Mount Eryx. Here he surprised the guard and seized both the Temple of Aphrodite, the most splendid of all temples in Sicily (where lies the modern village of Mte San Giuliano), and the old city of Eryx; he thus commanded all the roads to Drepana. It was a shrewd counterblow. Though Rome had lost control at sea, the only two towns still held by Carthage in Sicily were now cut off from the rest of the island.

Once again the position was one of stalemate. Each side required or took a breathing space. Rome faced her recent disasters by appointing a dictator, but she lacked generals of real distinction, and the annual change of magistrates continued to hamper efficiency in the field. The consuls elected for 248 were the cautious consuls of 252, and though no thoughts of peace were entertained, Rome was too exhausted to raise another navy, especially when the dangers of her Junior Service were becoming so obvious; she merely held on for the next six years. Carthage also let sleeping dogs lie. Instead of taking the offensive by sea and attacking Panormus or Syracuse, she concentrated on expeditions in the interior of Africa as far as Theveste. This policy arose partly from the prominence of Hanno the Great, the opponent of the Barcids and representative of the landed interests, partly from the desire to secure internal peace and prosperity before venturing further abroad. Carthage thus let slip a good opportunity of pressing home her success. In fact the only incident of note during 248 was that Rome renewed her treaty with the loyal king of Syracuse on easier terms; any tribute was remitted, his kingdom extended, and the treaty was made for all time.

Fresh life was again infused into the dreary struggle by the emergence of the energetic Hamilcar Barca, who raided the coast of southern Italy in 247. Rome replied by founding protective coastal colonies at Alsium, Fregenae and Brundisium; she abandoned the sea to the enemy, apart from the raids of some privateers on the African coast. In 246 Hamilcar struck at the rear of the Roman armies besieging Drepana and Lilybaeum by landing west of Panormus. He fortified a position on the mountain behind the city, named Heirkte,[18] and anchored his fleet at its foot, so that he was in good communication with the two besieged ports. From this mountain eyrie like an eagle he held the Romans at bay for three years and harassed their forces in frequent skirmishes, again raiding the Italian coast as far as Cumae. Still maintaining this guerrilla warfare he advanced in 244 to Mount Eryx in order to relieve pressure from the siege of Drepana. He captured the old town of Eryx on the northern slopes of the mountain, but the Romans retained the Temple of Aphrodite at the top of the mountain together with a lower point between the Temple and the town of Drepana, and so cut him off from interfering with the siege. Details of the two-year tussle are not known, but it was only terminated by the conclusion of the war.

The long years of Hamilcar's campaigns convinced Rome that the war could only be won at sea. As the treasury was exhausted, a loan was raised repayable only in event of victory. By this patriotic effort a fleet of 200 warships and many transport ships were constructed, the quinqueremes being of light build (without *corvi*). In the summer of 242 the new fleet sailed under C. Lutatius Catulus to Drepana, where he found no Punic navy to face him, partly perhaps because the home government was leaving the burden of war to Hamilcar, partly because they needed the crews for wars in Africa. An attack on Drepana failed, but provisions were running low in the besieged town. By March 241 the Carthaginians had with difficulty manned 170 to 200 vessels; they intended to land stores in Sicily and then, having embarked Hamilcar and his men in order to compensate for their lack of marines, to face the foe. But off the Aegates Islands they met the Roman fleet. Hampered by their inadequate equipment and heavy freights they were quickly defeated. The Romans sank 50 ships and captured 70 more. Further resistance was out of the question. Carthage had shot her bolt; the war was at an end.

The Carthaginian government gave Hamilcar full powers to negotiate for peace. The following terms were agreed upon by Lutatius, subject to ratification at Rome : Carthage was to evacuate Sicily, not make war on Hiero or his allies, return all prisoners, and pay 2,200 talents in twenty annual instalments. These terms were lenient: the indemnity was trifling in proportion to the wealth of Carthage and the war expenditure of Rome; but then Rome had won control of Sicily. They were flatly rejected by the Roman people. Ten commissioners were sent to consider the question on the spot, and they succeeded in tightening up the terms by adding 1,000 talents (to be paid immediately) to the indemnity and decreasing the time of payment of the rest to ten years ; all islands between Sicily and Italy (these would be Lipari and the Aegates) must be evacuated by Carthage ; neither side was to attack the allies of the other nor to recruit soldiers in the dominions of the other. Apart from the 1,000 talents the other clauses might seem advantageous to the ignorant populace at Rome, but they were in fact not a very serious addition. However, the alternative was to continue the war, and so the Roman people, doubtless heeding the authority of the Senate, accepted the terms, and peace reigned after twenty-four years.

So ended a struggle which was, wrote Polybius, 'the longest, most continuous and most severely contested war known to us in history'. Like the coming struggle with Hannibal, it was won by the moral qualities of the Roman people, by the patriotism of a citizen army, by the loyalty of the allies in Italy and of Hiero in Sicily, and by the steadiness of the senatorial government. The men of Rome vanquished the mammon of Carthage. Only in the crisis of the invasion of Africa had the citizens of Carthage drawn a sword in her defence. Her officers might be efficient, her gold might procure reliable mercenaries, but in the last resort she failed. Neither side produced a general of genius except perhaps Hamilcar, but the long years of disciplined warfare in Italy had given Rome an excellent fighting machine. True, she did not adapt it to meet the cavalry and elephants of the enemy and thus suffered defeat near the walls of Carthage; that reform was only achieved during the next struggle. But she did show great adaptability in taking to the sea; it was the old story of the struggle of the elephant and the whale, and she succeeded by determination rather than by technical skill. But the courage of the legions would have proved fruitless had the Italian troops failed them. The war showed clearly what the struggle with Hannibal proved beyond all doubt, that Rome's allies were bound to her by other ties than those of slave to mistress.[19]

VIII

THE ENTR'ACTE

The most obvious result of the First Punic War was that Rome had gained control of territory lying outside Italy. By driving the Carthaginians from Sicily she had become arbiter of the island's fate, and her decision opened a new chapter in her history. Two courses were open: either to apply in Sicily the methods that she had used in Italy or else to maintain the forms of administration with which the Sicilians were already conversant from the rule of Carthage and Syracuse.

In Italy the Romans had applied no theory of state ownership to conquered land; apart from the *ager publicus*, they exacted no tribute in the form either of the products of the earth or their equivalent in cash. Instead, they had demanded military service from the conquered whom they called allies and whom they allowed thereafter to share their victories and spoils. In Sicily they had at first adopted a similar policy, entering into alliances with Messana and Syracuse. Were they then to extend this system to the whole island, many of whose inhabitants differed from themselves in race, language and tradition? There were serious objections. The experience of many of the natives in political life was small, while their military qualifications were doubtful. Further, the Sicilians themselves would have considered it an intolerable burden to be dragged from their villages and farms to fight in wars about which they had no interest or knowledge. It would be easier for them to pay tribute as they had long been accustomed. And the existence of the practice was a strong factor in determining the policy of the Romans, who preferred to assimilate rather than to destroy; within limits, they were ready to adapt their machinery of government to current needs. To impose tribute was the line of least resistance; it was chosen perhaps without much thought of its implications or possible consequences, but in time it revolutionized the whole conception of government and changed the leader of an Italian federation into an imperial power which ultimately dominated the civilized world.

By establishing a new tribute-paying area Rome sowed the seeds from which her whole provincial system was to develop. But some parts of Sicily fell outside this district. The kingdom of Hiero, which comprised about a quarter of the island, was immune from taxation. By the alliance which he had concluded with Rome 'for ever' in 248, he was not even obliged to supply troops, though he voluntarily gave loyal support; but after his death in 215, and the revolt of Syracuse from Rome, Syracuse together with several of her subject cities was made tributary. Another ally of Rome was Messana, which, like many of the Greek cities of southern Italy, had to supply one warship; after the fall of Syracuse (212) Tauromenium and Netum were added to this class of *civitates foederatae*. To certain other cities Rome had promised autonomy and freedom from obligations in return for their help during the war; and she kept her promise. Halaesa, Centuripa, Segesta and Halicyae from the beginning of the war, and Panormus twelve years later, were all free from taxation though not allied to Rome (*civitates immunes*); this privilege, not confirmed by treaty, was dependent on their good behaviour and did not free them from Roman jurisdiction. At the other extreme from these free cities and allied cities was any land which the sovereign people of Rome might declare public property, *ager publicus*; the Roman censors then rented it on leasehold to its former holders. Probably, however, no territory apart from certain official Punic residences was disposed of in this way before the fall of Syracuse.

All these districts comprised about one half of the island. On the other half Rome imposed a regular annual tax, such as some cities had paid to Carthage, others to Syracuse. The dominant powers in Sicily had long collected tithes; Syracuse had done so from the days of Gelon. More recently Hiero had reorganized the assessment and administration of the taxes of his kingdom on very capable lines. He drew up a revenue code which in many respects resembled those of the great Hellenistic monarchies, especially Ptolemaic Egypt; yet it was probably his own work rather than a mere copy or adaptation of existing codes. So efficient was this Lex Hieronica that the Roman magistrates who first went out to govern Sicily decreed that the tithe should be collected on the lines laid down by this code, and the succeeding praetors maintained this practice, which was not embodied in law till the Lex Rupilia was passed in 131. But though Rome followed it in practice, she did not accept, nor perhaps realize, the theory on which it and the Oriental codes rested: that conquest involved full ownership of the conquered soil (*dominium in solo provinciali*). Instead, she regarded the revenue derived from Sicily as a tax paid by the governed to the state, not as rent paid by tenant to owner.[1]

The main form of taxation was a tithe on harvested crops (*decumana*). This system was very fair for an agricultural country, especially one that was subject to drought, for the amount of tithe would fluctuate with seasonal variations. Pasture land, which could not be taxed in this way, was liable to an annual monetary tax levied on every head of grazing stock (*scriptura*). Harbour-dues (*portoria*) were imposed on all imports and exports at the rate of 5 per cent. The Romans also reserved for themselves prior rights to buy additional wheat for the plebs at Rome (*frumentum emptum*), or for the Roman governor's household (*frumentum in cellam*). Such requisitions were later regulated by legislation (73 BC).

The collection of the tithe, which followed the methods of Hiero, was equitably managed and prevented Sicily from becoming the prey of Roman tax collectors, who later exploited other provinces. It was not farmed out by contracts let at Rome to individuals or companies, as were the harbour-dues; nor was it administered by state officials, which would have involved the creation of a civil service. Instead it was farmed out to the highest bidder in the province, whether native or Roman; agents of Roman companies were not allowed to bid. Local city magistrates were responsible for listing the farmers, their land and produce. On the basis of such schedules the contractor – often the town itself – could bid in the presence of the Roman magistrate with the prospect of $\frac{2}{5}$ per cent profit. He then fixed the exact amount of the tithe with the various farmers, who were protected against injustice, and deposited with the city magistrate copies of all agreements made. The local authorities thus became responsible for the correct delivery of the produce due, which was then paid to a Roman official. So efficient was the system that Cicero could write (*in Verr.*, II, iii, 8, 20): 'The law of Hiero is so carefully framed that neither in the cornfields, nor on the threshing floors, nor in the barns can the cultivator defraud the collector of one single grain without the severest punishment; nor is it possible for more than the tenth to be extorted from the cultivator against his will.'

The necessity of upholding law and order in the island led to the gradual creation of an administrative system. After her conquest of Italy

Rome had administered the annexed districts through the central government at Rome, not by installing permanent officials with *imperium* in the various localities. But it had been found necessary in the fourth century for judicial reasons to send to various districts legates of the urban praetor (*praefecti iure dicundo*); and in 267 four quaestors (*quaestores classici*) had been appointed to given districts to protect the financial interests of the state and to guard the coast. After the First Punic War one of these Italic quaestors was apparently sent to Lilybaeum, whence he could direct the administration of the island. But soon it became clear that the duties of such a governor required the possession of full *imperium*, which was not inherent in the quaestorship. A magistrate, such as the consul or praetor, was needed. And so in about 227, after Rome had gained control of Sardinia as well as Sicily, the annual number of praetors was raised from two to four; two of them continued to serve in Rome, while two went to the islands. From this time the word *provincia*, which meant the sphere within which a magistrate exercised his *imperium*, began to be applied more particularly to these foreign spheres outside Italy: her overseas provinces.

The provincial praetor exercised wide powers. He controlled the general administration of the province, the local authorities and all public works; he commanded all the land and sea forces within his province; and he was the supreme judge in civil and criminal cases. He was supported by a large staff, consisting of one subordinate magistrate, the quaestor (there were two in Sicily after 210), one or more senatorial *legati*, to whom he might delegate any business, and a number of 'comrades' (*comites*), young men whom he initiated in the routine of official life. Theoretically he remained the colleague of the other praetors and exercised less authority than the consuls. In practice, however, being far from the control of these magistrates, unchecked by the principle of collegiality, unhampered by the tribunician veto, with his judgments not subjected to the right of appeal (except in the case of Roman citizens), he wielded almost kingly power. And Verres proved to the unfortunate Sicilians towards the end of the Republic that a provincial praetor could become a local tyrant. But on the other hand his tenure of office was short, so that he could soon be called to task at Rome; he was checked by the local liberties granted to privileged cities under the official charter of the province (the *lex provinciae*); while the peaceful condition of a quiet province like Sicily precluded the use or abuse of much military power.

Under the strong hand of Rome, which had crushed the ancient struggle of Greek and Carthaginian in Sicily, the natives prospered. Their cities remained autonomous in local administration and they continued in increasing number to issue their own coinage. Within each city the popular assembly and the council still transacted business. Little attempt was made to adapt the municipal authorities to the Roman form, although the smaller membership of the councils made them easier bodies to deal with than the assemblies, thus giving a slightly anti-democratic bias. It is uncertain how far members of one community were forbidden the right to deal or hold property (*commercium*) or to marry (*conubium*) in another; Segesta was not allowed *commercium*, probably to safeguard her, while Centuripa was granted the somewhat doubtful privilege. The judicial machinery which was gradually created illustrates the fairness of the Roman rule. Cicero records (*in Verr.*, II, ii, 13, 32) that in a suit between citizens of the same state the trial should be held in that state and in accordance with the native code; this would not preclude an appeal to the governor. When a Sicilian sued a member of another state, the praetor chose the judge by lot (he could be a Roman citizen). In suits between an individual and a state not his own, the Senate of a third state became judge. In litigation between natives and Roman citizens, the judge was to be of the nationality of the defendant.

Such in brief was the scheme of taxation and administration which the Romans adopted in their first province, though many of the details were naturally only elaborated in the course of time and the quarter of the island which Hiero ruled was not added to the tithe-paying portion till after his death. With their interests protected the Sicilians prospered, and many must have realized that they were receiving considerable compensation for the tithe they now paid to Rome. They were freed from the heavy hand of Carthage who had sought to monopolize their trade; they were immune from exploitation by tax-gatherers; they were ruled efficiently by governors who for many years were just and honourable men; and when Rome again entered the lists with Carthage, their loyalty to Rome showed which of the two Republics they preferred as mistress.

2. CARTHAGE AND THE SARDINIAN QUESTION

The First Punic War had levied but a light toll in blood on the citizens of Carthage, but the Truceless War which followed endangered the city's very life. Twenty thousand mercenaries, who had returned from Sicily, mustered at Sicca Veneria (modern El Kef) and clamoured loudly for arrears of pay. This motley crew of Libyans, Iberians, Celts, Ligurians, Balearic Islanders and half-breed Greeks, who had found a common bond in their claims on Carthage, marched on Tunis under the joint leadership of a Libyan named Matho, and Spendius, who was said to be a runaway Roman slave. The standard of revolt was raised throughout the country. The subject Libyans rushed to arms against their oppressors. The Numidians swept over the western frontier. Utica and Hippo Diarrhytus, which alone remained loyal, were besieged; the mercenaries were masters of the open country and cut the communications of Carthage with the rest of Libya. Other mercenaries in Sardinia also revolted.

In desperate plight the Carthaginians raised an army under Hanno, who failed to relieve Utica (spring 240). Carthage was further isolated when Spendius camped at the only bridge over the river Bagradas, which ran between Utica and Carthage. Hanno's ill-success led to the appointment of his rival Hamilcar Barca, who had been eclipsed after the war with Rome, partly from dissatisfaction with the peace terms he had arranged and with his promises to the mercenaries, partly by the prominence of Hanno, who represented a party which saw the future of Carthage in expansion in Africa rather than in foreign exploitation which clashed with the interests of Rome.

By a decisive victory near the Bagradas Hamilcar opened up communications beyond the river. Then instead of joining his rival Hanno who was operating against Matho at Hippo he again tricked Spendius who was hanging on his heels. By showing great leniency after the victory Hamilcar tried to check the revolt, but Spendius destroyed all hope of compromise by torturing seven hundred prisoners. So the war was renewed with the utmost barbarity and cruelty on both sides.

When Utica and Hippo capitulated, the mercenaries moved against Carthage itself from their base at Tunis; but without the command of the sea they had little prospect of success. Carthage was further embarrassed by the revolt in Sardinia, but Hamilcar, who had been given the sole command after an ineffective attempt to co-operate with Hanno, soon rounded up and annihilated Spendius' force at Prione. Moving to Tunis he camped at the south end of the isthmus on which the town lay; Hannibal, whom he had left to cover Carthage, was at the north end. But Matho, goaded into action by the gruesome sight of the crucifixion of his fellow-mutineer, Spendius, and his companions, skilfully captured Hannibal's camp before Hamilcar could move. Hamilcar, thus forced to raise the siege of Tunis, withdrew to the mouth of the Bagradas to protect the communications of Carthage (239).

During the winter Carthage made her final effort. New troops were raised; Hamilcar and Hanno were reconciled. An energetic strategy gradually drew Matho to the neighbourhood of Leptis Minor; both sides wearied of guerrilla warfare and met on the field of battle, where the mercenaries were destroyed. The rebellious subject towns were reduced; Utica and Hippo surrendered after a short siege. Peace was restored after three years' fighting which far surpassed in cruelty and inhumanity any other struggle known to Polybius. The Carthaginians themselves had for once to fight for their city's preservation. The tenacious fury of the Semite had been roused to good effect; disciplined and scientific warfare had worn down the resistance of mercenaries whom common interests alone held together. But Carthage had paid a heavy price for victory, especially in her weakness after the war with Rome.[2]

During this life-and-death struggle Carthage had maintained friendly relations with Rome. True, some slight trouble had arisen when Italian merchants supplied arms and food to the rebels. The Carthaginians had captured 500 of them, but on receiving representations from Rome had released them. In return Rome sent back the Punic prisoners that were still in Italy, forbade further contraband running and allowed Carthage to trade with Italy and possibly to hire troops there. Possible friction was avoided for the moment in Sardinia, where the Punic mercenaries had revolted from Carthage and taken most of the island (240). They appealed to Rome for help, probably in 239, when Hamilcar's victory over Spendius suggested that Carthage was finishing her war in Africa. But Rome rejected their appeal and that of Utica which also proffered submission. She probably regarded the mercenaries as an international danger and preferred to respect the treaty of 241.

When Carthage had crushed the African rising, the mercenaries in Sardinia, being hard-pressed by the natives, again appealed to Rome (238). It was known that the Carthaginians would attack them soon, so that if Rome wished to prevent the reoccupation of the island by Punic forces, this was the time to act. For Carthage was worn out by her recent struggles; her fleet had been lost in the war with Rome and her revenues were reduced by the Truceless War. There was little likelihood that she would face another war if Rome insisted. The Romans, therefore, bluntly declared war on her when she objected to their claim to intervene in Sardinia.[3] In vain the Carthaginians protested that they had prior claims; in vain they offered to submit to arbitration (by Ptolemy III of Egypt?). Finally they were granted peace only at the price of 1,200 talents and the surrender of Sardinia; an additional clause was added, as it were, to the Peace of Lutatius. This act was strongly denounced by Polybius as 'contrary to all justice'. It would be idle to suggest that by abandoning

Sardinia for a year or more Carthage had forfeited her rights to it; the successful mercenaries could hardly claim to dictate the future of the island. Nor could it be classed among 'the islands between Sicily and Italy' which had been ceded to Rome by the treaty of 241, though Roman annalists patriotically may have tried to stretch the point. It may be true that the severe treatment by Carthage of Italian merchants, who continued to run contraband, gave Rome a pretext:[4] but it was no more than a pretext. Sardinia was so closely connected geographically with Italy that the Romans could not allow Carthage complete control of the island; the First Punic War had shown the danger which might arise from an enemy fleet based there. When the moment was ripe Rome acted with decision and without scruple and thus permanently embittered relations with her old rival just when they were becoming more friendly.

The Romans' troubles started when they set out to conquer Sardinia and with it Corsica whose capital they had taken in 258. The courage of the natives and the mountainous country rendered conquest a slow task. Ti. Sempronius Gracchus occupied the coastal cities once held by Carthage (probably in 237); but the conquest of the interior progressed slowly. Not till 231 was a semblance of peace imposed, when the consul gained a doubtful reputation by employing manhunting dogs against the natives. In the same year Corsica was pacified. In about 227 the two islands were constituted a Roman province like Sicily and a praetor was appointed annually to supervise them. This caused another revolt in Sardinia, which was, however, pacified by 225; by the Second Punic War the island was officially conquered, except for a few highland tribes. The province was administered like Sicily, except that no towns had obtained freedom or immunity. Apart from territory confiscated by Rome, a tithe on the products of the soil was levied on the rest, and Sardinia became, with Sicily, and later Africa, one of the three granaries of the Republic. This tax was not severe for a people which had been subjected to exploitation by Carthage, but the economic life of the island declined when its produce could no longer be shipped to the Punic markets of the west.

3. ROME AND THE GAULS

During Rome's struggle with Carthage the Italian federation had remained loyal; one exception merely emphasized the solidarity of the whole. Falerii waited till the end of the war and then revolted in 241; perhaps the occasion was the recent expiration of its fifty-years' alliance with Rome. But it did not have to wait long for its punishment. The consuls who had returned from Sicily stormed it in six days and forced the inhabitants to abandon their strong hill site (modern Civita Castellana) and to rebuild in the plain where the solitary church of Santa Maria di Falleri within the circuit of the Roman walls to-day preserves the name. Half the territory of Falerii was annexed as *ager publicus*, and a Latin colony was planted at Spoletium on the road to Ariminum and the north.

In contrast with the fate of Falerii, the loyalty of the Picentes and Sabines (p. 148) was rewarded by the grant of two wards in the Comitia Centuriata: two new tribes named Velina and Quirina were established in 241, bringing the total up to thirty-five, a number that was never increased. The fixing of the total had an important result, because the citizens of districts enfranchised thereafter had to be assigned to one of the existing tribes; this involved the gradual disappearance of the local significance of the tribes, which became merely administrative divisions. It is probable that the Comitia Centuriata was reformed at the time when these last two tribes were established, and that the reform was the work of the censors. Its main object was to correlate the centuries and tribes, possibly to make the Comitia Centuriata somewhat more democratic. The five 'Servian' classes were retained, but the centuries were rearranged. The first class was reduced from 80 to 70 centuries, two to a tribe, one of seniors and one of juniors (35 in each). Either the other four classes were treated similarly; if so, there would be 350 groups, and with the eighteen centuries of knights and five of proletarians, etc., a grand total of 373; or else the total number of centuries remained fixed at 193 and the ten centuries of the first class were redistributed among some or all of the other four (although the method of redistribution remains uncertain). The century which voted first (*praerogativa*) and generally had considerable influence on those that followed, was chosen by lot from the first class; then the knights and the five classes voted in order until a majority of the centuries' votes was obtained. But this would not be reached until at least part of the third class had voted; and if the voting was not solid for or against the motion even lower classes might get a chance to vote, whereas hitherto the knights and the first class had had a clear majority. Thus if the centuries numbered 350, the middle classes who predominated in the hitherto more democratic Comitia Tributa could now exercise a vote in the Centuriata. Probably the property ratings were adjusted at the same time. Wealth still remained predominant, though its influence was limited, while age received undue recognition since the number of *seniores* would be less than the *iuniores*. The will of the people still could not find such complete expression in the Comitia Centuriata as in the Tributa, but the working of the two assemblies was brought more into line.[5]

The peasant middle classes and the rural democracy were championed in 232 by a tribune named C. Flaminius, who attacked the patricio-plebeian nobility. He proposed that the *ager Gallicus (et Picenus?)*, the district south of Ariminum which had been confiscated from the Senones, should be divided into small allotments and distributed to poor citizens; and he forced this measure through the plebeian assembly in the teeth of bitter senatorial opposition. This was aroused partly perhaps by the consideration that it would be fairer to found a Latin colony on this territory, but more because individual senators were unwilling to lose their valuable leaseholds there, and above all because of Flaminius' disregard of the Senate and of the Comitia Centuriata. Tradition relates that this measure caused the beginning of 'the demoralization of the people' and hastened the Gallic invasion of 225 because it annoyed the Gauls. Of these statements, which derive from an aristocratic tradition hostile to Flaminius, the first is at least doubtful, for although in his disregard of the Senate Flaminius was the forerunner of the Gracchi, yet his measure was far from revolutionary. The second is demonstrably false: the Gallic invasion had threatened four years before and did not mature till seven years after the enactment, and the Gauls can have cared little whether territory so far south was occupied by individual Roman farmers or was controlled by wealthy Roman nobles. Flaminius' proposal was a timely measure of self-defence against the Gauls rather than a provocation.

Flaminius crossed swords with the Senate on another question. A tribune, Q. Claudius, carried a measure which prevented senators engaging in overseas trade to any extent: senators and their sons were forbidden to own ships other than small ones to transport the produce of their estates. Flaminius alone supported this measure in the Senate. It was designed to prevent private financial interests distracting or perverting the interests of the governing classes; it had the effect of forcing them to concentrate more on their lands. At the same time – the date is uncertain – senators were prohibited from taking state contracts.[6]

Flaminius' agrarian law focused attention on the north, where the Celts were restless. The Senones and Boii had taken to heart the bitter lesson taught by the campaigns which had ended in 282, and pro-videntially for Rome they remained quiet during her struggles with Pyrrhus and Carthage. But a new generation of Celts had now grown up and Rome was free to consider the safety of her northern frontier. During

the century the Ligurians, who had inhabited the sweep of hills from the
French Alps along the Italian Riviera, had thrust the Etruscans back from
Pisa and the River Arno, and had had dealings with their kinsmen in
Corsica, which Rome had determined to master. Further, Rome's friend
Massilia would be grateful to have the Tyrrhenian Sea cleared of the
pirates who frequented its shores. Thus many considerations led the
Romans to make some demonstration against the Ligurians, and we hear
of engagements in 238, 236, 234, 233 and 230, which led to the freeing of
Pisa, now probably a member of Rome's confederacy; the partial
submission of the Apuani; and the occupation of Luna. But the Ligurians
were not really overcome until after the Hannibalic War. More serious
were the movements of the Boii, who, reinforced by Transalpine tribes,
ventured to move against Ariminium in 236. But dissension among the
tribesmen led to the withdrawal of the army, so that the threat of a Gallic
peril was removed for the moment. Instead of taking the opportunity of
marching against the Boii and of advancing their frontier to the Po, the
Romans preferred peace. Skirmishes might continue against the Sardinians and Ligurians, but real warfare was at an end. In 235–234 with
due solemnity the gates of the Temple of Janus were closed for the first
time since the reign of Numa Pompilius.

During the next few years Rome's attention was directed towards the
Adriatic (see pp. 191–5), but it was sharply drawn back to the north
where the storm clouds lowered so ominously in 226 that Rome hastily
reached an agreement with Hasdrubal whose empire-building in Spain
was raising visions of renewed trouble with Carthage (see pp. 196 ff).
The Gallic clans were gathering. The Boii and the neighbouring
Lingones had summoned to their aid the war-like Insubres from beyond
the Po; from further west came the Taurini and the Gaesati from beyond
the Alps. Memories of Allia and the sack of Rome caused panic
throughout Italy. At Rome two Gauls and a Greek were buried alive in
the Forum Boarium in an attempt to anticipate literally a statement from
the Sibylline books that Rome 'must twice be held by a foreign enemy'. A
more sensible measure was the taking of a census of all the available forces
throughout Italy; the citizens amounted to 250,000 infantry and 23,000
cavalry, the allies to 350,000 men excluding reserves, the Bruttians and
Greek allies. Further, the Cenomani who dwelt north of the Boii did not
join their kinsmen, but with the non-Celtic Veneti of the north-east
remained at peace with Rome.

Rome hastened to defend Italy. One consul was absent in Sardinia, but
the other, L. Aemilius Papus, was stationed at Ariminum; Etruscan and
Sabine forces, commanded by a praetor, protected the passes of the

western Apennines; four legions covered Rome; two others guarded southern Italy and Sicily against the possibility of Carthaginian intervention. Instead of attacking Ariminum as they had done eleven years before, the Celts advanced over the Apennines into Etruria, their forces numbering 50,000 infantry and 20,000 cavalry. Devastating the country on their march they took the road to Rome and slipped past the two Roman armies. These hastened in pursuit, intending to converge at Clusium, where however the Gauls turned and tricked the praetor into battle near Montepulciano before the consul's arrival. Then, resolving not to face the consular army in battle, they retired with their booty to the Etruscan coast, south of the massif of Mte Amiata; it would have been too dangerous to retreat by the way they had come, while the coast route offered further booty and forage for their horses. From Orbetello they proceeded northwards, closely followed by Aemilius, when they were surprised to find another consular army facing them at Telamon. It was the legions of Atilius Regulus, who had been recalled from Sardinia and was marching south from Pisa. A great battle was fought. The Gauls formed two lines back to back to meet the double attack. The naked bodies of the Celts, their fine physique, their flashing gold necklaces and bracelets, the blare of their trumpets, all impressed the Romans. But discipline and superior equipment at length overcame their desperate valour. Though Atilius was killed, 40,000 Gauls were left on the field and 10,000 were captured; only part of their cavalry broke away. Never again did a Gallic army cross the Apennines.[7]

This unrest among the Gauls emphasized the fact that the Alps were the natural frontier of Italy and that the victory of Telamon must be followed up by the conquest of Cisalpine Gaul in order to ensure peace and a quiet frontier. After the battle Aemilius raided the Boii, who were completely subdued by the consuls of the following year (224). It fell to the lot of the popular leader C. Flaminius to lead the first Roman army across the Po against the Insubres. This daring and able politician, who had crossed swords with the Senate on the score of his land bill, reached the consulship in 223 and proceeded to display his not inconsiderable gifts as a soldier. With his colleague he crossed the Po near the Adda and then, instead of marching directly against the Insubres, he turned through the country of the friendly Cenomani and fell on the enemy from their exposed eastern flank. Hostile senators might point out the dangers of Flaminius' strategy, but it succeeded. In the country south of Bergamo and Brescia he encountered and defeated the enemy; the tradition, which assigns the victory to the efficiency of the Roman legions and tribunes in spite of their general's rashness, is not above suspicion. Flaminius is said to have left unread despatches which he received from the Senate before the battle, guessing that they contained an order to return without fighting. In any case he was recalled after the battle, and his colleague's refusal to disobey this summons prevented him from following up his victory. On his return he was voted a triumph by the people despite the Senate. After this honour he retired from office and thus allowed the consuls of 222 to enter on their duties on 15 March, a month earlier than usual; not till 153 did the consular year start on 1 January. Flaminius deserved a better tribute from his country than he received.

The Insubres sought peace on conditions which the new consuls, Cn. Cornelius Scipio and M. Claudius Marcellus, were unwilling to accept; they then prepared to renew the struggle with the help of 30,000 Gaesati. When the consuls attacked Acerrae, which commanded the passage of the river Adda, the Gauls made a counter-attack on Clastidium which had recently been occupied by Flaminius. The consuls separated. Marcellus marched to the relief of Clastidium, where he won a victory, charging on horseback the Gaulish chieftain Viridomarus whom he slew in single combat; he thus won the *spolia opima* for the last time in Roman history. Meantime Scipio captured Acerrae and advanced into the heart of Insubrian territory. At Mediolanum (Milan) he got into slight difficulties, until Marcellus arrived; together they routed the enemy and took the city.[8] The Insubres surrendered unconditionally and gave up some territory on which the colony of Cremona was soon founded. Lastly, the consuls of 221 and 220 finally overcame the native tribes of Istria and thus secured the north-eastern frontier up to the Julian Alps. Cisalpine Gaul was conquered and the way lay open for the infiltration of Roman culture. This was hastened by the extension of the road from Spoletium to Ariminum by Flaminius, who reached the censorship in 220; the whole route from Rome was reconditioned and the new Great North Road was called the Via Flaminia.

Two years later Latin colonies of 6,000 settlers each were planted at Placentia and Cremona to guard the passage over the Po against the Insubres, and a fortified outpost (rather than a citizen colony) was placed at Mutina (Modena) among the Boii. But hardly had peace been established when Hannibal appeared from over the Alps, and Cisalpine Gaul rallied to his banner.

4. THE ILLYRIAN PIRATES

Before and after, but luckily not during, Rome's struggle with the Gauls, her attention was diverted to Greece and a new world entered her purview.

Although in the course of the third century she had become arbiter of the destinies of a multitude of Greek towns in Magna Graecia and Sicily; although many of her nobles and many even of the general rank and file that had served abroad had become interested in Greek culture, nevertheless she had no direct dealings with Greece proper and no Roman embassy set foot in Greece before 228 BC.[9] But events occurred which forced Rome out of her indifference to the Hellenistic world. During the First Punic War an Illyrian chieftain named Agron had built up a very considerable kingdom, centred at Scodra (Scutari or Skhöder), and stretching from Dalmatia in the north down to the coast opposite the heel of Italy. In 231 by co-operating with Demetrius II of Macedonia he was enabled to interfere much further south, though the unwise celebration of a victory brought about his death. His widow, the queen-regent Teuta, aided by an unscrupulous chieftain, Scerdilaidas, carried on his imperialistic policy: in 230 they took Epirus and Acarnania and thus extended Illyria's sphere of control to the Corinthian Gulf.

It was not, however, the territorial expansion of Illyria that drew Rome's first glance across the Adriatic. The immemorial pursuit and chief industry of the Illyrians was piracy. Their rugged broken coast with its screen of islands formed a perfect base from which their light and speedy little galleys (*lembi*) could prey on passing merchantmen. Checked in earlier days by the fleets of various Greek cities, they now roved the seas unhindered until Rome at length assumed the role of policeman. As long as they victimized only Greek shipping in the Adriatic, Rome was unmoved. But when they ravaged the coast of southern Italy and ventured into the Ionian Sea to rob, capture and even kill Italian traders, popular indignation at last forced Rome's hand. But the Senate preferred diplomacy to force. Two envoys were sent to Teuta, who was busy besieging Issa in an attempt to annex all the neighbouring Greek cities not yet under her control (*aut.* 230). The queen repudiated responsibility for any outrages committed by her subjects and refused to guarantee the future safety of Italian commerce; angered by a threat from the ambassadors she broke off negotiations. On their return home the envoys were attacked by pirates and one of them was killed. Whether or not Teuta was directly responsible for this outrage, she sealed her doom by refusing to offer any explanation. But Rome was still slow to act. It was not until the queen had besieged and captured Corcyra and had defeated a relieving Greek fleet that a Roman navy sailed into Illyrian waters.[10]

In the summer of 229 Cn. Fulvius Centumalus sailed to Corcyra with 200 vessels. Resistance in face of this fleet was useless and even Teuta was not rash enough to attempt it. A Greek of Pharos named Demetrius, whom the queen had left in command at Corcyra, promptly betrayed the town to the Romans who received the willing surrender of the townsfolk. Fulvius then sailed to Apollonia where the other consul, L. Postumius Albinus, landed from Brundisium with 22,000 troops. Apollonia like Corcyra at once surrendered, and Epidamnus (Dyrrhachium) followed suit. The army advanced northwards perhaps to the Drilo (Drin) without meeting any serious opposition; the fleet received the surrender of Issa, Pharos and Corcyra Nigra. Teuta fled to her fortress at Rhizon where she held out till the spring of 228; her capitulation was inevitable, so that only one consul and 40 ships remained in Illyria during the winter. The terms granted her were that she should retain her crown, but pay tribute to Rome and renounce all claim to districts taken by the Romans; further, only two Illyrian vessels might sail beyond Lissus (Alessio), perhaps fixed as the southern limit of her kingdom.

Rome had thus freed the passage between Italy and Greece from the danger of Illyrian pirates. Future protection was secured by guarding the two flanks of the Illyrian kingdom. In the north the traitor Demetrius was given his native island, Pharos, together with other islands and mainland towns; here he reigned by permission of Rome. In the south the Romans themselves established a protectorate: a coastal strip from Lissus to the frontier of Epirus, together with the islands they had taken. The inhabitants of this district were made neither allies nor subjects; they were free from tribute and retained their autonomy, but had to supply troops on demand.[11] Thus almost without striking a blow Rome had confined Illyrian shipping to the Adriatic without destroying the kingdom, and had established a base on the Albanian coast from which she could keep an eye on her neighbour. The slowness with which she entered upon the war and the conditions she imposed after it are sufficient to disprove the theory that she deliberately cultivated an aggressive eastern policy. The Senate, although perhaps conscious that if the need arose the new protectorate would block Macedon, had only intervened when and in so far as it was necessary to maintain order.

After the war the Romans sent ambassadors to the Achaeans, Aetolians, Corinthians and Athenians to announce their victory and to explain their conduct; for the Greeks, no less than the Italians, had benefited by the suppression of piracy. Thus for the first time Rome came officially into contact with the leading powers of Greece by an exchange of diplomatic courtesies. The envoys were well received and Corinth admitted the Romans to the Isthmian Games, thus recognizing them as members of the Hellenic world. But no formal engagements were concluded, nor was any approach made to Macedon, which was now governed by Antigonus Doson, regent for the young Philip. Rome perhaps realized that the formation of her new protectorate had in fact annoyed the Macedonians, who in earlier days had controlled some of the Adriatic ports from which they were now excluded. Be that as it may, the Romans made no attempt to entangle themselves in Greek politics.[12]

During the next ten years Rome was too busy with the Gallic invasion and, as will be seen, with trying to check the growing power of Carthage in Spain, to think much of Greece where momentous events were taking place. Antigonus Doson had revived the power of Macedon and had asserted his hegemony in Greece; further, he had won the support of Demetrius of Pharos, who was quietly extending his power beyond the limits imposed by Rome. This adventurer, after the death or abdication of Teuta, had become regent for Agron's son, and with Prince Scerdilaidas controlled the Illyrian kingdom. With a rash disregard for his safety Demetrius continued on his reckless course of aggression even when the young Philip, who had succeeded Antigonus on the throne of Macedon, was distracted with internal difficulties and could give little help to his Illyrian ally. Nothing daunted, Demetrius in 220 proceeded with Scerdilaidas to attack Pylos with a fleet of 90 vessels, thus perhaps violating the treaty of 228, and then sailed into the Aegean, where his pirate squadrons ranged far and wide. Further, he invaded some territory under the Roman protectorate. This could not be overlooked, and the situation was aggravated in Roman eyes by a visit which King Philip paid to Scerdilaidas in Illyria in the winter of 220–219. Relations with Carthage were becoming strained and it would never do to allow eastern affairs to become threatening. What if Carthage should make overtures to Demetrius or Philip? So once again Rome sent a force to check Demetrius and his Illyrian pirates.

A whirlwind campaign laid Demetrius low. The consuls of 219, L. Aemilius Paullus and M. Livius Salinator, sailed to Greece. Demetrius intended to resist in the south at Dimale and in the north at Pharos, where he himself remained. But Aemilius stormed Dimale in seven days, with the result that the surrounding district hastened to surrender. The consuls then sailed to Pharos which they captured by strategy; a 'fixing' frontal attack covered the approach of a body of men who had disembarked at the rear. Demetrius fled to Philip. The consuls, anxious at the news which came from Spain, where Hannibal was besieging Saguntum, hastily made a settlement. Pharos and other districts were put on the same basis as the towns which had been placed under Roman protection ten years before. Scerdilaidas and the young king Pinnes were left undisturbed in Illyria.

Philip, deeply occupied in a struggle with the Aetolians and Sparta, had not raised a hand to help Demetrius, but welcomed him after his flight and later lent a ready ear to that adventurer's schemes for revenge on Rome. He also received help from Scerdilaidas who, disregarding his obligations to Rome, sailed south of Lissus to join him. Such happenings might have claimed Roman attention had it not been for Hannibal's distracting activity; as it was, the Romans did nothing. Scerdilaidas, however, decided with cheerful inconsequence to attack Philip, his erstwhile ally (217). But he soon came to grief and thus gave Philip control of more territory bordering on the Roman protectorate, so that when the moment was ripe the Macedonian king was more ready to make common cause with Hannibal. Thus Rome's two expeditions in eastern waters resulted in the suppression of piracy, the establishment of a protectorate in Lower Illyria and the stirring up of the enmity of Philip of Macedon.

5. THE PUNIC EMPIRE IN SPAIN

While Rome was engaged in Cisalpine Gaul and across the Adriatic, Carthage was fully occupied in the western Mediterranean. The friendly relations of Rome and Carthage during the war with the mercenaries were rudely shattered by Rome's seizure of Sardinia, and at Carthage the party which stood for hostility towards Rome again climbed into the saddle. If Carthage ever again intended to cross swords with Rome, clearly she must train and keep a standing army like other nations. Hanno's policy was to encourage expansion in Africa; and Numidia and Mauretania would have afforded good material. But there was better elsewhere. By reconquest and extended conquest Hamilcar proposed to make good the decline of Carthaginian influence in Spain, and thus to offset the loss of Sicily and Sardinia. In Spain Carthage could train and support an army with less fear of Roman intervention. It is unlikely that Hamilcar and the advocates of this policy of re-establishing Punic domination in the western Mediterranean aimed directly and deliberately at revenge. But certainly after Rome's handling of the Sardinian question those who saw the future of Carthage in Africa had to give place to an expansionist group. The tradition that Hamilcar conquered Spain against the wishes of his government is absurd. He was in alliance with Hasdrubal, the leader of the democratic party, and when money and booty began to pour in from the Peninsula Hanno's faction would become less vocal. The main part of the Punic government was behind the Barcids.

The cause, date and degree of the diminution of Punic influence in Spain is uncertain; but the application of the question *cui bono* would point to the implication of the Greek cities – especially Massilia. But Gades, at any rate, remained in Punic hands and thither Hamilcar Barca sailed in 237 with his nine-year-old son Hannibal whom he had just forced to swear that he would never be Rome's friend; this anecdote, which seems authentic, shows something of the mind of the father. Based at Gades, he proceeded to reconquer southern and eastern Spain. Andalusia soon fell to his sword and he advanced the Punic frontier to Cape Nao, building a dominating fortress at Akra Leuke (White Rock; probably modern Alicante). In 231 an embassy came to him from Rome, whose ally, Massilia, could ill afford to see the Punic frontier creeping so far north. The Romans themselves probably cared little what happened in southern Spain and were contented with Hamilcar's neat reply: that he was fighting the Iberians to get money with which to pay off the Roman war indemnity. But they had shown that they were keeping an eye on Carthaginian expansion and at some point they entered into friendly relations with the native city of Saguntum. Shortly afterwards Hamilcar, who was withdrawing from the siege of Helice (modern Elche) at the approach of the Orissi, met his death by drowning, but only after he had secured the safety of his son Hannibal and the officers with him (229–228). So fell a gallant soldier, of whom his country might justly be proud.

Hamilcar was succeeded by the leader of the popular party, his son-in-law Hasdrubal, who was chosen by the troops and afterwards received confirmation of his appointment from the people of Carthage. He avenged his predecessor's death by an expedition against the Orissi, and thus reached the Upper Guadiana. Though his army was reckoned at 50,000 infantry, 6,000 cavalry and 200 elephants, he achieved more by diplomacy than force. He married an Iberian princess and changed the Punic headquarters from Alicante to the site of Mastia, where he founded the city of New Carthage (Cartagena) on a peninsula which commanded one of the best harbours in the world; there were rich silver mines in the vicinity and the passage to Africa was easy. From this base he advanced up the east coast in the direction of the Ebro. In 226 he was met by ambassadors from the Romans, who feared that he might join hands with the rebellious Ligurians and Gallic tribes. A treaty was arranged by which Hasdrubal agreed not to cross the Ebro with an armed force and perhaps undertook not to help the Gauls; as a *quid pro quo* he possibly received the assurance that Rome would not interfere with his conquests south of the river. The attitude of Rome's ally Massilia to this arrangement is uncertain; though doubtless it was she who had warned Rome of Hasdrubal's encroachments. By the Ebro treaty she definitely lost her three colonies which the Carthaginians had taken: Hemeroscopium, Alonis and Alicante. But her two colonies north of the Ebro, Emporiae and Rhode, were saved from Hasdrubal's grasp.[13]

In 221 Hasdrubal was assassinated by a Celt and his place was filled by Hamilcar's twenty-five-year-old son, Hannibal, who was soon to enter the lists against Rome in one of the most epic struggles known to history. The new general reverted to his father's warlike policy, though, like Hasdrubal, he married a Spanish princess from Castulo. He at once attacked the Olcades who dwelt near the Upper Guadiana, and after wintering at New Carthage he stormed the highland tribes of the central plateau. Advancing along the westerly route to Salmantica (Salamanca) he defeated the Vaccaei and on his return the Carpetani, thus advancing the standards of Carthage beyond the Tagus (220). Though many of the more distant tribes south of the Ebro (e.g. the Celtiberians of the Upper Tagus and Douro, and the Lusitanians) were still unconquered, and though some of the nearer tribes (e.g. the Vaccaei and Carpetani) were only prevented from revolting through the hostages they had surrendered, nevertheless the Barcid generals had won a great empire from which Carthage could draw immense supplies of manpower and mineral wealth: 'an inexhaustible treasure-store for empire.'

But one city south of the Ebro still withstood Hannibal: the friend of Rome, Iberian Saguntum perched on its rocky plateau. When it became known that Hannibal intended to demand its surrender in the spring, Roman ambassadors ordered him to respect their ally. Receiving no satisfaction from the general, they proceeded to Carthage where they fared no better. The juridical aspect of their demand will be discussed later, when it will be seen that technically Rome was at fault and that Hannibal was under no obligation to respect their request. Further, he had been provoked by Rome. A quarrel of the Saguntines with the Torboletae, a neighbouring tribe, subject to Carthage, had led to political disturbances in Saguntum, and one party appealed to Rome to arbitrate (*c.* 221). The Romans, not unnaturally, decided in favour of the appellant party, which was put into power with some loss of life among the Punic faction. Disregarding Rome's representations, Hannibal advanced against Saguntum and championed the cause of his subjects, the

Torboletae (spring 219). Relying on help from Rome the Saguntines refused to surrender; but Rome was busy in Illyria, and Saguntum was left to face Hannibal's assault unaided. For eight months the blockade continued without thought of surrender, though Hannibal was ready to offer comparatively lenient terms. Finally, after a desperate and heroic resistance, the town fell by assault from the least inaccessible side, the west.[14]

Hannibal had thrown down the gauntlet. The fall of Saguntum fanned the sparks of rivalry into a blaze and made war inevitable. During the siege the Senate was probably unable to decide what ought to be done, especially as both consuls were absent on the Illyrian campaign – a preoccupation which the wily Hannibal did not overlook. It was only the fall of Saguntum that made action imperative. Had it held out through the winter, as the Romans hoped, the Hannibalic War might have been fought out in Spain (Pol., iii, 15). As it was, they temporized till late in March 218 or even longer, when an ultimatum was sent to Carthage demanding the surrender of Hannibal and his staff; this was virtually a declaration of war.[15] After some discussion the leading Roman envoy, the old *princeps senatus*, M. Fabius Buteo, held up two folds of his toga and cried: 'Here I bring peace and war; choose you which you will.' The Carthaginians bade him give them which he pleased; and Fabius dropping the fold of his toga replied: 'Then I give you war.' And the deadly gift was accepted.

6. THE CAUSES OF THE SECOND PUNIC WAR

The immediate cause of the Second Punic War was the Saguntine affair, which Polybius prefers to regard as the first incident in, rather than a cause of, the war. The question at issue was whether by attacking Saguntum Hannibal violated any treaty with Rome.[16] Patriotic Roman annalists (e.g. Livy, xxi, 2, 7; Appian, *Iber.*, 7) hastened to invent fictions to show that he had: for instance, they said that he broke the Ebro treaty by crossing the river to attack Saguntum, whereas the town lies a hundred miles south of the Ebro; or they suggest that a special clause was inserted in the Ebro treaty to the effect that Rome and Carthage should respect the neutrality of Saguntum. But it is not by such means that the blame can be assigned to Carthage.

There were two treaties which Hannibal's action might have infringed: that of Lutatius in 241 and the Ebro convention of 226. Rome's alliance with Saguntum was later than the treaty of Lutatius, so that the town was not included in the list of Rome's allies whom the Carthaginians had promised to respect. The latter, therefore, were quite correct in insisting that Hannibal had not violated this treaty. But what of the Ebro agreement? Unfortunately, it cannot be related chronologically to Rome's alliance with Saguntum with any degree of certainty; nor are its terms altogether clear. Even its validity has been questioned. It was a convention between Hasdrubal and delegates of the Roman Senate. It was probably ratified in Rome, and the Romans regarded it as legally binding on both parties, since the Carthaginians did not disavow their general who made it or his successor who, according to the Roman claim, transgressed it. The Carthaginians, however, denied that it had been ratified by their government. By its terms Hasdrubal renounced all hostile action north of the Ebro; his *quid pro quo* is not stated. Some suggest that he received little, others much. For instance, some allege that the treaty was unilateral and that as a member of a conquered nation Hasdrubal had to acquiesce in Rome's wish; or on the other hand, others hold that the Ebro treaty defined the spheres of influence of the two nations and that it imposed on the Romans, either explicitly or implicitly, the obligation not to interfere south of the river. Probably, however, the concession made by Rome in face of the Gallic peril was to leave Hasdrubal free to extend his Spanish empire up to the river. How this affected Rome's Saguntine alliance depends on the date assigned to the latter, which Polybius places 'several years before the time of Hannibal'. If, as seems more probable, the alliance was prior to the treaty, it was then virtually annulled by the spirit of the new covenant, and could not in fairness be used by the Romans as a handle to check Punic expansion in the south. If Rome accepted the alliance after 226, she was deliberately interfering in an area where she had in effect recognized Carthaginian control. Whichever date, then, is correct, Rome had no legal ground to restrain Hannibal from attacking Saguntum; indeed she made no military attempt to do this. However unwise the Carthaginian general may have been, he was within his legal rights and was no treaty-breaker.[17]

But if Hannibal's conscience was clear on the legal score, if he was merely returning the compliment for Rome's interference with the Torboletae, he could not turn a blind eye to the political aspect. He was attacking a town which was under the declared protection of Rome, and he had been warned that its capture would be regarded as a *casus belli*. Yet he persisted – and from no military necessity. The frontier quarrel between the Saguntines and Torboletae need not involve hostilities, unless Hannibal wished. True, the acquisition of Saguntum would remove an awkward thorn from his side in the event of war with Rome; but its military value was not sufficient to warrant the risk of war. Nor had the Romans thrown a protective garrison into the town, as they had into Messana in 264; such an act would have violated treaty rights, which they were unwilling to disregard till the fall of the town made action imperative. Hannibal therefore persisted for other reasons; because he judged war with Rome was inevitable and because by manoeuvring the Romans into a false position he had forced on them the onus of declaring war, so that he could expect the continued support of his home government. (The view of Fabius Pictor, refuted by Polybius (iii, 8) that Hannibal did not have the backing of the Carthaginian government either at this time or during the war, should be rejected.) His capture of Saguntum may not have been the cause of war, but it undoubtedly caused the outbreak of war at that moment.

The immediate cause of war was thus the action of Hannibal and his government, but what were the underlying causes? Polybius finds three. First, the hatred of Hamilcar towards Rome; after his forced surrender in Sicily he lived for revenge and his spirit survived him. Secondly, the bitterness felt at Carthage when Rome seized Sardinia and renewed the threat of war. Thirdly, resulting from this, Hamilcar's activity and the Carthaginian success in Spain.[18] Did the Second Punic War then owe its origin to the hatred of the house of Barca; was it a war of revenge? The answer must depend on the interpretation given to the motives of the Barcids in Spain. Were they building up resources and an army with which to hurl themselves against Rome or were they merely trying to compensate their country for its loss of Sicily and Sardinia; was the object of their empire-building offensive or defensive?

Hamilcar had gone to Spain immediately after his country had been humiliated by Rome in 237; he cannot have forgotten his enforced capitulation in Sicily; and he made his son swear never to be friends with Rome. These facts establish beyond doubt his hatred of Rome, but they do not prove that he contemplated revenge or that he went to Spain to plan it. Rather, he went with the intention of re-establishing his country's lost empire. He must have foreseen the possibility of renewed rivalry and he wanted to equip Carthage for the future, whatever that might hold. The fact that he did not rebuild a large Punic navy need not signify his pacific intentions (and anyway it would have been an unnecessary annoyance to Rome); it probably meant that in the event of war he planned to fight by land as Hannibal did when the day came. He wished to be prepared rather than to reopen the question. His successor Hasdrubal pursued still more clearly a defensive policy. When Rome was seriously engaged with the Gauls, so far from joining the attack on their side, he deliberately concluded a treaty with Rome which confined his activity to Spain. Hannibal, however, had to face somewhat different circumstances, for the Romans began to interfere in Saguntum. It is not likely that they acted with the desire of bringing a hornets' nest about their ears. But when they were freed from the Gallic peril, they began to look askance at the growing Punic power in Spain which they themselves had sanctioned; doubtless Massilia brought the situation to their notice. Their action at Saguntum was little more than a gentle hint to Hannibal to walk warily, but it was enough to fan his smouldering wrath to a blaze. He determined to make it a test case to see whether Rome would abide by her treaty; but he must have foreseen the result. The Barcids had remained true to a defensive policy till they feared, whether with good cause or not, a repetition of the Sardinian question. And this time the Carthaginians refused to bow their necks.

Hannibal had cleverly precipitated a crisis in which the Romans were technically at fault, but from which they could not retreat without loss of prestige. He was thus immediately responsible for a war which neither Rome nor Carthage had deliberately engineered. Yet it was improbable that the two Republics could have lived at peace indefinitely. A balance of powers, such as existed in the Hellenistic east, might have been maintained for a time, yet causes of friction would inevitably occur now that Rome had been forced to become a world power. But throughout the years between the first two Punic wars Rome had not followed a deliberately aggressive policy. It has been suggested that there was strong disagreement in the state between an agrarian party under Flaminius, which limited its outlook to Italy, and a capitalistic party which favoured a *Weltpolitik*. While admitting a real clash of interests, it is unlikely that the latter party formed any deliberate imperialistic policy. The Senate rather met practical difficulties with practical solutions than followed a consistent and carefully conceived scheme.[19] The seizure of Sardinia, which was the aggressive act of a nervous bully, represented a passing mood. The Gallic wars were defensive in spirit, though they caused Rome to safeguard her northern frontier. Her early action in Spain was due more to the apprehension of her ally, Massilia, than to a studied western policy. The intervention in Illyria was a necessary piece of police work. True, all these acts involved future responsibility. Once she had set her hand to the plough there could be no turning back. But Rome could hardly be expected to anticipate the ultimate result of each action. She dealt with each situation as it arose and if Hannibal chose to challenge her interference in Spain, she was willing to face the consequences and to determine the lordship of the western Mediterranean.

IX

HANNIBAL'S
OFFENSIVE
AND ROME'S
DEFENSIVE

1. HANNIBAL'S INVASION OF NORTHERN ITALY

When war was declared between Rome and Carthage, Rome's superiority at sea led her to suppose that she could choose the theatre for the new conflict. And she chose Spain and Africa. One consul, P. Cornelius Scipio, with some 24,000 men and 60 ships, was to conduct the war in Spain, while Ti. Sempronius Longus with about 26,000 troops and 160 vessels was sent to Sicily preparatory to crossing to Africa. The size of the African expeditionary force shows that Rome had no intention of striking immediately at Carthage itself. A demonstration could be made, the native tribes won over, the large estates of the nobles ravaged, and reinforcements for Hannibal intercepted; further support could be sent if events in Europe justified it. Meantime Hannibal must be watched. Naval inferiority would force him to seek the enemy by land either on the defensive in Spain or by an offensive in northern Italy. And because of the fiery spirit of the Barcid house and Hannibal's intrigues with the Gauls, the Romans might expect him to take the offensive, cross the Ebro, and advance gradually, consolidating his communications *en route*. So they decided to send an army to check him either in northern Spain or more probably in southern Gaul, since an immediate Roman offensive in Spain with no base and in face of the enemy's superior numbers would be hazardous. Resistance would be easier near the friendly Massilia and in reach of their base at Pisa, while Hannibal's strength would be less when he arrived there; after repulsing him at the Rhône, the Romans could launch an offensive in northern Spain. But whether they hoped to meet him in Spain or Gaul, they underestimated one factor – his genius.

Hannibal was not content to meet the enemy in Spain and Africa. He realized that a Roman victory in Africa would mean the loss of the war and that therefore he must strike first, while Carthaginian victories in Africa would not break the power of Rome, which could only be smashed beyond recovery by destroying her Italian confederacy. He determined therefore to cut off her source of strength by fighting in Italy and disintegrating the League. His chances of reaching Italy must have seemed meagre, as Rome guarded the seas and the land route was long and difficult, but he trusted in his ability to overcome the obstacles. Where he miscalculated was by assuming that Rome's allies were unwilling slaves of a tyrannical mistress. He hoped that they would rise to acclaim him as liberator, while Pyrrhus' career had shown that an army in Italy could seriously embarrass Rome. Further, he could count on the Gauls in northern Italy rallying to his banner; these traditional enemies of Rome, though recently defeated, were not completely crushed. So he formed the bold scheme of sacrificing his communications with Spain and Carthage and swooping suddenly on to northern Italy, which would form a base in place of Spain. He started with a veteran army of perhaps 35,000 or 40,000 men; for the defence of Africa there were some 20,000 men, while he left 15,000 in southern Spain and another 11,000 north of the Ebro.[1] The total forces which Carthage put into the field were about 80,000 soldiers, 100 ships and 25,000 marines; Rome mustered 70,000 men, 220 ships and 50,000–60,000 sailors. The seriousness of the struggle is shown by the numbers raised by the two Republics, although each of them could have doubled these if necessary. But Rome had two decisive factors in her favour: superiority at sea and the superior quality of the reserve troops which she could produce in her hour of need. The best troops of Carthage were already in the field.

At the end of April 218, Hannibal started on his crusade from New Carthage; he crossed the Ebro in early June when the spring flooding of the river had subsided, but he did not reach the Rhône till mid-August. This delay was hardly caused by a serious attempt to subdue the intervening tribes, because he had determined to sacrifice his communications. Possibly he encountered stronger opposition than he had anticipated, or perhaps he marched slowly to deceive the Romans, thinking that if he passed the Pyrenees by the end of July he could then dash forward and get through the Alpine passes before they closed in the autumn. In this way he would lull the enemy's suspicions and avoid the risk that the four consular legions might concentrate in northern Italy. At the Rhône he would have found P. Scipio waiting to contest his passage, had not the Roman plans miscarried. The Boii and Insubres around the new Latin colonies of Placentia and Cremona (p. 191) rebelled, doubtless at Hannibal's instigation, and the two legions which Scipio had prepared for Spain had to be directed to suppress the insurrection. However, Scipio raised two new legions and reached the mouth of the Rhône by the middle of August. Little realizing Hannibal's real intentions he sent out a cavalry detachment to reconnoitre. Meantime Hannibal, who had found his crossing of the Rhône challenged by hostile tribes on the further bank, sent a force under Hanno across the river higher up, and when they were ready to fall on the rear of the Gauls, he crossed over and won a victory. Scipio's reconnoitring force, after severely handling a Numidian scouting squadron, returned to headquarters to inform him that Hannibal had crossed the Rhône. Three days later Scipio arrived on the spot and found Hannibal's camp deserted and that he had crossed the river, elephants and all,[2] and was marching to the Alps. He then took a momentous decision. Instead of attempting a wild goose chase after Hannibal, he sent his army under his brother Gnaeus to Spain, where the enemy might be held at bay now that Hannibal's best troops had gone. Scipio himself returned by sea to northern Italy to assume command of the two legions there, and to await Hannibal's arrival. Though he has been criticized for neglecting the Italian front by sending his army to Spain, a truer appreciation shows that his cautious far-sighted conduct and his energetic initiative laid the strategic foundations by which victory was ultimately won.

Hannibal marched up the Rhône to the 'Island', where it is joined by the Isère (Isara), and then along this valley to Grenoble. Where he actually crossed the Alps always has been and presumably always will be a matter of uncertainty. The problem is literary even more than topographical. Polybius gives a graphic description, based partly on personal discussions with survivors and supported by a journey to the Alps to verify the geography. But even so his narrative does not fix the pass with certainty, while Livy's account, which derives in part from Polybius, introduces further difficulties. The majority of scholars look for the pass between the Little St Bernard and Mt Genèvre. But wherever the exact pass was, Hannibal's exploit has stirred the imagination of mankind.[3] The actual difficulty of crossing into Italy was not severe, for whole Celtic tribes often moved in this way. The real difficulties arose from the extreme hostility of the Alpine tribes and the fact that the descent was steeper than Hannibal had anticipated and was rendered more perilous by the snow and frost of the advancing autumn. If he had arrived somewhat earlier, many of the dangers would have been avoided. But in the circumstances it was a magnificent triumph of will and discipline over hardship and loss. And so he reached the plains of northern Italy, but with only 26,000 men. The Alps and their inhabitants had taken their toll.

When Hannibal had stormed the chief town of the Taurini (Turin) he was astounded to find that the legions in northern Italy were commanded by Scipio who had travelled nearly 1,000 miles in a month. Scipio crossed the Po near Placentia (Piacenza), hoping to meet Hannibal before his army had fully recovered from the rigours of its journey. He marched along the north bank of the river and encamped on the west of its tributary, the Ticinus. His cavalry engaged Hannibal's advance guard near Lomello, but was beaten back; he himself was wounded and his life was saved by his son, the future conqueror of Hannibal. A somewhat complicated series of manoeuvres followed, leading up to the battle of the Trebia.[4] Wishing to evacuate the open country, Scipio withdrew to Placentia, crossed to the south of the Po, advanced again westwards and encamped at Stradella, where he was less exposed to Hannibal's cavalry. Meantime Hannibal had advanced to the Ticinus, but found that Scipio had destroyed its bridge. Accordingly he retired westwards along the Po till he was able to cross above Tortona and then advanced towards Scipio and offered battle. But Scipio was forced by the desertion of his Gallic allies to retire to the Trebia just south of Placentia, where he awaited his colleague. Hannibal obtained by treachery the Roman post at Clastidium and then encamped opposite Scipio.

When news had reached Rome that Hannibal was marching against Italy, the African expedition was cancelled and Sempronius, who had captured Malta, was summoned to northern Italy. Leaving a squadron to protect Sicily, he hastened with his army to Ariminum and then joined Scipio at the Trebia in late November. Contrary to Scipio's advice Sempronius determined to fight, being buoyed up by a successful cavalry skirmish. On a bitter December day the Roman army was led breakfastless through the Trebia against the enemy. Hannibal's plan was for his centre to remain on the defensive and his wings to outflank and defeat the enemy, while his brother Mago, who lay in ambush in a scrub-covered gulley, charged out on their rear. All went according to plan, except that 10,000 Romans broke through Hannibal's centre of Celts and reached Placentia. But two-thirds of the Roman army was destroyed and Hannibal had won the first real battle of the war. Yet the Senate did not despair. The defeat was due to Hannibal's superior cavalry; the Roman legionaries of the centre had proved their mettle and were safe in Placentia. Winter would interrupt further operations, and next year their legionaries might yet assert the superiority in which they trusted.

2. HANNIBAL IN CENTRAL ITALY

'The Roman people', wrote Polybius, 'are most formidable, collectively and individually, when they have real reason for alarm.' The years which followed the battle of Trebia confirmed this. They put into the field for 217 eleven legions, some 100,000 men; five served as reserves in Rome, Sicily and Sardinia, two were assigned to Spain and four to North Italy. Scipio, who could not be blamed for Trebia, was continued in his command and sent to Spain; the new consuls, Cn. Servilius Geminus and the popular leader C. Flaminius, served in Italy. The election of Flaminius was a criticism by the people of the Senate's conduct of the war.

The Romans determined to abandon the plains of northern Italy, where Hannibal's cavalry and Gallic allies were most useful to him, and to defend central Italy; the fortresses in the Po valley could look after themselves. But they could not foresee where Hannibal would cross the Apennines. From Bononia (Bologna) to which he had advanced he could move either south-west, crossing by one of the numerous passes which led into Etruria, or south-east, marching to Ariminum (Rimini) and then along the via Flaminia. So the Senate wisely sent Flaminius to Arretium (Arezzo) to guard the western route while Servilius protected Ariminum, which was a strong strategic position where the Apennines reach the Adriatic and the northern plains terminate. From these two points the consuls could concentrate on any place at need and might even catch Hannibal between them. Though this division has been criticized, it was perhaps the wisest arrangement possible. The Romans might hope to hold fast to central Italy, where they had loyal allies, abundant supplies and knowledge of the country; and Hannibal would lack all these.

In May, when the passes were free from snow, Hannibal again abandoned his base and crossed the Apennines by the pass of Collina.[5] This route descends at Pistoia. Between here and Faesulae (Fiesole) Hannibal encountered great difficulties in the marshes which were swollen by the flooding of the Arno and the melting snows. Riding on the sole surviving elephant and suffering intensely from ophthalmia from which he lost the sight of one eye, he got his army through in four days, though with loss. After resting he recommenced his march southwards, ravaging the land as he went. Contrary to the advice of some of his staff,

Flaminius determined to follow; if he had waited for and joined Servilius, the combined Roman armies might have caught Hannibal between themselves and the troops in Rome. But Hannibal, reckoning on Flaminius' rashness, deliberately drew him on by exposing his flank as he marched to Cortona. The Roman, however, was not quite the headstrong fool that tradition has painted him; he declined battle and hung on Hannibal's tracks.[6] But to follow closely with his smaller force was dangerous, especially as Hannibal's superior cavalry could prevent adequate reconnoitring – a fact which in some way modifies the blame attaching to Flaminius for the disaster that befell. For Hannibal set yet another trap by suddenly swinging off the road to Rome eastwards towards Perugia along the north shore of Lake Trasimene. Here was a narrow defile with the hills coming right down to the lake except round a small plain over three miles long. On the hills above this plain Hannibal placed his troops in ambush.[7] Flaminius followed blindly. Early on a misty morning his army marched in column into the defile. Signalling from the hilltops above the mist Hannibal's troops rushed down simultaneously from all sides. For two hours the fight raged. Flaminius paid for his rashness by meeting a hero's death. Some 6,000 men in the front cut their way through the enemy but were later rounded up. The disaster was complete; nearly two legions were wiped out, although Hannibal granted the surviving Roman allies their freedom. There was no disguising the gravity of the occasion and in Rome a praetor announced laconically: 'We have been beaten in a great battle.'

Hannibal followed up the victory by sending his cavalry leader, Maharbal, against an advance guard of 4,000 of Servilius' horsemen who were riding hot-spur down the Via Flaminia. They were surprised and destroyed near Assisi.[8] But this crowning success must have been qualified for Hannibal by the obstinate fact that no towns of Umbria or Etruria opened their gates to him. A saviour from Rome's tyranny was at hand but they would have none of him. Knowing that an attempt on Rome itself would be vain, although the way thither lay open, he turned instead over the Apennines to Picenum, where he could rest men and horses. Then with fire and sword he blazed his way to Apulia and ravaged the territory of Luceria and Arpi. But once again the towns barred their gates.

The disaster of Trasimene caused such a crisis in Rome that the traditional remedy of appointing a dictator, unused for thirty years, was revived. As one consul was dead and the other cut off from Rome, the task was assigned to the Comitia Centuriata, which elected a man of wide experience and well-known caution, Q. Fabius Maximus. The Comitia, not the dictator, then appointed the Master of the Horse, M. Minucius Rufus. The essence of the dictatorship was absolute power, but now the power of the Master of the Horse, though subordinate, derived from the people and not from the dictator himself. Whatever the explanation of this hampering of the dictator's power may have been – distrust of reviving the office, popular demands, or the rivalry of the noble families – it did not work well. Fabius first restored the morale of the people by some religious celebrations, and then stated his policy: to dog Hannibal's heels and avoid pitched battles at all cost. He took over Servilius' army and marching to Apulia camped at Aecae near the enemy at Vibinum. Hannibal, unable to bring about a decisive outcome, struck through Samnium past Beneventum into Campania, one of the most fertile regions of Italy. Fabius followed and looked on while Rome's allies were unsupported and their land laid waste. Such a strategy of exhaustion was only justified as a temporary expedient; the Romans could still trust in the invincibility of their legions, so a breathing space was only permissible until Hannibal could be manoeuvred on to favourable ground. The situation was changed by the disaster at Cannae the following year, but now Fabius had to offer very solid recompense for the severe economic and moral loss which his strategy inflicted on the Roman cause. At length came the chance to prove the wisdom of his policy. Hannibal wished to withdraw to Apulia for the winter, but Fabius himself held Callicula, the pass by which Hannibal hoped to leave Campania.[9] Here was the opportunity to force him to battle on ground which would hinder his cavalry and where the Roman legions fighting in close order might anticipate success. But the over-cautious Fabius was outwitted as easily as the impetuous Flaminius. By a famous ruse, Hannibal at night drove 2,000 oxen with burning faggots tied to their horns towards Fabius' camp on the high ground; the pickets left the pass to investigate and under cover of the resultant surprise and confusion Hannibal slipped through. He marched back to Apulia, crossing the Apennines for the fourth time that year, and captured Gerunium near Luceria. Yet though his army was laden with booty, no city in Campania had revolted to him.

All this time opposition to Fabius' policy had been growing, though with courageous tenacity of purpose he had turned a deaf ear. No sooner was he summoned to Rome to confer with the Senate than Minucius, who had followed Hannibal to Gerunium, disobeyed Fabius' orders and attacked with considerable success, forcing Hannibal to change his camp. In Rome Fabius vainly tried to check popular discontent by getting Atilius Regulus elected consul in Flaminius's place, but the people demanded that Minucius should be made co-dictator with Fabius, an extraordinary undermining of the very nature of the dictatorship, which thus soon fell into disuse. When, after this political upheaval, Fabius returned to Minucius, the army was divided into two camps. Hannibal, counting on the discord of the Roman generals and on Minucius' desire for battle, soon drew him into an engagement which would, it is said, have proved disastrous but for the timely help of Fabius. Again the aristocratic tradition has perhaps exaggerated the danger of Minucius, the popular favourite, and the importance of Fabius' help; in any case Fabius allowed the Carthaginians to retire unopposed.[10] But Fabius' period of office soon expired, and the consuls, Servilius and Regulus, took over the command at Gerunium.

The consuls elected for 216 were the aristocrat L. Aemilius Paullus and the popular leader C. Terentius Varro who was a *novus homo*; the aristocratic tradition deals with him no more kindly than with his predecessors Flaminius and Minucius. He is represented as a radical demagogue opposed to the Senate, but his career shows that he enjoyed its confidence. Tradition made him the scapegoat of the disaster of Cannae, but he was scarcely more culpable than his colleague. He was decried as a butcher's son, as Cromwell was called a brewer, but he did not lack sterling qualities.

Suddenly came news that Hannibal had captured the Roman post at Cannae on the right bank of the Aufidus. Though he had carefully chosen a position in the plains by the Adriatic where his cavalry would have full scope, the Romans decided to give battle. The new consuls advanced to Cannae with their four legions slightly reinforced. Hidebound by tradition and hampered by practical difficulties, they probably did not unduly increase their usual force, as they still trusted in the quality of their troops. They outnumbered Hannibal's infantry, though they had few cavalry. Reaching the Aufidus they camped probably on the left bank not far from Cannae. Hannibal was encamped on the other bank some three miles higher up near Cannae. The Romans then formed a smaller camp on the right bank, as a protecting outpost. At this Hannibal transferred his camp to the north bank.[11] It was probably early in August that both armies crossed the river to battle. The Romans disposed their cavalry on the wings and massed their infantry in deep and close formation in the centre where they hoped to break the foe; they relied on their weight and push. To meet this Hannibal trusted the elasticity of his formation. He drew up his line in crescent shape. The Gauls and Spaniards held the centre; on their flanks *en échelon* behind them stood the African troops; the cavalry held the wings. As he expected, his cavalry was successful; the left wing of Spanish and Gallic horse defeated the Roman right, and began to surround the rear of the infantry, while a detachment was sent to help complete the defeat of the Roman left wing. Meanwhile the Roman infantry gradually forced back Hannibal's centre; if it broke before the cavalry could assail the Roman rear, Hannibal had lost the battle and probably the war. But the retreating Gauls held firm and the Roman centre was gradually drawn into a trap: Hannibal's crescent was now becoming a hollow, while the Africans began to encircle the Romans flanks. This encirclement was completed when the Carthaginian cavalry assailed the rear. The Romans, massed together and unable to move, were completely surrounded and cut to pieces. Aemilius, Minucius, Servilius and some 25,000 men fell; 10,000 were captured, while perhaps 15,000 escaped, including Varro. The enemy lost only 5,700. So ended the greatest battle the Romans had yet fought. Rome's prestige in Italy was shaken. Many towns in Samnium and Apulia and nearly all Lucania and Bruttium revolted to Hannibal; and, worse still, in the autumn Capua, the second city in Italy, and other Campanian towns followed suit. But the whole of Latium, Umbria and Etruria remained loyal. And Rome herself was safe; Hannibal dared not march against her walls

Cannae showed with tragic clearness that Rome must now abandon any attempt to seek out the main armed forces of the enemy and that Fabius' strategy of exhaustion must be rigorously followed. As Rome refused to accept defeat, Hannibal could only persevere in trying to break up her Italian Confederacy. But instead of asking his home government for further reinforcements for this task, he advised or acquiesced in a new Carthaginian strategy. This aimed at embarrassing Rome still further by extending the theatres of war and by raising up a circle of enemies around her. In the west the war was to be prosecuted vigorously in Spain and a landing effected in Sardinia; in the north were the hostile Gauls; in the east an alliance was sought with Philip of Macedon who would attempt to drive the Romans from Illyria; in the south the Greek cities of Sicily would be encouraged to revolt to Carthage, more readily when she was allied with Philip. Thus from all sides Carthage sought to encompass Rome, and before the fortunes of Hannibal in Italy are followed further, the new theatres of war in Spain, Sardinia, Macedon, and Sicily must be viewed.

3. THE SCIPIOS AND SPAIN

In Spain, where the war had started, the tide of war first rolled back on the Carthaginians. This country, where large armies starve and small armies get beaten, has always imposed similar difficulties and restrictions on invading armies. Only a small part was directly involved in the Hannibalic war, namely, the Mediterranean littoral with its hinterland; more particularly, the Ebro valley in the north and the rich valley of the Baetis (Guadalquivir) in the south, where lay the seat of Carthaginian power. These two valleys were linked by a coast road which passed through the two key towns of Saguntum and New Carthage (Cartagena), the latter being the Carthaginian war base. To an army invading Spain from the north-east three factors are necessary: control of the coast road, an adequate base and command of the sea. Thus Pompey's first plan of attack against Sertorius failed because he lacked the last two, while centuries later in different circumstances Wellington, entrenched at Torres Vedras with the command of the sea, threw into relief the vain attempt of Sir John Moore to advance inland without an adequate base. The three Scipios who fought in Spain realized the conditions of warfare which the country imposed, and thus succeeded where Napoleon failed; ultimately, to adapt Napoleon's vain hope, they were able 'to carry their victorious eagles to the Pillars of Hercules and drive the "Punic" leopard into the sea'.

The supreme importance of holding the enemy at bay in Spain was realized by P. Scipio, who despatched thither his brother Gnaeus in 218 and joined him the following year. Reinforcements from a country so rich in natural wealth and manpower must at all costs be prevented from reaching Hannibal. But events were to show that the Scipios, the two Thunderbolts of War (*duo fulmina belli*), aimed not merely at a defensive campaign of holding the line of the Ebro but at an offensive to break the enemy's power in the Peninsula.

In the late summer of 218 Cn. Scipio landed with two legions at Emporiae (Ampurias), from which base he marched south. His passage was uncontested till he reached Cissa, the enemy's base in northern Spain, where he defeated the commander Hanno. Cissa was taken, and Scipio advanced his fleet to Tarraco (Tarragona). Here the Roman naval camp was attacked by Hasdrubal, the Carthaginian commander of southern Spain, who arrived on the scene too late to help Hanno. Hasdrubal was repulsed and withdrew to his base at New Carthage. Thus in his first campaign Scipio prevented reinforcements reaching Hannibal, won a base and commenced the conquest of the district north of the Ebro. The next year, 217, was critical in Spain. Would Hasdrubal break through before the arrival of Roman reinforcements? With all his land forces and fleet he approached the mouth of the Ebro. Notwithstanding the smallness of his fleet Scipio decided to give battle, not only to avoid having his flank turned, but also because command of the sea was essential for further advance southwards, not to mention for precluding the shipping of help to Hannibal. Further, Scipio was reinforced by the Massilians, whose naval prowess was well known and who were eager to safeguard their trade with Spain by checking the power of Carthage at sea. So the Romans sailed forth and engaged and defeated the enemy's fleet off the mouth of the Ebro. This victory, besides enabling them to cross the Ebro in safety, affected the whole war and Hannibal's hopes of success. After a feeble demonstration off Italy in the same year, the Carthaginians abandoned any large-scale naval operations, so that Hannibal was left in Italy with Rome as mistress of the seas.[12]

When the proconsul Publius Scipio had joined his brother in Spain with reinforcements of 20 warships and 8,000 men, they advanced in the autumn across the Ebro and encamped near Saguntum. After this demonstration to impress the Spanish tribes they withdrew to winter-quarters north of the Ebro, having won and garrisoned Intibili and Iliturgi.[13] During the next year the war was at a standstill; the Romans consolidated in the north, while Hasdrubal suppressed a serious rising of the Turdetani in the south. But in 215 Hasdrubal, who had received reinforcements, advanced to try his chances. He met the Roman army near Ibera on the Ebro. The situation was critical. A Roman defeat would involve the loss of Spain and allow Hasdrubal to join Hannibal in Italy. Hasdrubal used the same tactics as his brother had at Cannae, but his weak centre of Spanish troops crumpled before his wings could outflank and surround the enemy. The Roman victory was crushing, since Hasdrubal's best African troops suffered most. The Scipios had won the first victory of the war in pitched battle; an achievement which might well hearten the home government in the gloom caused by Cannae. It strengthened Rome's prestige in Italy and still more in Spain, where other native tribes revolted from the Carthaginians.

To counteract this defeat the Carthaginians diverted to Spain an army under Hannibal's brother Mago, which had been destined for Italy. Native risings in North Africa under Syphax, however, involved the temporary recall of Hasdrubal, but by 212 the Carthaginians were able to maintain three armies in Spain under Mago, Hasdrubal Barca and Hasdrubal son of Gisgo. Meanwhile the Scipios had rested on their oars (215–213), because their strength was temporarily exhausted and further advance involved securing a new base and the coast road, while the further south they marched the deeper they penetrated into pro-

Carthaginian territory, where to win native support by force would alienate their allies, while to neglect it would endanger their communications. But by 212 their gradual advance was crowned with success, for they won the urgently needed base by capturing Saguntum.[14] They could now plan an offensive further south, although the superior forces of the enemy rendered it risky and further penetration would increase the distance from the centre of supplies. But to revert to a defensive policy would involve the sacrifice of their previous conquests and of their new Spanish allies. Trusting these, in 211 they advanced in two divisions against the enemy. This division was probably a mistake, as the united force might have crushed Hasdrubal Barca. They divided to put less strain on the natives of the districts from which they derived supplies. But Gnaeus was the first to learn the fickleness of their Spanish allies, who deserted when he advanced with one-third of the army against Hasdrubal. Forced to retire, he was harassed by the Carthaginian cavalry until the infantry came up and destroyed his forces at Ilorci (modern Lorqui), in a desolate plain surrounded by bleak and arid mountains in the hinterland of New Carthage. Meantime his brother Publius, penetrating probably to the upper courses of the Baetis, was cut off and his army was destroyed in an attempt to break away. Only a remnant under Fonteius at length reached the Ebro, where the soldiers elected as commander a Roman Knight, L. Marcius Septimus.

So fell the Scipios. But they had accomplished much. They had prevented reinforcements reaching Hannibal from Spain; they had inflicted two severe defeats on the enemy, by sea off the Ebro, by land at Ibera; then taking the offensive they had captured Saguntum, and advancing further south had won from Carthage a considerable part of her Spanish empire. But their last gallant attempt overstrained their inadequate resources. The Carthaginians, however, lamentably failed to drive home their victory, for each of the three generals wished to exploit the success for himself and would not co-operate with his colleagues. This saved Rome. Carthage lost a unique chance of sending help to Hannibal. The way was soon to be barred by the arrival of Nero and then barred still more firmly by the future conqueror of Spain.

4. THE EXTENSION OF THE WAR TO MACEDON

The Carthaginians also sought to embarrass Rome in Sardinia and Macedon. In 215 a force was despatched under Hasdrubal the Bald to Sardinia, where the natives were already restive under Roman rule, especially as the governor was ill. Rome energetically sent out a legion under T. Manlius Torquatus, who knew the island well. Landing at Cagliari he defeated the rebels before the arrival of Hasdrubal, who had been delayed by a storm. He then forced Hasdrubal's army to fight and won a decisive victory. Thus the Carthaginian attempt miscarried, and they made no further efforts to regain the island.

The extension of the war to Greece, known as the First Macedonian War, was little more than a side-show. Its ramifications belong rather to the history of the Greek world and its importance derives largely from the fact that it drew Rome closer to that world. For if Hannibal hoped that it would seriously distract Rome's attention, he miscalculated. Philip of Macedon, long suspicious of Rome's intervention in Illyria, was watching Hannibal's progress in Italy with keen self-interest. When he received news of Trasimene, he hastily terminated the war he was waging in Greece so as to have his hands free ; at Naupactus he concluded a peace with the Aetolians, many of whom viewed with apprehension 'the cloud rising in the west'. Driven on by dreams of conquest and by the advice of the pirate chief Demetrius, he built a fleet of light cutters which he launched in the Adriatic in 216 in order to obtain a naval base there and to reinstate Demetrius at Pharos. The approach of a Roman fleet caused his hasty withdrawal ; but he had shown his hand. When it was clear that Cannae would not end the war Philip took the decisive step of forming an alliance with Hannibal ; it was to be offensive during the war and defensive afterwards, when Hannibal would deal with Italy while Philip and Demetrius could assert their claims to Rome's Illyrian possessions and Corcyra.[15]

News of the alliance reached Rome through the capture of Philip's envoys and despatches. To meet the new danger on her flank, she ordered M. Valerius Laevinus, a praetor in command at Tarentum, to watch Philip and if necessary to cross to Illyria with 50 warships. In 214 Philip attacked the naval bases of Illyria, but Laevinus quickly recaptured Oricus, relieved Apollonia, forced Philip to burn his boats and retire to Macedon, and established himself on the Illyrian coast. Philip could only hope to dislodge him with the help of the Carthaginian fleet, for which he waited in vain, though he regained access to the Adriatic by capturing Lissus (213?). Laevinus, who feared the possible advent of a Carthaginian fleet, turned to a diplomatic offensive against Philip by stirring up war against him in Greece. In 211 he concluded an alliance with the Aetolians : they were to operate by land and keep any territory wrested from Philip ; Rome was to supply naval help and have the portable booty or part of it.[16] The alliance – the first concluded between Rome and a Greek people – was soon joined by many Greek states, Elis, Messenia and Sparta, by Attalus of Pergamum and by the chieftains of Thrace and Illyria. Not only was all possibility of Philip helping Hannibal in Italy averted, but by this skilful move the war in Greece was shifted largely on to the shoulders of the Greeks themselves.

In four campaigns Philip hurried with surprising energy from front to front (211–208). In 211 or 210 Laevinus was succeeded by P. Sulpicius Galba who celebrated his arrival in the Aegean by failing to relieve Echinus which Philip was besieging, although he captured Aegina. So the war dragged on, notwithstanding fruitless attempts by various parties to negotiate a peace. Throughout this war Philip in vain awaited naval help from Carthage and the growing realization at Rome that this support to their enemy was not forthcoming led to a gradual slackening of interest in this theatre of war. In 208 Attalus returned to Asia, and Rome did little in Greece; the Aetolians could be left to oppose Philip by themselves. This might suit Rome, but it did not suit the Aetolians, who ended the Hellenic War in 206 by making peace with Philip. This act, which Rome herself had made inevitable, at last stirred her to activity. In 205 P. Sempronius Tuditanus was sent out with a large force to succeed Sulpicius and to protect Illyria. But a successful demonstration there was not sufficient to rekindle the spirit of Aetolia against Philip. So Rome decided to abandon the war; she did not wish for a long single-handed struggle with Philip, especially at a time when, as will be seen, she was preparing to make her final effort against Carthage. Sempronius was ordered to decline battle and to come to terms. The Peace of Phoenice (205), which was concluded on the basis of *uti possidetis*, made only slight territorial adjustments. It was clearly an agreement for the mutual convenience of Rome and Philip. The Romans had been drawn into Greek affairs to meet a specific danger; with that removed they were ready to leave Greece to work out its own salvation. For Philip further resistance was futile, since no support came from Carthage. Further, the eastern world, of which Rome knew so little but was soon to learn so much, claimed his thoughts. Thus Carthage had signally failed to utilize her ally in Greece to the full in her struggle with Rome.

5. MARCELLUS AND SICILY

Events in Magna Graecia proved more formidable than those in Greece proper, for Sicily was suddenly swept into the war on the death of the aged Hiero (215). During his reign he had raised Syracuse to great prosperity and culture, and though the loyal ally of Rome, he had avoided the enmity of Carthage. Some of his subjects, however, including his own son, began to intrigue with Carthage and Rome's rebellious allies in Italy, while others desired to end the monarchy. But if they hoped for a glorious war of independence they forgot that the citizens of Syracuse lacked the resources and spirit which had made possible the resistance of their ancestors to the armada of Athens. Successful revolt from Rome could only lead to dependence on Carthage.

Since Hiero's son died shortly before his father, the kingdom fell to a grandson of the old king. This fifteen-year-old boy, Hieronymus, was soon entangled in the meshes of court intrigue. Two of Hiero's sons-in-law quickly usurped the regency of fifteen members which Hiero had appointed, and forced Hieronymus to approach Hannibal, whose agents, Hippocrates and Epicydes, arranged a treaty by which all Sicily was conceded to Hieronymus – notwithstanding the warning protests of the praetor Appius Claudius. A reaction of popular feeling against the monarchy quickly followed, and resulted in the murder of Hieronymus and nearly all the royal house (214); relations with Rome might yet be established. But suddenly the pendulum swung back again and the new republic chose as generals the two Carthaginian agents, Hippocrates and Epicydes. Meanwhile the Romans were alarmed, and sent the consul M. Claudius Marcellus to Sicily with an additional legion to join the two already there – the disgraced survivors of Cannae; the fleet was raised to a hundred sails. On Marcellus' arrival an attack on a Roman frontier post led to the outbreak of war. In reply Marcellus sacked Leontini with great severity. Hippocrates and Epicydes, who escaped to Syracuse, there massacred the Roman party and amid the utmost confusion prepared to defend the city against the might of Rome. It was a different beginning to the war from the one they had hoped for, when Syracuse, supported by the uprising of all the Siceliots, might have taken a glorious offensive; yet they could trust in the strength of their city, protected by the walls of Dionysius and the engineering skill of Archimedes.

Syracuse was situated partly on the 'island' of Ortygia, partly on the mainland. This latter settlement was divided into three separate regions: Neapolis (an extension of the old Temenitis) in the west, Achradina on the east coast, and Tyche to the north. The whole town nestled at the foot of the cliffs of the large plateau of Epipolae, around which ran the almost impregnable walls built by Dionysius, and guarded at their western extremity by the fort Euryalus. Nothing daunted, Marcellus approached with all speed and the Roman army camped in two divisions, one in the south at Olympeium, the other to the north of Epipolae near Hexapylon (Scala Graeca); thus they controlled the two main roads to the city. Then he launched an assault by land and sea from the north; Appius Claudius tried to storm the walls by Hexapylon, while Marcellus brought siege engines on his ships against the sea walls at Achradina. But the attack was beaten off, thanks largely to the efficiency of the artillery and contrivances devised by Archimedes; Marcellus had to desist and resign himself to a regular and lengthy blockade.[17]

Meanwhile Carthaginian reinforcements under Himilco had captured Agrigentum, where Marcellus arrived too late. But he won over some towns that had belonged to Hiero and cut to pieces a force which had slipped out of Syracuse to support Himilco. Reinforcements from Rome reached the army at Syracuse in safety, while the Carthaginian fleet, after an abortive demonstration by Bomilcar, did not try to relieve the city. But an ugly incident in central Sicily provoked considerable anti-Roman feeling: in attempting to hold Enna in face of treachery, the Roman garrison massacred the inhabitants. So ended the year 213; though Rome had lost much of the south coast and centre of Sicily, she had satisfactorily withstood the first shock of the revolt of the Greeks.

Throughout the winter the siege of Syracuse continued; no Greek or Punic army appeared to divert the besiegers. One night in the spring of 212, utilizing the preoccupation caused by the drunken revelry of a festival, Marcellus stormed part of the northern walls of Epipolae and advanced over the plateau. Tradition tells how when day broke he gazed over the beautiful city weeping with joy at his achievement and with sorrow at the impending doom. This was not long delayed. Descending the southern slopes of Epipolae, he camped between Tyche and Neapolis (near the necropolis of Groticelli) and overran the two suburbs. In his rear was the great fort of Euryalus, the impressive ruins of which still demonstrate its impregnable strength; but the commander surrendered in panic. Thus Marcellus had won all Epipolae. Counter-attacks by a sortie from Achradina, by Himilco, and by the fleet, all failed. Then, as so often in the history of Syracuse, Nature intervened. A pestilence swept through both armies; the Romans on the higher ground and with better sanitation escaped lightly, but Himilco's force perished. This decided the fate of Syracuse; the fall of the remaining portions, Achradina and Ortygia, was only a matter of time. In 211 Bomilcar arrived in Sicily with a Carthaginian fleet, only to panic and sail off again. Finally the city was betrayed by a Spanish mercenary captain; its rich artistic treasures were shipped to Italy, and Archimedes was killed during the looting of the city while absorbed in a geometrical problem. So after a siege of two and a half years fell a city which for three centuries had been chief among the Greek cities of the west.

The rest of the tale is soon told. Marcellus easily defeated a small Carthaginian force near Himera and then hastened home to enjoy an 'ovation'. A praetor continued to reduce the smaller towns, while late in 210 Valerius Laevinus took out fresh forces and conquered Agrigentum. Sicily was pacified. So by the persistent energy of Rome and the dash of Marcellus, through Carthage's lack of naval enterprise, fatal alike in Sicily and Greece, and above all because of the plague, a serious danger was averted. Sicily was the bridge between Italy and Africa, between Hannibal and his home government; the control of the bridge was of paramount importance.

6. FABIUS AND ROME'S DEFENSIVE

We must revert now to Rome's bitter hour after Cannae when the dark background served only to show up the splendour of her courage. She would not accept defeat though the flower of her manhood was slain, though southern Italy had revolted, though Hannibal was undisputed master in battle. The problem before the Senate was how to nullify Hannibal's tactical superiority, which lay in his cavalry, in the elasticity of his army as a whole and the co-operation of its parts, and in the skill with which he used the terrain. The answer was clear: the open battlefield must ever be avoided and his strength worn down by a 'strategy of exhaustion', which before Cannae was justified only as a temporary expedient and had earned for its advocate the abusive title of Cunctator, Delayer.

This strategy, though less spectacular than one of annihilation, required even more effort, and strained Rome's resources to the uttermost. Her naval supremacy must be upheld; this involved keeping nearly 200 ships afloat and some 50,000 sailors. All legions serving abroad must be maintained there, while as the theatres of war increased, so did their claims, so that by 212 Rome had in the field twenty-five legions; even slaves were allowed to volunteer in the dark months after Cannae. All this involved the utmost financial effort; in and after 215 the property tax (*tributum*) was doubled. Only by superior numbers and by time could Rome hope to win. But these forces must be applied wisely. Rome must conquer Hannibal, as she had conquered Italy, by her roads and fortresses. He must be worn down by marches and counter-marches.

But it was not enough to dog his heels. Roman armies, while avoiding open battles, must yet operate in the open; while one force acted on the defensive in face of Hannibal, another must take the offensive where he was not. By a wise use of the terrain parts of Italy could be protected and Hannibal's attempts to besiege towns could often be impeded, since his army was ill-equipped for siege work; he might capture Casilinum and Petelia, but he did not attempt bigger cities such as Naples, Cumae and Tarentum, still less Rome. When urged after Cannae by his cavalry officer to advance against Rome – 'for in five days we shall dine on the Capitol' – he knew the folly of such counsel. Further, small engagements, even if nominal tactical victories for Hannibal, were to Rome's ultimate advantage, because they all tended to whittle down his slender resources. Finally, though Hannibal had won much of southern Italy, which served as a base for recruiting, provisioning and wintering, it was also a responsibility: it crippled his freedom of movement, for he must protect his new allies. On such considerations rested Rome's policy, as advocated by Fabius. And Hannibal's only reply was to ravage the land mercilessly. But although this strategy of attrition might finally have brought a peace of sorts it could not humble Carthage and guarantee Rome's future security. It was only when Rome produced a military genius who could face Hannibal in the field that a lasting victory could be won. But until the *deus ex machina* appeared, it was only the great moral qualities of Rome that saved her – the tenacity of purpose of her citizens, the discipline of her soldiers, the prudence of her generals, and the wise directing force of her Senate.

After Cannae, as we have seen, news reached Rome of the revolt of Lucania, Bruttium, and Capua. Then came a report that Postumius had been surprised in Cisalpine Gaul; his force of two legions was cut to pieces, while the commander's skull was preserved for use in the temple rites of the priests of the Boii. To supervise Rome's defence a dictator was appointed, M. Junius Pera (consul 230 and censor 225) with Ti. Sempronius Gracchus as Master of the Horse. The people no longer challenged the political control of the Senate; the unfortunate careers of their own champions taught them to trust the Senate's judgment. Raising fresh forces Pera took up a position on the Via Latina near Teanum, covering the road to Rome. The Romans thus withdrew behind the line of the Volturnus so that Hannibal won over most of Campania except the coast towns and Nola, where he was frustrated by Marcellus. During the winter of 216–215 Hannibal besieged and finally captured Casilinum on the Volturnus. Later Roman annalists might delight in recounting that this winter, passed in luxurious quarters in Campania, undermined the discipline of Hannibal's army, but the Roman generals of the day knew better.[18]

The year 215 proved embarrassing to Carthage, as she sought to encircle Rome with enemies. Hannibal had to remain without help. The Scipios' victory at the Ebro necessitated diverting to Spain the reinforcements designed for Hannibal (p. 213). The rebellion of Syphax in Africa involved the recall of Hasdrubal from Spain. The ill-fated attempt of Hasdrubal the Bald in Sardinia was a useless dissipation of energy. In the summer Bomilcar landed a small force at Locri, but this was all the help Hannibal received. Only the arrival of reinforcements from Spain could change the complexion of the war; and this the Scipios prevented. In Italy the Romans again ventured across the Volturnus. Marcellus occupied a strong position (at modern Cancello) between Capua and Nola; Gracchus protected the coast near Cumae, while Fabius covered the way to Rome near Cales. Hannibal, who was thus surrounded on three sides, moved his camp from Capua to the hills above; at Mt Tifata he could command all the important roads and valleys, while a plateau suitable for his cavalry nestled among the peaks. From this stronghold, where centuries later Garibaldi also rested, Hannibal struck twice, but he struck in vain. His attempt on Cumae was thwarted by Gracchus; a second thrust at Nola was parried by Marcellus. But while he achieved little in Campania, his lieutenants were completing the conquest of Bruttium; Rhegium alone held out. Yet Rome showed her confidence in her generals by electing Fabius and Marcellus consuls for 214; the number of legions was raised from fourteen to twenty.

In 214 Hannibal, who had wintered in Apulia, returned to Mt Tifata and summoned Hanno from southern Italy. On his march via Compsa, Hanno found his path blocked by Gracchus who defeated him near the river Calor some three miles east of Beneventum and thus forced him to retire again to Bruttium. So Hannibal, who had in vain attacked Puteoli and Nola, abandoned his offensive in Campania. He failed to surprise Heraclea and then Tarentum, where the Roman fleet stationed at Brundisium was too quick for him. Meanwhile Marcellus had stormed Casilinum and the Romans had recovered Compsa and Aecae in Apulia, which meant that they could advance their base from Luceria to Herdonea. Hannibal was being pushed further and further south.

In 213 the Romans decided to concentrate on Apulia rather than to attempt the more difficult task of taking Capua. With four legions operating from a circle of fortresses they won over Arpi, but later a severe blow hit them. Not only had Syracuse transferred her allegiance and thus necessitated the removal of the energetic Marcellus from Italy, but now Tarentum followed her example; and in the wake of Tarentum came Metapontum and many other Greek cities in southern Italy. The Tarentines had been embittered by Rome's execution of some of their hostages who had tried to escape. Their town lay on a narrow peninsula, north of which stretched the best harbour in Italy (the Mare Piccolo); the site bears considerable resemblance to New Carthage (p. 226). By night two gates in the city's eastern wall were opened and when day broke two detachments of Hannibal's army had united in the Forum. The Roman garrison, however, retained the citadel, a strong hill which commanded the harbour entrance; this greatly diminished the value of Hannibal's success. He had to build a defensive wall between the town and citadel, and to drag the ships out of the harbour overland. So ended a dark year for Rome.

Many at Rome felt that their superior numbers were not being used to the best advantage; more boldness and vigour, greater clearness of purpose were required. Capua had been given a breathing-space which Marcellus' energy had denied to Syracuse. The people were tiring of Fabius (consul 215 and 214) and his son (consul 213). New men were elected consuls for 212: Q. Fulvius Flaccus (consul 237 and 224) and Appius Claudius Pulcher (praetor and propraetor in Sicily since 215); and all the commands in Italy, save only Gracchus', were changed. But most of the foreign commands remained unaltered. The number of legions was raised to its highest total of twenty-five; Rome braced herself for the effort and planned to start the siege of Capua. Though the consuls made their base at Bovianum instead of Beneventum or Casilinum in order to mask their intention, the Campanians suspected what was in store and asked Hannibal for supplies. Hanno was ordered to conduct convoys from Lucania. He advanced via Salernum towards Beneventum, which Flaccus entered secretly by night. Issuing forth, Flaccus surprised and captured Hanno's camp and supplies at Apollosa, three miles south-west of Beneventum, and thus thwarted the attempt to provision Capua. This success was counterbalanced by the surprise and death of Gracchus, probably in Lucania; this was the first Roman reverse in the field since Cannae, and Rome could ill afford to lose so brave and energetic a soldier. Hannibal himself marched into Campania, but could do little as provisions were already short. Three Roman armies closed round Capua and surrounded it with a double line of circumvallation.

In 211 the twenty-five legions were maintained and Flaccus, Appius

Claudius and Claudius Nero continued in the command at Capua. Hannibal made one last effort to relieve the city. He suddenly descended on it with a picked force, but the Roman entrenchments faced outwards as well as inwards, so that he could accomplish nothing when the Romans declined battle. He then made his final desperate throw : by marching on Rome itself he hoped to draw off the armies from Capua. Advancing through Samnium perhaps as far north as Amiternum he suddenly swept round to the south-west; crossing the Anio he camped four miles east of the city and rode up to the Colline Gate.[19] It was a terrifying moment; no enemy had approached the gates of Rome since the Gauls nearly two hundred years before. Beside the new recruits there were two of last year's legions in Rome. The walls were manned and a camp was formed about a mile outside, opposite Hannibal's. After a few days, when he hoped that part of the Roman army might be on its way from Capua he recrossed the Anio and marched by Tibur to Casinum after a slight skirmish with the consul Sulpicius Galba. By this route he would get between Capua and a Roman army advancing up the Via Latina. But at length, realizing that his bold stroke had miscarried and that the Roman armies were still beleaguering Capua, he did not return to Campania but swung off to Apulia, and left Capua to its fate. This was not long delayed; in despair the Capuans surrendered. Apart from some of the nobility, the people were granted their lives; the city was not sacked, but its land was confiscated; it was deprived of all municipal autonomy and was administered by a *praefectus* elected annually at Rome. The Senate's judgement of its defection was stern but just; politically Capua was destroyed, but materially it was allowed to live. It did not suffer the bitter fate of Syracuse.

The fall of Capua marked a turning point. The same year Syracuse also had fallen and an alliance had been negotiated with Aetolia. But news came from Spain of the disaster of the Scipios. Claudius Nero, who had served at Capua, was despatched with reinforcements to hold the line of the Ebro. Rome was exhausted. Hannibal might be confined to southern Italy, troops might come home laden with booty from Campania and Sicily, but the land of Latium and Samnium was still devastated and groaning for rest. So the legions were reduced to twenty-one and the year 210 passed comparatively uneventfully. Salapia was captured, though the consul Cn. Fulvius was trapped and killed near Herdonea in Apulia. His colleague Marcellus, the victor of Syracuse, did not attempt to storm Tarentum but contented himself by operating carefully near Venusia. But Rome's inactivity had a grave result in the autumn; twelve of the Latin colonies through war-weariness refused to send their contingents.

The year 209 opened with the gloomy prospect of further cautious advances gained at great sacrifice amid serious dissatisfaction among many of the allies; it finished, however, more successfully than could be anticipated. While Fulvius and Marcellus held Hannibal at bay, the cautious Fabius was to advance to Tarentum. Marcellus manoeuvred successfully against Hannibal near Canusium, Fulvius won back some hill towns; Fabius, aided by a fleet and by an attack on Caulonia to distract Hannibal's attention, moved against Tarentum which fell by treachery before Hannibal arrived. The city was sacked. Thus the long war dragged on in Italy. At stupendous sacrifice and with dogged perseverance Rome, after parrying Hannibal's offensive, had at length won Syracuse, Capua and Tarentum, and had confined Hannibal to southern Italy. But all might be in vain if the Italian Confederacy in the north began to break up. Not a moment too soon came news of young Scipio's brilliant success at New Carthage. The whole complexion of the war was changed; fresh courage and hope flowed in the veins of Rome and her allies. The conqueror of Hannibal had arisen.

X

SCIPIO
AND ROME'S
OFFENSIVE

1. SCIPIO'S CONQUEST OF SPAIN

After the disaster of the two Scipios in 211 the Romans lost all Spain
south of the Ebro, including presumably Saguntum, while the survivors
clung precariously to the Ebro line. Had the Scipios been killed a year
earlier, the situation would indeed have been calamitous; but the fall of
Syracuse and Capua facilitated the sending of reinforcements. The
appointment of Claudius Nero, who had long served in Italy under
Fabius' cautious strategy, suggests that the government envisaged a
purely defensive strategy in Spain. Indeed, with his few troops Nero
could hardly have acted otherwise. Landing late in 211 he tried during the
next year to secure the land north of the Ebro; his hold on the interior was
slender, though he possibly caused Hasdrubal Barca some trouble.

But a defensive attitude in Spain might not prevent the ultimate
breakthrough of overwhelming forces. A return to the offensive strategy
of the Scipios was indicated, if the man to direct it could be found; and
who was more fitting to avenge the Scipios than the son of Publius, the
future conqueror of Hannibal? Aged twenty-five, courageous, resource-
ful, self-confident and wise, the young P. Scipio had an extraordinary
power of inspiring confidence in others. His character was a blend of the
man of action and the religious mystic; his unusual enthusiasm was
moderated by Greek culture and Roman common sense. He had fought
in Italy, but as he had only held the aedileship (in 213) he was not qualified
for a high command. The details of his election are obscure, but he was
enthusiastically nominated by the people to a proconsular command in

Spain, and the Senate wisely acquiesced. Constitutional precedent was neglected; Scipio was the first *privatus* to be invested with proconsular *imperium*. His colleague, M. Junius Silanus, possessed only propraetorian *imperium*. Late in 210 he sailed with reinforcements to Spain where his total force, including the Spanish allies, was over 30,000 men.

Scipio spent the winter organizing his army and planning one of the most daring exploits of Roman history. So far from remaining on the defensive, he would strike at the enemy's heart by swooping on their base, New Carthage (Cartagena). Its capture would be of immense value. It contained the bulk of the Carthaginians' money and war material and their hostages from the whole of Spain; its harbour was one of the best in the western Mediterranean; and it would give Scipio a base from which to conquer the south. Inheriting the strategic ideals of his father, he realized that a base was essential and that his father had failed because Saguntum was not far enough south. His plan was possible because the three Carthaginian generals were still on bad terms and had wintered apart, Hasdrubal Barca in central Spain, the other Hasdrubal near the mouth of the Tagus, and Mago near Gibraltar; each was ten days' march from New Carthage. Thus one morning early in 209 the small garrison of the city awoke to find the town beleaguered by land and sea. For Scipio, leaving Silanus to guard his communications, had marched south with his main army at great speed and arrived at the same time as the fleet under his friend Laelius.

The town lay on a peninsula, which ran east and west, within a deep bay which faced south. On the east the peninsula was joined to the mainland by a narrow isthmus. On the west it was separated from the mainland by a narrow channel which ran north into a large lagoon which spread over the land immediately north of the town. The town was thus surrounded by water on three sides: by the lagoon in the north, by the canal in the west, and by the bay and open sea on the south. On his arrival Scipio encamped on a hill across the eastern isthmus. Next day after beating back a sortie he vigorously assaulted the town from the land side, while the fleet attacked from the south. The first assault failed, but later in the day he renewed the attack and simultaneously sent a party through the lagoon to storm the northern walls while the enemy's attention was engaged on the other fronts. This lagoon was shallow and in part fordable, but was probably not affected by any tidal action of the sea. When the wading party was about to start, a squall from the north suddenly sprang up and lowered the level of the lagoon by driving the water into the bay. Of this possibility Scipio who had made careful

topographical enquiries during the winter may have been aware. To the
men, however, it seemed like the direct intervention of heaven, not out of
keeping with the mystical self-confidence of their inspired leader. The
men raced through the now shallow waters and scaled the deserted
battlements, for all attention was focused on Scipio's frontal attack.
Sweeping along the northern wall the escalading party fell on the enemy
in the rear. At the same moment the whole defence was crumbling and the
naval detachment was scaling the southern walls. So fell the city.[1]

Thus Scipio had won the key position in Spain. Besides an immense
quantity of booty, money and munitions, he gained control of the local
silver mines and thus cut deep into the enemy's revenue. By his wise
treatment of the Spanish hostages and prisoners, he obtained more than
mere territorial advance. His romantic personality and his generous
outlook, like that of Sertorius later, fired the Spaniards' imagination, so
that many native princes came over to him. He spent the rest of the year
building up a new model army, drilling it in tactical reforms of far-
reaching effect and training it in the use of new weapons. He adopted the
Spanish sword and perhaps adapted the javelin (*pilum*) which led the
Romans to the mastery of the civilized world. Meanwhile the three
Carthaginian armies abandoned without a blow the eastern shore of Spain
and held on to the south and interior.

Scipio now had a base sufficiently far south to justify an offensive in
Baetica, where he marched early in 208. Hasdrubal Barca, who was
quartered near Castulo, advanced to a strong position south-east of
Baecula (Bailen) which he hoped would counterbalance the numerical
superiority of the Romans. Scipio occupied the hills opposite, but fearing
the arrival of a second Carthaginian army he decided to fight on the
ground chosen by Hasdrubal. This was a gradual hill, broken half-way up
by a flattish terrace; the front and rear were protected by rivers, the sides
by streams or watercourses. The Roman light-armed troops at first
engaged the enemy's covering force on the terrace, while Hasdrubal
began to lead his main forces out of the camp down towards it. Scipio sent
all his light troops to support the first attack and to engage the enemy's
attention. Meanwhile he divided his main army. Detachments swept up
the two valleys onto the terrace and fell on the Carthaginians' flank before
they had formed up. Seeing the day was lost Hasdrubal executed a
masterly withdrawal and retired with half or two-thirds of his army.
Crossing central Spain and the upper Ebro, he ultimately slipped through
the western passes of the Pyrenees on his way to Italy.

Though thwarted strategically, Scipio had won a glorious tactical victory, which was a real turning point in the development of the Roman army. The Romans were learning the lesson of Cannae and being trained to greater flexibility and individual initiative. Tactically the weak point at Baecula was that Scipio's light troops were not holding the enemy's main body during the outflanking movement. But that was soon to be remedied. Scipio has often been condemned by ancient and modern critics for allowing Hasdrubal to leave Spain. In the circumstances the charge is unjustified for three reasons. To follow Hasdrubal was too dangerous, if not impossible; and he could not hold all the passes of the Pyrenees. Secondly, Scipio's object in Spain was to subdue it, not to expose it to the other two Carthaginian armies while he went on a wild goose chase after Hasdrubal; indeed, it is doubtful whether as a mere *privatus cum imperio* he had the right to leave Spain without orders. Thirdly, the seriousness of Hasdrubal's arrival in northern Italy in 207 has been over-emphasized; Rome could and did cope with the danger. Scipio solved a difficult situation with marked success.[2]

After Hasdrubal Barca's departure for Italy, reinforcements were sent to Spain under Hanno, who joined Mago to recruit further in Celtiberia. They were checked by Silanus who captured Hanno, though Mago escaped and joined Hasdrubal Gisgo near Gades (207). With the threat to his flank now removed, Scipio could advance southwards, but Hasdrubal refused battle. His only hope was delay; so he turned to a Fabian strategy of exhaustion and distributed his army in various towns. Scipio did not waste time with a war of sieges, although as a demonstration his brother Lucius carried by assault a rich and valuable town, Orongis. In 206 the situation was changed. When Hasdrubal Gisgo heard that Hasdrubal Barca had been defeated and killed at Metaurus while seeking to join Hannibal, delay was useless; the fate of Spain must be staked on a pitched battle. Early in the year Scipio met the combined Carthaginian forces near Ilipa (Alcala del Rio, near Seville). For several days both armies faced each other in battle array with their best troops in the centre, their allies on the wings. Early one day Scipio drew up his troops in a different order with the Romans on the wings and a centre of Spaniards. A cavalry attack forced Hasdrubal to lead out his men in their usual formation, before he realized the altered Roman order. It was then too late to change. After a deliberate delay to weary the enemy, who had not breakfasted, Scipio stopped skirmishing and delivered the final blow. His centre advanced slowly, declining battle. Meanwhile his wings, by a complicated manoeuvre, were extended, advanced in column and then wheeled again into line, so that they outflanked the enemy, whose resistance soon crumpled. By a brilliantly rapid pursuit Scipio cut off the enemy's retreat; though Hasdrubal and Mago escaped, their forces were cut to pieces or else surrendered. No less brilliant were Scipio's tactics. He had rectified one of the weaknesses of Baecula; he now held the enemy's main forces while the wings carried out their outflanking movement.[3]

The rest of the year was spent in diplomatic arrangements and punitive expeditions. To prepare for the future, Scipio slipped across to Africa to interview Syphax, the Numidian sheikh who had been troubling Carthage. On his return he made an example of some Spanish towns, Ilurgia (Illorci), Castax and Astapa (Estepa near Osuna), capturing the first by a brilliant converging attack. A report that Scipio was ill caused a mutiny among troops stationed on his lines of communication at the Sucro, but this was promptly crushed. To steady his men he led them against two Spanish allies who had also profited by his illness to revolt. A brilliant Roman victory up the Ebro restored their loyalty and removed a dangerous threat to Scipio's flank. An interview with another African prince, Masinissa, and the founding of a colony at Italica (Santaponce, near Seville) for his veterans, completed Scipio's work in Spain. The final Carthaginian resistance at Gades collapsed and Mago, after a vain attempt on New Carthage, sailed off to the Balearic Isles, where he has left his name enshrined in Mahon, the capital of Minorca. So fell the Carthaginian Empire in Spain, while Scipio returned to Rome conquering and to conquer.

2. THE WAR IN ITALY

Meantime Rome had successfully weathered the storm in Italy. After the recapture of Tarentum in 209 the people were eager to make a final effort to end the war in Italy. The energetic Marcellus was elected consul for the fourth time for 208; his colleague, T. Quinctius Crispinus, had served under him at Syracuse. The two consuls encamped near Hannibal and it looked as if they might risk a battle. But while out reconnoitring they fell into an ambush; Marcellus was killed and Crispinus was mortally wounded.[4] In this unimportant skirmish Rome lost one of her best generals; it would be hard to replace the energy and dash of Marcellus, who alone seemed ready to cross swords with Hannibal. No further effort was made to renew the projected offensive, especially when news came that the commander at Tarentum had been defeated near Petelia, and later that Hannibal had driven off a Roman force which was besieging Locri. But the year was more successful abroad than in Italy. Laevinus, returning from a naval raid on the African coast, had defeated a Carthaginian squadron and captured 18 ships, and Scipio had won the battle of Baecula.

But news soon reached Rome that Hasdrubal had left Spain and was wintering in Gaul. True, Scipio was wisely keeping at bay the two other Carthaginian armies in Spain, but Hasdrubal might soon arrive in northern Italy with some 20,000 men. It was too hazardous for the Romans to attempt to check him, as they had tried to check Hannibal, at the Rhône, or even in the plains of northern Italy. Instead they must concentrate on central Italy and at all costs prevent him coming south to join Hannibal. The consuls elected for the critical year of 207 were C. Claudius Nero, who had served at Capua and in Spain, and M. Livius Salinator, who after conquering the Illyrians in 219 had withdrawn from public life. The legions, which for the last three years had dropped to twenty-one, were raised to twenty-three. While Nero held Hannibal at bay, Livius was to counter Hasdrubal's arrival.

By the end of May Hasdrubal had crossed the Alps, probably by the same pass used by his brother, and reached the Po valley, where he raised his numbers to 30,000 by recruiting Gauls. After failing to take Placentia, which would have been of great value, he advanced south in the summer when the fields of central Italy would provide corn for his troops and forage for his horses. As in 217, the Romans stationed two legions under Terentius Varro at Arretium in Etruria and two more under a praetor Porcius at Ariminum in the east; but they improved on the previous plan by placing Livius south of the two advance armies near Narnia, where he could support either according to Hasdrubal's movements. When it was clear that Hasdrubal was making for the Adriatic coast and the Via Flaminia, Porcius gradually withdrew while Livius hastened to join him, so that Hasdrubal found the united force of four legions awaiting him at the Metaurus.

Meanwhile Hannibal did not attempt to join his brother in northern Italy, and risk losing Bruttium, his only base in Italy. Instead the brothers hoped to meet in central Italy. Hannibal moved slowly northwards to Grumentum, where he found Nero and four legions.[5] Here, and again at Venusia, skirmishes took place which Roman tradition magnified into victories. Faced by four legions and with two more behind him at Tarentum, Hannibal could not advance beyond Canusium without serious risk. But events played into the hands of the Romans, who learned from the capture of Hasdrubal's despatch riders that the brothers intended to meet in Umbria. Claudius Nero then took a momentous

decision. Leaving four legions to watch Hannibal he determined to join
Livius in the hope of defeating Hasdrubal with their augmented forces
and of returning to his southern command before Hannibal had realized
his absence. He marched with 6,000 infantry and 1,000 cavalry along the
coast road, which was shorter and where provisioning was easier, amid
enthusiastic aid from the loyal population. At the river Metaurus he
entered Livius' camp by night, having covered 240 miles in six days
according to the pro-Claudian tradition. In the morning a double bugle-
call rang through the Roman camp and Hasdrubal knew that two
consular armies lay over against him.

The Romans had encamped probably south of Fanum and the
Metaurus where they could cover the coast road and watch the Via
Flaminia without being forced to fight on the level ground near Fanum,
where Hasdrubal had in vain offered battle to Livius. The arrival of Nero
changed the situation. In face of superior numbers Hasdrubal could not
force the coast road. He must either withdraw to northern Italy and await
events, or stake all on marching inland along the Via Flaminia in the hope of
joining Hannibal further south but with the risk of finding himself between
two Roman armies. It is not certain which plan he favoured, but probably
he chose the bolder one; he had before him the example of how Hannibal
had successfully thrown himself between Flaminius and Servilius at
Trasimene. In any case, Hasdrubal withdrew by night up the Metaurus
valley, where he was overtaken by the Romans before he could cross the
river. He was forced to fight. He posted his Gauls on a steep position on
the left and massed his other troops and elephants on the right where he
hoped to break the Roman line. But Nero, on the right wing, finding he
could not engage the Gauls because of the ground, led a force round to
support Livius on the left and thus outflanked the enemy. Seeing the day
was lost Hasdrubal charged into the thick of battle and died fighting.
'And it would not be just to take leave of this commander without one
word of praise,' wrote Polybius, who in a fitting tribute esteemed him a
worthy son of Hamilcar and a worthy brother of Hannibal.[6]

Victory was complete; Rome had won an open battle in Italy for the
first time during the war. The first serious attempt to reinforce Hannibal
had failed. The relief was tremendous and the effect on Rome's prestige in
Italy instantaneous. The battle of Metaurus was a decisive moment in
world history; it was Rome's 'Crowning mercy'. But had the result been
otherwise, it would scarcely have ended the war. Rome, that had stood so
much, could surely have braced herself for one more shock when the tide
of war was turning in her favour elsewhere. But the joy at Rome was

unbounded. Hastening back to the south, Nero, a member of the grim Claudian house, flung Hasdrubal's head into his brother's camp at Larinum. Thus learning the bitter news, Hannibal was forced to withdraw to Bruttium, unaided and alone.

The war in Italy began to hang fire and the centre of interest shifts to Africa, which the Romans were preparing to invade. In 206 the legions were reduced to twenty. Although there were thirteen in Italy itself, the consuls still feared to attack Hannibal, but the next year, while preparing for his African campaign, Scipio snatched Locri from Hannibal's grasp. At the same time the Carthaginian government made one last attempt to help Hannibal and to keep Scipio in Italy. Mago sailed from the Balearic Isles and captured Genoa, where he received reinforcements from Carthage.[7] This danger of a fresh invasion from the north was met by stationing armies at Arretium and Ariminum, as in 207. But Mago could not yet take the offensive; the Gallic tribes, abandoned by Hannibal and remembering the fate of Hasdrubal, were lukewarm, and it was a slow task to organize the hill tribes of Liguria. At length in 203 Mago advanced into the Po valley with some 30,000 men. One legion had been sent to Genoa, two more held the Boii at bay, while four advanced from Ariminum against him. After a serious engagement Mago withdrew wounded to the coast, where he found orders to return to Carthage, but he died on the voyage.

Meanwhile Hannibal had been holding on desperately in Bruttium like a lion at bay. Reinforcements from Carthage in 205 had been driven to Sardinia by a storm and there captured. Gradually one small town after another was wrested from Hannibal and he was even worsted in a skirmish near Croton, according to the Roman claim. All hope of success in Italy was dead; he could only try to prevent reinforcements being sent to Scipio who had invaded Africa, where success after success was reported. Finally, in the autumn of 203 he received orders to return home to defend Carthage. Having kept together a loyal army for fifteen years in an enemy's country, undefeated, he at last evacuated Italy more sorrowfully than an exile leaving his native land. He had failed in an attempt to which he had devoted his life. Yet all was not lost, and he must have felt some eagerness in the thought that he was going to face in battle the most brilliant general Rome had produced, and that when they parted the fate of the civilized world would be decided.

3. THE ROMAN OFFENSIVE IN AFRICA

On his return from Spain Scipio was elected consul for 205 amid great popular rejoicings, although he was not granted a triumph, which as a mere *privatus cum imperio* he could not claim It was now well known that he wished to carry the war into Africa. When the Senate discussed the allocation of provinces, strong opposition to Scipio's African project was led by Fabius; but finally a compromise was reached by which one consul should command in Sicily with the right to sail to Africa if he thought fit. As Scipio's colleague, P. Licinius Crassus, was Pontifex Maximus and could not leave Italy, Scipio had clearly won. But he was still further checked; he was given the command of only the two legions in Sicily, who were the disgraced survivors of Cannae. However, he raised 7,000 volunteers and the Italian allies supplied corn and material for the fitting out of 30 ships, so that he had a good nucleus with which to forge a weapon to strike at Carthage.

Fabius' opposition to Scipio's schemes was based on politics and strategy. Politically, he represented a class which did not look beyond Italy for Rome's future. Such men tried to stem the tide of Hellenism which was flooding Rome and wished to finish the war with all speed and to heal the wounds it had inflicted on the countryside of Italy.[8] The other view, as represented by the Scipios, was that a purely Italian policy was obsolete and that Rome must become a Mediterranean power. The military views of the two parties varied correspondingly. The object of the Fabians was 'limited': Hannibal was to be forced from Italy. Scipio's object was more 'absolute': the crushing of Hannibal and Carthage. He thought Rome would never be secure until Carthage was humbled and fettered – though not destroyed: the cry '*delenda est Carthago*' had not yet arisen. The strategy of each party represented its aims. Tactical inferiority forced on Fabius a defensive strategy, which had won him the title Cunctator. But a strategy of exhaustion seldom wins a war. Fabius could only hope that the war might 'fizzle out' and Hannibal retire. He could never conquer Carthage. But Scipio by his tactical reforms did not fear to meet Hannibal in the field and could use a strategy of annihilation. To defeat Hannibal in Italy might terminate the war, but Carthage would remain a danger. Hence he determined to disregard the enemy's main forces, strike at their base and so force Hannibal to return to Africa to fight the decisive battle. And this policy won the day.

Scipio began to train his new army in Sicily where his Hellenic sympathies and conduct won him ready support. His seizure of Locri from Hannibal had an unfortunate sequel, for Pleminius, the governor whom he left in charge, spent his time plundering the unhappy Locrians, and thus gave Fabius a chance to criticize the absent Scipio. A senatorial commission, headed by Scipio's cousin Pomponius, was sent to conduct an enquiry. Pleminius was condemned, but when the court began to

investigate Scipio's Hellenic manner of life, he skilfully turned the tables
by impressing them with his own military preparations. The Board,
which had come to criticize, remained to bless, and in the spring of 204
the expeditionary force, numbering perhaps 30,000 men, set sail for
Africa amid great enthusiasm.

Scipio landed according to plan at Porto Farina near Utica, which he
hoped to capture as a base. He was soon joined by Masinissa and his
cavalry, the young Numidian prince with whom he had wisely negotiated
in Spain, but not by Syphax, whom Hasdrubal had won to the
Carthaginian cause by giving him his beautiful daughter Sophonisba in
marriage. After a slight cavalry success Scipio advanced to Utica and
encamped on the hill behind the town. Meanwhile Carthage in alarm
prepared for a siege and sent out desperate appeals for help to Syphax and
Hasdrubal; the latter's son, Hanno, was busy recruiting. But Masinissa
decoyed Hanno's squadron past some hills to the south-west of Utica at
the Tower of Agathocles, while Scipio lay ambushed behind them.
Suddenly Scipio's troops burst forth over a flat saddle of the hills and fell
on Hanno's flank, while Masinissa wheeled round and attacked in front.
After this victory Scipio pressed forward the siege of Utica by land and
sea, but winter came on and the town still resisted. Threatened by
Hasdrubal and Syphax, Scipio withdrew for the winter to a sharp
headland projecting into the sea which was later known as the Castra
Cornelia.

The first season's campaign had been somewhat unspectacular and
Scipio was driven to an awkward position. His initial caution, however,
was quite justified and has been compared with that of Gustavus
Adolphus when he landed in Germany. He had wisely refused to
contemplate an attack on Carthage before winning an adequate base.
During the winter Syphax attempted to negotiate peace on the terms that
Carthage should evacuate Italy, and the Romans Africa. Though Scipio
had no intention of accepting conditions which would offer Rome no
compensation for all her sufferings, he prolonged negotiations in order
that his envoys might pay frequent visits to the enemy's quarters and
obtain detailed topographical information, for Syphax and Hasdrubal
were encamped during the winter on two adjacent hills; these formed the
southern termination of the ridge which in the north ended at the Castra
Cornelia, some six miles away.

In the spring of 203 Scipio broke off negotiations and renewed the
blockade of Utica. When the enemies' suspicions were lulled, he launched
an attack as sudden as his dash on Cartagena. One night he marched

under cover of the hills against the enemies' camps which he learnt were made of osier and reed. While he himself held back, Masinissa surrounded Syphax' camp and Laelius set fire to it. When the Carthaginians in Hasdrubal's camp, thinking the fire was accidental, rushed out to help, Scipio fell on this camp also. The two enemy leaders escaped, but a large part of their armies was destroyed. Polybius believed that no other disaster, even if exaggerated, could compare with the horror of this night. For the Romans success was complete. Instead of being confined to a narrow peninsula, Scipio had taken the offensive and with practically no loss had crushed superior forces.

At Carthage alarm prevailed, for Scipio was not only renewing the siege of Utica but now commanded the open country. Yet the bolder counsels of the war party predominated and it was decided to recruit a fresh army out of Scipio's reach. Within a month of the disaster Hasdrubal and Syphax had mustered some 20,000 men at the Great Plains (near Souk el Kremis) on the upper reaches of the Bagradas, seventy-five miles from Utica. They were still gathering strength in the quiet of the desert when suddenly Scipio struck. Leaving part of his army to continue the siege of Utica, he set out with some 12,000 men in light marching order, and in five days camped opposite the enemy. Trusting in their superior numbers and local knowledge the Carthaginians unwisely determined to fight; guerrilla tactics would have been safer. Thinking that they had Scipio within their grasp, they advanced to battle, with their Celtiberian mercenaries in the centre, the Carthaginians on the right wing, the Numidians on the left. Scipio placed his infantry in the centre in the usual three lines, the Italian cavalry on the right wing, Masinissa's horse on the left. At the first encounter the enemy's wings gave way and exposed the flanks of the centre which stood firm. Under cover of the first line the two rear lines of the Romans turned into column, half to right and half to left, and marched out to encircle the Celtiberians, who were cut to pieces. It was a great tactical victory. Not only were Scipio's troops more flexible, but he had used his legionaries (not merely the cavalry) to outflank the foe; at the same time the enemy's centre was not merely held at bay, as at Ilipa, but was actually engaged. Scipio could now do what Hannibal had done at Cannae; he had trained an army to meet the master tactician.

Scipio next captured Tunis, only fifteen miles from Carthage, where he could command the enemy's land communications. The Carthaginians made a desperate counter-attack on his fleet at Utica, but he marched there just in time to thwart it. He did not, however, return to Tunis immediately. Meantime Laelius and Masinissa had pursued Syphax to his own country and defeated him near Cirta (Constantine), which they captured. Syphax was taken prisoner, but his wife Sophonisba took poison.[9] The situation at Carthage was now desperate and Hannibal was at length recalled to defend his country. But the peace party of merchants and landowners prevailed and peace was sought. Scipio, who did not aim at the destruction of Carthage itself, offered terms: Carthage was to evacuate and renounce Italy, Gaul and Spain; surrender her navy, except 20 ships; pay an indemnity of 5,000 talents; and recognize the power of Masinissa in the west and the autonomy of the native tribes of Libya and Cyrenaica in the east. The terms were severe and would reduce Carthage to a purely African power, crippled in her trade, nominally independent, but in practice little more than a client state of Rome. But she accepted them, an armistice was made and the Senate after some delay ratified the treaty (winter 203–202). The delay was ominous for Scipio; it meant that rival noble families grudged him his success and were working against him. The war seemed at an end, but Hannibal was returning.

4. VICTORY AND PEACE

While terms were being discussed at Rome, Hannibal landed in Africa near Hadrumetum and was soon joined by Mago's army from Italy. When a storm drove a Roman convoy ashore near Carthage, the populace of the overcrowded and ill-supplied city seized the supplies. Scipio sent envoys to complain of this violation of the armistice, but they were dismissed and treacherously ambushed on their return voyage. Thus the war party at Carthage, trusting in Hannibal, again prevailed, and renewed hostilities just when the peace had been ratified at Rome.[10]

Scipio in anger stormed up the Bagradas valley, cutting Carthage off from her economic base. He hastily summoned Masinissa, who was fighting in western Numidia, and advanced further and further inland to meet him, as he dared not face the enemy without the Numidian cavalry. Thereupon Hannibal advanced from Hadrumetum to Zama, the western town of this name, hoping to cut Scipio's communications and to force him to fight without the cavalry. At Naraggara (Sidi Youssef) Scipio was joined by Masinissa and then advanced perhaps to the Ou.-et-Tine. After an ineffective interview between the two generals, the two armies faced one another for battle. Each side numbered between 35,000 and 40,000 men, the Carthaginians being slightly stronger in total, although weaker in cavalry; and each side was drawn up in three lines.[11] Hannibal placed his foreign mercenaries in his first line with a screen of light troops and elephants in front; the weak native Libyans and Carthaginians formed the second line; the third line was some distance from the first two and consisted of the Old Guard, Hannibal's veteran army from Italy; on the wings was the cavalry. The Romans were drawn up in their customary three lines, but the maniples of each line were stationed directly behind one another, not in echelon. The tactical aims of the two generals have not been fully recorded, but the following motives seem justified. Scipio counted on his superior cavalry to expose the enemy's wings; he then hoped to apply the outflanking movement which he had used with increasing skill and success at Baecula, Ilipa and Campi Magni. Hannibal, realizing his weakness in cavalry, probably ordered it to simulate flight and so draw its opponents off the field. He would then throw all his infantry in successive waves against Scipio's numerically inferior infantry, while he would thwart an outflanking movement by holding back his veterans as a reserve.

The battle opened with the charge of Hannibal's elephants, which miscarried. Some turned back on their own lines, others ran down the passages which Scipio had skilfully left in his ranks, others were driven off to the flanks. The Roman cavalry then charged and drove both Carthaginian wings off the field. The infantry closed, while Scipio, seeing Hannibal's third line remaining stationary, realized that an outflanking manoeuvre was impossible. The *hastati* drove back the first line of mercenaries, who were forced out to the wings by their second line which would not receive them; then, supported by the *principes*, they broke the Carthaginians of the second line. Scipio took the opportunity to break off the battle and both sides re-formed. Scipio lengthened his front by bringing up his two rear lines on the flanks of the *hastati*; Hannibal, whose front would thus be shorter than Scipio's, probably placed the survivors of his first two lines on the flanks of his veterans. Hannibal would need longer to reorganize, while Scipio would give him as long as he needed, hoping for the return of his cavalry. When the ranks again joined, it was hotly contested until the returning Roman cavalry fell on the enemy's rear. The cavalry had arrived in time to decide the course, not only of the battle, but of the world's history.

Hannibal's army was destroyed, although he himself escaped to Hadrumetum. Scipio received supplies at Castra Cornelia, and after making a demonstration at Carthage he received a peace deputation at Tunis, for Hannibal himself on his return to Carthage after thirty-six years was counselling peace, especially as news came that Syphax' son had just been defeated. Further resistance was useless and might involve the destruction of the city. Scipio also was ready for peace, because the siege of Carthage would involve fresh effort when Italy most needed rest, and because he wished to disarm but not to destroy.

A three months' armistice was concluded on condition that Carthage offered reparations for breaking the truce, gave hostages, and supplied corn and pay for the Roman troops during the armistice. According to the terms of the peace Carthage retained her autonomy, her territory within the 'Phoenician Trenches' (i.e. very roughly equivalent to modern Tunisia as far south as the Gulf of Gabes) and her control over trademarts like Emporia. She was to restore to Masinissa all his land and ancestral property. She was reduced to the state of a dependent ally of Rome, being allowed to make war on no one outside Africa and only with Rome's permission within Africa. This meant the end of her life as a great Mediterranean power and gave her no guarantee against future aggression in Africa. All her elephants and nearly her whole navy were to be surrendered, prisoners of war were to be given up and finally an indemnity of 10,000 talents was to be paid in fifty annual instalments, which would keep her weak and dependent on Rome for this long period (In fact when in 191 BC Carthage tried to pay the balance of her indemnity as a lump sum she refused.) In return the Romans would evacuate Africa in 150 days. And so the long war ended. The Senate ratified Scipio's terms and he returned victorious to Rome, where he was surnamed after the land he had conquered – Africanus.

The importance of the Second Punic War can hardly be exaggerated. It was a turning-point in the history of the whole ancient world. Its effect on Rome and Italy, on the constitution, on economic and social life, on religion and thought was profound. After it no power arose which could endanger the existence of Rome. The Hellenistic monarchies of the east still flourished, but at Rome's touch they fell like a house of cards. She was mistress of the fortunes of the civilized world and gradually introduced into that world a unity, unknown since the days of Alexander, which lasted some five hundred years. Further, the dramatic nature of the struggle has captivated the imagination of mankind. It was on this stage that one of the world's most glorious failures rose and fell, that one man pitted his resources against those of a nation. Not that Hannibal bore on his shoulders alone the whole weight of a war of revenge, unsupported by his home government, as popular fancy likes to paint the heroic figure; it was circumstances, or rather Rome's unceasing activity, that isolated Hannibal and forced him to fight unaided. And the causes of his failure

were largely the causes of Rome's success : Rome's superiority at sea, her
roads and fortresses, the unexpected loyalty of her Italian allies which
morally justified her conquest of the Italian peninsula, the unshaken
direction of the Senate, the loyal co-operation of the people and their 'will
to conquer' which survived disaster after disaster, the wisdom of a
strategy of exhaustion and the courage by which it was maintained while
the countryside bled, the blocking of reinforcements from Carthage and
Spain, the undermining of the enemy's resources in the Spanish
peninsula, and above all the superior quality of the vast manpower on
which Rome could draw in her hour of need. Finally, what turned the
hope of ultimate success against Hannibal into complete and devastating
victory against Carthage was the production of a military genius by
Rome, one who learning as a pupil from Hannibal himself forged out of
the Roman army a weapon which could be turned against the master.
Rome produced many generals of distinction but only one who dared face
Hannibal in open battle after Cannae. Fabius was called the Shield of
Rome and Marcellus her Sword, but Scipio's very name meant a Staff, on
which Rome could lean and with which she could thrash her foe. But the
brilliance of a Scipio would have been useless without that unswerving
loyalty and perseverance of the Senate and People of Rome. The
unavailing gallantry of the great house of Barca at length succumbed to
the solid moral qualities of the self-sacrifice of a nation at war. It was by
moral forces that Rome survived her ordeal: forces which were soon to
be blunted by ambition and avarice at home and by the contagious
corruption of the eastern world into which she was next drawn. Never
did the spirit of the Roman People shine forth brighter than in the dark
hours of the Second Punic War.

PART III

ROME AND THE MEDITERRANEAN

XI

ROME AND GREECE

1. THE HELLENISTIC WORLD

Hardly had peace been signed with Carthage when the Roman people was asked by the Senate to declare war against Philip, King of Macedon. Doubtless the ordinary Roman citizen was somewhat surprised and wondered what Greek politics had to do with Rome, but he was soon to learn that Rome's interests and obligations were no longer confined to Italy. The struggle with Carthage had broken down barriers which could not be raised up again, and Rome had become a world power. She had crushed one great power and must now align herself with the monarchies of the east. For the Greek world consisted of three great kingdoms, the remains of Alexander's empire, together with a number of Greek leagues and states more or less free. Throughout there reigned a balance of powers whose equilibrium could easily be upset. It only needed a spark to set the whole Hellenistic world ablaze. But before seeing how this conflagration was started we must glance round the eastern Mediterranean.

In Greece, since the days when the city-state flourished, many communities who wished to preserve their independence but were too weak to do this alone had combined into federations or leagues. The two chief of these were the Aetolian League in the north and the Achaean in the south. The former was loose and flexible in form and somewhat primitive in outlook; its unity derived largely from common interests in war. The plundering raiders from Aetolia had been severely checked for crossing Philip's path in 217. Smarting under this treatment they readily welcomed Roman intervention and fought with Rome against Macedon, only to be deserted by their ally and forced to patch up a peace with Philip (206). The Romans on their part also felt deserted by the Aetolians and so feelings had become very embittered. The Achaean League under the leadership of Aratus had become the predominant power in the Peloponnese, but had succeeded in defeating Sparta under Cleomenes only at the price of enlisting the help of Philip's predecessor, Antigonus Doson of Macedon (222), to whom the League surrendered its control of Corinth. But though Macedon guided their foreign policy the Achaeans still retained more of the old Greek outlook than did the Aetolians; and turning a deaf ear to Philip's call they maintained a policy of neutrality during the First Macedonian War.

In addition to these leagues, one of the old Greek city-states had shaken off the yoke of Macedon and regained its independence in 229: Athens. Though a shadow of her former self and little more than a university town with small military power, Athens still retained some influence, based partly on her glorious past; in politics she maintained a selfish neutrality. Of the other surviving Republics the most important was Rhodes, the Venice of the ancient world. This flourishing maritime state, whose control extended to the mainland of Asia Minor, had built up a prosperous trade. Her name was raised high among the nations by the good faith of her citizens and by her suppression of piracy; she consistently aimed at remaining on good terms with all men.

Of the three great powers which balanced their weight precariously against each other, Macedon had retained fitfully throughout the third century its old European dependencies and its control over the cities of Greece. On the accession of Philip V to the throne in 221 she held the three fortresses known as the 'Fetters of Greece', Demetrias, Chalcis and Corinth, and thus controlled Greek destinies without direct rule. As successor to the leadership of Antigonus Doson's Hellenic Federation Philip had by 217 reduced the Aetolians, who were the chief disturbers of the peace in Greece. The pirate chief Demetrius, angered at Rome's police raids in the Adriatic, had then involved Philip in a ten years' war with Rome. But his ambition for empire did not lead to a happy conclusion.

The second great monarchy, Syria, was at this time ruled by Antiochus III, surnamed the Great (223–187). His predecessors, the Seleucid kings, had failed to retain a large part of the eastern conquests of Alexander and had been constantly fighting with Egypt for the possession of southern Syria; Antiochus himself was defeated in a similar attempt at Raphia in 217. He aimed at reconstituting the old Seleucid empire and undertook an Anabasis in the Far East (212–205). The report of this adventurous expedition filled the Greek world with admiration, and Antiochus appeared as a second Alexander. His thoughts then turned again to Egypt, and he hoped to reverse the result of Raphia, but so far Rome was beyond his horizon.

Egypt, the third great monarchy, with its enormous resources and wealth had flourished materially under the Ptolemies, while Alexandria led the Greek world in learning, art and commerce. Abroad Egypt had gained wide control in Asia Minor and the Aegean; she had made her influence felt in Greece and, alone of the Hellenistic states, had entered into friendly relations with Rome, as early as 273, with a view to extending her commerce. Her success at Raphia in the fourth of the series of wars against Syria was followed by a period of degeneration. Internal dissension was reflected abroad and several of Ptolemy's foreign possessions slipped from his sluggish grasp.

Beside the three great monarchies there were other kingdoms. Bithynia, Pontus and Cappadocia paid only a nominal allegiance to Syria. Celtic tribes had set up the independent state of Galatia in the heart of Asia Minor. But the chief of these smaller kingdoms was Pergamum, where since 241 there had reigned a despot and merchant prince named Attalus, who differed much from the other rulers of the east. His sympathies with Greek culture and with the political aims of Athens and Rhodes drew him into the Greek world away from the great monarchs, who looked with jealous eye on the growing wealth and prosperity of the Pergamene kingdom.[1]

We must next trace how and why Rome was drawn into the vortex of eastern affairs and soon emerged riding the storm. Our sources record the facts clearly, but the motives of Roman policy are not so definitely stated. Hence it will be well to follow in some detail the incidents which led up to the war, because only so can we hope to lay bare Rome's policy and compare the varying constructions placed upon it by modern historians. First, then, the events, and secondly the policy that dictated them.

2. THE OUTBREAK OF WAR

The balance of the three eastern powers was upset by the death of Ptolemy Philopator and by the accession of a child to the throne of Egypt. In the winter of 203–202 Philip of Macedon and Antiochus of Syria formed a disgraceful alliance to share between themselves Egypt's possessions in Europe and Asia, although neither party probably intended to remain loyal to the terms of partition. As the lion's share was to fall to Antiochus, he was probably the moving spirit.[2] In the spring of 202 he invaded southern Syria, while Philip, at first avoiding a direct breach with Egypt, attacked with a newly built fleet some cities along the Bosphorus, some being free and independent while others were allied with or dependent on other communities: Lysimacheia, Chalcedon, and Cius were allies of Aetolia; Perinthus was a dependency of Byzantium; Thasos at this date was a free island. Philip's capture of Cius with the help of Prusias of Bithynia angered the Aetolians, displeased Antiochus, and led the Rhodians to decide to oppose Philip; their ambassadors had appealed in vain for the town and were forced to see it sacked. Then in 201 Philip annexed the Cyclades and occupied Samos. The precise order of subsequent events is uncertain, but Philip probably first suffered considerable losses in an indecisive naval engagement off Chios, then attacked Pergamum by land and ravaged its territory, next defeated the Rhodian fleet at Lade (near Miletus) and finally operated in South Caria where he was forced to winter.[3]

Philip's wanton atrocities against unoffending cities in peacetime had indeed stirred up a hornets' nest. The violence of his actions, which made war inevitable, may have been due to a desire to settle his accounts while Rome was still engaged with Hannibal. In that case he miscalculated, for Zama was being fought and the Romans would soon be free. But he may have derived some encouragement from the fact that in 202 (autumn) they had coldly rebuffed an Aetolian embassy, which had come to appeal on behalf of their wronged allies; Rome had not forgiven Aetolia for making peace with Philip in 206.[4] In the following autumn Attalus and the Rhodians also sent ambassadors to Rome to seek help. Rhodes' relations with Rome were somewhat strained: while remaining neutral in the First Macedonian War she had denounced Rome's interference. Attalus, however, was on good terms with Rome, but as he was not technically an 'ally' or perhaps even a 'friend', there was no legal ground for Rome to intervene. The Senate took no immediate open action but it suddenly reversed its earlier policy towards the eastern situation. One of the consuls elected for 200 was P. Sulpicius Galba, who had campaigned as proconsul in Macedon from 210 to 206; and when the new consuls entered office in March 200 Macedonia was allotted as a consular province to Sulpicius.

Why the Senate wanted war must be considered later, for it is a matter of conjecture rather than of proved fact. How the Senate precipitated war is the present question, for it had apparently to drive two unwilling

parties into conflict: the Roman people and Philip. Towards Rome
Philip's conduct had been legally correct and offered no formal ground
for reproach; and the Roman people unanimously rejected the consuls'
proposal, made in March 200, that war should be proclaimed.[5] It was then
decided to present Philip with an ultimatum, so strongly worded that he
would be unlikely to accept its terms; these were that he should make
reparation to Attalus (as if he, Philip, were the aggressor) and should not
make war on any Greek state (as if Rome was allied to any Greeks and
could demand their protection). Three ambassadors were sent, probably
in the spring of 200, to carry this ultimatum through Greece to Philip
who had returned to Macedonia; at the same time they were to stir up
pro-Roman feeling in Greece itself, to confer with Attalus and Rhodes,
and to visit Syria and Egypt with the object of mediating between the two
countries and sounding Antiochus' real intentions.[6]

In Greece the ambassadors were received none too cordially until they
reached Athens, where events played into their hands. By a selfish
neutrality the Athenians had kept out of the national movements of
Greece but had recently been forced to face the question of friendship or
enmity towards Philip. They had put to death two Acarnanian citizens
who had forced their way into the Eleusinian Mysteries (autumn 201),
and in the following spring the Acarnanians responded by devastating
Attica with help from their ally Philip. Athens did not reply by an
immediate declaration of war on Philip, but received help from Rhodes
and Attalus when a Macedonian squadron seized four of her warships.
Thus when the Roman ambassadors reached the Piraeus they met Attalus
who, with the help of Rome's promise to assist, persuaded Athens to
declare war on Philip (about May 200); however much Rome may have
contributed to this decision the responsibility must ultimately rest on
Athens herself. When Nicanor, a Macedonian commander, attacked the
suburbs of Athens, the Romans intervened and gave him Rome's
ultimatum to take to Philip. Then, as their anti-Macedonian appeals
found little favour with the Aetolians and Achaeans, the Roman embassy
went to Rhodes.

When the Athenians sent a certain Cephisodorus to Egypt, Rhodes,
Pergamum, Crete and Aetolia, he obtained little direct help and
proceeded to Rome which he reached in July, about the time when the
Senate again appealed to the Roman people to declare war on Philip, this
time with success.[7] Meanwhile Philip sent a general to ravage Attica, and
he himself after campaigning in Thrace besieged Abydos. Here he
received a formal *indictio belli* from Aemilius Lepidus, one of the Roman

ambassadors from Rhodes. In order to leave Philip no loophole, further demands were added to the previous ultimatum, namely, that he should make reparation to Rhodes as well as Attalus, and should respect all Egyptian dependencies. Philip accepted the challenge, stormed Abydos and returned home where he learnt that Sulpicius had landed near Apollonia with two legions. The Roman ambassadors meanwhile proceeded to Antiochus in the hope of securing his neutrality, and were met with cordiality and evasion. On their way back to Rome they called at Alexandria to report their failure to mediate with Antiochus.

3. THE CAUSES OF THE WAR

Events show that the Senate decided to fight Philip, but no authoritative statement supplies the reason. Thus the ground has been left free for modern historians to suggest the motives of Roman policy, which has been expounded as varying between the extremes of pure altruism and unscrupulous Machiavellianism. Two fundamental points are clear. First, the people did not want war. Their objection was natural enough: their numbers were depleted, agriculture was almost ruined, taxes were high, and they needed rest after the Hannibalic War. Secondly, there was little, if any, legal sanction for the war. The *ius fetiale* only allowed wars in defence of the state or of her oathbound allies (*socii*), while now the appellant peoples – Rhodes, Pergamum, Aetolia, and perhaps Egypt and Athens – were probably only *amici*, and some not even that, on whose behalf Rome was not bound to intervene. Rome had bound herself to her Italian *socii* by permanent *foedera* by which the ally supplied an annual military contingent and was not allowed to maintain neutrality. But in Greece and the east she found a different type of alliance: temporary alliance for a definite purpose and friendship in peacetime with the right to maintain neutrality. So Rome had adapted herself to her environment and had entered into relations of friendship (φιλία *amicitia*) with various states (e.g. with Egypt in 273 BC). Neither party was to fight the other; neutrality, if desired, must be respected; mutual help was not obligatory; such help, if supplied, would not be subordinate to Roman commanders, as were the contingents from *socii; amici* were formally enrolled but not by treaty. Now that Rome had adapted herself to Greek customs in dealing with Greek states, the question was raised: What was the position of *amici* in fetial law? When this was referred to the fetial priests it was decided to disregard the distinction between *amici* and *socii*, and for the occasion to extend the provisions of the *ius fetiale* over the *amici.* A phrase which had no legal standing was coined – *socius et amicus* – and the law was stretched a point to meet a present need.[8] But though perhaps by the Senate's wish the legal and religious difficulties were met, Rome did not in fact need to intervene on behalf of her 'friends' unless she so willed. Why then did she intervene?

The first and most obvious explanation is that Rome started a policy of systematic conquest: aggressive imperialism and militarism were the keynotes of the day. This theory, particularly in so far as it envisages desire for territory as Rome's object, must be rejected. After the Hannibalic War Rome annexed no Carthaginian territory in Africa; after this war with Philip she took no land and did not even claim Illyricum. If land was needed, the West offered better and richer ground for expansion. Spain, the Eldorado of the ancient world, had been left on her hands, while the colonization of the Po valley was uncompleted. But in fact the devastated land of Italy itself needed all her attention. There is little evidence to show that the spirit of military imperialism affected Rome's policy during the first decade of the second century – whatever its influence later. It was too soon after a life-and-death struggle, of which the issue had been uncertain almost to the end, for such a sense of power and superiority to arise which would drive on a people when they most needed rest. The day when Rome could justly be called 'that old unquestioned pirate of the land' was not yet. With militarism, commerce may also be rejected as an important cause of the war: the bulk of Roman trade was too small to influence her policy. Trade may have followed the flag, but it hardly pointed the way for it.[9]

To turn to the other extreme, the motive may have been an altruistic love of the Greeks, which led Rome to adopt what Tenney Frank has called 'sentimental politics'. The glory of the Greek world which was capturing the imagination of men, as it did again at the Renaissance, may have inspired the Romans to strike a blow in defence of the liberty of Greek states and thus gain for the 'barbarians' of the west the respect of the civilized world. A more cynical view, which rejects 'an over-romantic ardent sympathy for the Greeks', suggests that such a motive was used by Rome as a mere pretext. 'The Roman nobility had steeped itself in Hellenic culture, but had no tenderness for Greeks, as the late war had shown plainly enough. ... Their philhellenism confined itself to the things of the spirit . . . they were going to use a philhellenic policy against Philip . . . because it suited their purpose, not through love of Greece.'[10]

But between the extremes of militarism and philhellenism a middle course can be traced. Rome may have adopted a policy of defensive, rather than offensive imperialism. With the balance of powers upset in the east and with Philip launched on a career of conquest and trampling on his neighbours' rights, what guarantee had Rome that he would not turn against Italy when he was sufficiently strong, even if an immediate attack was improbable? May not Rome, through fear of ultimately being forced to fight in self-defence, have tried to forestall Philip? Livy at any rate describes how the consuls tried to stir the people to war by painting in lurid colours the dangers to be expected from Philip's aggression. The objection to this theory is that the Senate can hardly have had much real anxiety about Philip; it may explain how the Senate drove the people to war, but it hardly explains the Senate's own policy. To counter this difficulty it has been proposed to substitute Antiochus for Philip in the role of chief villain: it was fear of Antiochus that was the deciding factor with the Senate, who were suddenly converted to a warlike policy by the appeal of Rhodes and Attalus.[11] What these ambassadors brought home to the Senate was the danger of Antiochus' attitude: they were too skilful to emphasize their own grievances against Philip, which would hardly move the Senate, but having got wind of the coalition between Philip and Antiochus they used this information to scare Rome. Antiochus, the conqueror of the east, who had just returned from following the victorious route of Alexander to India, loomed large amid the mist of fears and rumours. What if he combined with Philip and concentrated in Greece as a base of operations against Italy? Now was the moment to intervene in Greece; not to subjugate it, which would have allowed the monarchs to pose as liberators, but to free it and then throw over it the aegis of permanent protection. If the Senate in appealing to the people harped on danger from Philip it was perhaps less because they themselves feared much from that quarter, than because they wished to use Philip's name as a handle where the more illusive and shadowy Antiochus would fail to touch a practical people. To this appeal to self-protection and self-interest the Senate may have added the claims of Attalus and Greek civilization and even perhaps of Athens. The idea of defensive imperialism, of establishing a protectorate over Greece for the mutual benefit of Rome and Greece (for it is unnecessary to deny any genuine feeling of interest in the welfare of Greece) was probably the determining cause of the Second Macedonian War.[12]

But it is perhaps a mistake to seek too cut and dried an explanation of the policy of a people who, like the British, proverbially had a genius for muddling through. Rome had sought to avoid interfering with the balance of powers: a policy which though selfish was reasonable and pacific. But circumstances were too strong. The desire to safeguard her future, possibly to punish Philip for his past conduct, possibly also to pose as the patron of the Greeks whose past glories she so admired, all swept her into the vortex of the eastern disturbance. Her actions were not the result of aggressive imperialism, commercial exploitation or territorial covetousness.

4. THE SECOND MACEDONIAN WAR

When Rome and Philip settled down to play the game of war, the dice were heavily weighted in Rome's favour, though the Greeks at first acted with great circumspection. Beside Rhodes and Pergamum, which could not put land forces into the field against Macedon, Rome only had the help of Athens, which provided a good naval base in the Aegean, and of the semi-barbarous princes of Illyria, Dardania, and Athamania in the north; the Aetolians were waiting to see which way the wind would blow. Philip's Greek allies were equally slow to rally to his banner. The Achaean League, his nominal ally, sent no material help, though some volunteers came from Boeotia, Acarnania and Epirus. The wealthier Greeks distrusted his ideas of social revolution, and the upper classes in most towns inclined rather towards Rome.[13] Finally, two savage raids on Attica in the autumn of 200 increased his unpopularity. The initial neutrality and caution of Aetolia and Achaea was natural, because the Hannibalic War had revealed the measure of Rome's strength. They could hardly doubt that ultimate victory would fall to Rome; by taking up arms they might delay this, but then they would have to face Rome's vengeance. Or even if they thought victory possible, what would they gain by it? Might it not make Philip's hand on Greece still heavier to bear? And Rome was coming, nominally at any rate, to protect a Greek city from Macedon.

The Romans can scarcely have anticipated great difficulty in launching an attack on Philip. Their naval supremacy allowed them to strike wherever they wished. They could devastate part of the enemy's land before Philip could concentrate his strength there. Their own and their allies' forces could surround him on most sides. True, if he made a spectacular start, he might hope to turn the balance in Greece in his favour and elicit help from Achaea and the continued neutrality of Aetolia; but otherwise he must expect to see more Greeks gradually rallying to the Roman cause and the net being drawn more tightly around him. Further, the Romans could count on their big battalions; if one expeditionary force was defeated, they could send out another, but Philip would find it very difficult to raise a second army if his forces were worsted in open battle. He was thus forced to renounce the offensive and plan a cautious but energetic defensive, however alien it was to his impulsive nature. He must try to wear down the Romans' patience. After all, they were weary of war, and the struggle in Greece was not vital, as they did not premeditate territorial expansion: possibly it might be fought to a standstill. The First Macedonian War provided good reason for such a hope; the Romans in weariness had left the Greeks to settle it by themselves; and their final intervention had been somewhat half-hearted. It had also trained Philip in the requisite strategy. Small fights, plundering raids, and surprise attacks had gradually exhausted both sides. But such a defensive strategy, although the best that Philip could devise, had many drawbacks: he must divide his forces to protect all fronts, and every loss he suffered, every unpunished devastation or strategic retreat would encourage his allies to desert and would drive the neutrals into the enemy's arms. But despite its shortcomings this plan was the only feasible reply to Rome's invasion. It was impossible to rally the Greeks to unite against a foreign invader. The Greek spirit had seldom permitted that, while now Rome was coming to protect Greece from Macedon. Thus Philip did not lack boldness in entering the lists in so unequal a contest.[14]

Landing with two legions near Apollonia in the autumn of 200, Sulpicius Galba sent a force to ravage the Macedonian frontier and a squadron to protect Athens. The former captured Antipatreia, the latter raided Chalcis *en route*. The next year Sulpicius planned to encircle Macedon; the Dardanians were to attack from the north, the Athamanes from the south, the navy from the east at Chalcidice. He himself advanced boldly from the west along the line of the later Via Egnatia and penetrated into Macedonia notwithstanding difficulties of commissariat and communications. Philip meantime advanced from Pella and after some manoeuvring gave battle at Ottolobus, where he suffered a slight defeat, which Sulpicius did not follow up. Though trivial, the engagement had the important result of deciding the Aetolians to support Rome. From the plain of Lyncestis (modern Monastir) Sulpicius might have turned north to join his Dardanian allies, but he preferred to march south, perhaps to join the Aetolians. Philip in vain contested his passage through the pass of Banitza and was again defeated. But hampered by practical difficulties in the heart of the enemy's country Sulpicius prudently turned westwards and returned to the Adriatic after completing a great circuit. Philip did not attempt to hinder him, for danger threatened on other fronts. His general beat back the Dardanians who had entered Paeonia, while he himself hurried south to Gomphi to drive back the Aetolians who had broken into Thessaly. The Roman naval attack in the Aegean, though unopposed by Philip, had produced only small successes apart from its capture of Oreus. Thus the year's campaign, notwithstanding Philip's activity, had seriously damaged his prestige in Greece; Aetolia had sided with Rome, while Achaea was tending in this direction and was only stopped by certain territorial concessions from Philip.

Sulpicius' successor found that Philip had occupied a strong position on his western front near Antigoneia, which controlled the Aoüs valley to Thessaly and covered the Drinus valley to Epirus, thus preventing the Romans from joining the Aetolians by either valley.[15] Evidently Philip realized the need to take the offensive, at least in appearance, and not to wait for a Roman army to invade his territory. The Roman commander, however, was almost immediately replaced by the consul T. Quinctius Flamininus, who arrived with reinforcements in the spring of 198. On the banks of the Aoüs the Epirotes arranged a meeting between Flamininus and Philip. Flamininus declared that Philip must abandon all the Greek states which he held and must offer compensation where actual restoration was impossible. Philip was ready to abandon what he had taken, but not what he had inherited, and to submit the question of indemnities to arbitration: that is, he was clearly prepared to sacrifice much. When Flamininus suggested that he should start with Thessaly, Philip indignantly broke off negotiations. From this it is clear, as it must have been clear to the Greeks, what Rome's intention was. Philip was to be driven out of Greece. The terms he offered might have prevented the war, but were inadequate to stop it when once started. If they were accepted Macedon would remain an autonomous great power, though humbled. But future peace and security could only be obtained by breaking the power of Macedon. As Scipio had realized that lasting peace could not be secured merely by driving Hannibal from Italy, so now Flamininus wished to conquer Macedon and to deprive her, like Carthage, of an independent foreign policy. His rousing proclamation not only expressed his own desire, but showed the official policy of the Senate.[16]

When negotiations had failed, Flamininus, unable to force Philip's position, turned it by guile. He learnt of a track which led round behind the enemy and by this means he was able during a battle to fall on their flank. Philip was forced to retire; after considerable loss he rallied his men and withdrew along the Aoüs valley and the Zygus Pass to the vale of Tempe. The Romans could now overrun Thessaly and central Greece.

Their allies, the Aetolians and Athamanes, promptly fell on Thessaly and captured Gomphi. Flamininus also approached through Epirus and the Peneus valley, but finding that many strongholds withstood him he turned south towards the Corinthian Gulf, where the allied fleet arrived after capturing Eretria. Here Flamininus brought pressure to bear on the Achaean League and at last won their support by promising to help them recover Corinth. However, Corinth and its Macedonian garrison unexpectedly resisted the attack, and shortly afterwards Argos seceded from Achaea to Philip.

With so much of Greece slipping from his grasp, notwithstanding events at Corinth and Argos, Philip was ready to seek terms; in November a conference was held at Nicaea in Locris. Polybius (xviii, 1 – 11) gives an interesting account of the proceedings, at which Philip's sardonic humour found full scope. It is unnecessary to follow the details : Rome clearly pursued the same policy, and though Philip was willing to concede more than earlier in the year he stubbornly refused to surrender the 'Fetters of Greece', Demetrias, Chalcis and Acrocorinth. But Rome, and still more her allies, insisted on the complete evacuation of Greece ; for the allies hoped to free Greece from Macedonian and Roman alike and so deprive Rome of the excuse or necessity for future intervention. The Senate refused to accept Philip's terms, broke off the negotiations and prolonged Flamininus' command.

Philip's desperate efforts to retain what he still held met with little success. Unable to protect Argos he handed it over to the tyrannical king of Sparta, Nabis, who betrayed his trust. After instituting a reign of terror in Argos, Nabis calmly threw in his lot with the Romans, who thus controlled the whole Peloponnese. Next Boeotia fell away from Philip, after Flamininus had thrown a body of Roman troops into the Theban assembly to influence the voting. Thus virtually all Philip's Greek allies, except Acarnania, Chalcis and Corinth, had been brought over to Rome ; the Hellenic League was broken. This success, which had been reached partly by arms, partly by diplomacy, was due largely to Flamininus. He was a genuine admirer of Greek culture and met the Greeks on their own ground. His magnetic personality, his enthusiasm, the tact and adaptability which he displayed instead of the Romans' all too common blunt and almost brutal self-assertiveness, all appealed to the Greeks. In his un-Roman qualities he resembled Scipio Africanus, though he lacked Scipio's strength and loftiness of character. If Rome wished to free Greece there were few men better suited than Flamininus to accomplish this with less loss of blood and without robbing the Greeks of their remaining shreds of self-respect. Here was a Roman consul seeking their friendship and promising their freedom, not spurning their ideals and exposing their weakness.[17]

The end was at hand. In 197 Philip marched south with 23,000 infantry and 2,000 horse. At Pherae he came into contact with the Roman army which was slightly larger. The ground was not suited for a battle, so both armies marched westwards on the opposite sides of a range of hills named Cynoscephalae (Karadagh). Near Scotussa detachments of the two armies met unexpectedly and a general engagement ensued.[18] On the rough ground on the southern slopes of Cynoscephalae the legion faced the phalanx. The right wing of each army was successful, the left was retreating. Victory hung in the balance, when an unknown tribune decided on his own initiative what ought to be done. Detaching twenty maniples from the two rear ranks of the victorious Roman right wing, he led them to the left where they outflanked the enemy and charged on them from the rear. The battle was won; to the astonishment of the Greek world the Roman legion had defeated the Macedonian phalanx. This was achieved partly owing to the nature of the ground and Philip's lack of cavalry, but mainly through the tactical flexibility which Scipio Africanus had given to the legion. The troops employed by Flamininus were largely composed of Scipio's veterans from Spain and Africa and there can be little doubt where the tribune had learnt his lesson in tactics. Flamininus was the victor of Cynoscephalae, but he was building on the foundations laid by another. And he was soon to realize that it was almost more difficult to make peace than war among the bickering states of Greece.

5. THE SETTLEMENT OF GREECE

After the battle the Aetolians, who had contributed largely to the victory of the Roman right wing, were eager to invade Macedon and to destroy its power once and for all. But this suited neither Rome nor Philip. Sweeping the Aetolians aside Flamininus announced that in answer to Philip's overtures and subject to the Senate's approval he had determined to make peace with Philip on the terms laid down at Nicaea, namely, that Philip should abandon all his dependencies outside Macedon. Philip was too clear-sighted to refuse. Further resistance might involve the extinction of the independent existence of Macedon. True, he might hope for the intervention of his ally Antiochus. But if, when the Syrian came, he was too weak to treat him as an equal, he would be regarded as a mere dependant like the kings of Bithynia and Cappadocia. How much better to retain his kingdom intact and to renew war on more equal terms if Antiochus did come later, than to risk all on a gambler's chance.

Flamininus also was ready for peace, not only for fear that he might be superseded in his command, but for very solid impersonal reasons. To destroy Macedon utterly was to court danger on all sides. It would remove the barrier which held back the barbarian Thracians, Illyrians and Gauls from the Greek frontiers.[19] If this barrier were to be removed either Rome or Greece would have to step in; but Rome was unwilling to undertake military occupation in the Balkan peninsula, while to allow the Greeks to advance in this direction would lead to interminable rivalry and confusion. Further, a prostrate Macedon would benefit not only Greek and barbarian but also Antiochus, who having wrested Coele-Syria from Ptolemy was free to re-establish his authority beyond the Taurus Mountains in Asia Minor and on the Asiatic shores of the Aegean. Although their relations with him had officially been friendly, the Romans could not but see that he had a formal right to intervene, since he was allied with Philip to share the Ptolemaic dependencies, while Rome had insisted on the restitution of the territory in Asia which Philip had occupied. But while Antiochus was not averse to seeing Macedon weakened, as that would give him supremacy in the Graeco-Oriental world, he can hardly have been eager to see the Macedonian control in the Balkans and Aegean merely replaced by that of Rome. Thus many motives, chief among them fear of Antiochus, induced Flamininus to meet Philip at Tempe, where despite the protests of Rome's allies an armistice was concluded during which all parties were to submit all details to the Senate. The Aetolians in particular were disillusioned and embittered; the Greeks were forced to see that Rome intended to settle affairs in her own way.[20]

Anxiety about insurrections in Cisalpine Gaul and Spain (pp. 292ff.) and still more about Antiochus, induced Rome to conclude peace with Philip on terms not unduly severe (winter 197–196). The terms, which were expounded in a senatorial decree, showed that the peace was more than a treaty with Philip; it was a manifesto to Greece and a warning to Antiochus: all the rest of the Greeks in Asia and Europe were to be free and governed by their own laws; the Greek cities subject to or held by Philip were to be surrendered to Rome; he was to evacuate and free certain cities in Asia Minor; all prisoners, deserters and his fleet to be surrendered; an indemnity of 1,000 talents to be paid, half at once, half by annual instalments. Yet Philip was not humbled as Carthage had been.[21]

In the spring of 196 ten commissioners were sent to Greece with the senatorial decree to settle affairs there with Flamininus, who had pacified some trouble in Boeotia by a show of force. They then published the Senate's decision, which was received with some uneasiness : what would happen to the 'Fetters of Greece' when surrendered to Rome? To allay this disquiet and to prove the sincerity of the Senate's intentions, Flamininus staged his famous declaration at the Isthmian Games. To the assembled Greeks a herald proclaimed that a number of Greek peoples whom he named were by order of the Roman Senate and the proconsul Titus Quinctius Flamininus declared free without garrisons or tribute to be governed by their own ancestral laws. Flamininus, his ambition at last sated, was almost mobbed by the enthusiastic crowd. The proclamation, together with the Senate's manifesto, was the high-water mark of Rome's philhellenic policy. She proclaimed freedom for Greece, and more, she proclaimed herself to be the permanent protectress of Greek liberty throughout the world, a liberty to be respected alike by the Greeks themselves, by the conquered Philip and by the aggressive Antiochus (see further p. 259).

This glorious moment was soon followed by a reaction in Greece. Although Rome imposed no tribute or garrisons, she was still the protectress and as such proceeded to 'settle Hellenic affairs'. The ten commissioners started on this disillusioning task and had accomplished enough by the end of the year to allow them to return to Rome, leaving Flamininus to complete the settlement. It is hardly necessary to follow the details : the Aetolians claimed back all their past conquests, but were only granted Phocis, Eastern Locris and part of Thessaly ; the rest of Thessaly was grouped into four small federal states, while Euboea was made into a separate league ; Corinth was added to the Achaean League. But before returning home the commission had accomplished two things of importance. An alliance was concluded with Philip, Antiochus' former ally, so that Rome might now hope to use him against Antiochus ; and secondly the disgruntled Aetolians, who were on the point of revolting, were persuaded to refer their troubles to Rome. But the commissioners could not advise the immediate evacuation of Greece, however ominous this might seem to the Greeks, who began to doubt Rome's integrity. Friendship with Philip, the pacification of Aetolia, the continued military occupation of Greece, all pointed in one direction – Antiochus, who had crossed to Europe.

In 195 Flamininus assembled delegates from all Greek states in Corinth to confer about liberating Argos from the clutches of Nabis of Sparta. All voted in favour of this crusade, except the Aetolians whose claims had not yet been settled. An allied army and navy was launched against Sparta and the power of Nabis was broken. But Flamininus would not go as far as his allies desired; as with Philip, he wished to cripple, but not destroy. Once again it was the Romans and not the allies who dictated the terms, which included the surrender by Nabis of Argos and other towns and of his fleet, an indemnity, and the renouncing of the right to make war or alliances. At the Nemean festival the freedom of Argos was proclaimed and the city re-entered the Achaean League. In the next year, 194, Flamininus persuaded the Senate, in spite of the danger from Antiochus, to redeem its pledge and to recall the army from Greece. He presided over a pan-Hellenic conference at Corinth, where he announced the Roman evacuation of Greece and amid much fatherly advice he urged the Greeks to make right use of their new freedom. The Roman garrisons were withdrawn from all towns, including the three 'Fetters', and Flamininus returned to Rome, where he celebrated a magnificent triumph. His ideals and ambitions were fulfilled. The Greeks were free, under a Roman protectorate. But they had paid a heavy price for their freedom and many besides the Aetolians looked askance at the settlement and the new regime. How they would respond to their fresh responsibilities the future alone would show.

XII

ROME AND
ANTIOCHUS

1. THE DIPLOMATIC CONFLICT

Antiochus had landed in Europe. After conquering Palestine, he turned to his hereditary possessions in Asia Minor and Thrace, now held by Ptolemy or Philip. In 197 he started a military promenade along the coast of Asia Minor. He was checked momentarily by Rhodes, who refused him the opportunity of joining his ally Philip. But when news of Cynoscephalae arrived, the danger was past and he easily bought over the Rhodians by some territorial concessions in Caria. He gradually made his way to the Hellespont, though respecting the boundaries which he had long ago guaranteed to Attalus.[1] Eumenes, Attalus' successor, however, was alarmed to find Pergamum surrounded on all sides by the advancing tide. At his advice the cities of Smyrna and Lampsacus, who had refused to submit to Antiochus and were being taken by force, appealed for protection to Rome, although they had no substantial claim on her. The appeal was welcomed and the Senate, which was concluding peace with Philip, issued its proclamation that 'Greeks in Europe and Asia were to be free and autonomous'. Beside this warning, which extended their philhellenic policy to Asia, the Senate tried to embarrass Antiochus by sending to him an ambassador who was to protect the interests of Egypt which Rome had conveniently neglected for three years. Undaunted, Antiochus crossed to Europe by the early summer of 196 and established himself on the Thracian coast. 'To him this was his last conquest, the recovery of the last piece of his heritage; but in the eyes of the Romans, Thrace could only be the first stage of an invasion planned to drive them from Greece.' (Holleaux, *CAH*, VIII, p. 184.)

A diplomatic duel followed which merely caused Rome and Antiochus to harden their hearts. Antiochus who had sent envoys to Flamininus at Corinth, received a brusque reply after the Isthmian Games: 'he must abstain from attacking autonomous cities in Asia and go to war with none of them; he must evacuate those which had been subject to Ptolemy or Philip; he was forbidden to cross into Europe with an army (which he had as a matter of fact already done); for no Greek henceforth was to be attacked in war or to be enslaved to any one; finally ambassadors would wait on Antiochus.'[2] These ambassadors, supported by the knowledge of Rome's alliance with Philip, explained the situation to Antiochus in much the same terms. The king replied that he could not understand the Romans interfering in Asia when he did not in Italy; he was merely recovering his ancestral kingdom in Thrace. He then played his trump card: the Romans need not worry about Ptolemy's possessions because he had just concluded an alliance with him. The Romans were outwitted. Though not admitting their claim to interfere, Antiochus took the wind out of their sails still more by offering to submit the cases of Lampsacus and Smyrna to the arbitration of Rhodes. Matters were thus brought to a standstill. The king would not admit, and the Romans would not abate their demands. Neither side wanted war and the question might have been settled amicably by an equitable recognition and definition of the king's 'sphere of influence' in Thrace. But Rome could neither believe that his intentions were pacific, nor tolerate a great power in the east which might one day grow to rivalry and hostility. The conference was interrupted by a report of Ptolemy's death. This was false, but it occasioned the ending of the king's minority and his accession to the throne as Epiphanes Eucharistos (an event celebrated on the Rosetta stone).

The next year, 195, Antiochus sent an offer to Flamininus to renew conversations about arranging a treaty of friendship with Rome; when told to deal direct with the Senate, he refused. Yet he had shown that he was ready to treat on his own terms and had no evil intentions against Rome. Rome's fears were increased by the movements of Hannibal, whose political opponents alleged, probably falsely, that he was intriguing with Antiochus. The Senate foolishly rejected Scipio's generous advice of non-interference and thereby drove Hannibal to join Antiochus (pp. 306f). This seriously complicated the eastern situation and fanned into a flame Hannibal's latent hatred of Rome. In 194 Scipio, elected to his second consulship, urged that Greece should remain one of the consular provinces, because he sincerely believed that it must be held a little longer as a barrier against the Syrian; to evacuate it would create a vacuum into which Antiochus with Hannibal behind him would inevitably be drawn. Scipio keenly supported a philhellenic policy, but he saw clearly the danger of pressing it to extremes. Yet to occupy Greece any longer would have strained to the breaking point the belief of the Greeks in Rome's sincerity. So the Senate followed Flamininus' advice and Greece was evacuated. But Scipio showed how deep his fears were by founding eight maritime colonies at unprotected sea-ports in southern Italy; if Hannibal should provoke an invasion of Italy, he should find it prepared.

In the winter of 194–193 Antiochus sent two envoys to propose a treaty of friendship with Rome. This was in effect an ultimatum of peace or war. If the offer was accepted, it would imply the recognition by Rome of Antiochus' authority in Thrace and Asia; if it was rejected, war might follow. But Flamininus, as the spokesman of the Senate, proposed a compromise: let Antiochus renounce his claims either to Thrace or to the autonomous Greek cities of Asia. Of the two alternatives, Rome apparently hoped to realize the evacuation of Thrace, since Flamininus told delegates of the Asiatic towns, then in Rome, that Rome would uphold their claims unless Antiochus withdrew from Europe. It is perhaps too severe to suppose that Rome's interference on behalf of these towns had been a mere diplomatic manoeuvre, but clearly Rome was willing to sacrifice their claims to avert war, especially as they might not suffer severely under Syrian rule. Yet it is difficult to believe that the Senate really anticipated that these terms would be acceptable to Antiochus; perhaps they were merely trying to postpone the evil day. The proposal is interesting, for it shows that Rome was now ready to adopt from the Greeks the theory of 'spheres of influence', and Antiochus was perhaps foolish in refusing to sacrifice his rather useless European annexe.[3] But such a compromise could only be lasting if Rome could once and for all overcome her mistrust of Antiochus. In any case little was achieved; the king's representatives, having no power to compromise, withdrew. The Romans contented themselves with sending an embassy to the east to obtain further information and to continue the negotiations. The sequel was not happy. After long delay a conference was held at Ephesus (193), where delegates from the Greek cities were instigated by Eumenes to speak out boldly.[4] This merely annoyed Antiochus further, negotiations again broke down, and when the embassy returned to Rome in the late summer war was looming large on the horizon. The same year the Aetolians invited Antiochus to liberate Greece.

When news reached Rome that Antiochus was preparing for war with the help of Hannibal, a commission headed by Africanus was sent to Carthage, where Hannibal's agent Ariston was fomenting trouble. Little could be accomplished because of the extreme delicacy of relations with Antiochus, but doubtless the current rumours were investigated. Hannibal was said to be urging Antiochus to give him 10,000 infantry, 1,000 cavalry and 100 ships. With this force he would stir up Carthage against Rome and then land in Italy; meanwhile Antiochus was to lead his main army into Europe and to paralyse Rome's efforts by taking up a strong position in Greece. It is uncertain what truth such rumour embodied: Antiochus certainly did not approve of a more ambitious scheme which Hannibal is said to have proposed later at a council of war at Demetrias. Probably the details of this first plan are exaggerated. Hannibal could scarcely have planned an immediate invasion of Italy with so small a force and such limited naval resources. It would be difficult to reinforce the infantry, as the Carthaginians, who were now without their Spanish and Numidian allies, would find it hard to raise mercenaries; and they would be attacked by Masinissa in their own country. The force landing in Italy could not expect to evoke widespread rebellion in the south before being overwhelmed, while if they landed in the north they would be too far from their base and from their objective, and might meet the fate of Hasdrubal or Mago. Hannibal may have suggested the invasion of Italy as an ultimate object; probably his immediate proposal was to stir up Carthage. This would satisfy his hatred and suit Antiochus' plan by distracting the attention of Rome away from Greece; if it succeeded beyond their hopes, Antiochus would welcome the rise of Carthage as a power to balance Rome in the western Mediterranean. Thus Antiochus probably encouraged Hannibal to make trouble in Carthage, but their *agent provocateur* failed and affairs in Greece soon claimed all Antiochus' attention and precipitated him into the war with Rome.[5]

2. THE WAR IN GREECE

The Aetolians, bitterly disappointed at the peace which Flamininus had imposed on Greece and at his casual treatment of themselves, sought relief by trying to combine the three kings, Philip, Nabis and Antiochus, against Rome (summer 193). Antiochus received their overtures, but did not seem disposed to take immediate action. Philip rebuffed them; he remembered how they had urged the Romans to overthrow his kingdom. Nabis, however, responded, but too quickly. Breaking his treaty with Rome he fell on the freed towns of the Laconian coast. The Achaeans under Philopoemen denounced Nabis' conduct to Rome and then defeated him in battle and blockaded Sparta.[6] The Romans sent a small squadron to operate against Nabis, while during the winter Flamininus went to Greece to bring his personal influence to bear; he was soon joined by Eumenes. He quickly ended the war in the Peloponnese on the basis of the *status quo* (spring 192). Nabis was lucky to have escaped so lightly, but the Achaeans were disappointed at not being allowed to press home their victory.

Despite the failure of their ambitious coalition the Aetolians continued on their course, buoyed up by the hope of winning Demetrias, where considerable opposition had been shown to Flamininus who had accomplished a disquieting journey through Greece. Further, Antiochus now seemed ready to take action, and his envoy announced that he was willing to join the Aetolians in restoring Greek freedom (March 192). They then formally asked him to deliver Greece and to settle their quarrel with Rome. Thus Antiochus could now play the same rôle of liberator to the cities of Greece as Rome had to the Greek cities of Asia: not yet by open war, but by armed mediation. This alarmed Rome. She hurriedly prepared 70 quinqueremes to protect Sicily and to form a reserve; an army was sent from Bruttium to Brundisium and an emergency force was levied. But while Rome prepared and Antiochus delayed, the Aetolians acted. They proposed to seize Demetrias and Chalcis to facilitate Antiochus' landing and to occupy Sparta in order to check the Achaeans. At Sparta they succeeded in assassinating Nabis, but were soon defeated and massacred; as a result Sparta was driven into the arms of the Achaean League. At Chalcis they failed completely. But they won Demetrias, and could thus offer Antiochus a secure base. But they had alienated Philip still more, for he had long coveted Demetrias. After further hesitation Antiochus landed a detachment of his army at Demetrias and marched to Lamia (autumn 192).

War, though not formally declared, was now inevitable. Antiochus, however, was not ready; he had only started preparing during the previous year, and it was a long task to mobilize the resources of his vast empire. But now that the Aetolians had precipitated the crisis, he must face a war which he did not really want. He was not going to fight in Greece from lust of conquest, nor even merely to assert his rights in Thrace. He desired that Rome should recognize him as an equal, and that he should be permitted to maintain his empire unhampered, and to develop it freely and in peace. To this end he had constantly tried to obtain friendship with the Romans, who failed to believe in the sincerity of his intentions and feared his increasing activity. To his offer of friendship they had replied by demands, unaccompanied by any concessions; that is, they insisted on asserting their superiority, not from militaristic aims but because they feared that the king, if recognized as an equal, would not be content to remain as such. Antiochus' aims were reflected in his method of war.[7] He did not wish to destroy Rome, but merely to make a military demonstration which would lead to his recognition as an equal power. Thus he rejected any idea of invading Italy, and while perhaps countenancing Hannibal's plan for Carthaginian co-operation he turned to a limited offensive in Greece. Here he could challenge Rome's supremacy with some prospect of success. If this was not immediately forthcoming he might hope that the Romans would tire of a long war in which their interests did not warrant great sacrifice. And even if they gained the upper hand they would hardly seek to destroy him root and branch: they had not pushed the First Punic War or their contest against Philip to this extreme. Thus he might hope for the success of his limited project, but he underestimated the perseverance and the distrust of Rome.

Although the smallness of the force with which the new liberator of the Greeks appeared caused much disappointment, he was somewhat grudgingly elected generalissimo by the Aetolians. Disturbances in his favour in many towns were soon checked. For instance, trouble at Athens was calmed by the presence of Flamininus and perhaps of Eumenes, supported by the eloquence of another Roman legate, M. Porcius Cato, who had advanced the Roman cause in Patrae, Aegium and Corinth. Antiochus was rebuffed by Chalcis and Boeotia, and in November Flamininus succeeded in persuading the Achaean League to declare war on the king and his Aetolian allies. But while Antiochus was busy storming Chalcis, a body of 500 Roman troops marching thither from the fleet on the Boeotian coast was attacked and almost annihilated by one of his generals at Delium. This act may have been justified from the military and legal point of view – for Rome's allies, the Achaeans, had now declared war on him – but Antiochus could no longer pretend that he had come to liberate the Greeks without fighting Rome. Further, now that he was technically the aggressor, Rome could start the war before it was formally declared by a vote of the people. Antiochus at last captured Chalcis so that the rest of Euboea and Boeotia went over to him. Then he conducted a successful campaign against Thessaly as far as Larissa, but the appearance of a Roman detachment at Gonni led him to suspend operations in January 191. The dramatic appearance of this Roman force was a severe blow: it revealed that Rome had entered the war and that Philip was siding with Rome, for only with Philip's consent could the troops have come through his country. Rome had in fact secured the support of Philip by promising that he might keep Demetrias and any other Thessalian cities which he took from the Aetolians. Hannibal was said to be urging Antiochus to a larger view: his son Seleucus should attack Macedon through Thrace to prevent Philip's co-operation with Rome; part of the fleet should attack the west coast of Italy, while part hindered the Romans crossing to Greece; Antiochus should advance to Apollonia to protect Greece and to seem ready to invade Italy. If ever Hannibal formulated this plan or hoped that Antiochus would follow it, his hopes were now effectively broken by Philip's declaration of friendship with Rome. The war must now be fought in Greece.

Realization of this affected the plans of Rome also. In the autumn of 192 a praetor named Baebius had crossed from southern Italy to Apollonia with only a few troops; until Antiochus' plans were known a large force could not be sent, as reserves must be held in Italy in case of diversions in Africa, Sicily or even Italy. But when Philip, actuated by self-interest and jealousy of Antiochus, had shown his hand, Rome could proceed with more energy and the Roman people formally declared war (at the beginning of the consular year 191, which by the Julian calendar was about November 192). Antiochus, however, had made the best of his opportunities. He held Demetrias and Chalcis, the whole of central Greece except Attica and Acarnania, and the greater part of Thessaly. Early in 191 he attacked Acarnania, but was soon recalled to Thessaly.

The consul M'. Acilius Glabrio landed at Apollonia with 22,000 troops in February 191, and was enabled to march at once towards Thessaly by reason of the mildness of the season and the preparations already made by Baebius and Philip. As town after town capitulated he gradually wrested all Thessaly from Antiochus. The king had received few reinforcements from Asia, while the Aetolians only sent 4,000 men; he was thus forced to fall back on Thermopylae which guarded the road to central Greece. In the famous pass he took up a position, not in the middle as Leonidas had done against the Persians, and the united Greeks against the Gauls in 279, but at the eastern gate where the sea was considerably further from the mountains than it had been in 480 BC. He strengthened his position by an earth rampart and a wall, and protected his flank by stationing half the Aetolians at Heraclea and the other half at the three forts guarding the mountain track by which the pass could be turned.[8] Acilius, who camped in the middle of the pass, launched a frontal attack but was easily beaten back, while the Aetolian force at Heraclea threatened his rear. But the inadequacy of the Aetolian contingent enabled the Romans to repeat the exploit of the Persian Hydarnes. Two ex-consuls, who were serving in the army, made the attempt by night. Valerius Flaccus, who advanced up the eastern track to join the main route over the mountains, was unable to pass the two forts. But Cato, taking the longer western route, swept past the defenders of the Callidromos path, where the Phocians had fled before the Persians three centuries earlier, and descended on the rear of the enemy's main army. The defeat was complete. Unlike Leonidas, Antiochus rode off, and collecting the panic-stricken survivors retired to Chalcis. Thence he set sail for Ephesus. The half-hearted support of his Aetolian allies and the slowness of his own mobilization thwarted his attempt to fight out the Syrian War in Europe. At one blow the Romans had driven their dreaded opponent from Greece.

The settlement of Greece was carried through the same year. Phocis, Boeotia, Chalcis and Euboea surrendered to Rome at once, but Aetolia remained obdurate. Acilius determined not merely to impose a peace on the Aetolians, from which they might recover to cause continued trouble, but to strike at the very roots of their power. When Heraclea, which commanded Thermopylae and had enabled the Aetolians to cut communications between northern and central Greece, was stormed by Acilius, the Aetolians sought peace, but they were offered such harsh terms that they determined to resist. Acilius struck a shrewd blow by laying siege to Naupactus, their principal port in the Corinthian Gulf. But such harshness was unwise, for it unduly benefited Philip, who was steadily regaining his power in the north, and it destroyed the ideal of a free Greece. Further, as a war of sieges must necessarily be protracted, it gave Antiochus longer to recover before Rome could square accounts with him. Flamininus, who meanwhile had been checking the cupidity of the Achaeans and imposing unity in the Peloponnese, ended hostilities in Aetolia by demonstrating to Acilius that the destruction of Aetolia involved the aggrandisement of Philip. He thus won for the Aetolians permission to appeal to the Senate and struck a blow at Antiochus, who still hoped for Aetolian co-operation.

3. THE WAR IN ASIA

In the war with Hannibal Scipio had maintained that future security demanded his decisive defeat, not merely his expulsion from Italy. The

Senate now believed with Scipio that Antiochus must not merely be driven out of Greece, but must be defeated in his own country and forced well back from the Greek cities of Asia Minor. Only by reducing his kingdom from the rank of a great power could permanent peace be guaranteed. There is no justification for assuming that the motive for this decision was aggressive militarism. The man best suited to face the great king was obviously Scipio Africanus, but he could not be re-elected consul without violating the constitution, since he had held this office only three years before. The consuls elected for 190 were his brother Lucius Scipio and his friend C. Laelius; the former obtained the province of Greece with the right to cross to Asia. As Lucius was less experienced, his brother Publius was 'associated' with him without specific duties and so the conqueror of Hannibal held the effective command against Antiochus.[9] The Scipios, who were to take over the two legions from Acilius, set sail with 8,000 reinforcements in March 190.

Meanwhile the Romans had determined to challenge Antiochus' supremacy at sea by preparing 100 battleships. With 50 of these C. Livius Salinator, son of the victor of Metaurus, sailed across the Aegean to join Eumenes. The Rhodians, who till then had remained neutral, had to decide their policy. If Antiochus predominated in the Aegean, their trade would suffer; but the Romans, if victorious, would hardly maintain a permanent squadron there. Further, Rhodes was ill pleased that Eumenes should derive all the advantages from victory and so she decided to cooperate with Rome, forgetting that when once the old balance of powers was destroyed, she would be virtually dependent on the goodwill of the victor. Antiochus, who was holding the Dardanelles against the possibility of a Roman invasion of Asia, sent his fleet to defeat Livius and Eumenes before they joined the Rhodians (September). An action was fought off Cape Corycus, between Ephesus and Chios, in which Antiochus' admiral, Polyxenidas, lost more than one-third of his ships. The Romans owed this important victory to their superior numbers and their grappling and boarding tactics: Antiochus was cut off from the Aetolians and deprived of the command of the sea, by which alone he might hope to contest the Roman crossing to Asia.

The Aetolian embassy which had come to Rome at the end of 191 had been offered hard terms: unconditional surrender or the immediate payment of 1000 talents and the renunciation of an independent foreign policy. Only by a decisive defeat could Rome expect to impose such conditions, which were naturally refused. Thus when the Scipios landed in Greece in April 190 they found that war had blazed out again and that

Acilius had recommenced his siege warfare by capturing Lamia and besieging Amphissa. Wishing neither to spend time breaking up the Aetolian League piece by piece nor to leave behind them an unbeaten Aetolia or a Greece in which Philip could expand freely, they offered Aetolia a six months' armistice. The Aetolians foolishly accepted, forgetting that further resistance would only be feasible if Antiochus remained unconquered; by this act they sacrificed any hope of help from him. The Scipios then despatched an energetic young man, Tiberius Sempronius Gracchus, the future son-in-law of Africanus and father of the Gracchi, to secure Philip's co-operation. Learning that the king had supplies ready, they proceeded safely through Macedon and Thrace to the Hellespont. The fact that Philip remained loyal when he had the chance of destroying the Roman army on its march through these wild countries is perhaps a testimony to the magnetic personality of Africanus, who quickly won his friendship, as shown not least perhaps by the personal letter which he wrote to Philip describing his Spanish campaigns.

At the same time a naval campaign was conducted to win control of the Hellespont and to secure communications. Antiochus had spent the winter enlarging his navy; he increased Polyxenidas' fleet to 90 warships, while Hannibal raised a second fleet in Phoenicia. A series of operations followed in which Livius and Eumenes were outmanoeuvred; Livius' successor, Aemilius Regillus, at first fared little better. Success at sea encouraged Antiochus to negotiate (May–June); he needed a breathing space before renewing the war, such as the Romans had obtained in Greece by their truce with Aetolia. But Aemilius was persuaded by Eumenes to reject the king's overtures. When news came that Hannibal was sailing up with another fleet, the Rhodians under Eudamus bravely sailed off to intercept him. Despite Hannibal's superior force Eudamus outmanoeuvred him off Side in Pamphylia and thus shared with Scipio Africanus alone the glory of having defeated Hannibal in battle. Antiochus then saw his opportunity. Only part of the Rhodian fleet under Eudamus had rejoined the Romans, while Eumenes was at Troas; so Polyxenidas was ordered to attack the numerically inferior enemy. The fleets met off Myonnesus. Eudamus skilfully prevented an enveloping movement against the Roman vessels and held the Syrians' wing while the Romans broke their centre. The battle gave the allies the command of the sea and opened the way for the Scipios to cross to Asia in safety.

Antiochus evacuated Thrace and did not try to contest the crossing to Asia. Avoiding all useless diversions he concentrated on mustering his army, summoning his allies of Galatia and Cappadocia. The Scipios, however, secured the neutrality of Bithynia.[10] After receiving the surrender of Lysimacheia, where a large supply of provisions had unwisely been left undestroyed, they crossed the Hellespont, as their communications by land and sea were secure For the first time a Roman army set foot in Asia. But the way was prepared by the number of allied or friendly states there: most of the Troad, Pergamum and Rhodes, and many cities on the Aeolian and Ionian coast. During a delay caused by the fact that as a Salian priest Africanus could not move for a month, Antiochus, clear-sighted and prudent, sent an envoy to offer terms. He would abandon Europe and break off relations with Aetolia; recognize the independence of Smyrna, Lampsacus and Alexandria Troas and of those Greek cities on the Aegean coast over which Rome wished to throw her aegis; finally he would pay half the cost of the war. These terms, which went considerably beyond what the Romans had claimed in 196, nevertheless left the power of Syria substantially intact. On his brother's advice Lucius Scipio replied that Antiochus must withdraw from Asia Minor north and west of the Taurus Mountains and pay full costs. Antiochus refused, while his envoys failed to win Africanus' co-operation by bribery and by offering to return his son who had been captured; incidentally thereby he provided Scipio's political opponents in Rome with good propaganda.

Proceeding down the Asiatic coast the Romans were joined at Elea by Eumenes; but here P. Scipio fell ill and had to be left behind. His brother advanced inland towards Thyatira while Antiochus retreated eastwards, not to avoid battle, but to seek suitable ground where his cavalry, chariots, elephants and superior numbers would have full scope. He had gathered a host of some 75,000 men to face the 30,000 Romans; their fighting quality was good but the variety of their equipment and training made co-operation of the parts difficult. In a carefully chosen position in the plain of Magnesia-ad-Sipylum he fortified a camp between two rivers, the Phrygius and Hermus. The Romans camped on the opposite (western) side of the Phrygius and then crossing over offered battle with their flanks covered by the two rivers. Antiochus drew up his army but would not advance against the strong Roman position. A third time the Romans moved their camp nearer the enemy's and again offered battle, though their right wing was unprotected; an engagement followed (probably in January 189).

The Roman weak spot was their exposed right wing in the south; here they massed their cavalry under Eumenes, hoping to defeat the enemy's armoured horsemen before or while these attempted to outflank the

Roman line. In this they succeeded. After the archers and slingers had scattered the Syrian scythe-chariots Eumenes charged home and thrust the cataphracts in confusion on to their own centre. Meantime Antiochus himself had led a successful charge of his Iranian horse on his right and had driven back the Roman left wing. But he repeated the error he had made at Raphia, by carrying on the pursuit instead of wheeling to support his centre or his broken left. The phalanx in the Seleucid centre had been drawn up with gaps between the columns and these had been filled with elephants. It stubbornly resisted the Roman legionaries until the elephants began to stampede and its flank was turned by Eumenes' successful cavalry charge. Gradually giving way to the legions under Domitius Ahenobarbus, who was the real commander in Africanus' absence, it was finally cut to pieces. The Syrian camp was captured and their losses were immense. Antiochus fled to Sardes and then to Apamea; when he saw his empire falling like a house of cards and the towns of Asia Minor surrendering to the Romans he laid down arms and sought terms. Thus the Romans had won Asia Minor, like Greece, at a single blow.[11]

4. THE SETTLEMENT OF THE EAST

Antiochus' ambassadors reached L. Scipio at Sardes, where he had been rejoined by his brother, Africanus, who proposed very similar terms to those demanded before the battle: the withdrawal of Antiochus beyond the Taurus, an indemnity of 15,000 talents, the payment to Eumenes of an old debt of 400 talents and a quantity of corn, and the surrender of Hannibal together with certain Greek agitators. When hostages had been given, an armistice was concluded. The terms were not crushing. The indemnity was large—the largest known to ancient history: Carthage had paid only 10,000 talents after the Hannibalic War—but it was not beyond Antiochus' power to pay. The surrender of Hannibal merely meant that he must leave Antiochus' territory; indeed Scipio, ever generous, may have inserted this clause to give him the opportunity of escape, an opportunity which Hannibal did not miss. The terms show that Scipio intended to leave Syria humbled but still alive and to give Rome no further occasion for interference and dispute. These terms were revised later by the Senate when ten commissioners were sent to make the final settlement with Cn. Manlius Vulso who succeeded Scipio in 189. The additional clauses were: Antiochus was not to war in Europe or the Aegean; if attacked by any of these nations he could resist, but he must not have sovereignty over them or attach them to himself as friends;

Rome should arbitrate in such disputes; he must surrender his elephants and fleet, except ten ships which were not to sail west of Cape Sarpedonium. Thus the Senate showed a jealous anxiety to exploit the victory and to rob the king of his armaments which would have been useful in the future against a neighbour like Egypt, in crushing internal troubles and in checking the expansion of the Rhodians who, not being allies of Rome, were left considerable scope for expansion. Unable to guarantee that he would not be attacked, Rome gave him the right to resist assaults but not to procure allies in the region from which he had been excluded. Scipio's more generous terms would have allowed him freedom for development within definitely prescribed limits; Syria could still have flourished under a Roman protectorate. In the Senate, however, there had been a reaction from the policies of the Scipios and the final peace meant that Syria would have little chance to develop a prosperous national life and that the weakening of the central power would hasten the breaking up of the state; Rome would be drawn into the east and the foundations were laid of that Roman predominance which was to last eight hundred years.[12]

Meanwhile other settlements were made by the consuls of 189, M. Fulvius Nobilior and Cn. Manlius Vulso, who superseded the Scipios. The Aetolians, once again rebuffed by the Senate, had renewed war against Philip during the winter. But their hopes were frustrated by news of Magnesia and then by the arrival of Fulvius with two legions (spring 189). Now for the first time Rome had four consular legions in the east, although the two in Asia were little more than garrison troops. After laying siege to Ambracia, Fulvius was persuaded to offer more lenient terms than unconditional surrender, and by the autumn the Senate had ratified a peace (a *foedus iniquum*), which subordinated the Aetolians to Rome and involved them in considerable territorial losses including Delphi, together with an indemnity of 500 talents. The long chapter of Aetolia's independent history was closed and Rome had accomplished in three years a settlement which Macedon had never been able to achieve. There was an epilogue to the war in Greece. Cephallenia had expressly been excluded from the peace. Rome wished to drive the pirates from this island and to gain this valuable base in the Ionian sea. After a four months' siege Fulvius took Same and subdued the island (January 188).

About the same time the final settlement of Asia was accomplished. The consul Manlius carried out an extensive expedition through the territory of the Galatians and reduced them to complete submission (189). The fact that Manlius acquired a staggering amount of booty and money by systematic extortion and warfare, and that the final defeat of the barbarians in their mountain strongholds of the Phrygian plateau involved great loss of life, tends to obliterate the real value of this achievement. It appears an act of wanton imperialism instead of a necessary piece of police work. The barbarians were a continual menace to the Greek and native communities of Asia Minor and only their complete submission would secure lasting peace, for the small army of Eumenes could hardly be expected to hold them back. The harsh and avaricious conduct of Manlius, who fought the barbarians with their own weapons, had turned a wise plan, well suited to Rome's protectorate mission, into a shameful blot on her good name.

In the spring of 188 Manlius joined the ten senatorial commissioners at Apamea and the final treaty was signed and honoured by Antiochus. As laid down by the terms, the king was confined to Syria. A great part of the territory ceded by Antiochus was divided between Eumenes and the Rhodians, with the river Maeander as the boundary between; the continental possessions of Rhodes were thus quadrupled, and the kingdom of Pergamum embraced more territory than the Italian federation including Sicily. The status of the Greek towns of the western seaboard proved a thorny question. Eumenes, the former champion of their liberty, now claimed sovereignty over them, but the Rhodians in jealousy urged their liberation, which had in fact been promised by the Scipios to those cities which surrendered. It was decided that cities previously subject to Antiochus were to be free (*liberae et immunes*), but those which had been tributary to Attalus and those which had opposed or seceded from the Romans during the war were to pay tribute to Eumenes; many individual exceptions were made. But since the liberated towns formed a barrier between Eumenes and the sea the king did not hesitate to claim Pamphylia, alleging that it was 'on this side Taurus', although he had been granted Telmessus, an enclave in Rhodian territory. Since the exact frontier was doubtful the Senate granted him western Pamphylia.

This settlement was a far cry from the proclamation of liberation for the Greeks with which Rome had entered the war. But it was a partial fulfilment, and showed clearly that the Romans themselves wished to wash their hands of Asia. In the autumn of 188 Manlius evacuated Asia, and after his army had been attacked by barbarians on its march through Thrace he arrived back in Italy, leaving Eumenes instead of a Roman army to be a bulwark against future disturbances. Pergamum would act as a wedge between Syria and Macedon, and at the same time limit the ambitions of the border states, Bithynia, Pontus, Cappadocia and Galatia. If Pergamum and Rhodes took a large share in frightening the Senate into war with Antiochus, it was certainly they, and not Rome, who reaped the main harvest. In little more than ten years Rome had overthrown the two great Hellenistic monarchies, but so far from having imperialistic aims, she had not left a single soldier behind in either Greece or Asia. She left the Hellenistic world free to abuse its liberty, and only when this occurred was she again unwillingly forced to intervene. But her patience was not inexhaustible.

XIII

ROME AND THE
EASTERN
MEDITERRANEAN

1. THE GROWING TENSION

During the forty years embraced by this chapter, Rome's foreign policy underwent a subtle change. Starting with the Greek particularistic principle of temporary alliances which had led to something like a protectorate system, Rome gradually turned to a policy of annexation in Greece. The philhellenic protectorate policy of the Scipios and Flamininus was abandoned in favour of a return to the old system of alliance, which really meant dependence. This reaction, led by Cato, was based on a dislike of things Greek and of the deleterious effect of eastern conquest on the character of Rome's generals. Further, the people looked askance at the increasing power which foreign conquest vested in the Senate and its prominent members. But beside this partly conscious reaction, Rome was driven on by circumstances. The view that she deliberately encouraged quarrels and rivalries in Greece in order to regain a foothold there is hardly acceptable, but having guaranteed the freedom of Greek cities, she could not disregard their quarrels and still more their appeals. The period shows a welter of disputes referred to the Senate. Rome showed herself slow to intervene, slow even to enforce her decisions, but it is little wonder if her patience was gradually broken down by this bombardment from the Greeks, whom she wished to ignore. We must now trace her relations first with Greece and then with Macedon till the outbreak of the Third Macedonian War.

Even before the Romans left Greece trouble was brewing in the Peloponnese. Though Philopoemen's dream of the whole Peloponnese united under the Achaean League was fulfilled, it was soon shattered by the revolt of Sparta and by Philopoemen's own lack of statecraft. Sparta had sent a force against her political exiles who after the recent social revolution were rallying in the liberated towns of the Laconian coast (189). When Philopoemen intervened, Sparta seceded from Achaea and offered Fulvius an explanation of its conduct which had infringed the Spartan-Roman Treaty. The question was referred to the Senate which being more concerned with Asiatic affairs replied ambiguously to an Achaean embassy. Thereupon Philopoemen stormed Sparta, massacred the anti-Achaean party, incorporated the city into the League, dismantled her walls, expelled the Helots, restored the exiles, and abolished the old Lycurgan constitution (188). But the Senate held back. Two years later the restored exiles ungratefully found grounds to complain to Rome about Achaea's conduct, but the Senate merely expressed disapproval.

In 185 a stiffening is noticeable in the Senate's conduct, due perhaps to the political decline of the Scipios and the growing ascendancy of Cato, and other political rivals of theirs, together with increasing anxiety concerning Philip's conduct. Having taken no action for four years despite much provocation, the Senate suddenly intervened. On his return from Macedon, Q. Caecilius Metellus (consul 206) rebuked Achaea for its treatment of Sparta and demanded that the League assembly should be summoned, but he was refused on the legal ground that he had no written instructions from the Senate. The Achaeans then received a sharp rebuke from the Senate, and Ap. Claudius Pulcher ordered a League assembly (184), which was marked by mutual recriminations. Thereafter Rome forced a settlement on Achaea, whose envoys had to sign it though thereby they broke the laws of their League: Achaea retained Sparta in the League at the price of restoring the exiles of 190 and rebuilding her walls. The League refused to endorse the settlement, but came to an agreement with Sparta whereby the exiles were not to be recalled. The Senate swallowed the insult.

In 183 Messene revolted from Achaea. The Senate warned the Achaeans, but did not prevent Italian blockade-runners helping Messene. Nothing daunted, Philopoemen defeated the Messenians, but was himself captured and poisoned. Thus died the 'last of the Greeks'. He was ultimately succeeded, not by the like-minded Lycortas, father of the historian Polybius, but by Callicrates, who advised the Senate actively to support the pro-Roman at the expense of the patriotic parties in the various cities. Then, relying on Rome's support, he persuaded the Achaeans to restore the Spartan and Messenian exiles and to allow the refortification of Sparta and the restoration of the constitution of Lycurgus (181). This action of Callicrates marked a new era in the relations of Greece and Rome, whereby Rome tended to support those who appealed to her authority whether right or wrong. As a result she had many flatterers but few friends. Callicrates is adjudged 'the initiator of great miseries to all the Greeks, but especially to the Achaeans, who because of their good faith had hitherto the privilege of dealing on something like equal terms with Rome.'[1] So ended the long Achaeo-Spartan imbroglio, the somewhat tedious details of which have been recorded because they illustrate the changing methods of Roman policy. Next, it will be seen how this was affected by the conduct of Philip.

Philip's loyalty to the Roman cause during the war with Antiochus was rewarded by the remission of the rest of his indemnity and by permission to keep the cities he had captured – but with a reservation. Glabrio had allowed him to retain those Thessalian cities which he took from the Aetolians, provided that such cities had sided with Aetolia voluntarily and not under compulsion. Though this settlement was in line with the policy adopted towards Eumenes in Asia, it obviously contained seeds of future unrest. Philip controlled a wide area which included the coastal strip of Magnesia with Demetrias, and towns on the Phthiotic coast, in Perrhaebia, in Hestiaeotis, and on the borders of Athamania and Dolopia, but the Romans had tried to limit his activity, and Glabrio's order to desist from besieging Lamia in 191 still rankled in his mind. If Philip felt aggrieved, Rome felt suspicious of his extraordinary activity in rebuilding the power of Macedon. By fresh taxation, by developing his mines, and by settling many Thracians in Macedon he strengthened his country's manpower and economic resources. His object may have been entirely pacific, but to Rome this presaged war. Indeed Polybius believed that Philip had decided to renew the war with Rome when his preparations were complete and that his successor Perseus merely followed in his father's footsteps. However this may be, the revival of Macedon increased Rome's suspicious fears.

Complaints soon reached Rome from various Thessalian cities that Philip was not observing the terms of the peace by withdrawing his garrisons. The details were very intricate, as it would not always be easy to determine whether a given city had gone over to the Aetolians of its own free will or not. The Senate dispatched a commission of enquiry, led by Caecilius Metellus. At a subsequent meeting at Tempe, although the Thessalians put forward a weak case, Philip foolishly let his tongue run away with him and observed that 'his sun had not altogether set'; nor did he improve his claims by adding that he knew that he would have to give up what he had received, whether or not his cause was just. He was then ordered to evacuate the cities which were appealing; they were to be added to the Thessalian League. A more serious situation, which had already arrested senatorial attention, arose from his occupation in 187 or 186 of two Thracian cities, Aenus and Maroneia, after their evacuation by Antiochus; Eumenes also on very slender grounds was putting in a counter-claim to these towns. The Roman commissioners required Philip to withdraw his garrisons from the two towns and referred the question to the Senate, which sent out a fresh mission under Appius Claudius and declared the towns free. This, however, so incensed Philip that he cruelly arranged a massacre in Maroneia. An enquiry was instituted and Philip's agent was summoned to Rome, but he mysteriously died on the journey. Rumour added that Philip was merely taking steps to hush up the affair.

To counter Rome's increasing suspicion, which was fed by a further mass of complaints from his neighbours in 184, Philip prudently sent his younger son Demetrius to Rome to protect his interests. Demetrius, who had made a good impression in Rome while there as a hostage after the Second Macedonian War, now obtained from the Senate a verdict in his father's favour which helped to relieve the tension between Rome and Macedon. But reports from Greece were not entirely reassuring, so a message which was sent to congratulate Philip on his compliance ended with a warning. The cause of Rome's suspicion was that the king, whose activity was now checked on the coast, had turned his attention to his northern boundaries where he planned new fortresses and shifted the population about. And even when he tried to add his name to the list of ancient explorers by climbing Mount Haemus a high peak in the Balkans (probably Mt Vitocha), to investigate a rumour that the Black Sea, the Adriatic, the Danube, and the Alps could all be seen thence, his action was interpreted as an attempt to plan an invasion of Italy. But if Philip's public affairs prospered, his private life was less happy. On the return of Demetrius to Macedon his elder brother Perseus accused him of plotting to win the succession to the throne and suggested that Flamininus and other Romans had been playing on his ambitions. Philip ordered the death of Demetrius and only later found that his fears had not perhaps been fully justified. Sick at heart at his own impetuous folly, he himself died soon afterwards (179). Though he did not live to see the dawn of that glorious day of which he dreamed, when Macedon once more should guide the world, he had raised his country to a height which it had not reached since the death of Alexander. Philip, rather than Philopoemen, might be called 'the last of the Greeks'.[2]

When Perseus ascended the throne of Macedon in 179 war was in the air, although the storm did not break for some years. He himself was not ready, and the number of Roman embassies to Greece showed that the Republic would welcome explanations rather than war. Perseus renewed 'friendship' with Rome and accepted his father's recent agreement with the Senate. At the same time he continued his father's policy of building up the power of Macedon. He subdued Dolopia and made a spectacular march through northern Greece to the oracle at Delphi. He repelled the attacks of Thracian tribes and strengthened his position by dynastic marriages; he himself married the daughter of Seleucus IV of Syria and he gave his sister in marriage to Prusias of Bithynia. He also won considerable popularity in Greece by appealing to the democratic and revolutionary elements in the cities. This attempt to pose as the champion of the oppressed and unprotected was not happy; it brought little really solid support and naturally annoyed the Romans, who tended to favour the law-abiding element in the Greek cities, which generally meant the aristocracy. The political parties in Greece were thus more sharply divided in their attitude to Rome and Macedon.[3]

During the first years of Perseus' reign many complaints reached Rome concerning his conduct, until in 172 Eumenes of Pergamum arrived with a detailed list of his crimes. Many of these were trivial, many unsubstantiated; and it need not be supposed that the Senate was over-credulous. But the visit of Eumenes was the deciding factor in Rome's attitude. Nor was Perseus' position made easier by the fact that on his return home Eumenes was nearly killed by a falling rock at Delphi. Perseus would hardly be foolish enough to precipitate matters by murder, but it served as good propaganda for Eumenes.[4] War could not be long delayed. Roman envoys were sent east to pave the way. The Achaean League was ready to support Rome – in fact it had anticipated events by severing relations with Macedon in 175. The Boeotian League hesitated, but under Roman pressure the component cities agreed to support Rome and the League broke up. Several Thracian rulers promised help, though Cotys remained loyal to Perseus. Syria, Egypt and Cappadocia were friendly, while Prusias of Bithynia claimed neutrality because of his relationship with Perseus. The support of Eumenes and Rhodes could be relied on. Finally, Q. Marcius Philippus interviewed Perseus (autumn 172) and tricked him into a truce until the next campaigning season; then war was declared on the ground that Perseus had attacked Rome's allies and was planning war on Rome (171).[5]

2. THE THIRD MACEDONIAN WAR

The consul P. Licinius Crassus landed on the Illyrian coast near Apollonia, where he had some 37,000 men, many of whom were recruits. The officers and men were less experienced than in earlier days; the generation which had fought with Hannibal was passing, while the wars with Philip and Antiochus had not afforded such a hard apprenticeship. Perseus mustered an army of 43,000 men, half of whom were the kernel of Macedon's power and formed the phalanx. This loyal force, which was larger than that with which Alexander the Great had crossed to Asia, was well-armed and well-disciplined by years of frontier warfare, though its officers lacked ability. But, like his father, Perseus was fighting for a lost cause and was the architect of his own downfall. Without the support of Greece, without naval power, he could not expect ultimate success; Rome's resources could stand defeat after defeat. Like Philip, he could only hope that the Romans, if wearied by initial failures, might drop the war as they had the invasion of Africa after the defeat of Regulus. Strategically, the Second Macedonian War had shown the difficulty of a Roman attack from the Adriatic coast up through the mountain valleys to Macedon. Perseus chose rather to defend his kingdom in the south, though he may have strengthened the forts in the western valleys. From Macedon to Thessaly ran the strong Olympus range which continued after the pass of Tempe as Ossa and Pelion. Here was a strong defensive position where he could control the passes to Macedon and from which he could take the offensive in the plains of Thessaly, when opportunity offered, and fight in the enemy's country.

Acting on this bold scheme, Perseus advanced past Tempe along the west of Ossa and took up a position near Larissa (spring 171). Here he was met by the Romans, who had advanced from the west past Gomphi. Near a hill named Callinicus the Romans were trounced in a severe cavalry engagement, but they refused Perseus' offer to treat, rejecting anything short of unconditional surrender. They retired northwards on the west of the Peneus, while Perseus marched up the east bank. A second engagement, which the Roman annalists magnified into a great victory, was fought near Phalanna, and Perseus withdrew from Thessaly for the winter, though he left garrisons at critical points. Thereupon Licinius marched off to Boeotia. His failure can be partly explained by the smallness of his force; also he had not been adequately supported by the Roman fleet. The Roman admiral, instead of operating on the Thessalian coast, had spent his time plundering Boeotia by land: possibly Rome wished to win the war by land and thus avoid any obligation to her naval allies, Pergamum and Rhodes.

The campaign of 170 was uneventful. Hostilius Mancinus, who failed to force the passes of the Olympus range and withdrew from Larissa to Pharsalus, tried to curb his marauding troops and to protect his allies, though the commander of the fleet captured Abdera with great cruelty. The Senate also took measures to right some of the wrongs suffered by the Greeks: several officers were punished. Perseus busied himself securing his communications with Epirus and campaigned successfully in the north against the Dardani, though his attempt to march south to win over the Achaeans failed. In 169 the consul Q. Marcius Philippus succeeded in reaching the Macedonian coast. Advancing north from Pharsalus he had the choice of three passes: Portaes, which led to the heart of Macedon; Pythion-Petra, which debouched near Pydna; and the pass of Lake Ascaris (Nezero) which reached the sea near Heracleum. All three passes together with Tempe were held by Macedonian troops. Marcius chose the third. Coming on the enemy's force he feigned retreat and then swung through a thick wood, Libethron (Ziliana), and reached the coast north of Heracleum. Perseus, who had scattered his forces to guard the passes from Tempe to Portaes and had only a small central force on the coast at Dium, thought that his men at Lake Ascaris had been defeated, and withdrew to Pydna where he concentrated his whole army. Thus the Romans had turned the Olympus range, but being short of provisions as the fleet had failed to co-operate they retired along the coast to Tempe. Perseus was thus enabled to move south again to a strong position near Dium on the Elpeus. This largely cancelled out Marcius' success in forcing the Olympus range, for the Romans only held a narrow strip of coast, of which the north end was blocked by Perseus' strong position.

These mediocre results caused considerable dissatisfaction among Rome's allies, some of whom began to waver in their loyalty, though the fragmentary state of the text of Polybius precludes a detailed judgement on their intrigues. The anti-Roman party at Rhodes got the upper hand and received envoys from Perseus; later they tried to mediate, but their envoys unfortunately arrived in Rome just after news of Perseus' defeat had been received, which naturally annoyed the Senate. Mysterious negotiations also took place between Perseus and Eumenes although they came to nothing. When the Achaean League offered the Roman army definite help, it was declined by Marcius, perhaps from mistrust (the historian Polybius, who was now the second officer of the Achaean League, took part in these negotiations). Perseus was also corresponding with Antiochus IV; and it is significant that the Macedonian navy began to operate off Asia Minor But amid much vague intrigue Perseus obtained one solid advantage, in the autumn of 169. He bought, though by a trick he avoided paying in full for, the support of Genthius, the Illyrian chieftain who reigned in Scodra (Scutari).

At Rome decisive action was demanded; an efficient general, L. Aemilius Paullus, consul of 168 and son of the consul who fell at Cannae, was sent to Macedon, and the legions were brought up to full strength. At the same time the praetor Anicius operated in Illyria. Taking the offensive against Genthius who had mustered an army and navy at Lissus, he stormed Scodra, captured the king, and then made a demonstration through Epirus. In thirty days he had fought the Third Illyrian War. Paullus had a more difficult task. He determined to turn Perseus' position by the Elpeus which he recognized was impregnable. Under cover of a movement which suggested that he was embarking a force at Heracleum, a body of about 8,000 men under Scipio Nasica retired to Tempe and round the Olympus range; then advancing over the Pythion-Petra pass they took Perseus in the rear. The king thereupon withdrew to a weaker position in the plain south of Pydna, for he wished to retain the ability to give battle if he judged fit. Paullus joined Nasica and advanced against the enemy; wisely refusing to fight the same day, he encamped for the night. Perseus, who let slip this chance of attacking the enemy, was in a desperate situation; Paullus could penetrate Macedonia, while Anicius after defeating the Illyrians could advance from the north as Galba had in 199. The next day, 22 June 168, the two armies were drawn up for battle. Between them flowed a shallow stream, the Leucus. Paullus resolutely refused to attack. At midday Perseus withdrew to his camp, hoping to induce the enemy to advance; but the Romans remained stationary, if indeed they had yet been drawn up in battle array. Later in the day a skirmish took place between some advance guards by the river which was crossed by some of Perseus' Thracians. He thereupon determined to fight, and one after another his detachments advanced over the river. His left wing, composed of the Thracians and light troops, was quickly vanquished by the Roman allies, strengthened by twenty-two elephants. The Macedonian phalanx in the centre at first made headway against the legions, but it was disordered by the broken ground when it advanced up towards the Roman camp. The legionaries showed great flexibility and brilliance in manoeuvre, by hurling themselves into its gaps or round its flanks where their Spanish swords made short work of enemy spearmen. The fate of the northern wings is unknown; perhaps they were not even engaged. The Macedonian losses were terrific. Perseus fled to Pella and thence to Samothrace where he was finally betrayed to the Romans.[6]

The war was over and the towns of Macedonia surrendered in quick succession. It remained to make a settlement. This was carried out by Paullus and a senatorial commission. The guiding principle was unchanged: freedom for Greece and Macedon and no annexation of territory. On this the various parties in the Senate were united though for different reasons. Paullus represented the old policy of Flamininus and the Scipios, who wished Greece to be free, although his outlook had been tempered by the disillusioning passage of time. Cato also argued that 'Macedonia must be set free, since we cannot guard her' because he wished to have nothing to do with eastern conquest and its demoralizing influences. Consequently a proclamation was made that the Macedonians should be autonomous, that they should pay to Rome annually half what they had paid to their king in direct tax, that the royal mines and estates should be closed and that the land should be divided into four Republics. A general disarmament was imposed, but frontier tribes might maintain armed forces to check the barbarians. This was a generous decision. The tribute was merely another form of war indemnity, which could not be exacted when the central government no longer existed. The importation of salt and the exportation of timber were also forbidden; the measure was not for the benefit of Italian merchants, but to secure for the people the monopoly which the kings had exercised. The king's personal estate, which now became Rome's public property, was not managed by Roman agents. The gold and silver mines were temporarily closed, but the iron and copper ones were worked by contractors, probably Macedonians. The four Republics were formed in accordance with the geographical features of the land. They were to be independent, without political or economic interconnections with each other. Thus Rome, by imposing a freedom on the Macedonians which perhaps they did not much desire, violated their sense of nationality. But the charters which were given to individual cities and states were sound enough to outlast two centuries. Further, an interesting experiment was tried regarding the constitution of the Republics. The Senate of each state was elected by the separate communities, while the chief magistrate was chosen by the direct vote of a popular assembly. Representative government had been tried by Achaea,

Aetolia and Arcadia, and in the old Boeotian League, but there the representative body had been limited by other bodies; in the Macedonian Republics the local Senate was the primary authority.[7]

The settlement of Illyria was similar. Freedom from taxation was granted to those towns which had been loyal to Rome; the rest paid about half of the former royal land tax. Their territory was abandoned by the Romans and divided into three separate regions. In Greece it was proposed to make no radical alterations, but if the country was again to be abandoned it must be taught the full weight of Roman authority. The cities were cleared of all Macedonian sympathizers in a brutal putsch. In Aetolia five hundred of the anti-Roman party were put to death after a farcical trial, and throughout northern Greece the predominance of Rome was explicitly recognized; Athens alone received preferential treatment. In Achaea, on the advice of the infamous Callicrates one thousand men were deported to Italy on the pretext of being tried at Rome; among them was the historian Polybius. In Epirus Rome's treatment was still more brutal. Aemilius Paullus was ordered to plunder the country systematically; at one fell swoop 150,000 Epirotes were carried off to the Roman slave market and the country was left desolate. This inexcusable barbarity shocked even a world on whose conscience cruelty did not lie heavily.[8]

Thus Paullus settled Greece and returned to hold the greatest triumph yet witnessed in the streets of Rome (September 167). Greece was left free and beyond light taxation in lieu of war indemnity Rome made no attempt to exploit her victory. But her attitude had changed. True, she still preferred diplomacy to war, but the old philhellenic policy was dead, killed by the unending bickerings of the Greeks themselves and by Rome's apprehension, which gradually turned to a tired desire to wash her hands of all things Greek, accompanied by a steady deterioration of the character of many of her outstanding men.

3. THE HELLENISTIC EAST[9]

In Asia Minor the power of Eumenes of Pergamum had not been unchallenged. In 186 Prusias of Bithynia, who at Rome's bidding had remained neutral during the war with Antiochus, attacked Eumenes and welcomed Hannibal, but he quickly obeyed an order from the Senate to cease hostilities; Hannibal took his own life to avoid extradition (183). Thereafter Bithynia caused little trouble. Prusias II (c. 181–149) showed his humility by appearing in Rome dressed as a freedman. When later he

GREECE and the
AEGEAN AREA

0   25   50   75   100 miles

0   50   100   150 km

MAP III

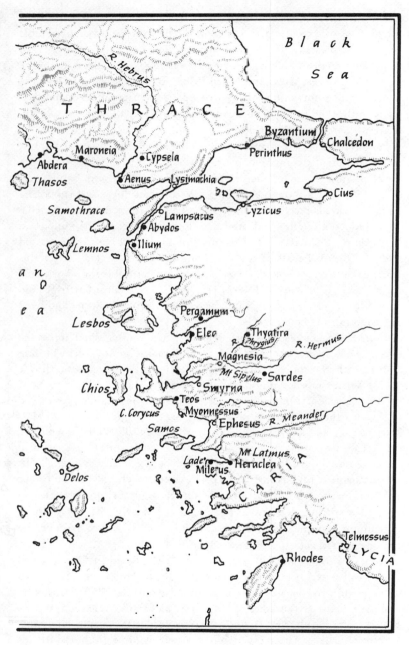

attacked Pergamum after Eumenes' death Prusias had to face a hostile coalition of other states and was soon forced to make an unfavourable peace in the presence of three Roman commissioners (154). Attalus II of Pergamum retaliated a few years later by inciting Nicomedes to dethrone his father, Prusias, who appealed to Rome. But the Senate was so slow sending out commissioners that Nicomedes anticipated them by murdering his father and ruling in his stead; as this involved the renewal of good relations between Bithynia and Pergamum, Rome acquiesced (149).

Pergamum suffered further hostility from King Pharnaces of Pontus, whose imperialistic aggression was curbed in a four years' war by a coalition of Pergamum, her erstwhile foe Bithynia, and Cappadocia (183–179). For although Ariarathes IV of Cappadocia had supported Antiochus in his recent war, the good offices of Eumenes had secured a large reduction in his indemnity to Rome: in return he supported Pergamum. Pharnaces, though undaunted by Rome's half-hearted intervention on behalf of the coalition, was duly checked. After this neither Pontus nor Cappadocia gave Rome much trouble for many years. Mithridates III of Pontus (169–121) helped Rome against Carthage, and Ariarathes V (163–c. 130) maintained friendship with Rome and even died fighting for her cause.

Eumenes' secret dealings with Perseus naturally discredited him in the eyes of the Romans, who repaid this seeming lack of good faith by hinting to his brother, Attalus, that he might aspire to the Pergamene throne (167). When Eumenes announced that he was coming to Rome to plead his cause, the Senate immediately decreed that no king should be received in Rome, though King Prusias had just been welcomed. Attalus, however, remained loyal to his brother, who lived till 159. His own reign (159–138) was marked only by a defensive war against Prusias, which Rome approved; nor did he incur the Senate's displeasure by his encouragement of Nicomedes (see above). In fact, this client prince served Rome well, and diplomatic pressure through such an agent proved a good substitute for armed intervention. Indeed, the kingdom of Pergamum remained undisturbed until it was jolted out of existence by the unexpected action of Attalus III in bequeathing it to Rome (133).

Rhodes sank into obscurity even sooner. The Rhodians had received Lycia and Caria for helping Rome against Antiochus (189), but unfortunately the Senate had not specified the status of the Lycians, who regarded themselves as allies of Rhodes, while Rhodes regarded them as subjects. This resulted in war and Lycia appealed to the Senate, who ruled that the Lycians had been given to Rhodes not as a free gift but as friends and allies (177). The attitude of Rhodes became somewhat frigid, and during the war with Perseus the anti-Roman faction became more prominent, but there was as yet no open breach. In 168 an unfortunate episode occurred: Rhodes sent an embassy to Rome to try to mediate in the quarrel with Perseus. When the ambassadors learnt that news of Perseus' defeat at Pydna had just arrived they did their best by hastily substituting a congratulatory speech in place of the one they had come to deliver; but it was not convincing. A praetor even proposed that war should be declared, but Cato promptly quashed the idea; the Rhodians in gratitude sent a golden crown and humbly sought alliance with Rome. This was not granted till after a dignified interval (165). Meanwhile the Senate punished Rhodes by declaring that the Lycian and Carian cities assigned to her in 188 should be free and by creating commercial competition at Delos, which was handed over to Athens on condition that no harbour dues should be imposed. Both these measures struck hard at Rhodes' revenue, and the greatness of the island began to fade. Rome was later hoisted on her own petard when the pirates whom Rhodes had long kept in check became the scourge of the eastern Mediterranean. The chief centre of piracy was Crete, which was distracted by internal dissensions; Rome had intervened to settle these in 189 and 174 with little effect. When in 155 a united Crete fought against Rhodes, Rome failed to help her sister Republic, who could no longer keep the seas clear for her trade.

After the battle of Magnesia the Seleucid monarchy, despite the loss of Asia Minor, Armenia, Parthia and Bactria, gradually revived. More isolated from the western world, it began under Antiochus IV Epiphanes (from 175) to strengthen its authority in the east, to check internal disintegration and nationalistic movements, and finally was ready to break another lance with Egypt for the age-long debated possession of Coele-Syria. Rome's relations with Egypt were slightly strained: antagonized by the alliance of Egypt with Antiochus III in 196, she had not rewarded Egypt at the settlement of Apamea, although she had originally been anxious to protect Egyptian dependencies. Further, Egypt had made some tactless overtures to the Achaean League in 185 and 183, but native revolts kept the country out of European politics. By 170 Egypt was planning to renew the invasion of Coele-Syria, when Antiochus IV crashed through her frontier defences. The young Ptolemy VI Philometor was captured and the Alexandrines replaced him by his brother Ptolemy VII, Euergetes Physcon. But instead of fighting his way back to the Egyptian throne, as Antiochus hoped, the deposed king came to terms and set up a joint kingship with his brother. Antiochus, who had withdrawn, thereupon re-entered Egypt and seized Cyprus (168). Rome had been too busy in Macedon to assist either of the Ptolemies, although a centenary renewal of the friendship between Rome and Egypt had been effected, but after Pydna the Senate sent a peremptory order to Antiochus to evacuate Egypt and Cyprus. The Roman envoy, Popillius, handed the Senate's despatch to the king, who asked for time to consider; but Popillius merely drew a circle round Antiochus in the sand and bade him answer before stepping out of it. The king meekly obeyed and withdrew from Egypt.

The two Ptolemies did not reign in amity for long. In 164 Philometor was expelled from Egypt and appealed to Rome, making a theatrical appearance in the Senate-house dressed in a suppliant's rags; the Senate intervened by diplomacy alone. After another reconciliation between the brothers, Philometor obtained Egypt and Cyprus, Euergetes Cyrene, but when soon afterwards Euergetes appeared in Rome to ask for Cyprus (162), the Senate agreed but took no military action to enforce his claim and merely broke off diplomatic relations with Philometor. Later Euergetes alleged that his brother had tried to murder him, and in 154 he returned to Rome where he supported his accusation by displaying to the Senate some knife-marks on his body. Before leaving Cyrene, however, he had tried to propitiate the Romans and to show his subjects that a revolt during his absence would not lead to freedom or union with Egypt: he set up a public inscription stating that should he die without legitimate heirs he bequeathed to the Roman people his rightful realm, the protection of which he entrusted to them. This document, the earliest known testament of a Hellenistic king in favour of Rome, did not, in fact, become operative, but it illustrates the humility which the Hellenistic world now adopted towards the rising sun of Rome.[10] In reply to his friendly gesture and Ptolemy's personal appeal, the Senate ordered their eastern allies to co-operate in restoring Cyprus to him. But when the promised help did not materialize, it seems that the king attempted to reinstate himself and was captured. He was, however, generously restored to Cyrene by his brother Philometor, who continued to reign in Egypt and Cyprus at peace with Rome, where Cato supported his cause. Though Polybius (xxxi, 10) criticizes Rome's policy towards Egypt as an example of how she profited by the mistakes of another, it is in fact noticeable that Rome seemed to procrastinate and often did not insist on the immediate execution of her requests. Indeed, her hesitancy towards Egypt may have inspired Carthage and the Achaean League with unwarranted hopes.

Further trouble arose in Syria on the death of Antiochus IV (163). The rightful heir to the throne was his nephew Demetrius, the son of his predecessor Seleucus IV; but Antiochus left his son Antiochus V to succeed him. The Senate ordered commissioners to settle the difficulty. When they proceeded to enforce some disarmament clauses of the Peace of Apamea an insurrection broke out, in which the angry crowd at Laodicea mobbed the embassy and killed its leader (162). Further, Demetrius, who was a hostage at Rome, escaped to Syria without the Senate's permission, and recovered his father's kingdom.[11] He secured the death of Antiochus V, but had to face a pretender, Timarchus, governor of Babylonia, who had won verbal recognition from the Senate. Perhaps with a view to checking his power the Senate received the overtures of Judas Maccabaeus from Jerusalem and concluded a treaty with the Jews, promising Roman help and friendship if they were attacked (161).[12] The next year Demetrius, who had overthrown the rebel Timarchus, at length obtained official recognition from the Senate through the good offices of Tiberius Gracchus. Rome continued to avoid active intervention in Syria. About 150 a pretender, Alexander Balas, gained recognition from the Senate and overthrew Demetrius, who was constantly making trouble and enemies. In 147 a son of Demetrius challenged Balas and was supported by Ptolemy VI. When the people of Antioch offered Ptolemy the Seleucid crown, fear of provoking Rome sufficed to make him decline it, and he withdrew in favour of the young Demetrius, who requited him by seizing Coele-Syria at his death; so ended the long struggle between the Ptolemies and Seleucids (145). Thus in the years which followed the death of Antiochus the Great, Rome often exerted diplomatic pressure against Syria where she liked to see a weak king on the Seleucid throne. But as Syria became weaker and her revival less possible, indifference took the place of that suspicion and fear which had often driven Rome to intervention and once to arms.

4. THE END OF GREEK INDEPENDENCE

The four Macedonian Republics for some time proved a successful experiment, especially considering that the people were not used to self-government. In 158 the Senate reopened the royal mines and allowed the Republics the right of coinage. The first serious trouble arose from a pretender to the Macedonian throne. This adventurer, named Andriscus, who claimed to be a son of Perseus, at first failed to gain support in Macedon or Syria, and even when aided by Thracian troops and money he only climbed to the throne of Macedon after two victories in the field

(149). Rome was slow to act, especially in view of the lack of Macedonian enthusiasm for the pretender. But he was soon strong enough to defeat a small Roman force which was sent against him. In 148 Caecilius Metellus arrived with two legions and quickly ended Andriscus' career. To prevent similar disturbances in the future, Rome took a momentous departure from her old policy of leaving Greece free and ungarrisoned. Macedon was declared a Roman province governed by a Roman magistrate, and Illyricum and Epirus were added to his sphere of administration.[13] But it was not intended to alter the conditions of the local communities as fixed by Aemilius Paullus; the tribute probably was not increased, while the restrictions between the now abolished Republics were removed. With her frontiers severely guarded Macedon entered on a period of comparative peace, and before the death of Polybius the Via Egnatia had been completed from Epidamnus on the west coast to Cypsela near the Dardanelles, a length of 535 miles; but her independent history was ended.

In Greece, as in Macedon, permanent changes were at length introduced. The Senate's refusal to free the thousand deported Achaeans was a bitter pill for the League to swallow; to free them would be to admit that their detention had been unjust. Only after sixteen years was the remnant set free (151/50). Meantime the League had been robbed of its most experienced statesmen and had been at the mercy of the hated pro-Roman Callicrates, whom even the children in the streets called 'traitor'. The Senate in vain tried to compensate for detaining the prisoners by ensuring that her envoys in Greece were men of character and by allowing the League or its cities to arbitrate in disputes between Sparta and Megalopolis in 164 and between Athens and Oropus in 156. When Callicrates died in 150 the last check on the anti-Roman party was removed and the Achaeans' anger blazed forth, fanned by the extremist Diaeus. Mistaking Rome's conciliatory attitude for weakness they saw their opportunity for revenge now that Roman armies were engaged in Spain, Africa and Macedon. The cause of the outbreak was Achaea's attempt to coerce Sparta, who had seceded from the League. When Sparta complained at Rome the Senate ordered the Achaeans to restore full independence to Sparta, and to Corinth and Argos who did not desire it (148). At Corinth, where anti-Roman feeling ran strong among the proletariat, the Senators bearing the decree were mobbed and the punishment of those responsible was refused. A conciliatory message from the Senate caused a second hostile demonstration at Corinth. Achaea then declared war on Sparta and Heracleia-ad-Oetam, and there was a general rally among the masses in Boeotia and Euboea in her favour. But the Achaeans' action was aimed at Rome, and while their new general and dictator, Critolaus, was busy storming Heracleia instead of organizing his defences, a Roman army under Metellus descended from Macedon and swept him aside (146). A second army, raised by Diaeus, checked Metellus at Corinth, but in vain. His successor, Mummius, arrived with four legions and routed the enemy at the Isthmus; he then entered Corinth.[14]

For a moment Rome's patience broke under the strain and she decided to punish Corinth for violating the sanctity of her ambassadors and to make an example of her to all Greece. Mummius was ordered to sell the remaining inhabitants into slavery and to level the city to the ground; her artistic treasures were shipped to Rome, whether or not there is truth in the anecdotes which told how the troops played dice on famous masterpieces and how the matter-of-fact Mummius contracted that any lost on the voyage should be replaced. Details of the Senate's settlement are obscure. Individuals were punished. The Achaean and at least all hostile leagues were temporarily dissolved. The cities, at any rate those which had remained loyal to Rome, were probably immune from taxation, while the prohibition of *commercium* between cities was probably only a temporary restriction. Democracies were abolished and timocracies established in those parts of Greece which had been reduced in war. As Greece had no frontiers to be protected, she was not made into a province till a century later. But she was placed under the supervision of the governor of Macedonia who was responsible for settling disputes and maintaining order.

The punishment of Corinth was cruel but effective. There is little evidence to support the view that it was dictated by commercial jealousy. It was a lesson to all Greece that Rome was tired of her quarrels, and the lesson was not in vain. That an oligarchical state should seek to impose an aristocratic form of government on Greece was natural enough, especially as it facilitated the transaction of business; at the same time the Greeks retained considerable local autonomy. Indeed, after some years the commercial barriers between cities were removed and even the leagues were revived on a social and religious basis. The long chapter of Greek independence was ended. But peace did not necessarily bring prosperity or happiness. Hellas had fallen from her high estate. And it is more just to charge Greece herself with slow suicide than to accuse Rome of murder or even homicide.[15]

XIV

ROME, ITALY
AND THE
WESTERN
MEDITERRANEAN

1. THE NORTHERN FRONTIER

After the Second Punic War Rome had to face the challenge of the barbarian, as well as of the civilized, world. Cisalpine Gaul must be recovered, subdued and secured. In Spain the natives must be driven back to render the Roman occupation safe; having wrested the Peninsula from Carthage, the Romans no more thought of giving it back to the natives than the Allies after the First World War thought of letting German colonial possessions revert to a native administration. Yet Rome had not entered on a systematic career of conquest; perhaps it would have been better for the native populations if she had. Distracted by eastern affairs and exhausted by the Hannibalic War, she only fought as need arose. A systematic conquest, followed up by the spreading of Roman civilization, could have been accomplished in a few years. Instead, slow wars dragged on interminably, often with little plan, under mediocre or ambitious generals; useless cruelty and great losses were endured by both sides, until at length a semblance of order was imposed. Although the final settlement of these barbarian tribes was only completed by Augustus the peacemaker, yet in the fifty years which followed the Hannibalic War Rome had asserted her suzerainty, not only in Corsica, Sardinia and the highlands of central Spain, but also on her northern frontier from near Marseilles, along the sweep of the Alps to Istria and thence down the western coast of the Balkan peninsula.

At Hannibal's approach many of the Gauls of the valley of the Po who had just bowed the knee to Rome had rallied to his standard. But they had not given him adequate support; not till the end of the war did his agent succeed in fomenting a serious Gallic revolt, and then it was too late; the golden opportunity of 218 BC had been lost The loyalty of the Veneti and Mantua, Cremona and Placentia gave the Romans an invaluable foothold in the north against Gallic unrest, which only came to a head in 201 when the Boii defeated a Roman detachment (near modern Forli), while the consul Paetus was trying to secure an important pass over the Apennines by the Sapi (Savio) valley. Encouraged by the victory, instigated further by Hamilcar, and supported by the Insubres and Cenomani, they fell on Placentia (200 or 199). The praetor Furius Purpureo arrived too late to save the town, but he parried a Gallic thrust at Cremona where he defeated the Insubres.[1]

When affairs in Greece began to shape better the Senate decided on more drastic action in the north. The consuls of 197 converged on Cisalpine Gaul from opposite directions. Cornelius Cethegus approached from Venetia and found the Cenomani ready to acknowledge Rome's suzerainty once more, while he defeated the Insubres on the banks of the Mincio near Mantua. Meantime his colleague Minucius Rufus, who marched from Genoa over the Apennines, burnt Clastidium as punishment for its defection in the Hannibalic War, and mastered the country around Litubio; but the Gauls and Ligurians would not meet him in open battle. In 196 both consuls again took the field. Marcellus, the son of the victor of Syracuse, crossed the Po and finished the war in Transpadane Gaul by defeating the Insubres near Comum. They signed a treaty by which no Insubrian was ever to receive Roman citizenship; soon afterwards the district of Mediolanum (Milan) was occupied by Italian settlers. Although the Boii were thus isolated, they withstood the other consul in Cispadane Gaul and perhaps even attacked Marcellus on his return journey. As their submission was expected shortly, little effort was made; the various battles, recorded by Roman annalists, amount to little, and no general won a triumph. In 192 Lucius Flamininus and Domitius Ahenobarbus, the victor of Magnesia, tried in vain to outshine their predecessors. But the next year P. Cornelius Scipio Nasica, cousin of Africanus, won a striking and final victory over the Boii, who ceded half their territory and gradually withdrew to Bohemia or else were absorbed by the spread of Roman civilization.

The conquered district was soon organized. In 190 Placentia and Cremona were both reinforced by 6,000 Roman and Latin settlers. The next year Bononia (Bologna; the old Etruscan Felsina) received 3,000 colonists who were given large allotments of 50–70 *iugera*. In 183 Parma and Mutina were settled as Roman colonies; the large number of settlers, 2,000 at each, and the traditionally small allotments of 5–8 *iugera* emphasize the military need. Meanwhile the consuls of 187, Aemilius Lepidus and C. Flaminius, were linking up these new districts with roads that bore their names: the Via Aemilia, running from Ariminum through Bononia to Placentia, and the Via Flaminia from Arretium over the Apennines to Bononia. Thus the whole of Cisalpine Gaul in the region of the Po gradually came under Roman influence, from the Adriatic to the Sesia in the west.[2] Beyond this river the Romans did not venture; the Salassi of the western Alpine valleys around Aosta long retained their independence.

The Romans then addressed themselves to the problem of the tribes on either side of Cisalpine Gaul: the Ligurians and the Istri. The Ligurians who dwelt in the Apennines from the Arno to Savoy were a hardier race than the Gauls of the northern plain. From their mountain heights they threatened alike the valley of the Po and the plains and ports of Tuscany, and even challenged the commerce of Massilia. Their two chief tribes were the Apuani above Luna (Spezia), and the Ingauni north and west of Genoa. By making peace with the latter in 201 the Romans secured control over the important ports of Luna and Genoa, and were in no hurry to undertake the systematic reduction of the Italian Riviera. Minucius Rufus marched through Ligurian territory in 197, and Minucius Thermus forced back the Apuani, who threatened Pisa in 192, and made a demonstration beyond the Auser.[3] The Senate did not take active measures till after the wars with Philip and Antiochus. While constructing a road from Pisa to Genoa in 186 the consul Marcius Philippus ventured with two legions into the mountain fastness of the Apuani and was destroyed in a pass which received his name – Saltus Marcius. The following year one consul proceeded against the Apuani, the other against the Ingauni who had broken their alliance. But the resistance of the Ligurians was slow to weaken. In 181 Aemilius Paullus, the future victor of Pydna, reduced the Ingauni to allegiance; the consuls of 180 defeated the Apuani and transported 40,000 of them to near Beneventum in Samnium. In the vacant territory the Romans probably established a Latin colony at Luca (*c.* 178) and in 177 Luna received 2,000 Roman citizens.[4]

But the Ligurians were far from pacified. A violent revolt occurred near Mutina and campaigning continued till 175. Thereafter fighting was sporadic, and Roman generals found an easy way to win a triumph. Though ambition and cruelty sometimes went hand in hand, the Senate with the zealous Cato at its elbow often checked unlawful activity; for instance, in 172 Popillius Laenas was forced to release prisoners whom he had taken in his campaign against the Statielli. Later the Romans in securing a road to Massilia and Spain came into contact with the more westerly Ligurian tribes. Victories were reported from the Maritime Alps in 166, 158 and 155 BC. In 154 the Oxybian Ligurians raided the Massiliote ports at Antipolis (Antibes) and Nicea (Nice) and assaulted a Roman embassy which had been sent at the request of Massilia. Punishment was quickly meted out by the consul Opimius and part of their territory was given to Massilia. Thus the land route to Spain was secured and a few years later Genoa was linked with the northern plains by the construction of the Via Postumia to Cremona and Aquileia.

As a result of these Ligurian and Gallic campaigns the Romans obtained, either by direct possession or through their Latin colonies, about half of the 18,000 square miles south of the Po. Although they planted only two citizen colonies, Mutina and Parma (and Dertona, about 120), in this district, individual settlers were encouraged to migrate northwards by the granting of plots of land to applicants (e.g. in 173, to citizens 10 *iugera*, to allies 3 by viritane assignation).[5] The success of this movement can be traced in the rapid extension of local centres for trade and administration (*fora* and *conciliabula*) and by the growth of the tribe Pollia in which many such colonists were enrolled. With the colonists there came order, prosperity and civilization. The land was reclaimed and improved; in addition to main roads many branch roads were constructed; these served also as embankments against flood, and alongside them ran ditches which helped to drain the land. Nor did the migration stop south of the Po. Roman and Italian farmers gradually bought up a large part of the land to the north and thrust the Celtic tribes steadily towards the foothills of the Alps. The way was thus gradually prepared for the inclusion of Cisalpine Gaul within the sphere of Roman administration, with all that it has meant to later history.

The natural frontier in north-east Italy was the arc of the Cornic and Julian Alps terminating in the Istrian peninsula. This district, which had been subdued before the Hannibalic War, had been lost during that upheaval, but the Romans, whose flank was protected by the friendly Veneti, postponed reasserting their authority until after they had dealt with the Po valley and Liguria. Warnings, however, were sent to the raiding tribesmen from the mountains, and in 181 a Latin colony was founded at Aquileia as a permanent bulwark on this frontier. Three thousand colonists, mostly veteran soldiers, were sent out; in 169 another 1,500 families followed. Exceptionally large allotments, from 50 to 140 *iugera*, were granted in order to attract better-class farmers who would run their estates with hired or slave labour and would thus be free to act as a garrison if necessary. When peace was secured Aquileia developed into the most important commercial city in the north, thanks to its nodal position. But its foundation stimulated the angered Istri to further raids, so that an expedition was launched against them under Manlius Vulso in 178.

Manlius advanced from Aquileia over the Timavus and took up a position in the enemy's country; his two legions camped separately, while 3,000 Gallic allies formed a third camp.[6] When the Istrians swept aside his outposts and stormed his camp, the troops fled in a panic to the Roman fleet which was stationed nearby on the coast. Manlius at length steadied his men and then retrieved the day by carrying out a converging attack on the Istrians from his other two camps. After wintering at Aquileia, Manlius advanced before his successor arrived into the Istrian peninsula and won a victory perhaps on the Quieto. While he was besieging the survivors who had rallied in the south at Nesactium near Pola, Claudius Pulcher arrived with a new army to take over the siege, which he soon completed. After he had stormed two other towns, resistance was stamped out and Istria was conquered as far as the Arsia.

After the war with Perseus and Genthius the Romans had secured the Dalmatian coast as far north as the Narenta. It only remained to reduce the strip from there to Arsia to turn the Adriatic into a Roman lake. When the Dalmatae, the chief tribe of this coastal strip, began to harry certain neighbouring tribes and Greek colonists, the Senate intervened. A Roman embassy was insulted and the consul C. Marcius Figulus was sent to Dalmatia (156). After an initial defeat, he ravaged the country and besieged the capital, Delminium.[7] But, like Manlius at Nesactium, he was not allowed to complete the task, which fell to the lot of his successor, P. Scipio Nasica. Meanwhile L. Cornelius Lentulus had advanced in the north from Aquileia into Pannonia, perhaps to Siscia (156). As this demonstration was not followed up, there was still a small gap left between the Roman possessions on the Adriatic coast – from Arsia to the Titius, which was not dealt with till 129. But with this trifling exception Rome had now extended her authority from the Ligurian tribes near Marseilles, round the sweep of the Alps to Istria and thence down the western coast of the Balkan peninsula.

Sardinia and Corsica had remained at peace for twenty years after the Hannibalic War – a period marked by the governorship of Cato, who banished all moneylenders and reduced the exactions made on behalf of the Roman governor (198). But during Rome's preoccupation with the Ligurians the two islands revolted, perhaps in conjunction with the mainlanders (181). Corsica soon submitted, but the Sardinians held out longer, until brought to heel by Ti. Sempronius Gracchus, who doubled their tribute (177–176). Occasional fighting flared up again in Corsica until its final submission in 163; and even then brigandage occasionally lifted its head in the interior.

2. CATO AND GRACCHUS IN SPAIN

The Romans had not fought the Hannibalic War to win Spain, but once having stepped into the shoes of Carthage, they intended to keep the spoils of victory. They had won only a small but the most valuable, part of the whole Peninsula: the lower Ebro valley, the east coast and the Baetis valley. They then had to decide whether to disregard or to conquer the highland tribes of the interior, who had remained untouched by the Carthaginians apart from Hannibal's lightning campaign; though the Romans ended by conquering them, they did not necessarily start with that intention. The desire for law and order on the frontiers and the need for further conquests to protect previous ones partly explains the long series of wars waged in Spain. But the rich resources of the land excited Rome's cupidity at a time of exhaustion when she had to rally her strength to meet the demands of the eastern wars. So she began to exploit her new province, which naturally evoked increasing discontent among, and ultimate conflict with, the natives of the interior. These wars, which continued till 133 BC, were waged by both sides with much cruelty and treachery, albeit often with great courage, and brought to the surface many of the baser elements of the Roman character.[8]

Scipio Africanus had conquered Spain, not as a regular magistrate, but merely as a *privatus* on whom the Roman people had conferred proconsular *imperium*. His successors were nominated in a similar way (205–198). But Rome soon adapted her machinery of government and from 197 BC the annual number of praetors was raised from four to six; two were sent to Spain with proconsular rank, with twelve lictors in place of the six granted to their colleagues. Each administered one of the two separate provinces (Hispania Citerior and Ulterior) into which Spain was now divided in order to surmount the difficulty of maintaining communications throughout the land. Nearer Spain comprised the valley of the Ebro and the east coast to a point south of Cartagena; in the northern part the natives were unused to foreign rule. Further Spain consisted of the far richer Baetis valley south of the Sierra Morena, where the inhabitants had long been accustomed to a foreign yoke.

In general Rome took over the reins of government from Carthage, and the Spaniards who had at first welcomed the Romans as protectors soon found that they had merely exchanged masters. Special treaties were granted only to larger communities and to certain Phoenician and Greek towns such as Gades and Emporiae. The colony of Italica, founded by Scipio Africanus, retained its Roman citizenship, and in 171 a Latin colony was founded at Carteia. Communes and towns were encouraged at the expense of larger tribal units, while native chiefs were no doubt controlled. The Romans levied auxiliaries and imposed tribute in the form of a fixed tax (*stipendium*), not a tithe; this was paid partly in natural products, such as corn, but mostly in bullion or in coined money; to this end the natives were encouraged to mint silver and copper on a Roman monetary standard. But it was the extortion of the Roman governors, rather than the tribute itself, which galled the natives most and which opened a shameful page in the history of Roman provincial adminis- tration. As the Spaniards themselves in the sixteenth century fell on the riches of Mexico and Peru, so with like avarice and cruelty the Romans exploited their new Eldorado. Scipio Aemilianus at Numantia is reported to have levied 40,000 auxiliaries, while in ten years (206–197) 130,000 lb of silver and 4,000 lb of gold were transported to Rome. The result of this continued maladministration was that in 171 the first court to try cases of extortion (*repetundae*) was set up and in 149 it was established on a permanent basis.[9]

As a protest against Roman policy a vast insurrection swept through Spain in 197, starting in the south among the Turdetani; it included the Phoenician cities of Malaca and Sexi, which doubtless had suffered from Roman governors since even Rome's ally, Gades, had to endure a Roman *praefectus*. The revolt spread rapidly over the central highlands to the north, where a praetor Tuditanus was defeated. In 196 Rome herself was too busy in Greece and Cisalpine Gaul to reinforce the Spanish praetors, who nevertheless won a success in Turdetania and probably brought the Phoenician coast towns to heel. In the following year it was decided to raise the legions in Spain to four (about 50,000 men, excluding native allies), by despatching a consular army under Cato. Though welcomed by the Greek settlement at Emporiae, he had to face a grave situation: in the north only the Ilergetes remained loyal. He took care to support his army from the land, remarking to the army contractors that 'war feeds itself', and then advanced against the enemy whom he defeated in battle. Consequently the rebellion in the north subsided enough to allow the praetor at Tarraco to join his colleague in the south where together they checked the less warlike Turdetani. When this tribe was strengthened by 10,000 Celtiberian mercenaries Cato himself marched south. Here he tried to buy over the Celtiberians and achieved little: a signal failure considering the size of his army. Marching back through the highlands he unsuccessfully attacked Segontia and Numantia, although he was not technically at war with the Celtiberians.[10] This campaign consequently thus destroyed all hope of peace and ushered in the Celtiberian wars which lasted intermittently till 133; but perhaps open war was better than a state of peace under cover of which the Celtiberians could ravage Roman territory by serving other tribes as mercenaries. Returning down the Ebro, Cato pacified the restless mountain tribes of Catalonia, and after reorganizing the working of the mines there he led his army back to Rome to receive a triumph. His campaign benefited the treasury, but it did not crush the spirit of revolt; indeed the interest which attaches to his personality has led to the magnifying of his exploit. Valuable geographical knowledge of the Celtiberian theatre of war may have been gained, but what might not a Hannibal or a Scipio have accomplished with Cato's forces?

The war continued, and even spread to the Lusitani (in southern Portugal) who were defeated by Scipio Nasica near Ilipa in 194. Then the Romans advanced from the south against the central highlands of Old Castile, subjugating the Oretani and Carpetani and capturing Toledo (193–192). Indecisive hostilities dragged on: for instance, Aemilius Paullus, who was defeated by the Lusitani in the Saltus Castulonensis in 190, retrieved the situation the next year. In 186 the Senate supplemented the inadequate forces by raising the number of legions in Spain to four, and maintained this strength till 179. Although the Roman praetors defeated the Lusitani, who were aided by the Celtiberi, in Carpetania in 185, they were reluctant to risk penetrating into the heart of the little-known districts of Lusitania and Celtiberia, notwithstanding their 40,000–50,000 men.

In 181 the Lusones, a Celtiberian tribe, tried to migrate into Carpetania. Their southward advance was checked at Aebura by Fulvius Flaccus, who after severely trouncing them in battle marched northwards, captured their capital, Contrebia, and took the district which the Romans called Celtiberia Citerior (i.e. south and east of the plateau of Almazan and the Sierra del Moncayo). The following year he started to attack Celtiberia Ulterior, but was recalled by the arrival of his successor, Ti. Sempronius Gracchus ; while returning to the coast he was assailed in the Saltus Manlianus (Jalon valley) but turned the tables by winning a fresh victory. Meanwhile Gracchus advanced up the Ebro and snatched Caravis (north-west of Saragossa) from the clutches of the Celtiberians, against whom he planned a converging attack. His colleague, Postumius, assailed the Vaccaei in the west and then advanced along the upper Douro towards Celtiberia, while Gracchus himself penetrated up the Jalon valley from the east. After a victory near Contrebia Gracchus made a treaty with the southern Celtiberians, by which they furnished auxiliaries and tribute, while in Further Celtiberia the warlike Arevaci concluded a favourable alliance. Like the elder Scipio and Hasdrubal, but unlike so many other generals, Gracchus sought to win over the natives by sympathy rather than by force ; and his name was long honoured in Spain for fair dealing and wise moderation. He even made some attempt to Romanize the conquered country by founding Graccuris on the Upper Ebro; later another town, Corduba, was established in southern Spain as a centre of Roman civilization (168 or 151). This First Celtiberian War (181–179) had resulted in the subjugation of the southern tribes and alliance with the northern. Comparative peace reigned for twenty-five years, so that Rome could devote herself to the Istri (178–177), the Sardinians (177–176) and above all to Perseus (172–168).

3. THE CELTIBERIAN AND LUSITANIAN WARS

For many years Roman governors administered and plundered Spain, and the provincials appealed, often with success, to Rome for justice. But in 154 war again broke out among the Lusitani and raged till 138. Meantime the Celtiberians made a bid for independence in 153 but were crushed by 151; this short Second Celtiberian War will be described before the longer struggle with Lusitania. The interest of these wars derives from the emergence of a national hero, whose brilliant guerrilla warfare recalls another great national leader, Owain Glyndwr; from the heroic resistance of the Celtiberians; from the demoralizing effect which they exercised on the Roman character; and finally from their link with the present, for many of the camps which were built during them have been uncovered this century.[11]

Stimulated by the rebellion of the Lusitanians, the Belli in 153 refused to stop fortifying their town of Segeda in the upper Jalon valley, and encouraged the neighbouring tribes in Nearer Celtiberia to revolt. The

Senate assigned four legions to Spain and sent the consul Q. Fulvius Nobilior, son of the victor of the Aetolians, against the Celtiberians. When he advanced up the Jalon valley, the Belli abandoned Segeda and took refuge with the Arevaci, thus spreading the disturbance into Further Celtiberia. Nobilior left a supply post at Ocilis and advanced to Almazan, twenty miles south of Numantia, where his summer camp still survives.[12] But while his army threaded its way through the defile to Numantia it was attacked by the Arevaci; 6,000 legionaries fell near Monte de Matamala on 23 August, the day of the Vulcanalia. The Roman cavalry, however, succeeded in driving back the victors to Numantia. Nobilior followed and camped on a mountain named Gran Atalaya near Renieblas, some four miles east of Numantia, where he commanded the approaches to the Ebro. Communications with his base at Ocilis would be difficult; after his recent defeat he evidently mistrusted the route thither and preferred to rely on the Ebro valley. In the summer he failed to storm Numantia, notwithstanding the use of elephants, and the neighbouring Uxama (Osma), so that he was forced to encamp for the winter (153–152) at Gran Atalaya amid great cold and hardship; his impressive winter camp still exists (Camp III).

In 152 he was succeeded by M. Claudius Marcellus, who took Ocilis and the revolted Jalon valley. By the offer of favourable terms many tribes, including the Arevaci, were induced to send embassies to Rome. But the Senate, now accustomed to the obsequious compliments of the Greeks, was in no mood to listen to tribesmen who spoke as free men conscious of their rights; Scipio Africanus, with his courteous sympathy towards the Spaniards, was long dead and Rome had drunk too deep from the cup of military power and domination. After negotiations had broken down Marcellus encamped on a hill (Castillejo), just north of Numantia, where later Scipio Aemilianus camped. He then made peace with the Numantines in return for a very large sum of money; the terms were probably the same as those formerly imposed by Gracchus. When the new consul L. Licinius Lucullus arrived in 151 and found peace established, he savagely turned against the unoffending Vaccaei. He took the town of Cauca by treachery; but his brutality merely stiffened the resistance of Intercatia and Pallantia, which he assailed in vain. He then withdrew to Further Spain to help the equally unscrupulous Galba against the Lusitanians. For seven years peace reigned in Celtiberia.

Meanwhile in 154 the Lusitanians had raided Roman territory, defeated two praetors and stirred the Vettones to arms. The following year they discomfited Mummius, the future destroyer of Corinth, and

sent the captured Roman standards as an incentive to the Celtiberians;
next, they attacked the Conii, raided Baetica and perhaps crossed to
North Africa, but soon afterwards Mummius and his successor turned
the tables on them. Consequently they made a treaty: only to break it the
next year and to defeat Sulpicius Galba in a notable victory (151). Galba
was reinforced by the arrival of Lucullus, but he found treachery more
expedient than arms. After inducing the Lusitanians to submit, he
disarmed, separated and finally butchered them. This cold-blooded
atrocity was even more treacherous than Lucullus' treatment of the
Vaccaei, who had received no formal pledges from Rome when they
surrendered. Rome's name was dishonoured; such cruelty had never
before stained her annals. On his return Galba was brought to trial, but
though Cato, now aged eighty-five, supported the prosecution, a wise use
of his ill-gotten gains and the tears of his little children obtained his
acquittal. Rome truly was falling from her ancient greatness, as the ruins
of Corinth, Carthage and Numantia were soon to testify.

Among the survivors of Galba's massacre was a shepherd named
Viriathus.[13] He persuaded some 10,000 Lusitanians, who had been cut off
by the praetor Vetilius, to fight for their liberty instead of surrendering.
Under his leadership they broke away and for eight years he withstood
the arms of Rome. First he adopted guerrilla tactics without any definite
fortress for a base; in a narrow pass of the Sierra Ronda he trapped and
defeated the praetor Vetilius who followed him south from Urso in the
valley of the Guadiaro, some twenty-five miles south of Ronda (147). He
then established himself nearer home in a strong position in Carpetania
on the Hill of Venus (Sierra S. Vincente; forty miles north-west of
Toledo). From here he long dominated the surrounding district, striking
northwards to Segovia, and eastwards to Segobriga; finally he won a
number of towns near Corduba in the south (146–141). The Roman
forces continued to meet with defeat, even after 145 when a consular
army of two legions was sent out. In 141/0 Fabius Maximus Servilianus
was surrounded, but Viriathus unexpectedly accepted a treaty and
allowed the Roman army to withdraw. Though the terms were ratified at
Rome, Servilianus' successor, Servilius Caepio, took upon himself to renew hostilities. The last phase of the war opened, in which Viriathus was
forced back on the defensive. Caepio advanced into Lusitania from the
south (a Castra Servilia has been found north of Caceres) and after a defeat
suborned three of Viriathus' friends to cut his throat as he lay sleeping in
full armour in his tent (139). This terminated the war, although Caepio's
successor, D. Junius Brutus, penetrated further north. In 138 he subdued

Portugal up to the Douro and the next year while his fleet advanced along the coast he reached Galice and defeated the wild Callaici beyond the Oblivio (Minho). He fortified Olisipo (Lisbon) and settled the veterans of Viriathus at a place named Valentia (Valença do Minho?). His treatment of the natives was marked by a greater moderation than many of his predecessors had displayed.

So fell Viriathus, a great national leader and hero, by a fate similar to that of Sertorius whom he much resembles. His courage, his skill in guerrilla warfare, his inspiring and magnetic personality, all alike command respect. But like many leaders from the elder Scipios to Wellington, he underestimated the volatility of the Spanish temperament. He failed to discipline his men adequately, to obtain the co-operation of the Celtiberians and to weld the various tribes into a nation.

4. THE NUMANTINE WAR

Encouraged by the initial success of Viriathus the Celtiberians had again broken into rebellion in 143. This Third Celtiberian, or Numantine, War was centred around Numantia, which was situated on a hill at the junction of two rivers which run through heavily forested valleys. It had been founded on the site of earlier settlements by the Iberians who penetrated the Celtic highlands about 300 BC. The Iberian element was responsible for the town wall with an inner ring of houses, while the centre was laid out in accordance with Greek principles. The population gradually spread beyond the walls, and when the town was attacked in 153 the larger settlement would be protected by a palisade.[14] Though their civilization was somewhat backward and their pottery coarse, the Numantines had magnificent iron weapons. Through scarcity of corn they continually raided the valleys of the Ebro and Jalon; they derived supplies from the Vaccaei and found pasturage among the Arevaci.

At the beginning of the war Numantia remained inviolate. Q. Caecilius Metellus Macedonicus conquered the tribes of the Jalon valley in Nearer Celtiberia (143), and then advanced against the Vaccaei in the north-west in order to cut off the Numantines' source of supplies (142). He was succeeded by an inefficient soldier, Q. Pompeius, who encamped on the hill Castillejo at Numantia, but although he commanded 30,000 men he failed to storm Numantia with its 8,000 defenders. Thereupon he advanced to annoy the walls of Termantia on the Douro, but in vain. Returning to Numantia, he attempted a blockade and even essayed to flood the eastern plain (140). But at the approach of winter his troops suffered from dysentery and intense cold, so that he was ready to induce the Numantines to accept terms. On the arrival of his successor, Popillius Laenas, in 139, Pompeius repudiated the terms, which had not yet been ratified by the Senate, but he carefully kept the money he had demanded for arranging the treaty; though later he was court-martialled at Rome he escaped the consequences of his treachery. Popillius campaigned against the Lusones, but his attack on Numantia miscarried (139–138). The year 137 was marked by disaster and further disgrace. The commander Mancinus was cut off in the pass of Tartajo near Nobilior's former camp at Renieblas while attempting to withdraw from Numantia to the Ebro. He surrendered with 20,000 men, and the young Tiberius Gracchus, who was trusted for his father's sake, undertook responsibility for the fulfilment of the terms. The Senate disgracefully refused to accept the conditions and with shameful hypocrisy made a scapegoat of Mancinus by sending him back to Numantia, naked and with his hands bound behind him. The Numantines with dignity refused the offering. They had lost the chance of a signal victory over their enemies through treachery. Rome's name was again dishonoured, and one more incident could take its place alongside those for which Lucullus, Galba and Pompeius were responsible. Mancinus' successors left Numantia alone and were content to plunder the Vaccaei. So the war dragged on, until in 135 the Roman people again elected to the consulship (before the legal interval had elapsed) the recent conqueror of Carthage, Scipio Aemilianus, son of Aemilius Paullus the victor of Pydna and adopted grandson of Scipio Africanus the Elder.

Instead of regular reinforcements Scipio took to Spain a number of volunteers and a corps of five hundred friends and dependants as a kind of private bodyguard to protect him while he redisciplined the army. This cohort, devoted to the person of its general, gave him personal protection and was in essence the prototype of the later imperial Praetorian Guard. Scipio's first task was to restore efficiency among the demoralized troops in Spain. Camp-followers, women and soothsayers were sent packing; the men were vigorously dragooned and made to use the spade as well as the sword. But such an army, though redisciplined, could not take Numantia by storm, so that Scipio determined to reduce it by blockade and starvation. But first he cut off its source of supplies. Marching up the Ebro to Deobriga he turned westwards against the Vaccaei and reduced Pallantia and Cauca. Then he approached Numantia from the west along the Douro, scouring the fields as he went (autumn 134).

Behind a defensive palisade he built seven camps around the town and linked them together with a strong wall set with towers, so that Numantia was completely invested. The two chief camps were at Castillejo in the north where he had his headquarters, and at Peña Redonda in the south; each held a legion, while the other camps were manned by Italian and Iberian allies. Scipio's forces numbered some 20,000 Italians and 40,000 Iberians. Although the besieged were not more than 4,000, they held out with heroic and tragic courage for eight months, resorting in their desperation even to cannibalism. All attempts to break through Scipio's iron ring failed, though finally a chief and four companions slipped out on a cloudy night and even got their horses over the wall by a folding scaling-bridge. But in vain. They could not rouse the countryside to arms again. Scipio refused to accept any terms short of unconditional surrender. Finally famine did its work and the heroic Numantines capitulated. Without consulting the Senate Scipio burnt the town to the ground, as a red layer of burnt material still bears tragic witness (August 133). Many famous men saw the smoke and flames of Numantia rising to the sky: Scipio's brother-in-law, Gaius Gracchus; a young cavalryman, Gaius Marius; the poet Lucilius; the young Numidian prince Jugurtha; two military tribunes Asellio and P. Rutilius Rufus, who both wrote histories of the war; and perhaps Scipio's friend, the historian Polybius.

The fall of Numantia established beyond question the dominion of Rome in Spain. The story is a painful one and Rome's methods of diplomacy had deteriorated. But this declension from her pristine standards of honesty resulted in part from contact with more barbarous races than those encountered in Italy or the east. Differences of custom may often have led to misunderstanding. The Spaniards when forced to come to terms did not always intend to keep them, and so Rome learnt to meet treachery by treachery and to fight with Spanish weapons. Further, the Senate was jealous of its power and reserved the right to revise arrangements made by its generals, so that treaties made in good faith in Spain might not always be ratified at Rome The Senate may have underestimated the difficulty of campaigning in Spain and good generals may have fought shy of the province, but Rome's chief mistake was her failure to understand the Spanish character. The successes of Scipio Africanus the Elder, the elder Gracchus and Sertorius show that more could have been accomplished by sympathy and moderation than by brute force. Yet Rome gave Spain something, although at the point of the sword, which she could not give herself: out of the blood and tears of conquest a new race painfully raised itself on the first steps of civilized life.

By lifting the conquered to the same level of culture as the conquerors Rome abolished the need for opposition and laid the foundations of that great prosperity which Spain enjoyed under the Roman Empire.

5. CARTHAGE AND MASINISSA

The terms imposed on Carthage after Zama had put an end to her independent political life, but within the prescribed limits she could still develop her territory and foster her commerce. She was hampered less by external circumstances than by internal moral weakness. Her oligarchical government was selfish and corrupt. Though she paid her annual indemnity to Rome, notwithstanding the loss of her Spanish mines, it was the lower classes that bore the burden. The exploitation by a vicious oligarchy of a state whose treasury was nearly empty could not continue indefinitely: at last the people called on Hannibal to cleanse the administration. Elected Sufete in 196,[15] he at once struck at the power of the oligarchs. He skilfully manoeuvred an official appeal to the people by getting at variance with the Senate. In the popular assembly he vigorously attacked the Council of One Hundred and Four Judges and passed a law which made membership subject to annual election by the people, with the proviso that no judge should hold office for two consecutive years. At one blow the tyrannical control of the oligarchs was undermined. Hannibal followed up this triumph by a masterly re-organization of the public revenues and by encouraging commerce and agriculture. So happy were his reforms that by 191 Carthage could offer to pay off the rest of her war indemnity in a lump sum, whereas the instalment of 199 had been paid in such poor silver that the Roman quaestors had rejected it.

But Hannibal's very success caused his downfall. Though supported by the people, he could hope for little mercy from the disgruntled oligarchs, who setting party before state appealed to Rome on the pretext that Hannibal was intriguing with Antiochus. A stir was caused in political circles. Cato had just entered office (195) and the anti-Barcid faction had unwittingly provided him with powder and shot to attack his enemy, Scipio Africanus. It would be argued that Scipio's generous peace terms had enabled Hannibal to overthrow the nobility of Carthage and to seize the helm himself: with the east so unsettled, what might this not mean? Scipio himself maintained that it was beneath the dignity of the Roman people to meddle with the party politics of Carthage or to treat as a common criminal the man whom they had defeated in open war. This was the wiser, as well as the more generous, policy, for there is no evidence, beyond the accusations of his political opponents, that Hannibal had any far-reaching designs. As it was, Scipio's rivals won the day and succeeded in driving Hannibal into the arms of Antiochus, thereby creating the very situation they were trying to avoid. They sent three commissioners to Carthage, nominally to arrange a frontier question between Masinissa and Carthage, but actually to complain to the Carthaginian Senate that Hannibal was intriguing with Antiochus. Hannibal perceived their real purpose and fled by night from the city, ultimately reaching the court of Antiochus; that he sought asylum beyond the reach of Rome does not prove that he had previously been intriguing with the king. The Punic government then humbled itself and formally exiled its greatest citizen.

After sacrificing Hannibal to Punic jealousy and Roman revenge, the Carthaginian government would long keep the anti-Roman party under its heel; indeed Hannibal himself had aimed at avoiding giving any cause of complaint to Rome. He received no encouragement from Carthage when plotting with Antiochus. With continued humility Carthage sent large quantities of corn to support the Roman armies in Greece and Asia, and as Rome's ally, promptly gave military and naval assistance when required. True, in 174 and 171 BC Masinissa accused Carthage of plotting with Perseus, but the suspicions were unfounded. During the first half of the second century Rome and Carthage lived, if not in harmony, at least in unbroken peace. Roman policy was non-aggressive, while trade and the coming and going of embassies taught the two peoples to know each other better. The final breakdown was caused not by Carthage, but by the ambitious Masinissa.

Masinissa, who was thirty-seven years old at Zama, preserved his vigour into a ripe old age : at eighty-eight he still commanded his army in battle, mounting his horse unaided and riding barebacked. But he had other outstanding qualities besides physical vigour. Fearless and unscrupulous, diplomatic and masterful, he conceived the tremendous ideal of welding the native tribes of North Africa into a nation. He successfully developed agriculture and commerce, and encouraged the spread of Punic civilization. His fame soon exceeded the confines of Africa; he cultivated relations with the Greek world, and at Delos at least three statues were erected in his honour. Throughout he remained the faithful ally of Rome, aiding her with supplies and troops in her eastern and Spanish wars. But his territorial aggressions soon caused friction with Carthage.[16] After Zama he had been rewarded with the Numidian empire of the defeated Syphax and with any territory which either he or his ancestors had held. With this exception Carthage had retained her possessions inside the Phoenician Trenches and her control of Emporia.[17] Obviously difficulties would arise in interpreting Masinissa's claim within the Trenches, and these would be increased by the fact that Carthage was forbidden to wage war on any ally of Rome in Africa. Masinissa gradually but systematically proceeded to occupy Emporia, other maritime colonies of Carthage, and much territory within the Trenches. Whenever he rattled the sabre, Carthage always declined the challenge and merely appealed to the Romans, who sent out boundary commissions, but these always decided in the king's favour or else left the question unsettled (e.g. in 193, 182, 174 and 172 BC). Finally Carthage became restive, and after a series of razzias Masinissa occupied a district in the Great Plains called Tusca (perhaps the modern Dougga). Again Carthage appealed to the Roman Senate, with the usual result that a commission headed by Cato left the question undecided (probably in 153). But not all the Senate was willing to follow the revengeful advice of Cato, who now urged the destruction of Carthage. The next year another commission was despatched under Scipio Nasica who forced Masinissa to withdraw a little way.

In Carthage party strife was rife and the popular party succeeded in exiling the leaders of the faction which desired to come to an agreement with Masinissa (151–150). When the king tried to insist on the reinstatement of these exiles, the patience of the Carthaginians broke down and they declared war, unmindful of the restrictions of the Zama treaty. A fierce engagement gave a slight victory to the Numidians, so that the Carthaginians were ready to negotiate for terms through the good offices of Scipio Aemilianus, who had just arrived from Spain in order to obtain some elephants. Negotiations, however, broke down, and Masinissa managed to cut off his enemy's supplies. Starvation and disease at length forced the Carthaginians to capitulate; they agreed to cede the debated territory and to pay 5,000 talents in fifty years. But as the survivors marched out they were treacherously attacked by the king's son, Gulussa; few escaped to Carthage. The attempt to check Masinissa's advance had thus proved abortive; it had merely established the king in more territory and had roused the anger of Rome.

6. DELENDA EST CARTHAGO

The African question had long evoked much thought at Rome, until out of ugly suspicions and rumours of war there gradually crystallized two opposing policies. As is well known, whenever Cato was asked his opinion in the Senate he used with untiring importunity to add: 'I am also of the opinion that Carthage should cease to exist.' He is also said to have emphasized the dangerous proximity of Carthage by dramatically displaying in the House a ripe fig which he declared had been gathered at Carthage only three days before. But while the old man, obsessed with this one idea, was inciting the warmongers, P. Cornelius Scipio Nasica, a noble of considerable weight who had twice been consul, supported the Carthaginian cause, traditionally on the ground that fear of a strong political rival was a salutary discipline for Rome; but his motives are more likely to be found in a different political outlook combined with a more generous spirit. Neither party immediately gathered enough strength to win a political victory, and the scales remained balanced: in 152 Cato could arbitrate against Carthaginian interests, while the next year Nasica forced Masinissa to draw in his horns. But suddenly the Carthaginians threw themselves into the scales – on the wrong side. By attacking Masinissa they had given their foes in Rome the pretext they were seeking. And amid the cries of '*Punica fides*' which rang so pleasantly in Cato's ears, the more generous voice of Nasica was drowned.

The cause of the Third Punic War was, as Appian rightly states, the infringement of the Zama treaty by Carthage when she attacked Masinissa. Livy, following the patriotic efforts of Roman annalists to justify their city, declares that Carthage had prepared for war against Rome since 154 and that the Senate was very long-suffering. But if Roman ambassadors or spies saw hoards of munitions in Carthage, these were being prepared to settle accounts with Masinissa, not with Rome. There were, however, causes more deep seated than the juridical case which Rome used as a mere pretext. Some have supposed that economic factors were at work; but the view that commercial jealousy affected Rome's policy and that the Senate was influenced by vested interests has not met with favour. Political motives, however, were more potent. During his visit to Africa, Cato had been deeply impressed by the apparent prosperity of Carthage; he feared a possible revival of Rome's old enemy, especially when by paying the last instalment of the war indemnity in 151 the Carthaginians were seemingly less dependent on their conqueror. But the need for precautions against a Punic *revanche* were reinforced by misgivings about the growing strength of Masinissa, who having encircled Carthage might next covet the city itself. Suppose that the new Numidian kingdom, which had already upset the balance of power in Africa, should absorb Carthage, and that Masinissa, no longer content to play the role of watch-dog, should begin to growl at his master. Fear and hatred increased at Rome and men only awaited the opportunity.[18]

Nor had this been long delayed. By attacking Masinissa the Carthaginians gave the war party in Rome a pretext, a *justa causa*. Learning that troops were being levied in Italy they hastily condemned their military leaders to death, and then sent to Rome to complain of Masinissa and to shift the blame on to the shoulders of the condemned leaders. At this a Senator bluntly asked why they had not condemned the officers at the beginning of the war. On asking how they could atone, the Carthaginians were told that they must satisfy the Roman people, but the nature of this satisfaction was not defined, so that while Carthage debated Rome completed her preparations. Early in 149 Utica deserted Carthage and surrendered unconditionally to Rome. War was declared on Carthage, and a force of perhaps 80,000 men crossed to Utica: M'. Manilius, a well-known orator, commanded the land forces, while his philosophically-minded colleague, L. Marcius Censorinus, was in charge of the fleet. Among the military tribunes was P. Cornelius Scipio Aemilianus, who three years later destroyed Carthage. Meanwhile, when five deputies arrived in Rome to announce that the Carthaginians had decided that their only hope of safety lay in unconditional surrender, they found that war had been declared and that the consuls had already sailed.

By this formal act of surrender (*deditio*) Carthage had atoned for her breach of the Zama treaty and thus deprived the war party in Rome of any excuse for prosecuting hostilities. But at the same time she had put herself completely at the mercy of the Romans: she had given them a blank cheque, and if they cared to insert '*delenda est Carthago*' she could hardly complain. But it was the calculating and almost diabolic manner in which the Roman diplomats played their cards that roused the passion of the Carthaginians and the disgust of a large part of the civilized world. For in the Senate the Punic ambassadors were told that they would be allowed to retain their freedom, laws, territory and other property, both public and private, provided that they surrendered three hundred noble hostages and obeyed 'such commands as should be imposed on them by the consuls'. It was significant, as a certain Mago pointed out at Carthage, that no reference was made to the city, but it was too late to retract, and the hostages were duly handed over. Still keeping their real mission secret the consuls demanded the surrender of all arms and weapons; 200,000 panoplies and about 2,000 catapults were obediently given up, though the Carthaginians ventured to point out that they could not protect themselves against their erstwhile general Hasdrubal who had escaped execution and had collected 20,000 troops. The grim reply was that Rome would provide. Next, thirty leading citizens were ordered to go to Rome to hear the Senate's final orders. At long last the consuls announced the Senate's decision: the inhabitants must evacuate Carthage, which would be destroyed; the could settle where they liked provided that it was ten miles from the sea.

The Romans had skilfully attained their object, whether Carthage submitted or not. For if she refused she would thereby break the agreement made at the moment of her *deditio* and thus give them the legitimate excuse to proceed by force of arms. That Rome was technically correct is probable; she had skilfully used two pretexts, the infringement of the Zama treaty and of the act of *deditio*, to enforce her will. True, there might be room for more than one interpretation, the Romans regarding the act of *deditio* as a unilateral agreement, the Carthaginians as a bilateral. But nothing except the plea of expediency can excuse the deceit with which Rome first obtained hostages, then disarmed the city and only finally announced her real intentions. The shrewd historian Polybius, who was indirectly involved, shows clearly by his conduct that he regarded the surrender of Carthage as the end of the war; but he misjudged either the intention of the Senate or the fury of the Semite.

7. THE FALL OF CARTHAGE

Carthage with magnificent, if blind, resolve refused to submit. When the Roman consuls had sternly rejected an eloquent appeal for mercy, voiced by Banno, all the pent-up passions of hate and fear and despair were let loose in the city. Amid scenes of wild confusion the gates were closed and the walls manned. The slaves were freed and two generals elected: the exiled Hasdrubal was prevailed upon to forget the past, while the defence of the city was entrusted to another Hasdrubal, a grandson of Masinissa. A request for a month's truce was rejected by the Romans. Within the city all toiled night and day, the very temples being used as workshops for the manufacture of fresh arms. The walls were strengthened, supplies were received from Hasdrubal who controlled the open country, and though most coastal cities rebelled like Utica, the subject Libyans remained loyal. For some time the consuls waited patiently for the unarmed city to surrender. Meanwhile Masinissa caused slight anxiety. It was a grandson of his that was organizing the defence of Carthage, and the king himself, who saw the fruit of his ambitions now snatched from his grasp, was somewhat cold when asked for assistance; when later he proffered it, he was told abruptly that the Romans would let him know when they needed help.

At length Manilius and Censorinus moved against the city with their army and navy (summer 149). But they found that they had a harder nut to crack than they had anticipated. The walls of Carthage were well-nigh impregnable and her natural position was very strong. The city lay on the southern half of a peninsula which projects from the west into the Gulf of Tunis; its northern flank is protected by steep hills. South of these hills were the suburbs of the city, called Megara, then the Byrsa hill on which lay the citadel, next the lower ground with the market place and harbours, and finally beyond the southern walls a sandy spit of land which formed a bar across the inland lake of Tunis. The isthmus connecting the peninsula with the mainland was narrow, and across it ran the triple fortifications of the western wall of the city, which was forty-five feet high and thirty-three broad.[19] On the north of this isthmus Manilius encamped in order to cut off reinforcements from the interior, while Censorinus was stationed with the fleet on its southern shore by the lake of Tunis. After a vain assault from this isthmus, a regular blockade was instituted, but in the summer the unhealthiness of the stagnant lake forced Censorinus to move across the sand-bar to the sea, where his fleet was damaged by the Carthaginians. After he had returned to Rome to hold the elections, the enemy attacked by night the camp of his isolated colleague, Manilius, and the situation was only retrieved by the skill of Scipio.

Scipio again displayed conspicuous ability when during the winter Manilius led two unsuccessful expeditions against the Carthaginian forces near Nepheris, some twenty miles south-east of Tunis. He was once again in the limelight when the aged Masinissa, now on the point of death, asked that the grandson of his friend Africanus should arrange the future of his kingdom; Scipio decided to divide Numidia between the king's three sons and thereby averted the danger which a united Numidia had presented. Trusting in his increasing fame and popularity, Scipio then returned to Rome to seek office, while the consul of 148, L. Calpurnius Piso, with the admiral L. Hostilius Mancinus, arrived in Africa to take over the command. Warned by their predecessors' failures against Hasdrubal and Carthage, they attacked the towns which still remained loyal to Carthage, but they achieved little. Consequently the Carthaginians regained confidence: they were in touch with the Mauri in the west and with the pretender Andriscus in Macedonia (p. 289), while Masinissa's sons were no longer sending help to the Romans. Further,

Mancinus had got into difficulties. Having landed on the coast north of Carthage, near Sidi bou Saïd, he had penetrated into the suburb Megara, but was cut off in a perilous position. His urgent dispatches to Utica for help arrived only just in time. Scipio, who had that very evening returned to Africa, succeeded in rescuing him the next day.

In Rome there was such dissatisfaction with the conduct of the war that when Scipio intended to stand for the curule aedileship, he was nominated and elected consul by the people on account of his military record, though he was under the legal age and had not held the praetorship. The opposition of the consul in charge was swept aside by a tribune, and when Scipio's colleague C. Livius Drusus demanded that the provinces should be allocated by lot, another tribune intervened. As at the election of his adoptive grandfather, the constitution had to give place to the will of the people; like the Spartans after Leuctra they said: 'Let the laws sleep today.' Even old Cato went so far as to quote Homer and praise a Scipio by bluntly admitting that Aemilianus was 'the only sage among the flitting shades'. Among the companions who accompanied the new consul to Africa were the historian Polybius and the younger Laelius, whose father had accompanied the elder Africanus.

On his arrival in Africa, which was not a moment too soon to rescue Mancinus, Scipio at once determined to starve out the beleaguered city by an unbroken blockade. But while he was busy re-establishing the lax discipline of his army, Hasdrubal, who had been recalled, had taken up a strong position on the isthmus before the western wall of the city. Scipio encamped opposite; then in order to win control of the isthmus, and thus to cut off Carthage from the mainland, he made a night attack on the north-west corner of the walls. Some 4,000 men penetrated into Megara; this caused such a panic that Hasdrubal hastily fled from his advanced post into the city (spring 147). Scipio, his immediate object thus achieved, extricated his men from the suburb, where they were finding the ground very difficult, and then constructed a double line of earthworks right across the isthmus, close to the city wall. Hasdrubal's only reply was to mutilate his Roman prisoners and throw them from the walls.

Carthage was now entirely cut off from supplies by land, but occasionally a ship succeeded in running the blockade by sea. To complete his cordon Scipio established his fleet and many soldiers on the sand-bar south of the city; from here he began to construct a mole out to sea across the entrance of the Punic harbour. When the Carthaginians saw this work progressing they feverishly built fifty warships from old

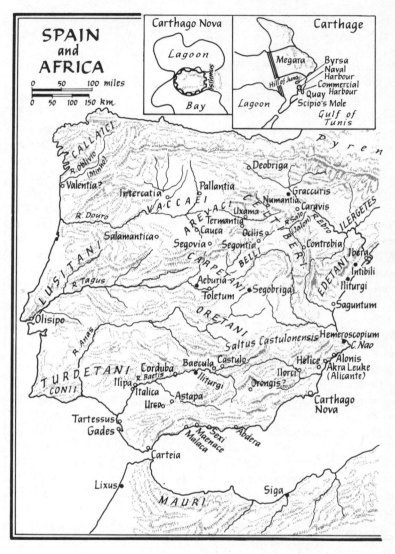

MAP IV

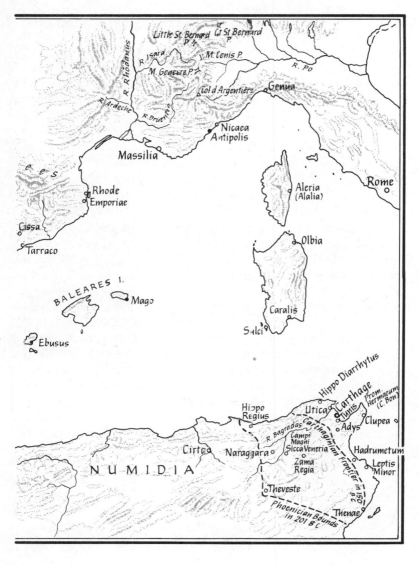

Little St Bernard P.

Gt St Bernard P.

R. Isara

M. Cenis P.

R. Rhodanus

M. Genevre P.

Col d'Argentier

R. Po

Genua

R. Ardeche

R. Druentia

Nicaea

Antipolis

Massilia

Aleria
(Alalia)

Rome

Rhode

Emporiae

Cissa

Olbia

Tarraco

BALEARES I.

Mago

Caralis

Ebusus

Salci

Hippo Diarrhytus

Carthage

Prom.
Hermaeum
(C. Bon)

Hippo
Regius

Utica

Tunis

R. Bagradas

Carthaginian Frontier in 150 B.C.

Adys

Clupea

Cirta

Naraggara

Campi
Magni
Sicca Veneria

Zama
Regia

Hadrumetum

Leptis
Minor

N U M I D I A

Theveste

Thenae

Phoenician Bounds
in 201 B.C.

material and cut a new channel from the inner harbour eastwards to the sea. The high walls around the arsenal screened their actions, so that the Romans were astounded to see this new fleet put to sea. The Punic commanders, however, foolishly waited to test its quality instead of taking the Romans by surprise. Three days later an engagement was fought off the harbour; the Romans finally prevailed, while the enemy either tried to re-enter the narrow entrance of their harbour or else were driven on to the quay and destroyed. After a desperate fight Scipio established himself on the quay where he fortified a position commanding the harbours. Carthage was now completely surrounded. Her last hope was thwarted during the winter when Scipio defeated a small force at Nepheris and captured the town. The Libyan tribes hastened to surrender to Rome. The final agony of Carthage was at hand.

In the spring of 146 Scipio gave orders for the final assault. While Hasdrubal fired the southern part of the harbour where he expected the attack, Laelius succeeded in piercing the wall further north on the seaward side of the inner harbour. Hence he advanced to the market-place, while the defenders fled to the Byrsa hill. For six days and nights the Romans fought their way step by step up the hillside amid the houses which they burned and destroyed one after another. On the seventh day the citadel surrendered and 50,000 men and women came forth to slavery. A final stand was made in the temple of Esmun by 900 Roman deserters, together with Hasdrubal's wife, who, unlike her husband, disdained surrender and perished amid the flames of the temple. For ten more days the fires of Carthage burned; the ruins were razed; a plough was drawn over the site; salt was sown in the furrows; a solemn curse was pronounced against its future rebirth; Carthage had been destroyed.

The cities which had remained loyal to Carthage were destroyed; those, like Utica, which had embraced the cause of Rome, were declared free and received territorial concessions. The rest of the land which Carthage had controlled at the beginning of the war was made into the new Roman province of Africa, the boundaries of which were marked out by a vast fosse. His work done, Scipio Aemilianus returned to Rome to celebrate his triumph and to follow the example of his grandfather by adopting the name of Africanus (Minor).

The fall of Carthage evoked varied comments in the Greek world. Some men commended the Romans for their statesmanlike policy in removing a perpetual menace; others believed that they had been corrupted by lust for power. Some contrasted the earlier civilized methods of Roman policy with their present stratagems and deceits;

others again denied that they were guilty of treachery or injustice. But few can read the account of the fall of Carthage given by Appian, who followed Polybius closely, without a feeling that Rome also had fallen from her pristine greatness. Rome's conduct may have been juridically correct, but she was forgetting those moral qualities which had made her great. Even the order to abandon the city of Carthage might have been anticipated, for others such as the people of Falerii and Ligurian and Spanish tribes had been moved from their homes; and as Rome itself was more than ten miles from its port, the agriculturally-minded Senators would be less prepared to consider that the future they proposed for Carthage was unduly severe. It was rather the callous and calculating way in which the order was enforced, together with the nervous bullying which had originally goaded Carthage into retaliating against Masinissa, that casts a shadow over Rome's good name. The horrors of the siege excite pity, but they are not unparalleled in the history of the ancient world. Scipio might weep over the burning city, but his thoughts were rather brooding over the mutability of human affairs and the possible fate of his own city as he quoted the lines of Homer:

> That day shall be when holy Troy shall fall
> And Priam, lord of spears, and Priam's folk.

And though, in another poet's vision, Hannibal had arisen to avenge Dido, the fall of Carthage was not avenged and Scipio's fatalistic fears were not realized until centuries later the Vandal brought the Imperial City to her knees; and then the flourishing *Carthago rediviva* of the Empire followed her imperial mistress under the spear of the barbarian.

XV

ROMAN POLICY
AND THE
GOVERNMENT

The real government of Rome during the second century was the Senate, the instrument of the nobility, whose power rested on custom and not on law. We must first consider what policy this governing authority pursued in home affairs, towards the old Confederacy; and secondly, its foreign policy and provincial administration. Then we must examine the basis of the power of this senatorial oligarchy, its control of all branches of public life, the cliques into which it was divided, and the tendencies which these represented.

1. HOME POLICY

By the Lex Claudia of 218 (p. 188) senators were forbidden to own ships other than small ones to transport the produce of their estates. A sharp distinction was drawn between land and trade, between the governing and commercial classes. A senator could get round the law by allowing his freedmen to trade for him or by loans on bottomry, but in the main the distinction remained real. During the strain of the Hannibalic War the government, which relied largely on private enterprise for supplies, had to excuse from military service three companies of nineteen men who supplied the Spanish army on credit (215). Two of the contractors scuttled their ships, which had been filled with rubbish, and demanded compensation from the state which had undertaken responsibility for sea-risks. Despite the Senate's desire to maintain unity at home, two tribunes brought a capital charge against them; during their trial their fellow-contractors rioted and used violence. The war thus helped to make the commercial classes conscious of their unity and importance.

The capitalists were known as equites. This term strictly refers to two classes of people: either young nobles, members of the eighteen equestrian centuries, who ceased to be effective cavalry and became an honorary corps; or members of ignoble (non-official) families whose incomes were equivalent to those of the equites, but who were not enrolled in the equestrian centuries. In the third century the censors had drawn up a list, supplementary to the eighteen centuries, of those whose property warranted cavalry service at their own expense; probably in the second century this *census* was fixed by law. It was these men who were then commonly called equites. With the conquest of the Mediterranean world they gained an extended field for their activities. Many of them formed joint-stock companies of limited liability, and to such corporations the censors usually let contracts for the performance of public works and the collection of certain taxes. The equites were also permitted to collect the tithes and the grazing tax on public lands in Italy, together with harbour dues. They took over the operation of the Spanish mines about 178 and of the Macedonian mines in 158. Though the military supplies and equipment for the eastern wars were primarily the responsibility of the regular magistrates, these must often have had recourse to the co-operation of traders. Thus by helping the state to exploit its extensive real estate, by contracting for public works, by collecting certain taxes, a body of rich and intelligent men was created. These *publicani* were backed by smaller *negotiatores*, who went in for money-lending, banking and trading, and on occasion even by senators who borrowed from them or speculated with their help. If any of them wished later to turn to a public career they might by serving as military tribunes or *praefecti sociorum* get their feet on the lowest rung of an official career, but they seldom succeeded in climbing to the top. But included in the *ordo equester* were the country gentry of the towns of Italy who preferred the interests of their landed estates and the affairs of their local communities to both the glamour of political life in Rome and the risks of business. These men in part came from the same social background as the senators: although wealthy enough and with the right family connexions to compete for office, they chose to stand aloof. As tensions with the senatorial order developed, it was the *publicani*, described by Cicero as the 'flower of the equestrian order', who in the main began to clash with the Senate in the political arena. How the equites became increasingly politically self-conscious is a story that belongs more to the revolutionary age of the Gracchi, but before then they had become an important factor in Roman life.[1]

The policy of the Senate towards this new class was to use it commercially, instead of creating an adequate civil service, but to disregard its political claims. This naturally occasioned a certain friction and jealousy between the classes. In Cato's censorship of 184 his letting of state contracts was so severe that the leading contractors complained to the Senate and got their contracts cancelled. In 169 a real quarrel broke out between the Senate and equites. The censors refused to accept tenders from contractors, who had been employed by the previous censors, on the ground of their exorbitant profits. The cause of the excluded publicans was taken up by a tribune. When one of the censors tried to intervene at a meeting, both were accused of high treason (*perduellio*) and only just escaped condemnation through the exertions of the nobles and the popularity of Ti. Sempronius Gracchus. It is noteworthy that the censors, backed by the Senate, succeeded in defying the power of the tribune, but the incident also shows the important part now played by the capitalist class in Roman life; as the Senate usurped more judicial power the breach between senators and equites widened until C. Gracchus precipitated a political crisis.

Secondly, the government had to define a policy towards freedmen. The conquest of the Mediterranean was flooding the slave markets and consequently there was an increase in the number of freedmen, who with their children swelled the mass of clients. After the liberal attempt of Appius Claudius had failed, those who possessed no land, whether rich or poor, had been placed in the four urban tribes (304), but between the First and Second Punic Wars, perhaps when the Comitia Centuriata was reformed, all freedmen were confined to the urban tribes, irrespective of whether they possessed land. But the Hannibalic War had emphasized their importance, so that in 189 Q. Terentius Culleo carried a liberal measure enrolling sons of freedmen, *libertini*, in the rustic tribes. At the same time (or in 179) freedmen with land valued at more than 30,000 sesterces, that is, those whose *census* was equal to that of the first or second class of the centuries, could also be enrolled in the rustic tribes; in 179 those who had sons and land in a rustic tribe received the same privilege. But in 169 the censors provided that those freedmen who had not 30,000 sesterces were in future to be confined to one urban tribe (the Esquilina). In sum, this policy to liberated slaves was very generous compared with that of other ancient states; for they became so numerous that, had their votes not been limited, they might have outvoted the citizens living outside Rome. But the infusion of this element into the state threatened the old standards of morality and it must have embittered those Latins who in vain tried to gain or retain Roman citizenship.[2]

The Italian confederacy had been tested in the fire of the Hannibalic War and it emerged changed. The old feeling of unity and equality was shattered: Rome held whip and reins alike. Those allies that had revolted were not treated with undue harshness. In 210 Capua had felt the strength of Rome's hand, but her punishment was not unjust; the original owners were generally allowed to remain as tenants on their land when it had been annexed by Rome. Further south the Romans had confiscated more land from the rebels, especially from Bruttium, Thurii and Tarentum, perhaps some 4000 square miles, which they could dispose of as they liked, by founding colonies or by viritane assignments. Two small Latin colonies were settled at Copia (193) and Vibo (Hipponium; 192), but as the Latin towns could supply few colonists, the founding of Latin colonies would mainly redound to Rome's advantage. But the shortage of men was widespread and there was more attractive land than the devastated south nearer Rome; so the censors rented out large estates of 500 *iugera* to any Roman, Latin or ally who had the means to undertake the venture. In this way southern Italy recovered something of its old prosperity, but the growth of large ranches where cattle, sheep and horses were reared mainly by slave labour soon seriously affected the economic life of Italy.[3]

Latin colonies were still founded for some time, and Latins were even allowed to share in the citizen colonies to make up the numbers, for example, at Buxentum in 194, but when colonists from Ferentinum claimed that participation in a citizen colony automatically granted Roman citizenship, the Senate refused the claim. Roman franchise was becoming more valuable, and a quick method of winning it had been for a Latin to participate in a Roman colony instead of settling in Rome long enough to be enrolled by the new censors in the ordinary way. The Romans also were becoming unwilling to surrender their citizenship by going to Latin colonies. At first they were attracted by the grant of larger allotments than the 5–10 *iugera* of Roman colonies: at Copia commoners received 20 *iugera*, equites 40; at Bononia 50 and 70 respectively; at Aquileia 50 and 140. After 178 BC, however, no more Latin colonies were founded, partly because Rome felt she could not afford to lose more citizens by settlement in Latin colonies and partly because later the military need declined. When in 173 Boian land was distributed *viritim*, 10 *iugera* were given to citizens but only three to allies. Indeed, very few Roman colonies were settled in Italy after this date. When the *tributum* was discontinued in 167 the Senate became more dependent on its revenue from rents from *ager publicus* and was less willing to grant land for colonies of any sort. But the burst of colonization after the Hannibalic War had been useful. The citizen colonies formed military centres which strengthened the confederation; the Latin colonies became centres of agricultural development; and all hastened the unification of Italy.[4]

Latin claims for Roman citizenship also caused friction. The Romans remembered how to be generous when in 188 they raised Arpinum, Formiae and Fundi from half- to full citizenship and the Capuans to a probationary stage. The rest of the cities enjoying half-franchise may gradually have been promoted (how gradually we do not know: some may have continued until the Social War), but no effort was made to enfranchise the Italian allies. Complaints reached Rome from various Latin cities which could not fulfil their military obligations because so many of their citizens had settled in Rome.[5] In 193 a consul tried to meet the difficulty by summoning contingents of allies in proportion to the number of men fit for service in each town, instead of in accordance with the old fixed quota. In 187 the Latins asked that those who had migrated to Rome should be repatriated: twelve thousand men were struck off the citizen-roll and sent back to their own colonies. This alien act was for the benefit of the Latin communities and to the disadvantage of Rome, but it must have caused much discontent among the ejected and it infringed the *ius migrandi*. When the Latin cities appealed again, a Lex Claudia, passed in 177, was enforced by the censors of 173, who expelled more of those who had wrongly been registered at Rome.

The Latins and allies found other causes for complaint. The spoils of empire, the revenue from the tithes, harbour dues and mines, and tribute of the provinces went into the Roman Treasury and did not enrich the Latins. Similarly, the bulk of the sum raised from the sale of war booty was paid by successful generals into the Roman Treasury; at first the small donative given from the booty to the rank and file was shared by Roman and Latin alike, but after the Histrian War in 177 the Latins received only half as much as Romans. Though Italian merchants often followed the flag it was the Roman governors that received the fruits, whether honest or corrupt, from the provinces. Further, by an enactment of a tribune, P. Porcius Laeca (199), Roman citizens in Italy and the provinces were safeguarded against the almost unlimited *imperium* of the governor by the right of appeal; the scourging of Roman citizens without appeal was forbidden by Marcus Porcius Cato (198 or 195); and Lucius Porcius Cato (?154) prohibited summary execution by military officers.[6] But over the Italians that served with the Romans and over the Italian traders and residents the governor still retained powers of life and death and the right to scourge.

Direct interference by Rome in Italian affairs was small. For instance, in 193 a Lex Sempronia virtually instructed the *praetor peregrinus* to apply Roman laws of usury to all Latins and Italians in their dealings with Roman citizens. This limitation of the *ius commercii* was quite fair in practice, but the measure emphasized the difference in political status between Romans and allies. A more striking instance of interference was the enquiry caused by the Bacchanalian conspiracy (pp. 400 f.). The spread of mystic cults from southern Italy led to the formation of secret associations for their celebration. The resultant immorality and disorder forced the Senate to stamp out the evil (186–181). The cult itself was legalized for individuals, but all secret associations were disbanded. It is noticeable that police measures were first taken in Rome itself and then conducted largely in *fora*, that is, citizen territory, and only in allied districts in the last resort. In fact the Senate made itself responsible for public security in Italy, and thereby might technically infringe its treaties with the various cities, but it interfered as little as possible. More annoying was the later interference by Roman magistrates who, in touring the country, illegally imposed burdens on cities. In 173 Postumius demanded free entertainment when passing through Praeneste. It was symptomatic that a Roman magistrate should apply to an honoured allied city in Italy treatment which had been reserved for subjects; also that the Praenestines dared not refuse. The abuse increased. The story of how the chief magistrate of Sidicinum, an allied city, was scourged because he was slow in clearing a public bath for a Roman magistrate's wife is well known.[7]

In sum, Rome's relations with her confederacy underwent a gradual change in the second century. During the first decade or so a certain generosity remained, which was later throttled by self-interest and aggressiveness. As the franchise was coveted, so it was withheld. Latin colonies ceased; Latins received smaller assignments of land. The Empire was exploited for Rome rather than for Italy, and Roman magistrates became more overbearing. The distinction between the privileged Latins and the other Italians had broken down. The Latins realized that they were to be treated like the rest, and all found their condition sinking from alliance to dependence, if not to subjection. It was not until after the smouldering discontent had blazed forth in the Social War that Italy really became one.

2. FOREIGN POLICY AND THE PROVINCES

The Hannibalic War forced the world to think in international terms. 'Hitherto', wrote Polybius, 'the world's history has been, so to speak, a series of disconnected transactions . . . but after this epoch history becomes a connected whole.' All civilized countries had to face the fact that the two halves of the Mediterranean were now linked by the central power in Italy. It was long before Rome finally won the whole Mediterranean world, but the battle of Zama sealed her primacy and by the year 146 she had six provinces – Sicily, Corsica and Sardinia, the two Spains, Macedonia and Africa; five of these had fallen to her as the result of wars with Carthage. She had ties of alliance or friendship with Numidia, Massilia, Illyria and the rest of Greece, the kingdoms of Asia Minor, Syria and Egypt; in reality these countries formed a Roman protectorate. A superficial glance at this great achievement might give the impression that the Romans had been driven on by a lust for conquest which would not be satisfied until it embraced the whole world; but that this was not so is clear from an examination of the circumstances in which they acquired their various dependencies. Indeed, for many years they tried not to annex territory and wished either to avoid foreign complications or else to exercise influence rather than rule abroad. The early growth of the Empire falls into two clear divisions : the period from 241 to 197 and then after a gap of fifty years the period around the year 146. What then did this changing policy mean, why did Rome acquire an empire and how did she adapt her machinery of government to meet it?

During the first period of annexation Rome had been dominated by fear of Carthage, and her four earliest provinces were annexed mainly with the object of excluding the Carthaginians from them. Although the Romans had not thought it wise to extend their confederacy to include these countries, from which they exacted some form of taxation in place of military service, they had not deliberately tried to build up an empire. The word *provincia* only meant the sphere of work allotted to any magistrate; Italy itself could form such a 'province', as when it was assigned to a consul in 171 BC. As the need to send magistrates abroad increased, the number of praetors was raised to four (*c.* 227) and then to six (197). After this the Romans were unwilling to extend the Empire, and the reasons are not far to seek.

Annexation involved administrative, financial and military problems which strained the institutions of a city-state. To govern an empire a civil service of permanent officials had gradually to supersede annual magistrates, and a citizen militia, commanded by officers who often had little military experience or aptitude, gave place to a professional army. The Hannibalic War had moulded the army in the direction of professionalism: the periods of service, the foreign theatres of war, the difficulty of control by the home government, the length of the generals' commands, had all increased. But it was followed by a reaction to the more amateur system of earlier days. Rather than create a standing army for provincial defence, or allow the provincials themselves to guard their own frontiers, the Romans preferred to allow foreign kings to protect their interests. But the problem of administration influenced Roman policy even more than that of imperial defence. The Romans were unwilling to create the necessary machinery beyond raising the number of praetors to six, two of whom served in Rome, the others in the four provinces. But though no more provinces were added, Rome had to fight, arbitrate and govern in the Hellenistic world. This required magistrates, and so the device of prolonging an annual magistracy, first adopted in the Samnite Wars and used frequently during the pressure of the Hannibalic War, was afterwards used more frequently, and when Macedonia and Africa were annexed the problem of provincial administration was solved by the extended use of the pro-magistracy. It became more usual for pro-magistrates to govern the provinces, until in Sulla's time it was the regular custom, if not a legal necessity.

It has been suggested that the Senate adopted an anti-expansionist policy in order to secure its exclusiveness at home.[8] To have increased the number of provinces would have meant increasing the number of magistrates and hence of admitting more men into its upper ranks, while to create a new type of magistracy which did not carry with it the right to a seat in the Senate would have been equally injurious to the senatorial nobility in the long run. When, however, the pro-magistracy became more common, the Senate was able to plan a second period of provincial annexation (146–121). Doubtless this desire to maintain its exclusiveness was a real factor in the policy of the Senate, which was especially jealous of provincial governors whom it found difficult to control. But if for other reasons annexation seemed desirable, the Senate might well have devised the method of *prorogatio imperii* fifty years earlier; the commands of the Scipios and Flamininus were striking examples in wartime of a method which could have been adapted to peace. The government had other objections, beside the peril to its own exclusiveness, against increasing the number of provinces. Early in the second century fear of eastern complications forced the Senate to define a policy towards the

Hellenistic world; it followed the line of defensive imperialism, but its opinion was divided. The more liberal outlook of a number of philhellenic nobles led to the establishing of 'friendship' and ultimately to the formation of a protectorate system. A reaction followed, led by Cato, who wished to interfere as little as possible in foreign affairs, thinking that foreign conquest was undermining Roman character. But both schools of thought were opposed to annexation. Thus many considerations militated against the formation of further provinces: the inadequacy of Republican institutions; the lack of permanent officials and a professional army; the Senate's dislike of increasing the number of magistrates and widening the basis of the nobility; its mistrust of distant commands; and the wish of some to protect but not to rule the Greek world, and of others to neglect it.

The protectorate system gradually broke down in Greece, and ties of friendship and temporary alliance soon hardened into permanent alliance, which meant Roman leadership in external affairs. After 187 Roman policy deteriorated, but even after Pydna an attempt was made to patch up the old system. The Romans tried to uphold a protectorate in Macedonia, as in Illyria, by deposing the king and breaking up national unity. But their brutal treatment of Aetolia and Epirus revealed their attitude. The punishment of Corinth showed clearly what a Roman protectorate meant when the Greeks still refused to set their own house in order. In Spain too, methods of policy deteriorated. Neither of the two departures from the protectorate system, the formation of the provinces of Macedonia and Africa, was caused by the desire to annex. In Macedonia, where Roman patience was exhausted, annexation seemed the only method of securing peace; local conditions were changed as little as possible. The destruction of Carthage was caused by misplaced jealousy and fear. The creation of the province was a measure of self-protection, whether necessary or not. Only some 5,000 square miles were annexed, of which a large part was assigned to seven free cities which paid no taxes to Rome. Indeed, the Romans seemed desirous of maintaining a protectorate system wherever possible, as later, after the Jugurthine War. The policy of annexation was due less to the senatorial nobility than to the military captains of the last century of the Republic. But protection meant in fact control. Equal alliance and friendship could not be maintained between two parties of such different weight. The kings of Asia Minor were virtually client kings. It has been seen that Rome was slow to intervene in the east and that the initiative was often taken by the Greeks themselves, but insensibly the Romans came to dominate their friends and allies as effectively as their subjects; and the fault belonged as much to the suicidal folly of the Greeks and to the deterioration and weakness of the east, as to Rome. But to measure the decline in Rome's policy it is only necessary to consider first the brave declaration of freedom to Greece in 196, and then the smouldering ashes of Corinth, Carthage and Numantia, or the crowd of princes and envoys that waited obsequiously in the lobby of the Senate-house.

The change in Roman policy is sometimes attributed to the growth of a capitalist class in whose commercial interests Rhodes was humbled in 167 and Corinth and Carthage were sacked in 146. Little evidence can be found in support of such a proposition.[9] The stipulation in Rome's treaty with Ambracia in 189 requiring exemption from port dues appears unusual; the clause in the constitution of the Macedonian Republics, restricting the exportation of timber and the importation of salt, was probably designed to protect Macedon; the request of Rhodes in 169 for permission to buy grain in Sicily may imply some control by the Senate over the Sicilian market, but even supposing such control was permanent, it was more probably exercised for political than for commercial motives. The Romans declared Delos a free port when handing it over to Athenian control; their motive, however, was probably political, to punish Rhodes, and the inscriptional evidence shows that, although Italian merchants benefited, Orientals benefited still more. The destruction of Corinth aided Delos, but the Romans would hardly have undertaken its destruction to benefit Italian merchants so indirectly; and the motives which led to the overthrow of Carthage were probably political. The Romans took few measures to aid their merchants and did not trouble to keep the seas free from pirates. Many Italians went to the provinces to seek their fortune in trade or business, partly because of agricultural depression in Italy; a capitalist class was created; and trade followed the flag. But there is little evidence to show that such classes were influential enough to mould Roman policy or to shape the political decisions of the Senate. The equites and the merchants of southern Italy reaped, but it was the Senate that sowed.

Roman policy, guided by political rather than commercial or economic motives, deteriorated partly because of an increasing tendency to exploit the provinces and theatres of war.[10] In theory the burden imposed on the provincials was not severe; as a general rule instead of giving their lifeblood like the Italian allies, they merely paid some form of tax, either a tithe as in Sicily or a fixed tribute (*stipendium*) as in Spain, Africa and Macedon. Notwithstanding the Spanish mines, it is doubtful whether the revenue from Spain paid for the cost of occupation, and in such warlike provinces the task of administration must often have seemed thankless. The annexation of Sicily, Sardinia and Corsica was advantageous since they were fairly peaceful and supplied the Roman market with corn. But while in theory the administration might be beneficial to Rome and fair to the provincials, in practice much depended on the character of the governor, who with the tax-collectors could fleece the provinces if he wished. It must be remembered that his position was unpaid, that he had had to bear the cost of reaching office and that, if a praetor, he was probably hoping to obtain the consulship on his return to Rome. Roman society was becoming more luxurious and a political career involved increasing expense. The Senate in theory discountenanced cruelty or oppression in the provinces, since disorders caused trouble and expense; but in fact the governor, far from its watchful eye, had to be allowed considerable rope – and he did not often hang himself. Further, it would increase his future electioneering prospects if he adopted a lenient attitude towards the Italian merchants and businessmen who invaded the provinces, and to whom, whether as individuals or as partners in, or agents of companies, the Roman government found it convenient to farm the collection of harbour dues and the tax on pasturage. In the provinces that paid a fixed *stipendium*, which could have been collected direct by the governor's quaestor, *publicani* were still able to collect the secondary taxes and the revenues from public lands and mines; they could also do business for local governing bodies which were responsible for the collection of taxes. A governor would seldom wish to offend the agents of the great companies at Rome.

Thus, although the provincial system was theoretically fairly sound, it was open to abuse by unscrupulous governors. The abuses increased in the years after 146 until they reached their climax in the governorship of a Verres, but that they were not unknown in the earlier part of the second century is clear from the appeal of the unhappy Spaniards in 171. Little was done to counter the disgrace until, by a Lex Calpurnia *de repetundis* in 149, a permanent court was established to try cases of extortion. Jurors were empanelled by the praetor from the Senate and the court was more expeditious than the cumbersome tribal assembly; yet as corrupt governors were judged by members of their order, the verdict might not always be unbiased. But there was a brighter side to the picture; extortion, at any rate during the earlier part of Rome's imperial career, was the exception rather than the rule, and most magistrates were men of honour. Polybius wrote that 'if a single talent is entrusted to a Greek statesman, ten auditors, as many seals and twice as many witnesses are required for the security of the bond, yet even so faith is not observed; while a Roman official or diplomat who handles vast sums of money keeps faith through the mere moral obligation of the oath he has sworn . . . amongst the Romans the corrupt official is as rare as the financier with clean hands among other people' (vi, 56; he also admits a deterioration of Roman character, xviii, 35; xxxi, 25).

3. THE SENATORIAL OLIGARCHY

In the classic description of the Roman constitution in his sixth book, Polybius concludes that it contained three fundamental principles, monarchy, aristocracy and democracy, which were excellently mingled and balanced: the consuls represented regal power, the Senate aristocratic, and the people democratic. (Polybius, vi, 11−18. One may compare the English Cabinet *vis-à-vis* the Crown, Lords and Commons.) Such was the theoretical distribution of power, but in fact it was the Senate that drove the chariot of state and seldom did the magistrates or people try to kick over the traces. The Senate had come out of the Hannibalic War with flying colours and its functions widened with the extended scope of Roman policy. The increasing complication of judicial affairs could have been met by establishing paid jurymen from the people, as at Athens, but instead the people allowed the Senate to appoint judicial commissions to deal with matters that concerned the safety of the state and to supply the jury when the first *quaestio perpetua* was established. The Senate's control of the chief military commands, of finance and of foreign policy, was unquestioned till the time of Tiberius Gracchus; any objections raised by the people, as when they refused to declare war on Philip in 200, were generally overruled. It also took over from the people the right to prorogue a magistrate's command, and occasionally it dispensed with the use of sortition in assigning duties to magistrates. The extent of its powers will be seen best by considering its relations with the people and with the magistrates.

Between the Lex Hortensia of 287, which had asserted the sovereign authority of the Roman people, and the close of the Hannibalic War, the voice of the people was heard occasionally. The democratic leaders of the new nobility may have urged the people to decide on the Mamertine alliance, while part of the Senate procrastinated, and the people stiffened up the terms imposed on Carthage after Aegates Insulae. The popular leader Flaminius enjoyed a striking career despite senatorial hostility, and when the Hannibalic War broke out the people were inclined to question the leadership of the Senate and to elevate their own nominees to command the armies. Flaminius, Minucius Rufus and Terentius Varro were not perhaps the military fools that the aristocratic tradition has depicted, but they were unfortunate. After their defeats the people acquiesced in the Senate's direction of the war and only once again expressed their will forcibly, this time more wisely, by electing Scipio Africanus to the Spanish command. The prestige which the Senate thus won by its conduct of the war remained unshaken in the next century. The people were now willing to acquiesce, since their own representatives, the tribunes, could keep an eye on proceedings in the Senate. Also much of the legislation of the second century was carried through the tribal assembly by tribunes; this was due partly to the frequent absence of the consuls abroad, but it had the effect of keeping the people busy and giving them the impression that they were the main legislative body, whereas probably most of the measures had already been shaped in the Senate. Until the end of the Spanish wars little protest was heard from the people.

Beside encroaching on the judicial and indirectly on the legislative functions of the people, the Senate also won over their magistrates. The tribunes, who had originally been outside the Senate, were gradually absorbed into it and became an instrument of the senatorial oligarchy, for among the ten there would normally be some partisans of the Senate. They gained the right, perhaps by the Lex Hortensia, of convoking the Senate, and they gradually became in effect magistrates of the *populus* and not merely of the *plebs*, the office being held between the quaestorship and praetorship; thus a tribune, Ti. Sempronius Gracchus, intervened at the trial of the Scipios to help one of the old patrician families. One function of the tribune was that of public prosecutor. But the Senate, jealous of outstanding personalities, was often quite as interested as the people in calling magistrates to book, so that in the second century we find tribunes undertaking prosecutions in their own or senatorial interests rather than on behalf of the people. As cliques developed within the Senate, members of one faction would use this method to attack their rivals; Cato, for instance, is said to have been prosecuted forty-four times and he probably returned blow for blow by using the services of tribunes. Such prosecutions would often be dropped during the proceedings when once the political object had been attained, and generally some tribune could be found to veto his fellow. Another symptom of the decline of the tribunate was the use made of it by ambitious young men, who, lacking other means of attracting notice, would attack prominent men for personal or party ends, and so gain notoriety and impress the electorate. Occasionally tribunes may have tried to oppose the will of the Senate; such an attempt may have led to the Lex Aelia et Fufia, which gave magistrates the right to obstruct plebeian assemblies by announcing unfavourable omens (*obnuntiatio*) (*c.* 150 BC). But in the main the tribunes had become tools of the Senate.[11]

The war with Hannibal had two opposite results: it increased both the oligarchical power of the central administrative body, the Senate, and the dictatorial power of the executive magistrates. The need for continuity of command led to the suspension of the rule that forbade re-election to the consulship within ten years. During the war Q. Fabius Maximus, already twice consul, held the office three times (215, 214, 209), M. Claudius Marcellus four times (215, 214, 210, 208) and Q. Fulvius Flaccus twice (212, 209); they also held pro-magistracies. Even more revolutionary was the career of Scipio Africanus, who acted as proconsul in Spain for five years (210–206) and in Africa for three (204–201) and in the interval was consul (205); so that he was in command for ten consecutive years. Besides this threat to the annual magistracy, the principle of collegiality weakened; the complication of business involved a division of labour, and when regular governorships were established in the provinces collegiality abroad had disappeared in fact and in law. Indeed, the power of the consuls had grown immensely: they exercised semi-independent control in distant lands, they commanded large armies, they had to take decisions which determined the fate of countries, they dictated terms to subjects and allies. At home the use of the overriding power of the dictatorship had lapsed, so that the way was open for the ambitious general to aim at personal rule. But the kingly position won by Scipio Africanus after the battle of Zama engendered rivalry at home, and the jealous nobility found means to check the over-popular or over-ambitious general and to reduce genius to the level of mediocrity.

There were many ways by which the influence of the magistrates could be checked. The use of lot in assigning provinces prevented an ambitious candidate from emphasizing to the electorate his suitability for a given appointment. There was a tendency to keep the consuls in Italy when possible and to use praetors and propraetors for duties abroad. True, the increase of provinces necessitated prorogation of command, and a further move was taken in that direction by the Lex Baebia which reduced the praetorships in alternate years from six to four, chiefly to allow praetors in Spain a longer command to avoid the waste of time caused by the long journey to and from Spain; this law was, however, quickly repealed. But prorogation did not become a danger because the Senate gradually took over from the people the right to decide the matter. Consequently, after 200 BC few commands were prolonged for more than one year; that of Flamininus (198–194) was exceptional. Similarly, the method of investing *privati* with *imperium*, which had been applied to Scipio Africanus and to his successors in Spain, was discontinued when the number of praetors was raised in 197. But the Senate's strongest hold over the magistrates was gained by restricting re-election and establishing a fixed sequence of office. In the fourth century tenure of the consulship for two consecutive years and re-election to the same office within ten years had been forbidden, and before the Second Punic War it became necessary for a year to elapse between the tenure of the aedileship, praetorship and consulship. Though in wartime the rule had to be disregarded, a fixed order of office became customary. This was regulated by statute in 180, and a two-years' inverval between offices probably was prescribed (Lex Villia Annalis).[12] Office must be held in the following order: quaestorship, aedileship, praetorship, consulship. The aedileship was not an essential stage, but was sought after as it gave the chance of winning popularity with the mob by a lavish display of public games. The minimum age limit for office was also fixed, and ten years' military service was a necessary qualification for the quaestorship; thus the consulship could not be reached before the age of thirty-four, or, if the aedileship had been held, of thirty-seven. Later the minimum age for the consulship was fixed at forty-two and re-election was forbidden (perhaps *c.* 150). Thus the Senate was able to curb undue ambition, and any danger to the constitution arising from the practical abolition of collegiality and from the powers of provincial commanders was averted.

The Senate, the stronghold of the nobility, controlled not only the magistrates and people but was itself controlled by an inner circle of nobles, the descendants of those who had held the consulship (or perhaps, in the third and early second centuries, any curule magistracy may have sufficed). Men outside this group might reach the quaestorship, but they seldom climbed much higher; when they succeeded in gaining a consulship they were acclaimed 'new men' (*novi homines*). The effective government was in the hands of some ten or twenty families. Of the 108 consuls between 200 and 146 BC only eight came from new families, and perhaps only four were strictly *novi homines*, two of whom were helped by aristocratic friends, Cato (195) by Valerius Flaccus, Glabrio (191) by the Scipios (the two others were Cn. Octavius, 165, and L. Mummius, 146).

Sallust remarks that the nobility passed on the consulship from one to another.[13] Of the 200 consuls who held office from 234 to 134 BC, 159 were members of twenty-six families, 99 of ten families. The old difference between patrician and plebeian had disappeared, and in 172 both consuls were plebeians for the first time, but a new exclusiveness had grown up. This was partly due no doubt to deliberate policy, but partly also to difficulties inherent in the nature of the Roman magistracy: a candidate must be wealthy and yet have no connection with trade, and it was difficult for him to attract the notice of the electorate if he was outside the charmed circle of noble families whose exploits were on all men's lips.

4. THE RIVAL FAMILIES

Party politics in a modern sense were unknown at Rome. The electorate did not vote for party candidates who represented definite policies, although exceptionally when an individual was known to favour a certain policy his chances of election might be affected by this: for instance, Scipio gained office partly on the strength of his strategic programme for invading Africa. In the main, however, men were elected as the result of the strength of their social backing, which derived from family, *gens*, friends and clients. But the nobility, which comprised the families of those candidates who had successfully reached the consulship, was not generally of one mind. Schisms and factions would naturally arise from political or personal causes, and the leading senatorial families would tend to fall into cliques. The extent to which an elaborate system of groupings and counter-groupings emerged has been differently estimated but it can hardly be denied that such groups formed the real, if unadvertised and unofficial, basis of Roman public life. The subject cannot be traced in any detail here, but a few examples may be given.[14]

The five chief *gentes* at the beginning of the Hannibalic War were the Fabii, Claudii, Cornelii, Aemilii and Valerii. Until Cannae a coalition of the Scipios (Cornelii) and Aemilii held sway, but then gave place to the Fabian faction. By 212 the Claudii, supported by Fulvius Flaccus, had become more prominent, but the fortunes of the Scipios began to rise again when young Scipio succeeded Claudius Nero in Spain. The influence of the Scipios grew steadily, though challenged by Fabius and the 'die hards', but while Scipio was in Africa a coalition of the Claudii, Fulvii, and Servilii jealously tried to undermine his position by political intrigue at Rome. His victory at Zama gave Scipio the most powerful position yet held by a Roman general, and men may have wondered whether this popular hero would challenge the senatorial oligarchy and try to establish a tyranny by overthrowing his rivals at home. He was, however, content to sink back into the life of a private citizen, but his personal influence was great. He was elected censor and made *princeps senatus* in 199, and many relatives and friends held office during the first decade of the second century. There is no doubt that his sympathies were philhellenic. Not only had his ready adoption of Greek habits in Sicily annoyed Cato, but when in the east he visited Delphi and Delos where he dedicated gifts to Apollo and received the honour of proxeny. Apart from his personal interest in Greek culture, epigraphic evidence demonstrates that he supported a philhellenic policy. During the war with Antiochus he and his brother proclaimed freedom for the Greek cities in Asia, as Flamininus had for those in Greece: they would liberate all cities which had supported the Roman cause or which surrendered at once. In a letter recognizing the autonomy of the inhabitants of Heraclea-by-Latmus, the Scipios emphasized their goodwill towards all the Greeks and promised similar treatment to all who surrendered. The freedom granted was genuine, for a few years later Heraclea was allowed to carry on a war with Miletus without interference from Rome.[15]

Clearly Scipio Africanus supported the philhellenic policy of the Senate, and the man who had won Spain, Africa and Asia would realize the impossibility of putting the clock back and of trying to limit Rome's interests to Italy, as some of his contemporaries wished. Indeed, it is probable that his was one of the first minds to wrestle with the problem of Rome's imperial mission. The terms he imposed on Rome's enemies together with his philhellenic tendencies give the clue to his policy: the Greeks were to be free, the barbarians to be crushed; the old monarchies were to be humbled, but not completely overthrown; client princes were to guard against their possible revival; in short, a balance of powers was to be established, all dependent on Rome, who was to allow free life to flourish under her protecting aegis. Hannibal and Antiochus could both bear witness that their conqueror's policy was moulded by the two thoughts that were later formulated by Virgil as '*parcere subiectis et debellare superbos*'.

The extent of the opposition which Scipio encountered is a matter of debate. An attempt to range the Roman nobility in two camps, a philhellenic group and a group opposed to Hellenism, results in over-simplification, since it is far from certain that all the philhellenists were united. Scipio at first possibly helped Flamininus with the political object of weakening the Claudii and the national object of applying a more genuine philhellenic policy, but the situation was changed when his political opponents drove Hannibal to the Court of Antiochus. Military necessity, as he conceived it, led him to criticize Flamininus' scheme for the complete evacuation of Greece.[16] But while the philhellenists were quarrelling, the old conservative element of the Fabian group was championed by Cato. Born at Tusculum in 234 of good yeoman stock, Cato spent the earlier years of his life, when not on military service, in working on his own estate like a Cincinnatus. His ability, combined with rugged honesty, simple living and dogged perseverance, soon attracted the notice of Valerius Flaccus, who helped him to a political career in Rome. He reached the quaestorship in 204, when his enmity towards Scipio was engendered, and the aedileship in 199; his praetorship in Sardinia in 198 was marked by the suppression of usury. His upright character and oratorical ability won for him the consulship in 195, and all the conservatively-minded Romans who wished to restore the ancient simplicity of earlier days found a rock to cling to amid the surging seas of Hellenism. But though Cato might oppose the repeal of sumptuary laws and check magisterial abuses, his narrow nationalism was doomed to failure. Notwithstanding his victories in Spain, he failed to break the influence of his opponents, and in 195 Africanus descended into the political arena and won a resounding victory for himself and his family at the polls. Led on by fear of Antiochus, a motive which may have contributed to Scipio's desire to seek office and to his successful candidature for the consulship of 194, he urged that Greece should be held as a barrier against the king. This policy, which was not adopted, annoyed both Flamininus and Cato, though for different reasons. In the elections for 192 Flamininus' brother Lucius defeated Africanus' cousin Nasica; this points to a desire to continue a policy of non-interference in Greece. But before the year was out Antiochus had landed in Greece; Flamininus' diplomacy was good in its place and he was allowed to carry on in Greece, but the warnings of Africanus appeared to be coming true, so that his group again leapt into the saddle. The consuls for 191 were P. Scipio Nasica and Manius Acilius Glabrio, a *novus homo* and supporter of the Scipios. The year was marked by success. Acilius drove Antiochus from Greece; Livius, another supporter of the Scipionic group, defeated the King's navy; and Nasica crushed the Boii. Relying on this rising tide of popularity, Africanus could urge the necessity of pushing home the victory against Antiochus. He could not seek the consulship again without violating the constitution, but when his brother Lucius and his friend C. Laelius, another *novus homo*, were elected consuls for 190, he was associated with the eastern command. The Scipionic group was at the height of its power. But while the fate of Asia was being decided on the plains of Magnesia, Cato and his fellows were securing the decline and fall of the victors.

In 190 Cato prevented Minucius Thermus, a supporter of the Scipios, from celebrating a triumph over the Ligurians. The next year he introduced scandal as a political weapon in the elections for the censorship. Glabrio, Scipio's friend and the most popular candidate, was accused of having misused some booty taken at Thermopylae. The prosecution was supported, or even instigated, by Cato, his fellow candidate, who had served on his staff. Proceedings were dropped as soon as Glabrio's reputation and election chances had been undermined; but Cato himself failed to win office despite, or because of, this effort. In the same year the Scipios were superseded, Asia being allotted to Manlius Vulso and Aetolia to Fulvius Nobilior. Neither lacked opponents and they were recalled later through the efforts of Aemilius Lepidus, the consul of 187, who censured Fulvius' conduct at Ambracia, while L. Aemilius Paullus blocked Vulso's demand for a triumph. If Lepidus and Paullus were supporters of the Scipios, rather than agents of Cato, the Scipionic group apparently had begun to revive. Cato, however, decided to hunt bigger game.

In 187 two tribunes, the Petillii, were instigated by Cato to demand in the Senate that L. Scipio should render an account of 500 talents which he had received from Antiochus as pay for his troops. Africanus, who knew the shaft was really aimed at himself, disdained reply and indignantly tore up the account-books in the Senate. The question turned on whether the money formed part of the 'booty' at the general's own uncontrolled disposal or whether it was part of the war indemnity approved by the Senate and Roman people to whom an account should be rendered. The attack was not directly an accusation of maladministration, nor was the Senate a court of law; a demand was merely made to put the matter in order. When the Scipios maintained the correctness of their behaviour, the matter was dropped: the Senate thus supported Africanus against tribunician interference in financial affairs. Nothing daunted, Cato took steps to enforce his demand elsewhere. Another tribune, Minucius Augurinus, formally accused Lucius Scipio of refusing to render an account; he imposed a fine and demanded surety which Lucius refused to pay, perhaps from pride. When Lucius was threatened with imprisonment if he persisted in his refusal, Africanus persuaded another tribune, Sempronius Gracchus, to veto proceedings, so that the matter fell through. The question of Lucius' guilt hardly exists; it was a matter of definition. The next year he gave splendid games in an attempt to retrieve the falling popularity of his house. In 184 an attack was launched against Africanus himself. The accusation, made by a tribune, M. Naevius, was perhaps treasonable dealings with Antiochus (p. 269). Africanus merely replied that it ill befitted the Roman people to listen to any accusations against one to whom the accusers owed it that they had the power of speech at all. At this the people dispersed and the charge was not perhaps pressed home. But Africanus realized that his influence was gone; his brother failed to win the censorship; his own health was bad and neither his brother nor son were competent to take his place. So he withdrew to Liternum near Naples into political exile away from a country which had grown tired of its saviour. He died the next year, as did another who had devoted his life to his own country's service – Scipio's old foe, the exiled Hannibal.[17]

In 184 Cato and his patron L. Valerius Flaccus were elected censors and the latter succeeded Scipio Africanus as *princeps senatus*. The recent scandal of the Bacchanalia may have weakened the position of the liberal philhellenes, so that Cato was now able to lead a reaction. He tried to check luxury and he revised the list of the Senate and the muster-roll of the equites with severity. If in his censorship he was too reactionary and accomplished little permanent reform, he at least drew attention to some of the evils of his day and tried to re-establish a greater sense of moral responsibility, which was the necessary preliminary to any far-reaching reforms. But he was after all a *novus homo* and despite his influence Roman policy must have been largely shaped by a middle bloc of nobles, representing average senatorial opinion. This was led during the next few years by the Fulvii, perhaps in alliance with Aemilius Lepidus who was censor with Fulvius Nobilior in 179. By about 173, however, the influence of the Fulvii had declined and new leaders emerged from such families as the Postumii and Popillii, whose more aggressive policies and methods shocked some of the older patrician nobility. But after some stormy clashes and the national victory over Perseus, greater concord was established within the Senate and the fiercer quarrels of earlier days were forgotten. Cato might continue to the end of his long life to attack his political opponents, but many of these tussles were fought more for social or personal than political causes. Not until the end of our period do we find a serious political clash, when once again he crossed swords with a Scipio, the younger Nasica, who opposed his desire to destroy Carthage and who could remark sarcastically that thanks to the Senate's merciless policy there were no longer any nations before whom Rome need either fear or blush.[18]

PART IV

ROMAN LIFE AND CULTURE

XVI

ECONOMIC
AND SOCIAL
ORGANIZATION

1. AGRICULTURE

Agriculture was the primary industry of the Roman people. The peasant-farmer was the backbone of the state, and Rome's conquest of Italy, which was won by the sword, was consolidated by the plough. Later Romans identified the ideal citizen of early days with a Cincinnatus who was called from the plough to the dictatorship or a Manius Curius whom Samnite envoys found cooking his own meal of herbs. The early festivals of Rome, the predominance of the later rustic tribes over the urban tribes, and many personal names such as Fabius (Beanman) and Lentulus (Lentilman), all testify to the pre-eminence of agricultural interest. Whether the earliest settlers on the Palatine were primarily given to pasturage or agriculture, it was the latter manner of livelihood that prevailed in historical times and was doubtless encouraged under the Etruscan domination. It is unlikely that many farmers in Latium sank to a condition of serfdom or that the overthrow of the Etruscans seriously affected agricultural conditions. But even if the economic distress of the fifth century was not caused by an attempt of serfs to become free peasants and members of the plebeian class, the early political history of Rome was dominated by the land question (pp. 81ff.). The need to create a military organization to preserve the state forced the nobles to make political and economic concessions to the lower classes. The farmer-soldier extended the frontiers of his city, and land-hunger was satisfied by founding new 'tribes' and fortress colonies which spread the Roman system of peasant husbandry throughout Italy.

In early days agriculture was not regarded as a means by which the state could exploit the natural resources of Italy: it was a domestic matter under the direction of the paterfamilias who was responsible for the support of his family. The farmer lived on his plot of land which he cultivated with the help of his sons and sometimes of clients or slaves. Since such slaves were mainly Italian, they were regarded as humble dependants and part of the family, not as mere chattels. The arable land around the homestead was chiefly devoted to the production of spelt (*far*) for food and oats for fodder. The staple diet was a kind of porridge, prepared from ground meal, water and salt, together with such garden vegetables, as beans, lentils, onions and garlic. In the fifth century wheat and bread began to supersede the earlier porridge. Figs, grapes, apples, pears, nuts, milk and honey swelled the menu; little meat and practically no fish was eaten, though bacon was highly esteemed. A rough wine was produced and the cultivation of the olive was gradually introduced from southern Italy. Agricultural methods were primitive, governed by tradition and rule of thumb. The ox and ass supplied labour. Tools and appliances were simple: the plough long remained unimproved. Irrigation and drainage, which had been fostered by the Etruscans, became less effective under private enterprise. In course of time the more skilful or fortunate farmers outstripped their neighbours and consequently a gradual inequality in the size of estates became apparent, so that the amount of land held by one man was limited by statute (p. 116).

Pasturage, though less important than agriculture, was widely practised. In early times the peasants could supplement the produce of their small allotments by grazing animals on common land. Some parts of Italy were more suited to pasturage than the production of corn; when the Romans gained control of the upland country, which provided good summer pastures, they could keep larger flocks and herds by changing the grazing ground according to season, as is done in Italy today. In time this led to the growth of large estates, for the small farmer would not find it worth while to send a few beasts to distant pasturage. But before the Punic Wars the farmer devoted his time chiefly to tilling the soil, apart from grazing a few animals on the wastes and commons near his farm.[1]

Rome's conquest of Italy involved the disappearance of earlier conditions with the advance of Roman peasant husbandry[2]. The Greek cities of southern Italy had formed part of the capitalist system of the Hellenistic world; with Sicily and Sardinia they long remained one of the world's richest grain markets. They exported much grain to Greece, while Etruria and Carthaginian Sicily and Sardinia supplied the Punic cities of Africa, which concentrated on commerce and the production of wine, olive oil, and fruit for the western markets. The Greeks of Italy and Sicily also produced wine and oil in competition with Greece itself and North Africa. While metal industries flourished in Campania and Etruria, wool was produced particularly in Apulia. In central Italy, where there were few towns, conditions of life were more like those in Latium, though tribal grazing was perhaps more common than individual ownership of land and agriculture. In Etruria the conquering aristocracy had reduced many of the inhabitants to serfs, who worked on their large estates or in industry. Further north were Celtic shepherds and peasants with pasturage predominating. Rome's conquest involved fewer changes in the north than south. The Celts were driven back. Part of Etruria was colonized, part may have continued its old manner of life. Most Greek cities in the south, succumbing to the Samnite tribes and Roman colonization, became cities of peasants ; few remained centres of the more progressive economic life of earlier times. Thus Italy became mainly a nation of small farmers.

Rome's conquest of the Mediterranean had greater economic repercussions on Italy itself than on the provinces, where conditions remained much the same as before. War and provincial administration filled the pockets of senators and equites, who often returned to Italy and looked around for safe investments. Land attracted most of their capital, and it so happened that the state had much land of which to dispose. The Hannibalic War had resulted in a great increase of Rome's *ager publicus*, while the land had been so devastated that it was difficult to attract the small farmer back to it. Apart from the foundation of a few colonies, the state was ready to lease out large allotments to any who had the capital and vision to undertake the venture. A slow revolution took place : land now became an object of speculation to be exploited as a regular source of profit. The owner no longer lived as a farmer on his estate, but entrusted it to the management of a steward (*vilicus*). As the ravages of war in Italy had created a shortage of free men willing to settle on the land, and as foreign wars had flooded the Italian slave markets, servile labour soon began to oust free labour on the bigger estates. Thus in many parts of Italy, especially in the south, peasant husbandry gave place to a capitalist system of large estates worked by cheap labour and devoted to pasturage and stock-rearing or to the cultivation of the vine and olive. The absentee owners swelled the ranks of the aristocracy and the well-to-do middle class of Rome and the Italian cities.

We have far more knowledge of agricultural conditions in the second, than in preceding centuries, thanks to the survival of Cato's book on agriculture which gives a vivid picture of life in Italy. He appears to advocate grazing as the most profitable use of land, at any rate in certain districts; the demand for horses and wool was increasing, while more mutton and beef was eaten. In discussing his preference in crops Cato, who was probably thinking chiefly of the district around Rome and parts of Campania, advocates viticulture, vegetable gardening and the raising of osiers for basket-weaving and vine-props (when the estate was near a town), olive plantations, meadow land for fodder, and lastly cereal culture. There was a decreasing supply of olives from Greece and an increasing demand in Italy; their cultivation required little labour except at harvest-time when the resident slave labour of the estate would be supplemented with free workers operating under contract. Further, much of the land of an olive plantation could still be used for grain or sheep-grazing. The low esteem in which Cato holds cereals is partly due to the restricted district which he was considering. Wheat from the Sicilian tithes in no way swamped the markets of Rome, but supplied a very small part of the needs of Italy. After Zama wheat was cheap, but during the wars of the second century army requirements prevented much provincial grain reaching the open market at Rome, so that cereal culture was helped rather than hindered by the foreign wars. The effect on the home market of competition caused by the importation of foreign corn was very limited.[3] In the uplands pasturage spread at the expense of arable farming because it was more profitable, and cereal farming was left to the small farmer or to the tenants or serfs of the great landowners in certain districts.

Thus in many parts of Italy capitalist farming, on both a large and small scale, replaced peasant husbandry. Agricultural methods on the large estates differed little from the old, apart from the introduction of servile labour, though some of the slaves would have knowledge of the more scientific estates of the east. Arable land was fertilized with manure and legumes, which in some years were ploughed under as cover crops or used in rotation with wheat. Apart from this it is uncertain whether attempts were yet made to relieve exhausted soil by rotation of crops, except that land might be allowed to stand fallow for a year as rough pasturage. More important than any improvements in method, more important even than changes in production, was the increase of servile labour which drove numerous free workers off the land. Some might be absorbed by commercial enterprise abroad, but many drifted to the towns and the capital itself. Since no Industrial Revolution took place to engage their activity they soon became a useless mass of unemployed, until Tiberius Gracchus sought to give them a new start by raising the cry, 'Back to the land'.

2. WARFARE

The early Roman had to spend much time fighting in defence of the fields he tilled. Every property owner was expected to fight for his city, which had no professional army, only a citizen militia, called up as need demanded. The primitive organization, based on Thousands, soon proved inadequate for military purposes, and by the Servian reform the community was organized as an army and the 'nation in arms' became the chief political assembly. The complex question of the development of the early army has already been discussed (pp. 71ff. and relevant notes), and we have seen how military, political, economic and social needs led to the introduction of a battle-line of heavily armed infantry (hoplites). This new levy (*Legio*) was at some point divided into two groups or legions, though it is uncertain whether this occurred at the time of the fall of the monarchy (to provide each consul with a command) or in the difficult days after the Gallic invasion. During the siege of Veii (i.e. *c.* 400 BC) pay was introduced in order to enable the yeoman soldiers to keep the field throughout the year: the first step towards turning a citizen militia into a professional army had been taken. Then, as Rome's territory and population increased, it was found necessary in the Second Samnite War to levy two consular armies of two legions each.

The introduction of pay meant that each man could now arm himself, and it was not necessary to place the wealthier men in the first line. Gradually experience, skill and age supplanted wealth and the census as the basis of military arrangement. The heavy infantry was drawn up in three lines, *hastati, principes* and *triarii*, though the light-armed troops were still recruited on a strict census basis from the two lowest classes. All three lines had practically the same armour; helmets, breastplates, shields, greaves, javelins and swords. The front line, despite its name, did not consist of spearmen (*hastati*), and the second line (*principes*) had ceased to form the front of the battle array; the *triarii* were a third supporting line of veterans, with slightly lighter armour. This important reorganization was accompanied by a fundamental change in tactics: the phalanx gave place to the manipular system which endured till the last century of the Republic. The legion was divided into 30 maniples, each comprising 120 men. Intervals were left between the maniples in each line, and the maniples of the second line covered the spaces of the first. The object of the reform was to give greater elasticity than the mass-tactics of the phalanx. The army was thus divided horizontally into three lines and vertically into maniples. A corresponding change was made in equipment; the most important introduction was the *pilum*, a javelin $6\frac{1}{2}$ feet in length, half wood and half iron, which replaced the spear (*hasta*) in the two front lines. The date of these changes is disputed. Some assign them to the years after the Gallic invasion and to the wisdom of Camillus. Others suppose that the flexible manipular formation was forced upon the Romans when operating in the rough hill country of Samnium; also that the *pilum* derived from Samnium.[4] Further, contact with the gaily-dressed cavaliers of Campania and Samnium may have helped to transform the mounted infantry of Rome into real cavalry. But Roman cavalry was always weak, so that the Romans depended more on their allies; and even Italian cavalry from the time of the Hannibalic War was supplemented by hiring foreign auxiliaries. The allies sent forces to the Roman armies; the maximum levy of each state was fixed by its treaty, though normally the whole contingent would not be called out. The allied troops served with the legions under Roman officers (*praefecti sociorum*).

Such in brief was the army that conquered Italy; but before it conquered the Mediterranean world it was reformed still further. Manipular tactics had ousted the rigid phalanx, but the battle-line was not sufficiently flexible; it still relied on mere push and weight and could not wheel or turn with any ease. When faced by a mobile enemy, the Roman legions collapsed. Cannae showed with tragic clearness the vulnerability of the legions, which broke because they could not bend, and the inadequacy of Roman cavalry; once the wings had been swept clear of the covering cavalry the infantry was outflanked and surrounded before it could break through the enemy's centre. This weakness was gradually rectified by the genius of Scipio Africanus, the first Roman general as such, who went to Spain, not as consul or praetor, but as an army commander with proconsular power, to campaign not for a year but until victory was won. There he built up his new model army. He threw over the close maintenance of the triple line and created lines which operated independently. This more flexible weapon was used with increasing skill, at Baecula, Ilipa and Campi Magni, until it crushed Hannibal at Zama. Scipio also made the individual more effective when he had broken away from the compact mass by adequate training in arms drill. The Spanish sword with its well-témpered point was adopted, and the *pilum* may have been improved from Spanish models. Rome's lack of cavalry was counteracted by alliance with the native princes of Spain and Numidia. But Scipio's greatest tactical contribution was that he made the units more self-reliant and thus led on to the next development of Roman tactics when the cohort, a grouping together of three maniples, became the unit; possibly some experimental tactical use of cohorts already may have been made by Scipio himself.

The Hannibalic War tended to professionalize the Roman army, but it was followed by a reaction to the more amateur methods of earlier days and many men were glad to return to civil life. Despite easier conditions of service and under some commanders a dangerously lax discipline, there was a marked reluctance for military service on the part of some. But others had gained an appetite for soldiering and did not wish to settle back on the land. The wars of conquest and long periods of service offered such men a profession, though a precarious one, as there was no standing army: forces were still raised from the propertied classes as need demanded and demobilized when operations were over.[5] Conditions of life are well illustrated by a speech which Livy puts into the mouth of a veteran volunteer in 171 BC: 'I am Spurius Ligustinus, and I come from the Sabine country. My father left me less than an acre of land and a small cottage in which I was born and bred; I live there now . . . I have six sons and two daughters, both now married . . . I became a soldier in the consulship of P. Sulpicius and C. Aurelius [200 BC] . . . I served in the ranks for two years against King Philip. In the third year as a reward for bravery T. Quinctius Flamininus made me a junior centurion. Discharged after Philip's defeat, I at once went to Spain as a volunteer with M. Porcius [195] who thought me worthy of promotion to a higher rank among the centurions. A third time I again enlisted as a volunteer in the army which was sent against the Aetolians and King Antiochus; I was promoted by M'. Acilius [191] . . . We were brought back to Italy and then I served in two legions which were raised for a year. Then I served in Spain, once under Q. Fulvius Flaccus [181] and again under Ti. Sempronius Gracchus. Four times within a few years I have been first centurion of a legion; I have been rewarded thirty-two times for bravery by my generals; I have received six civic crowns. I have served in twenty-two annual campaigns, and I am over fifty years old' (Livy, xlii, 34).

During the Republic there was no standing navy; ships were built and fitted out as required. Before the First Punic War the navy was small and a few ships were supplied by the Italiot towns; but the war forced Rome to become a great sea power. In their amateur but successful manner the

Romans put one or both of the consuls in command of the fleet. During part of the Hannibalic War the fleet sometimes formed the separate 'province' of a praetor; sometimes it was commanded by a consul or his deputy (*praefectus*). The oarsmen and sailors were supplied by the allies and maritime colonies, and after 217 by *libertini* also. The marine troops were usually drawn from the Roman proletariat, the sixth class, or occasionally from allies and Latins. Naval service was not popular. The standard vessel was the quinquereme; the trireme and quadrireme were also used, as well as lighter craft such as the Illyrian *lembi*. As the admiral's flagship one of the great Hellenistic ships might be used. Although the Roman navy played an important role in her conquest of the Mediterranean world, it did not adequately police the seas in times of peace, so that piracy became a real danger to Italian shipping.

3. COMMERCE AND INDUSTRY

The peasants who tilled their fields around Rome were long oblivious to the fact that they were sandwiched in between two commercial peoples, the Etruscans and the Greek colonists. From the eighth century Etruria enjoyed an active trade with Greece and with some centre from which wares of Egyptian and Assyrian style were shipped to Italy. Fine gold and silver work to adorn the princely tombs at Caere and Praeneste was brought from the east in exchange for the copper of Tuscany and the iron of Elba. Gradually an Etruscan school of artists arose who found their inspiration in the imported models; previously the early Italian coppersmiths had only produced simple geometric designs, but now native Etruscans manufactured works of art for the home market and export. In the seventh century Corinthian wares dominated the Etruscan markets (and indeed the whole western Mediterranean) and Corinthian influence was paramount in Etruscan art. Early in the sixth century Attic pottery reached Etruria, and for the next hundred years Greek imports and influences so predominated that it is often impossible to distinguish Greek and Etruscan work, at any rate in the minor arts. Etruscan potters still manufactured *bucchero* ware, the black surface of which gives the appearance of metal; but Greek styles were increasingly popular, whether made by Etruscans or Greek settlers. The sixth century witnessed many other events of commercial importance: the Greek colonization of Massilia, the rise of Carthage, the subsequent alliance of Etruria and Carthage against the Greeks, the downfall of Greek competition in the west, the growth of the Punic policy of a *mare clausum*, and the Etruscan domination of Latium which temporarily swept the Romans into a world of trade and industry.

Reference has already been made to the spread of Etruscan and Greek civilization in Latium (see pp. 39ff.). Industry was doubtless stimulated in many cities, though it is not always possible to determine whether a given object is of native workmanship or imported. Praeneste, for instance, became an industrial centre; the gold fibula, which dates from about 600 and bears the earliest known Latin inscription ('Manios made me for Numasios'), points to a local metal industry, while in the sixth century mirrors were manufactured there under Etruscan influence. Commerce passed along a land route from Etruria to Praeneste, while Greek and Phoenician wares entered Latium through the port of Satricum, which was in close touch with Cumae by sea; Greek imports for Falerii and southern Etruria probably passed up the Tiber through Rome. The temples of the seventh or sixth centuries at Velitrae, Ardea, and Satricum show clearly the development of industry and art in Latium. But the country's lack of mineral wealth clipped the wings of commerce, for there was little with which Latium could pay for foreign wares. The skill of local metal workers may have formed a source of wealth, while pasturage would produce some hides, wool and swine for export, and parts of Latium grew timber. But it is unlikely that a surplus of grain could be grown for export or that trade became very flourishing except under Etruscan encouragement.

The relation of Rome to Italian commerce must remain somewhat obscure. The warrior's tomb with chariot and armour on the Esquiline (p. 46) gives a tantalizing glimpse of the mid-seventh century, but the predominant preference of the Romans for incineration rather than inhumation, together with the continuous occupation of the site for so many centuries, has lessened the chance of the survival of gold or silver objects. However, with the coming of the Etruscans the villagers of Rome became the citizens of a rich and powerful city, and to a limited extent they must have shared in the wider life of their rulers. As we have seen, temples and other public buildings, equal to or surpassing those of other Latin cities, sprang up. Industry flourished, in the hands of both immigrant Etruscan workers and the native craftsmen whom they inspired. The tradition that there were eight labour guilds in the regal period (goldsmiths, carpenters, dyers, leather-workers, tanners, bronze-smiths, potters and flute-blowers) is reasonable, as it excludes those activities which still remained domestic, such as the weaving of clothing and the baking of bread, while the existence of guilds is mentioned in a clause of the Twelve Tables. It is uncertain how far these workers manufactured more than was required for the Rome market by the soldiers, farmers and householders or by the luxurious court of their overlords. But however the Romans paid for it, they undoubtedly imported large and increasing quantities of Greek pottery (pp. 60, 76). Further, her geographical position enabled her to control the trade in salt which was collected at the flats near Ostia and sold to the hill tribes, and also to levy dues on goods moving between Etruria and Campania. But the long-deferred recourse to the use of minted money, and the complete indifference shown towards commercial interests in the first treaty with Carthage, suggest that the primary interest of early Rome was not commerce. When Etruscan rule was withdrawn Rome was not completely cut off from the Greek culture of Campania, but the import of Greek vases gradually dwindled and the building activity of the early fifth century died down. By the mid-fifth century it was clear that Rome was reverting to a simpler state: agriculture and warfare rather than industry or commerce filled life. With the disappearance of court life industry naturally lagged: the Twelve Tables forbade extravagant funerals, and Etruscan luxury gave place to the simpler native usages. Some workmen may have found their employment gone and have swelled the ranks of the discontented plebeians, but even if their numbers were not large they will have increased the social difficulties of the time.

By *c.* 400 BC, after a period when Roman interests were largely domestic, she moved into the ken of Greek historians, and was soon described by Heracleides of Pontus as 'a Greek city situated on the shore of the great sea'. In the course of the fourth century after the Gallic invasion Rome became a powerful city. The newly-built 'Servian' walls enclosed an area of about 1,060 acres, which was more than twice that of Capua and about five times that of Ardea; not all the enclosed area, however, may have been thickly populated. The construction of the wall involved much labour, as some five million cubic feet of cut stone must have been used. A few temples were built, but they were probably small.

At the same time military needs resulted in Rome's intrusion both north and south into areas where Greek influence predominated. In Campania pottery was manufactured on Attic models, and the paintings of the fourth-century tombs at Paestum and Capua show the influence of Greek art. At Capua also Etruscan gold workers continued their trade. A successful pottery industry flourished at the Latin colony of Cales. At Praeneste a vigorous bronze industry is attested by the beautiful mirrors and boxes (*cistae*) engraved with scenes from Greek mythology and decorated with ornamental handles; perhaps the old Etruscan industry was in part carried on by Campanian-Greek workmen. In Etruria itself, where activity slackened on the downfall of their empire, artistic effort and Greek influence were renewed in the fourth century. The wall paintings might be more sombre, but many bronze statues (e.g. the Mars of Todi) and sarcophagi of real artistic merit were produced. After the fall of Veii, pottery was manufactured at and exported from Falerii, where two old temples were redecorated in Hellenistic style; two new temples adorned Volsinii. A pair of Panathenaic amphoras, dated 336, attest the spread of Attic influence at Caere.

Indirect contact with Greek art through direct relations with Etruria and Campania may have stimulated emulation by the Romans, but the evidence suggests that it was not extensive. A number of temples were built, especially after the great Samnite War. They were probably adorned with terracotta revetments and pediments like the contemporary Etruscan temples, and some were decorated with paintings, but the artists may have been imported. Thus a military scene from a third (?)-century tomb on the Esquiline depicts negotiations between Q. Fabius and an enemy general, M. Fannius: perhaps an episode in the Samnite Wars. The buildings of Rome can scarcely have been less imposing than those of many of the towns that she conquered. One of the most beautiful boxes of the Praenestine type (the Ficorini *cista*) was made at Rome and bears a Latin inscription: '*Novios Plautios med Romai fecid*' ('Novius Plautius made me at Rome'). But this is not sufficient evidence to suggest widespread industry. The local pottery was not notable enough to export: transport was too dear. Cheap black Campanian ware is found in the Esquiline graves. The legislation of Appius Claudius implies the existence of a fairly large free industrial class at Rome, but this may have merely supplied weapons for the army, agricultural implements for the farmers and domestic furniture for the householder. If warfare stimulated industry, colonization checked it by draining the population. And still the Romans remained uninterested in commerce. When their treaty with Carthage was renewed in 348 they allowed the Carthaginians to extend the area of the *mare clausum* and left their own port open to foreign traders. About the same time a small fortress was established at the Tiber's mouth at Ostia. The colony may have been designed to protect and facilitate commerce, but it equally well may have been a military post against sea raiders from Antium.[6] The general inexperience of the Romans at sea before the First Punic War confirms the supposition that their main activities were directed landwards.

The Roman conquest of Italy secured for the citizens benefits which included *commercium*, but the conquest of the Mediterranean opened up vaster fields. The Romans, however, were content to step aside and leave commercial enterprise to the Greeks of southern Italy. The governing class did not seek fresh markets for the products of Italian industry. Provincial administration proved more profitable. Unfortunately we have little evidence of the progress of Roman industry in the third century. The wars with Carthage must have stimulated the production of arms and military equipment which were presumably supplied in the main by Rome and the municipal towns of central Italy. In Campania the production of pottery declined, but metal industries continued to prosper. In southern Italy Rome's conquest weakened local industry and Hannibal's invasion wrought untold damage: Tarentum never recovered its pristine prosperity. The towns of Etruria were more prosperous, though artistic inspiration declined. Mirrors, similar to those from Praeneste, were manufactured, and the increasing popularity of in- cineration encouraged the production of urns of alabaster, marble and travertine. In 205 Scipio received supplies of grain and timber from Caere, Volaterrae, Perusia and Clusium, cloth from Tarquinii, iron from Populonia and manufactured weapons from Arretium.

In the second century similar conditions prevailed. Romans of good family still left industry to the lower classes, but slave labour slowly tended to supplant free. Plautus refers to a large number of skilled workers: workers in gold, iron, wood and leather; makers of boxes, leather bottles, shoes, ropes and shields; dealers in wool and linen; carpenters, potters, dyers, fullers, millers, bakers, weavers. Cato's list of agricultural implements required for his olive orchard and vineyard is both long and instructive. He also suggests the best shopping centres (*de agr.*, 10f; 135): Rome for clothing, jars and bowls, heavy ploughs, yokes, locks, keys and baskets; Cales and Minturnae for iron agricultural implements; Venafrum for spades, ropes and tiles; Suessa for wagons and threshing sledges; Capua for light ploughs, bronze utensils, ropes and baskets; Pompeii and Nola for mills and olive crushers; Nola for bronze utensils. Pottery was still exported from Cales to central Italy, but the industry declined. The so-called Megarian ware made in southern Umbria was sold chiefly locally and in southern Etruria. The great slag heaps at Populonia near Elba indicate that an average of a hundred thousand tons of iron ore were treated each year during the last centuries of the Republic. Some of the pig-iron was forged on the spot and at Arretium; some was sent to Puteoli as the local timber supply decreased. Copper, tin, and lead also were mined in Etruria, but after Cato had organized the Spanish mines, Etruscan mining and metal working declined, though farming flourished and the slave-worked plantation system spread in Etruria.[7] In general, the small shop system, which is revealed at Pompeii, prevailed. The shopkeeper generally made and sold his goods in the same small room.[8] Cattle, fish and vegetables were sold in separate *fora* in Rome, while special market days were held every eighth day. A trader might hawk his wares around neighbouring towns, but the slowness and cost of transport precluded a far-flung trade in cheap goods. An ox team covered little more than ten miles a day and it has been reckoned that to haul an olive mill for twenty-five miles would add a sixth to the original cost of the mill. River transport would be used where possible, and the Roman roads which spread over Italy for military purposes served also commercial ends. Nevertheless trade in Italy, for the most part, remained local.

Overseas trade, especially with the east, increased in the second century, but it had little interest for Roman nobles or influence on Roman policy (pp. 327). For instance, the Romans allowed Gades to grow fat on the Atlantic trade of the Carthaginians instead of claiming the legacy for themselves; similarly, no commercial treaty was struck with Masinissa. Ostia's heyday was after Gracchan times, though a Roman tariff station was set up at Puteoli in 199. The Roman naval transport service was responsible for the transhipment of large quantities of grain, and the cost of freightage precluded a vigorous trade in ordinary commodities as grain, oil and wine. But the increasing demand for luxuries in Rome would promote trade, and the equites gradually became a Third Estate. Yet the aristocracy retained its vested interests in land, and 'labour' had no adequate political means of expressing its will.

4. CURRENCY AND FINANCE

The Greek cities of southern Italy coined silver: Tarentum from the mid-sixth century, Cumae from *c.* 500 BC, Naples and the Etruscans from *c.* 450 BC; but the Romans were slow to develop a monetary system of their own. The view that Roman coinage began about 340, when Capua issued the so-called Romano-Campanian series for Rome, has now been generally abandoned and the development of Rome's early coinage is set later.[9]

In early times values were estimated in terms of oxen and sheep; hence the word *pecunia* (money), derived from *pecus*. The Romans were content to barter or to use copper weighed in the balance (*aes rude*); about 430 BC a law was passed by which for the collection of fines 100 pounds of bronze was equated with ten sheep or one ox. It was not until 289 that the office of triumvirs of the mint was established, probably for the purpose of casting the so-called *aes signatum*, bronze in bars weighing some six pounds each and bearing types on each side (such as a shield and sword, trident, anchor, elephant, sow, ox); only one of those that survive bears a legend, ROMANO (RUM). Since these bars lacked a mark of value and had to be weighed, they were money rather than coins, but probably at the same time real coins were issued: circular bronze *asses*, marked I (one *as*) and weighing a pound. The first of these libral *asses* was probably the series that had the heads of Janus and Mercury on its two sides. It was followed by other series, which include that with a wheel as a constant reverse type on all denominations (a reminder of Rome's interest in road construction and starting perhaps in 269) and the more famous Janus/prow series (probably *c.* 225) which remained the normal type of Roman bronze coinage throughout Republican times. It was the war with Pyrrhus and closer contacts with southern Italy and its silver coinage that led Rome to produce in a southern mint two issues of silver coins, marked ROMANO (RUM), for war purposes: the types were Mars/horse's head, and Apollo/horse. Then in 269 the mint officials produced a silver coinage in Rome with the same legend and showing Hercules/wolf and twins; this was soon followed during the First Punic War by another series showing Rome/Victory (both with corresponding bronze). Meantime the old *aes signatum* was falling into disuse and struck bronze began to replace the cast *aes grave*. Then after the war followed four silver issues marked ROMA, of which the fourth (*c.* 230: 235, 225?) depicted a young Janus and Victory in a chariot (*quadriga*) and became known as a *quadrigatus*. At much the same time came the libral bronze prow series. Thus although Rome had been slow to adopt a coinage, under the stimulus of the Pyrrhic and First Punic Wars she not only accepted this civilized medium of exchange but took to it with open arms. Traders and Roman soldiers serving in southern Italy and Sicily would benefit, and Rome's international status was enhanced.

The Hannibalic War had sharp effects on the coinage. The weight of the *as* declined steeply: to a semi-libral standard near the beginning and then rapidly to a triental and (214?) quadrantal. Soon after 215 the *quadrigatus* was replaced by a smaller *victoriatus* (with reverse type of Victory). A year or so earlier an emergency gold issue was made (Janus/oath-scene) when Naples, Paestum and Syracuse sent gifts of gold to Rome, and then *c.* 211–209 a second gold issue (Mars/eagle): after the defection of the Latin colonies 4,000 lb of gold were taken out of the reserve. In or about 211 a radical change was made with the introduction of a new silver *denarius* (= 10 *asses,* and showing Roma/Dioscuri on horseback), linked to a sextantial bronze system. This new bimetallic system remained the basis of Rome's coinage throughout the rest of the Republic.

Thus Roman coinage was issued to meet the requirements of war rather than of trade. Practical needs were met by practical solutions, not by constructing economic theories. Hence wartime difficulties forced the Senate partially to repudiate its debts by reforming the coinage instead of by establishing a permanent war debt to be funded and repaid over a long period. The financial policy of the state followed the lines of its political development. In Italy Roman colonies would naturally use Roman coins, while many independent Greek states and some Latin colonies issued coins in early times. But Roman coinage gradually predominated and after the Hannibalic War the Romans claimed a monopoly. In the provinces no uniform policy was enforced. In the west convenience generally led to the establishment of a Roman monopoly. A policy of enlightened self-interest was shown in Spain where beside Roman coinage native silver (*argentum Oscense*) was allowed to circulate in the second century, partly as a medium for the payment of tribute and partly to facilitate commerce within Spain. Carthage also continued to issue money. In the East where the Romans found a variety of issues existing they did not interfere with local coinage. Their wars there rather served to bring the money of the East to Rome. So great was the flow that many Eastern nations were forced to go off the silver standard, although Roman exactions may have been a contributory rather than the chief cause of this.

The late invention of Roman coinage attests the simplicity of the financial problems of early Rome. But her intrusion into the Mediterranean world and the strain of the Punic Wars forced the Roman treasury to shoulder heavier responsibilities. Towards the end of the First Punic War when the treasury was exhausted and taxes could not be increased, the government followed the example of a Greek 'liturgy' or a modern war loan: a fleet was raised by public subscription, but with the understanding that the state would refund the money in event of victory. The main source of income was taxation. The usual *tributum simplex* was a one-mill tax (one-tenth of 1 per cent of property values); this might be increased in wartime. Other sources were rent from public land, an indemnity of 100 talents from Hiero, and profits from the sale of prisoners and booty. The cost of the war to the Roman treasury has been estimated at some 100 million denarii. The Hannibalic War strained the treasury still further. In 216 an acute shortage of money led to the appointment of *triumviri mensarii* and a slight inflation by reducing the weight of the *as*. In 215 double *tributum* was levied; later this may have been still further increased. When cash was exhausted, credit alone remained; in the following winter the praetor called on war-profiteers to offer supplies for Spain by contract on indefinite credit, and three companies of nineteen men responded. In 214 crews were supplied by 'liturgy', state building contracts were undertaken on undated promises to pay, slaves were bought on credit for military service, trust funds of widows and orphans were taken over by the state, many knights and centurions refused their pay. To meet a fresh crisis in 210 the state borrowed the savings of the citizens: much jewellery, plate and precious metals were voluntarily contributed. In 209 the reserve sacred treasury was used, and when twelve of the Latin colonies refused to supply further troops or pay, the other eighteen offered more. After Metaurus had relieved the strain, the twelve defaulters were punished in 205–204 by the imposition of direct taxation, based on a census, in addition to their other obligations. From this taxation two-thirds of the voluntary contribution of 210 was repaid in 204 and 202; the third instalment was paid in land in 200 when the Macedonian War claimed financial support. Scipio's African expedition was largely financed by voluntary help. The treasury receipts during the war have been reckoned at 286 million denarii (citizen tribute, 65 million; tithes of Sicily and Sardinia, 24; port dues, etc., 10; booty, 65; sacred treasury, 5; loans, contributions, super-taxes, etc., 117). The corresponding expenses of 286 million are estimated at: army stipends, 180 million; food for allied troops, 36; land transport, 15; arms, 20; navy and transport, 35. The average annual expense of the war was about $3\frac{1}{2}$ times greater per annum than during the First Punic War.[10]

During the first half of the second century national wealth rapidly increased. Roman property, which may have been worth some one thousand million denarii in 200 BC, was doubled or trebled in value by 150 BC, while the population had increased about 50 per cent.[11] War indemnities, booty, and the Spanish mines formed new items of income. In 187 Manlius Vulso persuaded the Senate to repay all the outstanding *tributum* still owing from the Hannibalic War; this perhaps only included the super-tax over and above the *tributum simplex*. By repaying $25\frac{1}{2}$ *tributa* the government finally liquidated its war debt. In 167 citizen taxes were discontinued and ten years later the treasury had a balance of $25\frac{1}{2}$ million denarii in its vaults. Professor Tenney Frank has worked out the budget of the period as follows. Income, 610,600,000 denarii (war indemnities 152,100,000; booty and Spanish mines, 159,500,000; citizen tax, 60 million; rents from public land, 63; provincial tithes, 130; other vectigalia, 46). Expenses are reckoned at 555 million denarii (army stipend, 300 million; food for allies, 64; transport, 50; navy, $58\frac{1}{2}$; public buildings, 20; super-tax repaid, $22\frac{1}{2}$; other expenses, 40). These figures may well be 50 per cent too high or low, but at any rate they give a valuable idea of the scale of Roman finance for a period when 77 per cent of the national income was devoted to military costs.

The evidence for the purchasing power of money is still more slender. It has been reckoned that in the second century a bushel of wheat cost 3 denarii; olive oil, 10 denarii an amphora (26 litres); ordinary wine, half the price of oil; beef, perhaps 2 or 3 *asses*: a complete suit, 100 denarii; a lady's wardrobe 1000 denarii; farm slaves, about 500 denarii; a plough ox, 60–80 denarii. Wages were low. A slave could be hired out at $\frac{1}{2}$ denarius a day; free labour may have earned a little under a denarius. Thus a labourer who earned 300 denarii a year might be able to feed and clothe himself and his wife on two-thirds of his income, leaving the meagre balance for house rent and extras. At the other end of the social scale the estate of Scipio Africanus may have been worth a million denarii.[12]

5. SLAVERY

The Etruscan chieftains who settled in Italy reduced many of the natives to serfdom and doubtless acquired alien slaves by trade and piracy. There is no definite evidence that serfdom survived in Etruria in Roman times, but it still existed before the First Punic War when some serfs at Volsinii, who had been freed by their masters for military service, seized the government, and thus brought Roman punishment on their own heads, and were perhaps reduced to slavery. Whether in early days the Etruscans had introduced serfdom into Latium is uncertain. But in the difficult years that followed the fall of Etruscan power the plight of the small Roman farmer was wretched and some citizen debtors must have lost their freedom in the economic struggle. In law, of course, a slave was not a person but *res mancipi*, the property of his owner who could inflict any punishment, including death, unfettered by any legal limits. The extension of Roman power throughout Italy had two results: the condition of the Roman peasants improved, and the number of slaves, created by conquest, increased. But the slave was not yet regarded as a profit-making machine, though occasionally skilled workers might be used for profit. As he and his master generally belonged to the same or similar races, he was treated as a servant of the family and worked by his master's side in the fields. He shared in certain festivals and was allowed to keep his savings (*peculium*) with some hope of eventually buying his freedom. Emancipation was frequent and in 357 a law was passed imposing a 5 per cent tax on manumission. Since 4,000 lb of gold had accumulated in the treasury from this source by 209, an average of some 1,350 slaves may have been freed each year. The political generosity of the Roman government towards this freedman class which in general took the place of clients attached to the great houses is discussed elsewhere (p. 320); at the end of the third century Philip of Macedon, writing to the inhabitants of Larissa, called attention to the liberal policy of the Romans in granting full citizenship, including the right to hold office, to liberated slaves (Dittenberger, *Sylloge* II, 143).

Before Rome's conquest of the Mediterranean world slavery was not such a grievous blot on her civilization as it became after her contact with Carthaginian, Hellenic and Oriental ideas. The supply of slaves was maintained, partly by children born to slaves in the house (*vernae*; who were usually treated with particular kindness), but more especially by warfare. It has been reckoned that the First Punic War produced some 75,000 slaves whose sale brought the Roman treasury 15 million denarii. During the Hannibalic War the capture of Tarentum alone produced some 30,000 prisoners, while the war captives of the first half of the second century may have numbered 250,000. The demand was increasing, both for mere labour in the country and for more educated slaves for domestic work in the town. After Cannae slaves had been freed for military service, while landowners called to the front would require slaves to run their farms in their absence. With the growth of the plantation system in the second century, slave labour largely supplanted free on the big estates, since free labourers were liable to be called away from agriculture to the army.

The increasing prevalence of slavery in the second century had a deteriorating effect both on Roman character and on the conditions of the slaves themselves. Carthaginians, Spaniards, Greeks, Macedonians and Syrians poured into the slave markets. As manumission was common many foreign freedmen or their descendants achieved full Roman citizenship; lower moral standards from the east crept into Italy and ultimately the Orontes flowed into the Tiber though only the beginnings of the movement are visible in our period The more educated slaves would be used in the towns, where they often alleviated their lot by pandering to the increasingly luxurious tastes of their masters, who were frequently less cultured than they were; others drove much free labour out of the manual trades. In the country gangs of the more barbarous slaves worked the *latifundia* under the control of slave-bailiffs. They were often treated as mere beasts and sometimes worked in chains. Cato, who in his early days had toiled with his slaves, showed a revolting callousness, working them till they dropped or selling them when they became useless. He allowed them a blanket, a tunic and a pair of wooden shoes every second year. Still more wretched were those who worked in the mines of Spain or Macedon. Such conditions led to insecurity in Italy: runaway slaves naturally turned to brigandage, and conspiracies became more common. Punic slaves in some Latin cities tried to rebel in 198; two years later a legion was required to suppress an outbreak in Etruria; others rioted in Apulia in connection with the Bacchanalian conspiracy (186–180); the serious revolts in Sicily, however, belong to a later period. This brutal and degrading system was a canker that gnawed at the healthy life of Italy; it remained for Stoicism and Christianity to remind men that a slave was a fellow human being.[3]

6. FAMILY LIFE[16]

The Greek lived in a house, the Roman in a home. It was a Greek who said, 'The city trains the man'; a Roman probably would have said that a man was taught by his family and the state. From the earliest times the family formed the basis of Roman society and provided for each future citizen his grounding in education and morality in a community which knew neither school nor church. The paterfamilias held in his 'hand' (*manus*) the whole *familia*, which included wife, children, dependants and estate. Over them he exercised absolute and life-long power (*patria potestas*), including the right of life and death (*vital necisque potestas*). This authority was in practice limited to private affairs, as a father could not control a son who was holding a magistracy, but it remained a reality: towards the end of the Republic a father slew his son for participating in Catiline's conspiracy. It was the father who decided after the birth of a child whether to rear or expose it, though in this he was restricted by religious prohibitions. But the very survival of the *patria potestas* shows that it can seldom have been abused: it was a healthy discipline, remote from Oriental despotism. Further, before taking action a father would generally consult a family council of relatives whose advice might act as a moral, though not a legal, restraint. As the head of each family must be a male, the father usually adopted a son if he had not one of his own. Children born to his sons or brothers were 'born to him' (*adgnati, agnati*), but the children of his daughters and sisters only 'shared in his birth' (*cognati*) and legally belonged to the families of their fathers or husbands.

Within the household the women, especially the *materfamilias* or *matrona*, who played such an important part in upholding the family, attained a dignified and influential position. Unlike the women of Greece the Roman lady pursued her daily occupation in the *atrium* or main room, not in Oriental seclusion. Her chief occupations were to bring up the children, to manage the household work, and to make wool for weaving the family clothes. She could attend religious festivals or banquets and had complete social liberty. This practical freedom contrasts strangely with her theoretical dependence on her husband. Legally a woman had no personal existence and on marriage she merely passed from the protection of her father to the *manus* of her husband. But the emancipation of women was begun early; they were allowed by the Twelve Tables to hold property. There was also a development of the marriage ceremony. Beside the ancient patrician rite of *confarreatio* which gave the husband complete authority over his wife, marriage by *coemptio* was recognized: this implied an equal partnership and the wife could say, 'Where you are master, I am mistress' ('*Ubi tu Gaius, ego Gaia*'). Marriage by *usus* was established by a year's uninterrupted cohabitation. By a law in the Twelve Tables a wife could avoid the legal control of her husband by passing three nights during each year away from her husband's house. Finally there was free marriage, based on mutual consent, which gave the husband no authority over his wife. It was the payment of dowry rather than a legal ceremony that marked the intended permanence of a union. As marriage was more a personal affair than the concern of the state, divorce was also personal and easily obtained (by the husband, though not by the wife!). And yet it was infrequent. Where affection failed, the conservative tendencies of a dignified aristocracy must often have tended to uphold the continuity of family life. But even in an age of loosening family ties, the numerous sepulchral monuments of Imperial Rome attest the prevalence of happy married companionship (e.g. 'She loved her husband with her whole heart, she bare two sons . . . cheerful in

converse, dignified in manner, she kept the house, she made wool.'
C.I.L., I, 1007; cf. the formula S.V.Q. '*sine ulla querela*'. Still more must
similar conditions have prevailed in the earlier and more austere days
whose monuments have perished.

Roman education was a family concern. In early days the object of
training was to form character rather than to promote culture; to fit a
child to become a good citizen. Though religion was divorced from
morality, the simple daily religious ceremonies of the household would
often produce in a child a sense of responsibility and awe towards the
unseen. But the greatest influences in the building of character and the
enforcing of morality were the parents, home life and the *mos maiorum*.
The ideal Roman was a *vir fortis et strenuus*. The qualities to be evoked
were *gravitas, continentia, industria, diligentia, constantia, benevolentia, pietas,
simplicitas*, and above all *virtus*, manliness. The mother was responsible
for the children's earliest training, and her influence was great. The older
boys constantly attended their father at his duties in home and state and
received from him instructions in the three Rs, as well as in physical
training. They were taught to respect the traditions of their family and of
the state. Thus a dignified, patriotic and self-sacrificing character was
formed, but often at the cost of a certain conservative narrowness and
unadaptability. The first school is said to have been opened in Rome
about 250 BC. From that period onwards Greek influences increased.
Rhetoric and slavery began to get a stranglehold on Roman life, despite
the opposition of Cato, who wrote in large letters an account of the
legends of early Rome for his son to learn and who studied Greek
literature in order to teach his son and to save him learning from a slave.
Family life remained uncorrupted and a source of Rome's greatness as
long as men could say with Cato that 'a wife and a son are the holiest of
holy things'.

7. GREEK INFLUENCES

For centuries the Romans had no literature, philosophy or history, and
the achievements of Hellenistic science were unknown. During the regal
period they saw something of Greek art through contact with Etruria and
Campania, but afterwards they relapsed into a parochial state. The
conquest of southern Italy gave them a glimpse of the Greek world, and a
Greek playwright, Andronicus, was taken from Tarentum to Rome
where he translated the *Odyssey* and Greek plays. Then the First Punic
War opened the floodgates of Greek culture. Roman soldiers campaigned

for years in Sicily where they saw the luxurious court life of Hiero and the amenities of the Greek cities. They watched Greek plays in the theatres and picked up so much of the language that later their own writers, Naevius and Plautus, could venture to introduce Greek puns and colloquialisms in their plays for popular consumption. Duilius not only received the honour of a column and a laudatory rhetorical inscription in the Forum, but also was thenceforth escorted home at night through the streets of Rome with torches and music, as if returning from a revel in a Greek city. In the Hannibalic War Roman soldiers crossed to Greece itself, while others campaigned again in Sicily. The nobility and to some extent the people were waking up to the glory that had been Greece. A new world was swimming into their ken and they became self-conscious. They realized that they counted in a larger world, where they were still regarded as barbarians, and they hastened to imbibe some of the culture of their neighbours. Greek literature and thought captivated the imagination of many: Marcellus transported to Italy works of art from captured Syracuse, and Scipio Africanus excited the anger of the old-fashioned Fabius because of the enthusiasm with which he threw himself into the cultural pleasures offered by that city. A group of philhellenic nobles was formed of whom the chief were Scipio and Flamininus.

But Greece displayed not only the greatness of her past but also the decadence of her present. In the second century more Roman soldiers and businessmen met the Greeks at home and familiarity bred contempt. The idealism of any philhellenists appeared impracticable, Roman policy became more realistic, and Greek independence was finally extinguished. But Rome not only gave, whether freedom or peace; she also received. Throughout the century Greeks poured into Italy: statesmen, traders, craftsmen, artists, and above all teachers and slaves. Cato, who with narrow nationalism had withstood the liberal policy of the Scipios, now set himself to stem the tide that threatened to sweep away the simplicity of Roman life. Greek men of culture aroused his puritanical suspicions; the corruption of others was only too patent; and all were tarred with the same brush since they threatened to undermine the *mos maiorum*. In every field a bitter struggle was waged between the nationalists and the Hellenists, each of whom saw only one side of Greek culture. But Cato fought a losing battle; despite his fulminations a younger generation of enthusiasts received the torch of Hellenism unquenched. Around Scipio Aemilianus there gathered a number of friends, including the historian Polybius, Panaetius the Stoic philosopher, Laelius the 'Wise', the dramatists Terence and Pacuvius and the satirist Lucilius. This 'Scipionic circle' formed a centre of the new enlightenment and a brilliant social coterie; amid great freedom of thought and discussion an attempt was made to blend the best elements of Greek and Roman life.

The direct influence of Greek culture on Roman literature and art, philosophy and religion is discussed elsewhere. It remains to refer to its less beneficent effect on society and life. Not all the ills of the second century can be laid at the door of the Greeks, but most are due indirectly to Rome's conquest of the Hellenistic world and the lowering of her moral standards. Whether Greece was the cause or the first victim of Rome's corruption can scarcely be decided: the two cultures reacted on one another with some good results, such as peace for Greece and culture for Rome, but the last state of both nations was worse than the first.[15]

During the second century family life declined. The census statistics show an unhealthily small increase. Female and infant mortality was doubtless high. As early as 234 BC complaints were heard that celibacy was increasing. The number of children in the great families declined, so that recourse was often had to adoption, to prevent their extinction. Divorce became more common. Girls married young, often at the age of twelve; old men sometimes married young girls, and it was not unknown for father and son to marry two sisters. The emancipation of women proceeded apace. Instead of reverting to the control of their own families on the death of their husbands, they had often persuaded their husbands to decree by will that they should be allowed to nominate their own guardians. An attempt was made to check their extravagance and to prevent their gaining control of large amounts of capital by passing a law (Lex Voconia) in 169 forbidding a testator of the highest property class to make a woman his heir and limiting legacies to a sum less than that received by the heir. This attempt to secure a male succession and to preserve the large estates in the hands of the nobles was easily thwarted by the invention of legal fictions. An earlier bill, the Lex Furia Testamentaria, probably of 183, had limited bequests to 1,000 *asses* in cases where the legatee was outside a certain degree of affinity. This also could be obviated, as numerous bequests might exhaust the estate and leave the heir penniless.

Changes in family life inevitably affected education which remained a domestic matter, though Polybius censured the state for not assuming control. The father was often less able or willing to train his children to meet the needs of the day. Consequently Greek slaves were employed as tutors in large houses, as were private chaplains by noblemen in Elizabethan England; and the number of schools increased. The influence of a slave on a growing boy was a poor substitute for a father's instruction in the *mos maiorum*, and character necessarily suffered. But the change was not entirely bad, for the curriculum was widened and the father often chose the teachers with great care. Aemilius Paullus, the victor of Pydna, devoted especial care to the education of his children, and Cornelia, the daughter of Scipio Africanus, trained her sons, Tiberius and Gaius Gracchus, with a wise intermingling of Roman virtues and Greek enlightenment. Even Cato in his old age was forced to realize that the coming generation must be trained to meet a larger world than that faced by their fathers. Greek language, literature and thought were studied; public speaking was practised and rhetoric began to get its fatal hold on Roman life.

Educated Romans learnt to speak Greek in quite early times. Thus in 282 BC L. Postumius Megellus, an ambassador to Tarentum, addressed the council in Greek; true, his audience laughed at his faults in language, but perhaps it was not too bad since they went on to insult him in other ways and were obviously out to be obstreperous. A century later Flamininus and the father of the Gracchi were excellent Greek speakers, and Aemilius Paullus in his diplomatic interviews with Perseus switched easily from Latin to Greek, while P. Licinius Crassus, consul in 131, in dispensing justice in Asia Minor could even reply to Greek petitioners in five different dialects. Further, as we shall see (p. 385), Roman writers were composing histories in Greek before the end of the third century, and so by the next century probably most Roman nobles were becoming bilingual. This gave them an advantage in their diplomatic dealings with the Greeks, who by contrast appear to have failed to learn Latin.[16]

Life became more luxurious as money poured in from foreign conquests and contact with the east awoke fresh needs. It is easy to exaggerate the extent of this change in the first half of the second century: the pictures drawn by Plautus reflect Athens of the New Comedy period, not Rome; Roman conservatism acted as a brake and luxury remained rather primitive. Though Cato could complain that Rome was the only city in the world where a jar of preserved fish cost more than a yoke of oxen, his strictures on Roman customs were doubtless exaggerated by his moralizing zeal. But changes were taking place. The growth of town at the expense of country life involved a rise in the price of property and rents in the city. Domestic architecture was adapted to fresh needs and the *atrium* became a hall rather than the centre of the house. Works of art were collected to adorn the dwellings of the rich. Manlius Vulso brought back from Asia bronze couches, costly coverlets, tapestry and other fabrics, pedestal tables and silver salvers. The Greek bathroom (*balneum*) began to supersede the old washroom (*lavatrina*), and public baths existed at Capua during the Hannibalic War. Banquets became more luxurious, and cookery an art. Baking became a trade instead of the housewife's task, and bakers' shops are heard of in 171. Ennius wrote on the *Art of Pleasant Eating* (ἡδυφαγητικά) and drunkenness increased. In vain Cato opposed the repeal in 195 of the Oppian law, a wartime measure of 215 which had limited the amount of jewellery and plate that could be used by individuals. As censor in 184 he laid heavy taxes on luxuries, especially women's ornaments and dress, vehicles and slaves. In 181 a Lex Orchia limited the number of guests that might be invited to entertainments, and in 161 a Lex Fannia fixed the maximum expenditure on banquets at the Megalesian Games. The very frequency of such sumptuary legislation points to its ineffectiveness. The nobility indulged their wealth and leisure, but their luxury only seemed excessive in contrast with their earlier austerity. (Less than a hundred years earlier, in 275, P. Cornelius Rufinus, who had twice been consul and had celebrated a triumph, was expelled from the Senate for possessing 10 lb of silver vessels!) Two pictures of the wife and daughter of Scipio Africanus give us an intimate glimpse of social life. Aemilia, his wife, 'used to display great magnificence, whenever she took part in the religious ceremonies of the women. For apart from the richness of her own dress and the decorations of her carriage, all the baskets, cups, and other utensils of the sacrifice were of gold or silver and were borne in her train on such solemn occasions, while the number of maids and servants in attendance was correspondingly large' (Polybius, xxxi, 26). Of the *salon* of his daughter Cornelia, Plutarch writes, 'She had many friends, and kept a good table that she might show hospitality, for she always had Greeks and other literary men about her, and all the reigning kings interchanged gifts with her' (*c. Gracchus*, 19). Among these the King of Egypt in vain sought her hand and offered her the crown.

The urban mob, which was growing in Rome as slave labour drove free off the large plantations, had to be amused. There were six regular festivals; the duration and richness of these were increased. Horse and chariot races had formed the main item; scenic displays were staged in 364 and became regular features after 240. But in 186 Greek athletes and wild beasts were introduced into the Circus, though attempts to build a permanent theatre were fruitless and one which was commenced was pulled down in 154. Still more degrading was the introduction of gladiatorial contests in 264. These were private displays, staged in the

Forum to adorn a funeral. For instance, at the funeral of Flamininus in 174 thirty-seven pairs of swordsmen fought. Though such displays were regarded as examples of courage, they soon had a brutalizing effect. Schools of gladiators were established, though no amphitheatres yet existed in Rome. Terence's *Hecyra* could not hold an audience when rumours of gladiators were heard; and the Romans turned a concert given by some famous Greek artists into a coarse burlesque (167): they did not accept the best that Greece offered. In the race for wealth and popularity the nobles lavished more and more on public games, and an aedile might well waste his fortune and have to recoup himself later when he served abroad. Italian allies and provincials sometimes made 'voluntary' contributions to amuse the mob at Rome.

Such were some of the symptoms of the changing spirit of Rome. Below there was a deep spiritual unrest. Cato complained that the Greek spirit questioned everything and settled nothing. Old landmarks were being overthrown. Nobler minds sought refuge in Greek culture and philosophy. Others, recoiling from the formalism of the state religion, fled to the enthusiastic eastern cults. Some made ambition, wealth and power the end of life; some turned to self-indulgence, with or without a Greek cloak of hedonistic theory. Though the sturdy common sense and conservatism of the Romans withstood many temptations, contact with the Greek spirit brought one revolutionary change. In earlier days the individual had worked only to take his proper place in the community; few men of brilliance or creative genius emerged; the portraits of Rome's early heroes seem painted with the same brush. Ennius could truly write: '*Moribus antiquis res stat Romana virisque.*' But later individuals arose, conscious of their own rights and potentialities. Scipio Africanus was one of the earliest leaders who did not quite conform to type; and it was the outstanding individual who at the head of a devoted army threatened and finally overthrew Republican Rome. But as yet the individual hesitated to hurl himself against the rock of the senatorial oligarchy, which did not totter till many had dashed themselves to pieces against its strength.

8. THE CITY[17]

Our earliest glimpse of Rome reveals a picture similar to the sight beheld by Aeneas on his arrival at the seven hills, as portrayed in the eighth book of the *Aeneid*. Amid forest clearings there nestled primitive huts whose appearance is now revealed by the remains on the Palatine and by the hut-like ossuary urns, while their form is still reflected in the straw *capanne* of the modern peasants of the Roman Campagna. We have seen (pp. 42ff.) how these early settlements gradually coalesced into a united community. Then came a period of amazing urban growth and building under the Etruscans, and a final spurt of temple construction, under Greek influences, in the early years of the fifth century (p. 82), after which public building languished. The next stage in the city's history is marked by the invasion of the Gauls, who sacked the town, though sparing some of the temples. The greater part had to be rebuilt and protected by a stone wall (p. 104); so pressing was the danger that the houses were rebuilt with little thought to town planning. Indeed, in the fifth and fourth centuries the Romans were too busy fighting and building roads and colonies in Italy to give much thought to decorating their own city. However, they did not entirely overlook the need for public works: in 312 Appius Claudius constructed a new aqueduct, largely underground, but it was followed in 272 by an aqueduct some forty miles long, the Anio Vetus, which brought supplies from the Sabine hills. War booty helped victorious generals to vow and build several new temples after 350, and in 338 the consul Maenius enabled the public to watch something of the life of the Forum, including public ceremonies, by building balconies on the upper floors of some of the surrounding *tabernae* (small shops with open fronts, which often masked the larger town houses of the nobility). Shortly afterwards the orators' platform was adorned with the 'beaks' (*rostra*) of the ships captured from Antium; it became known as the Rostra.

The next era of building was after contact with Sicily had awakened a desire for a new type of architecture. In the second century Rome began to assume a fresh appearance. New temples were built, some in the Tuscan style, others in a new Hellenistic manner with walls of tufa covered with bright stucco, like the buildings of the 'tufa' period at Pompeii. Basilicas, porticoes and triumphal arches arose to adorn the capital; the drainage system was improved, roads were paved with stone, and in 144 a new high-level aqueduct, the Aqua Marcia, was erected. Private houses, which formerly had been mean, were now built by the nobles to match at any rate the smaller atrium-houses of the 'tufa' period of Pompeii; and tenement houses, the forerunners of the blocks of 'sky-scrapers' of the Empire, were erected for poorer citizens. Some of this building was haphazard, but many of the newer districts were developed on a symmetrical plan, even though this could not be applied to Rome as a whole. At the very end of our period significant innovations were made. About 146 BC two temples were built of Greek marble; a vein of limestone called travertine was discovered; and concrete was introduced or used more freely.

The appearance of the city in 146 BC may perhaps best be realized by taking an imaginary tour round it. On the Janiculum west of the river, for ever made famous by the defence of another Roman Republic, there were no serious fortifications. The Tiber was bridged by the old wooden Pons Sublicius, south of the island; between bridge and island were the stone piers of the Pons Aemilius (179), but stone arches were not constructed till 142. On the island, which was probably connected with both banks by bridges, stood the temples of Aesculapius (291) and Faunus (194). The Pons Sublicius debouched into the Cattle Market (Forum Boarium) where the 'Servian' wall came down to the river. It is hardly necessary to follow the course of the wall as since the Hannibalic War it had been losing importance. Through the Forum Boarium flowed an open drain, the Cloaca Maxima, running between the Capitol and Palatine from the Roman Forum where it drained the surrounding hills. In the market stood the old altar of Hercules Invictus and the round temple of Hercules Victor, decorated with frescoes by the poet Pacuvius; also two temples attributed to Servius Tullius – Fortuna and Mater Matuta, which contained a picture of Ti. Sempronius Gracchus' Sardinian campaign and a map of the island. In front were two arches with gilded statues erected by L. Stertinius in 196.[18]

In the valley which ran from the market south-eastwards between the Palatine and Aventine was the Circus Maximus, the chief amusement place of the city. Founded by Tarquinius, it still remained a wooden construction; at the north end were painted *carceres*, the starting-point for the chariots, and down the centre ran a *spina* decorated with statues and equipped with *ova* to record the laps. Nearby was the temple of Juventas, vowed by Livius Salinator at Metaurus, and at the southern end the altar of Corisus, an old Italic agricultural deity. On the slopes of the Aventine stood the temple of Ceres, Liber and Libera (496); its terracotta decorations by Greek artists were in a lighter style than the older Etrusco-Latin type. It was the headquarters of the plebeian aediles and contained their archives as well as copies of *senatus consulta*. On the Aventine itself, a plebeian quarter, were two famous temples: that of Juno Regina, dedicated by Camillus, who brought the wooden cult statue of the goddess from Veii (392), and that of Diana, ascribed to King Servius, which contained a bronze copy of the compact with the Latins and the Lex Icilia of 456. Over the hill ran the Clivus Publicus from the Forum Boarium, and the end of the Appian aqueduct; on the top was an open space, Armilustrium, where lay the traditional tomb of Titius Tatius. At the foot of the western slope of the Aventine below the 'Servian' wall along the river ran the Porticus Aemilia (193), a large market-hall, designed to receive and distribute goods and foodstuffs brought up the Tiber. It was restored in 174 and, if the identification with the present remains is correct, it is important as providing the earliest known use of concrete, which was soon to revolutionize Roman building. At its north end rose the Column of Minucius, erected by popular subscription to the *præfectus annonae* of 439. On the Caelian Hill, east of the Aventine, there were few buildings of importance.[19]

North-east of the Circus Maximus rose the Palatine with its fortifications and many early buildings and sanctuaries, though few of them are known. Apart from archaic burials and cisterns, there were the greatly venerated Hut of Romulus and the Lupercal, a cave at the south-west corner of the hill near the site of the fig tree where Romulus and Remus had been washed ashore; a monument representing the wolf and twins was erected here by the Ogulnii in 296. From here an ancient stairway, Scalae Caci, led down to the Circus Maximus, perhaps serving as a short cut to the Clivus Victoriae, the ascent to the Palatine from the Velabrum on which stood the Temple of Victory (244) and a shrine of Victoria Virgo built by Cato (193). The picturesque ilex-covered ruins of the temple of Magna Mater (191), which contained the black stone from Pessinus, are the only remains of the early Palatine temples. Of the private houses on the Palatine reference is made to that of Cn. Octavius, consul of 165.[20]

North-east of the Palatine, on the Velia, the Sacred Way started on its track down through the Forum. Near where the arch of Titus now stands were the Temples of Jupiter Stator (294) (Flavian remains), of Penates Dei (Augustan remains), and of Lares, indicating the approach to the heart of the Roman state. If in imagination we descend the Via Sacra we can see the monuments in the southern and northern halves of the Forum. On the south were the precincts of Vesta in whose round temple the sacred fire of the state was kept perpetually burning by the Vestal Virgins whose house (Atrium Vestae) lay just to the south. Within the precinct were the Domus Publica, where the Pontifex Maximus lived; opposite lay the Regia, his headquarters, and its shrine of Mars.[21] Nearby is the Spring of Juturna where Castor and Pollux watered their horses after the battle of Lake Regillus and where they appeared also after Pydna. Their temple, dedicated in 484 and rebuilt in 117 in a Hellenized style, was often used as a meeting place for the Senate; its remains, of the Augustan Age, form a landmark in the Forum. In front stood an equestrian statue of Tremulus, consul in 306, commemorating his victory over the Hernici. Here the main road to the Forum Boarium along the west of the Palatine started; it was called the Vicus Tuscus, perhaps after a settlement of Etruscan workmen, and contained a statue of the Etruscan god Vortumnus. It was a busy quarter with an unsavoury reputation. To the west were the Old Shops, the centre of the bankers and moneylenders; behind them, on the site of the house of the elder Scipio Africanus the Basilica Sempronia was built in answer to the needs of a new age (170): a roofed hall with colonnades, in which much public business was transacted. Then, beyond the Vicus Jugarius, which also led to the Forum Boarium, stood the Temple of Saturn at the foot of the Capitol. Coeval with the Republic, it contained the state treasury; the treasury offices were in the Area Saturni nearby, until the Tabularium was built in 78. From the temple a portico ran up along the Clivus Capitolinus, the main paved approach to the Capitol (part of the paving of 174 BC survives).

Before climbing the Capitol, we must return to the Velia and the northern half of the Forum. Here were the New Shops, a business centre which had originally been let by the state to tenants, especially provision merchants and butchers; but these had been moved north to the Macellum before 310. Next were the Basilica Aemilia (179), where a water-clock was installed in 159 (some remains of the earliest period survive); a shrine of Cloacina, coeval with the Cloaca Maxima; and the Temple of Janus, the gates of which were only closed in peacetime. Here the Argiletum led northwards to the Macellum, a central building surrounded by shops, which in 179 had absorbed the local fish and other markets, and to the slums of Subura. Nearby were a statue of Marsyas, perhaps brought from Apamea by Vulso in 188 because of the legendary connection of the town with the tomb of Aeneas; the praetor's judgment-seat (tribunal), transferred from the Comitium about 150; and the Lacus Curtius. Next was the Comitium, the open assembly place of the Roman people, bounded on the north by the Curia, on the west by the *carcer* and Basilica Porcia, and on the south by the Rostra; it was consecrated ground and the political centre of Rome till the second century. In front of it stood the Rostra, adorned with the beaks of the ships captured from Antium in 338, from which orators addressed the people, and the Graecostasis, an open platform used as a tribunal for foreign ambassadors, especially Greeks; on it was a small bronze shrine to Concordia, erected by Cn. Flavius (304). Here were the Tomb of Romulus and the column of Duilius with an archaic inscription celebrating his naval victory of 260. Other old monuments were the Fig Tree and statue of Navius, a puteal, a statue of Horatius and the Volcanal, from which kings and magistrates addressed the people before the Rostra was built. At the back of the Comitium stood the Curia Hostilia, the original Senate-house (on the side wall was a painting of Messala's victory of 263), and nearby was the censors' office (Atrium Libertatis). Westwards lay the Basilica Porcia, erected by Cato in 184, in which the tribunes held court. The column of Maenis recalled the victor of Antium. At the foot of the Capitol were the subterranean prison (*carcer* or Tullianum) which could only be entered by a hole in the roof and which probably dates back to regal times; the Temple of Concord, vowed by Camillus in 367; and the Porticus Deorum Consentium (the existing remains are Flavian). Hence the Clivus Capitolinus leads up to the Capitol; at its summit stood an arch erected by Scipio Africanus together with seven statues and two marble basins.

The Capitoline hill consisted of two peaks, the Area Capitolina and the Arx. The former was an open space around the temple of Jupiter Optimus Maximus; it was surrounded by a wall and portico (159). Within the area was Rome's most famous temple (pp. 57f.); gilt shields adorned the pediment (193), its walls and columns were covered with stucco (179) and later it received a mosaic floor and gilded ceiling (142). In front of the temple steps was an altar on which sacrifices were offered at the beginning of the year and at triumphs. A colossal statue of Jupiter, erected by Sp. Carvilius in 293, could be seen from the Alban Mount. There were statues of Hercules, Mars, and the kings and heroes of the Republic, and so numerous were the trophies of victory that they were removed in 179. There were other temples, including that of Fides, built *c.* 250, which was often used by the Senate; on its walls were international agreements. Other state archives were kept in the Atrium Publicum, and the Curia Calabra afforded another assembly hall. On the Arx was the temple of Juno Moneta, which occupied the site of the house of Manlius Capitolinus (344). It contained the *libri lintei* and the mint which was perhaps established in 269. The sacred geese were kept nearby. At the north-east corner was an open grassy space with a thatched hut, the Auguraculum, where the public auspices were taken.[22]

Below the Capitol outside the city wall and *pomerium* the Campus Martius stretched to the Tiber. It was used for pasturage and military exercises, but had been encroached on by a few individuals; the elder Scipio had a villa and garden there. The west side was marshy and contained an oak grove, Aesculetum, where the Assembly had met to pass the Hortensian laws, and a district called Tarentum where there were hot springs and an altar of Dis Pater and Proserpine. The south-eastern portion was named Prata Flaminia. Here was situated the Circus Flaminius, built in 221 for the plebeian games; it was probably a circular area rather than a stadium and it also served as a market place. There was an altar of Mars which dated to the regal period; a portico led from it to the nearest city gate (193). The Ovile was a large enclosed area divided into aisles in which the Comitia Centuriata met to vote. The Villa Publica (built in 435 and enlarged in 194) was used as the headquarters for state officers engaged in taking the census or levying troops, for generals desiring a triumph, and for lodging foreign ambassadors. Near the Circus Flaminius was the Temple of Bellona, vowed by Appius Claudius Caecus in 296, where the Senate often met to receive victorious generals; nearby was an assembly place for senators (Senaculum) and the Columna Bellica, a boundary stone over which the fetial priest formally hurled a spear on declaration of war. There were many temples, including that of Apollo (431), from which a portico later ran to the river (179). Between the Campus and the Forum Boarium was the vegetable market (Forum Holitorium) with temples to Spes, Juno Sospita and Janus; the remains of these have recently been exposed from the surrounding church of S. Nicola in Carcere.[23]

Finally, reference may be made to some outlying monuments. On the Quirinal was the Temple of Semo Sancus (466) containing the shield bearing the treaty with Gabii, and bronze wheels from the destruction of Privernum in 329. Outside the Colline Gate were temples to Honos, Virtus (third century) and Venus Erucina (181). Within a grove on the Cispius stood the Temple of Juno Lucina (375) where gifts were offered for new-born children. On the Esquiline was a Temple of Tellus (268) which was sometimes used by the Senate, and here came the aqueduct bringing water from the Anio. On the Appian Way outside the Porta Capena were temples of Tempestates (259) and Mars (388) where troops assembled on setting out for war. In 189 the Appian Way was paved to this point. Beyond the Servian wall was the family tomb of the Scipios, who preferred inhumation to cremation. It was hewn out of the rock and its passages have been cleared. Many famous members of the family were buried here, and it contained a statue of Ennius.

The crowds that thronged the buildings are of more interest than the city itself, but of these we catch only a few glimpses. Plautus in the *Curculio* gives a vivid description of the Forum: 'If you wish to meet a perjurer, go to the Comitium; for a liar and braggart, near the Temple of

Venus Cloacina; for rich married wasters, the Basilica. There too will be harlots and men ready to haggle. Members of dining-clubs, you'll find in the fish market. In the lower Forum reputable and wealthy citizens walk about; in the middle, near the canal, the merely showy set. Above the Lacus Curtius are those impudent, talkative, spiteful fellows who boldly decry other people without reason and are themselves open to plenty of truthful criticism. Below the Old Shops those who lend and borrow at interest. Behind the Temple of Castor are those whom you would do ill to trust too readily. In the Tuscan street are men who sell their services; in the Velabrum bakers, butchers, soothsayers.

9. LAW

The purpose of this section is to refer briefly to the principles and method of Roman law, not to the details of particular institutions. Roman law is a peculiar manifestation of the Roman spirit, and its history 'affords a unique example of the juristic method of legal development, of law not simply positive, but existing of right and co-ordinated and developed by reason . . . a consistent body of reasoned doctrine, essentially not created by the State, though sanctioned by its protection'. In this one department of thought the Romans proved superior to the Greeks, despite the richness of Greek jurisprudence. Here Greece did not take Rome captive, but Rome merely accepted from her a few individual ideas. The Greeks 'enter into the legal history of Europe only by their contribution to the cosmopolitan jurisprudence of Rome.'[24]

Our chief concern is with private law. Of the two principal divisions of public law, the development of constitutional law has been treated in connection with Rome's political history; of criminal law, which was not scientifically handled by the Romans themselves till Hadrian's day, little need be said. In the Twelve Tables it was not distinguished from private law and though it was marked off when *iudicia privata* were assigned to a praetor (366), much of the field covered by modern criminal law (e.g. theft and assault) fell within the ambit of the civil law of delict. Crimes, such as murder, treason, evasion of military service and certain religious offences, came within the jurisdiction of the magistrates (quaestors, aediles, tribunes) and the assemblies of the people. This procedure by which the accused, if a citizen, could appeal from a magistrate's sentence to the Comitia Centuriata (whose function resembled that of the English Crown rather than of the Court of Criminal Appeal) and could escape the death penalty by exile, long sufficed, but in the second century it was reinforced by the appointment of special '*ad hoc*' *quaestiones*. These served as precedents for the later *quaestiones perpetuae*, of which the first was established in 149 (p. 329).

We must now turn to the development of civil law (*ius civile*), the legal customs of the Roman citizens. Early customary law, based in part on religious sanctions, changed very slowly in both its secular (*ius*) and religious (*fas*) aspects. It was interpreted by an exclusively patrician college of pontiffs, who advised the king as a council on religious questions, while its individual members could give professional advice (*responsa*) on matters of private law (*ius*); their function was thus advisory, not judicial. The first breach in this monopoly was made by the publication of the Twelve Tables in reply to popular demand. This code, which marks the beginning of historical Roman law, remained the fundamental statute of the Republic. It is primarily secular and concerned with private law, and is a remarkable testimony to the legal genius of the Romans in that they detached law from religion at so early a date. A small community of peasant-proprietors had established a body of law which found its sanction not in the authority of a divine or human lawgiver, but in a sense of justice and equity which was inherent in the peculiar genius of the Latin race.

This great achievement outlasted the national period during which Rome conquered Italy, but it naturally had to be adapted to fresh needs. The method of change, or the 'source of law', which for English Common Law is statute (Act of Parliament) and precedent (principles established by individual judges), among the Romans was statute, jurisprudence (or *interpretatio*), and magisterial edict. The original statutes of the Twelve Tables were modified, exceptionally by fresh legislation (as for example by the Lex Canuleia of 445), and constantly by interpretation, first by pontiffs and then by professional jurists. The privileges of the pontiffs were gradually whittled down. Men would still have to consult them after the publication of the Twelve Tables in order to learn the correct legal formalities, but their decisions would now have to square with a public code. The next attack came from Cn. Flavius, who in 304 published the correct forms of procedure, and four years later the College of Pontiffs was opened to plebeians (p. 122). The first plebeian Pontifex Maximus, T. Coruncanius (253), *primus profiteri coepit*; this apparently means that he admitted the public, or at any rate students, to his consultations. There thus grew up a class of men known as *iuris consulti*, or *iuris prudentes*, who interpreted the law to the changing needs of their age. These jurists were professional lawyers in a limited sense; they received no fees and were public men who shared in the administration of the state, e.g. Coruncanius who as consul took the field against Pyrrhus in 280, Publius and Sextus Aelius, the consuls of 201 and 198, and M'. Manilius who attacked Carthage in 149. They were in practice recruited from the *nobilitas*, and they regarded jurisprudence as part of the art of government, so that they developed Roman law to keep pace with the needs of the state. Their chief service was to give advice (*responsa*) either to individuals (cf. our 'opinions' of counsel) or to magistrates or judges (*iudices*) who were laymen more like our jurymen than judges. Such opinions, though theoretically only persuasive, were in fact generally accepted as binding precedent by custom, though not by law, and so Roman law was modified and built up much like the 'judge-made' law of England. As an example of 'interpretation' and of the extraordinary adaptability of Roman institutions the development of the emancipation of children from their father's power may be cited. The Twelve Tables enacted that a son who had been sold by his father three times should be free from his control. This measure, which was designed to punish the misuse of *patria potestas*, was 'interpreted' to emancipate a son by a fictitious threefold sale. Further, it was extended to the emancipation of daughters who need be 'sold' only once, since the Twelve Tables demanded three sales for sons and did not mention daughters.

After some 250 years of development which was mainly juristic, fresh need stimulated new methods. The chief need was created by contact with foreigners and the method used was the magisterial edict. Theoretically the *ius civile* applied only to citizens, and foreigners had no rights or duties under it. Commerce demanded that this condition should cease. After extending their rights to the Latins and concluding special treaties with Carthage the Romans had appointed a special *praetor peregrinus* (*c.* 242) to deal with disputes in which foreigners were involved and to relieve the *praetor urbanus* of this duty. With the acquisition of provinces the sphere of foreign jurisdiction was immensely widened; the magistrate had to develop a method of his own, since the Roman *legis actio* procedure was not available, and to decide what law to apply, since the *ius civile* was designed only for citizens. To build up a code of 'private international law' would prove too cumbersome, and in practice the *praetor peregrinus* and the provincial governor issued edicts, stating what principles they would adopt. These would naturally be based mainly on Roman law, but Roman formalism was tempered by foreign, especially Greek ideas. Thus a system was created which was not the Roman *ius civile*; it governed all free men, irrespective of nationality. This led to the conception of *ius gentium*, or 'that part of the law which we apply both to outselves and to foreigners'. Later in the first century under the influence of Aristotle's division of law into 'man-made' ($νομικόν$) and 'natural' or 'common' ($φυσικόν: κοινόν$), and of Stoic ideas of 'life according to nature', the *ius gentium* was identified with the law of Nature or a law common to all peoples. This creation of *ius gentium*, or commercial law, was a magnificent achievement by which Roman law was modernized. It was made possible by the praetorian edict.

As the English legal system comprises common law and equity, so beside the Roman *ius civile*, which was formed by statute and interpretation, there was created a counterpart to the earlier English equity: a system of magisterial law (*ius honorarium*) grew up from the edicts in which higher magistrates, especially praetors, proclaimed their orders and intentions. Though such edicts were valid only for the year, each magistrate would in practice take over the bulk of his predecessor's proclamation. Since the praetor could not legislate, his edicts were not statutes, but they were nevertheless an important source of law; he could not give a right but he could promise a remedy, and this in turn implies the existence of a right. According to Papinian the function of the *ius honorarium* was to 'aid, supplement or correct' the civil law. It is uncertain when the praetors attained this full right: indeed this is one of the most controversial questions of Republican law. For many years the early system of *legis actiones* and purely civil law prevailed, until the Lex Aebutia (*c*. 150) substituted for the stereotyped *legis actiones* a formulary system of procedure by which cases were tried in a form of words which depended on the praetor. It would seem probable that this law was preceded by a period in which a praetor, who had public opinion behind him, could exercise some influence, but he was not legally given a free hand until the enactment of the Lex Aebutia, which marks the beginning of the great period of the praetorian edict. The *ius civile* was gradually amended by the *ius praetorium*. Thus the law of a city-state was adapted to meet the needs of an empire, and Roman law became one of the chief civilizing forces in the history of mankind, and the basis of a large part of modern European law.

XVII

LITERATURE AND ART[1]

1. EARLY LATIN

In early days a great variety of languages was spoken in Italy, but by the end of our period Latin predominated, though such dialects as Oscan survived till the first century AD, while Greek was adopted by educated Romans as a second tongue. Apart from Etruscan all these languages were Indo-European and thus akin to one another: in the north was Celtic and the Ligurian speech, which linguistically is intermediate between Celtic and Italic; on the Adriatic coast a group of 'Illyrian' dialects is found (Messapic, Venetic, Rhaetic and perhaps 'old Sabellic'); Greek was spoken in the cities of Magna Graecia; in central Italy the Italic dialects prevailed. These last fall into two main classes: Latin and Faliscan; and Umbro-Sabellian including Oscan and minor dialects. Apart from affinities with Greek and Celtic which derive from a distant common Indo-European origin, the Latins borrowed much from their neighbours' speech in historical times, from Sabine, Oscan, Greek, Etruscan and even Celtic. Of the ten thousand Greek words which came into Latin use, a considerable number was introduced by the actual process of intercourse in speech. The Latins borrowed their alphabet from the Greeks by way of Etruria. But out of a tongue which was uncouth and heavy the Romans by borrowing and still more by adaptation wrought a language which became the medium for one of the noblest literatures; one that outlived the Roman Empire, and became the servant of learning and religion and the direct ancestor of a great portion of the languages of modern Europe.

Few traces of early Latin survive. They include the inscription written alternatively up and down the Forum *stele* under the Lapis Niger (sixth century?), that written (*c.* 600 BC?) from right to left on the Praeneste fibula: '*Manios med fhefhaked Numasioi*' = *Manius me fecit Numerio*, and that on the Duenos bowl (fourth century) found on the Quirinal which shows Greek influence (*Duenos med feced*). Somewhat earlier than the Hannibalic War is a dedication from Tusculum: '*M. Fourio C.f. tribunos militare de praidad Maurte dedet*' (*M. Furius C.f. tribunus militaris de praeda Marti dedit.*) To the same period belong the epitaphs in Saturnian verse of Scipio Barbatus, consul of 298, and his son, consul in 259: '*Honc oino ploirume consentiont* R(*omai*) − (*Hunc unum plurimi consentiunt Romae*)− *Duonoro optumo fuise viro*'−(*Bonorum optimum fuisse virum*)−'*Luciom Scipione*' − (*Lucium Scipionem*). It is uncertain to what extent certain literary remains have been corrupted and how far their archaic Latin is genuine. Examples are the fragments of the litany of the Salii, which was unintelligible in Horace's day, the hymn of the Arval Brethren which begins, '*Enos, Lases, iuvate*' (*nos, Lares, iuvate*), and the Twelve Tables.

The beginning of Latin prose may be found in official documents such as the Twelve Tables, priestly Commentarii, Acta, Fasti and Annales, and early laws and treaties. Speeches in the Senate and funeral orations stimulated the development of Roman oratory. Early poetry is represented by the hymns already mentioned, by didactic proverbs (e.g. '*Hiberno pulvere, verno luto,/Grandia farra, camille, metes*'), lullabies (e.g. '*Lalla, lalla, lalla: i aut dormi aut lacta*'), wedding or funeral songs, and by the words chanted by workers in the fields or women at the loom. Whether any real poetry was conceived is uncertain. Varro records that at banquets boys used to sing lays celebrating the deeds of great men; Cato says that the banqueters themselves contributed songs. On such evidence Niebuhr proposed, and Macaulay popularized, the theory of the existence of an early popular ballad literature, from which Livy derived many details of the legends of early Rome. Though Rome produced no Homer to sing the glory of heroes (κλέα ἀνδρῶν), clearly songs were sung in early days, and the mead-hall of Caedmon's day had its Roman counterpart. But such *carmina* probably had little influence upon later historiography.[2] The metre of these early songs and litanies was the native Saturnian, which Ennius depised as crude in contrast with his own Hellenic hexameters: '*quos olim Fauni vatesque canebant*'. Popular drama originated in Fescennine verses, *satura*, and Atellan farce. Livy (vii, 2) describes how performances with musical accompaniment called *saturae* were enacted by Etruscans in Rome in 364 and replaced the earlier

Fescennine banter; the 'satire' was in turn superseded by the more regular drama on Greek models introduced by Livius Andronicus.[3] Fescennine verses were rough jests, improvised and sung at harvest and vintage festivals to avert the evil eye; they long survived at marriages and triumphs. These crude jests may have developed into dialogue, but they remained amateur efforts. The term originates from Fescennium in Etruria or from 'fascinum,' a phallic symbol to avert the evil eye. The dramatic nature of *satura* has been questioned by some who see in Livy's account a reflection of Aristotle's view of the origin of Greek comedy. With Ennius *satura lanx*, a mixed dish, became a literary miscellany, but it may have started its career on the stage. The *fabulae Atellanae* were Oscan farces, originating at Atella in Campania. When introduced into Rome, perhaps in the third century, they became popular and were acted by amateurs who did not suffer from that stigma which was later attached to professional actors at Rome.[4] The characters were stock figures: Maccus the Fool, Pappus the Dotard, Bucco the Glutton, Manduccus the Champer, and Dossennus (probably a glutton rather than a hunchback). From such crude beginnings did Latin literature spring.

2. THE POETS

Horace considered that Roman literature began with Livius Andronicus, that is at the time when Rome had conquered Italy and was asserting her supremacy throughout the Mediterranean.[5] National victory stimulated artistic production. The Romans, suddenly brought face to face with the literature of Greece, became conscious of the crudeness of their own early efforts. True, they tended to regard literature rather as an extra than a fundamental part of life and were slow in losing the suspicion that thought delayed action. Further, the perfection of Greek literature in all genres might have deterred a less practical people. But when the Romans conceived a desire for literature they determined to get it quickly, starting with pure translation from the Greek and adapting their language to this end. Increasing contact with the Greek world stimulated their desire to accept the legacy of Greece and to shape it to their national needs.

Livius Andronicus (*c.* 284–204), though cavalierly dismissed by Cicero and Horace, was a great pioneer if not a great poet. He was a Greek from Tarentum who served in the household of Livius Salinator. Traditionally a slave freed by Salinator, he more probably gained citizenship through Salinator's patronage. He taught Latin and Greek and translated the *Odyssey* into Latin Saturnians. In 240 he was chosen by the aediles to translate in varied metres a comedy and a tragedy for performance at the Ludi Romani that year. In 207 he was entrusted with the composition of a Processional Ode for a ceremony of purification of the state. This success resulted in the establishment by the government of a club or academy for literary men on the Aventine. Livius might be called the father of epic and lyric poetry, of tragedy and comedy at Rome, if the outstanding genius of Ennius had not a greater claim. His translation of the *Odyssey* became a schoolbook, which the youthful Horace had occasion to connect with the cane of his master Orbilius, yet it must have opened up a wonderland of romance and adventure for boys who had been accustomed only to learning by heart the Twelve Tables. It is easy to blame the translator for defective renderings and for falling far short of the noble hexameters of his original; it is less easy perhaps to envisage the greatness of his contribution. The titles of eight of his tragedies have survived; they point to the three great tragedians, especially Sophocles, as the source, and show a preference for stories from the Trojan cycle, which had interest for the Romans who had a natural concern about the background to the story of their own Trojan origin. A Roman dramatist could not reproduce the Greek chorus (which indeed had gradually dropped out of Greek tragedy after Euripides' day) since he could not provide a trained chorus of twelve singers and dancers; so Livius (and later Naevius) increased the number of monodies and thus made Roman tragedy more like modern opera than Greek tragedy had been. He acted in his own plays. His comedies are based on the New Comedy, not on Aristophanes. Examples of his rugged vividness may be taken from the *Aegisthus*:

> *Tum autem lascivom Nerei sumum pecus*
> *Ludens ad cantum classem lustratur (? choro);*

(Then Nereus' wanton snub-nosed flock in fun
Frolic to music choir-like round the fleet.)

or from his *Andromeda*: '*Confluges ubi conventu campum totum inumigant*'. (When the waters in their concourse congregate to flood the plain) (J. Wight Duff).

More has survived of the work of Naevius (*c.* 270–199), an Italian whose outspoken comments on the nobility, especially the Metelli, led to his imprisonment towards the end of the Hannibalic War. He wrote two plays in prison retracting his remarks, and so was released, but he later died in exile at Utica. His first plays were produced in 235. Titles of seven of his tragedies from Greek mythology survive. He first 'contaminated' plays by adopting features from two originals,[6] and he set a new fashion by writing historical plays (*fabulae praetextae*): an *Alimonia Romuli et Remi* and *Clastidium*, celebrating the exploits of Marcellus in 222. His comedies and epic poetry, however, achieved greater fame. We have the titles of thirty-four comedies, which were apparently amusing, mordant and outspoken. Some were based on Greek New Comedy (*palliatae*), others on native life (*togatae*): from *The Girl from Tarentum* (*Tarentilla*) there survives a vivacious description of the wiles of a flirt. Even more important was his epic in Saturnians, the *Bellum Punicum*, describing the first war in which Naevius himself fought; the earlier part recounts the legendary origin of Rome and Carthage by way of introduction. This work had considerable influence on Ennius and Virgil. Naevius' style is sometimes rigorous, sometimes bald (cf. his famous 'noble Duke of York' lines: *Marcus Valerius consul|Partem exerciti in expeditionem|Ducit*). But his fondness for compound words (as *arquitenens, frundiferos*) shows that a poetic diction was being created. His genius was essentially Latin; 'full of Campanian (or as we should say "Castilian") pride,' he composed his epitaph which claimed that after his death men forgot to speak the Latin tongue at Rome: '*Oblitei sunt Romai loquier lingua Latina*'. At any rate he had laid the foundation of the national epic.

Q. Ennius (239–169), Rome's soldier-poet who more truly than Livius can claim the title of father of Latin poetry, was born in Calabria and was brought to Rome from military service in Sardinia by Cato in 204. There he taught and wrote, winning the friendship of Scipio and Fulvius, and ultimately attaining full citizenship. He spoke Greek, Messapic and Latin and showed great versatility of gifts. He took a large part in introducing Greek thought to Rome; in southern Italy he had absorbed much of the thought of Pythagoreanism, Epicharmus, Euhemerus and Epicurus. It is a paradox of fate that this Hellenist should have been brought to Rome by Cato. His comedies were slight, but he adapted at least twenty Greek tragedies, especially plays of Euripides whose critical spirit thus spoke from the Roman stage; he perhaps reintroduced the chorus into tragedy. He excelled in presenting moving situations, such as Alcmaeon hounded by the Furies, Cassandra's sorrows, or the emotional farewell of captive Andromache:

> *O pater, O patria, O Priami domus,*
> *Saeptum altisono cardine templum.*

In his *Saturae* Ennius developed a new type of literature, a general commentary on life in the form of narrative, anecdote, fable or dialogue. To the *satura* may belong his *Euhemerus* and *Epicharmus*, his *Scipio* which honoured his patron Africanus, and perhaps his *Ambracia* which celebrated the exploits of Fulvius Nobilior. Ennius' greatest contribution was the eighteen books of his *Annals*, an epic account of Rome from earliest times down to 172 BC, written in hexameters. His description of the First Punic War was slight, as Naevius had already covered the ground in Saturnians. Whether the mixing of epic poetry and contemporary history was successful or not, Ennius provided Rome with a national epic which found its unity, not in its form, but in its conception of the grandeur of Rome's expanding greatness. The attempt by one who claimed to be the Roman Homer to adapt the Latin language to a Greek dactylic metre was bound to result in a certain roughness of form (e.g. the famous tmesis '*Saxo cere comminuit brum*' for '*Saxo cerebrum comminuit*'); but there were flashes of real beauty and impressive sonority: *ingenio maximus, arte rudis*. Many lines epitomize the spirit of early Rome: '*qui vincit non est victor nisi victu' fatetur*'; '*moribus antiquis res stat Romana virisque*'; Curius '*quem nemo ferro potuit superare neque auro*'; and Fabius, '*unus homo nobis cunctando restituit rem*'. The measure of Ennius' success is the measure of the debt that Lucretius, Virgil and other poets owed him:

> *Ennius ut noster cecinit qui primus amoeno*
> *detulit ex Helicone perenni fronde coronam.*

Later generations could with truth repeat the epitaph of such a poet:

> *Nemo me dacrumis decoret nec funera fletu*
> *Faxit. Cur? Volito vivu' per ora virum.*

And Quintilian could say: 'Let us worship Ennius like groves hallowed by age, where the great old oaks are not so much beautiful as awe-inspiring.'[7]

M. Pacuvius (*c.* 220–130), the nephew of Ennius, was a painter and writer. Beside *saturae* and a *praetexta*, named *Paullus*, he composed tragedies based on the Greek tragedians. His language was at times stilted and quaint, as in his description of dolphins as '*Nerei repandirostrum incurvicervicum pecus*', but he had a vivid pen and was regarded in the Ciceronian age as Rome's tragic poet. The other claimant to this title was his junior L. Accius (170–*c.* 86), after whom the writing of tragedy declined.

T. Maccius Plautus (*c.* 254–184) specialized in comedy. His early hardships in Rome, where at one time he worked as an actor or stage carpenter, at another in a flour mill, have been questioned, but his later popularity doubtless stabilized his position. One hundred and thirty plays masqueraded under his name, until Varro drew up a canonical list of twenty-one, of which all survive, though one only in fragments. A few were written towards the close of the Hannibalic War, the majority in the second century. Plautus drew on Philemon, Diphilus, Menander and other writers of Greek New Comedy, but he did not reproduce them in detail. New Comedy of Athens was a comedy of manners far removed from the vigorous Aristophanic caricature of individuals. A certain variety was displayed in this social satire, but the characters and plots tended to conform to type: the young lover, the confidential slave, the parasite, the courtesan, the pander and the braggart soldier. To transpose this immoral world on to the Roman stage would have shocked some and bored others, but Plautus wrote for his audience with great skill. By retaining the Greek background he was able to convince his hearers that they were witnessing life in a foreign land; and many would enjoy a display of the weakness of human nature or the antics of an impudent Greek slave, if they thought it would not corrupt their own national life: '*Licet haec Athenis nobis*' (Plaut., *Stich.*, 448). By imposing a Roman touch here and there Plautus interested his audience, who heard Roman characters generally referred to as 'barbarians', but who also saw Roman military and legal customs prevailing in a Greek setting and heard Latin puns as well as occasional references to contemporary events. Plautus cared nothing for consistency, just as Shakespeare when following Plutarch did not hesitate to let Theseus appear in English court dress. He played to his gallery still further by replacing the polish of his models with a coarse and boisterous Roman humour of a knockabout type: the banging of doors, the beating of slaves, scenes of rioting, eating and drinking, or the elephantine tread of a man disguised as a bride would appeal more to a Roman than to a Greek playgoer. Finally, Plautus, perhaps developing a movement introduced by Livius and Naevius, changed his models into something approaching a modern comic opera. Menander's plays were written mainly in iambic senarii which were spoken by the actor, but Plautus retained this metre only for about one quarter of each play; the rest was brisker, either delivered as a recitative accompanied by a flute or else pure lyrics which were sung. A Greek visiting a Roman theatre would have found the Plautine version of a play that he knew very different from the original.

Of the plays themselves little can be said here. Apart from the

Amphitruo (imitated by Molière and Dryden) which is a tragicomedy influenced by South Italian humour rather than a *fabula palliata*, they fall into various types as well as into 'plays pleasant and unpleasant'. Many are comedies of intrigue, others are character plays (as the *Miles Gloriosus*), some are based on cases of mistaken identity (e.g. the *Menaechmi*, imitated in Shakespeare's *Comedy of Errors*), others on the motive of recognition (ἀναγνώρισις); the *Captivi* is unique in containing no female characters. The appeal of Plautus lies primarily in his *vis comica* expressed in racy language. As in the New Comedy there was an underlying element of universal appeal, so Plautus strikes a semi-serious note at times, as in the treatment of his central theme of love. Though he lacks the lyrical sweetness of Aristophanes, he has something of the great master's joy in living; his exuberant fun is not far removed from the full-blooded energy of the Elizabethans. Here lies his wide appeal to which even St Jerome and Luther responded.

Among other composers of *palliatae* was Caecilius Statius (*c.* 219–168), an Insubrian war captive who became the first Celtic author in Rome. In language he naturally fell short of the Latinity of Plautus or Terence, but his plots were considered first-class, either because he indulged in 'contamination' less than his contemporaries or perhaps because, like Terence later, he created an element of surprise by not disclosing the outline of the plot in his prologues. Better known through the survival of six plays, written between 166 and 160, is the younger poet whose work Caecilius encouraged: P. Terentius Afer (*c.* 195–159), an emancipated slave from Africa who became an intimate member of the Scipionic circle. By Terence's day the attitude of Roman society to things Greek was changing, so that he found it possible to hellenize the *palliatae* still further. His plays are more homogeneous and lack the Roman element introduced by Plautus; the lyric parts are reduced in favour of spoken iambic parts; his interweaving of two plots is more skilful, so that Julius Caesar could call him 'Menander halved'. The society and morality which he depicts is the same as in Plautus, but the tone is more refined; there is less coarseness and less comedy. The plots tend towards monotony; the reader never laughs and sometimes forgets to smile. But Terence shows a greater human interest and kindliness than his predecessor. His language is not an echo from the street, but from a cultured society. His neatness of expression has enshrined many a famous thought, as '*fortes fortuna adiuvat*', '*modo liceat vivere, est spes*', '*quot homines, tot sententiae*', or '*homo sum : humani nihil a me alienum puto*'. 'A lover of pure Latin' (*puri sermonis amator*), Terence clothed Latin comedy most nearly in its original Attic grace. But in doing this he nearly killed Graeco-Latin comedy: Plautus had made it popular by partial nationalization, but Terence destroyed any chance of it becoming a popular national growth. The refinement and charm of his language and the dexterity of his plots might appeal to the educated Hellenists, but the common people, for whom the plays were really staged at the festivals, soon grew tired and found rope-dancers and gladiators more attractive than *The Mother-in-Law* (*Hecyra*).

This reaction against *palliatae* favoured the production of *togatae*. Titinius, a late rival of Plautus, solved the difficult problem of presenting the love story of Greek comedy in a Roman setting without offending Roman taste by choosing for his scene the free society of Italian village communities. The recovery of his lost plays, such as *The Lady of the Dye Shop* or *The Dancing Girl of Ferentinum*, would throw a welcome light on social conditions on which we have little contemporary evidence.

3. PROSE WRITERS

At Rome, as elsewhere, prose developed more slowly than poetry. It served law and government, legal and annalistic purposes, but it was long before history was written in Latin. The first Roman historian, Fabius Pictor, wrote an account of Rome from its origins in Greek, partly because his own language had not become flexible and partly as propaganda to impress the Greek world with the growing importance of the Roman people. His example was followed by Cincius Alimentus, who had been captured by Hannibal, by the son of Scipio Africanus, by Albinus the consul of 151, and by Acilius. Some of these works were later translated into Latin. Poetry might be left to freedmen, but those who had contributed to the making of Roman history naturally wished to leave some record of Rome's struggles.

The father of Latin prose was Cato the Censor. He wrote a history in Latin, thereby setting an example which was followed by the annalists of the Gracchan era. This account of Rome's development from early times down to Cato's own time was called the *Origines* (see p. 410). Cato wrote other books, including an encyclopaedia which contained treatises on rhetoric, medicine and agriculture, and probably also on military affairs and law. His only surviving work is the *De agri cultura*, a practical manual of household economy and estate management; its style, modernized by later copyists, was prosaic, terse and simple. Of his speeches about 150 were known to Cicero; the style is blunt, vigorous and vivid, and Cato followed the advice which he gave to his son: '*rem tene, verba sequentur*'. We hear of orators who preceded him: for instance, the stirring speech in which Appius Claudius denounced treating with Pyrrhus remained a Roman classic. Appius' other literary activities included the authorship of *Sayings* inspired by Pythagorean doctrine, and a reform of Roman writing. Reference is made to the funeral speeches delivered by Fabius Cunctator for his son and by Q. Caecilius Metellus for his father. Ennius hailed Cethegus, the consul of 204, as 'the very heart of persuasion' (*suadae medulla*), while the elder Scipio, Sempronius Gracchus and Aemilius Paullus had good reputations as orators. Sextus Aelius Paetus, consul of 198, composed a legal handbook named *Tripertita*, which contained the text of the Twelve Tables, their interpretation, and forms of lawsuits. The work was regarded as the 'cradle of the law' (*cunabula iuris*).

That early Roman prose was as formless as the English prose of Chaucer is shown by early inscriptions, the rambling Duilian inscription or a passage from Ennius' *Euhemerus* quoted by Lactantius. But the necessity of public debate in the Senate-house, Forum and law courts forced men to argue lucidly and to dignify their expressions in accord with the gravity of their themes. Cato might care little for the sound or rhythm of his words, but his earnestness to drive home his points must have shaped his words more keenly than a mere academic study of Greek rhetoric would have done. It was Roman public life, more than the inspiration of Greek models, that moulded the early prose into a language which under Cicero's genius became 'the prose of the human race'.

4. ART[8]

The enthusiasm for Greek art in the nineteenth century obscured the existence of Roman art, which was regarded as a pale and debased reflection of its Hellenic prototype. Even after Wickhoff's discovery that Roman art had a separate existence, it was usually identified with the art of the Empire. But this is no longer possible. The existence of the primitive Italic stock, on which Etruscan and Greek shoots were grafted, has been recognized, though it is not always easy to see it distinctly through the luxuriant foreign growth. The Romans were not an artistic people in the same sense that the Athenians had been; their individualistic instincts might offend Greek aesthetic canons, but their realism was no less an expression of national character than was Greek idealism. The products of the Bronze Age and the Villanovans may not have reached a high standard of artistic perfection, but at least they contained the germs of a native art. This was fertilized by the Etruscans whose art had developed rapidly as a result of wider foreign contacts. But the evolution of Etruscan art was carried through on Italian soil and it is impossible to determine the share taken in this process by peoples of early Italic stock. Even if Etruscan art is set at its lowest level as deriving its whole vitality from Greece (and many would demur from so harsh a criticism), yet it cannot be denied that by fidelity to Ionic models it stimulated artistic production in many parts of Italy; and others would concede that the Italic background gave it something of value.[9] It was through the Etruscans that Rome first came into contact with Greek art, but early in the fifth century she saw something of it first-hand. During the fifth and most of the fourth century Etruscan art was depressed, but it revived towards the end of the fourth. Rome's widening influence then brought her first into Campania, where a flourishing Osco-Samnite variety of Italic art had succeeded the earlier culture of Etruscans and Greeks, and secondly into Magna Graecia and Sicily. But though 'captive Greece overcame her savage conqueror and introduced the arts into rustic Latium' she did not entirely overwhelm native characteristics.

Of the individual arts reference has been made elsewhere to architecture: to the development of temple and city architecture under the Etruscans at Rome, where the high Italic *podium* and round hut-like temples were not entirely superseded; to the Greek style used for the temple of Ceres, Liber and Libera; and to the victory of the Hellenistic over the Tuscan style in the second century when Greek basilicas and temples began to adorn the city. The appearance of early Roman statues, the *ars statuaria vetustissima* mentioned by Pliny, may be judged from the Etruscan Apollo of Veii, which despite its Ionian inspiration and technique retains an Italic accentuation of force and violent effort. Besides gods whom the Etruscans anthropomorphized in statuary, men and women were modelled. The great merit of Roman portraiture under the Empire was not achieved in a day; indeed the origin of the portrait bust and the portrait statue goes back to the 'canopic' urns from Chiusi which were roughly shaped into human busts. The Etruscan sarcophagi of the early period and of the third and second centuries and the peculiar ash-chests of Volterra afford numerous examples of vivid portraiture. There are many Italic portrait heads of terracotta, limestone and bronze, which are 'examples of naturalism untouched as yet by Greek idealism or by the Roman insistence upon detail' (E. Strong, *CAH* IX, 812). The famous bronze head of Brutus, the first consul, illustrates the Roman love of realism. The production of such works was stimulated by the custom, practised by the noble houses of preserving wax *imagines* of their ancestors in the halls of their houses. These portrait galleries must have greatly influenced the development of Roman portraiture, which was marked by a pitiless realism, far remote from the idealistic strivings of the Greeks to portray a type. The carvings, no less than the figures, on Etruscan sarcophagi and ash-chests influenced Roman work in relief which attempted to grapple with the third dimension; where the Greeks had used a background as a mere screen, the Etrusco-Italic reliefs used it to emphasize the corporeity of the figures. The fondness for human everyday subjects and the beginnings of the fresco-like 'continuous' style go back to the pre-Roman period of Italic art. The achievement of native Roman art, freed from specifically Etruscan and Greek influences, is seen in an alabaster urn of the third or second century, now in the British Museum, depicting in relief an equestrian procession, perhaps the parade of Roman Knights which commemorated the battle of Lake Regillus.

How far the excellence of Etruscan metal work was imitated at Rome is uncertain, but we know that the Ficorini *cista* was made there, and its engravings, though Greek in subject and manner, contain Latin details. Many of the Praenestine mirrors and *cistae* depict scenes from Greek mythology, but others show homelier or comic episodes of Latin life: a girl and youth playing draughts or the kitchen scene of the *cista* Tyszkiewicz. Among the minor arts a series of engraved gems shows distinct Italic workmanship, differing from the Etruscan and Graeco-Roman gems.[10] The subjects are often religious and reproduce votive pictures set up in shrines or temples as thank-offerings.

The numerous references to painting in Plautus show that in his day this art was popular in Rome. Pliny records seeing paintings in the Latin temple at Ardea which he declared to be older than Rome itself, while only its friable plaster prevented the emperor Claudius from removing a painting from a temple at Lanuvium. The appearance of these early paintings may be guessed from surviving Etruscan paintings which it is often difficult to distinguish from the different Italic groups. Our earliest Roman example is the military fresco from the Esquiline (? third century); in draughtsmanship and arrangement it displays Hellenic influence, but its details are Italic.[11] It is akin to the work of the Osco-Samnite school of Campania, which is illustrated by the splendid Samnite Knight from Capua (*c.* 300), the gaily-caparisoned cavaliers with plumed helmets and cloaks returning home from war from Paestum, or the two gladiators, fighting to the last gasp, from Capua. Painting became increasingly popular when in the third century generals set up in temples mural pictures of themselves as triumphator or of their military exploits. Portable pictures of victories were carried in triumphal processions and were also used as political propaganda by electioneering candidates. The poet Pacuvius was famed as a painter, while Demetrius of Alexandria, who came to Rome in the second century, started a vogue in maps and geographical pictures, which may have encouraged the growth of a school of landscape painters; the demand for such work, however, probably did not become extensive until the first century. Further, the claims of religion were answered by votive pictures from the humble, as well as by the self-advertising magnificence of the nobility. Naevius caustically refers to a certain Theodotus who painted with an ox's tail figures of dancing Lares on altars of the Compitalia; recent excavations at Delos have revealed examples of such rough but vigorous little sketches of the Lares. The poster advertisement for gladiatorial shows, which Horace's slaves admired, may have been used before the end of our period (Horace, *Sat.*, ii, 7, 96). But it is difficult to determine whether all these efforts represent the influence of a distinctive Italic national school of painting or, as is perhaps more likely, merely reflect contemporary Hellenistic art.

Roman art owed much to Greece, but it was not purely imitative. It was eclectic and adapted to its own genius what others might offer. Greek architects were primarily concerned with religious buildings, but the Romans devoted as much attention to secular. In two branches the Roman spirit was pre-eminent: in portraiture and later in historical monuments. Thus it is possible to trace, though dimly, the strivings of a practical, but not altogether unimaginative people to assimilate the glories of Greek art: that the waves of Hellenism did not entirely overwhelm the impulses of the native spirit testifies to a rugged independence that developed realistic tendencies which an idealistic Greek might have despised.

XVIII

ROMAN RELIGION[1]

1. THE RELIGION OF THE FAMILY

During the centuries that separated the early beginnings of the peoples of Italy from the days of their supremacy in the Mediterranean their religious experience was naturally varied. From an animistic stage in which many traces of magic and taboo survived they passed to anthropomorphism and polytheism, and the state relieved the individual of many of his responsibilities to the unseen powers of the universe. There was no prolonged period of national suffering, such as the Jewish Captivity, to break down the barriers of formalism which state ritual erected around real religious feeling, but gradually foreign ideas and rites overlaid the old Roman religion and men sought refuge from scepticism or an empty formalism in the more emotional and mystic beliefs of Greece and the Orient or in the nobler teaching of the later Greek philosophers.

Roman religion was so free from the baser forms of magic and taboo that it is probable that these were deliberately excluded by the state. Yet some traces of earlier beliefs survived in historical times. Totemism, which belongs to a tribal form of society in which family life is unknown, was naturally absent from a people whose life centred around the family. Like the Jews, the Roman authorities tried to eradicate magic as a social factor, but they could not prevent individuals from practising it except under those forms which were harmful to the community. For instance, a spell which aimed at transferring the fertility of the lands of a neighbour to a man's own fields was expressly forbidden in the Twelve Tables, which also banned anyone who 'chanted an evil charm' ('*Qui fruges excantassit, qui malum carmen incantasset*', Pliny, *N.H.*, xxviii, 17). But individuals still continued to inscribe spells (*carmina*) and curses (*dirae*) on tablets (*tabellae defixionum*) for the undoing of their enemies, and Cato could advocate a process of sympathetic magic accompanied by a charm to cure a dislocated limb. Another form of harmless private magic was the survival of the use of amulets, particularly the *bulla* worn by children to avert such danger as the evil eye, and the little swinging figures (*oscilla*) which were hung up at certain festivals to protect the crops. It is improbable that these figures were substitutes for an original human sacrifice, a rite from which the Romans were mainly free. Magical practices also managed to survive here and there in public ceremonies, as, for instance, two forms of sympathetic magic designed originally to procure rain: at the *aquaelicium* a stone (*lapis manalis*) was carried in procession to form the centre of a 'rain-making' rite, and on the Ides of May straw puppets were thrown into the Tiber by the Vestal Virgins from the Pons Sublicius. A magical method of increasing fertility survived in the ceremonial whipping during the Lupercalia, well known from Shakespearean allusion; and 'telepathic' magic is seen in the reputed power of the Vestal Virgins to stop a runaway slave from leaving Rome by a spell. A belief also in taboo, that a mysterious power in certain objects made them dangerous or unclean, survived at Rome in some aspects, together with the corresponding need for purification or disinfection. Though few traces are found of a blood taboo, many things were considered unclean or holy: new-born children, corpses, strangers, iron, certain places such as shrines or spots struck by lightning, and certain days, particularly thirty-six in the year (*dies religiosi*). The unlucky priest of Jupiter (Flamen Dialis) was subjected to numerous taboos: amongst others he might not touch a goat, horse, dog, raw meat, a corpse, beans, ivy, wheat, or leavened bread: his nails and hair must not be cut with an iron knife, and he must have no knot on his person. But such primitive beliefs in taboo or magic were scarce in historical Rome.

Religion has been defined as 'the effective desire to be in right relations with the Power manifesting itself in the universe'. This Power seemed to the early Romans to manifest itself in the form of impersonal 'spirits' (*numina*), which had local habitations, as springs, rivers, groves or trees.[2] Some dwelt in stones which, however, had probably been worshipped as sacred objects in days before an indwelling spirit was conceived: for instance, boundary stones, the *lapis silex* in the shrine of Jupiter Feretrius, and the *lapis manalis* already mentioned. The *numina* gradually assumed functional as well as local aspects, and then received names in an adjectival form to denote their functions. Later the spirit approached more nearly to a definite personality and the priests drew up 'forms of invocation' (*indigitamenta*) assigning minor spirits to all the sub-divided activities of human life from Cunina, the spirit of the cradle, to Libitina, that of burial.

Early religious practice was centred in the family, the economic unit of an agricultural people, and was associated with the house and fields, especially the boundaries. Every important part of the house had its own spirit. The spirit of fire, Vesta, dwelt in the hearth; each day during the chief meal part of a sacred salt cake was thrown into the fire from a small sacrificial dish. The store-cupboard (*penus*) had its guardian spirits, the Penates. The door was the seat of Janus, who when conceived in the image of man faced both ways. The door was particularly important, since evil spirits might enter the house through it: hence a dead man was carried out of the house by night feet first, so that he might not find his way back. The Genius of the head of the family was also worshipped: this conception was probably that of the procreative power of the family on which it depended for its continuance. The religion of the family was an attempt to maintain peace with these spirits; if the powers were duly propitiated there was nothing to fear from the divine members of the *familia*. Apart from 'family prayers' at the beginning of the day and the offering to Vesta, ritual centred around birth, marriage and death. At the birth of a child three men struck the threshold with an axe, pestle and broom, agricultural implements, to keep out the wilder spirits of whom the chief was later named Silvanus. Many ceremonies accompanied marriage; for instance, a bride from another family might offend the household spirits and be dangerous as a stranger; so at the critical moment of entry she smeared the door posts with wolf's fat and oil and was carried over the threshold. It was necessary to perform certain rites exactly (*iusta facere*) to ensure that the dead did not 'walk'. Although perhaps even in Palaeolithic times man was thought to survive death, and the Neolithic folk had fairly definite ideas of a future state, the dead had little or no individuality. The great throng of the dead were identified with the Di Manes, the Kindly Gods, who were perhaps originally chthonic deities. At the festival of the Lemuria in May the head of the household could get rid of ghosts by clashing brass vessels and by spitting out black beans from his mouth, saying nine times, 'With these I redeem me and mine'; when the ghosts behind had gathered up the beans, he expelled them with the ninefold formula '*Manes exite paterni*'. In the later Parentalia the element of fear was diminished and graves were decorated by the living members of the family.

The religion of the family, though centred in the house, naturally extended to the fields. Boundary stones not only had to be set up with due ceremony, but were the object of an annual festival, the Terminalia, in which they were garlanded by the farmers whose lands adjoined. It was also necessary to beat the bounds in order to purify, protect and fertilize the fields. This was done at the Ambarvalia in May in a solemn procession which culminated in prayer and the sacrifice of a pig, sheep and bull (*suovetaurilia*). The spirits of the fields, Lares, were placated at the Compitalia at places where paths bounding farms met. This joyful ceremony was shared by the slaves, who had no part in the worship of the house; later they introduced the worship of the Lares into the house where it was adopted by the whole household.[3] Other festivals were celebrated by the *pagus* as a whole at seed-time and harvest.

It was long before these vague, aniconic spirits were conceived in human form or as personal beings with human characteristics. This development was only finally achieved under foreign influence and through the establishment of state-cults of the various deities. But from the first some emerged above the rest. Apart from Janus and Vesta, Jupiter, the sky-god of the Indo-Europeans, transcended the limits of animism, as did Mars who was originally an agricultural deity as well as a war god and thus manifested two kinds of *numen*: indeed Mars was probably the chief deity of the primitive Romans. With them is linked Quirinus, perhaps the war god of the Quirinal settlement or the god who presided over the assembled citizens; later legend equated him with Romulus.[4]

2. THE RELIGION OF THE STATE

The religion of the family, though the expression of a group rather than of individuals, might have led to an advancement of man's knowledge of the Divine, had not a development taken place which tended to deaden its reality. That feeling of awe and anxiety towards the unknown which the Romans called *religio* had led men to evolve certain rites by which they maintained the *pax deorum*, a peace or covenant with their divine neighbours. As the city grew, the state stepped in and undertook this responsibility on behalf of the community. Traditionally in the reign of Numa a calendar was drawn up to fix a routine of festivals and to divide the days of the year into those on which it was religiously permissible to transact civil business and those on which it was not (*dies fasti et nefasti*). It reflects the transition of a rural people to the political and military life of the city-state; but agricultural life is still its basis. But as the town dweller would gradually lose interest in the details of country festivals and as the calendar gradually got out of gear with the agricultural year, this fixed form of ritual, though saving the individual from anxiety, soon lost all religious meaning for the people of the city. Many survivals of magic, grossness and barbarism were doubtless excluded from the new state cult, which required permanent officials to perform its ceremonies and to take charge of the *ius divinum*. In the regal period the king was the state priest, the paterfamilias of the community; at the fall of the monarchy his ceremonial duties devolved chiefly upon the Pontifex Maximus and partly upon the Rex Sacrorum, who retained his title. Under the priest-king were the priesthoods. Of these the chief were the two great colleges of augurs and pontiffs. Whatever their origin, the pontiffs of the Republic took over the administration of the state cults and the legal aspect of religion, and their leader, the Pontifex Maximus, was installed in the king's palace, the Regia. In addition there were individual priests, Flamines, attached to particular deities; the chief was the Flamen Dialis, the priest of Jupiter. And there were group-priests: the Fetiales, Luperci, Salii and the Vestal Virgins.

Some attempt was made to maintain the reality of the earlier practices which the state took over. For instance, the Compitalia or festival of the Lares was celebrated at cross-roads instead of where properties had adjoined. Other festivals were held outside the sacred boundary of the city, the *pomerium*, as the Terminalia at the sixth milestone of the Via Laurentina, and the beating of the bounds, Ambarvalia, at the fifth milestone on the Via Campana; this latter rite gave rise to a ceremony of Amburbium, by which the boundaries of the city were purified. But many of the old festivals lost all meaning for the town dwellers and became mere ritual for the priests. The domestic deities, however, were more easily adapted. Janus, the spirit of the house door, was worshipped at the doorway of the state at a gateway in the Forum, which was only closed in peacetime; he soon became the god of beginnings, and later gave his name to the first month of the year. Vesta became the hearth of the state on which the sacred fire must be kept alight; her round temple in the Forum reproduced the shape of the primitive huts of Latium, and near by dwelt her priestesses, the Vestal Virgins. Her worship illustrates the reality and continuity of Roman religious feeling; no statue was ever placed in her temple.

The object of Roman ritual was, as has been said, to maintain the *pax deorum*. The methods adopted were sacrifice, prayer, expiation, purifi-

cation and vows. Sacrifice or the making of anything *sacrum*, the property
of the deity, was designed partly to honour the deity and partly to expiate
sin by means of offering and prayer; there appears little trace of
sacramental sacrifice, whereby the worshipper enters into communion
with the deity. The offering consisted of food, such as the salt meal given
to Vesta. Blood offerings in early times appear confined to the ceremonies
of lustration and *piaculum*, but in the state cult were used in *sacrificium*. The
commonest victim was the pig, to which on important occasions the
sheep and ox were added. It was essential that both the priest, who in the
days before the state cult was the paterfamilias of the household, and the
victim, should be acceptable. Minute details were laid down regarding
the condition and behaviour of the victim; while it was being sacrificed
pipers played lest any unlucky sound or word should mar the worship.
The priests stood with veiled heads. After the slaughter, the victim's
internal organs were examined in case of any defect. The idea behind the
sacrifice is shown by the common formula which occurs in the
accompanying prayer: macte esto. The deity's strength is to be increased
(? cf. the root of *magnus, magis*), so that his glory and goodwill towards
the worshippers may also be increased. This idea probably marks a stage
between the earlier conception that the gods actually partook of the
offering and the later view that the offering was merely an honorary gift.
The prayers, as seen in the *carmina* of the Arval Brothers or those preserved
by Cato, mark a transition between magic and religion; in their
repetitions and in the emphasis on the exact wording, they retain the
outward characteristics of spells which bind the deity. But the substance
of the prayer is petition rather than compulsion or bargaining. The god
may withhold the request, though, in fact, if he is invoked in the correct
formulae, it would be thought unreasonable and contrary to his nature
for him to do so. As an example the prayer of a Roman farmer in clearing a
wood may be quoted: 'Be thou god or goddess to whom the wood is
sacred, as it is right to make expiation by the offering of a pig because of
the clearing of this sacred wood, for this cause that all may be rightly
done . . . I make pious prayer that thou wouldest be kind and gracious to
me, my home, my household and my children; for which cause be thou
enriched (*macte esto*) with the sacrifice of this pig for expiation' (Cato, *de
agr. cult.*, 139). This prayer illustrates the expiatory type of sacrifice or
piaculum which is atonement for an offence committed, and an act of
compensation to the god, rather than a free-will offering like the ordinary
sacrificium. Generally a blood offering was made. If any slip or omission
occurred in the ritual of a sacrifice, it was necessary to renew the

ceremony and to make a *piaculum*. Characteristically the practical Roman often insured against any slip by a prior piacular sacrifice which was to atone in anticipation. Thus when the Arval Brethren, who suffered from a taboo on iron, had to take an iron implement into their sacred grove, they offered a *piaculum* beforehand.

Purification (*lustratio*) was closely akin to, or indeed a form of, piacular sacrifice. The object was to keep away hostile spirits by means of processional rites, which still survive in the ritual of the Roman church, though changed in form and meaning. These processions, which culminated in acts of sacrifice and prayer, marched round the boundaries of the farm and village. For instance, the Lupercalia was in origin a lustration of the Palatine settlement. When the city was established it too must have its sacred boundary (*pomerium*) within which only the gods of the city might dwell. Little is known of the lustration of the boundaries of Rome in the festival of Amburbium, but full details are recorded in the inscriptions of Iguvium concerning the lustration of the citadel of this Umbrian town.[5] Such a process of purification was extended from the boundary line of farm or city to the human beings within, to the whole people or the army together with its weapons. Even the trumpets were purified at the Tubilustrium in March. It is not unlikely that triumphal arches and the custom of forcing a surrendered army under a ritual yoke of spears derive from the primitive desire to get rid of all dangerous contagion. But like many other ceremonies, the act of purification became formalized: the prayers were murmured and unheard by the people, and the lustration of the army developed into a political census. Finally, the gods were approached by means of vows (*vota*). The legalistic language in which private vows are often couched cannot obscure the fact that they are prayers accompanied with the promise of an offering if they are heard: they are not legal transactions which bind both parties. Public vows, which were taken in the name of the state, were a later development and were, to some extent, a covenant in the name of the state. Other vows, such as to found temples or give games, and even the vow of the *ver sacrum* were acts of self-renunciation rather than contractual covenants.

Much of the state ritual was taken over from, and was an elaboration of, the rites of the orderly worship of the household. But the general effect of the organization of religion by the state was to rob it of its real meaning and smother the spiritual possibilities inherent in an advanced animistic belief. The simple ritual of the household and farm, which though without much direct influence on conduct yet engendered a sense of duty within the family and a sense of spiritual union between neighbours, survived long in country districts. But the individual citizen as such was relieved of all need to worry about the gods: the state priesthoods deadened his religious and moral instinct. The formalism of Jewish worship was quickened by a burning monotheism and by the moral earnestness of the prophets. The early Romans had priests but no prophets. The state religion may have helped to preserve family life by maintaining a sense of law and order, but it could not satisfy the cravings of the individual who, in times of stress, sought relief in foreign religious ideas.

3. FOREIGN CULTS

The development of spirits (*numina*) into gods (*dei*) was gradual. Its beginnings cannot be traced, but they go back in part to the Indo-European period before the Italian and Greek races separated. Some deities, as Jupiter, Mars and Juno, are found in the worship of many Italian towns, others are more local. When the Romans came into contact with the cults of neighbouring towns, they tended to assimilate any new deities which might meet needs unanswered by their native deities.[6] For instance, Minerva, an Italian goddess of handicrafts, was imported to meet needs created by the growth of trade and industry in the regal period; Diana of Aricia was installed on the Aventine for political motives (p. 55); Fortuna, originally perhaps an agricultural deity, from Praeneste or Antium, and Venus, originally the protectress of gardens, perhaps from Ardea. But not all the new deities were Italian in origin. Contact with Etruria and the Greeks brought many new gods into Latium and ultimately to Rome.

The influence of the Etruscans on Roman religion was profound, yet transitory. They hastened the change of spirits into gods fashioned in the image of man, but they did not impose their own gloomy beliefs on the Roman people. Hitherto spirits had been worshipped at holy places, where an altar of turf might be erected – but not in temples made with hands. But from Etruria the Romans derived the idea of housing a deity in a temple and of providing him with a cult statue. When this was done the transition to anthropomorphism was complete. The most famous of Rome's temples was that begun on the Capitol by Tarquinius and dedicated in the first year of the Republic to the Etruscan Triad, Tinia, Uni and Minerva. Of these deities, however, two were Italian, Juno and Minerva, while Tinia was identified with Jupiter. The temple was built by Etruscan workmen in Etruscan style, and it contained a terracotta cult statue made by an Etruscan artist, but its Etruscan connections were soon forgotten and it became the abode of Jupiter Optimus Maximus, the god who centralized the worship of the Roman people and became the presiding genius of the whole state. But the Romans were slow to apply rigorously the ideas they adopted. Mars and Hercules had long to be content with altars in the Campus Martius and Forum Boarium; and cult statues of native gods were few before the Hannibalic War. 'For more than 170 years', wrote Varro, 'the Romans worshipped their gods without images. Those who first made images of the gods, both removed fear from their states and added error.' But while anthropomorphism led to scepticism, the adoption of Etruscan methods of divination led to superstition. This art was practised by the Romans before contact with Etruria: auspices were taken from the flight of birds and sometimes from the behaviour of lightning. But under Etruscan influence the Roman state elaborated augury, instituted a college of augurs, and used Etruscan experts in divination from the entrails of animals. The darker side of Etruscan religion, its morbid preoccupation with death and its elaboration of the tortures of the damned, had little effect on Roman belief, but did unfortunately influence Roman conduct. The practice of slaughtering prisoners who were led in triumphal procession, and the institution of gladiatorial shows in 264 BC, derived from a people who may well have introduced human sacrifice into Italy.

Contact with Greek religious ideas, which came to Rome through Etruria and Latin towns and later by direct intercourse with the Greek cities of southern Italy, had a far greater influence on Roman religion. If the Asiatic origin of the Etruscans be granted, they must long have been conversant with Greek ideas, with which, at any rate, they were familiar before their contact with Rome. From Latin cities also, which had been brought by trade into contact with Greek colonies, the Romans received anthropomorphic deities. Perhaps from Tibur came Hercules, whose worship as a patron of commerce was conducted in Greek fashion with unveiled head at the Ara Maxima in the Forum Boarium, where his wide reputation might secure safety for all traders. Traditionally in 499, the cult of Castor and Pollux was introduced from Tusculum and a temple was erected (cf. p. 369) in the Forum; their association also was commercial. During the regal period Apollo was established in a precinct outside the Porta Capena, probably as a god of medicine to deal with a plague; in 431 a temple was built for him. Apollo's connection with the oracle of the Sibyl at Cumae directed Rome's attention thither. The story of how Tarquin bought the Sibylline books is well known; even if a permanent collection of oracles did not exist in Rome at so early a date, it is probable that the Romans sent to consult the oracle in times of stress, such as famine. It was in obedience to the Sibyl's directions that a temple was built on the Aventine to Ceres, Liber and Libera: the Romans thus adopted the cult of the Greek corn deities, Demeter, Dionysus and Kore, beside seeking corn from Cumae. By 367 there was probably a permanent collection of Sibylline oracles at Rome, under the care of *decemviri sacris faciundis*, who consulted them in times of difficulty to discover how to maintain the *pax deorum*. Their importance is that they led to the reception of new Greek deities, such as Mercury, Neptune and Aesculapius in their Latin names, and of the *Graecus ritus*. These new gods, however, had less religious significance than the new ceremonies of *lectisternia* and *supplicationes*. In 399, when a pestilence raged during the siege of Veii, the Sibylline books ordered that for eight days images of three pairs of gods should be exhibited on couches before tables spread with food and drink. Here was novelty indeed. Appeal was made not to the old *numina* but to Greek gods; the whole population was to share in the ceremony; and the eight days were kept as holidays. Doubtless the ceremony was partly an attempt to divert the attention of the people from their hardships, but it was also an appeal to the emotional expression of religious feeling. Five *lectisternia* were decreed in the fourth century. Connected with them was the *supplicatio* in which the whole people went garlanded in procession around the temples of the city and there prostrated themselves in Greek fashion, the women 'sweeping the altars with their streaming hair'. The dignified attitude of the early Roman was forgotten and the chilling effect of the formal state religion led to these outbursts of popular emotion in foreign rites in which the individual could again take his part. The Roman state was forced to respond to the new needs, but in doing so it prepared the way for the even wilder worships of the east.

Apart from such occasional outbursts the general effect of the predominance of an official priesthood was to bring the old religious forms into contempt, so that we find Claudius Pulcher daring to drown the sacred chickens (p. 175). But the disasters of the Hannibalic War reawoke religious fears and anxiety. The number of prodigies that was noticed and recorded in the books of the pontiffs testifies to the renewal of superstitious dread. The state tried to comfort and distract the people by giving public games in accordance with Sibylline instructions; in 217 Ludi Magni and in 212 Ludi Apollinares were celebrated. After Trasimene and Flaminius' disregard of the *pax deorum* sterner remedies were taken; a *ver sacrum* was vowed and a *lectisternium* was held on a large scale (see p. 19). Twelve pairs of gods, Greek and Roman alike, were displayed and the old distinction between native and foreign deities was disregarded: the advice of the Sibylline books and the decemvirs was esteemed higher than the old *ius divinum* of the pontiffs. Cannae evoked even greater religious panic, which was quietened by burying alive two Greeks and two Gauls in the Forum Boarium *minime Romano sacro*, and by despatching an embassy to seek advice at Delphi. In 213 there was a fresh outbreak of religious emotionalism among the women, and the praetor was instructed to rid Rome of all private priests and prophets, who were undermining the state religion by introducing foreign rites. When Hasdrubal's invasion threatened, the pontiffs took special precautions to secure the *pax deorum*: twenty-seven maidens chanted a *carmen* composed by the poet Livius Andronicus and an elaborate ritual procession was staged. After Hasdrubal's defeat at Metaurus an extraordinary wave of thankfulness to heaven swept over the people. During the last stage of the war it was found in the Sibylline books that Hannibal would leave Italy if the 'Great Mother' of Phrygia was brought to Rome. So in 204 the cult stone was shipped from Pessinus to Ostia, where it was received by Scipio Nasica and Roman matrons who escorted it to the temple of Victory on the Palatine. There it remained until a temple was built for the Magna Mater in 191. Thus the first Oriental deity was officially introduced into Rome in a desperate attempt at novelty when the ordinary Greek deities had become familiar. It is unlikely that the magistrates realized at first the ecstatic and orgiastic nature of the cult; later Roman citizens were forbidden to take part.

Twenty years later the introduction of the worship of Bacchus caused a serious scandal. Dionysus or Bacchus had long been recognized at Rome as Liber, but it was not till 186 that the orgiastic features of the Dionysiac ritual reached Rome from southern Italy, mediated through Etruria and Campania. Revelry may have occurred at native Italian rural festivals, but the celebration of the Bacchanalia introduced drunkenness, crime and immorality of all kinds. The cult spread like wildfire until the Senate authorized the consuls to stamp it out throughout Italy. It was treated as an offence against the state, not against religion; as a conspiracy or rebellion against which police measures must be taken. Morality was the concern of the state rather than of Roman religion from which it was divorced. With characteristic shrewdness the Senate legalized the cult when its excesses had been suppressed: if anyone desired to continue this worship, he must obtain permission from the praetor who would seek the

Senate's sanction that no more than five persons might celebrate the cult together. Death was the penalty for infraction. Worship which did not endanger public morality was a matter for individual wishes, not for the state : an important precedent was established by a state which later had to deal with Christianity.[7]

The Romans went after foreign gods and imported *externa sacra* because they desired something better than the old religious forms which had lost their meaning. But the 'enthusiastic' cults which answered the need of the individual merely stirred up emotional frenzy and moral degradation. The state tried to check the evil which it had at first encouraged, but the way was open for the numerous oriental cults that came to Rome in the later Republic and the Empire. In 181 an attempt was made to introduce other religious ideas which offered the individual the hope of attaining happiness in the next world by initiation and mystic purification in this. Orphism and Pythagorean beliefs spread northwards from Magna Graecia and some forged writings were 'discovered' in the tomb of Numa. The books were burnt as subversive of the state religion, but Orphic ideas were doubtless reaching Rome, and Ennius' influence helped their circulation; they had, however, greater effect in the later Republic.[8]

The fusion of Greek and Roman religion, or rather, the overlaying of the old Roman beliefs with Greek mythology, was completed by the increasing influence of Roman literature. Under the spell of Greek models Roman writers, who found their early history barren of sagas of gods and heroes, took over a large part of the mythology of Greece and thus accelerated the process by which the old Latin *numina* were identified with the gods of Greece. The anthropomorphic tendency was complete : Roman deities, identified with their Greek counterparts in the Olympian hierarchy, were now paired off as husbands and wives, and the mythological foibles of the gods were even shown on the Roman stage : the amours of Jupiter and the misdoings of Mercury were parodied before a Roman audience in the *Amphitruo* of Plautus. At Rome Ennius popularized the teaching of Euhemerus on the human origin of the gods, which held that they were merely great men deified. So complete was the fusion of the Graeco-Roman mixture that it is only comparatively recently that the native worship of early Rome has been cleared of its foreign accretions and its real nature understood. One scholar who has taken a large part of the work of reconstruction points out that at the end of the Hannibalic War the divine inhabitants of the city were as much a *colluvies nationum* as the human population itself. 'Under such

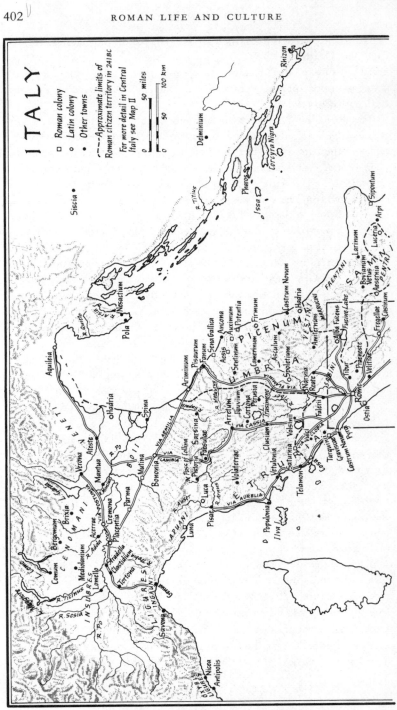

MAP V

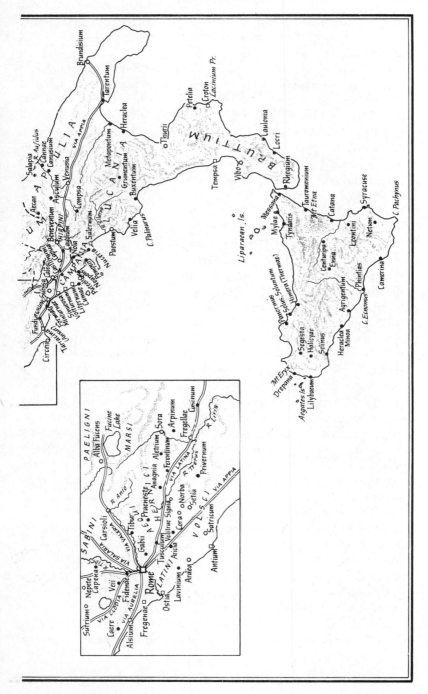

circumstances neither the old City-state nor its religion could any longer continue to exist . . . . In the next two centuries Rome gained the world and lost her own soul.'⁹

But the picture is not entirely black. The old Roman religion might develop into formal sacerdotalism upheld by an urban aristocracy, but its vitality was not extinguished among the common people of the countryside. Graeco-Roman mythology might give rise to widespread scepticism, but the educated could seek salvation in Greek philosophy, which now penetrated into Rome. In 173 two Epicurean philosophers were expelled from Rome and in 161 philosophers and rhetoricians in general suffered the same fate. The practical Roman did not take naturally to philosophy, mistrusting its abstract teaching, especially of those who held the object of life to be pleasure, albeit those pleasures of reflection chosen by reason rather than physical pleasures. In 159 (or 168) the Stoic Crates, delayed at Rome by an accident, started to lecture. It was impossible to stem the tide from Greece. In 155 the heads of the three great philosophic schools, Critolaus the Peripatetic, Diogenes the Stoic and Carneades the Academic came to Rome on a political embassy. While waiting they gave lectures and Carneades startled his respectable audience by accepting principles one day which he refuted the next and by propounding the theory that justice was a convention. This new teaching aroused the interest of the 'intellectuals' of the Scipionic circle, which was joined by the Stoic Panaetius about 144 BC. The manner in which the teaching of the Porch was adapted to Roman life is a subject which falls beyond the scope of this volume.¹⁰ Suffice it to add that Stoicism taught the Romans a new doctrine of the relation of man to God; and even more influential than its theological and moral theories was the fact that it offered men a new way of life. Its appeal lay largely in the possibility of the practical application of its teaching to everyday life. The comprehensiveness of the Stoic ideal exercised a profound and inspiring influence in the Roman world at a time of religious bankruptcy, and it reinforced men's moral reserves, until another religion from the Orient, very different from the earliest eastern cults that reached Rome, brought a still broader view of the universal brotherhood of man and offered a different way of life from that laid down by the Stoic sage. If the promise of the early religious experience of the Roman people was not fulfilled, at any rate the early Christian Church had to reckon with many of the phases of its development, besides receiving into its own vocabulary such words as 'religion', 'piety', 'saint' and 'sacrament'. Roman Stoicism made its contribution to the thought of Christianity; the organization of the old state religion impressed itself on that of the new priesthood; and even the petty *numina* of the countryside survived long enough to influence the Roman Catholic conception of the division of function among the saints and to provoke the derision of the Church Fathers.

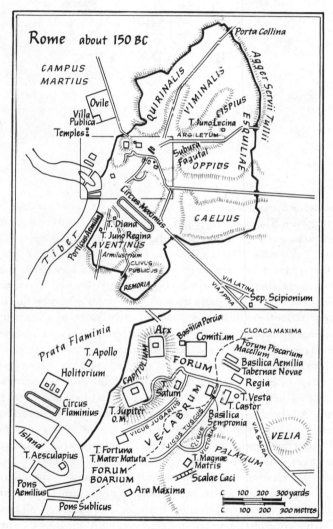

MAP VI

XIX

SOURCES AND
AUTHORITIES

1. ARCHAEOLOGY AND INSCRIPTIONS

Archaeological material provides the main basis of our knowledge of the prehistory and ethnology of Italy. The nature of Etruscan civilization and the appearance of early Rome and other Italian towns has been revealed largely by the spade. The result often confirms in a striking manner the later literary tradition which can thus be tested and controlled at many points, though elsewhere much of the early history must remain hypothetical. There has been a reaction from the hypercritical and destructive attitude displayed towards early Roman history at the beginning of this century by E. Pais, who later indeed himself somewhat modified his earlier views; and this reaction is due in part to the new light shed by archaeological research. The material provided also illustrates later phases of Rome's conquests in Italy and the Mediterranean world. As examples there may be cited the discovery of a Chalcolithic settlement and Iron Age huts at Rome, of the site of Politorium, of the thirteen altars and the probable 'tomb of Aeneas' at Lavinium, of the *castrum* at Ostia which dates the Roman colony to the mid-fourth century; excavations which reveal the early prosperity of Ardea and its decline after the Samnite Wars; the Greek, Lucanian and Roman phases exemplified in the splendid fortifications and other buildings at Paestum; the Etruscan, Greek, Samnite and Roman stages in the development of Pompeii; the early growth of colonies, as Minturnae, Cosa and Alba Fucens. Beside the laying bare of cities and buildings archaeologists have supplemented the literary tradition by the discovery of coins (p. 353 ff.) and inscriptions.

Apart from those inscriptions which illustrate the dialects, constitutions and religious history of Italian towns, the majority which survive are concerned with Roman contacts with the Hellenistic world.

Of the laws, treaties and public documents some survived long enough to be recorded by ancient historians; others have been unearthed in modern times. Examples of the former are the Twelve Tables, the *foedus Cassianum*, and Rome's early treaties with Carthage, recorded by Polybius. The latter are illustrated by the surviving Forum inscription; the treaty with Aetolia; the *Senatus consultum de Bacchanalibus* of 186 BC and that relating to Thespiae in 170; the decree of Aemilius Paullus, granting freedom to a small Spanish town; the letters of the Scipios to Colophon and Heraclea.[1]

2. CALENDARS AND FASTI

In early days the Pontifex Maximus drew up a list of days on which it was *fas* or *nefas* to transact business. This calendar gave the names and dates of those religious festivals which concerned the whole state. Examples of such calendars survive; though nearly all date from the Empire and contain the calendar as revised by Caesar, they nevertheless reproduce the skeleton of the original calendar, which was ascribed to Numa, and form a main source of our knowledge of early religious practice. In the absence of any system of eras the year to which the calendar referred would be denoted by affixing the names of the chief magistrates. The Pontifex at first probably recorded on the calendar any outstanding event of the year, but when these events became numerous he set up in the Regia a white tablet to record the names of the magistrates and the events of the year, such as wars, triumphs, temple foundations, eclipses and portents. These Tabulae Pontificum were probably first collected and published in eighty volumes of *Annales Maximi* by Mucius Scaevola, the Pontifex Maximus of 130 BC. How many other lists of magistrates existed we do not know; we hear, for example, of *libri magistratuum* on linen rolls (*libri lintei*) which an annalist, Licinius Macer, said he found in the temple of Juno Moneta. These lists clearly formed a primary source for annalists when they first desired to reconstruct and write up the history of Rome. Many chronological tables were in circulation towards the end of the Republic; for instance, Cicero's friend Atticus compiled a *liber Annalis*. In the reign of Augustus two important lists were set up on the triumphal arch of Augustus in the Forum at Rome: the Fasti Consulares which recorded the names of the consuls, censors, dictators, masters of the horse, decemvirs, and consular tribunes from the beginning of the Republic, and secondly the Fasti Triumphales which listed the magistrates and pro-magistrates who had obtained triumphs from the time of Romulus. Of these lists we have considerable fragments, now called the Capitoline Fasti because they are preserved in the Palazzo dei Conservatori Museum on the Capitol; the missing portions can be reconstructed from other sources, such as an anonymous compiler known as the Chronographer of AD 345. That similar lists existed in Rome before the time of Augustus is shown by the discovery of a calendar and list of consuls and censors on the walls of a private house of *c*. 70 BC at Antium.[2]

The crucial question is how far the Fasti of the fifth and fourth centuries are reliable; for the later period their authenticity is not doubted. The credibility of the whole of early Roman history depends to a considerable extent upon the answer. It is admitted on all sides that the early lists are not free from errors and falsifications. Mommsen's belief in their substantial reliability was succeeded by the hypercritical attitude of Pais who denied them virtually any value. A reaction followed, led by the saner counsels of De Sanctis, and even Pais somewhat modified his earlier views, but unanimity is far from being reached. A primary consideration is the possibility of the survival of early documents after the sack of Rome in 390. It has sometimes been maintained that all the old temples perished in the fire. Archaeological research has shown that this is not true in the main, though in the case of the Regia itself a verdict of 'not proven' must be returned.[3] And if the Gauls spared the temples they probably spared the archives and records which they contained. It is noteworthy that though Athens was burnt by the Persians in 480 and 479 a list of eponymous magistrates of the city going back two centuries earlier survived. But though the probability of the survival of early records be admitted, the errors of the Fasti cannot be overlooked. Both Livy (viii, 40) and Cicero (*Brut.* 62) tell how tradition was impaired by funeral eulogies and family pride which appropriated to itself the glory of exploits belonging to others. It is sometimes said that since the plebeians did not hold the consulship until 367 all plebeian names in the Fasti before that date must be forgeries due to the class and family pride of the great plebeian families; and an occasion for the falsification is found in the Lex Ogulnia (*c*. 300) which admitted plebeians to the college of pontiffs (p. 122). This raises the question: when were the Tabulae of the pontiffs begun and when were they first publicly exposed? They may not have been made public earlier than *c*. 300 when popular demand became vocal, because before then the nobility had other ways of getting any information they required. This, however, does not mean that the *annales* started then. Cicero (*de orat.*, II, 12, 52) expressly says that they went back to the beginnings of the Roman state. Beloch, however, denies this; on the evidence of the only genuine fragments of the *annales* which refer to an eclipse, also mentioned by Ennius, he assigns the beginning of genuine records to a little before 288, which is the date he conjectures for the eclipse which must have been the first in a series. But the evidence is far from satisfactory and Beloch himself can only find a few interpolations in the consular Fasti of 486–364 BC and has accepted the Fasti Triumphales as a useful source.[4] In the Fasti of the fifth century many names occur which were unknown in later times; there can be little reason to suppose that these are interpolations. Further, since patricians and plebeians often had the same names in early times and as original patrician names sometimes passed over to plebeian families, it is not necessary to assume that all the names in the Fasti which were later plebeian need be plebeian inventions. Thus it is not unreasonable to suppose that the Fasti are substantially sound from the beginning of the fifth century and that, despite some later inventions, a reliable list of names is to be found. It is also easy to exaggerate the extent to which the lists used by the later Roman annalists differed from one another.

3. THE HISTORIANS[5]

The first historian to take serious notice of Rome's history was curiously not a Roman but a Greek, Timaeus of Tauromenium in Sicily (*c.* 350–260 BC) who was impressed by Rome's defeat of Pyrrhus which showed the Greek world that a new power was arising in the west. Timaeus, who was exiled from Sicily, lived mainly in Athens, where he wrote a history of Sicily and also a history of Pyrrhus. In his historical work he discussed Rome's origins and dated its foundation to the same year as that of Carthage; he also referred to the introduction of coinage, the census classes and Roman customs such as the sacrifice of the October horse, while he personally questioned the inhabitants of Lavinium about the Roman Penates there. He was later fiercely criticized by his fellow Greek historian Polybius, who aimed at becoming Rome's chief historian, but his work remained popular. However, before the days of Polybius the Romans had decided that it was time for them to begin to write their own history.

The earliest Roman historians were Q. Fabius Pictor, L. Cincius Alimentus, Postumius Albinus and Acilius (p. 385), but they too all wrote in Greek. They were senators whose purpose was in part to expound and justify the Roman way of life in the light of past history to the Greek world with which Rome was then coming into contact. They recounted the legends of the regal period for what they were worth, but they probably did not elaborate their accounts of the first two centuries of the Republic for which reliable evidence was limited. There is little reason to suppose that men who as consuls argued the merits of laws and treaties in the Senate or who as praetors sat in judgment in the courts, lost all their critical faculties when they came to write history. They knew the value of documents and though they presumably had a natural pro-Roman and aristocratic bias, their accounts were essentially trustworthy. The most important of this group of senatorial historians was probably Fabius Pictor, who may be exonerated from the charge recently brought against him that he falsified Rome's early history by antedating the period of her power vis-à-vis the Latins (p. 472). He struck a moralistic and didactic note, emphasizing Rome's moral code in domestic and public life, and history was to him a serious business, not unworthy of the leisure time of a Roman senator. His influence was considerable, since his work was used by Polybius, not least for his account of the First Punic War and for the causes of the Second. Fabius and these other historians wrote in Greek partly in order to explain Rome to the Greek world, but partly also because the Latin language had not yet been sufficiently moulded as a vehicle for historical prose. This was the achievement of Cato.

The seven books of Cato's Origines, written from c. 168 to 149, followed Hellenistic historians who dealt with the founding of cities (ktiseis), but they were written in Latin; Cato created Latin history. His treatment of his theme in the Origines varied considerably in different parts: the first three books dealt with the origins of Rome (book i) and of the other cities of Italy; books iv and v covered the events from the First Punic War to 167 BC, but in the last two books Cato extended his scale and even inserted some of his own public speeches, thus approaching autobiography. His treatment was discursive (capitulatim); he used local legends and Hellenistic traditions, as well as Fabius' work. He did not spare his own political opponents or minimize his own exploits, but (unlike the senatorial historians) he wrote with an anti-aristocratic bias which suppressed the names of famous generals, though he ironically recorded that of Surus, the bravest Carthaginian war elephant. Although this idiosyncrasy was not followed by later writers, the Origines formed a link between the work of his predecessors and that of the group of 'older' annalists who began a fresh reconstruction of Roman history. They are represented by Cassius Hemina and Calpurnius Piso (consul in 133).

The publication of the Annales Maximi by Scaevola then established the 'definitive' form of this material which was used by the 'later' annalists from Cn. Gellius to the Sullan annalists (Claudius and Valerius) and Livy. These men wrote for a wider public which had become acquainted with the rhetorical histories of Greek writers, and many were influenced by party interests. They wrote too on a larger scale : by making greater use of the material in the Annales Maximi, by utilizing the traditions preserved (partly orally) in the great families, and by rhetorical treatment, Gellius devoted 20 books to the events of 500–300, which Piso more soberly had recorded in two (with an average of perhaps some twelve lines to a year). Q. Claudius Quadrigarius (c. 78) may partly have avoided this danger by starting his history with the year 390, but his contemporary Valerius Antias ran to at least 75 books of rhetorical and unreliable historical romance. In the Ciceronian age the demand for more reliable reference books was met by antiquarians who wrote commentaries and en-cyclopaedias on legal, constitutional and religious institutions. Their researches led to the discovery of a number of constitutional documents of considerable antiquity and value, but their object was not always purely theoretical and historical ; they often sought to find precedents to justify existing procedure. Among the annalists Licinius Macer and Aelius Tubero claimed to have undertaken documentary research. Licinius found in the temple of Juno Moneta some books written on linen, *libri lintei*, which contained lists of senior magistrates. His political views and family connections will have affected his interpretation of the past : as a *popularis* and a plebeian tribune in 73 BC, he saw the struggle of the orders in the light of contemporary events, and as a Licinius he will not have minimized the importance of the Licinian rogations.

We now come to the historians proper, who based their work on the annalists. Of these the greatest is Livy who, while Augustus was restoring the state, wrote an account of the Roman people from the landing of Aeneas to 9 BC in 142 books; of these books i–x (to 293 BC) and xxi–lxiv (218–167) survive. The success which he achieved is due partly to his greatness as a writer, partly to his co-operation with Augustus' attempt to restore the ancient Roman virtues, for above all Livy's history is a pageant of the worthies of the Roman state. His honesty and fairness stand out in contrast with the fabrications of an Antias. His value as a historian depends on the sources which he used in any given part of his narrative; where he follows Polybius or the older annalists he is trustworthy, where he uses Claudius and Valerius (as he does in a large part of the fourth and fifth decades) he is less so. He recounted the legends of early Rome, but he did not mistake them for historical fact. One grave charge against him is his neglect to consult original sources and documents; he was content to use published accounts. This may be explained, if not excused, when the practical difficulty of consulting unclassified and uncatalogued documents is realized, especially since the historian was writing a work about three times the length of Gibbon's *Decline and Fall*. For the lost books we have 'tables of contents' (*periochae*); fuller epitomes existed, of which a fragment has been found in a papyrus from Oxyrhynchus. Dionysius of Halicarnassus lived in Rome at the same time as Livy and wrote in Greek a *Roman Antiquities* in 20 books, of which 10 survive intact, the rest in extracts. The work covers the period from the foundation of Rome to 264 BC and was published in 7 BC. In his first book Dionysius used Greek writers, in later books the annalists, especially the more recent ones; his attitude towards his sources was uncritical. Another Greek historian of Rome is Cassius Dio, consul in AD 229. His *History of Rome* from early times down to his own consulship was completed in 80 books. The first 35 of these are lost, but we have an *Abridgement* made by Zonaras in the twelfth century AD. For the older period he used annalistic sources, which resemble Dionysius more than Livy; for the second century he made some use of Polybius.

Beside annalistic accounts historians wrote monographs. Philinus of Agrigentum composed in Greek an important account of the First Punic War, which was one of the main sources used by Polybius. An important monograph was the *Bellum Punicum* of Coelius Antipater (*c*. 120 BC), who used Fabius, other annalists, Silenus (a Geek historian who campaigned with Hannibal) and Polybius. Coelius' work was one of Livy's main sources in his third decade; though praised by Cicero (not least for its literary style), it appears from the existing fragments to be marred by rhetorical exaggeration. Among the writers of monographs may be classed Appian, an Alexandrine Greek (*c*. AD 160) who composed a Roman history in 24 books, divided on a geographical principle; he dealt with wars in Italy, Spain, Africa, etc., in separate books. For the Hannibalic War he relied mainly on the later annalists, for the second century on Polybius and the annalistic tradition.

Of historians of the world Polybius is the most important. This statesman of the Achaean League was deported to Rome in 167 where he gained the intimate friendship of Scipio Aemilianus with whom he witnessed the fall of Carthage and perhaps Numantia. Of his 40 books the first five survive complete, the rest in excerpts of considerable length. He realized that Rome's conquest of the Mediterranean world had given history an organic unity it had never before possessed. His theme was to show how the Romans had subdued the whole inhabited world in less than fifty-three years. His aim was truth; to attain it he eschewed the attractive rhetoric of many of his contemporaries and wrote a pragmatic account, to which he devoted the critical faculties of a trained historian and the wisdom of an experienced and widely-travelled statesman. After a sketch of the events of 264–220 he treats in detail world history from 220 to 167; he later continued his account down to 145. He has been hailed by Mommsen as the 'sun in the field of Roman history', and by T. R. Glover as 'the first true historian of Rome'. Of the 40 books of the *Universal History* of the Sicilian Diodorus (*c.* 30 BC) books i–v, xi–xx (the last from 480 to 302 BC) survive in complete form. He is more concerned with Greek than Roman history. His notices of early Roman history may derive from some chronological table, but it is quite probable that he used as his chief source one of the earlier Roman annalists, e.g. Fabius Pictor, and thus preserves a better tradition than Livy or Dionysius; for the period after 200 BC he used Polybius.

Biography was first popularized at Rome by Varro. The *Lives* of Nepos (99–24 BC) are not of great historical value, those by Plutarch are more important. Plutarch does not claim the title of historian; his object is rather to point a moral and adorn a tale, but he provides some valuable material. He used various sources; antiquarian studies for the lives of *Romulus* and *Numa*; Dionysius for *Coriolanus*; Fabius Pictor, Ennius and Greek historians contemporary with Pyrrhus for *Pyrrhus*; Polybius, Coelius, annalists and Livy for *Fabius, Marcellus* and *Aemilius Paullus*.

Finally, reference may be made to the valuable information contained in the works of such writers as Cicero and Varro, and to the far less valuable sketches and epitomes by Florus (*c.* AD 130), Eutropius (fourth century) and Orosius (AD 417), who mainly reproduce the Livian tradition.

4. SOURCES

It may be found useful to provide a list of some of the more important literary sources for this period. To attempt to give a complete list, and still more to add references to the epigraphic, archaeological and numismatic material, would far exceed the scope of this short note. But the following references may help to put those readers, who do not already know the way well, on the track of some of the more important literary sources for the narrative portions of this book. Authors' names are given in full in the first reference, but are then generally abbreviated (note, L. for Livy, and P. for Polybius).

Chapter I The Land and its Peoples

7 THE ETRUSCANS. Appian, *Lib.*, ix, 66; Dionysius of Halicarnassus, i, 26–30; Herodotus, i, 94; Justin, xx, 5; Pliny, *N.H.*, iii, 50, 51; 112 f., 133; Strabo, v, 2, 1–2; 2, 4; Tacitus, *Ann.*, iv; 55, xi, 14; Thucydides, iv, 109; Livy, v, 33.

Chapter II Regal Rome

2 THE FOUNDATION OF ROME; THE LEGENDS. Dionys., i, 72–4; Festus, *s.v.* Roma; Cicero, *de rep.*, ii, 3; 5–7; 10, 18; Plutarch, *Romul.*, 12; Velleius Paterculus, i, 8; Solinus, i; Orosius, ii, 1.

3–4 THE EARLY KINGS. THE SIXTH-CENTURY KINGS. L., i, ii, 1–15; Dionys., ii–v, 36; Cic, *de rep.*, ii, 1–30; Plut., *Romul.; Numa; Poplicola*; App., *Basilic.*, 1–12; Dio Cassius, i–iv; Zonaras, vii, 1–12; Eutropius, i. 1–11; Florus, i, 1–2; 4.

Chapter III The New Republic and the Struggle of the Orders

L. ii–iv (see especially ii, 1; 8; 18; 32–5; 41–2; 52; 54–7; iii, 20, 7; 30, 7; 33–59; iv, 1; 6–8; 12–16; 24; 43–4; 54); v, 12; 7–13; Dionys., v–xi (see esp. v, 19; vi, 89; ix, 41–9; x, 55–61; xi, 1–46); Cic., *de rep.*, ii, 31–7; *de leg.*, iii, 3, 8–9; 7, 16–17; 8, 19; 10, 24; Dio, iv–vi (frgs); Zon., vii, 13–20; Tac., *Ann.*, xi, 22; Asconius, *in Cornelianam*, p. 76 Cl.; Diodorus, xii, 24–6; Pliny, *N.H.*, xviii, 4.

Chapter IV The Roman Republic and its Neighbours

1 THE TRIPLE ALLIANCE. L., i, 50; ii, 19–20; 22; 25–6; 33; 40, 12–41, 1; Dionys., v, 61; vi, 4–13; 95; viii, 69; Cic.*pro Balbo*, 23, 53; P., iii, 22.

2 THE SABINES, AEQUI AND VOLSCI. L., ii–iv (see esp. ii, 16; 22; 25–6; 30–1; 33–49; 53; 58–60; 62–5; iii, 1–8; 15–18; 22–30; 42; 60–3; 66; 69–70; iv, 9–11; 26–30; 37; 43; 45–7; 51; 56–7); Dionys., ii, 49; v–xi (*passim*); Plut., *Poplicola*, 20–2; *Coriolanus*; Diod., xi, 40, 5; xii, 30, 6; 34, 5; 64; xiii, 42, 6; xiv, 11, 6; Dio, v (frgs); Zon., vii, 16–18; App., *Ital.*, 5–7 (frgs).

3 THE DUEL WITH VEII. L., ii, 42–50; iv, 17–23; 30–34; 57–61; v, 1–8; 13–32; Diod., xi, 53, 6; xii, 80, 6–8; xiv, 16, 5; 43, 5; 93; 98, 5; 102, 4; Plut., *Camill.*, 1–13; Zon., vii, 20–1; Dionys., xiii, 1–2.

4 THE GALLIC CATASTROPHE. L., v, 33–49; P., i, 6, 2–4; ii, 14–18; Diod., xiv, 113–17; Plut., *Camill.*,14–30; App., *Celt.*, 1–9 (frgs); Dio, vii, 25; Dionys., i, 74; xiii, 6–10; Flor., i, 7.

5 THE RECOVERY OF ROME. L. v, 50–5; vi, 1–10; 22–33; 42; vii, 7–27; P., ii, 18, 6–8; Plut., *Camill.*, 31–43; Zon., vii, 24.

6–7 ROME'S WIDENING HORIZON. THE END OF THE LATIN LEAGUE. L., vii, 27, 2; 29–42; viii, 1–14; P., iii, 22–7; Oros., iii, 7; Diod., xvi, 15; 45, 8; 69, 1; App., *Samn.*, 1–2; Dio, vii, 35; Zon., vii, 26.

Chapter V The Union of the Orders and the Constitution

L., vi, 11; 14–21; 34–42 (see esp. 35, 4–5 (cf. x, 13, 14 and 23, 13), 42, 11–14); vii, 1; 15, 13; 16, 1; 17, 6; 21, 5; 22, 6–10; 27, 3–4; 41; 42, 1–2; viii, 12, 14–16; 15, 9; 23, 12; 28; ix, 20, 5; 29, 5–11; 30, 1–4; 33–4; 42, 1–3; 46; x, 6–9; 22, 9; *Epit.*, xi; xii; Dionys., xiv, 12; Diod., xv, 61, 1; xx, 36; Fest., p. 288L; App., *BC*, i, 8; Gellius, xv, 27; Gaius, i, 3; Dio, viii, 37, 2–4; Zon., viii, 2; Pliny, *N.H.*, xvi, 10, 37.

Chapter VI Rome's Conquest and Organization of Italy

1–3 ROME AND THE SAMNITES. THE GREAT SAMNITE WAR. ROME'S TRIUMPHANT ADVANCE. L., vii, 15–17; 19–27; 29–31; 36–40; ix, 1–29; 31–2; 35–45; x, 1–5, 10–21; 25–46; *Epit.*, xi; xii; P., ii. 19–20; App., *Samn.*, 4–6; Dio, viii, 36, 8–24; 28–32; Diod., xix, 10, 1–2; 65, 7; 72, 3–9; 76; 101; xx, 26, 3–4; 35; 44, 8–9; 80; 90, 3–4; 10, 4–5; Dionys., xv–xviii (frgs); Eutrop., ii, 9–10; Flor., i, 11–12; Velleius, i, 14, 3–6; Zon., vii, 26; 8, 1.

4–6 THE GREEKS OF SOUTHERN ITALY. THE ITALIAN ADVENTURE OF PYRRHUS. THE END OF PRE-ROMAN ITALY. App., *Samn.*, 7–12; Dio, ix–x; Diod., xx, 104; Dionys. xix–xx; Flor., i, 13–16; P., iii, 25; Justin (ep. Trog.), xviii, 1–2; L., *Epit.*, xii–xv; Plut., *Pyrrhus*; Velleius, i, 14, 7–8; Zon., viii, 2–7.

Chapter VII The First Struggle

P., i, 5–64; L., *Epit.*, xvi–xix; App., *Sic.*, 1–2; *Lib.*, i, 1–4; Dio, xi; Diod., xxii–xxiv (frgs); Eutrop., ii, 18–28; Flor., i, 18; Oros., iv, 7–11; Zon., viii, 8–17.

Chapter VIII The Entr'acte

2 CARTHAGE AND THE SARDINIAN QUESTION. P., i, 65–88; iii, 10; L. *Epit.*, xx; App., *Sic.*, ii, 3; Zon., viii, 18.

3 ROME AND THE GAULS. P., ii, 17–35; L., *Epit.*, xx; Dio, xii, 50; Flor., i, 19–20; Zon., viii, 18; 20.

4 THE ILLYRIAN PIRATES. P., ii, 2–12; iii, 16; 18–19; L., *Epit.*, xx; App., *Illyr.*, 2, 7–8; Dio, xii, 49; 53; Flor., i, 21; Zon., viii, 19–20.

5–6 THE PUNIC EMPIRE IN SPAIN. THE CAUSES OF THE SECOND PUNIC WAR. P., ii, 1; 13; 36; iii, 10–15; 17; 20–30; 33; App., *Iber.*, 1–2; Dio, xii, 48; Diod., xxv, 9; Justin, xliv; Zon, viii, 19; L., xxi, 1–3.

Chapter IX Hannibal's Offensive and Rome's Defensive

1, 2, 6 HANNIBAL'S INVASION OF NORTHERN ITALY. HANNIBAL IN CENTRAL ITALY. FABIUS AND ROME'S DEFENSIVE. P., iii, 33–94; 100–18; vii, 1; viii, 26–36; ix, 3–8; 22–6; 44; x, 1; L., xxi, 1–59; 61–2; xxii, 1–18; 23–61; xxiii, 1–25; 30–9; 42–9; xxiv, 1–3; 7–20; 43–9; xxv, 1–22; 40; xxvi, 1–16; 21–4; 26–40; xxvii, 1–16; App., *Han.*, i–viii, 49; Dio, xiii–xv (frgs); Eutrop., iii, 7–23; Flor., i, 22; Nepos, *Hannib.*; Oros., iv, 14 ff.; Plut., *Fab.; Marcell.*; Zon., viii, 21–ix, 6.

3 THE SCIPIOS AND SPAIN. P., iii, 76; 95–9; ix, 11; L., xxi, 60–1; xxii, 19–22; xxiii, 26–9; xxiv, 41–2; xxv, 32–9; App., *Iber.*, 3; Zon., ix, 3.

4 THE EXTENSION OF THE WAR TO MACEDON. P., vii, 9; x, 25; 41; L., xxiii, 33; 40–1; xxiv, 40; xxvi; 24–6; xxvii, 29–33; xxviii, 5–8; xxix, 12; Zon., ix, 4.

5 MARCELLUS AND SICILY. P., vii, 2–8; viii, 5–9; 37; ix, 10; 27; L., xxiv, 4–7; 21–39; xxv, 23–31; 40; xxvi, 40; App., *Sic.*, iii–v; Zon., ix, 4–5.

Chapter X Scipio and Rome's Offensive

1 SCIPIO'S CONQUEST OF SPAIN. P., x, 2–20; 34–40; xi, 20–33; L., xxvi, 17–20; 41–51; xxvii, 17–20; xxviii, 1–4; 12–38; xxix, 1–2; App., *Iber.*, 4–7; Dio, xvi (frgs); Eutrop., iii, 15; Zon., ix, 7–10.

2 THE WAR IN ITALY. P., x, 32–3; xi, 1–3; L., xxvii, 20–9; 33–50; xxviii, 9–12; 38–46; xxix, 5–11; 13–23; 36–8; xxx, 1–2; 18–24; 26–8; 38–45; App., *Han.*, viii, 50–ix, 61; Dio, xvi–xvii (frgs); Plut., *Fab.; Marcell.*; Zon., ix, 8–9.

3–4 THE ROMAN OFFENSIVE IN AFRICA. VICTORY AND PEACE. P., xiv, 1–10; xv, 1–19; L., xxix, 3–4; 23–36; xxx, 3–17; 24; 29–38; App., *Lib.*, ii, 7–ix, 66; Dio, xvii (frgs); Eutrop., iii, 20–3; Zon., ix, 12–14.

Chapter XI Rome and Greece

P., xv, 20–5; xvi, 1–12; 24–35; xviii, 1–12; 18–39; 42–8; L., xxxi, 1–9; 14–18; 22–47; xxxii, 1–25; 28; 32–40; xxxiii, 1–21; 27–35; xxxiv, 22–41; 48–52; App., *Maced*, iv–ix, 4; Dio, xviii, 57–60; Flor., i, 23; Plut., *Flamininus*; Zon., ix, 15–16; 18.

Chapter XIII Rome and Antiochus

1– THE DIPLOMATIC CONFLICT. THE WAR IN GREECE. P., xviii, 49–52; xx, 3; 7–11; xxi, 1–5; L., xxxiii, 38–41; xxxiv, 57; xxxv, 12–13; 15–19; 25–83; 42–51; xxxvi, 1–35; App., *Syr.*, i, 1–iv, 21; Flor., i, 24; Plut., *Cato*, 13–14; Zon., ix, 18–19.

3–4 THE WAR IN ASIA. THE SETTLEMENT OF THE EAST. P., xxi, 6–48; L., xxxvi, 41–5; xxxvii, 1–45; 52–7; 60; xxxviii, 1–41; App. *Syr.*, v, 22–vii, 44; Flor., i, 27; Zon., ix, 20–1.

Chapter XIII Rome and the Eastern Mediterranean

1 THE GROWING TENSION. P., xxii, 1–4; 6–15; 18–19; xxiii, 1–18; xxiv, 1–3; 6–13; xxv, 2; L., xxxix, 23–9; 33–7; 46–53; xl, 2–16; 20–4; 54–8; xli, 22–5; xlii, 5–6.

2 THE THIRD MACEDONIAN WAR. P., xxvii, 1–11; 14–16; xxviii, 3–15; xxiv, 1–11; 13–21; xxx, 6–15; 22; 29; 32; L., xlii, 25–67; xliii, 7–12; 17–23; xliv, 1–13; 16; 18; 20–46; xlv, 4; 6–9; 17–18; 26–34; App. *Mac.*, xi–xix; *Illyr.*, ii, 9–10; Dio, xx (frgs); Flor., i, 28; Plut., *Aem. Paullus*; Zon., ix, 22–4.

3 THE HELLENISTIC EAST. P., xxii, 5; 16–17; xxiv, 1; 5; 14–15; xxv, 1; 4–6; xxvi, 1; xxvii, 3–4; 7; 17–20; xxviii, 1–2; 16–23; xxix, 2; 22–7; xxx, 1–5; 16–21; 23–8; 30–1; xxxi, 1–20; 30–3; xxxii, 1–12; 15–16; xxxiii, 1–7; 11–19; xxxv, 6; xxxvi, 14–15; xxxix, 7; L., xli, 20; xlii, 11–17; 45; xliii, 6; xliv, 14–15; 19; xlv, 3; 10–13; 19–26; 44; *Epit.*, xlvi–liii; Zon., ix, 25.

4 THE END OF GREEK INDEPENDENCE P., xxxvi, 10–11; 17; xxxviii, 9–18; xxxix, 2–6; L., *Epit.*, xlix; lii; Flor., i, 30–2; Pausanias, vii, 11–16; Zon, ix, 28; 31.

Chapter XIV Rome, Italy and the Western Mediterranean

1 THE NORTHERN FRONTIER. P., xxxii, 9; 13; xxxiii, 8–10; L., xxxi, 2; 10; 29; xxxii, 29–31; 36–7; xxxiv, 46–8; xxxv, 3–6; 11; 22; xxxvi, 38–40; xxxix, 1–2; 20; 54–5; xl, 16; 25–8; 38; 41; 53; xli, 1–4; 10–12; 17–19; xlii, 7–9; App., *Illyr.*, ii, 11; Dio, xviii; Flor., i, 26; Zon., ix. 15.

2–4 CATO AND GRACCHUS IN SPAIN. THE CELTIBERIAN AND LUSITANIAN WARS. THE NUMANTINE WAR. P., xxxv, 1–5; L. xxxiii, 21; xxxiv, 8–21; xxxv, 1–2; 22; xxxix, 20–1; 30–1; xl, 16; 30–3; 35–6; 39–40; 47–50; xli, 26; App., *Iber.*, viii, 39–xvi, 98; Dio, xxii–xxiii (frgs); Flor., i, 33–4; Plut., *Cato*, 10; Zon., ix, 17.

5–7 CARTHAGE AND MASINISSA. DELENDA EST CARTHAGO. THE FALL OF CARTHAGE. P., xxxi, 21; xxxvi, 1–9; 16; xxxviii, 7–8; 19–22; L., xxxi, 11; 19; xxxiii, 45–9; xxxiv, 60–2; xxxv, 14; xxxix, 51; xl, 17; xlii, 23–4; xlv, 13–14; *Epit.*, xlviii–liii; App., *Lib.*, x, 67–xx, 135; Flor., i, 31; Zon., ix, 18; 26–7; 29–30.

Chapter XV Roman Policy and the Government
P., vi, 11–56; L., xxxiii, 27, 6; xxxiv, 1; 45; xxxvii, 57; xxxviii, 42–60; xxxix, 8–19; 40–4; 55; xl, 19; 34; 37; 44; 51–2; xli, 9; xliii, 2–5; xlv, 15; Cic. *de rep.*, ii, 54; *de offic.*, ii, 75; *Brut.*, 106; Cato, *Speeches* (frgs); Gellius, x, 3, 13.

5. CHRONOLOGY

Many of the difficulties of Roman chronology derive from the long-continued absence of a generally accepted era. The main points chosen by the Romans were the foundation of the city, the first consulships, and the sack of Rome by the Gauls. Attempts to establish these dates were made by two methods, either by synchronizing them with Greek Olympiads or Athenian archonships, or by standardizing the list of Roman magistrates. By the former method the foundation of Rome was set in 752 (Cato), 751–750 (Polybius and Diodorus), 748 (Fabius) or 729–728 (Cincius); the first consulship in 508–507 by Polybius and 508 by Dionysius; and the sack of Rome in 387 by Polybius and Dionysius. The list of magistrates, however, was not quite long enough to span these periods, so that various expedients were devised by Roman antiquarians. Five years of anarchy (*solitudo magistratuum*) were interpolated into the period of the Licinian laws (so Livy and Fasti; Diodorus gives only one); or the same college of magistrates was repeated (those of 391–387 repeated after the Gallic invasion by Diodorus), or four years were interpolated during which dictators and masters of the horse were the chief magistrates (in 333, 324, 309, 301; Fasti). Finally, the foundation of Rome was set in 754–753 by Atticus and Varro; this date was officially accepted and so fixed chronology could be established *ab urbe condita*. In modern times the Varronian system is generally accepted as a convenient convention and is used in this volume; thus the sack of Rome is placed in 390 rather than more accurately in 387. The year of the foundation is usually set in 753 in order to allow only the 119 years which the Capitoline Fasti establish between the first consulship and the sack of Rome.

Though the dates from the third century can be established with adequate accuracy, the Roman calendar remained confused, because the Roman year of twelve lunar months was too short and constantly got out of gear with the solar year. To counterbalance this the pontiffs used to intercalate an extra month of 22 or 23 days after February every two years. But this was not satisfactory, especially during the Hannibalic War which engrossed all attention, and in fact the Roman calendar had advanced far ahead of the Julian, perhaps by some four months, though some calculations would put it at only one or two; the problem hinges on how many intercalations were in fact made (however, an eclipse which occurred on 14 March 190 happened according to the Roman calendar on 11 July). In 191 Acilius Glabrio passed a law to regulate intercalations, but this provisional remedy proved inadequate: thus the Roman date of an eclipse which occurred on 21 June 168 was 3 September, although intercalation had been made in 169. It needed the political scandals of the last century BC and the statesmanship of Julius Caesar to set the matter right.[6]

CHRONOLOGICAL TABLE

This table is designed to emphasize some of the outstanding events in early Roman history. The Varronian dating (pp. 418ff.) has been followed. Prior to 390 BC many of the dates are merely traditional and some of the facts (e.g. the foundation of colonies) are not above suspicion.

A. THE REGAL PERIOD

Growth of Rome

c. 800(?) BC	Roma Quadrata; settlement on Palatine.
c. 750–670	Septimontium; union of settlers of Palatine, Velia, Fagutal, Cispius, Oppius, and Caelius.
7th cent.	City of the Four Regions; addition of Quirinal, Viminal, and part of Forum.
7th cent. end	Last Forum burials.
6th cent.	'Servian' City, including Capitol and Esquiline.

Traditional Dates

753–715	Romulus.
715–673	Numa Pompilius. Established cult of Vesta, etc.
673–642	Tullus Hostilius. Destruction of Alba Longa.
642–616	Ancus Marcius. Extension of Rome's power to coast.
616–579	L. Tarquinius Priscus. Forum drained.
579–534	Servius Tullius. 'Servian' organization begun. Treaty with Latins. Temple of Diana on Aventine.
534–510	L. Tarquinius Superbus. Capitoline temple. Treaty with Gabii. Ager Romanus extended to c. 350 sq. miles.

B. FROM THE FOUNDATION OF THE REPUBLIC TO THE GALLIC SACK

509	**Fall of monarchy;** institution of two annual magistrates. First treaty with Carthage.

	War with Porsenna (who captures Rome ?).
504	Migration of Claudii to Rome.
501	First dictator appointed.
496	Battle of Lake Regillus fought by Rome against Latin League.
495	Cult of Liber, Libera and Ceres on Aventine. Latin colony at Signia.
494	First secession; plebeians assert their rights (or 471). Latin colony at Velitrae.
493	**Treaty of Spurius Cassius with the Latins.**
492	Corn imported from Cumae. Latin colony at Norba.
491	Raid of Coriolanus.
486	Sp. Cassius proposes agrarian law. Treaty of Rome with Hernici. **Wars with Aequi and Volsci intermittently for fifty years.**
484	Latins recover Tusculum from Aequi and Volsci.
483–474	War with Veii.
479	Battle of the Cremera.
474	Etruscans defeated off Cumae by Hiero.
471	**Lex Publilia Voleronis.** Concilium Plebis and tribunes officially recognized.
462	Agitation of Terentilius Harsa.
459 ?	Tribunes raised to ten.
458 ?	Minucius defeated by Aequi at Mt Algidus. Aequi defeated by Cincinnatus.
456	*Lex Icilia de Aventino publicando.*
451–450	The decemvirates. **Publication of the XII Tables.**
449	Secession of the plebs. **Valerio-Horatian Laws.** Rights of tribunes legally defined.
447	Quaestors elected by the people. Comitia Tributa Populi perhaps instituted.
445	**Lex Canuleia. Military tribunes with consular power replace consulship.**
444	Treaty with Ardea.
443	**Censorship established.**
442	Latin colony at Ardea ?
439	Minucius deals with corn supply of Rome.
433	Temple of Apollo founded.

431	**Decisive defeat of Aequi on the Algidus.**
428–425	Rome wins Fidenae from Veii.
421	**Quaestorships raised to four: opened to plebs.**
418	Roman garrison (colony ?) at Labici.
409	Three quaestors plebeians.
406	Anxur reduced.
404	Velitrae receives garrison.
399	Lectisternium decreed.
396	Military pay introduced.
	Fall of Veii. Peace with Volsci.
393	Latin colony at Circeii.
390 ?	Latin colony at Sutrium.
390	**Battle of Allia. Gauls sack Rome.** (387 acc. to Polybius.)

C. THE CONQUEST OF ITALY

388	Aequi defeated at Bola.
387	Creation of four rustic tribes on ager Veiens (making total of 25).
386–385	Latins, Volsci and Hernici defeated.
385	Latin colony at Satricum.
383 ?	Latin colony at Nepete.
382	Latin colony at Setia.
381	Tusculum pacified.
378	'Servian' Wall begun.
377	Latins defeated after their capture of Satricum.
	Licinius and Sextius start their agitation.
367	**Laws of Licinius and Sextius passed. Consulship restored.** Creation of curule aedileship.
366	**First plebeian consul. Creation of praetorship.** Curule aedileship to alternate annually between patricians and plebs.
361	Romans capture Ferentinum.
359	Tarquinii revolts.
358	Hernici readmitted to alliance. **Renewal of treaty with Latins.** Two new tribes created on land from Antium (total 27).
357	Government tax on manumission. Rate of interest fixed. Falerii revolts. Gallic raid on Latium.

356	**First plebeian dictator.**
354	**Alliance of Rome and Samnites.**
353	Caere defeated: 100 years' truce: receives half-citizenship (or later).
352	Quinqueviri mensarii established.
351	**First plebeian censor.**
	Tarquinii and Falerii reduced: forty years' truce.
348	Renewal of Rome's treaty with Carthage.
346	Gallic raid checked (or 349). Defeat of Antium and Satricum.
343	Falerii receives permanent alliance.
	Latin attack on Paeligni.
343–341	**First Samnite War** (very doubtful).
342	Military mutiny and secession. **Leges Genuciae.**
340–338	**Latin revolt.**
339	**Leges Publiliae.**
338	**Latin League dissolved.** Lanuvium, Aricia, Nomentum, Pedum and Tusculum receive full citizenship. Fundi, Formiae, Cumae, Capua, etc., receive half-citizenship. Roman colony at Antium and Ostia (?). Land confiscated from Veltrae.
337	**First plebeian praetor.**
336	Teanum granted alliance.
334	Latin colony at Cales.
332	Acerrae receives half-citizenship. Two new tribes created in Latium (total 29).
	Rome's treaty with Tarentum (or 303).
332–331	Rome makes thirty years' truce with Senones.
c. 330	Roman alliance with Fabrateria and Frusino.
329	Privernum captured and receives half-citizenship. Roman colony at Tarracina (Anxur).
328	Latin colony at Fregellae.
326	**First use of prorogatio imperii. Lex Poetilia** concerning debt (313).
	Roman alliance with Neapolis, Nuceria and the Apulians.
	Rome captures Rufrium and Allifae.
326–304	**Second Samnite War.**
321	Roman defeat at **Caudine Forks.** Peace. Rome surrenders Fregellae.

318	Two tribes (Falernia and Oufentina) created in northern Campania (total 31).
	Alliance with Teanum (Apuli) and Canusium.
	Roman prefects sent to Capua and Cumae.
316	Samnite War renewed.
315	Luceria captured. Samnite victory at Lautulae. Revolt of Capua and Aurunci to Samnites.
314	Roman victory at Tarracina. Capua and Aurunci reduced. Latin colony at Luceria.
313 (or 312)	Fregellae and Sora recaptured. Nola and Calatia made allies. Latin colonies at Suessa Aurunca, Pontia, Saticula, Interamna.
312	**Censorship of Appius Claudius.**
	Romans capture Peltuinum and Allifae. Via Appia started. Aqua Appia.
311	**Duoviri navales appointed.**
310	Naval landing at Pompeii fails. Roman advance into Etruria. Roman treaties with Cortona, Perusia, Arretium.
308	Alliance with Tarquinii renewed for forty years. Alliance with Camerinum and Ocriculum.
307	Revolt of the Hernici.
306	Anagnia stormed; receives half-citizenship.
	'Philinus' treaty with Carthage.
304	Repeal of reform of Appius Claudius. **Flavius publishes the 'legis actiones'.**
	Aequi defeated. Samnite War ended. Alliance with Marsi, Paeligni, Marrucini, Frentani.
303	Latin colony at Alba Fucens (or 300) and Sora.
	Half-citizenship to Arpinum and Trebula.
	Temple of Salus dedicated.
302	Latin colony at Carsioli (or 298). Alliance with Vestini.
300	Lex Valeria de provocatione. **Lex Ogulnia,** opening priestly colleges to plebeians.
299	Two new tribes, Aniensis and Terentina (total 33).
	Latin colony at Narnia (Nequinum). Alliance with Picentes.
	Gallic raid in Roman territory.
298–290	**Third Samnite War.**
298	Rome captures Taurasia, Cisauna, Bovianum Vetus, and Aufidena.

296	Samnite raid in ager Falernus. Roman colonies at Minturnae and Sinuessa.
295	Roman victory over Samnites, Gauls and Umbrians at **Sentinum.**
294	Forty years' treaty with Volsinii, Perusia, Arretium. Samnite victory near Luceria.
293 (?)	Lex Maenia. Cult of Aesculapius imported. . Roman victory over Samnites at Aquilonia.
292	Falerii reduced; truce.
291	Venusia stormed: Latin colony there.
290	Peace with Samnites. Sabines granted half-citizenship. Latin colony at Hadria and Roman (?) colony at Castrum Novum Piceni.
289	Mint and triumviri monetales established.
287	**Lex Hortensia.**
284	Senones defeat Metellus at Arretium. Revolt of Vulci, Volsinii, and some Samnites and Lucanians. Senones driven out of ager Gallicus. Roman colony at Sena.
283	**Boii defeated at Lake Vadimo.**
282	Boii defeated near Populonia, Roman garrisons sent to Thurii, Rhegium and Locri. **Roman fleet attacked by Tarentines.**
281	Roman embassy at Tarentum.
280	Alliance with Vulci, Volsinii, Rusellae, Vetulonia, Populonia, Volaterrae, and Tarquinii.
280–275	**War with Pyrrhus.**
280	Pyrrhus lands in Italy, and defeats Romans at Heraclea. (Winter) Negotiations with Pyrrhus.
279	Battle of Asculum.
278	Peace negotiations fail. Rome's treaty with Carthage. Pyrrhus leaves Italy.
276	Pyrrhus returns to Italy.
275	**Pyrrhus defeated** near Malventum; returns to Greece.
273	Latin colonies at Paestum and Cosa. Caere mulcted of some territory. Roman friendship with Egypt.
272	Livius Andronicus brought to Rome. Anio Vetus aqueduct. Alliance with Velia, Heraclea, Thurii, Metapontum. Surrender of Tarentum.
270	Capture of Rhegium.
269	First silver coinage minted at Rome. Revolt of Picentes.

268	Picentes reduced: half-citizenship. **Sabines receive full citizenship.** Latin colonies at Beneventum and Ariminum.
	Capture of Sarsina.
267	War with Sallentini. Capture of Brundisium.
266	Apulia and Messapia reduced to alliance.
264	First gladiatorial show at Rome.
	Latin colony at Firmum. Capture of Volsinii.
263	Latin colony at Aesernia.

D. THE FIRST AND SECOND PUNIC WARS

264–241	**First Punic War.**
264	Roman alliance with Mamertines. **Roman army lands in Sicily.**
263	Hiero becomes Roman ally.
262	Capture of Agrigentum.
260	**Naval victory off Mylae.**
259	Roman occupation of Corsica.
258	Naval victory off Sulci.
257	Naval victory off Tyndaris.
256	Naval victory off Ecnomus. **Regulus lands in Africa.**
255	Defeat of Regulus' army. Naval victory off Cape Hermaeum.
	Roman fleet wrecked off Pachynus.
254	Romans capture Panormus.
253	Roman fleet wrecked off Palinurus.
250	Victory at Panormus. Siege of Lilybaeum.
249	Claudius' naval defeat at Drepana. Roman transport fleet wrecked.
247	Hamilcar Barca starts Carthaginian offensive in Sicily.
244	Latin colony at Brundisium.
243	Roman fleet built from voluntary loans.
242	**Institution of praetor peregrinus.**
241	**Naval victory off Aegates Insulae. Peace. Roman occupation of Sicily.** Falerii reduced. Latin colony at Spoletium. Two tribes created in Picenum (total 35).
241 ?	**Reform of the Comitia Centuriata.**
238–225	Occupation and reduction of Corsica and Sardinia.

238–230	Intermittent campaigns against the Ligurians.
236	First play of Naevius.
	Gallic raids in the North.
c. 235	The quadrigatus introduced.
235–234	Temple of Janus closed.
232	**Distribution of ager Gallicus carried by Flaminius.**
231	Roman embassy to Hamilcar in Spain.
229–228	**First Illyrian War. Roman protectorate established on the Illyrian coast.**
228	Roman envoys in Greece.
227	**Praetorships raised to four. Sicily and Sardinia under praetors.**
226	Roman embassy to Hasdrubal in Spain; **Ebro treaty.**
225	**Invading Gauls defeated at Telamon.**
223	Flaminius defeats Insubres.
222	Battle of Clastidium. Insubres surrender.
221–220	**North-eastern frontier secured to Julian Alps.**
c. 221	Saguntines appeal to Rome.
220	Construction of Via Flaminia.
219	**Second Illyrian War; Demetrius defeated.**
	(aut.) **Hannibal storms Saguntum.**
218 ?	**Lex Claudia.**
	Latin colonies at Placentia and Cremona.
	Roman ultimatum to Carthage. **War declared** (spring).
218–201	**Second Punic War.**
218	Hannibal in northern Italy. Battles of Ticinus and Trebia.
217	Roman naval victory off the Ebro. Battle of Lake Trasimene.
216	**Battle of Cannae.** Revolts in central Italy, and of Capua.
215	Tributum doubled.
	Hannibal in South Italy. Hasdrubal defeated at Dertosa.
	Alliance of Carthage with Philip and Syracuse.
214	Roman successes in Spain.
214–205	**First Macedonian War.**
213	Hannibal occupies Tarentum. Roman siege of Syracuse.
212	Siege of Capua.
	Ludi Apollinares introduced.

212–211	The denarius introduced.
211	Hannibal's march on Rome. Fall of Capua and Syracuse. Roman alliance with Aetolia. The Scipios defeated in Spain.
210	Twelve Latin colonies refuse contingents. Fall of Agrigentum. Scipio Africanus lands in Spain.
209	Recapture of Tarentum. Capture of New Carthage.
208	Death of Marcellus. Battle of Baecula.
207	**Hasdrubal defeated at Metaurus.**
206	Battle of Ilipa. **Final reduction of Spain.** Aetolians make peace with Philip.
205	Scipio in Sicily. Peace of Phoenice (or 204).
204	Ennius brought to Rome. Cult stone of Mother Goddess brought from Asia Minor. **Scipio lands in Africa.**
203	Syphax defeated. Battle of the Great Plains. Armistice broken. Defeat of Mago. Hannibal recalled in winter.
202	First prose history of Rome by Fabius Pictor. **Scipio's victory at Zama** (aut.).
201	**Peace.** Masinissa king of Greater Numidia. **Carthage becomes a client state.** Appeal of Attalus and Rhodes.

E. EXTENSION OF EMPIRE

200–196	**Second Macedonian War.**
200	War declared on Philip. Insubres sack Placentia.
199	Lex Porcia, limiting imperium of governors. Death of Naevius.
198	Flamininus' victory at the Aoüs. Achaeans join Rome.
197	**Praetorships raised to six. Spain organized as two provinces.** Cethegus defeats Insubres. **Battle of Cynoscephalae.** Peace between Philip and Rome (winter). Revolt of Turdetani in Spain.
196	Final defeat of Insubres by Marcellus. **Flamininus' proclamation at Corinth.** Appeal of Smyrna to Senate.
195	Repeal of Lex Oppia. Lex Porcia, forbidding scourging of citizens. Hannibal exiled. **Masinissa starts his raids on Punic territory.** Cato in Spain. War against Nabis.
194	Roman colonies at Volturnum, Liternum, Puteoli,

Salernum, Pyrgi, Sipontum, Tempsa, Croton, Buxentum.

Lusitani defeated; war drags on intermittently.

Evacuation of Greece.

193   Latin colony at Copia.

192–189   **War with Antiochus.**

192   Latin colony at Vibo. The Apuani checked. War declared on Antiochus, who lands in Greece (Oct.).

191   Lex Acilia, concerning the calendar.

Boii defeated by Scipio Nasica. Antiochus defeated at Thermopylae. War in Aetolia. Antiochus' fleet defeated off Corycus.

190   Placentia and Cremona resettled. The Scipios in Greece.

Antiochus' fleet defeated at Side and Myonnesus.

189   Libertini enrolled in rustic tribes.

Latin colony at Bononia. Campanians enrolled as citizens. Fall of Ambracia Peace with Aetolia.

Defeat of Antiochus at Magnesia. Manlius raids Galatia.

188   Full citizenship granted to Arpinum, Formiae, Fundi. Treaty of Apamea. **Settlement of Asia.**

187   Government liquidates war debt. **Attacks on Scipios.** Non-citizens expelled from Rome.

Via Aemilia and Via Flaminia.

186   Senatus consultum de Bacchanalibus.

Ligurians defeat Philippus.

184   Cato censor. Death of Plautus. Exile of Scipio Africanus. Roman colonies at Potentia, Pisaurum. Philip sends Demetrius to Rome.

183   Lex Furia Testamentaria. Death of Scipio Africanus. Roman colonies at Parma, Mutina, Saturnia.

181   Lex Baebia. Lex Orchia (sumptuary). Latin colony at Aquileia. Roman colony at Graviscae. Ingauni defeated. End of Achaeo-Spartan quarrel.

Revolt in Corsica and Sardinia.

181–179   **First Celtiberian War.**

180   **Lex Villia Annalis.**

Latin colony at Luca. Apuani defeated. Foundation of Graccuris in Spain.

179	Accession of Perseus.
178	Expedition against Istri.
177	**Latins expelled from Rome.**
	Roman colony at Luna. Annexation of Istria.
177–176	Sardinia reduced.
173	Latins expelled from Rome. Two Epicurean philosophers expelled.
	Envoys sent to arbitrate between Masinissa and Carthage.
172	**Two plebeian consuls.**
172–167	**Third Macedonian War.**
171	**Temporary court de repetundis.**
	Latin colony at Carteia in Spain.
169	Lex Voconia. Freedmen confined to one urban tribe.
	Quarrel between Senate and Equites.
168	**Defeat of Perseus at Pydna.** Romans capture Scodra. Antiochus checked. Delos declared a free port. Foundation of Corduba in Spain (or 151).
167	**Tributum discontinued.** Perseus' library brought to Rome. Epirus plundered. **Macedon divided into four, Illyria into three protectorates. 1,000 Achaeans deported to Italy.**
166–159	Production of Terence's comedies.
163	Final reduction of Corsica.
161	Lex Fannia (sumptuary). Expulsion of Greek philosophers.
	Treaty with Jews.
159	Law against bribery.
157–155	Roman campaigns in Dalmatia and Pannonia.
155	Carneades in Rome.
154	Oxybian Ligurians defeated.
154–138	**Lusitanian War.**
153–151	**Second Celtiberian War.**
151	Carthage declares war on Masinissa.
150	Return of Achaean exiles to Greece.
c. 150	Lex Aelia Fufia. **Lex Aebutia,** establishing a formulary system of legal procedure.
149–146	**Third Punic War.**
149	**Permanent court** de repetundis (Lex Calpurnia). Publication of Cato's Origines.

SELECT BIBLIOGRAPHY

A full bibliography of earlier works will be found in *The Cambridge Ancient History*, vols iv (1926), vii (1928), viii (1930), and more detailed works are cited in the following notes.

A. GENERAL HISTORIES

J. B. BURY, S. A. COOK, F. E. ADCOCK and M. P. CHARLESWORTH, *The Cambridge Ancient History*, vol. iv, chs 12 and 13; vol. vii, chs 10–18, 20, 21, 24–6; vol. viii, chs 1–15; vol. ix, chs 10, 20, 21 (Cambridge, 1926–32).

M. CARY and H. H. SCULLARD, *A History of Rome*, edn 3 (London, 1975).

G. DE SANCTIS, *Storia dei Romani*, 4 vols (Turin, 1907–64).

T. FRANK, *A History of Rome* (New York, 1923).

T. FRANK, *Roman Imperialism* (New York, 1914).

L. HOMO, *Primitive Italy* (London, 1927).

TH. MOMMSEN, *Römische Geschichte*, edn 12 (Berlin, 1920); Eng. trans., W. P. Dickson (London, 1901).

C. NICOLET, *Rome et la conquête du monde méditerranéen 264–27 avant J.-C.* (Paris, 1977).

E. PAIS, *Storia di Roma dalle origini all'inizio delle guerre puniche*, 5 vols (Rome, 1926–8).

E. PAIS and J. BAYET, *Histoire romaine*, vol. i (in Glotz, *Histoire générale*, edn 2 Paris, 1940).

L. PARETI, *Storia di Roma*, i–iii (Turin, 1951–3).

A. PIGANIOL, *Histoire de Rome*, edn 4 (Paris, 1962).

A. PIGANIOL, *La conquête romaine*, edn 5 (Paris, 1967).

M. ROSTOVTZEFF, *Rome* (*A History of the Ancient World*, vol ii) (Oxford, 1927 and 1960).

B. CONSTITUTIONAL AND POLITICAL

F. E. ADCOCK, *Roman Political Ideas and Practice* (Michigan, 1959).

E. BADIAN, *Foreign Clientelae (264–70 B.C.)* (Oxford, 1958).

J. BLEICKEN, *Das Volkstribunat* (Munich, 1955).

G. W. BOTSFORD, *The Roman Assemblies* (New York, 1909).

T. R. S. Broughton, *The Magistrates of the Roman Republic*, 2 vols and Supplement (New York, 1951–60).

F. Cassola, *I gruppi politici romani nel iii sec.a.C.* (Trieste, 1962).

J. Crook, *Law and Life of Rome* (London, 1967).

F. de Martino, *Storia della costituzione romana*, vols i–ii, edn 2 (Naples, 1972).

D. Earl, *The Moral and Political Tradition of Rome* (London, 1967).

K. von Fritz, *The Theory of the Mixed Constitution in Antiquity* (Columbia, 1954).

J. Hellegouach, *Le Vocabulaire latin des relations et des partis sous la république* (Paris, 1963).

M. Gelzer, *The Roman Nobility*, Eng. trans. (Oxford, 1969).

A. H. J. Greenidge, *Roman Public Life* (London, 1901).

L. Homo, *Roman Political Institutions* (London, 1929).

E. Meyer, *Römischer Staat und Staatsgedanke*, edn 2 (Zürich, 1961).

Th. Mommsen, *Römisches Staatsrecht*, 3 vols (Leipzig, 1887–8); French trans., *Le Droit publique romaine*, 7 vols (Paris, 1887–91).

F. Münzer, *Römische Adelsparteien und Adelsfamilien* (Stuttgart, 1920).

J.-C. Richard, *Les Origines de la plèbe romaine* (Paris, 1978).

H. H. Scullard, *Roman Politics, 220–150 B.C.* edn 2 (Oxford, 1973).

A. N. Sherwin-White, *The Roman Citizenship*, edn 2 (Oxford, 1973).

E. S. Staveley, *Greek and Roman Voting and Elections* (London, 1972).

L. R. Taylor, *Roman Voting Assemblies* (Michigan, 1966).

L. R. Taylor, *The Voting Districts of the Roman Republic* (Rome, 1960).

P. Willems, *Le Sénat de la république romaine*, 3 vols (Paris, 1878).

C. MILITARY AND NAVAL

F. E. Adcock, *The Roman Art of War* (Harvard, 1940).

P. Connelly, *Hannibal and the Enemies of Rome* (London, 1978).

P. Couissin, *Les Armes romaines* (Paris, 1926).

J. Kromayer and G. Veith, *Antike Schlachtfelder*, vols, ii–iv (Berlin, 1903–31).

J. Kromayer and G. Veith, *Heerwesen una Kriegführung der Griechen und Römer* (Munich, 1928).

J. Kromayer and G. Veith, *Schlachten-Atlas zur antiken Kriegsgeschichte, Römische Abteilung*, i–ii (Leipzig, 1922).

J. H Thiel, *A History of Roman Sea-Power before the Second Punic War* (Amsterdam, 1954).

J. H. Thiel, *Studies of the History of Roman Sea-Power in Republican Times* (Amsterdam, 1946).

D. ECONOMIC AND SOCIAL

E. Badian, *Publicans and Sinners* (Otago, 1972).

J. P. V. D. Balsdon, *Life and Leisure in Ancient Rome* (London, 1969).

S. F. Bonner, *Education in Ancient Rome* (London, 1977).

P. A. Brunt, *Italian Manpower, 225 B.C.-A.D. 14* (Oxford, 1971).

A. Burford, *Craftsmen in Greek and Roman Society* (London, 1972).

T. Frank, *An Economic History of Rome*, ed 2 (Baltimore, 1927).

T. Frank, *An Economic Survey of Ancient Rome*, vol. i, *Rome and Italy of the Republic* (Baltimore, 1933).

W. E. Heitland, *Agricola* (Cambridge, 1921).

H. Hill, *The Roman Middle Class* (Oxford, 1952).

P. Louis, *Ancient Rome at Work* (London, 1927).

C. Nicolet, *L'Ordre équestre à l'époche républicaine*, 2 vols (Paris, 1966–73).

I. Shatzman, *Senatorial Wealth and Roman Politics* (Brussels, 1975).

K. D. White, *Roman Farming* (London, 1970).

E. SPECIAL PERIODS

(i) Early Ethnology

L. Barfield, *Northern Italy before the Romans* (London, 1971).

L. B. Brea, *Sicily before the Greeks* (London, 1957).

F. Von Duhn, *Italische Gräberkunde*, 2 vols (Heidelberg, 1924–39).

A. Forni, ed., *Civiltà del Ferro* (Bologna, 1960).

P. G. Gierow, *The Iron Age Culture of Latium*, 2 vols (Lund, 1964–6).

T. E. Peet, *The Stone and Bronze Ages in Italy and Sicily* (Oxford, 1909).

S. Puglisi, *La civiltà apenninica* (Florence, 1959).

D. Randall-MacIver, *The Iron Age in Italy* (Oxford, 1927).

D. Randall-MacIver, *Italy before the Romans* (Oxford, 1928).

G. Säflund, *Le Terremare* (Lund, 1939).

D. H. Trump, *Central and Southern Italy before Rome* (London, 1966).

J. Whatmough, *The Foundations of Roman Italy* (London, 1937).

(ii) The Etruscans

L. Banti, *The Etruscan Cities and their Culture* (London, 1973).

R. Bloch, *The Etruscans* (London, 1958).

G. Dennis, *The Cities and Cemeteries of Etruria*, 2 vols, edn 3 (London, 1883).

P. Ducati, *Le probleme étrusque* (Paris, 1938).

R. A. L. Fell, *Etruria and Rome* (Cambridge, 1924).

W. V. Harris, *Rome in Etruria and Umbria* (Oxford, 1971).

H. Henken, *Tarquinia and Etruscan Origins* (London, 1968).

J. Heurgon, *Daily Life of the Etruscans* (London, 1964).

K. O. Müller and W. Deecke, *Die Etrusker*, 2 vols (1877).

M. Pallottino, *The Etruscans* (London, 1975).

D. Randall-MacIver, *The Etruscans* (Oxford, 1927).

D. Randall-MacIver, *Villanovans and Early Etruscans* (Oxford, 1924).

H. H. Scullard, *The Etruscan Cities and Rome* (London, 1967).

D. Strong, *The Early Etruscans* (London, 1969).

G. E. W. WOLSTENHOLME, (ed.), *Medical Biology and Etruscan Origins* (Ciba Foundation Symposium, London, 1959).

(iii) Early History of Rome and Italy

A. ALFÖLDI, *Early Rome and the Latins* (Michigan, 1964).

K. J. BELOCH, *Römische Geschichte bis zum Beginn der Punischen Kriege* (Berlin, 1926).

R. BLOCH, *The Origins of Rome* (London, 1960).

P. DE FRANCISCI, *Primordia Civitatis* (Rome, 1959).

E. GJERSTAD, *Early Rome*, 6 vols (Lund, 1954–73).

W. V. HARRIS, *Rome in Etruria and Umbria* (Oxford, 1971).

J. HEURGON, *The Rise of Rome* (London, 1973).

W. HOFFMANN, *Rom und die Griechische Welt im 4. Jahrhundert* (Leipzig, 1934).

P. LEVÊQUE, *Pyrrhos* (Paris, 1957).

R. M. OGILVIE, *Early Rome and the Etruscans* (London, 1976).

E. PAIS, *Ancient Legends of Roman History* (London, 1906).

E. PAIS, *Storia di Roma dall' età regia sino alle vittorie se Taranto e Pirro* (Rome, 1934).

I. S. RYBERG, *An Archaeological Record of Rome from the seventh to the second century B.C.* (London, 1940).

E. T. SALMON, *Roman Colonization* (London, 1969).

E. T. SALMON, *Samnium and the Samnites* (Cambridge, 1967).

J. W. SPAETH, *A Study of the Causes of Rome's Wars from 343 to 265 B.C.* (Princeton, 1926).

A. J. TOYNBEE, *Hannibal's Legacy*, 2 vols (Oxford, 1965).

(iv) Rome and Carthage

K. CHRIST, (ed.), *Hannibal* (Darmstadt, 1974).

T. A. DOREY and D. R. DUDLEY, *Rome against Carthage* (London, 1971).

R. M. ERRINGTON, *The Dawn of Empire: Rome's Rise to World Power* (London, 1972).

E. GROAG, *Hannibal als Politiker* (Vienna, 1929).

S. GSELL, *Histoire ancienne de l'Afrique du Nord*, vols i–iv (Paris, 1913–21).

U. KAHRSTEDT, *Geschichte der Karthager von 218–146*; vol iii, O. Meltzer, *Geschichte der Karthager* (Berlin, 1913).

R. P. LAPEYRE and A. PELLEGRIN, *Carthage punique* (Paris, 1942).

J. F. LAZENBY, *Hannibal's War* (Warminster, 1978).

G. CH. and C. PICARD, *Daily Life in Carthage at the Time of Hannibal* (London, 1960).

G. CH. and C. PICARD, *The Life and Death of Carthage* (London, 1968).

H. H. SCULLARD, *Scipio Africanus in the Second Punic War* (Cambridge, 1930).

H. H. SCULLARD, *Scipio Africanus: Soldier and Politician* (London, 1970).

B. H. WARMINGTON, *Carthage*, edn 2 (London, 1969).

(v) Rome and the Mediterranean World

A. E. ASTIN, *Cato the Censor* (Oxford, 1978).

A. E. ASTIN, *Scipio Aemilianus* (Oxford, 1967).

M. CARY, *A History of the Greek World from 323 to 146 B.C.*, ed 2; vol. iii, *History of the Greek and Roman World* (London, 1963).

G. COLIN, *Rome et la Grèce de 200 à 146 avant J.C.* (Paris, 1908).

E. V. HANSEN, *The Attalids of Pergamon*, edn 2 (Cornell, 1972).

M. HOLLEAUX, *Études d' épigraphie et d' histoire grecques*; vol. iv, *Rome, la Macédoine et l'Orient grec* (Paris, 1952).

M. HOLLEAUX, *Rome, la Grèce et les monarchies hellénistiques au IIIme siècle avant J.C. (273 205)* (Paris, 1921).

D. MAGIE, *Roman Rule in Asia Minor* (Princeton, 1950).

P. MELONI, *Perseo* (Rome, 1953).

S. I. OOST, *Roman Policy in Epirus and Acarnania* (Dallas, 1954).

E. PAIS, *Storia di Roma durante le grandi conquiste Mediterranee* (Turin, 1931).

E. PAIS, *Storia interna di Roma dalle guerre Puniche alla rivoluzione Graccana* (Turin, 1931).

M. ROSTOVTZEFF, *Social and Economic History of the Hellenistic World*, 3 vols (Oxford, 1940).

H. H. SCHMIDT, *Rom und Rhodos* (Munich, 1957).

A. SCHULTEN, *Numantia*, 4 vols (Munich, 1914–31).

A. SCHULTEN, *Geschichte von Numantia* (Munich, 1933).

F. W. WALBANK, *Philip V of Macedon* (Cambridge, 1940).

E. WILL, *Histoire politique du monde hellénistique*, 2 vols (1966–7).

F.   LITERATURE AND ART

A. BOETHIUS and J. B. WARD-PERKINS, *Etruscan and Roman Architecture* (Harmondsworth, 1970). Revised edn part I (1978).

M. S. DIMSDALE, *A History of Latin Literature* (London, 1915).

J. WIGHT DUFF, *A Literary History of Rome from the Origins to the Close of the Golden Age*, edn 8 (London, 1953).

T. FRANK, *Life and Letters in the Roman Republic* (Cambridge, 1930).

A. GRENIER, *The Roman Spirit* (London, 1926).

P. LEJAY, *Histoire de la littérature latine des origines à Plaute*, 2 vols (Paris, 1925).

F. LEO, *Geschichte der römischen Literatur*, vol. i (Berlin, 1913).

L. R. PALMER, *The Latin Language* (London, 1954).

E. PULGRAM, *The Tongues of Italy* (Harvard, 1958).

H. J. ROSE, *Handbook of Latin Literature*, edn 2 (London, 1950).

M. SCHANZ, *Geschichte der römischen Literatur*, vol. i, edn 4 by C. Hosius (Munich, 1927).

E. STRONG, *Art in Ancient Rome*, 2 vols (London, 1929).

E. STRONG, in *Cambr. Anc. Hist.*, Vol. ix, ch. 20.

J. M. C. TOYNBEE, *Roman Historical Portraits* (London, 1978).

(On individual writers see above, ch. xix, notes.)

G. RELIGION

F. ALTHEIM, *A History of Roman Religion* (London, 1938).

C. BAILEY, *Phases in the Religion of Ancient Rome* (Oxford, 1932).

R. S. CONWAY, *Ancient Italy* (Cambridge, 1933).

G. DUMEZIL, *Archaic Roman Religion* (1970).

W. WARDE FOWLER, *The Religious Experience of the Roman People* (London, 1911).

W. WARDE FOWLER, *The Roman Festivals* (London, 1899).

A. GRENIER, *Les religions étrusque et romaine* (Paris, 1948).

W. R. HALLIDAY, *History of Roman Religion* (Liverpool, 1922).

K. LATTE, *Römische Religionsgeschichte* (Munich, 1960).

R. M. OGILVIE, *The Romans and their Gods* (London, 1969).

H. J. ROSE, *Primitive Culture in Italy* (London, 1926).

H. J. ROSE, *Ancient Roman Religion* (London, 1949).

G. DE SANCTIS, *Storia dei Romani*, IV, 2, i (Florence, 1953).

G. WISSOWA, *Religion und Kultus der Römer*, edn 2, (Munich, 1912).

H. GEOGRAPHICAL

M. CARY, *The Geographic Background of Greek and Roman History* (Oxford, 1949).

A. VAN DER HEYDEN and H. H. SCULLARD, *Atlas of the Classical World* (Edinburgh, 1959).

G. SCHMIED T, *Atlante aerofotografica delle sedi umané in Italia*, vol. ii (Florence, 1970). This is a magnificent series of aerial photographs of ancient sites in Sicily and Italy.

See further Addenda on p. 529.

ABBREVIATIONS

Kromayer-Veith,   J. Kromayer and G. Veith, *Antike Schlachtfelder*
Schlachtfelder   (1903–31)
Kromayer-Veith,   J. Kromayer and G. Veith *Schlachten-Atlas*
Atlas   *zur antiken Kriegsgeschichte*, Römische
   Abteilung (1922)

Latte, *Röm. Relig.*   K. Latte, *Römische Religionsgeschichte* (1960)
Lewis-Reinhold,   N. Lewis and M. Reinhold, *Roman Civilisation*
Rn. Civ.   (1951–5)
MEFR   *Mélanges d'archéologie et d'histoire*
   de l'École française de Rome

Momigliano, *Secondo,*   A. Momigliano, *Secondo, Terzo, Quarto, Quinto*
Terzo, Quarto,   *Contributo alla storia degli*
Quinto, Contrib.   *studi classici* (1966–)
Mommsen, *Staatsr.*   T. Mommsen, *Römisches Staatsrecht* (1887–8)
Münzer, *Röm.*   F. Münzer, *Römische Adelsparteien und*
Adelsparteien   *Adelsfamilien* (1920)
Nash, *Pict. Dict.*   E. Nash, *Pictorial Dictionary of Ancient*
Anc. Rome   *Rome* (1961–2)
Num. Chron.   *Numismatic Chronicle*
Ogilvie, *Livy*   R. M. Ogilvie, *Commentary on Livy, Books*
   i–v (1965)
Ogilvie, *Early Rome*   R. M. Ogilvie, *Early Rome and the Etruscans* (1976)
OGIS   W. Dittenberger, *Orientis Graeci Inscriptiones*
   Selectae (1903–5)
PBSR   *Papers of the British School at Rome*
Par. Pass.   *La Parola del Passato*
PW   Pauly Wissowa, *Real-Encyclopaedie der Klassischen*
   Altertumswissenschaft (1893–)
Proc. Cambr. Phil. Soc.   *Proceedings of the Cambridge Philological Society*
RA   *Revue archéologique*
Riccobono, *Fontes*   S. Riccobono, *Fontes Iuris Romani Ante-*
   Justiniani, i (1941)
Riv. Fil.   *Rivista di Filologia*
Röm. Mitt.   *Mitteilungen des deutschen archäologischen*
   Instituts, Römische Abteilung
Sherwin-White,   A. N. Sherwin-White, *The Roman Citizenship*
Rom. Cit.   edn 2 (1973)
St. Etr.   *Studi Etruschi*
TAPA   *Transactions of the American Philological Association*
Walbank,   F. W. Walbank, *A Historical Commentary on*
Polybius   *Polybius* (1957–79)

NOTES

CHAPTER 1 THE LAND AND ITS PEOPLES

1. ITALY. In general see M. Cary, *The Geographic Background of Greek and Roman History* (1947). In detail see H. Nissen, *Italische Landeskunde*, 2 vols (1883, 1902).

2. EARLY MAN. In general, see A. M. Radmilli, *Piccola guida della preistoria Italiana*[2] (1974), an excellent analytical account from Palaeolithic down to Villanovan times. Also a general survey by J. Whatmough, *The Foundations of Roman Italy* (1937). For more detail see *Popoli e civiltà dell'Italia antica*, 8 vols, ed. M. Pallottino *et al.* (1974). Two recent studies in English are L. Barfield, *Northern Italy before Rome* (1971) and D. H. Trump, *Central and Southern Italy before Rome* (1966). An older work is T. E. Peet, *The Stone and Bronze Ages in Italy* (1909). G. Daniel and J. D. Evans (*CAH*, II, 2 (1971), ch. xxxvii) provide a survey of conditions in western Mediterranean countries, while J. Heurgon (*The Rise of Rome* (1973), ch. i) sets the Mediterranean scene for Rome's emergence.

3. NEOLITHIC ITALY. See chs iii of the books by Barfield and Trump, and *Popoli*, I, ii, cited in previous note. For the Neolithic settlement in Apulia see J. Bradford and P. R. Williams-Hunt, *Antiquity*, 1946, 191 ff.; 1950, 84 ff; also R. Whitehouse, *Proc. Prehist. Soc.*, xl, 1974, 203 ff.

4. COPPER AND BRONZE AGES. See R. Peroni, *L'antica età del bronzo* (1971), and the books cited above, with detailed bibliographies: Barfield, Trump and *Popoli*, I, ii.

5. BELL BEAKERS IN ITALY. See D. Ridgway, *Antiquity*, 1972, 52.

6. APENNINE CULTURE. See Trump, op. cit., 107 ff. and S. M. Puglisi, *La civiltà apenninica* (1959). On transhumance as an economic stimulus in promoting the interchange of goods in *early* Italy (which declined with the later growth of the road system) see J. E. Skydsgaard, *Analecta Romana Instituti Danici*, vii, 1974, 7 ff. On the comparative rarity of bronze in the Apennine culture see G. Barker, 'The first metallury in Italy', *Bollettino di Palentologia Italiana*, vol. 80, 1971, 183 ff. Excavation of an Apennine settlement (*c.* 1600–800 BC) at Luni, 50 miles north of Rome, which included the discovery of five Mycenaean sherds, has thrown much light on the development of this culture: see C. E. Östenberg, *Luni sul Mignone* (1967).

7. MYCENAEANS IN THE WEST.   See Lord William Taylour, *Mycenaean Pottery in Italy* (1958). Metapontum: Strabo, 264; G. Pugliese Carratelli, *Par. Pass.*, 1958, 205 ff., *Atti del I congr. di studi sulla Magra Grecia* (Naples, 1962), 137 ff. On Luni see Östenberg, op. cit., n. 6 above Cf. also note 18 below.

8. AUSONIAN CULTURE. LIPARI.   See Diodorus v, 7. L. Bernabò Brea, *Sicily before the Greeks*, edn 2 (1966). D. H. Trump, *Central and Southern Italy before Rome* (1966), 133 f., 142 f., unlike Brea, would associate Diodorus' Ausonians with the later period.

9 VILLANOVAN CULTURE.   See n. 2 above and D. Randall-MacIver, *Villanovans and Early Etruscans* (1924), *The Iron Age in Italy* (1927); *Civiltà del Ferro* (Bologna, 1960); L. Barfield, *Northern Italy* (1971). M. Pallottino (e.g. *The Etruscans* (1975), 37 ff.) objects to the use of such phrases as 'Terramara folk' or 'Villanovans', whom he considers to be archaeological inventions or modern myths, since these terms really represent cultural areas and not ethnic units. However, if they are understood as groups of people sharing a similar culture (and after all culture cannot exist unless embodied in a 'folk') and not as monolithic ethnic blocks, then perhaps no great harm comes from using such convenient modern labels.

10. URNFIELDS.   See H. Müller-Karpe, *Beiträge zur Chronologie der Urnenfelderzeit, nordlich und sudlich der Alpen* (1959).

11. EARLY VEII. See J. B. Ward-Perkins, *PBSR*, 1961.

12. SALERNO DISTRICT.   See P. Sestieri, *St. Etr.*, 1960, 73 ff., E. Lepore, *Par. Pass.*, 1964, 144 ff., B. D. Agostino, *St. Etr.*, 1965, 671 ff., M. Napoli, id., 661 ff., J. de la Genière, *Recherches . . . Sala Consilina* (Naples, 1968), *MEFR*, 1970, 571 ff. G. B. Modesti (ed.), *Seconda Mostra della preistoria e' della protostoria nel Saliternita* (Salerno, 1974) describes recent finds.

13. SITULAE.   See O. H. Frey, *Die Entstehung der Situlenkunst* (1969).

14. THE ITALIC LANGUAGES.   For a general survey of the problems see E. Pulgram, *The Tongues of Italy* (1958), L. R. Palmer, *The Latin Language* (1954), G. Devoto, *Gli antichi Italici*, edn 3 (1968). For the material see R. S. Conway, *The Italic Dialects* (1897), E. Vetter, *Handbuch der italischen Dialekte* (1953), A. Ernout, *Le dialect ombrien* (1961), J. W. Poultney, *The Iguvine Tablets* (1959). On Indo-European in general see R. A. Crossland, *CAH*, I, ii (1971), ch. xxvii, G. Devoto, *Origini indeuropee* (1961).

15. OSCAN AND UMBRIAN.   It may be of interest to quote examples. From an Oscan inscription on a boundary stone between Nola and Abella in Campania, regarding a temple of Hercules : '*ait pust feihuis pus fisnam amfret, eisei terei nep abellanus nep nuvlanus pidum tribaramattins*' = '*post muros autem qui fanum circumeunt, in illa terra neve Abellani neve Nolani quidquam aedificaverint*' = 'but regarding the walls that surround the temple, on that ground no man from Abella or Nola is to build anything.' Umbrian is represented by the inscription from Iguvium (Gubbio) containing the liturgy of a sacred brotherhood: thus, e.g. '*vitlu vufru pure heries facu, eruhu ticlu seste, urfeta manuve habetu. estu iuku habetu: iupater sace, teje estu vitlu vufru sestu*' = '*vitulum votivum cum voles facere, illa dedicatione sistito Iovi patri. Cum sistis, orbitam in manu habeto.*'

Istum sermonem habeto: "*Iuppiter sancte, tibi istum vitulum votivum sisto*"'
= 'when you wish to sacrifice a calf as a votive offering, let it be consecrated
in that dedication to father Jupiter. When you consecrate it, hold a round
cake in your hand. Use these words : "Holy Jupiter, to you I consecrate this
calf as a votive offering".'

16. VER SACRUM.   See Festus, 150, 424, 519 L; Dion. Hal. i, 16; Livy, xxii, 10,
xxxiii, 44, xxxiv, 44. J. Heurgon, *Trois Études sur le Ver Sacrum* (1957).

17. AUTOCHTHONOUS VILLANOVANS AND LANGUAGE.   M. Pallottino believes
that there was no basic ethnic change among the Villanovans: his views are
summarized in *The Etruscans* (1975), 80 f. He also believes (op. cit. 49 ff.,
58 ff.) that waves of Indo-European dialects reached Italy from the east
across the Adriatic and pushed earlier languages (Ligurian and Tyrrhenian)
to the north and west.The first proto-Latin wave arrived before *c.* 2000 BC and
was later pushed westwards by the subsequent wave of Umbro-Sabellian
dialects which established themselves within 'Apennine' southern-central
Bronze Age Italy. A third, Illyrian, wave got no further than the east coast.

18. CONTINUING GREEK TRADE?   See F. G. Lo Porto, *Bollettino d'Arte* (1964),
67 ff., on the excavation of the acropolis at Porto Saturo, which may be
identified with Satyrion where the Spartan leader of the colony to Tarentum
landed in the late eighth century. Iapygian protogeometric and geometric
pottery and other evidence suggest continued occupation, while Strabo (vi,
3, 2), based on Antiochus of Syracuse (the fifth-century historian of Sicily and
Italy), states that the Spartan leader was welcomed by the barbarians and
Cretans living there: this may reflect a memory of Greeks surviving at
Tarentum.

19. PHOENICIAN COLONIZATION.   The general importance of the Phoenicians
has been overrated at some times (e.g. during the last century) and
underrated at others. The early dates which tradition assigned to some
colonies (e.g. *c.* 1100 BC to Lixus, Gades and Carthage) must be abandoned
(though the alternative date of 814 for Carthage, which Timaeus derived
from Tyrian documents, may be only one or at most two generations too
early). A few Phoenician traders may have ventured into the west between
1100 and 900, but no large *settlements* are likely to have been founded.
Archaeology suggests settlements at Motya in western Sicily in the eighth
century, Utica possibly in the eighth, Sardinia in the eighth (though a Punic
inscription at Nora seems to belong to the ninth), Lixus in the sixth (at
Mogador Greek pottery of *c.* 650 BC has been found, indicating the
Phoenicians as middlemen, and trade rather than settlement). In Spain the
earliest surviving evidence at Gades is late sixth century, but two interesting
settlements in the area of Malaga have recently been excavated which are
considerably older and go back to the late eighth century: Torre del Mar
(probably Maenake) and Almunecar (ancient Sexi). See in general D. Harden,
The Phoenicians (1962), S. Moscati, *The World of the Phoenicians* (1968), J.
Heurgon, *Rise of R.*, 57 ff., with bibliographies, 287 ff. In particular, V.
Tusa, *Mozia*, 1–vi (1964–72); B. S. J. Isserlin, *Antiquity*, 1971, 178 ff.; A.

Jodin, *Mogador* (Rabat, 1966); M. Pellicar, *Madrider Mitteil*, 1963, 9 ff.; *Arch. Anzeiger*, 1964, 476 ff. For possible Phoenician pottery in Italy at the time of the first Greek colonization see M. B. Ingrassia, *Magna Graecia*, xiii, 5–6, 1978, 12 ff.

There is now evidence of Phoenician residents at Pithecusae (Ischia): a child burial in a local amphora with an Aramaic inscription, and a Phoenician inscription on a local vase: see M. W. Frederiksen, *Arch. Reports*, 1976–7, 44.

20. PHOENICIANS AT ROME? See A. Piganiol, *Hommages à A. Grenier* (1962), 1261 ff., D. Van Berchem, *Rendiconti della Pontificia Accad. di Archeologia*, 32 (1959–60), 61 ff. (cf. *Syria*, 1967, 73 ff., 307 ff.), and, for an extreme view, R. Rebuffat, *MEFR*, 1966, 7 ff. J. Heurgon, *JRS* 1966, 2 f.; *Rise of R.*, 73 ff. is somewhat more cautious: 'all this still remains very obscure'.

The cult of Hercules (Greek Heracles) spread widely in Italy from the south to Etruria (cf. J. Bayet, *Les origines de l'Hercule romaine*, 1926) though it is impossible to define the precise point from which it reached Rome (so judges K. Latte, *Röm. Relig.*, 214). The cult at the Ara Maxima was traditionally established by Hercules himself or by Evander; it was in private hands (members of the *gentes* Potitii and Pinarii) until taken over by the state in 312 BC. It is true that Hercules was popular with merchants, and was later equated with Melqart, while the ritual had some oriental features (e.g. a tithe), though the idea that 'Potitii' originally meant 'those possessed by the gold' (cf. Katochoi) is very doubtful (possession is not a feature of early Roman religion). True also, the recent discovery of the Punic dedication to Astarte at Pyrgi and that of the Greek Sostratus to Hera at Gravisca (pp. 31; 23) makes foreign dedications in Etruria or Rome more probable. But a Phoenician settlement so far inland as Rome is out of character, and even if the cult was established by easterners it might have been the work of Carthaginians rather than Phoenicians, i.e. at a later date than that originally put at 600 BC or earlier. However, the theory must remain a pure hypothesis as yet, since no decisive evidence has been found to support it.

21. GREEK COLONIZATION. See T. J. Dunbabin, *The Western Greeks* (1948), A. G. Woodhead, *The Greeks in the West* (1962), J. Boardman, *The Greeks Overseas* (1964), 175 ff. The vexed questions of basic causes, priority and chronology belong primarily to Greek rather than to Roman history and so need not be discussed here. On the recent important excavations at Pithecusae see D. Ridgway, 'The first Western Greeks: Campanian Coasts and Southern Etruria', in *Greeks, Celts and Romans*, ed. C. F. C. Hawkes (1973), 5 ff., with full bibliography, p. 30 ff. See also G. Buchner, *Arch. Reports for 1970–1*, 63 ff. and Buchner and Ridgway, *Pithekoussai*, I (forthcoming).

22. HOMERIC REFERENCES. 'Nestor's Cup': see *Iliad* xi, 632 ff.; for the inscription see R. Meiggs and D. Lewis, *A Selection of Greek Historical Inscriptions* (1969), n.l. Tataie inscription: see A. G. Woodhead, op.cit., n. 21, p. 36 with illustration. Shipwreck: this shows an upturned ship and the crew in the water with fish; see J. S. Morrison and R. T. Williams, *Greek*

Oared Ships (1968), 34 and pl. 60. On the legends of Odysseus in the west see E. D. Phillips, *JHS*, 1953, 53 ff. (cf. for a briefer statement J. B. Bury and R. Meiggs, *A History of Greece* (1975), 74).

23. GRAVISCA AND SOSTRATUS. Sostratus: Herodotus. iv, 152. If not actually Herodotus' man, this Sostratus will have been a member of the same family. Excavations and the inscription: D. Ridgway, *Arch. Reports for 1973–4*, 49 ff., A. W. Johnston, *Par. Pass.*, 1972, 416 ff. and F. D. Harvey, ibid., 1976, 206 ff., who dates the inscription to the latter part of the sixth century and points out that an Aeginetan selling Attic pottery in Etruria thus provides evidence for the existence of an 'international merchant class' as early as the sixth century. See also M. Torelli, *Par. Pass.*, xxxii, 1977, 398 ff. The large quantities of Greek pottery include dedications to Hera (12), Aphrodite (2) and Demeter (1), and there is evidence for a cult of the Etruscan deities: Uni (an inscription on a silver bowl) and Turan (four inscribed Etruscan sherds).

24. DEMARATUS. Pliny, *NH*, xxxv, 16, 152; Strabo, v, 219. A. Blakeway, *JRS*, 1935, 129 ff. showed the reliability of the archaeological background: Corinthian pottery dominated the Etruscan market in the first three quarters of the seventh century, and there is evidence that Greek artists were producing vases in Etruria. But cf. G. Vallet, *Rhégion et Zancle* (1958), 185.

   Pliny says that Demaratus was accompanied by three workers in clay, who introduced modelling to Italy: one was named Diopus. This name has not been attested elsewhere until the recent discovery at Camerina in Sicily of a mid-sixth-century antefix, inscribed with the name of Diopus. This raises many problems, but at very least strengthens the probability of the historical existence of Demaratus. See M. W. Frederiksen, *Arch. Reports*, 1976–7, 71.

25. CELTS. In general see T. G. E. Powell, *The Celts* (1958); A. Grenier, *La Gaule celtique* (1945), *Les Gaulois* (1945); H. Hubert, *Les Celtes et l'expansion celtique* (1932), *Les Celtes depuis l'époque de la Tène* edn 2, (1950). Cf. J. Heurgon, *Rise of R.*, 34 ff., with modern bibliography, 277 ff.

26. THE ETRUSCANS. Two old books are still valuable: K. O. Müller and W. Deecke, *Die Etrusker*, 2 vols (1877, reprinted 1965) for source material, and G. Dennis, *The Cities and Cemeteries of Etruria* edn 3, 2 vols (1883) for the geographical background. General surveys include M. Pallottino, *The Etruscans* (1975); D. Strong, *The Early Etruscans* (1969); H. H. Scullard, *The Etruscan Cities and Rome* (1967), = *Le città etrusche e Roma* edn 2 (1977) with updated bibliography); L. Banti, *The Etruscan Cities and their Culture* (1973); J. Heurgon, *Daily Life of the Etruscans* (1964); E. Richardson, *The Etruscans: their Art and Civilization* (1964); J. Heurgon, *Rise of R.*, 40 ff., 280 ff.

27. ETRUSCAN ORIGINS. P. Ducati, *Le problème étrusque* (1938) surveys various views up to that date. M. Pallottino, *L'Origine degli Etruschi* (1947) examines the evidence in detail. Cf. J. B. Ward-Perkins, *Harvard Studies in Classical Philology*, 1959, 1 ff.; A. Toynbee, *Hannibal's Legacy* (1965), vol. i, 356 ff.,

L. A. Foresti, *Tesi, ipotesi e considerazioni sull' origine degli Etruschi* (1974). Also the works cited in n. 26 above.

The two chief views are expressed by Herodotus, i, 94 (from Lydia) and Dionysius of Halicarnassus, i, 26–39 (autochthonous). Another view, that the Etruscans arrived in Italy overland from the North over the Brenner Pass, has now been generally abandoned (it rests on, for example, some similarities between Etruscan and the Raetian language of the Central Alps). A fifth-century historian, Xanthus of Lydia, apparently did not mention any Lydian settlement in Italy or a Lydian ruler named Tyrrhenus, but we know little of his work, and he does not appear to have been very reliable; cf. H. H. Scullard in E. Badian (ed.), *Ancient Society and Institutions* (1966), 225 ff. M. Pallottino is the most weighty exponent of the theory of formation on Italian soil. For some medical approaches to the problem see G. E. W. Wolstenholme and C. M. O'Connor (eds), *Ciba Foundation Symposium on Medical Biology and Etruscan Origins* (1959). It is scarcely possible to discuss details of the problem here.

28. ETRUSCANS AND NORMANS. If the Etruscans arrived as a small conquering alien aristocracy, a parallel may be seen (as suggested by J. B. Ward-Perkins and others) with the Norman invasions of southern Italy and England. The parallel of course cannot be pressed in detail (thus the Anglo-Saxon state in pre-conquest England was highly organized, unlike the political structure of the Villanovans in Etruria), but the achievement of the Normans suggests the kind of development that *might* have taken place in Etruria. C. H. Hoskins (*Normans in European History* (1915), 247) wrote that the Normans 'did their work pre-eminently not as a people apart, but as a group of leaders and energizers, the little leaven that leaveneth the whole lump. Wherever they went, they show a marvellous power of initiative and assimilation: if the initiative is more evident in England, the assimilation is more manifest in Sicily.' Again, R. H. C. Davis (*The Normans and their Myth* (1976), 103) writes: 'At Hastings . . . apparently as the result of one day's fighting England received a new royal dynasty, a new aristocracy, a virtually new Church, a new art, a new architecture, and a new language.' Invasion, followed by intermingling and speedy fusion of two stocks: it happened in England, but had it happened also in Etruria?

29. ETRUSCAN CITIES AND ARCHITECTURE. See the books quoted in n. 26 above, especially L. Banti (287–300 for detailed bibliography) and H. H. Scullard; also A. Boethius and J. B. Ward-Perkins, *Etruscan and Roman Architecture* (1970). It is not possible here to give a detailed bibliography of the individual cities, but two sites may be mentioned: for Tarquinii see H. Hencken, *Tarquinia, Villanovans and Early Etruscans*, 2 vols (1968) and a shorter book, *Tarquinia and Etruscan Origins* (1968): for Veii, J. B. Ward-Perkins *PBSR*, 1961.

The major Etruscan cities controlled large areas of land beyond their city walls: thus the ager Tarquiniensis included several large settlements or towns at Norchia, Musana, Tuscania, Bieda and Visentum. Some of these smaller towns have been revealed only by field work and archaeology, as San Giovenale inland from Tarquinii, or Luni nearby (C. E. Östenberg, *Luni sul Mignone* (1967), Acquarossa near Viterbo, or at Poggio Civitate near Murlo and Siena (Cf. D. Ridgway, *Arch. Reports for 1973–4*, 56 f; this excavation is throwing much light on varied aspects of Etruscan life of the seventh and sixth centuries.)

30. ETRUSCAN ART.   See P. J. Riis, *An Introduction to Etruscan Art* (1953). Two finely illustrated books are R. Bloch, *Etruscan Art* (1959) and M. Moretti and G. Maetzke, *The Art of the Etruscans* (1970). Cf. also M. Santangelo, *Musei e Monumenti Etruschi* (1960). Two small but useful books on painting are A. Stenico, *Roman and Etruscan Painting* (1963) and R. Bartoccini, *The Etruscan Paintings of Tarquinia* (Milan, 1959). Bibliography in L. Banti, *The Etruscan Cities* (1973), 281–6. L. Bonfante, *Etruscan Dress* (1976).

31. ETRUSCAN RELIGION. C. Clemen, *Die Religion der Etrusker* (1936); L. Ross Taylor, *Local Cults in Etruria* (1923); C. O. Thulin, *Die Etruskische Disciplin*, 3 vols (1906–9); F. de Ruyt, *Charun, démon étrusque de la mort* (1934); A. J. Pfiffig, *Religio Etrusca* (Graz, 1975).

32. ETRUSCAN LANGUAGE.   The majority of inscriptions have been published in *Corpus Inscriptionum Etruscarum* (1893-, still in progress). New material appears in the annual periodical, *Studi Etruschi*. M. Pallottino, *Testimonia Linguae Etruscae*, edn 2 (1968) provides a collection of over 900 inscriptions. For general treatment see M. Pallottino, *The Etruscans* (1974), chs 10–12; R. A. Staccioli, *La lingua degli Etruschi*, edn 2 (1969).

The Pyrgi inscriptions were written on sheets of gold leaf, two in Etruscan and one in Punic; they were found between two early fifth-century temples. They record a dedication by Thefarie Valianas, ruler of Caere, to Uni-Astarte, a Phoenician goddess, and belong to *c.* 500 BC. Their linguistic value is great, even though they do not provide a strictly bilingual inscription since their content is only similar and not exactly the same. The dedication of a shrine by an Etruscan to a Punic deity suggests very close relations between Caere and Carthage, and probably the existence at Pyrgi of a small settlement of Carthaginian merchants. Of the large bibliography which has grown up since the discovery of the tablets in 1964 reference may be made to J. Heurgon, *JRS*, 1966, 1 ff.; J. Ferron, *Aufstieg NRW*, I, i, 189 ff.

33. ETRUSCAN LITERATURE.   See especially J. Heurgon, *Daily Life of the Etruscans* (1964), ch. viii, who emphasizes its volume, and W. V. Harris, *Rome in Etruria and Umbria* (1971), ch. i, who circumscribes its extent. On Claudius the Etruscologist see A. D. Momigliano, *Claudius*, edn 2 (1961), 11 ff., 85 f., 128. The François tomb painting at Vulci: Momigliano, op. cit., 85; for the date 340–310 see M. Cristofani, *Dialoghi di Archeologia* 1967, 186 ff. Elogia: see M. Torelli, *Elogia Tarquiniensia* (1975) and the discussion of this by T. J. Cornell, *JRS*, 1978, 167 ff. On Etruscan historiography see Cornell, *Annali di Pisa*, iii, 6 (1976), 432 ff.

34. ETRUSCAN MAGISTRATES.   A model iron axe with *fasces* of *c.* 600 BC was

found in a tomb at Vetulonia, the very place where this symbol of power was said by the ancient sources to have been invented. When the twelve cities of the Etruscan League united for a common enterprise, the twelve rulers of the cities each carried one axe; this was probably the origin of the twelve *fasces* carried by lictors in front of the kings and consuls of Rome. Funerary sarcophagi from southern Etruria and alabaster urns from Volterrae depict processions of Etruscan magistrates, generally riding in chariots, with attendants carrying *fasces*. See R. Lambrechts, *Essai sur les magistratures des républiques étrusques* (1959), with illustrations. On the constitutional aspect of the magistrates see J. Heurgon, *Historia*, 1957, 63 ff.

35. THE ETRUSCAN LEAGUE. Its strength or weakness, its composition and functions and other problems are briefly discussed by Scullard, *Etruscan Cities*, 231–6.

36. ETRUSCAN SOCIAL STRUCTURE. See J. Heurgon, *Latomus*, 1959, 3 ff.; S. Mazzarino, *Historia*, 1957, 98 ff.; Scullard, *Etruscan Cities*, 236 ff. Military reforms: A. M. Snodgrass, *Arms and Armour of the Greeks* (1967), ch. iii.

37. ETRUSCAN EXPANSION. Cato, *Origines*, ii frg. 62P. For more detail and references to the ancient and modern authorities on Etruscan expansion in Italy see Scullard, *The Etruscan Cities and Rome* (1967), ch. vi (in the south) and vii (in the north). On Etruscan influence in northern Italy see L. Bonfante, *Archaeological News*, v, 1976, 93 ff.

38. ALALIA. See Herodotus, i, 163 ff.; Diodorus, v, 13; Strabo, v, 2, 7.

39. ETRUSCO-CARTHAGINIAN TREATY. See Aristotle, *Politics*, iii, 9; 1280a35.

40. ARISTODEMUS AND CUMAE. The history of Aristodemus is recorded by Dionysius of Halicarnassus, vii, 2–12 (cf. Jacoby, *FGrH*, no. 576). Whatever other elements have gone into this story, these include a local chronicle of Cumae which may be regarded as essentially reliable. This has wider implications, since it provides an account which is independent of the Roman tradition and bears testimony to the general historical background of events in Roman history connected with the fall of the monarchy there, with Porsenna and the Latins before the end of the sixth century.

The battle of Cumae was celebrated in one of Pindar's Odes to Hiero, and by the spoils that Hiero sent to Olympia: these include two surviving Etruscan helmets, inscribed: 'Hiero and the Syracusans (dedicated) to Zeus the Etruscan spoils won at Cumae.' See Pindar, *Pythian*, i, 71 and (for the helmets) Meiggs and Lewis, *Greek Historical Inscriptions*, vol. 1 (1969), n. 29, p. 62.

41. ETRUSCANS IN NORTHERN ITALY. In general see G. A. Mansuelli and R. Scarani, *L'Emilia prima dei Romani* (1961), especially ch. vi; *Mostra dell'Etruria Padana*, edn 2, 2 vols (1961). An introduction to Marzabotto is provided by G. A. Mansuelli, *Marzabotto. Guida alla Città* (Bologna, 1966). On Spina see S. Aurigemma, *Il Museo naz. arch. di Spina in Ferrara* (1957); P. E. Arias and N. Alfieri, *Spina* (1958).

42. LATIUM. Theophrastus, *Hist. Plant.*, v, 8, 3. See T. Ashby, *The Roman Campagna in Classical Times* (1927, reprinted 1970); B. Tilley, *Vergil's Latium*

(1947). Traces of the primitive forests survive in the Forests of Castel Porziano and of Circeo, while Romans of later days could be reminded of the numerous lakes, lagoons and ponds of early times when they looked at the Lacus Curtius in the Forum or the low-lying ground occupied by the Circus Maximus or the Colosseum.

43. LATIAL CULTURE. The archaeological evidence is published in a massive corpus by P. G. Gierow, *The Iron Age Culture of Latium*, I (1966), II, i (1964). See also the catalogue of the exhibition in Rome in 1976 entitled *Civiltà del Lazio primitivo*, published under the direction of G. Colonna. For comparison with southern Villanovan culture see Gierow, I, 483 ff. It is not certain whether the hut-urn type of ossuary spread from southern Etruria to Latium or vice versa. Gierow supposes that Latial culture arrived in two waves, first to the Alban Hills, Rome, Ardea, and perhaps Antium and Tibur, the second to Satricum and Praeneste. The early evidence from the Alban group corresponds to that of the Palatine group at Rome, while the south Latin group is linked to the Esquiline settlement. Those who argue for a long chronology (from the tenth century) include H. Müller-Karpe and R. Peroni, while E. Gjerstad and P. G. Gierow are among the proponents of the short chronology (starting *c.* 800).

44. DECIMA AND OTHER SETTLEMENTS. For these Latin cities and recent excavations see *Civiltà del Lazio primitivo* (1976). Decima is most probably to be identified with Politorium, on which see Livy, i, 33, 1, Cato, frg. 54P and Pliny, *NH*, iii, 68–9. Pliny says that it had long since disappeared without trace (*sine vestigiis*) and that it had been a member of the Alban League. For the excavations see *Civiltà del Lazio primitivo* (1976), 252 ff., D. Ridgway, *Arch. Reports 1973–4*, 45 f. and *Par. Pass.* xxxii, 1977, 241 ff. Ficana: *Civiltà*, 250, Ridgway, 46, *Par. Pass.*, 1977, 315 ff. La Rustica and Osteria dell'Osa: *Civiltà*, 153 ff. and 166 ff. Other sites (e.g. Alban hills, Rome, Gabii, Tivoli, Praeneste, Lavinium, Ardea, Anzio, and Satricum) are discussed in *Civiltà. Arch. Laziale*, i, 1978, 35 ff. (Ficana), 42 ff. (Gabà), 65 ff. (Satricum). On Gabii see F. Castagnoli, *Comptes Rendus*, 1977, 468 ff.: a sanctuary (to Juno?) existed from the seventh to the second century, its origin going back to the period of Gabii's independence. On Decima see now *Archaeologia laziale*, 1979.

45. PRISCI LATINI. See Livy, i, 38, 4; Dion. Hal. iii, 49–50; Pliny, *NH*, iii, 68–9. Dionysius reckons the number of communities sharing in the festival of Jupiter Latiaris in the sixth century at forty-seven. A. N. Sherwin-White, *Rom. Cit.*, 9, equates Livy's Prisci Latini with those living between the Anio and Tiber. See also A. Bernardi, *Athenaeum*, 1964, 223 ff.

46. THE LATIN LEAGUE. See A. N. Sherwin-White, *Rom. Cit.*, 11 ff.

47. ETRUSCAN LATIUM. See briefly H. H. Scullard, *The Etruscan Cities* (1967), 170–7. Praeneste in the fourth century had eight tributaries among the lesser Latin communities: Livy, vi, 29, 6. On the Manios inscription (*Manios med fhefhaked Numasioi*) see *Civiltà del Lazio primitivo*, 376 ff.; A. E. Gordon, *The Inscribed Fibula Praenestina. Problems of Authenticity* (University of California Publications: Classical Studies, vol. 16, 1975); D. Ridgway, 'Manios

Faked?', *BICS*, 24, 1977, 17 ff., who traces the ambiguous history of the fibula in modern times and concludes : 'I see the question of authenticity in terms of precisely a "50–50" chance'.

48. ALTARS AT LAVINIUM. The two earliest of the thirteen (8th and 13th) probably date to the sixth century. 'The full complement of twelve altars was reached in the fifth-fourth centuries, by which time the thirteenth had been abandoned and the eighth reconstructed': D. Ridgway, *Arch. Reports 1967–8*, 34 (fig. 5 provides a photograph). See also C. F. Giuliani and P. Sommella, *Par. Pass.*, xxxii, 1977, 356 ff; F. Castagnoli, *Comptes Rendues*, 1977, 464 ff. For the inscription ('*Castorei Podluqveiqve Qvrois*) see S. Weinstock, *JRS*, 1960, 112 ff.

CHAPTER II REGAL ROME

1. THE TIBER. See J. le Gall, *Le Tibre* (1953) L. A. Holland, *TAPA*, 1949, 281 ff. Although the site of Rome offered the best crossing-place, the Etruscans could cross the river a little further north at Fidenae (near Veii) and Lucus Feroniae and thus reach Campania via Praeneste and the route of the later Via Latina.

2. THE ARCHAEOLOGICAL MATERIAL. This is published in the monumental work of E. Gjerstad, *Early Rome*, vols i–vi (1953–73): vol. iv is partly resumptive of vols i–iii; vol. v deals with the literary evidence and vol. vi provides an historical survey. As a corpus of material it is unsurpassed, but not all Gjerstad's interpretations of it have won general acceptance (p. 465 n. 49). For an assessment of the problems involved see A. Momigliano, *JRS*, 1963, 95 ff. (= *Terzo Contrib.*, 545 ff). For discussion of many other aspects of early Rome see *Terzo Contrib.*, 545–695, *Quarto*, 273–499 and *Quinto*, 293–331. See also G. Poma, *Gli Studi recenti sull' origine della repubblica romana, 1963–73* (Bologna, 1974) for various aspects of recent archaeological work see several writers in *Per. Pass.*, xxxii, 1977. A general sketch is given by R. Bloch, *The Origins of Rome* (1960), while much of great value is contained in Ogilvie, *Livy*.

3. THE ARGEI. See Varro, *De Lingua Latina*, v, 45–54. They were straw puppets which were thrown into the Tiber on 14 May as a purificatory sacrifice, *possibly* being surrogates for human victims of earlier times.

4. SEPTIMONTIUM. The derivation from Saeptimontium is proposed by L. A. Holland, *TAPA* (1953), 16 ff. One problem is that the sources give 8 not 7 hills, but this can be explained, e.g. by eliminating Subura because it was a valley or a gloss on Caelius, or Germalus might be rejected and Palatium applied to the whole hill. It is noteworthy that Septimontium belonged to a group of *sacra publica* named *pro montibus* and that these seven hills were called *montes*, whereas the excluded Quirinal and Viminal were *colles*. R. Gelsomino, *Varrone e i sette colli di Roma* (1975), argues that, although the festival was old, it was not connected with *septem* until this derivation was propounded by Varro in 52–51 BC.

5. JANUS. L. A. Holland, *Janus and the Bridge* (1961) has argued that the god

Janus was a *numen* attached to water-crossings, *Janus* meaning gateway. In later times the gateways and temples of Janus were opened in war and closed in peace: Mrs Holland explains that originally the Janus was opened by removing the bridge (*Ianus invius*) when war threatened, and closed (*Ianus pervius*) by replacing the bridge in times of peace. Her book is full of ingenious ideas and her thesis has been accepted by e.g. E. Gjerstad (cf. *JRS*, 1963, 229 f.) and (apparently) J. Heurgon (*Rise of R.*, 32). A major obstacle is that the ancient sources do not seem to connect Janus with water-crossings.

6. FOUNDATION LEGENDS.   See especially Dion. Hal., i, 72–4; Livy, i, 1–7 (with Ogilvie's *Livy*). A full up-to-date bibliography of the large modern literature on this topic is given by T. J. Cornell, *Proc. Cambr. Phil. Soc.*, 1976, 1, n. 2 (note also two recent discussions: H. Strasburger, '*Zur Sage von der Gründung Roms*', *Sb. Heidelb. Akad.*, 1968, and G. K. Galinsky, *Aeneas, Sicily and Rome* (1969)). Cornell's article, 'Aeneas and the Twins: the Development of the Roman Foundation Legend' (op. cit. *supra*) is a valuable and thoroughly documented discussion. He argues that the story of Romulus and Remus was the original authentic Roman version of the founding of the city. He counters the arguments of Strasburger who believes in a late literary origin for the twins (early third century) and that the story was invented as anti-Roman propaganda by an unknown Greek author (the story had unsavoury episodes, such as the murder of Remus and the rape of the Sabine women). The evidence is extremely complex, so reference must be made to Cornell's article for further detail. On the myths of early Rome in general see M. Grant, *Roman Myths* (1973).

7. AENEAS IN ETRURIA.   See G. K. Galinsky, op. cit, n. 6, ch. iii; and A. Alföldi, *Early Rome and the Latins* (1965), 287. For recent attempts to lower considerably the date of the Aeneas statuettes in Etruria see M. Torelli, *Roma medio-repubblicana*, 335 f., *Dialoghi di Arch.*, 1973, 339 ff., and for the consequential dating of the whole legend of Aeneas in Italy see T. J. Cornell, *Liverpool Classical Monthly*, 4, April 1977, 75 ff.

8. LAVINIUM AND ALBA LONGA.   See F. Castagnoli (ed.), *Lavinium*, i (1972), ii (forthcoming), *Par. Pass*, xxxii, 1977, 340 ff. Timaeus: Dion. Hal., i, 67; Jacoby, *FGrH* 566 F 59. Inscription to Lar: S. Weinstock, *JRS*, 1960, 114 ff; doubts about the reading have been raised by H. G. Kolbe, *Röm. Mitt.*, 1970, 1 ff. which though countered by M. Guarducci, ibid., 1971, 73 ff., still persist (see Cornell, op. cit *supra*, n. 7). Heroon: Dion. Hal, i, 64; P. Sommella, *Atti pont. accad. rom. arch. Rendiconti*, xliv (1971–2), 47 ff.; *Civiltà del Lazio primitivo* (1976), 305 f., (bibliography in Cornell, op. cit. *supra*, n. 6, p. 14 n. 3; photograph in *Arch. Reports 1973–4*, 47). For some difficulties in accepting the identification with the shrine described by Dionysius and an origin of the cult in the sixth century see Cornell, *Liverpool Cl. Monthly*, April 1977, 79 ff.

Aeneas was linked with Alba Longa as well as with Lavinium. In rivalry, Alba twice unsuccessfully tried to transfer the Penates from Lavinium to itself (Dion. Hal., i, 67), and a Greek mythologer Conon (first century BC) preserved a version that Aeneas had settled in Alba, not Lavinium; in Ennius and Naevius Aeneas may have married the daughter of the king of Alba, not Lavinia. Further, according to legend Aeneas was led by a sow (with thirty piglets, symbolizing the thirty Latin peoples) to the site of Lavinium (so e.g. Timaeus) or alternatively to the site of Alba, which got its name Alba from a *sus alba* (so Fabius Pictor, frg. 4, Peter). Though no archaeological evidence supports the claim that Rome was settled by Alba (as has often been believed), yet Alba may well have exercised some leadership (through the religious league) in Latium before she was destroyed in the mid-seventh century, and as such would be thought to have claims as strong as Lavinium. On Alba's claim to Aeneas see Galinsky, *Aeneas, Sicily and Rome* (1966), 43 ff.; Alföldi, *Early Rome and the Latins*, 271 ff.

9. THE EARLY KINGS AND DUMÉZIL. Attempts to dismiss the early kings as gods or as personifications of the seven hills have been demolished by G. De Sanctis, *SR*, 1, 358 ff. With great ingenuity and in a large number of books G. Dumézil has developed novel ideas about early Roman society, its gods, and kings. These are based on the assumption that, since the Romans shared with Indians and Celts a common Indo-European ancestry, it is legitimate to seek help in these other areas in order to solve problems and obscurities in early Rome. Thus he believes that early Roman society, like early Indian, was divided into three classes : the priests (who included the kings), the warriors, and the producers or farmers, corresponding respectively to religious sovereignty, military strength and fertility. This tripartite division was seen in early Rome in the three tribes of Ramnes (priests), Luceres (warriors) and Tities (producers). In religion Jupiter, Mars and Quirinus were responsible for the three functions, with their corresponding priests (*flamines*). In many legends and myths a 'terrible' type of king (who was also a magician) was contrasted with a more just ruler: in India they are Varuna and Mitra, in Rome they are the gods Jupiter and Fides (or Divus Fidius) and the earthly kings the terrible Romulus and the pious and peaceful Numa. The second, military, function produced Indra, Mars and Tullus Hostilius; the third, fertility, produced Quirinus and Ancus Marcus. Later, Tarquin contrasted with Servius Tullius. It is unnecessary here to list the numerous works in which Dumézil has argued his views, except his synthesis, *Archaic Roman Religion*, 2 vols (1970): these views have had considerable influence especially among French historians of religion, but for rejection see, e.g., H. J. Rose, *JRS*, 1947, 183 ff., or A. Momigliano, *Terzo Contrib.*, 581 ff., who concludes that 'not only is his evidence weak, but his theories are unnecessary'.

For discussion about the legends concerning the kings, and indeed on all aspects down to 390 BC see above all R. M. Ogilvie, *Livy*. This work is indispensable for any study of this period but since reference cannot be made to it at all relevant points, this general direction of the reader's attention to it must be emphasized. See also Ogilvie's shorter synoptic work, *Early Rome and the Etruscans* (1976).

A. Alföldi, *Die Struktur des voretruskischen Römerstaates* (1974) is 'essentially a work of comparative anthropology, not history': so writes R. M. Ogilvie in his review of this book (*Cl. Rev.*, 1976, 240 f.). It tries to discern the society of the Latins while they were still living in a nomadic state when they passed, so it is supposed, from a matriarchy with triadic institutions to a patriarchy with binary institutions: see A. Momigliano, *Rivista Storia Italiana* (1977), 160 ff.

10. SABINE SETTLEMENT. Long ago Mommsen dismissed a supposed early union of some Sabines and Romans as an anticipation of the granting of Roman citizenship to the Sabines in the third century. The most recent exponent of this negative view is J. Poucet: at length in *Recherches sur la légende sabine des origines de Rome* (1967), at medium length in *Aufstieg NRW*, i, i (1972), 48–135, and more briefly in *L'Ant. Class.*, 1971, 129 ff., 293 ff. With Mommsen, Poucet believes the whole story was designed to justify the dual magistracy at Rome; also that the fighting in Rome was based on the capture of the Capitol by the Sabine Appius Herdonius in 460 BC (Livy, iii, 15) and on the battle with the Samnites at Luceria in 294 (if the former of these supposed precedents is possible, the latter is almost certainly to be rejected). For a criticism of Poucet's views (including his assumption about Livy's sources) see R. M. Ogilvie *Cl. Rev.*, 1968, 327 ff. From the historical point of view the important question is not so much the details of the legends but rather whether a vague tradition of a real infusion of Sabines into early Rome is likely to have survived into later times.

11. TARQUINIUS PRISCUS. A tomb of the Tarchna family has been found at Caere, with the Latin equivalent of the name as Tarquitius, which is probably the same as Tarquinius. Thus the Tarquins may have come to Rome from Caere rather than from Tarquinii. See M. Cristofani, *La tomba delle iscrizioni a Cerveteri* (1965), appendix 1. Additional support is given to Priscus' existence by the consideration that Etruscan influence is shown by archaeology to have continued at Rome throughout the sixth century: so why not two Tarquins, as the Romans believed?

12. THE VULCI PAINTING AND MASTARNA. For the painting see F. Messerschmidt, *Nekropolen von Vulci* (1930), A. Momigliano, *Claudius* (1961) 11 ff., 85 f., A. Alföldi, *Early Rome and the Latins* (1965), 220 ff., M. Cristofani, *Dialoghi di Archeologia*, 1967, 186 ff. The emperor Claudius in a speech (the Table of Claudius, discovered at Lyons in 1528: *ILS*, 212, Smallwood, *Documents . . . of Gaius, Claudius and Nero* (1967), 369; cf. Tacitus, *Ann.*, xi, 23 ff.) quotes the Roman tradition that Servius Tullius was the son of Ocresia, a war captive, but prefers the Etruscan version that Servius was the same as Mastarna who came to Rome after his friend and leader Caelius Vibenna had been killed, and was honoured when one of the hills was named the Caelian after him. The Etruscan version is illustrated by the Vulci painting, though not all details are clear. Three other groups in the painting show single combats in which men from Volsinii, Sovana, and (?) Falerii, are being killed by three warriors who presumably came from Vulci (their names, and those of the towns of the vanquished, are painted in). One

important aspect of the painting is that it reveals the existence of Etruscan historical traditions, separate from the Roman: thus Mastarna became known to the Romans only much later, though his discoverer is uncertain: see T. J. Cornell, *Amali di Pisa*, iii, 6 (1976), 432 ff.

There is no need to follow G. De Sanctis (*SR*, I, 375, 446 ff.) who regarded Mastarna as a duplicate of Lars Porsenna (p. 75), or L. Pareti (*St. Etr.*, v, 154 ff.) who carried the argument further by identifying Mastarna with both Porsenna and Servius Tullius, who are considered to be reduplications of one person, as are the two Tarquins whom they succeeded.

Macstarna is the Etruscan form of the Latin word *magister*, and therefore appears to be a title rather than a personal name. That, however, does not necessarily mean that this anonymous hero did not perform the acts attributed to 'Macstarna', while if Claudius was right his name will have been Servius and he may well stand in that part of the sixth century to which tradition assigned Servius. Ogilvie (*Early Rome*, 88), however, is inclined to place him, together with the Vibennae, in the late rather than the earlier sixth century and to regard him as an adventurer who seized the superior magistracy at Rome during the chaos following the fall of the Tarquins.

For the Vibenna inscription from Veii and two others (from Bolsena and Vulci) see M. Pallottino, *St. Etr.*, xii, 455 ff. and the works listed by W. V. Harris, *Rome in Etruria* (1971), 11, n. 7.

A. Alföldi, *Early Rome and the Latins* (1965), ch, v, has put forward the imaginative theory that Rome was in fact ruled by a series of conquering Etruscan kings from Tarquinii, Caere, Vulci, Veii and Clusium. It is perhaps sufficient here to refer to A. Momigliano's review of this book (*JRS*, 1967, 211 ff. = *Quarto Contrib.*, 487 ff.) and on this point to his conclusion that 'the theory . . . seems to me to be without the slightest foundation in our evidence'. For Alföldi's restatement of his theory see *Römische Frühgeschichte* (1976), 168 ff.

13. DIANA'S AVENTINE TEMPLE. The attempt by A. Alföldi (*Early Rome*, 85 ff.) to assign this temple to a date after 500 BC as a mere imitation of the federal sanctuary at Aricia has been rejected by A. Momigliano (*Terzo Contrib.*, 641 ff.) and R. M. Ogilvie (*Livy*, 182 f.). This is only one item in Alföldi's main thesis, namely that Rome in fact gained predominance among the Latin cities only in the fifth century, and that the picture of Rome's earlier leadership which is given by Livy is a deliberate and false invention by the annalist Fabius Pictor which has imposed itself on later writers. For discussion and rejection of this ingenious theory see A. Momigliano, *Quarto Contrib.*, 487 ff, Ogilvie, *Cl. Rev.*, 1966, 94 ff, A. N. Sherwin-White, *Rom. Cit.*, edn 2, 190 ff. and M. Pallottino, *Comptes Rendus*, 1977, 216 ff. Pallottino's article provides an excellent survey of the recent archaeological work which demonstrates the economic and cultural importance of sixth-century Rome and also assesses the historicity and achievements of Servius Tullius. See further below, p. 471 n1.

Granted that the Aventine cult of Diana goes back to Servius and the sixth

century, its temporal relation to the Arician cult remains uncertain.
Momigliano argued that it was the original cult, designed to unite Latium in a
common bond with Rome (thus, e.g., old excavations at Aricia provided
little evidence for cult before *c.* 500 BC); however, the evidence does not
seem sufficiently conclusive to dismiss the priority of Aricia (cf. Ogilvie,
Early Rome, 68). Ogilvie also stresses the connection between the Aventine
cult and the Greek city of Massilia: Strabo (iv, 180) records that Diana's
statue was set up in the same way as that of Artemis (= Diana) at Massilia,
which in turn derived from Ephesus. The emperor Claudius referred to rites
which should be paid to Diana 'according to the laws of the king (Servius)
Tullius' (*ex legibus Tulli regis*, Tacitus, *Ann.* xii, 8); these rites may therefore
have been influenced by the federal cult of Artemis at Ephesus and more
directly by that at the Greek colony at Massilia.

14. THE REGIA.   See F. E. Brown, *Les Origines de la République romaine* (*Entretiens
Hardt*, xiii (1966), 47 ff. (Cf. some qualifications by A. Drummond, *JRS*,
1970, 200); *Rendiconti Pont. Accad. di Arch.*, xlvii, 1974–5, 15 ff. The
interpretation of the sixth-century developments remains uncertain. It
seemed (cf. Brown, op. cit.) that only in the rebuilding of *c.* 500 was the plan
established which the Regia then retained throughout the Republic, but this
now seems less certain (cf. *Rendiconti*). On the *rex sacrorum* see below,
p. 467 n. 5.

15. COMITIUM AND VOLCANAL.   See F. Coarelli, *Par. Pass.*, xxxii, 1977, 166 ff.

16. TEMPLES AT SANT'OMOBONO.   Beside Gjerstad, *Early Rome*, see A. Sommella
Mura, *Par. Pass.* xxxii, 1977; M. Pallottino, *Comptes Rendus*, 1977, 216 ff.;
and G. P. Sartono and P. Virgili, *Archelogia Laziale*, ii, 1979, 41 ff.

17. ETRUSCAN INSCRIPTIONS IN ROME.   For the three inscriptions see E.
Gjerstad, *Early Rome*, iv, 494; M. Pallottino, *Testimonia Linguae Etruscae*,
edn 2, (1968), 24; *Stud. Etr.*, xxii (1952–3), 309. A bowl of *c.* 525 BC
carries the words *ni araziia laraniia*, while the name *uqno* is inscribed on
another fragment and may recall Aucno, the legendary founder of Mantua.
For a fourth inscription see p. 529.

18. THE TRIUMPH AND SPOLIA OPIMA.   On the triumph see L. B. Warren, *JRS*,
1970, 49 ff.; H. S. Versnel, *Triumphus* (1971), on which cf. D. Musti, *JRS*,
1972, 163 ff. The triumph may have developed from a simpler ceremony in
which a victorious king dedicated as a trophy the armour of a defeated foe to
Jupiter Feretrius at a shrine on the Capitol. The nature of such trophies is
obscure: there were said to be three *spolia opima, prima, secunda*, and *tertia*
(?offered to Jupiter Feretrius, Mars and Quirinius): Varro, *Festus*, 202L. The
early shrine or temple of Jupiter Feretrius was very small and contained only
a sceptre and a flint (*silex*); the latter was used in the fetial ceremonies for the
declaration of war (p. 66). The epithet was probably derived from *ferre*
rather than *ferire* (cf. *foedus ferire*): cf. Ogilvie, *Livy*, 70 f. A denarius of 50 BC
shows Marcellus, the conqueror of Syracuse, standing in the temple and
holding the *spolia opima* (Crawford, *RRC*, n. 439).

19. GAMES.   Several Etruscan tomb paintings show Games which resemble the
traditional Roman Games, e.g. the Tomb of the Augurs (wrestlers) and the

Tomb of the Olympiads (runners, horse racing) at Tarquinii, and the Tomb of the Monkey (horsemen, wrestlers, athletes, boxers) at Clusium. The early fifth-century Tomb of the Bigae at Tarquinii shows not only a variety of games but also wooden stands for the spectators at each side. See, e.g., A. Stenico, *Roman and Etruscan Painting* (1963), plates 7, 17–19, 34–43.

The Ludi Romani, which were attributed to the Tarquins (Livy, i, 35, 7; Dion. Hal., vi, 95) were celebrated annually on 13 September, the birthday of the Capitoline temple. Before they started, the images of the gods were carried in procession through the streets to the Circus. Beside these regular Games, special votive games might be held to celebrate some special victory or occasion (seven such are recorded before 350 BC).

20. THE SERVIAN WALL. For the existing remains see G. Säflund, *Le mure di Roma* (1932); E. Gjerstad, *Early Rome*, iii, 26 ff.; E. Nash, *Pict. Dict. Anc. Rome* (1962), ii, 104 ff; *Roma Medio-Repubblicana* (1973). The greater part of the remains belong to the fourth century (an earlier wall is presupposed in Varro, *de Ling. Lat.*, v, 48). On the strength of a piece of Attic red-figure pottery Gjerstad would date the *agger* to *c.* 475. But this sherd could be three or four decades earlier and there is evidence for an earlier phase of construction, so that the first *agger* could well have been built by Servius Tullius, as tradition demands.

21. VITICULTURE. Pips of grapes are not found before Gjerstad's period IV, commencing *c.* 625 BC: thus viticulture was probably introduced by the Etruscans. See Gjerstad, *Early Rome*, iv (1966), 342 f.

22. GREEK POTTERY IN ROME. See E. Gjerstad, *Early Rome*, iv (1966), 514 ff.

23. OSTIA. Considerable remains of the Roman colony planted at Ostia in 338 BC survive, but nothing much earlier has yet been found. This does not rule out earlier settlements which would have lain outside Roman Ostia and near the medieval salt-beds. See R. Meiggs, *Roman Ostia*, edn 2 (1973).

24. THE FALISCANS. The early development of the Faliscans resembled that of the Romans: inhumers had mingled with Villanovan incinerators. Their language was very close to Latin. Their chief city was Falerii Veteres (Città Castelana). See M. W. Frederiksen and J. B. Ward-Perkins, *PBSR*, 1957, 67 ff. Closely related was Capena, and not far off was Lucus Feroniae (at Scorano), a market town which lay at an important river crossing, where an annual festival (in honour of Feronia, an Italic woodland goddess) and market were held. See G. D. B. Jones, *PBSR*, 1962, 191 ff. On Decima cf. p. 448 n. 44.

25. GABII. Gabii lay near Torre di Castiglione, some twelve miles from Rome. Existing remains are not earlier than the third or fourth century, but seventh-century pottery resembles Alban pottery (cf. the tradition that Gabii was a colony of Alba: Dion. Hal., i, 84). Cf. L. Quilici, *Civiltà del Lazio primitivo*, 186 f. Gabii was too strong to be absorbed by Rome without negotiation and an agreement (Livy, i, 54; Dion. Hal., iv, 57). The tradition is confirmed by Gabii's later peculiar relationship to the Roman state: *ager Gabinus* remained juridically distinct from *ager Romanus*, and the Gabine robe (*cinctus Gabinus*) was worn by Roman officials as a sacred vestment on certain occasions.

Ogilvie (*Livy*, 209 f.), however, is inclined to believe that the shield is more likely to have been a trophy from the capture of Gabii after its revolt in the Latin War in 338 BC. On the site see now *Archaelogia Laziale*, 1978. 47 ff.

26. EARLY ROMAN SOCIETY AND INSTITUTIONS. See H. Stuart Jones, *CAH*, vii, ch. xiii; P. de Francisci, *Primordia Civitatis* (1959), a very detailed work in Italian; papers by A. Momigliano in *Terzo* and *Quarto Contributi*; F. De Martino, *St. d. cos. rom.*, 1, edn 2 (1972), which may overemphasize economic and class-division factors (cf. E. S. Staveley, *JRS*, 1960, 250 ff.) but often provides useful summaries of other scholars' views together with bibliographies.

The vexed question of the priority of *familia* or *gens* need not concern us here. Cf. De Martino, op. cit. 4 ff.

27. PRIVATE PROPERTY. Not only the belief of the later Romans but also the need to explain the differentiation between patricians and plebeians require the assumption that private property was widespread if not completely unrestricted in early Rome. Possibly some land may still have been entailed within the *gentes*. The implications of the words *heredium* and *mancipatio* are not clear. In the Twelve Tables *heredium*, hereditary estate, meant 'orchard' (*hortus*), not 'fields' (Pliny, *Nat. Hist.*, xix, 50), while *mancipatio* could be thought to have implied originally that only moveable objects (*manu capere*) could be sold.

28. PATRICIANS AND PLEBEIANS. Political distinction: see Livy, i, 8, 7; cf. i, 34, 6; iv, 4, 7; Cicero, *de rep.*, ii, 8, 14; 12, 23; Dion. Hal., ii, 8, 1–3; 12, 1. Racial or conquered: see, e.g., J. Binder, *Die Plebs* (1909); W. Ridgeway, *Proc. Br. Acad.*, 1907; R. S. Conway, *CAH*, iv, 466 ff.; A. Piganiol, *Essai sur les origines de Rome* (1916); rejected by H. Stuart Jones, *CAH*, vii, 421 ff. and by H. J. Rose, *JRS*, 1922, 106 ff., who has disposed of the view that the plebeians were matrilineal, the patricians patrilineal, together with many other social and religious differences which are often taken to denote differences of race (the patricians themselves consisted of a blend of races). Mommsen: see *Röm. Forsch.*, i (1864), 69 ff., *Röm. Staatsr.*, iii (1887), 3 ff. F. De Martino (*St. d. cos. Rom.*, edn 2, (1972), i, 66 ff.) discusses various views that have been advanced from the time of Machiavelli to those of Alföldi and Momigliano (on the last two see below n. 39). See now also J. C. Richard, *Les Origines de la plèbe romaine* (1978).

29. ECONOMIC DIFFERENCES. This aspect is stressed in most recent discussion. See E. Meyer, *s.v.*, Plebs, in Conrad (ed.), *Handwörterbuch d. Staatswissenchaft*, E. Meyer, *Röm. Staat und Staatsgedanke*, edn 2 (1961), 33 f.; F. De Martino, *St. d. cos. Rom.*, edn 2, (1972), i, 79 ff. The view of K. J. Neumann (*Die Grundherrschaft d. röm. Rep.*) followed by Ed. Meyer (*Kleine Schriften*, i (1924), 351 ff.), that the Etruscans introduced serfdom into Latium, has not been generally accepted.

30. DIVISION INTO ORDERS. Although some passages (e.g. Livy, x, 8: '*vos [patres] solos gentem habere*') seem to point to the original exclusion of the plebeians from the citizen body, this view cannot be maintained: see, e.g. H.

Stuart Jones, *CAH*, vii, 417 f. Similarly the general consensus of opinion now inclines to a late date (fifth century) for the real hardening of the class distinctions between patricians and plebeians; see the basic article by H. Last, *JRS*, 1945, 30 ff. This is so completely accepted by P. de Francisci that in his large study of pre-Republican Rome (*Primordia Civitatis*) he does not even discuss the question except, in passing, at the end (pp. 777 f). Such a view, however, should not be allowed to obscure the fact that during the regal period the patricians claimed many special privileges, even if the sharpest confrontation developed only after the fall of the monarchy. Cf. J. Heurgon, *Rise of R.*, 110 ff. For the recent view of A. Momigliano and further discussion see p. 459 n. 39.

31. THE FETIALES. See Livy, i, 24, 4 f., 32, 5 ff. (with Ogilvie, *Livy*, 110 ff, 127 ff.). The procedure described by Livy is undoubtedly very old, but the formulae which he preserves were mediated to him via a second-century antiquarian tradition and so have been subjected to some distortion. Negotiations for making peace treaties were handled by two Fetiales: the *pater patratus* (presumably the 'father' acting for the state as a whole) and the *verbenarius* who carried sacred grasses which had been torn, with earth, from the citadel, thus providing the envoy with a piece of his own country which he could take as protection against foreign influences in enemy territory. How later Romans adapted this primitive procedure to later needs, including wars overseas, has been discussed by F. W. Walbank, *JRS*, 1941, 86 ff., *Cl. Ph.* 1949, 15 ff. and by J. W. Rich, 'Declaring War in the Roman Republic in the period of Transmarine Expansion', *Latomus*, vol. 159, 1976, 56 ff.

32. THE THREE TRIBES. The names Ramn(ens)es, Titi(ens)ses and Luceres were derived by later annalists from Romulus, Titus Tatius and perhaps an Etruscan king Lucumo. See J. Heurgon, *Rise of R.*, 120. f. for pre-Etruscan origin (contrast Ogilvie, *Livy*, 80, for Etruscan origin).

33. THE CURIAE. See Dion. Hal., ii, 7; 3–14; 21–3. See A. Momigliano, *JRS*, 1963, 109 ff. (= *Terzo Contrib.*, 571 ff.); F. De Martino, *St. cos. rom.*, 1, edn 2, 146 ff; R. E. A. Palmer, *The Archaic Community of the Romans* (1970). Momigliano lucidly poses the problems involved. De Martino, in line with his view of the early evolution of Rome, sees the *curiae* as a stage in the slow process of the transformation of a gentile structure into a unitary form. Palmer sees the *curiae* as originally separate ethnic groups which gradually fused together to form the earliest community of Rome (cf. Ogilvie, *Early Rome*, 51 f.); they were not *phratries*, clans or military units; but were earlier than the three tribes which were military non-ethnic units, under the later kings and early Republic the reactionary Comitia Curiata dominated by the patres is to be contrasted with a progressive Comitia Centuriata headed by its officers, later consuls. For a criticism of Palmer's often very speculative views see A. Drummond, *JRS*, 1972, 176 ff. For the view that the Comitia Curiata had been preceded by a Comitia Calata (which later seems to have been a special form of both Comitia Curiata and Comitia Centuriata; cf. Aulus Gellius, xv, 27) see J. Heurgon, *Rise of R.*, 123 f.

34. PATRES CONSCRIPTI. The implications of this term have been endlessly debated in both ancient and modern times. The general view was that the *patres* were the original patricians (members of the *maiores gentes*) and the *conscripti* the plebeians later added to the Senate. It is uncertain whether the phrase means 'enrolled fathers' (*conscripti* being an adjectival qualification) or *patres et conscripti* (cf. the phrase *qui patres qui conscripti*). In the former case early virtual automatic membership (the privilege of certain families) will have been supplemented by the inclusion of other important members of the community, and then the whole body was enrolled as *patres*. Alternatively the Senate came to comprise *patres*, who did not need formal enrolment, and non-*patres* who had to be enrolled (*conscripti*): these need not be identified with the *minores gentes* nor strictly with the plebeians, who may not have been so clear-cut a group in the very early period. For the latter view see A. Momigliano, *Quarto Contrib.*, 423 ff.: the existence of a group of *conscripti*, who were neither patricians nor plebeians (but who later merged with the plebeians) would help to explain the presence in the Fasti of the early Republic of names of consuls that are apparently plebeian: they would have been *conscripti* (cf. ch. iii, n. 2). Ogilvie (*Early Rome*, 59) believes that under the monarchy all members of the Senate were automatically patricians, but that this ceased with the establishment of the Republic, when patrician status was restricted.

35. THE TRIUMPH. See above, n. 18. The king in his triumphal *insignia* in some sense represented Jupiter, but (despite much debate) the idea of divinization was probably not involved. In the early days of the Republic a minor form of triumph was developed, the *ovatio*; this may approximate more closely to the early pre-Etruscan form of celebration before the Etruscans had elaborated the ritual (e.g. the general went on foot or horseback, not a chariot). In the late third century generals who were refused full triumphs by the Senate might hold unofficial ones on the Alban Mount during the Feriae Latinae. For later developments (241–133 BC) see J. S. Richardson, *JRS*, 1975, 50 ff.

36. THE CALENDAR. Since 'Numa's' reform does not refer to the dedication of the temple of Jupiter Capitolinus in 509 BC it must have been earlier than that, while if Aprilis is an Etruscan word the reform probably was made in the sixth century. A. K. Michels, *The Calendar of the Roman Republic* (1967), however, attributes this pre-Julian calendar to the decemviral period, but this view is contested by R. M. Ogilvie, *Cl. Rev.*, 1969, 330 ff. (cf. A. Drummond, *JRS* (1971), 282 f.). Ogilvie (*Early Rome*, 42) also suggests that although the lunisolar calendar was established during the Etruscan period, it was not openly published, for all to see and read, until the time of the Decemvirate. The introduction of the new month of January is not generally thought to have resulted in changing the beginning of the Roman year from March to January until 153 BC. Mrs Michels, however, believes the change to be older and that in 153 what happened was only the bringing into line of the official consular year with the older calendar year. On the calendar see, besides Mrs Michels's book, E. J. Bickerman, *Chronology of the Ancient World* (1968), 43 ff.

and A. E. Samuel, *Greek and Roman Chronology* (1972), ch. v. On the calends and the king's proclamation: Macrobius, i, 15, 9–13; cf. Lydus, *de mens*, iii, 10.

37. LEGES REGIAE. A collection of laws ascribed to the kings existed in the second century AD (Pomponius, *Digest*, i, 2, 2, 2). It was called *ius Papirianum* because it was allegedly composed under Tarquinius Superbus by a Sextus Papirius, while a C. Papirius, the first Pontifex Maximus, was said to have restored a collection, made by Ancus Marcius, of some laws of Numa which had been recorded on tablets in the Forum and become illegible (Dion. Hal., iii, 36). All such *leges regiae* preserved in the ancient writers have been collected: see, e.g, Riccobono, *Fontes*, i, 1–8. They deal chiefly with religious matters and may reflect early rules of the regal community, even if they were not published in the Forum as were the later Twelve Tables, though the survival of the inscription under the Lapis Niger shows that publication cannot be quite excluded. For a defence of their basic historicity see A. Watson, *JRS*, 1972, 100 ff.

38. DUOVIRI PERDUELLIONIS.   A. Magdelain, *Historia*, 1973, 405 ff., has attempted to show that these officials were invented by later annalists.

39. THE EARLY CAVALRY.   A. Alföldi, *Der frührömische Reiteradel und seine Ehrenbezeichnen* (1952), identified the patriciate with the 300 cavalry. This view has been challenged by A. Momigliano, *Quarto Contrib.*, 377 ff. and the discussion has been continued in *Historia*, 1963, 385 ff., 444 ff. De Martino, *St. d. cos. rom*, edn 2, I, 197 ff., believes that the equestrian centuries *were* reserved for patricians, but that to argue that the patricians had acquired their political privilege from their monopoly of the cavalry is to view the problem wrongly: the patricians derived their power rather from the *gentes*. For the dissociation of the mysterious *proci patricii* from the *sex suffragia* see Momigliano, op. cit, 377 ff. Ogilvie (*Early Rome*, 44 ff.) believes that in the earliest army cavalry was more important than infantry, but he rejects (56 ff.) Alföldi's identification of the patricians with an aristocracy of knights who formed the royal cavalry.

40. HOPLITE WARFARE.   The archaeological evidence suggests the introduction of hoplite tactics in the mid-sixth century: see A. N. Snodgrass, *Arms and Armour of the Greeks* (1967), 74 ff. This provides a conclusive argument against those (e.g. M. P. Nilsson, *JRS*, 1929, 4 ff.) who dated the 'Servian' reform to the mid-fifth century as the organizational means of introducing a Greek hoplite system. Further, our sources (Diodorus, xxiii, 2 and the *Ineditum Vaticanum*, 3) say that it was the Etruscans who taught the Romans to fight 'with bronze shields and in a phalanx'.

41. REFORM OF THE ARMY.   It is widely agreed that the manner in which (though not necessarily the date at which) the army reforms were made has been solved by P. Fraccaro, *Atti del sec. Congr. Naz. di Stud. Rom.*, iii (1931), 91 ff. (= *Opuscula*, II (1957), 287 ff). Cf., e.g., J. Heurgon, *Rise of R.*, 150 ff.; for a general sketch of the evolution of the legion see A. J. Toynbee, *Hannibal's Legacy*, I (1965), 505 ff.

There are, however, still champions of a much later and slower development. Thus G. V. Sumner (*JRS*, 1970, 76 ff.) argues that Servius created a centuriate organization of the army of 3,000, based on the 30 *curiae* and the 3 original tribes. When the new territorial tribes were created in the mid-fifth century (so Sumner believes), a phalanx of 3,000 hoplites in 30 *centuriae* was established; at the same time the new model army was adapted for political purposes as a new Comitia Centuriata, no longer based on the *curiae*. This *legio* was increased to 4,000 *c.* 431 BC, and to 6,000 *c.* 405 when the Comitia Centuriata took on its classical form of five classes. After 367 it was divided into two legions, and by 311 the four-legion manipular army had been created.

42. CLASSIS AND INFRA CLASSEM. The supposition of a division between *classici* and those *infra classem* is based on Cato (*apud Gellium*, vi, 13, 1) and Festus, p. 100, L). It has been supported by Beloch, *Röm. Gesch.*, 291, A. Bernardi, *Athenaeum*, 1952, 3 ff. and A. Momigliano, *Terzo Contrib.*, 596; *Quarto*, 430 ff., but it has been questioned by E. S. Staveley (in a valuable paper on work done on the early Roman constitution 1940–54 in *Historia*, 1956, 79) who argues that Gellius does not prove or even imply that there were ever less than five *classes* in the centuriate organization and that Cato's remark derives not from fifth-century records but from an unclear distinction of his own day when *classicus* may have indicated social standing.

43. THE TRIBES. After 241 BC the total number of tribes was, and remained at, 35. Fabius Pictor (frg. 9P) attributes to Servius the creation of 4 urban and 26 rustic tribes; Livy (i, 43, 13) ascribes the four urban tribes to Servius at the time of the institution of the census but does not mention the rustic ones; but elsewhere (ii, 21, 7) he says that 21 tribes were formed in 495 BC. Probably 20 of these (the 4 urban and 17 rustic, i.e. excluding the tribe Clustumina) should be attributed to Servius. A fragment by an unknown writer on the Servian constitution (*Papyrus Oxyr.*, 17 (1927), n. 2088) refers to Servius' division into tribes. In general see L. R. Taylor, *The Voting Districts of the Roman Republic* (1960).

44. DATING THE COMITIA CENTURIATA. Early views are discussed by G. W. Botsford, *The Roman Assemblies* (1909), more recent ones by E. S. Staveley, *Historia*, 1956, 74 ff. For later discussions see P. Fraccaro, *JRS*, 1957, 64; P. de Francisci, *Primordia Civitatis* (1959), 672 ff; L. R. Taylor, *Voting-Districts of the Roman Republic* (1960), 3 ff.; A. Momigliano, *Terzo Contrib.*, 594 ff.; R. M. Ogilvie, *Livy*, 166 ff.; G. V. Sumner, *JRS*, 1970, 76 ff.; F. De Martino, *St. d. cos. rom.*, edn 2, I, ch. vii.

As an example of those who accept Fraccaro's explanation of the growth of the army (see n. 41 above) but reject his dating we may quote briefly the position of De Sanctis (*Riv. Fil.*, 1933, 289 ff.) who maintains that the Servian order cannot be earlier than the end of the fifth century or the beginning of the fourth: if it existed in the regal period it would imply a population of 200 inhabitants to a square kilometre, which De Sanctis rejects as impossible. He also emphasizes the improbability that Rome could put

6,000 men into the field at so early a period. He distinguishes three periods of development: (a) The earliest of 3,000 infantry and 300 cavalry with three praetors (this accords with his theory that three praetors and not two consuls, or praetors, took the helm as the monarchy declined). (b) This army, based on Thousands and the old tribes and *Curiae*, was gradually increased. In 444 when three military tribunes took supreme control in the state, the army still contained only 3,000 men. The increase in the number of these military tribunes (three or four from 426 to 406, six from 405 to 367) implies an increase in the Thousands of the army. It was at this period, sometime between 405 and 367, that the new 'Servian' order was introduced, probably immediately after the Gallic sack. (c) In 366, when consuls were substituted for military tribunes, the legion of 6,000 men was divided into two separate legions, each under six tribunes; six were nominated by the consuls, six elected by the people. When the number of legions and tribunes was later increased the additional tribunes were elected by the people. Fraccaro's explanation of the method of transition from one to two legions is to be followed.

The chief merit of De Sanctis' argument seems to be that it explains the fluctuating number of military tribunes: they varied with the number of Thousands of men levied annually. But since one of them sometimes remained in the city, their numbers may not depend strictly on the military organization. De Sanctis also implies that the 'Servian' order was introduced after the Gallic sack; it is difficult to see how this arrangement based on sixty centuries would square with the occasional appointment of seven, eight, or nine military tribunes (and De Sanctis himself rejects Beloch's elimination of the odd numbers from the Fasti as arbitrary). Again, not all De Sanctis' arguments are irrefutable. For instance, if Frank's calculations are accepted *Econ. Survey of Anc. Rome.*, I (1933), 19 ff., there is no objection on the score of population to placing the 'Servian' reform early. But even if these are rejected, the existence of a given number of centuries need not imply that at any given time they all contained 100 men. As De Sanctis says, a century of the census must have contained two or three times more people than a century of the legionary army. Is it not then possible that, accepting Fraccaro's position, the primitive Romulean centuries were doubled by 'Servius' for census purposes; that each military century formed a part only of the census century of a full 100 rather than that the census century exceeded the military century of a full 100; and that the military centuries only gradually reached a full total which would produce an infantry of the line of 6,000 men? Other objections to De Sanctis' views have been advanced by Fraccaro (*Athenaeum*, 1934, 57 ff. = *Opuscula*, II (1957), 293 ff.) that he and Beloch have been forced to imagine a Comitia Centuriata earlier than the 'Servian' one, of which tradition records no trace; and that if the 'Servian' reforms had been later than the regal period, their chronological position would have been mentioned (e.g. the decemviral legislation is not referred to Romulus or Servius!).

45. SEXTUS TARQUINIUS. For the suggestion that the *praenomen* of Gnaeus Tarquinius Romanus depicted on the tomb at Vulci (p. 452) is wrong and that the man being killed is Sextus rather than his father or brothers see Ogilvie, *Livy*, 230. If the Tarquin family did come from Caere (p. 452), this city would be a natural place for them to seek refuge.

46. HORATIUS, SCAEVOLA AND CLOFLIA. According to Livy, Horatius after his heroic defence of the bridge swam to safety, but Polybius (vi, 55) says that he was drowned. Scaevola, after failing to kill Porsenna, showed his indifference to pain by holding his right hand in a fire: Porsenna was duly impressed. Cloelia was a Roman girl, given as a hostage to Porsenna; she escaped across the Tiber, either by swimming or on horseback, but was returned to Porsenna who admired her bravery and handed her back. For a discussion of the origin of these stories, which may well be linked with statues of Horatius and Cloelia in Rome, whose meaning was misunderstood, see Ogilvie, *Livy*, 258 ff.

47. PORSENNA. For the view that he came from Veii, not Clusium, see E. Pais, *Storia di Roma*, II, 97 ff. Pliny, *NH*, ii, 140 derives him from Volsini. For his capture of Rome see Tacitus, *Hist.*, iii, 72. He is said to have tried to keep the Romans in subjection by forbidding the use of iron weapons (as the Philistines had dealt with the conquered Israelites). E. Gjerstad (*Opuce. Rom.* (1969), 149 ff.) believes that his main target was Cumae rather than Rome. Ogilvie, (*Early Rome*, 88 f.) suggests that Porsenna's move south was activated by pressure upon Clusium by the hill tribes of central Italy (Gallic pressure from the north had scarcely started so early as this).

48. THE CUMAEAN CHRONICLE. Whether Dionysius derived his information on Cumaean and Latin affairs from a local chronicle or from a writer, Hyperochus of Cumae, is uncertain. Only recently has the significance of this independent Greek tradition been emphasized. See A. Momigliano, *Terzo Contrib.*, 664 f.; E. Gabba, *Les Origines de la Rep. Rom.*, (*Entretiens Hardt*, xiii (1966), 144 ff.); A. Alföldi, *Early Rome and the Latins* (1964), 56 ff.

49. MONARCHY AND REPUBLIC. The conventional view (as expressed, e.g., by Mommsen) is that when Tarquin was suddenly expelled two annually elected magistrates (consuls, though probably first called praetors) succeeded to his position: this dual office was designed to prevent a recurrence of monarchical rule. But many historians reject a sudden change and believe in evolution rather than revolution. Some argue that the power of the kings declined gradually, as at Athens. The title *rex*, like *basileus* survived in the person of a priest-king (*rex sacrorum*), but his power was limited by the creation of three praetors who originally commanded the three military contingents of the Ramnes, Tities and Luceres. Their duties were gradually differentiated and the one left in Rome to administer justice sank to an inferior position; on this view, the traditional account of the creation of the praetorship in 366 arose from the fact that the names of the third 'praetors' were first recorded from then onwards. Such a theory, which cuts clean across all that the Romans themselves firmly believed about the fall of the monarchy, does not win a ready acceptance.

Other historians turn to Etruria and Italy rather than to Greece to illuminate Rome's constitutional development, but their contribution is not conclusive. On the analogy of the Etruscan magistrate called *zilath* (translated into Latin as *dictator*) and of the dictator who was the chief magistrate in such Latin cities as Aricia and Lanuvium, it has been suggested that the earliest magistrate at Rome was the dictator, whose original title was *magister populi*, together with his subordinate, the *magister equitum*. This view, although solving some difficulties, totally contradicts the tradition that the Roman dictatorship was an extraordinary non-annual magistracy. In Etruria a regular sequence of office (*cursus honorum*) may have been established when the monarchy gave place to the local aristocracy, while among the Italian peoples a magistracy was shared by more than one person. The Umbrians had two Marones, the Sabines eight Octovirs, and the Oscans two Meddices. But it is not certain whether any of these groups represent the principle of collegiality: possibly the first pair of Octovirs had equal authority, nothing is known of the Marones, while the Oscans definitely had a Meddix Tuticus and a Lesser Meddix. Thus it cannot be ascertained whether the Romans borrowed or invented the principle of two collegiate magistrates, and the comparative study of other institutions has hardly produced results sufficiently conclusive to justify the rejection of what the Romans believed concerning the nature of their earliest magistracy.

K. Hanell (*Das altrömische eponyme Amt* (1946)) has advanced the view that the Romans were wrong in linking the establishment of the Republic with that of the eponymous magistracy; the latter might have existed under the monarchy, and in Hanell's view it came into being at the same time as the adoption of the pre-Julian calendar which is to be associated with the foundation of the Capitoline temple. These eponymous magistrates will have been *praetores maximi*, since praetors and dictators are postulated in the regal period as helpers and deputies respectively of the king; such conditions prevailed until the Decemvirate, when the monarchy ended. This ingenious attempt to support the evolutionary theory (cf. De Sanctis, above) has not been widely accepted, even by other scholars who are dissatisfied with the traditional account. These, although ready to accept that the end of the monarchy was sudden and revolutionary, are not willing to believe that the dual consulship was devised suddenly in 509 as an anti-monarchical safeguard: it will have resulted from an evolutionary process, and prototypes of the consuls will have been, e.g. two auxiliaries of the king, legionary commanders called praetors (so A. Bernardi, *Athenaeum*, 1952, 24 ff.). Other scholars have assumed a period between the monarchy and the appearance of magistrates with *par potestas*, when one magistrate, or a college of magistrates in which one predominated, exercised control, e.g. a *praetor maximus* (on whom see A. Momigliano, *Quarto Contrib.*, 403 ff.). According to the antiquarian Cincius (Livy, vii, 3, 5) the *praetor maximus* every year drove a nail into the wall of the temple of Jupiter Capitolinus, presumably to mark the passing of one year; this will have started in the first year of the Republic when the temple was dedicated. The nature and history of the office remain very obscure. It could be an alternative title to *maior consul*, the consul who held the *fasces*. Another view is that of De Martino (*St. d. cos. rom*, edn 2, I, 234 ff.) who believes that until 451 the chief magistrate was a *dictator annuus*; he was replaced in the struggle of the orders by an annually elected board of ten, which two years later was followed by two unequal praetors, who thereafter were sometimes replaced by military tribunes, until the dual consulship was established in 367. This view is criticized by E. S. Staveley, *JRS*, 1960, 251 f. The main thesis of a massive work by R. Werner, *Der Beginn der römischen Republik* (1963), has not been readily accepted (for criticism see A. Momigliano, *Terzo Contrib.*, 669 ff. and R. M. Ogilvie, *Cl. Rev.*, 1965, 84 ff.). Werner's conclusion is that Tarquin was expelled and the dual consulship established *c.* 472: this is based on his view that time was first reckoned by the nail-ceremony in the temple of Jupiter and not by eponymous consuls, the latter system being adopted only in the third century when the pontiffs equated the Capitoline era with the era based on the expulsion of the kings; this involved a large-scale interpolation of names in the consular Fasti (which Werner regarded as unreliable) to fill the gap between 507 (dedication of Capitoline temple and start of the nail-ceremony) and *c.* 472 (beginning of the Republic and consuls); Ogilvie (op. cit., 87) accepts that the Romans originally reckoned their years by nails rather than by magistrates, but does not accept Werner's main thesis.

These various theories have been mentioned in order to give some indication of the direction of recent enquiries, rather than to suggest their success. A most useful guide to some of this work, together with a sane and balanced assessment of it, is given by E. S. Staveley, 'The Constitution of the Roman Republic, 1940–1954', *Historia*, 1956, 74 ff, especially 90 ff.

A major chronological problem which affects both the beginning and end of the monarchy remains to be mentioned. As we have seen, the distinguished Swedish archaeologist, E. Gjerstad, has established the main lines of the growth of the city: a pre-urban period (divided on the evidence of pottery into four periods, 800–750, 750–700, 700–625, 625–575), followed by the epoch of the Archaic city (Early, 575–530, Middle, 530–500, Late, 500–450). These results seem to many to support the traditional literary evidence to a remarkable degree: thus the pre-urban period corresponds with the Latin kings, the Early and Middle Archaic with the Etruscan kings, and the Late Archaic with the gradual decline of Etruscan influences after the explusion of the Tarquins. However (unfortunately, as it will seem to many) Gjerstad has accepted the view of Hanell in putting the end of the monarchy well into the fifth century, in fact to the mid-century and the time of the Decemvirate. In brief, Etruscan rule in Rome was *c.* 530–450 rather than *c.* 616–510. This theory, apart from the difficulties of correlating archaeological evidence with constitutional changes, involves transferring to the regal period many events which tradition assigned to the early Republic, e.g. the struggle of the orders and the treaty of Cassius. Dislocation and the telescoping of events on this scale seem unacceptable and indeed quite unnecessary, since the archaeological evidence does not appear to be at essential variance with the literary tradition.

Gjerstad's views are of course expounded at length in his great work, *Early Rome*; shorter statements in his *Legends and Facts of Early Roman History* (1962) and in ch. i of *Entretiens Hardt*, xiii (1966). For criticism see M. Pallottino, *St. Etr.*, 1963, 19 ff.; A. Momigliano, *Rivista Storica Italiana*, 1961, 802 ff.; 1963, 882 ff., *JRS*, 1963, 95 ff. (= *Terzo Contrib.*, 661 ff., 545 ff.); R. M. Ogilvie, *Cl. Rev.*, 1964, 85 ff; F. de Martino, *Aufstieg NRW*, I ii, 1972, 217 ff.

CHAPTER III THE NEW REPUBLIC AND THE STRUGGLE OF THE ORDERS

1. THE FIRST CONSULS. Tradition associates no less than five consuls with the first year of the Republic, fitting them all in by means of violent deaths or forced retirements. It is more probable that they were connected by popular legend with the birth of liberty and that subsequently their names were included in the Fasti, than that their names were originally in the early Fasti and that later legends were devised to connect them with the establishing of the Republic. It is difficult to assert, but arbitrary to deny their historicity. Three names perhaps may be removed: L. Tarquinius Collatinus as a 'doublet' of the king; Sp. Lucretius because of his connection with Lucretia; P. Valerius Publicola as a reduplication of another Valerius who also held office with a Horatius in 449 BC (legends connected with Valerius were designed partly to explain the name Publicola and partly to glorify the Valerian *gens* which later numbered among its members a very unreliable annalist, Valerius Antias). Of the two remaining names M. Horatius Pulvillus, who consecrated the Temple of Jupiter Capitolinus built by Tarquin, may be a 'doublet' of the consul of 449, invented in order that a Republican magistrate might share the glory with the hated tyrant. But since Polybius dates the first treaty between Rome and Carthage 'in the consulship of Brutus and Horatius', the magistracy of Horatius, if invented, was invented early. Similarly, attempts to dispose of Junius Brutus have not been totally successful: to turn him into some kind of divinity because of the similarity of his name with Juno is absurd, while the fact that the Junii were later a plebeian family does not preclude an original patrician stock. In addition to the reduction of the five consuls to two, another point in the traditional account needs correcting: their original title probably was *praetor* (*prae-itor*, a leader; στρατηγός in Greek writers); since they called their colleagues together they were named *praetores consules*, and later, when another praetor was established to administer justice, the adjective *consules* was used as a noun to distinguish them from the new *praetor*. But though the traditional account is encrusted with legend and has been written in the light of later developments, it need not for that reason be completely rejected. An

important archaic inscription from Satricum has just been published by C. de Simone, *Archelogia laziale*, i, 1978, 95 ff. It appears to date from *c.* 500 BC, and after eleven letters whose meaning is obscure, it runs '*Popliosio Valesiosio suodales Mamartei*', and may mean something like 'the *sodales* (i.e. the members of a priestly college) of Publius Valerius dedicated this to Mars' (the god's name being in the Oscan form). It must apply to a member of the Valerian *gens*: could it be Publius Valerius Poplicola, consul in the first years of the Republic (another was consul in 475)?

2. EARLY PLEBEIAN CONSULS? The general problem of the Fasti and their reliability is discussed elsewhere (ch. xix), but we must face here the question of the apparently plebeian names in the early Fasti. At one time they were totally rejected even by many who believed that in other respects the lists might be more or less reliable: the ground of the rejection was the belief that no plebeian could have held the consulship at this time of patrician privilege, and that therefore their presence was due either to later interpolation arising from family pride (to have ancestors who 'came over with the Normans') or else that they were in fact names of patrician *gentes* who later died out and then reappeared as plebeians. In more recent years many have been prepared to grant them greater credibility, based partly on the assumption that the political distinction between patricians and plebeians had not reached its peak so early (see, e.g., A. Bernardi, *Rendicont. Istituto Lombardo*, lxxix (1945–6), 1 ff.; H. Last's paper in *JRS*, 1945, 30 ff. was important as emphasizing the late closing of the patrician ranks). A neat solution would be to suppose that these consuls were *conscripti*, neither patricians nor plebeians, if the theory of A. Momigliano could be accepted: see above, ch. ii, n. 34. The difficulty of disentangling the patrician or plebeian status of certain families at different periods of history is examined by I. Shatzman, *Cl. Qu.*, 1973, 65 ff., in regard to the Veturii in the context of the early Fasti.

The Fasti give 12 plebeian consuls for 509–486, none in the years 485–470 (when the Fabii dominated the scene with consulships in seven consecutive years, and no Etruscan names appear), one in 469, none again until 461, and five in the 450s; then the Decemvirate interposed. The early years of the Republic were obviously very disturbed with the intervention of Porsenna and with pro- and anti-Etruscan groups no doubt in competition (not to mention the effect of external Latin threats on internal politics). Thus J. Heurgon (*Rise of R.*, 164 f.) would explain the Fasti as representing a compromise which resulted from an alliance between plebeians and some of the Etruscans *vis-à-vis* the patricians, Whatever may be thought of this, once the new Republic began to settle down the patricians clearly strengthened their hold upon the supreme magistracy, at any rate until 461, whether or not plebeians had any legal claim to it.

3. PROVOCATIO. According to Livy (ii, 8, 2) P. Valerius Publicola carried a law in 509 which established the right of appeal (*provocatio*) from the magistrates to the people (*iudicium populi*, i.e. the Comitia Centuriata acting as a court of law in capital cases). But since similar laws were said to have been passed later

(Twelve Tables, 450; Valerian-Horatian laws, 449: Lex Valeria of 300) many scholars believe that the right was not established as early as 509. The procedure was that a victim of a magistrate's *coercitio* appealed to the people which either confirmed or rejected the magistrate's sentence. Some suggest that the magistrate at first did not pass judgement but referred the question of guilt direct to the popular assembly, while W. Kunkel (*Untersuchungen zur Entwicklung des röm. Kriminalverfahrens* (1962) has argued that only political offences against the state were referred to the *iudicia populi* and that ordinary crimes were handled by a praetor or a *triumvir capitalis*. A. H. M. Jones (*The Criminal Courts of the Roman Republic* (1972), ch. i) has defended the traditional viewpoint. For the various laws de *provocatione* see E. S. Staveley, *Historia* (1955), 412 ff.

4. IMPERIUM.   On the nature of *imperium* see E S. Staveley, *Historia*, 1956, 107 ff.

5. REX SACRORUM.   See A. Momigliano, *Quarto Contrib*, 395 ff., *Quinto Contrib.*, 309 ff. The *reges sacrorum*, found in other Latin towns (Tusculum, Lavinium, Velitrae, and perhaps Alba), may have been established there at the time when they were losing their kings, as at Rome. The word *rex* was found on a *bucchero* vase found in the Regia in recent excavations. The *rex* was chosen by the Pontifex Maximus in the second century BC (Livy, xl, 42), yet he retained precedence in processions where the pontifex maximus took only fifth place, and pontifical decisions in 270 were still dated by the name of the *rex* (this also suggests that years in the regal period had been numbered as regnal years, as happened at Caere where the Pyrgi inscription refers to the third year of Thefarias; cf. Momigliano, op. cit.).

6. PATRICIAN NUMBERS   K. J. Beloch, *Röm. Gesch.*, 221, reckons the patricians as less than one-tenth of the free population of Rome *c.* 500 BC.

7. DICTATORSHIP.   On its origin and the various modern theories about this see E. S. Staveley, *Historia*, 1956, 101 ff.

8. GREEK POTTERY.   See E. Gjerstad, *Early Rome*, (1966), 514 ff. Athenian trade with the Etruscan cities also declined, but not to the same extent as that with Rome.

9. USURY.   According to Tacitus (*Ann.*, vi, 16, 3) the decemvirs in 451 BC fixed the minimum rate of interest at *unciarium fenus*, which if the interest was annual amounted to $8\frac{1}{2}$ per cent, if monthly to 100 per cent. Livy, however, assigns the law to 357 BC. A passage in Cato (*de agri cultura, ad. init.*) may imply that he thought that loans at usury were forbidden in early Rome.

10. NEXUM.   Details are obscure, partly because the system was abolished towards the end of the fourth century. It was very difficult for the bondsman (*nexus*) to escape from his condition, which was permanent until a third party could be found to buy back the bondsman from the creditor and so release him. See M. I. Finley, *Revue d' Histoire du Droit* (1965), 159 ff. and Ogilvie, *Livy*, 296 ff. Cf. also A. Watson, *Rome of the XII Tables* (1976), ch. ix.

11. FOOD SHORTAGES AND DISEASE.   Corn shortages are recorded for the years 508, 496, 492, 486, 477, 476, 456, 453, 440, 433 and 411. Despite some

possible inaccuracies the main record is likely to be true, since Cato tells us (frg. 77 P) that corn shortages were registered in the *annales*, i.e. the Tabula Pontificum. In the 490s the cult of the corn goddess Ceres, whose centres were at Cumae and Sicily, was established at Rome, while trade with western Sicily, which was under Punic control, will have been helped by Rome's treaty with Carthage. The account of a Roman embassy sent to Sicily in 491–0 (Dion. Halic., vii, 1–2) may well be reliable, since it probably derives from a Greek source independent of the Roman tradition. See Ogilvie, *Livy*, 256 f., 291, 321.

Epidemics are recorded in 490, 466, 463, 453, in six years in the 430s, and in 428, 412, 411, 399, 392, and 390 (malaria, anthrax?); for references and discussion see Ogilvie, *Livy*, 394 f.

12. MAELIUS, SERVILIUS AND MINUCIUS. The story of Maelius is quite probably historical since it antedates the troubles arising from the corn supply in the time of Gaius Gracchus: it was recorded by Cincius *c.* 200 BC. Servilius acted either as a private citizen or (according to a later tradition) as a Magister Equitum: see A. W. Lintott, *Historia*, 1970, 12 ff. Minucius was *praefectus* (? *urbi*) in 440 and 439 according to the *Libri Lintei* (these were early lists of magistrates, written on linen and kept in the temple of Juno Moneta: see R. M. Ogilvie, *JRS* (1958), 40 ff.). He was later honoured with a column and statue for a subsequent distribution of corn: the column is depicted on *denarii* of *c.* 134 BC (Crawford, *RRC* (1974), 242–43), but was not set up before the fourth century (Momigliano, *Quarto Contrib.*, 329 ff.). A later Minucius (M. Minucius Rufus, consul in 110) built a porticus Minucius which was used for corn distributions in the Roman Empire. Thus both Maelius and Minucius may be accepted as historical figures, though the connection between them is not beyond doubt. See Ogilvie, *Livy*, 550 f.

13. SP. CASSIUS. For an analysis of his story see Ogilvie, *Livy*, 337 ff. A. W. Lintott, *Historia*, 1970, 18 ff. argues that in the original story Cassius was put to death by his father by virtue of the latter's *patria potestas*, and that his formal trial and conviction for treason (*perduellio*) was a later form.

14. THE FIRST SECESSION. The historicity of this movement is defended by Ogilvie, *Livy*, 309 ff.

15. LEX PUBLILIA. In view of the importance of what was enacted in 471, Publilius Volero may well be a historical character, although some have seen in him only a doublet of Publilius Philo, dictator in 339. Livy ii, 56, 2 says that the right to elect plebeian magistrates was given to the Comitia Tributa; this should probably be the Concilium Plebis. Perhaps the concessions attributed to Publilius were the result of a secession.

16. COMITIA TRIBUTA POPULI. The existence of this Comitia, as distinct from the purely plebeian Concilium Plebis Tributum, was first shown by Mommsen. For the evidence see A. H. J. Greenidge, *Roman Public Life* (1901), 443 ff; E. S. Staveley, *Athenaeum*, 1955, 3 ff. Some scholars, however, maintain that there was only one tribal assembly, from which the patricians were excluded: they are therefore forced to postulate that the patricians were admitted at some unrecorded date, perhaps in 287.

17. THE TRIBUNES. See G. Niccolini, *It tribunato della plebe* (1932). According to Varro (*de ling. Lat.*, v, 91) they derived from the military tribunes, but E. Meyer (*Kleine Schriften*, i, 333 ff.) argued that they had been administrative officers of the tribes.

18. THE DECEMVIRS. The problems involved are discussed by Ogilvie, *Livy*, 451 ff. Cicero (*de rep.*, ii, 61 ff.) and Dionysius state that the decemvirs remained in office for three years. Cicero tells nothing of the fierce struggle that led up to their establishment. On Appius and the plebeians see De Sanctis, *SR*, ii, 47 ff.

19. THE TWELVE TABLES. Their authenticity has withstood the attacks of modern scholars, e.g. of E. Pais (*Ricerche sulla storia e sul diritto pubblico di Roma*, i (1915)) who assigned them to the end of the fourth century, and of E. Lambert (*Revue hist. de droit franc. et étranger*, 1902) who placed them at the beginning of the second. The original tables, set up in the Roman Forum, have of course perished, but the code has been partially reassembled from quotations in ancient writers. These fragments are collected in Riccobono, *Fontes*, 23 ff., and elsewhere; for a translation see Lewis-Reinhold, *Rn. Civ.*, i, 102 ff.; for discussion, H. F. Jolowicz, *A Historical Introduction to the Study of Roman Law*, edn 2, (1972), chs vii–xii, F. Wiencker, 'Die XII Tafeln in ihrem Jahrhundert', *Entretiens Hardt,* xiii (1966) 293 ff. See also A. Watson, *Rome of the XII Tables* (1976), which deals with the law of persons and property.

20. THE VALERIO-HORATIAN LAWS. According to Livy (iii, 55) these laws (a) restored the right of appeal, (b) gave *plebiscita* the force of law, (c) reaffirmed the sacrosanctity of the tribunes:

(a) *provocatio*: since the right of appeal (cf. p. 466 n. 3 above) is said already to have been restored by the Twelve Tables, its inclusion in the Leges Valeriae-Horatiae may be an anticipation of the Lex Valeria of 300. E. S. Staveley may well be correct in his analysis of these various laws (*Historia*, 1955, 412 ff.): the right was not granted in 509, and although its possible use was conceded in the Twelve Tables by the patricians in order to check indiscriminate use of tribunician *ius auxilii*, no magistrate was *compelled* to grant an appeal against his *coercitio* until the Lex Valeria of 300 BC. A. W Lintott (*AufstiegNRW*, II, i (1972), 226 ff.) has surveyed the history of *provocatio* from the beginning to the principate. He considers that it arose from self-help when a private individual, assailed in some way called aloud on his fellow-citizens to bear witness and give help; in later times such an appeal to the self-help of the plebs was usually made through its spokesmen, the tribunes. The first law to afford support to *provocatio* as such was that of 300.

(b) *plebiscita*: this second measure is the most controversial of the three, because if it was true it would have given the plebs legal power to realize their aims and to end the struggle. Livy's words are '*ut quod tributim plebs iussisset, populum teneret*' (55); i.e. what was voted by the plebs should be binding on the whole people. But he also says that the law of Publilius Philo of 339 BC laid it down '*ut plebiscita omnes Quirites tenerent*' (viii, 12), while according to Gellius (xv, 27) the Lex Hortensia of 287 decreed '*ut eo iure, quod plebs statuisset, omnes Quirites tenerentur'* : that is, the same law was enacted three times. Many of the theories evolved to meet the difficulty are scarcely tenable. Clearly such an important law would not have continually fallen into disuse so as to require re-enacting; nor is it practical to suppose that the plebs gained power in some matters in 445, in others in 339, and in all in 287. Another suggestion is that some limiting conditions may have been omitted, for instance, that the plebs might pass resolutions which could go before the Comitia Centuriata if first approved by the Senate; that the *auctoritas patrum* was dispensed with in 339, and that in 287 reference to the Comitia was made unnecessary. According to Mommsen Livy mistook his authority and *populus* is meant instead of *plebs*; the reference then is not to the Concilium Plebis but to the Comitia Tributa which he supposes was established in 449. Since there is no evidence for any of these views De Sanctis and others regard the law of 449 as a quite unhistorical anticipation of the later law. The objection to this last view, which is by far the simplest, is that certain important laws (the Lex Canuleia of 445, the Licinio-Sextian rogations of 367 and the Leges Genuciae of 342) were passed by the plebs before 339 BC. It has therefore been suggested (by Sir H. Stuart Jones, *CAH*, vii, 484) that a law of 449 did give validity to *plebiscita*, which the patricians long contended were not binding on them because enacted without their consent, and disregarded *de facto*. Alternatively it is possible that no law was passed in 449 to this effect, but that the plebs asserted their right to issue binding laws and that the other authorities were forced by circumstances to pass through the usual channels the subsequent legislation which had originated with the expressed will of the people: in that case later historians might regard the measures as legally binding *plebiscita*, when in fact they were only resolutions of the people which were made law by the whole state; that is, they were not laws *per se*. E. S. Staveley's view (*Athenaeum* (1955), 3 ff.) is that in 449 all measures carried by a tribal system of vote, i.e. *plebiscita* in the Concilium Plebis and *leges* in the Comitia Populi Tributa, were made valid, subject only to the *auctoritas patrum*, and that this patrician right to veto legislation was cancelled in regard to (i) the Comitia Tributa by the Lex Publilia of 339, and (ii) the Concilium Plebis by the Lex Hortensia of 287.

(c) *The tribunate*: according to Livy's third law the *caput* of any man who harmed the tribunes or aediles should be devoted to the gods and his goods confiscated and sold at the temple of Ceres, Liber and Libera. This view, which affirms the sacrosanctity of the plebeian officers in law, may derive from a tradition designed to explain away the revolutionary character of the tribunate. Nevertheless, it is quite possible that the tribune's rights, which hitherto had been based on a *lex sacrata* sworn by the plebs, were now confirmed by law. Diodorus (xii, 25) records that one of the provisions of the Valerio-Horatian laws was that ten tribunes should be chosen annually to guard the liberty of the citizens. (He adds that one of the consuls must be a plebeian and that the tribunes on pain of being burnt alive must appoint their successors before going out of office. The former clause is an anticipation of fourth-century conditions; the latter is a plebeian agreement, not a legal pact between plebeians and patricians.) Though Diodorus is obviously wrong in supposing the tribunes were first created in 449 (he has indeed already referred to their existence in 471) and though the date when their number was raised to ten is uncertain (Livy put it at 457 but 449 is quite possible), he may be right in supposing that the patricians in 449 first recognized in law the tribunate which they had long been forced to recognize in fact. This would help to explain why the Valerio-Horatian laws were regarded as a milestone on the plebeian advance to success. Otherwise, especially for those who reject the view that they legalized *plebiscita*, their importance would seem obscure. Such a concession may well have been won as the result of a secession.

21. MILITARY TRIBUNES WITH CONSULAR POWER. Beloch's view that all the plebeian names in the Fasti from 444 to 367 are interpolations is too drastic. Cf. *CAH*, vii, 520. In 22 years between 444 and 367 BC consuls, not military tribunes, were elected. The view that consular tribunes were created for military needs or for administrative convenience (cf. K. von Fritz, *Historia*, 1950, 37 ff.) has been rejected by E. S. Staveley (*JRS.*, 1953, 30 ff.) who champions Livy's explanation that the purpose was political, designed to appease plebeian agitation for the consulship. F. E. Adcock (*JRS.*, 1957, 9 ff.) finds no *single* explanation satisfactory: in the years 444–406, when there was much oscillation between consuls and consular tribunes, different reasons will have operated at different times; in the years 405–367 the preference for consular tribunes reflected the balance of supply and demand in regard to approved generals and administrators. A. Boddington (*Historia*, 1959, 365 ff.) suggests that at first the consular tribunes were supplementary colleagues of the consuls, appointed at any time of the year to meet unexpected military needs, and only later (probably after 390) did they form an alternative magistracy to the consulship. See also R. Sealey, *Latomus* (1959), 521 ff; J. Pinsent, 'Military Tribunes and Plebeian Consuls: The Fasti from 444 to 342', *Historia-Einzelschriften*, Heft 24 (1975), who examines the chronological basis of the ancient tradition; but on Pinsent see A. Drummond, *JRS*, 1978, 187 f.

22. THE CENSORSHIP. In general see J. Suolahti, *The Roman Censors* (1963).

CHAPTER IV THE ROMAN REPUBLIC AND
ITS NEIGHBOURS

1. ROME AND THE LATINS. The Roman tradition has naturally stressed Rome's increasingly dominant position *vis-à-vis* the Latins, and it may well be that this domination took longer to achieve than the later Romans liked to recognize. Thus the 'Roman' colonies founded in the early fifth century were in fact federal 'Latin' colonies, in which Rome shared, and perhaps she did not dictate the policy leading to their foundation (see p. 95). While the Latins continued as long as possible to maintain a belief in the sovereignty of their federal organization, the Romans increasingly tended to minimize any

feeling of dependence on the Latins. However, a recognition of some pro-
Roman bias in the Roman sources need not lead to acceptance of the far-
reaching views of A. Alföldi, who in his stimulating and ingenious book,
Early Rome and the Latins (1964), argued that the whole picture of early Rome
in relation to the other Latin cities which is given by Livy was deliberately
invented by Fabius Pictor in an attempt to show that sixth-century Rome was
the leading Latin city, whereas in fact (so Alföldi argues) Rome only gained
the predominance in the later fifth century, after having been dominated by
Alba Longa and Lavinium and then by a string of Etruscan cities (cf. 453
n. 12 above). This large-scale deliberate falsification by Fabius can scarcely
be accepted: for its decisive rejection see A. Momigliano, *Quarto Contrib.*,
487 ff. (= *JRS*, 1967, 211 ff.), Ogilvie, *Cl. Rev.* (1966), 94 ff., and A. N.
Sherwin-White, *Rom. Cit.*, edn 2, 190 ff.

Alföldi has now restated his position and replied to his critics in *Römische
Frühgeschichte* (1976). His detailed arguments cannot be examined here:
whether he is right or wrong on this point or that, the basic question is
whether he is right both on a sufficient number of points to provide any
justification for so radically reconstructed a picture of early Rome and in his
belief that it is more likely to be true than the more traditional one (whether
or not this hypothetical picture was invented by Fabius Pictor or found in
part by him in his earlier sources). The matter must be left to future debate,
and here it can only be said that in the writer's view this attempt to undermine
the traditional structure has failed: too many of the foundations on which the
latter rest remain unshaken: Etruscan Rome survives as a great and powerful
city.

2. LAKE REGILLUS. Despite the story of the help given to the Romans by the
horsemen gods, Castor and Pollux, the battle seems to have been a hoplite
affair, since Livy (ii, 20, 10) records that the Roman cavalry, after riding to
the battlefield, dismounted and fought on foot. Some ten years after the battle
a temple of Castor and Pollux was dedicated in the Roman Forum. The battle
and the divine epiphany were also commemorated by a parade of horsemen
(*transvectio equorum*), which was held on 15 July during the later Republic and
was revived by Augustus. On the importance of the cult of the Dioscuri in
early Latium see p. 40.

3. THE CASSIAN TREATY. See Livy, ii, 33, 4; Dion. Halic., vi, 95. The text
survived in the early days of Cicero (*pro Balbo*, 53). The thirty Latin cities may
represent a later total of the League (some time before 338 BC) rather than the
number at the time of signing the treaty. Livy (ii, 22, 5) may suggest that the
treaty was made in 495 by Cassius as a fetial priest rather than in 493, the year
of his second consulship, where Livy later (ii, 33, 4) places it; closer to the
battle would make better sense. Radical attempts to question the traditional
date are scarcely supported by valid evidence, e.g. by Beloch (*Röm. Gesch.*,
189 ff.) who places it in 358 when Livy says it was renewed. Any attempt to
place it after 338 is ludicrous, as the Latin League had no political existence
then. The only possible date, other than the traditional one, is the period after

the Gallic invasion, when Roman authority was weakened. But an early date is supported by its internal evidence. This suggests that Rome was not more powerful than the Latins, as she afterwards became; and as the booty was to be divided into two parts, neither party can have had allies, i.e. it is prior to Rome's alliance with the Hernici. For a defence of the tradition see A. N. Sherwin-White, *Rom. Cit.*, edn 2, 20 ff. On the machinery of the League and arrangements for military leadership (which are uncertain) see Ogilvie, *Livy*, 400.

4. THE HERNICI.   Their ethnic affinities are uncertain. Beloch (*Röm. Gesch.*, 197 ff.) would place the Hernican, like the Latin, alliance in the fourth century.

5. SABINE CONQUEST OF ROME?   This is the view of E. Pais, *Ricerche sulla storia e diritto*, Ser. i, 349 ff. Details about Herdonius are confused (Livy, ii, 15–18). Since the episode of a corps of Tusculans intervening on behalf of Rome does not look like a complete invention, there may be a core of truth in the story, but see Ogilvie, *Livy* 423 ff. (who thinks that the Sabines had an understanding with Etruscan Veii). The view of Mommsen is that the Romans on the contrary even annexed some Sabine territory, a view that is thus diametrically opposed to that of Pais.

6. THE CLAUDII.   The migration to Rome is placed in 504 by Livy, ii, 16, 4, Dion. Hal., v, 40 and Plutarch, *Publ.* 21, in the time of Romulus by Suetonius, *Tib.* 1, and in that of the Tarquins by Appian, *Reg.* 12. Considerations of family prestige or of the creation of new patricians might point to either of the earlier dates, but the disturbed conditions of *c.* 504, together with the probable creation of a new tribe, the Claudia, in 495, support the later date.

7. PRISCAE LATINAE COLONIAE.   This is the best title for these early federal settlements. They are discussed by E. T. Salmon, *Roman Colonization* (1969), 40 ff. and in more detail in *Phoenix*, 1953, 93 ff. and 123 ff. The early foundation of such colonies is denied by some (e.g. E. Meyer) and their establishment is dated at the end of the fifth century, but the fact that they were captured later by Rome does not mean that they were not originally pro-Roman: they may have changed hands more than once in the course of the century. Excavations at Norba suggest that the smaller sixth/fifth-century walls were superseded about 340 by a larger circuit: see G. Lugli, *Rend. Lincei*, 1947, 294.

8. CORIOLANUS.   See H. Last, *CAH*, vii, 498 f., E. T. Salmon, *Cl. Quart.*, 1930, 96 ff., and Ogilvie, *Livy*, 314 f. (On Plutarch's treatment of the story see D. A. Russell, *JRS* 1963, 21 ff.)

Festus (180 L) preserves the fragmentary record of an inscription which originally recorded the names of nine Romans (seven being ex-consuls) who fell in a battle against the Volsci (c. 487 BC?) and were cremated and buried in the Circus Maximus.

9. ARDEA.   Although excavation has not substantiated the tradition of the colony, there is no need to reject it (with Beloch, *Röm. Gesch.*, 147, who does,

however, accept the *foedus Ardeatinum*). A similar treaty with Lavinium (and perhaps with Aricia), outside the framework of the Cassian treaty, shows that Rome was beginning to add a limited series of local alliances to her general confederation with Latium as a whole. Cf. A. N. Sherwin-White, *Rom. Cit.*, edn 2, 26.

10. THE CREMERA DISASTER.   The traditional date of 479 is suitable: when later the Romans had to bear the full weight of the Volscian push they were free from complications in Etruria. The exact date accords with the fact that the name Fabius which appears in the Fasti of the seven years 485–479 is missing for the next eleven years; this in itself helps to confirm the tradition. The nature of the engagement has been used to suggest that hoplite tactics had not yet been introduced. However, during the disturbed days of the early Republic (with episodes like those of Porsenna's activities) disciplined phalanx warfare may well have given place temporarily to more 'heroic' methods of fighting, or, more probably, an irregular formation was deliberately used on a mission aimed at raiding and seizing an enemy strongpoint on the frontier, a mission for which the Fabii may well have volunteered (possibly because of their local interests in the district).

11. FIDENAE.   Velthur Tolumne, a member of the family of the Tolumnii, is mentioned in an inscription (?sixth-century) from Veii: B. Nogara, *Not. d. Scavi* (1930), 327 f. Augustus corrected the popular view that Cossus won the *spolia* as military tribune in 437 by discovering that the breastplate referred to Cossus as consul. Unless Augustus misrepresented the facts in order to justify his refusal of the *spolia opima* to M. Crassus, governor of Macedonia, or misread an abbreviation of the name Cossus as consul, the date of the war must have been the consulship of Cossus, i.e. 428 BC. Serious doubts must arise when it is recalled that in this early period the chief magistrate was called praetor not consul, and that *cognomina* were not officially written; however, the original inscription might have been restored sometime during the four centuries before Augustus saw it. The record of the first war may be due to the *cognomina* of the consul L. Sergius Fidenas and of the dictator Q. Servilius Fidenas; these may have been given because these men owned property around Fidenae rather than because they had won triumphs. It is, however, possible that they were involved in earlier operations around Fidenae, though the details of the war of 437 undoubtedly belong to 428–425.

12. THE SIEGE AND FATE OF VEII.   On the site of Veii see J. B. Ward-Perkins, *PBSR*, 1961 (and for the *ager Veientanus*, ibid., 1968). On Livy's account of the siege see Ogilvie, *Livy*, 626 ff. (he dates the fall to 392–1). Archaeological evidence shows that the natural defences were artificially strengthened at the end of the fifth century against the Roman attack: the tufa wall was cut back and elsewhere a wall of stone and earth was built. The story of the capture by driving a tunnel under the citadel must be rejected, but it may have arisen from the presence of numerous drainage tunnels (*cuniculi*) in the neighbourhood. In fact at the Roman camp in the north-west the newly-built wall was constructed over *cuniculi* which had been filled in with earth and stones.

The Romans could possibly have used these to enter the city but not the citadel, which was solid underneath. The story of the draining may or may not have some connection with this episode: the *emissarium* of the Alban Lake, an engineering work some two thousand yards long, was certainly not constructed later than the siege of Veii. After the fall of Veii the Romans solemnly transferred the statue and cult of Juno Regina by a ritual of *evocatio* to Rome: the statue was installed by the victorious Camillus on the Aventine. The dedication of the golden bowl at Delphi may be accepted: though stolen en route by the Liparians, it was restored, only to be melted down later by Onomarchus; however, the bronze base remained. The dedication is important because it shows the early friendship of Rome and Massilia (on their early relations see G. Nenci, *Riv. di stor. Ligure*, 1958), and Rome's interest in Greece and Apollo. It is not surprising that Rome should send a gift to Delphi when her neighbour Caere maintained a treasury there.

After its destruction Veii maintained only a trickle of life, while the resettlement of its territory is marked by the pottery found on the farms: on one hundred sites examined, the cessation of black-glazed ware at about one third indicates the end of their occupation, while the spread of this ware to other sites indicates the farms of the new Roman masters.

13. FALERII. The one fact that emerges from the story of the Faliscan schoolmaster (Livy, v, 27; Dion. Halic., xiii, 1–2) is that Falerii was not stormed (despite Diod., xvi, 96). It was saved by its precipitous position.

14. SUTRIUM, NEPETE, VOLSINII. Diodorus (xix, 98): Sutrium, 390; Nepete, 383 (cf. Livy, vi, 3, 2; 21, 4). But Velleius (i, 14) gives: Sutrium, 383, Nepete, 373. 'To go to Sutrium' remained a proverbial phrase meaning 'to be ready for war'. It was an exposed outpost. Cf. Plautus, *Casina*, 524. The tradition (Livy, v, 3–2; Diod. xiv, 109) of a Roman war against Volsinii (392–391) is hardly reliable: at most it represents a frontier raid. Rejected by De Sanctis (*SR*, ii, 149), it is accepted by E. Meyer, *Gesch. d. Altertums*, v, 316.

15. ROME AND LATIUM. On their relations see De Sanctis, *SR*, ii, 151 ff., A. J. Toynbee, *Hannibal's Legacy* (1965), i, 115 ff.

16. BATTLE OF ALLIA AND THE SACK OF ROME. The Gauls advanced not perhaps down the Tiber valley, which was too swampy, but round through Sabine territory to Reate and thence by the Via Salaria: see Kromayer and Veith, *Atlas, Röm. Abt.*, Blatt. 1. The numbers are also given as 70,000, against 40,000 Romans (cf. Diod., xiv, 113, 114; Plut. *Camillus*, 18). The battle is placed on the left or eastern bank of the Tiber by all ancient writers except Diodorus who places it on the right bank. The main objections to the right bank are (1) the Allia which gave its name to the battle is on the left bank, (2) a flight to Veii would be unlikely if the Romans were forced back on the right bank, (3) it is *a priori* probable that the Gauls would advance on the Roman side of the Tiber. Mommsen, followed by E. Meyer, argued for the right bank. See Kromayer, *Schlachtfelder*, iv, 449 ff. and Schachermeyr, *Klio*, 1929, 277 ff. who support the left bank. O. Skutsch, *JRS*, 1953, 77 f. and 1978,

93 f., has drawn attention to traces of a tradition (observable perhaps in Ennius, *Annales*, frg. 164, Tacitus, *Ann.*, xi, 23, and in Silius Italicus, *Pun.*, i, 525 f.; iv, 150 f.; vi, 555 f.) that the Capitol actually fell to the Gauls. This tradition, however, must be rejected. For traces of the devastation see L. G. Roberts, *Mem. Amer. Acad. Rome*, 1918, 55 f. and E. Gjerstad, *Early Rome*, vol. iii (1960), index, *s.v.* Gallic invasion; they include a layer of roof-tiles on the site of the Comitium in the Forum. Livy (v, 40, 9 f) tells how in the evacuation of the *sacra* the Vestals had been helped by a certain Lucius Albinus, while Plutarch (*Camill.*, 22, 4) says that Aristotle mentions a Lucius as the man who saved Rome. This is important both as confirming the tradition and also as showing that it is earlier than the later building up of Camillus as the saviour-hero of Rome.

17. SOME LEGENDS OR FACTS.   As to the story of the senators, Ogilvie (*Livy*, 725 f.) is inclined to accept it as a deliberate act of *devotio*. He also points out that although geese were not sacred to Juno, birds were kept on the Capitol for purposes of divination (hens, used later, may only have been imported in the fourth century). The real reason for the withdrawal of the Gauls was probably a report that the Veneti were attacking Cisalpine Gaul (Polybius, ii, 18, 3), while Livy (v, 48, 1) refers to pestilence among the Gauls. Diodorus (xiv, 117, 7) records that the Gauls were defeated not by the Romans but by the Caeretans in Sabine territory and the gold was thus recovered. Livy, however, had no difficulty in turning Rome's disaster to Rome's glory: after Brennus' insolence, Camillus appeared as a *deus ex machina* and routed the enemy. Livy puts in his mouth a fine speech (v, 51–4) appealing for the preservation of Rome and its glory; this may reflect fears at the end of the Republic that the capital of the Empire might be transferred from Rome either by Julius Caesar or Mark Antony, fears which Augustus finally allayed. Lastly, we may note that according to one tradition, Hellenic perhaps in origin, the friendly Greeks of Massilia had advanced the ransom money (Justin, xxiv, 4, 3).

18. THE 'SERVIAN' WALL.   T. Frank (*Roman Buildings of the Republic*, 1924) had supposed that it was built by the Roman army with Veientane captives serving as quarrymen. But see G. Säflund, *Le mura di Roma repubblicana* (1932); Nash, *Pict. Dict. Anc. Rome*, ii, 104 ff. (with bibliography); *Roma Medio Repubblicana. Aspetti culturali di Roma e del Lazio nei secoli iv e iii a.C.* (1973). However, the quarry-marks on the wall seem now to be archaic Latin and not Greek: see F. Castagnoli, *Stud. Rom.*, 1974, 431, n. 14, J. Reynolds, *JRS* 1976, 177.

19. THE WARS.   Accepted in general by e.g. L. Homo, *CAH*, vii, ch. xviii; rejected by Beloch (*Röm. Gesch.*, 319).

20. ETRUSCAN CONTACTS.   In *I rapporti romano-ceriti* (1960) M. Sordi, who has tried to distinguish traces of Etruscan historiography in the surviving tradition, finds strong Etruscan influences in Rome in these years, arising from friendship with Caere. This friendship is placed in a wider setting: it helped to counter Rome's weakness in Latium, to check the expansionist

policy of Dionysius of Syracuse into Italy, to contain Gallic threats, to support Rome's expeditions to Sardinia and Corsica, and to promote friendship with Massilia and the Carthaginian treaty of 348, while internally in Rome a pro-Etruscan plebeian group was strengthened and supported the Licinian reforms. Such a reconstruction, even if the evidence is too weak to give it full support, at least emphasizes the widening horizon that Rome was being forced to face (though Etruscan influence on Roman politics at home is much less likely). But some of the items in Rome's alleged overseas interest at this time are somewhat suspect: attempts to found colonies in Corsica (attested by Theophrastus, *Hist. Plant.*, v, 8, 2, at some unnamed date, but before he wrote in the late fourth century) and in Sardinia *c.* 377 BC (Diod., xv, 27, 4), and the treaty of alliance with Massilia which Justin (lxiii, 5, 10) set as early as 386. Rome's supposed growing Mediterranean interests, arising from her friendship with Etruscan Caere, as expounded by M. Sordi, are taken seriously by J. Heurgon, *Rise of R.* 183 ff.

21. VOLSCIAN DEFEATS. Beloch (*Röm. Gesch.*, 315 ff.) regards the victory of 389 as a fictitious counterblast to the battle of Allia, and those of 386 and 381 as reduplications of that of 389.

22. CAERE. See A. N. Sherwin-White, *Rom. Cit.*, edn 2, 53 ff.; De Sanctis, *SR*, ii, 256 ff.; Beloch, *Röm. Gesch.*, 363 ff. For a defence of a grant in 386 see M. Sordi, *I rapporti romano-ceriti* (1960), 36 ff.; W. V. Harris, *Rome in Etruria and Umbria* (1971), 45 ff. A. J. Toynbee, *Hannibal's Legacy* (1965), i, 410 ff. and P. A. Brunt, *Italian Manpower* (1971), 515 ff. give full discussions and follow Beloch in dating *civitas sine suffragio* to 274–273. For the wider implications of Rome's relations with Caere see n. 20 above.

23. FURTHER GALLIC RAIDS. Polybius (relying on Fabius Pictor) records that in 357 some Gauls reached the Alban Mount unopposed and that in 346 or 345 they returned to the attack but withdrew when challenged by the Roman army; Livy (drawing upon later annalists) attributes a Roman victory to Camillus' son in 349 when the picturesque incident of the intervention of the raven (*corvus*) on behalf of M. Valerius Corvus took place. Perhaps the events recorded in 349 and 346 refer to one affair, while Livy's raid of 360 may be equated with the Polybian incident of 357.

24. SABELLIAN CAMPANIA. For the occupation of Campania by the Sabellians see T. J. Cornell, *Museum Helveticum*, 1974, 193 ff.

25. RAIDS ON CENTRAL ITALY. In 384 Dionysius I raided Pyrgi and sacked the rich Etruscan temple of Leucothea or Eileithyia (Diodorus, xv, 14). Traces of his raid survive: see *Arch. Class* 1957, 213. There seems no good reason to doubt Livy's references (vii, 25, 4; 26, 13) to raids in Latium in 349.

26. THE SAMNITES. On their culture and history see E. T. Salmon's standard work, *Samnium and the Samnites* (1967). M. Sordi, *Roma e i Sanniti nel IV secolo A.C.* (1969) takes full note of the 'international' background, but is speculative, not least in chronological reconstruction (cf. J. Pinsent, *JRS*, 1971, 271 f.).

27. ROMAN VICTORIES? The capture of Sora on the Upper Liris and the victory

over the Aurunci attributed to 345 (Livy, vii, 28) are probably anticipations of the events of 314: see De Sanctis, *SR*, ii, 266.

28. THE FIRST SAMNITE WAR.   F. E. Adcock, who rejects the war, writes (*CAH*, vii, 588) that to accept it one would have to postulate 'folly in the Romans, blindness in the Latins, a short memory for benefits in the Campanians and a short memory for injuries in the Samnites'. De Sanctis (ii, 269 ff.), however, accepts the war as historical in outline; though rejecting the alleged *deditio* of the Campanians to Rome, he believes in a Romano-Campanian alliance and in the two Roman victories at Suessula and Mt Gaurus, but he rejects the battle at Saticula as an anticipation of Caudium. If the war is accepted, Rome's motives may include a desire to get a foothold in the rear of the Volsci, Aurunci and discontented Latins, to win control of one of the wealthiest cities in Italy and to prevent the Samnites from strengthening their position in Campania: so S. W. Spaeth, *The Causes of Wars, 343–265* (1926), 20. The historicity of the war is also defended by E. T. Salmon, *Samnium and the Samnites* (1967), 195 ff. (cf. also A. Bernardi, *Athenaeum*, 1943, 21 ff.) and E. S. Staveley, *Historia*, 1959, 419 ff. Staveley believes that behind Rome's desire to extend her influence southwards into Campania lay a growing interest in trade and industry, and that this Campanian policy was promoted by a group of men who included Q. Publilius Philo, M. Valerius Corvus, Sp. Postumius Albinus, C. Maenius and later the great Appius Claudius. On the other hand Salmon finds the advocates of this southern policy in a group of patricians, though with the support of some plebeian leaders (*Samnium*, 203 ff.). While it is clear that a group of senators successfully continued to advocate a more active policy towards Campania, the extent to which military motives were reinforced by commercial interests must remain doubtful.

29. CAMPANIAN POLICY. If the First Samnite War and the Roman-Campanian alliance are accepted, this sudden change in the Campanians has to be explained. De Sanctis (*SR*, ii, 274) suggests that as they were allies of the Roman-Latin alliance they had to choose between the two and chose to support the weaker side because they could thus hope to preserve their independence in the event of being victorious. The relations of Rome and Capua between 343 and 338 are discussed by A. Bernardi, *Athenaeum*, 1942, 88 ff., 1943, 21 ff. On early Capua see J. Heurgon, *Capoue préromaine* (1942). (On Republican Capua see M. Frederiksen (*PBSR*, 1954, 80 ff.), who also discusses the (Greek) origin of the Campanian cavalry, *Dialoghi di Archeologia*, 1968, 3 ff.)

30. THE LATIN WAR.   Livy, viii, 3–14. See F. E. Adcock, *CAH*, vii, 589 ff. Livy's account (vii, 42–viii, 1) of how the consul of 341 defeated the Volscians of Privernum who had raided Setia and Norba is probably an anticipation of the incident of 329. Manlius' route in 340 is uncertain (cf. Salmon, *Samnium*, 207, n. 3); the route mentioned in the text is supported by Adcock (*CAH*, vii, 590), but rejected by De Sanctis (*SR*, ii, 276). The battle of Trifanum (whose precise site is unknown) was clearly fought not far from Capua. Diodorus (xvi, 90, 2) puts it near Suessa. Livy (vii, 6, 8; 11, 8) gives

two battles, which should be reduced to one. Since Trifanum is unknown, perhaps the battle should be called that of Suessa. After the battle in 338 near Antium, the prows (*rostra*) of the ships of Antium were taken to adorn the Comitium in the Forum at Rome.

CHAPTER V   THE UNION OF THE ORDERS AND THE CONSTITUTION

1. A LAND BILL IN 367?   This is rejected by De Sanctis, *SR*, ii, 216 ff. and Beloch, *Röm. Gesch.*, 344, but defended by Münzer, *PW*, xiii s.v. Licinius Stolo, by H. Last, *CAH*, vii, 58 ff., by T. Frank, *Econ. Survey*, i 27 f. and by De Martino, *St. d. cos. rom.* 1, 396 ff. A clause limiting the number of sheep and cattle which could be kept on public pastures may have been included. The provision of a certain proportion of free labour is obviously an anticipation. G. Tibiletti in his discussion of *possessio* of *ager publicus* (*Athenaeum.* 1948, 173 ff., 1949, 1 ff., 1950, 245 ff.) accepts a Licinian law *de modo agrorum* but argues that it admitted plebeians to *possessio*; it is doubtful, however, whether this right was hitherto restricted by law to patricians. He also believes that a law establishing 500 *iugera* and limiting pasturage was passed after the Hannibalic War.

2. DEBT REMISSION?   This measure is defended by H. Last, *CAH*, vii, 543.

3. LEX POETELIA.   See Cicero, *de rep.*, ii, 59. E. Pais. *Ricerche sulla storia e sul diritto publico di Roma*, iv, 44 ff.

4. LICINIAN-SEXTIAN ROGATIONS.   On the reorganization of the Roman government in 366 see K. von Fritz, *Historia*, 1950, 1 ff., who emphasizes the influence of administrative needs.

5. CAMILLUS AND CONCORD.   See A. Momigliano, *Cl. Qu.*, 1943, 111 ff. (= *Secondo Contrib.*, 89 ff.). The temple lay in the north-west corner of the Forum. The surviving remains belong to a restoration made by Tiberius and dedicated in AD 10.

6. PLEBEIAN CONSULS.   Münzer's view (*Röm. Adelsparteien*, 30) that at this time the consulship alternated annually between the Orders is improbable. However, possibly the Leges Liciniae-Sextiae had made one plebeian consulship merely permissive and it was not made obligatory until the Lex Genucia in 342.

7. PLEBISCITA.   See above, p. 469 n. 20. Possibly it was enacted in 339 that the consul must bring *plebiscita* before the Comitia Centuriata for confirmation or rejection. It is not very likely that they were ever subject to the *auctoritas patrum*: cf. *CAH*, vii, 483.

8. NEWCOMERS.   Cicero, *pro Plancio*, 19. Not all the cases advanced by Münzer (*Röm. Adelsparteien*, 46 ff.) are acceptable: see *CAH*, vii, 548; L. R. Taylor, *Voting Districts of the Roman Republic* (1960), 287 f.; F. Cassola, I *Gruppi politici*, (1962), 152 ff; A. J. Toynbee, *Hannibal's Legacy*; (1965), 340 is more favourable.

9. APPIUS CLAUDIUS. Tradition is weighted against him: it may derive from Fabius Pictor whose clan was hostile to the Claudii. His censorship is dated to 312 by Livy (ix, 29, 6) and to 310 by Diodorus (xx, 36, 1). Livy records that he refused to resign his office; according to some annalists he was still censor when he was elected consul in 308. This hostile tradition may have arisen from doubt about the date of his office. He may also have suffered from the reputation of his tyrannical ancestor, the Decemvir. See A. Garzetti, *Athenaeum*, 1947, 175 ff.; E. S. Staveley, *Historia*, 1959, 410 ff.; E. Ferenczy, *From the Patrician State to the Patricio-Plebeian State* (Budapest, 1976), 144–217; on his tribal reforms see also P. Fraccaro, *Athenaeum*, 1935, 150 ff. (= *Opuscula*, ii, 1957, 149 ff.) and L. R. Taylor, *Voting Districts of the Roman Republic* (1960), 11 and 133 ff. (Fraccaro has shown that the landless *were* enrolled in any tribe.) Appius Claudius was a cultured patrician and a legal expert. The motives that led him to champion radical reform have been variously interpreted. Niebuhr regarded him as the leader of the patricians against the new patricio-plebeian nobility. Mommsen went to the other extreme and saw in him a democratic demagogue and would-be Caesar. To Garzetti he was a moderate who by building up his *clientela* hoped to succeed to the position that Publilius Philo had enjoyed. Staveley sees him as trying to change a basically agricultural community into one in which agriculture and commerce played an equal part. Ferenczy takes an even more radical view of Appius' tribal reform: all citizens were allotted to their tribes, irrespective of their place of domicile or financial resources, both for political reasons and to strengthen the army.

CHAPTER VI ROME'S CONQUEST AND ORGANIZATION
OF ITALY

1. NEAPOLIS. Livy (vii, 22–6) wrongly says that there were two cities in one at Naples. The quarter of the oldest inhabitants, Palaeopolis, corresponds with Pizzofalcone in the modern city (cf. *Par. Pass.*, 1952, 250, 269 f.); on the city in general see M. A. Napoli, *Napoli greco-romana* (1959). Despite difficulties in Livy, it is too radical to reject the siege entirely (as is done by T. Frank, *Roman Imperialism* (1914), 45). One fact at any rate is above suspicion: the resultant alliance with Rome. On Rome's relations with Naples see also W. Hoffmann, *Rom und die Griechische Welt im vierten Jahrhundert* (1934), 21 ff.

2. LUCANIA AND APULIA. Livy (viii, 25, 3; 27, 2) says that Rome concluded alliances with the Lucani and Apuli. The Lucanian alliance should probably be rejected (Livy, viii, 27, 5–10, says the Lucanians later repudiated their treaty), while that with Apulia must remain uncertain (it is rejected by E. T. Salmon, *Samnium and the Samnites* (1967), 215). But cf. M. W. Frederiksen, *JRS*, 1968, 226, and R. M. Ogilvie, *Cl. Rev.*, 1968, 331.

3. THE CAUDINE FORKS. The exact site of the disaster is uncertain. See Kromayer, *Schlachtfelder*, iv, 481 ff. and *Atlas, Röm. Abt.*, col. 2 ff.; P.

Sommella, *Antichi campi di battaglia in Italia* (1967), 49 ff. Three main sites have been suggested: (a) the pass between Arienzo and Arpaia, (b) the more open ground between Arpaia and Montesarchio, and (c) between S. Agata dei Goti (Saticula) and Moiano. (a) is traditional and the most probable (it contains a locality still named Forchia), and is supported by Kromayer and by Salmon (*Samnium*, 226); cf. D. Adamesteanu, *Atti II Conv. di Studi sulla Magna Grecia* (1963), 57; for (b) see De Sanctis, *SR*, ii, 307 ff.; (c) is advocated by F. E. Adcock, *CAH*, vii, 599.

4. PEACE OR WAR? Livy's story of the repudiation of the peace, which is probably based on the Senate's attitude to the capitulation of Mancinus in Spain in 137 BC (p. 304), should be rejected. E. T. Salmon (*JRS*, 1929, 13) believes that in 318 the Romans prolonged the *pax Caudina* by forming a two-years' truce with Samnium, as alleged by Livy (ix, 20). This truce, however, could have been invented by the annalists who rejected the *pax Caudina* in order to account for the peacefulness of these years. In any case the Second Samnite War (which was the First if the struggle of 343 is rejected) in practice consisted of two wars, from 326–321 and 310–304.

5. SATRICUM AND ARDEA. Livy (ix, 21) says the Romans attacked Saticula, but this has probably been confused with Satricum: see E. T. Salmon, *TAPA*, 1957, 99 ff. The raid on Ardea is recorded by Strabo (v, 232): traces of the catastrophe appear to survive: see *Bollet. Stud. Mediterr.*, 1931, 15.

6. THE ETRUSCAN WAR. The accounts of these campaigns in Livy, ix, and Diodorus, xx, 35, 1–5; 44, 8–9, are full of difficulties which have led some historians to extreme scepticism: thus, e.g., Beloch (*Röm. Gesch.* 413 ff.), rejects Fabius' victory as a reduplication of the events of 295; he limits operations to a fight between Q. Aemilius and the Etruscans at Sutrium (Livy, ix, 37; Diod. xx, 35) and places the alliances with Cortona, etc. in 294 BC, with Camerinum and Ocriculum in 295. Such hypercriticism is unjustified. For a more balanced and moderate assessment, see W. V. Harris, *Rome in Etruria and Umbria* (1971), 49 ff. Unless the whole campaign of 311 is merely a doublet of that of 310, the Etruscan attack on Sutrium will have started in 311.

7. BOVIANUM. It is generally believed that there were two Samnite towns named Bovianum: B. Vetus and B. Pentrorum. The latter is modern Boiano, while the former has always been identified with Pietrabbondante. However, in the light of recent excavations at Pietrabbondante it has been suggested that this was not the site of Bovianum Vetus, which in fact may not have existed: see Salmon, *Samnium*, 13, n. Regarding the campaign of 305, Livy says (ix, 44) that the Romans penetrated to Bovianum; if this is accepted the site will in any case be that of Boiano. Diodorus on the other hand places the Roman success at Bola (an ancient Latin town of unknown site).

8. ROME AND ALEXANDER. Bruttians, Lucanians and Etruscans visited the court of Alexander the Great at Babylon. The story that the Romans also sent envoys (Pliny, *NH*, iii, 57) is probably rightly doubted by Arrian (vii, 15, 5–6). Alexander's alleged idea of sending an expedition to Italy and the west

(Diod., xviii, 4, 3) is also doubted by many, but in fact his final plans are simply not known: see E. Badian, *Harvard Stud. Cl. Phil.*, 1967, 204. Later Romans probably believed in this threat and Livy patriotically argues that if he had invaded Italy, Alexander would have met the same fate as Pyrrhus (ix, 17). Strabo (v, 232) alleged that Alexander, and later Demetrius Poliorcetes, protested to Rome about Italian pirates; this may be true.

9. THE PHILINUS TREATY.   Polybius (iii, 26, 3 f.) denied the assertion of the pro-Carthaginian historian, Philinus of Sicily, that there was a treaty between Rome and Carthage which forbade the Romans to enter Sicily and the Carthaginians Italy. If Philinus, however, was right (cf. A. J. Toynbee, *Hannibal's Legacy* (1965), i, 543 ff.; R. E. Mitchell, *Historia*, 1971, 633 ff.), the treaty should probably be dated to 306. See further for its place in the context of Romano-Punic treaties pp. 160, 486.)

10. THE THIRD SAMNITE WAR.   The theory of Beloch (*Röm. Gesch.*, 426 ff.), that the war of 298–290 was mainly fought against the Sabines rather than the Samnites and that the Roman tradition has confused the names, has not met with much support (cf. F. E. Adcock, *CAH*, vii, 615; Salmon, *Samnium*, 259). For the war see Salmon, op. cit., 255 ff. and, for Etruscan involvement, W. V. Harris, *Rome in Etruria and Umbria* (1971), 61 ff. The alleged capture of Bovianum by M. Fulvius in 298 is probably a duplicate of its capture in 305, while his alleged campaign in Etruria *may* be a duplicate of that in 295. The inscription on the sarcophagus of Scipio Barbatus claims that he 'subdued all Lucania' (Dessau, *ILS*, n. 1). A. La Regina (*Dialoghi di Arch.*, 1968, 173 ff.) suggests that the Lucani conquered by him were a small northern group in the Sango valley in Samnium.

11. SENTINUM.   Polybius (ii, 19) mentions only Samnites and Gauls. Livy (x, 27, 3) adds Etruscans and Umbrians (cf. Diod., xxi, 6); if true, their numbers are likely to have been small. Beloch naturally converts the Samnites into Sabines. The story of the *devotio* of Decius to the Gods Below is told of three Decii: his father at Veseris in 340, and his son at Asculum in 279. The matter is uncertain. Beloch would even rob this Decius of his death at Sentinum and believes that he fought later in Samnium. Sentinum was situated at Sassoferrato, to the north of which the battle is placed by P. Sommella, *Antichi campi di battaglia in Italia* (1967). A contemporary Greek historian, Duris, put the casualties at 100,000! (Diod, xxi, 6, 1).

12. MANIUS CURIUS DENTATUS AND 284 BC.   He had terminated the Third Samnite War in 290 and was a man of considerable distinction: on him see G. Forni, *Athenaeum*, 1953, 170–240. On the events of 284 see Polybius, ii, 19; Walbank, *Polybius*, i, 188 ff.; E. T. Salmon, *Cl. Ph.*, 1935, 23 ff.; W. V. Harris, *Rome in Etruria* (1971), 79 f.; J. H. Corbett, *Historia*, 1971, 656 ff.; M. G. Morgan, *Cl. Qu.*, 1972, 309. Harris argues strongly (op. cit., 85 ff.) that Rome's final post-war settlements with the Etruscan (and Umbrian) cities were based on *foedera* (not *indutiae*).

13. THE TARENTINE TREATY.   Its date is uncertain, whether 348 (Mommsen), 332 (M. Cary, *J. Philology*, 1920, 165 ff.), 315 (Burger, *Der Kampf zwischen Rom und Samnium* (1898)), or 303 (De Sanctis and Beloch).

14. AGATHOCLES. During his intervention in Italy the tyrant of Syracuse engaged Samnite, Etruscan, Celtic and Campanian mercenaries, but it is uncertain whether he had any relations with Rome, though this is not impossible. Beloch (*Griechische Geschichte*, IV, i, 205) regarded Venusia as a Roman outpost against Agathocles.

15. ROMAN POLICY. Some (e.g. T. Frank, *CAH*, vii, 641) have attributed Rome's policy of intervention in the south to the plebeian leaders, now strengthened by the Lex Hortensia. E. T. Salmon (*Samnium*, 281 ff.), however thinks that the 'southern lobby' in the Senate comprised, as earlier, a faction of the patricio-plebeian nobility, and included Ap. Claudius Caecus, P. Cornelius Rufinus, P. Valerius Corvus, L. Papirius Cursor, and C. Aelius (who proposed that aid should be sent to Thurii in 286/285). See also F. Cassola, *I gruppi politici Romani* (1962), 159 ff.; he argues for a sharp division of interest between those nobles who championed the rural plebs and those who backed the merchant class, thus probably overemphasizing economic influences in Roman policy. R. E. Mitchell stresses the possible effect on Carthage of Rome's involvement in southern affairs from 326 onwards (*Historia*, 1971. 633 ff.).

16. PYRRHUS. In Plutarch's *Life of Pyrrhus* there is a substratum of sound material which he derived from the historian Hieronymus of Cardia, who in turn made use of Pyrrhus' own *Memoirs*. A detailed modern account is given by P. Lévêque, *Pyrrhos* (1957). G. Nenci, *Pirrho, aspirazioni egemoniche ed equilibrio mediterraneo* (1953), is primarily concerned with Pyrrhus' policy: Nenci believes that Pyrrhus was supporting a supposed anti-Carthaginian policy of the Ptolemies and that therefore the primary target of his western adventure was Carthage rather than Rome. But see J. V. A. Fine, *AJPhil.*, 1957, 108 ff. It is not possible to discuss here the many controversial details raised by Pyrrhus' battles in Italy, but on one aspect of these battles (his use of 'Lucanian oxen', as the Romans nicknamed his elephants) see H. H. Scullard, *The Elephant in the Greek and Roman World* (1974), ch. iv (with notes); his Indian elephants are depicted on a painted dish, on a coin of Tarentum and on early Italian *aes signatum* (cf. Scullard, plates vii a, xiv a and b).

17. PEACE NEGOTIATIONS. These are a matter of dispute. The main possibilities are that Cineas went to Rome (a) in 280, (b) in 279 after the battle of Asculum, (c) twice, in 280 and 279 (cf. W. Judeich, *Klio*, 1926, 1 ff.), (d) once only in 280, but that peace negotiations were conducted in Campania early in 279 (G. N. Cross, *Epirus* (1932), 115 ff.). See further, A. Passerini, *Athenaeum*, 1943, 92 ff.; P. Lévêque, *Pyrrhos* (1957), 341 ff., 404 ff.; M. R. Lefkowitz, *Harvard St. Cl. Ph.*, 1959, 147 ff.

18. THE ROMANO-CARTHAGINIAN TREATY. Polybius, iii, 25. See Walbank, *Polybius*, i, 349 ff.; P. Lévêque, *Pyrrhos* (1957), 409 ff. The treaty is usually dated 279/8. E. Will (*Histoire politique du monde hellénistique* (1966), i, 106 ff.), however, argues for 280, while Nenci, *Historia*, 1958, 261 ff., believes in two agreements, in 280 and 278 (but see Lefkowitz, *Harvard St. Cl. Ph.*, 1959, 170). According to R. E. Mitchell (*Historia*, 1971, 646 ff.) the essence of the negotiations of 279/8 was to reaffirm the Philinus treaty and to arrange

conditions under which any possible joint action might be taken against Pyrrhus (not with him, as often assumed). This interpretation of Polybius (iii, 25) is also reached by K. Meister, *Riv. Fil*, 1970, 408 ff. and in *Historische Kritik bei Polybios* (Wiesbaden, 1975).

If the Romans received any financial help from Carthage, they may have used some to mint their first silver coinage, just as earlier they may have used some of the vast amount of bronze that they received in 290 at the end of the Third Samnite War for producing their heavy cast *aes grave*.

19. PYRRHUS' NAVAL DEFEAT. This battle was interpreted by Beloch (*Griechische Gesch.*, IV, i, 556) and Cross (*Epirus*, 120) as an attempt by the Carthaginians in pursuance of their treaty of 278 to relieve Rhegium, which they suppose was being blockaded by Pyrrhus immediately after the king had landed in Italy.

20. BENEVENTUM. The battle was traditionally fought at Beneventum. Beloch (*Gr. Gesch.*, IV, ii, 476 and *Röm. Gesch.*, 466 ff.), however, questions this and argues in favour of a site near Paestum, the Campi Arusini (cf. Orosius, iv, 2, 3). The idea that the Romans faced Pyrrhus so far north scarcely squares with the traditional account of their recent victories in the south.

21. LOCRI. Twenty-seven bronze tablets, recently discovered, record annual loans made by the temple of Zeus to the city; they include expenses to meet the demands during Pyrrhus' occupation: see A. de Franciscis, *Klearchos*, 1961, 17 ff.; 1962, 66 ff.; 1964, 73 ff.; 1965, 21 ff.; *Atti d. Congr. intern. di Numismatica, 1961* (1965), 21 ff. Locri celebrated her return to Rome by issuing coins which depicted Rome crowned by Pistis (= Fides, Loyalty).

22. THE CAMPANIANS AT RHEGIUM. The date, nature and number of this garrison are uncertain. They were sent by Rome perhaps in 282 and rebelled in 280. Polybius (i, 7, 7) gives 4,000, but other authors differ (confusion may have arisen from the 500 men sent in 278). They were Campanians, under a Campanian commander. The story is told from the Roman point of view (deriving from Fabius Pictor), but some have suspected that Rome was not so innocent or the Campanians so guilty as suggested. Thus F. Cassola (*I gruppi politici romani*, 171 ff.) even argues that Rome, suspecting disloyalty in Rhegium, carried out a preventative massacre. Cf. also A. Toynbee, *Hannibal's Legacy* (1965), i, 101 f. For discussion of sources see Walbank, *Polybius*, i, 52 f.

23. VOLSINII. A recently found inscription, from S. Omobono in Rome, commemorates the dedication of the booty captured in 264 at Volsinii by M. Fulvius Flaccus: *M. FOLV (IO. Q. F. COS) OL. D. VOLS (NIO). CAP (TO).* See *L' Année Epigraph.*, 1964, 72; J. Reynolds, *JRS*, 1971, 138. Cf. Pliny, *NH*, xxxiv, 34.

24. TWELVE LATIN COLONIES. In future Latin colonies the *ius migrandi* was probably limited by the proviso that any Latin settling in Rome and claiming citizenship must leave a son behind him; this measure would check any decline in Latin manpower and thus strengthen the Confederacy. A group of twelve Latin colonies is sometimes referred to as having *ius Arimini* or the *ius*

duodecim coloniarum (Cicero, *pro Caecina*, 102). See Sherwin-White, *Rom. Cit., edn. 2*, 102 ff.; E. T. Salmon, *Roman Colonization* (1969), 92 ff.; and A. Bernardi, *Studia Ghisleriana*, Ser. I, 1948, 237 ff. who suggests that the twelve colonies with *ius Arimini* were the Latin colonies founded in and after 268, Ariminum to Aquileia, which preserved some of the prerogatives of Roman citizenship as *ius conubii* and *commercii* (and with no restriction on *ius migrandi*).

25. MUNICIPIA. So A. N. Sherwin-White, *Rom. Cit.*, edn 2, 59 ff. *contra* H. Rudolf, *Stadt and Staat in röm. Italien* (1935). On the word *municipium*, J. Pinsent, *Cl. Qu.*, 1954, 158 ff. On the municipal organization of Italy see also A. J. Toynbee, *Hannibal's Legacy*, i, 189 ff., 397 ff.

26. MILITARY SERVICE. Allied troops were called up in accordance with a roll (*e formula togatorum*) kept at Rome. This was either a list of the maximum number of troops that the Romans might levy from each ally (so Toynbee, *Hannibal's Legacy*, i, 424 ff.) or a sliding scale, which Rome could vary, indicating that each ally must supply a fixed number of men for each legion that Rome raised for any given year (so P. A. Brunt, *Manpower*, 545 ff., who also discusses the varying proportion of allies to Romans, 677 ff. Cf. also V. Ilari, *Gli Italici nelle strutture militari romane* (1974)).

27. POPULATION. On these figures, which were naturally only general calculations, see Beloch, *Griech. Gesch.*, IV, i, 662 and *Bevölkerung d. Gr.-Röm. Welt* (1886), esp. 367: De Sanctis, *SR*, ii, 425 and 462 ff., III, i, 331; T. Frank, *CAH*, vii, 811 and *Econ. Survey*, i, 56 ff. In addition there were the slaves whose numbers even at this early period cannot have been inconsiderable (p. 358). A. Afzelius, *Die römische Eroberung Italiens, 340–264 v. Chr.*, (1942), has examined the population of Italy and attributes Rome's successful conquest of Italy mainly to her growing superiority in manpower and to her political skill in applying this to the best advantage. See too P. A. Brunt, *Italian Manpower, 225 BC–AD 14* (1971), which though concerned with later periods is especially relevant to this book for the years 225–146 BC.

CHAPTER VII   THE FIRST STRUGGLE

1. CARTHAGE. On Carthage and Carthaginian civilization see S. Gsell, *Histoire ancienne de l'Afrique du Nord*, 8 vols (1914–28); O. Meltzer, *Geschichte der Karthager*, i–ii (1879–96), iii (by U. Kahrstedt, 1913); B. H. Warmington, *Carthage*, edn 2, (1969); G. and C. Charles-Picard, *Daily Life in Carthage* (1961) and *The Life and Death of Carthage* (1968); G. Picard, *Carthage* (1964).

The date of its foundation is still uncertain. The earliest deposit of proto-Corinthian pottery found in the sanctuary of Tanit belongs to *c.* 725 BC, while some Punic pottery is probably slightly older. This comes within sight of the traditional date of 814, and of course earlier tombs may still await discovery. See also p. 518 n. 19.

2. TARTESSUS. A description of the Spanish coast and Tartessus is given in Avienus' *Ora Maritima* which embodies the *Periplus* (sailing directions) of a

sailor from Massilia about 520 BC. A flourishing trade was carried on with Brittany, the British Isles and the northern coasts in tin and amber, while a high degree of culture was attained. Tartessus was probably the biblical Tarshish. See A. Schulten, *Tartessos* (1922) and *CAH*, vii, ch. xxiv; J. M. Blasquez, *Tartessos* (1968); A. Arribas, *The Iberians*. On Phoenician influence in this area see above, p. 442 n. 19. The destruction carried out by the Carthaginians *c*. 500 BC was so effective that later writers confused Tartessus and Maenace with Gades and Malaca. Archaeological evidence attests Punic influence through Andalusia as far north as the Sierra Morena from *c*. 500 BC. Whether this involved political domination (as Schulten believed on the strength of Polybius' remark (ii, 1) that Hamilcar 'recovered' (*anektato*) the district in 237) or merely commercial domination is uncertain. Any direct control would probably be confined to coastal areas and would weaken inland.

3. THE EARLY TREATIES BETWEEN ROME AND CARTHAGE. The contents of the treaties between Rome and Carthage before the First Punic War have been briefly summarized in the text above (p. 160), but their date and number is a matter of great dispute. Polybius (iii, 22 ff.) quotes three and declares that there were only three: these may be called P1, P2 and P3. P1 is dated 508–507, P2 is undated, P3 belongs to the Pyrrhic War in 279–278. Polybius also rejects as false the statement of the pro-Carthaginian Sicilian historian Philinus that there was another treaty which forbade the Romans to enter Sicily and the Carthaginians Italy. Diodorus (xvi, 69) gives only one treaty before that of 279; this he said was the first treaty. According to his chronological system it is placed in 344–343, although this may perhaps be corrected to 348. Livy records a treaty in 348, the fact of a Punic embassy at Rome in 343, another treaty in 306 and again in 279.

The first main problem is the date of P1. The Polybian date of 508 is defended concisely by H. Last (*CAH*, vii, 859 ff.). The conditions implied by the treaty and their considerable difference from those of P2, as well as the archaic language of the treaty (Polybius says that Roman scholars found it difficult to decipher), point to the sixth-century date. If this is accepted, P2 may be dated in 348 in accordance with Livy's first treaty.

Many scholars, however, reject the early date and place P1 in 348. In that case P2 is placed either in 343 (on the assumption that the Carthaginian ambassadors received a treaty in return for their complimentary gift of a golden crown weighing 25 lb) or in 306 (on the assumption that conditions had not altered sufficiently between 348 and 343 to justify a fresh treaty). However, the situation in Italy after 310 militates against placing P2 in the last decade of the fourth century. The date of P3 is not disputed.

The second main problem is whether Polybius' statement that there were only three treaties must be accepted and whether his denial of the treaty recorded by Philinus is valid. Both these points, together with the condition of the Roman state archives, their accessibility, completeness and reliability, are discussed by M. Cary ('A Forgotten Treaty between Rome and Carthage', *JRS*, 1919, 67–77) who makes out a very strong case for accepting the Philinus treaty and placing it in 306; (P1 is then assigned to 348 and P2 to 343). It is argued that Polybius probably had no first-hand acquaintance with the Roman archives which would hardly contain a complete collection of Rome's past treaties. The Philinus treaty is also indicated by Servius (*Ad Aen.*, iv, 628) who probably follows a tradition independent of Philinus. Further, the treaty of 279 implies that certain barriers existed which precluded the Carthaginians from landing in Italy and the Romans from crossing to Sicily; it thus confirms the existence of an earlier treaty which put these territories out of bounds. Polybius denied its existence, but then his pro-Roman sources had good reason to overlook it. The ban may have been military and political rather than commercial: compare the Ebro treaty which forbade the Carthaginians to cross the Ebro, but only ἐπὶ πολέμῳ (Pol., iii, 30, 3). Cary, however, later became more sceptical about the Philinus treaty (*A History of Rome* (1954), ch. xii, n. 8) and was inclined to follow F. Schachermeyr (*Rheinisches Museum*, 1930, 350 ff.), who believes it is a misunderstanding of the pact of 279 which he assumes to have been a 'gentlemen's agreement': the Carthaginians received an informal assurance of a free hand in Sicily. Walbank (*Polybius*, i, 354) thinks it may have been an unpublished agreement toward the end of the war with Pyrrhus.

It is impossible here to enter into details or to refer to all modern theories, e.g. the elaborate suggestion of A. Piganiol, (*Musée belge*, 1923, 177) that Polybius has inverted the order of the first two treaties and that P2 belongs to 348 and P1 to *c.* 327. The present writer is inclined to accept the Philinus treaty of 306, but to place P2 in 348 and P1 in 508. Once it is admitted that the number of treaties has not been irrevocably fixed by Polybius' *ex cathedra* statement, it is impossible to determine the precise number. It is probable that Carthage had treaties with Etruscan Rome and would seek to maintain relations with the new Republic. If it is thought that the phrase 'quarto renovatum' which Livy applies to 279 means literally '*renewed* a fourth time', then a treaty may well be placed in 343, making five in all: in 508, 348, 343, 306 and 279. But more important than the precise number is the fact that the early treaties were commercial, and the last two political.

Amid a great number of recent discussions see Walbank, *Polybius*, i, 337 ff.; ii, 635; iii (1979), 766 f.; and A. J. Toynbee, *Hannibal's Legacy* (1965), 519 ff. For a recent reaffirmation that the Fair Promontory was west and not east of Carthage see R. Werner, *Chiron*, 1975, 5, 21 ff. On the identification hangs the area forbidden to Roman shipping: it was probably west of Carthage and included the northern shore of Africa from Tunisia to Morocco rather than east (which would have interdicted the Syrtes).

For a full discussion of the evidence and modern theories see Walbank, *Polybius* i (1957), 337 ff. and Toynbee, *Hannibal's Legacy* (1965), i, 579 ff. The latter is able to take account of some views (e.g. of R. Werner, *Der Beginn der römischen Republik* (1963)) published later than Walbank's discussion. See also on the first two treaties K. E. Petzold, *Aufstieg NRW*, I, i, 364 ff., and on the last two K. Meister, *Riv. Fil.*, 1970, 408 ff. and *Historische Kritik bei Polybios* (1975) and R. E. Mitchell, *Historia*, 1971, 633 ff. Mitchell, like Toynbee, accepts the Philinus treaty (and incidentally that of the early Republic); he also sees the treaties of 306 and 279/8 as proofs of Rome's growing strength rather than of weakness or disinterest, a strength which provoked Punic suspicions.

4. THE CARTHAGINIAN NOBILITY.   De Sanctis, *SR*, i, 50, 54 argued for an ever-open caste, Groag (*Hannibal als Politiker* (1929), 19) for a closed caste. The nobility becoming interested in land: see U. Kahrstedt, *Geschichte der Karthager* (1913), 138 ff., 582 ff. and Cavaignac, *Histoire de l' Antiquité*, iii, 162 ff.; criticized by Groag, op. cit., 18 f.

5. CARTHAGINIAN FINANCE.   The calculations of Kahrstedt (op. cit., 133 ff.) have been rejected by De Sanctis, *SR*, III, i, 81.

6. CARTHAGINIAN RELIGION.   Many personal names imply the favour of Ba'al: Adherbal, Hasdrubal, Hannibal. Urns have been found in the Sanctuary (Tophet) of Tanit containing the calcined bones of young children, probably victims 'passed through the fire'. See B. H. Warmington, *Carthage*, edn 2, (1969), 147 ff.

7. QUOTATION.   From F. N. Pryce, *Universal History of the World*, iii, 1942.

8. THE TARENTINE INCIDENT.   This is not recorded by Polybius, but by Livy, *Epit.*, xiv (cf. xxi, 10, 8); Diod, frg. 43, 1; Orosius, iv, 3, 1 and others. It has been rejected completely by Beloch (*Griech. Gesch.*, IV, i, 642); Frank (*CAH*, vii, 656) rejects the implication of *Punica fides*, on the ground of Polybius' silence and the improbability that Carthage would risk war with Rome for the sake of one Italian harbour – but she did later for one Sicilian town, while Polybius, who did not record the Roman siege of Tarentum, might overlook an incident which did not technically infringe existing treaties and so could not honourably be cited as an act of Punic treachery.

9. WAR MOTIVES.   Rome's difficulty in maintaining a balance of power: see De Sanctis, *SR*, III, i, 101. Popular leaders; T. Frank, *CAH*, vii, 670 f. If, in line with the Philinus treaty, Rome had obligations not to intervene in Sicily, no reference to this would be likely to be enshrined in the work of Fabius; and the official account current in Polybius' day would not paint Rome as a treaty-breaker. If Polybius found any such reference in his pro-Carthaginian sources it would automatically be rejected together with the Philinus treaty. See also F. Hampl, *ANRW*, I, i, 412 ff. A. Heuss (*Hist. Zeitschrift*, 1949, 457 ff.) (= *Der erste punische Krieg*, edn 3, (1970) believed that Carthage had no hostile designs on Italy, and that by intervening at Messana the Romans would face Syracuse rather than the Carthaginians as their primary enemy. In line with this J. Molthagen has argued (*Chiron*, 1975, 89 ff.) that the Romans feared the expanding interest of Syracuse (not of Carthage) in southern Italian affairs: at first the war was essentially between Syracuse and Rome, and only in the winter of 263/2, when the Romans showed that they did not intend to leave Sicily, did the Carthaginians take effective hostile action. This was not the view of Polybius and it can hardly be doubted that the Romans did declare war on Carthage in 264.

10. THE OUTBREAK OF THE FIRST PUNIC WAR.   The part played by C. Claudius, a military tribune, is doubted by some: cf. Walbank, *Polybius*, i, 61. Polybius (1, 11, 11) places the embassy sent by Appius Claudius after his arrival in Sicily, but see Diodorus xxiii, 1, 3 (cf. Livy, xxxi, 1,4). Ennius refers bluntly to the fact: '*Appius indixit Karthaginiensibus*'. T. Frank suggests that Claudius went beyond the Senate's wishes and was for this reason denied a triumph: but the Senate showed no sloth in prosecuting the war, and it is not certain that the tradition of Claudius' success is correct: see next note. On the problems of the formal declaration of war see J. W. Rich, *Declaring War in the Roman Republic* (Collection Latomus, vol. 149; 1976), 119 ff.

   Basic for the study of the Punic Wars are Walbank, *Polybius*, i, and De Sanctis, *SR* iii. Two general accounts are D. R. Dudley, *Rome against Carthage* (1971) and R. M. Errington, *The Dawn of Empire: Rome's Rise to World Power* (1972).

11. APPIUS CLAUDIUS.   Polybius records that Claudius' two engagements were successful and that afterwards he marched against Syracuse; this march is probably a doublet of that of Valerius in 263 (Beloch, *Griech. Gesch.*, IV, ii, 533 ff.). Polybius rejects the account of Philinus, according to whom the two Roman engagements were unsuccessful, because he cannot explain the retreat of the Syracusans on this evidence. Polybius' authority is not unimpeachable: he admittedly gives only a sketch of the First Punic War. Probably both sides claimed the victory and the issue was uncertain. The suggestion of De Sanctis (*SR*. III, i, 109 ff.) that Hiero did not retreat till 263 when faced by the increased forces of Rome is attractive; the failure of Claudius would explain much: the Senate's displeasure with him, the discontent of the people at the conduct of the war, and the reason why it was his successor Valerius that won the title 'Messalla' (the first Roman to adopt such a 'triumphal' place name).

12. THE TWO NAVIES.   (a) *Speed of Roman construction.* The timbers of the Punic ship found off Marsala (see *e* below) were numbered by letters and suggest mass-production. The keel was of maple, the ribs of oak and the planking of pine; it was carvel built, i.e the outside planks were assembled first and the ribs inserted afterwards; the hull was covered with lead sheeting and the ram with bronze. A bag of cannabis was found, suggesting the need to relieve the hardships of rowing. (b) *Triremes and quinqueremes.* W. W. Tarn, *Hellenistic Military and Naval Developments* (1930), held that the trireme did not have three banks of oars, but oars in groups of three, with one man to each oar; the quinquereme had five men to each out-rigged oar, but like the trireme only one bank of oars. Against this view of the trireme is that of J. S. Morrison and R. T. Williams (*Greek Oared Ships, 900–322* BC (1968), 169 ff.) who believe that it was rowed by oarsmen at three levels (cf. Morrison, *Mariner's Mirror*, 1941, 14 ff., *Cl. Qu.*, 1947, 122). A less probable arrangement for the quinquereme is a group of three men to an upper oar and two to a lower. (c) *The corvus.* Tarn (op. cit., 149) believes that the *corvus*, as described by Polybius (i, 22) would have caused a quinquereme to turn turtle: it was rather an improved grapnel. *Per contra* J. H. Thiel (*Studies on the History of Roman Sea-*

power (1954), 432 ff.) argues that the 'crow' *was* a boarding-bridge, that its use was abandoned between 255 and 249 because of the resultant naval losses suffered through storms, and that its revival was impossible when a lighter type of quinquereme was built from 242 onwards; see also H. T. Wallinga, *The Boarding-bridge of the Romans* (1956). (d) *Size of fleets*. See Tarn, *JHS*, 1907, 48 ff. and Thiel, op. cit.; there was a tradition that by a supreme effort Carthage could raise 200 vessels, and this is probably correct; the limitation would be imposed by the difficulty of raising crews, not of building ships. (e) *Surviving ships*. A Punic warship has recently been found off Marsala in western Sicily and has been 'excavated'; see H. Frost, *Int. J. Naut. Arch.*, 1972, 113 ff., *Mariner's Mirror*, 1973, 229 f. A Roman mid-third-century ship has been found off Terrasini, west of Palermo; it contained amphorae, but also two Roman swords (a merchantman with a military guard aboard or a troop transport?): see V. Giustolisi, *Le navi romane di Terrasini* (Palermo, 1975). (f) *Early representations*. The prow of a ship became the normal type of the obverse of the Roman bronze coinage, which was probably first issued between 260 and 235; it may have commemorated a specific battle or Rome's naval success in the war as a whole. A Punic ship is depicted on the coinage issued by the Carthaginians (Mago?) in Spain (see, e.g., Scullard, *Scipio Africanus* (1970), pl. 14).

13. DUILIUS.   An imperial copy of the laudatory inscription on the column still survives (Dessau, *ILS*, 65). Both it and the Fasti Triumphales imply that the liberation of Segesta preceded the battle of Mylae; Polybius and Zonaras invert the order. The Carthaginian naval defeat recorded by Polybius (i, 21, 11) might be a doublet of the battle of Mylae (from Philinus' account).

14. ECNOMUS.   The formation of the Roman fleet is uncertain. Polybius says that it advanced in wedge shape, the first two lines forming the spearhead, the second two forming a double base to the triangle. This formation is accepted by Kromayer (*Atlas*, col. 15), but is rejected by De Sanctis (*SR*, III, i, 140 f.) and Tarn (*Hellenistic Military Developments*, 151) who says that it is 'quite impossible; no captains, let alone Roman captains, could have kept station. What happened was that the Roman centre pressed forward.' If the first two squadrons sailed in line ahead and then deployed into line abreast, or if they sailed in line abreast and then advanced with all speed, so that the swifter ships of the centre got ahead of the wings—then, in either case, from the enemy's point of view they would appear in wedge-shape formation. See further, Walbank, *Polybius*, i, 83 ff.

15. REGULUS.   The story that Regulus was later sent on parole to Rome to negotiate, that he refused to advise the Senate to accept conditions and returned voluntarily to Carthage to suffer torture and death, became a national epic (see e.g. Horace, *Odes*, iii, 5) but its historicity is doubtful. It could have been invented to counterbalance the story that he died in captivity and that his widow tortured some Carthaginian prisoners in Rome: the barbarity of the Carthaginians was invented to exculpate the barbarity of this Roman matron. T. Frank (*Cl. Phil.*, 1926, 311 ff.), however, defends the

peace mission, and although Polybius almost certainly did not know the Regulus story, it is as least as old as the annalist Sempronius Tuditanus (Aul. Gell., *NA*, vii, 4, 1) who was quaestor in 145 and consul in 129; according to him the embassy was concerned only with an exchange of prisoners, though Livy (*epit.*, xviii) adds peace. If the story was completely without foundation, would a man of affairs like Sempronius have recorded it? The history of the 'Regulus legend' is discussed by E. R. Mix, *Marcus Atilius Regulus, Exemplum Historicum* (1970).

16. NAVAL NUMBERS.   See W. W. Tarn, *JHS*, 1907, 48 ff. At the Hermaean Promontory Polybius gives: Roman fleet 350, Romans capture 114; this does not square with his account of the losses off Camerina. Diodorus says that the Romans captured 24; this, however, would involve accepting Polybius' figures of 350 for the Roman fleet, which is on other grounds thought to be too high. In the storm it is suggested by T. Frank (*CAH*, vii, 685) that 15 per cent of Italy's able-bodied men went down. This stupendous figure however, presupposes that all the rowers were free men.

17. METELLUS AND THE ELEPHANTS.   On the date see M. G. Morgan, *Cl. Qu.*, 1972, 121 ff. After the battle Metellus transported, with difficulty, the captured elephants to Rome, where they were displayed in the Circus, thus giving the Roman people their first sight of African elephants (those of Pyrrhus having been Indian). Thereafter the Caecilii Metelli adopted the elephant as a kind of family badge, which was often used on coins issued by members of the family who became mint-masters. See H. H. Scullard, *The Elephant in the Greek and Roman World* (1974), 151 f.

18. HEIRKTE.   The site of Heirkte has been sought on Mte Pellegrino, just north of Palermo, or Mte Castellaccio to the west; De Sanctis (*SR*, III, i, 181) argues for the former, Kromayer, *Schlachtfelder* III, i, 4 ff. for the latter. V. Giustoli, *Le navi romane di Terrasini e l'avventura di Amilcare sul Monte Heirkte* (Palermo, 1975), has found traces of a camp on Monte Pecoraro (west of Mte Castellaccio), with associated pottery of the first half of the third century; this he suggests was Heirkte.

19. ROME'S ALLIES.   It is noteworthy that in 242 despite wartime difficulties Rome allowed two of her *foederati* in Italy (Naples and Elea) and two Sicilian cities to receive invitations to a festival of Asclepius in Cos: see H. Bengtson, *Historia*, iii (1954–5), 456 ff.

CHAPTER VIII   THE ENTR'ACTE

1. PROVINCIAL LAND.   See T. Frank, *JRS*, 1927, 141 ff., who shows that no theory of state ownership of provincial land was recognized till after the reign of Claudius. Although the lawyer Gaius asserted that the *dominium* in all provincial soil was vested in the Roman people or the emperor, this was a late theory and had little practical importance: cf. A. H. M. Jones, *JRS*, 1941, 26 ff. (= *Studies in Roman Government and Law* (1960), 141 ff.). On the Lex

Hieronica and the taxation of Sicily see especially J. Carcopino, *La Loi de Hiéron et les Romains* (1919).

2. THE TRUCELESS WAR.   Polybius (iii, 75 ff.) gives a full account, on which Flaubert based his vivid historical novel, *Salammbô*. The mercenaries in effect established a separate state, since they issued a considerable coinage, including gold (see E. S. G. Robinson, *Num. Chron.*, 1943, 1 ff.; 1953, 27 ff.; 1956, 9 ff.; Jenkins and Lewis, *Carthaginian Gold and Electrum Coins* (1963), 43); after using Carthaginian types, they invented their own: Head of Hercules/Prowling lion, inscribed 'of the Libyans'. The site of Prione is uncertain: Veith, *Schlachtfelder*, III, ii, 550 ff., located it near Sidi Jedidi not far from Hammanet, but this is doubtful. The site too of the final battle is unknown: Polybius, whose account is pro-Barcid, deals summarily with the campaign in which Hanno took a prominent part.

3. WAR ON SARDINIA.   On the adaptation of the fetial procedure for the declaration of war against overseas enemies see F. W. Walbank, *Cl. Phil.*, 1949, 15 ff. and J. W. Rich, *Declaring War in the Roman Republic*, Collection Latomus, vol. 149 (1976).

4. ROMAN PRETEXT.   Cf. Appian, *Lib.*, 5; *Iber.*, 4 and Polybius, iii, 28, 3; this tradition may derive from Fabius, while the censure of Rome which Polybius repeats may come from the writer who continued the work of Philinus.

5. REFORM OF THE COMITIA CENTURIATA.   This reform is described by Cicero (*de rep.*, ii), Livy (i, 43, 12) and Dionysius (iv, 21, 3), but much remains obscure, especially regarding its nature, purpose and date.

(a) *Nature.* Either the centuries remained at 193 or else *all* 5 classes were made into 70 centuries, giving (with equites, etc.) 373 centuries. Mommsen, who believed in 373 centuries, thought that they were grouped into 193 *ad hoc* voting units. His view has received some support from the discovery of the Tabula Hebana, which shows that such a system *could* work (cf. G. Tibiletti, *Athenaeum*, 1949, 223 ff.); this document, a *rogatio* of AD 19 in honour of Germanicus, found at Heba (Magliano) in Etruria, shows that under Augustus temporary voting groups called centuries were formed from 33 tribes in an assembly of senators and equites which took part in the electoral process for appointing consuls and praetors. But that is not to say that the reformed Comitia in the third century *did* work in the way that Mommsen envisaged: see E. S. Staveley (*AJPhil.*, 1953, *Historia*, 1956, 112 ff, *Greek and Roman Voting and Elections* (1972), 126 ff.) who rejects the 373 centuries, discusses recent views and argues that the co-ordination of centuries with tribes was neither confined to the first class nor extended to all five classes, but was applied in the first and second class, with the abolition of the distinction between *seniores* and *iuniores* in the second class. J. J. Nichols and L. R. Taylor (*AJPhil.*, 1956, 225 ff., 1957, 337 ff., *Roman Voting Assemblies* (1966), 87 ff.), however, have supported Tibiletti and Mommsen's general position. For a brief summary of the evidence see Walbank, *Polybius*, i (1957), 683 ff.

(b) *Purpose.* This has been regarded by many as democratic: thus Mommsen saw the hand of Flaminius behind it (cf. E. Schönbauer, *Historia*, 1953–4,

31 ff.). But if this was the purpose, the result was not democratic (cf. De Sanctis, III, i, 344), since *inter alia* the Fasti show that in the later third century the *nobilitas* strengthened rather than relaxed its hold upon affairs. Thus some would argue that the reform was promoted by the nobility to restrict the influence of the wealthy trader who was enrolled in the urban tribes (so E. S. Staveley, *AJA*, 1953). Cf. L. R. Taylor (*AJPhil.*, 1957), who believes that the nobility found the tribes easier to manipulate than the centuries : hence the reform in their interest.

(c) *Date.* Fresh light may be afforded by an inscription from Brindisi, an *elogium* which records the achievements of someone who '*primus senatum legit et comiti [a ordinavit]*,' apparently in the consulship of Aemilius Barbula (and Iunius Pera) in 230; if so, the subject may be Q. Fabius Maximus who was censor in 230 (cf. G. Vitucci, *Riv. Fil.*, 1953, 42 f.), and the reference may be to the reform of the Comitia Centuriata. There is, however, the possibility that the subject was a local magistrate of the Latin colony of Brundisium who was concerned with the local constitution (so E. Gabba, *Athenaeum*, 1958, 90 ff. ; cf. T. R. S. Broughton, *MRR*, Suppl., 1960, 2) and that therefore the inscription has no bearing upon the Comitia at Rome.

6. FLAMINIUS. On his career see K. Jacobs, *Gaius Flaminius* (1938, written in Dutch), and Z. Yavetz, *Athenaeum*, 1962, 325 ff. De Sanctis (*SR*, iii, i, 334) argued that Flaminius was responsible for a law limiting the amount of public land to be held by an individual and that the agrarian Lex Licinia of 367 was merely an anticipation of this. But see p. 479 n. 1.)

7. TELAMON. For the site of the battle and finds in the district see P. Sommella, *Antichi campi di battaglia in Italia* (1967), 11 ff.

8. MARCELLUS. Polybius' account (ii, 34) is pre-Scipionic and the danger which Scipio incurred is minimized; for the part played by Marcellus see Plutarch, *Marcell.*, 7. Was Scipio's advance any less dangerous than that of Flaminius which the aristocratic tradition so heartily condemns?

9. ROME AND GREECE. Polybius, ii, 12, 8. The alleged Roman treaty with Rhodes in 306, her alliance with Apollonia in 266, and her intervention on behalf of Acarnania in 239 may all be dismissed as fictitious. See M. Holleaux, *Rome, la Grèce et les monarchies hellénistiques* (1921) and *CAH*, vii, 822 ff. General contacts had of course existed intermittently since Etruscan times, but not specific political commitments. See F. W. Walbank, *JRS*, 1963, 2 f.

10. ILLYRIA. See Polybius, ii, 2–12; iii, 16, 18–19 and Walbank, *Polybius*, i, *ad loc*. On Illyrian piracy see H. J. Dell, *Historia*, 1967, 344 ff. On Roman policy, Holleaux, op. cit. above, E. Badian, *PBSR*, 1952 (= *Studies in Greek and Roman History* (1964), 1 ff.), N. G. L. Hammond, *JRS*, 1968, 1 ff., K. E. Petzold, *Historia*, 1971, 199 ff., P. S. Derow, *Phoenix*, 1973, 118 ff.

11. THE ILLYRIAN SETTLEMENT. The legal position of the Greek towns is doubtful. They were not *dediticii*, enjoying *libertas precaria*, as Holleaux (*CAH*, vii, 836). De Sanctis (*SR*, iii, i, 301) believed that Issa, Dyrrhachium and Apollonia were recognized as allies, Issa having a *foedus aequum*, and Corcyra being *immunis et libera*. But see E. Badian, *PBSR*, 1952, 72 ff.: all were free *amici*, with no treaties, and extra-legal *clientela* of Rome.

12. ROMAN POLICY.   Holleaux (*CAH*, vii, 837 ff.) has rejected the view that the Romans formed an imperialistic policy against Macedon or even that they negotiated in Greece as a precaution against Macedon. His views have been widely accepted. However, N. G. L. Hammond (*JRS*, 1968, 1 ff.) has revived the view of Rome as imperialistic and anti-Macedonian: at the end of the first war Roman control in Illyria was not dictated by revenge or anti-piratical desires, but to gain power there, and Rome was careful to send embassies to Macedon's enemies, the Achaean and Aetolian Leagues and not to Macedon; a cold war was developing. It is hardly to be expected that Macedon would smile on Rome's intervention in the Balkans, but Roman policy in 228 is scarcely likely to have envisaged the idea of dominating or destroying Macedon.

13. MASSILIA.   T. Frank (*CAH*, vii, 810) assumes that a trilateral treaty was signed by the two parties and a willing Massilia. But A. Schulten, (ibid., 788) believes that Massilia would not welcome Rome's concessions. Yet had it not been for her alliance with Massilia Rome might have been content to fix the limit of Hasdrubal's aggressions at the Pyrenees. On Massilian diplomacy see F. R. Kramer, *AJPhil.*, 1948, 1 ff. The further implications of this treaty are discussed on pp. 198 ff.

14. SIEGE OF SAGUNTUM.   Polybius, iii, 17. Livy's account is highly coloured and cannot be trusted in detail. His statements regarding the embassies to Hannibal are confused, because his source (Coelius?) has tried to justify Rome's lack of support to Saguntum. The assault on Sagunto (Murviedro) by Marshal Suchet in 1811 confirms the probability that resistance weakened in the west.

15. A SENATORIAL DEBATE?   Dio (Zon., viii, 22) says that on the fall of Saguntum there was a senatorial debate in which L. Cornelius Lentulus proposed an immediate declaration of war, Fabius the sending of an embassy. Polybius (iii, 20) ridicules this tradition which derives from Chaereas and Sosylus 'whose compositions are more like the gossip of the barber's shop than history.... There was no debate on the question of war'. De Sanctis, however, has shown (III, ii, 197) the probability that this tradition is reliable. Prompt action might have been wiser, for the embassy merely succeeded in showing up the weakness of Rome's juridical position (unless the embassy did not reach Carthage until after Hannibal had actually crossed the Ebro, as W. Hoffmann, *Rhein. Mus.*, 1951, 77 ff.; cf. H. H. Scullard, ibid., 1952, 212 ff. both reprinted in *Hannibal*, ed. K. Christ (1974). 134 ff., 156 ff.). The leader of the embassy was more probably M. Fabius than Q. Fabius Maximus. J. W. Rich (*Declaring War in the Roman Republic*, Collection Latomus, vol. 149 (1976), 28 ff., 109 ff.) attributes the Senate's hesitation even after the fall of Saguntum to a practice, which he believes obtained, namely that it regarded itself as entitled to postpone wars until the new consuls entered office (*ad novos consules*).

16. WAR GUILT.   For the immense literature on this topic prior to 1930 see *CAH*, viii, 724. For more recent discussions of the sources and modern views see Walbank, *Polybius*, i (1957), esp. 168 ff., 310 ff., 327 ff. and F.

Cassola, *I gruppi politici romani* (1962), 250 ff. Five more recent discussions are G. V. Sumner, *Harvard Stud. Cl. Ph.*, 1967, 204 ff., *Latomus*, 1972, 469 ff., A. E. Astin, *Latomus*, 1967, 577 ff., R. M. Errington, *Latomus*, 1970, 26 ff., F. Hampl, *ANRW*, I, i, 427 ff. Two well-known older papers, by W. Otto and G. De Sanctis, are reprinted in *Hannibal* (ed. K. Christ, 1974).

17. THE SAGUNTINE ALLIANCE. This has long been regarded as a formal alliance based on a treaty (*foedus*): thus Polybius refers to the Saguntines as σύμμαχοι of the Romans. But he also says that they placed themselves in the *fides* of the Romans. Thus it has been suggested (see J. S. Reid, *JRS*, 1913, 179 ff.; E. Badian, *Foreign Clientelae*, (1958), 49 ff., 293; Errington, *Latomus*, 1970, 41 ff.) that the action was a *deditio in fidem* (rather than a formal treaty) which imposed moral but no legal obligations on Rome (cf. T. A. Dorey, *Humanitas*, 11, 12, 1959–60, 2 f.), while A. E. Astin (*Latomus*, 1967, 589 ff.) goes even further in supposing that there was not even a formal *deditio* but a looser acceptance into Roman *fides*. Equally controversial is the date of the agreement. The early date implied by Polybius is rejected by E. Groag (*Hannibal als Politiker* (1929), 17 ff.) who assigns the alliance to 221–220: the Saguntines appealed to Rome while Hannibal was campaigning in central Spain. A late date is also proposed by R. M. Errington (*Latomus*, 1970, 43 f.), reviving the idea of J. S. Reid (*JRS*, 1913, 178 ff.) that the agreement was reached when the Romans arbitrated in the internal quarrel at Saguntum, but this does not seem very probable. Against a late date (which would make the alliance an infringement of the Ebro treaty) is the fact that the Romans were eager to discuss the treaty, but the Carthaginians refused (Polybius, iii, 21; 29). For an analysis and discussion of modern views see also F. Cassola, *I gruppi politici romani nel iii sec.a.C* (1962), 244 ff.

18. PERSONAL VENDETTAS. For Polybius' three reasons see iii, 9, 6–10. He also says that Fabius Pictor gave two causes for the war: Saguntum and the imperialist ambitions of Hasdrubal (whose policy was rather, as we have seen, pacific). Livy on the other hand has little to say about the arguments of Polybius or Fabius: for him Hannibal is the villain, '*non dux solum, sed etiam causa belli*' (xxi, 21, 1).

19. ROMAN POLICY. Agrarian versus capitalist: E. Meyer, *Kleine Schriften*, ii, 375 ff. Modern views continue to fluctuate: thus G. V. Sumner (see n. 16 above) believes that the Romans were entirely concerned with curbing Carthaginian expansion, while at the other extreme Errington dismisses the 'wrath of the Barcids' as unknown to Fabius Pictor and thinks that Roman policy to Spain was essentially apathetic.

CHAPTER IX HANNIBAL'S OFFENSIVE AND
ROME'S DEFENSIVE

1. HANNIBAL'S FORCES. Polybius (iii, 33) quotes the figures for the Spanish and African armies. He himself saw at the Lacinian promontory in Bruttium a

bronze tablet on which Hannibal had inscribed these particulars. The same source (iii, 56) guarantees the numbers with which Hannibal arrived in Italy, but the numbers assigned to him on his departure from Spain are exaggerated by Polybius or his source: cf. De Sanctis; *SR*, III, ii, 83 ff.

2. CROSSING THE RHÔNE.   For this picturesque incident see Pol., iii, 42, Livy, xxi, 28. The crossing cannot be located with certainty. Napoleon (*Commentaires*, vi, 159) was probably right in setting the limits between the Rhône's tributaries, the Durance and the Ardèche. For discussion and bibliography see Jullian, *Histoire de la Gaule*, i (1908–9), 464, who, however, favours a crossing further south at Tarascon. Cf. also De Sanctis, III, ii, 70, Walbank, *Polybius*, i, 378. On Hannibal's elephants here and elsewhere see H. H. Scullard, *The Elephant in the Greek and Roman World* (1974), 154 ff. There is no doubt that the main herd comprised African elephants, though there is a possibility that Hannibal may have had one or two Indian beasts in addition.

3. THE ALPS.   The topographical evidence given by Polybius (iii, 50–6) and Livy (xxi, 31–7) does not allow any conclusive identification of the pass used by Hannibal. For older discussions it will suffice here to mention the bibliography in *CAH*, viii, 725 and to list the more probable passes and some of their advocates: (a) Little St Bernard: Niebuhr, Mommsen, Lehmann, Viedebandt; (b) Mt Cenis: Napoleon, Osiander; with the variant of Col du Clapier: Azan, Colin, Wilkinson; (c) Mt Genèvre: Neumann, Fuchs, Marindin, De Sanctis; with the variant of Col de Malaure: Bonus; (d) Monte Viso (Monviso): Col d' Argentière and variants: Freshfield. See further De Sanctis, *SR*, III, ii, 65 ff.; Walbank, *Polybius*, i, 382 ff. The views of Sir Gavin de Beer, *Alps and Elephants* (1955), more ingenious than convincing, have been refuted by Walbank, *JRS*, 1956, 37 ff., and A. H. McDonald, *Alpine Journal* 1956, 93 ff. A balanced survey of the problem is given in D. Procter's excellent *Hannibal's March in History* (1971). If any trend can be detected, it perhaps leans towards the Col du Clapier (cf. also E. Meyer, *Museum Helveticum*, 1958, 227 ff.).

4. TREBIA.   Scipio's movements after Ticinus have caused much difficulty, partly owing to Livy's inferior account which places the battle on the right of the river. The account given in the text follows De Sanctis and Kromayer. When Scipio had recrossed the Po (presumably at Placentia; according to Lehmann, *Hist. Zeitschr.*, 1916, 101 ff., a little further west and according to Fuchs near Pavia) he camped περὶ πόλιν Πλακεντίαν (Pol., iii, 66, 9): on the east or west of the Trebia? Topography and strategy suggest on the west; i.e. the left bank, some way off at Stradella; Lehmann and Fuchs place the camp nearer Placentia at Rottofreno, but this is in the open plain. The old view of Grundy (*Journ. Phil.*, 1896, 83; *Cl. Rev.*, 1896, 284) though rejected by later critics (e.g. Kromayer) has been revived by Beloch (*Hist. Zeitschr.*, 1915), who places Scipio's camp on the east bank of the Trebia. This view alters the whole topography of the battle which followed; according to it, after the desertion of his allies Scipio then

withdrew and camped on the left of the river, while Hannibal encamped on the right and the battle was fought on the right bank. Scipio's retreat over the Trebia becomes, on this theory, an advance, while Beloch even regards it as a doublet of his retreat after the battle of Ticinus. The view has been rejected by De Sanctis, Lehmann, and Kromayer, and the old view that Scipio camped with Sempronius on the right, Hannibal on the left bank and that the battle was fought on the left bank also may be retained. Laqueur's theories (*Polybius*, 99) are not happy; see De Sanctis' criticism (p. 98). Tenney Frank (*JRS*, 1919, 202 ff.) believes that Placentia before it was refounded in 190 was near Stradella: a theory which solves many difficulties, but is supported by no evidence. It may be added that Livy (xxi, 57-59) gives a long account of campaigning during the winter, but this may safely be rejected as reduplication. See also Walbank, *Polybius*, i, 404 ff.

5. HANNIBAL CROSSES THE APENNINES. The route suggested in the text is supported by Kromayer (*Schlachtfelder*, iii, 104-47) and De Sanctis (III, ii, 104-9). It involves the supposition that there were then marshes between Pistoia and Florence, which is highly probable. The four days mentioned by Polybius present a difficulty, which is not insuperable. Routes further north and west are too long and too near the sea and would lead through marshes which were impassable for ancient armies before the land was drained; routes further east were not marshy and would bring Hannibal too near Flaminius at Arretium. The marshes were probably subject to flood, and Veith refers to similar conditions suffered by the Austrians at Muzakja in Albania in the winters of 1916-18.

6. FLAMINIUS. The extant tradition, which is aristocratic in outlook, depreciates such popular leaders as Flaminius and Varro, but an impartial estimate of their careers goes far to modify such criticism. Tradition asserts that Flaminius refused to co-operate with Servilius, which the facts contradict. He acted rashly but did not fall into every trap that Hannibal set. He was probably hastening south, not to fight, but to join Servilius further south, instead of awaiting him in the north.

7. TRASIMENE. The various hypotheses suggested for the actual site of the battle all agree that it was on the north shore of Trasimene; but various positions are chosen: (1) Borghetto-Passignano. This view has been adopted in the above text: see Fuchs (*Wien Stud.*, 1904, 134), Pareti (*Riv. di Fil.*, 1912, 383), De Sanctis (109) and Hallward (*CAH*). (2) Passignano-Monte Colognola: here the mountains are much nearer the sea. The view of Henderson (*J. Phil.*, 1897; 1899), Kromayer and Walbank; criticized by De Sanctis. (3) Borghetto-Tuoro; a very confined space – see Grundy (*J. Phil.*, 1896, 83; 1897, 273), Reuss (*Klio*, 1906, 226), M. Caspari (*Eng. Hist. Rev.*, 1910, 417). (4) Up the river Sanguineto. This improbable view presupposes that Flaminius was not surprised on the march by Hannibal, but saw the enemy above the Sanguineto and advanced against him in battle formation – see Sadée (*Klio*, 1909, 48) and Lehmann (*Jahresber. d. phil. Vereins Berlin*, 1915, 81). A recent attempt to identify the site from the finding

of what were alleged to be the ashes of the dead by G. Susini is criticized by Walbank, *JRS*, 1961, 232 ff (cf. *Polybius*, ii, 638).

8. SERVILIUS. See De Sanctis, *SR*, III, ii, 122 ff. Appian, *Iber.*, 9, 11, who follows an inferior tradition, places the defeat at the lake of Plestia (Pistia) east of the Via Flaminia.

9. CALLICULA. The pass probably lay between Cales and Teanum (cf. De Sanctis, *SR*, III, ii, 124 ff; Hallward, *CAH*, viii, 50); less probably further north at Mte Caievola, as Kromayer.

10. MINUCIUS RUFUS. On his office see T. A. Dorey, *JRS*, 1955, 92 ff. On the topography see De Sanctis, *SR*, III, ii, 54; Kromayer, *Schlachtfelder*, iii, 248.

11. CANNAE. *Numbers*. The Roman forces considerably outnumbered those of Hannibal, though they probably did not amount to the 80,000–90,000 men that Polybius and Livy give (Livy also knew of other assessments). Cf. De Sanctis, *SR*, III, ii, 131, B. H. Hallward, *CAH*, viii, 52. The basic reliability of the number of legions in the field in the years 218–167 given by Livy is defended by De Sanctis and by P. A. Brunt, *Manpower* (1971), 416 ff., 645 ff. against the criticism of M. Gelzer, *Kleine Schriften*, iii, 220 ff. *Site*. Two main solutions of the difficulties in fixing the site are offered: (1) It lay on the north, i.e. left bank of the Aufidus, with the Romans facing roughly east and the Carthaginians west. This is the view of Delbrück, De Sanctis and Hallward. An improbable variant, with the armies almost north and south, was proposed by Lehmann (*Klio*, 1917, 162), though later retracted (*Klio*, 1930, 71). Judeich (*Hist. Zeitschr.*, 1927, 1) places the armies facing north-west and south-east; criticized by Kromayer (*Schlachtfeld.*, iv, 611). (2) It lay on the south bank, i.e. the right. This school falls into two divisions: (*a*) those who place the battle to the west of Cannae, with the armies facing very roughly north and south; this view is very improbable. It is proposed with individual variations by Arnold, Hesselbarth and Reusch (who alters the course of Aufidus) and recently by Lehmann in his recantation (*Klio*, 1930). (*b*) those who place the battle east of Cannae with the Romans backing the sea some three miles distant. This view, adopted in the text above, is that of Kromayer (proposed in *Schlachtfeld.*, iii, and defended in iv, and *Atlas*), Kahrstedt, Cornelius, etc. The discovery of a large cemetery south of the Aufidus (*Arch. Anzeiger*, 1938, 717; M. Gervasio, *Iapigia*, ix) seemed to have established that the battle was fought on the south bank, but these burials appear to be medieval (see H. H. Scullard, *Historia*, 1955, 474 f.; F. Bertocchi, *Rendic. Ac. d. Lincei*, xv, 337). For full discussions of Cannae, see especially Kromayer, De Sanctis and Walbank *Polybius*, i, 435 ff. Cornelius' 'Cannae; das militärische u. das literarische Problem' (*Klio*, xxvi, 1932) contains much of interest, but his main contention is untenable: namely, that in the Polybian account the Romans broke through the Gallic-Spanish line and were caught behind that line by the Africans held in reserve. The Gallic line bent but did not break; nor were the Africans a reserve.

Six deep grain depositories, which may have formed part of the rich granaries captured by Hannibal, have been found: see *The Times*, 2 August 1930.

12. NAVAL BATTLE OFF EBRO. For the naval aspect of the war see J. H. Thiel, *Studies on the History of Roman Sea-Power in Republican Times* (1946). A description of the battle of the Ebro is probably found in a fragment of the Greek and pro-Carthaginian historian Sosylus: see F. Jacoby, *FGrH*, 176 F. Our five sources all give different reasons for the victory. Polybius (iii, 95–6) gives the nearness of the Carthaginians to their infantry on the shore; for Livy (xxii, 19–20) it is surprise; Frontinus (*Strat.* iv, 7, 9) tells of the throwing of burning projectiles; Zonaras, of the destruction of the Carthaginian sails; while Sosylus says the skill of the Massiliotes foiled the enemy's manoeuvre. The reasons given by Polybius, Livy and Sosylus are not mutually exclusive.

13. THE SCIPIOS IN 217. Traces of their camps have been found at Almenara, five miles north of Saguntum; the accuracy of Polybius' topographical description is thus strikingly confirmed: see A. Schulten, *Arch. Anz., 1933, 622 ff.*, and, for photograph, Scullard, *Scipio Africanus* (1970), plate 24. In Cibili lay near Benicarlo, and Iliturgi in Catalonia at Cabanes west of Oropesa: see A. Schulten, *Hermes*, 1928, 288 ff. The site of the more famous southern Iliturgi in Andalusia is now shown by an inscription (in honour of its *deductor* Ti. Sempronius Gracchus) to have been near Mengibar in the province of Jean: *A. Espan. Arch.,* 1960, 193 ff.

14. THE SCIPIOS' ADVANCE. It is very improbable that the Scipios also penetrated into Andalusia and captured Castulo, as Livy, xxiii, 49; xxiv, 41 f. Such annalistic accounts, which Livy derived from Valerius Antias, may contain elements of truth, but it is safer to reject them. Strategic considerations make an advance and victories in southern Spain very improbable. However, this idea has been revived by E. C. Sanchez, *Habis*, 1975, 213 ff., who placed the defeat of Publius Scipio near the river Genil, southwest of Corduba.

15. PHILIP'S TREATY WITH HANNIBAL. On the terms and Philip's subsequent war with Rome see F. W. Walbank, *Philip V of Macedon* (1940), 70 ff. The terms of the treaty are given by Polybius, vii, 9, who provides a Greek translation of the Punic document which fell into Roman hands. E. Bickerman, *TAPA*, 1952, 1 ff. equates the oath with a Hebrew covenanted treaty (*berit*). See also A. H. Chroust, *Classica et Med.*, 1954, 60 ff.; Walbank, *Polybius*, ii, 42 ff. It is noteworthy that the terms imply that Hannibal's war aims were limited and that he does not appear to have aimed at the complete destruction of Rome.

16. THE AETOLIAN TREATY. The terms are summarized by Livy, xxvi, 24. Part of a copy of the text, in Greek, was found in 1949 inscribed on a stone in Acarnania. See G. Klaffenbach, *S.-B. Berlin*, 1941, 13 ff.; A. Momigliano, *Quinto Contrib.* 977 ff.; A. H. McDonald, *JRS*, 1956, 153 ff.; E. Badian, *Latomus*, 1958, 197 ff.; Walbank, *Polybius*, ii, 162, 179 ff., 599 ff.; and G. A. Lehmann, *Untersuchungen zur hist. Glaubwürdigkeit des Polybios* (1967), who deals with the problems at length. See also E. Badian, *Titus Quinctius Flamininus* (1970), 49 ff.; J. Briscoe, *Commentary on Livy xxxi–xxxiii* (1973), 273 f.; D. Musti, *Aufstieg NRW*, I, ii (1974), 1146 ff. The terms were

probably agreed by Laevinus and the Aetolians in the autumn of 211 and ratified in Rome two years later.

Livy records that if the Romans took any cities they were to have the movable booty while the cities and their territories fell to the Aetolians. But the inscription adds two further clauses (the second fragmentary): booty from cities taken jointly by Romans and Aetolians should be shared, and any cities that went over voluntarily to the Romans or Aetolians could be received into the Aetolian League. This last clause causes problems in regard to Flamininus' settlement of Greece in 197 when he denied the Aetolians any right to four Thessalian cities on the ground that they had surrendered to him. Questions of Flamininus' honour or Polybius' accuracy may be involved, but possibly in the lost part of the inscription there was some further qualification about the cities that surrendered voluntarily under which Flamininus' demand might be justified (cf. Walbank, op. cit, 600).

17. SYRACUSE.   On the topography see K. Fabricius, *Das Antike Syrakus* (1932), who showed that the city did not extend on to the plateau of Epipolae; also H.-P. Drögemüller, *Syrakus* (1969). Polybius, viii, 6–8, describes the catapults of varied range, the huge beams and cranes which swung over the walls to drop weights, the mechanical arms which capsized the Roman boats, etc. In general see E. W. Marsden, *Greek and Roman Artillery* (1969), and for Archimedes pp. 109 ff. A. W. Lawrence, *JHS*, 1946, 99 ff. discusses the siting of Archimedes' artillery. Archimedes is also said to have focused the sun's rays by means of bronze mirrors in order to set fire to the Roman ships: recent experiments, carried out by modern Greek sailors, suggest that this may have been possible: see *The Times*, 7 November 1973.

18. CAPUA.   The rebel cities, Capua, Atella and Calatia, issued coins (mainly bronze) as an act of independence: some depict elephants (see Scullard, *The Elephant in the Greek and Roman World*, 70 ff. For Hannibal's coinage in Italy see E. S. G. Robinson, *Num. Chron.*, 1964, 37 ff. The coins issued by the Barcids in Spain, with probable portraits of Hamilcar, Hannibal, Hasdrubal and Mago, may be mentioned here: see E. S. G. Robinson, *Essays in Roman Coinage* (ed. R. A. G. Carson (1956), 34 ff.) On the sources see J. von Ungern-Sternberg, *Capua im zweiten punischen Krieg: Untersuchungen zur römischen Annalistik* (1975).

A report in the *Daily Telegraph* of 2 February 1976 refers to the discovery near Santa Maria Capua Vetere of what appears to be a military encampment (?Hannibal's camp).

19. HANNIBAL'S MARCH AGAINST ROME.   According to Polybius (ix, 5) Hannibal marched through Samnium and crossed the Anio; Coelius (Livy, xxvi, 11) sent him through Samnium, the Paelignian Sulmo, Amiternum and Reate: but Livy (xxvi, 7–11) thought he advanced direct along the Via Latina. E. W. Davies, *Phoenix*, 1959, 113 ff., argues for the Via Latina, but the longer route is supported by E. T. Salmon, *Phoenix*, 1957, 153 ff., who attributes Livy's mistaken route to confusion (by Valerius Antias) of Paelignian with Volscian Sulmo. See also Walbank, *Polybius*, ii, 121 ff. Traces

of Hannibal's sack of the temple at Lucus Feroniae (Livy, xxvi, 11) survive:
R. Bloch, *Rev. Phil.*, 1953, 75.

CHAPTER X SCIPIO AND ROME'S OFFENSIVE

1. NEW CARTHAGE AND SCIPIO.   For this episode and Scipio's Spanish and
African campaigns see H. H. Scullard, *Scipio Africanus in the Second Punic War*
(1930) and, more briefly, *Scipio Africanus, Soldier and Politician* (1970); also
Walbank, *Polybius*. On the topography see Scullard (1930), 289 ff. This and
Polybius' account of the storming of the city abound in difficulties. Although
Polybius had visited New Carthage and based his account on a letter from
Scipio to king Philip V, his description raises many problems, some of which
arise from his rationalistic outlook, which refused to recognize anything
extraordinary either in nature or in the character of his hero Scipio. Thus the
sinking of the waters in the lagoon may seem miraculous, but it was a miracle
in the sense of a coincidence in time rather than a violation of natural law.
Many parallels in history can be found, the most striking being that related in
Exodus: 'And the Lord caused the sea to go back by a strong east wind all the
night and made the sea dry land' (if the early account is disentangled from
later miraculous elements, we find a perfectly natural explanation of the
passage of the Red Sea; see H. H. Scullard, *Expository Times*, November
1930, 55 ff.). By Polybius' time, and perhaps even during Scipio's lifetime,
popular tradition about Scipio was growing into a 'legend'. This arose from
Scipio's exceptional personality and his apparent belief in divine help,
especially from Jupiter in whose temple he used to commune (a very un-
Roman habit). Polybius the rationalist might regard Scipio's conduct as a
way of winning popular confidence, but in fact his beliefs may have been
genuine and he should not be dismissed as a hypocrite. On the 'legend' see
R. M. Haywood, *Studies on Scipio Africanus* (1933); F. W. Walbank, *Proc.
Cambr. Phil. Soc.*, 1967, 54 ff.; H. H. Scullard, *Scipio* (1970) 18 ff., 235 ff.

2. BAECULA.   On the topography see Scullard, *Scipio* (1930), 300 ff.; (1970),
258 ff. and Veith, *Schlachtfelder*, iv, 503 ff. (the site suggested by Scullard is
accepted by R. Thouvenot, *Essai sur la province romaine de Bétique* (1940), 89
n. 3). Scipio is sometimes criticized and Baecula minimized to a mere
rearguard action (e.g. by Ihne, ii, 380), but for a defence see Scullard, op. cit.,
and B. H. Hallward, who writes (*CAH*, viii, 87), 'the censure ignores the
lesson of all campaigning in Spain'. R. C. Sanchez (*Habis*, 1975, 213 ff.)
rejects the usual identification of Baecula with Bailen and seeks it west of
Castulo south of the Baetis at Betula, but he does not offer any precise site for
the battle.

3. ILIPA.   Date: Livy's chronology is followed above, but many (e.g. De
Sanctis, *SR*, III, ii, 496) transfer Ilipa to 207, because of the number of events
to be crowded into 206 (for an attempt, however, to accomodate them all see
Scullard (1930), 304 ff.). On the site of the battle and of the Roman and

Carthaginian camps see Scullard, *JRS*, 1936, 19 ff. (cf. A. Schulten, *Arch. Anzeiger*, 1940, 113 ff.; 1943, 51). In line with his proposal to shift the campaigns of the elder Scipios and Publius further to the south-west (cf. p. 449 n. 14; and n. 2 above), R. C. Sanchez rejects Alcala del Rio as the Ilipa of the battle and seeks an Ilipa somewhere around Munda south of the Baetis, but is not very specific.

4. MARCELLUS. Hannibal is said to have buried Marcellus with full military honours, though he kept his signet ring. He tried to capture Salapia by means of a forged dispatch sealed with this ring, but the trick miscarried and he lost 300 men, who on entering the city were cut off by the dropping of a portcullis. Marcellus, the 'Sword of Rome', had shown more initiative than most of his contemporaries, as attested by the annalistic exaggerations of his exploits. His faith is seen in his dedication of temples to Honos and Virtus, his appreciation of Greek culture in his sending the artistic treasures of Syracuse to Rome. For his portrait see Crawford, *RRC* n. 439.

5. GRUMENTUM. On the topography of the fight at Grumentum see Kromayer, *Schlachtfelder*, III, i, 414 ff., and *Atlas*, col. 28, 9.

6. METAURUS. The battlefield is uncertain and the fixing of it affects the strategy attributed to Hasdrubal. Two main theories may be distinguished: (*a*) the Romans camped near Fanum Fortunae (Fano) and the battle was fought on the north of the Metaurus; then Hasdrubal's march by night was an attempt to reach central Italy; (*b*) the Romans and Carthaginians camped near Sena Gallica (Senigallia) and the battle was fought south of the Metaurus; in this case Hasdrubal's march was a retreat either to northern Italy or to reach a defensive position beyond the Metaurus. A third solution, that of Kahrstedt, seeks to cut the Gordian knot by rejecting the night march as an annalistic invention; the battle would then have been fought near the camps, but this is very improbable. Of the two main views the first has been adopted in the above text. The chief objection to it is that Livy places the camps at Sena; but this hardly excludes the district around Sena. It is impossible here to enter into the controversy, but the main exponents may be listed (for details see the bibliographies in Kromayer-Veith, *Schlachtfelder*, III, 424 ff., *CAH*, viii): (*a*) north of Metaurus, moving westwards from Fano: Vaudoncourt (La Lucrezia), De Sanctis (M. Sterpeti), Lehmann (Calmazzo), Tarducci (San Silvestro); (*b*) south of Metaurus. Pitalluga and Oehler and with slight variations Kromayer (San Angelo), Bottini Massa (Cerasa), Marcolini (M. Maggiore) and recently in two pamphlets, G. Rossi (Montebello) to which A. Bianchini has replied (Tombacchia and Vago Colle). Cf. G. Buroni, *Le diverse tesi sulla battaglia del Metauro* (1953), and Walbank, *Polybius*, ii, 267 ff.

7. MAGO. J. H. Thiel, *Roman Sea-Power* (1946), 144 ff., suggests that in view of her available naval forces Rome was culpable in allowing Mago to land, as earlier Scipio was in allowing his escape from Spain.

8. A PEACE PARTY? E. Meyer (*Meister der Politik*, i, 101, 131 ff.; *Kleine Schriften*, ii, 353, n. 2) suggested that Fabius and his supporters were ready in

205 to compromise with Carthage and allow her to keep her African possessions in exchange for peace. W. Schur (*Scipio Africanus* (1927), 47) summarizes their policy as the freeing of Italy, the reconquest of the lost Po valley and its colonization by farmers.

9. SOPHONISBA.   The romantic story of her relations with Masinissa and her death is recorded by Livy, xxx.

10. PEACE NEGOTIATIONS.   A fragment of papyrus of the second century BC deals briefly with the negotiations of 203–202 (*Catalogue of Greek Papyri, J. Rylands Library*, iii, n. 491, ed. C. Roberts). The author is unknown but was nearly contemporary and possibly more pro-Carthaginian than other writers. See Walbank, *Polybius*,ii, 442; Scullard, *Scipio* (1970), 270.

11. ZAMA.   The decisive battle of the Hannibalic War, traditionally known as Zama, has more recently been dubbed Naraggara (e.g. by De Sanctis) or Margaron (by Veith), although this is only to exchange one uncertainty for another. The ancient accounts of the battle bristle with difficulties regarding the topography, strategy, tactics, numbers, chronology, etc. The account given in the text is based on the present writer's views as expressed in *Scipio Africanus* (1930). For a criticism of some of these views, cf. P. Fraccaro (*Athenaeum*, ix, 1931, 428–38) who would seem to smooth over the difficulties in Polybius' account somewhat too easily. Two traditions are extant, the better one of Polybius and Livy, the inferior one of Appian and Dio; the latter finds an advocate in Saumagne. In matters of strategy and tactics it is not chiefly the facts which are questioned, but the motives of the leaders. Polybius' authority must be final in questions of fact, but it appears legitimate to assign motives from the data which he gives when he does not do so himself, or even to suppose that the motives he does supply may be wrong – for his account presents difficulties and contradictions which necessitate some criticism. The account given above adheres closely to Polybius in facts and attempts to avoid the supposition of a gap in the present text of Polybius (as Veith) or an alteration in his order of the movements in the battle (as De Sanctis).

There were probably two towns named Zama in North Africa (a third at Sidi Abd el Djedidi north-west of Kairouan was probably not called Zama). Zama Regia was most probably Seba Biar, while this settlement may have declined and the Zama of the Roman Empire have lain at modern Jama: see Scullard, *Scipio* (1970), 271 ff. Provided the general neighbourhood of Zama can be established, the precise sites are less important for the campaign, since Zama was clearly only Hannibal's camp before his final advance westwards to the battlefield. Similarly, Scipio camped at Naraggara (Livy; Polybius gives Margaron, which is otherwise unknown) but no suitable battlefield can be found there. The most probable site is that suggested by Veith (*Atlas*, col. 40, *Schlachtfelder*, iv, 626 ff.) in the plain of Draa-el-Metnan some eight miles from El Kef and about half way between Naraggara and Zama (Seba Biar). A visit to this site has confirmed the present writer in his belief in its suitability on physical as well as literary grounds. Most of the modern literature on the subject is criticized by Veith, *Schlachtfelder*, iii, 599 ff. and iv, 626 ff., although he curiously neglects the valuable account by De Sanctis, *SR*, III, ii, 549 ff., 588 ff. which appeared before he published his fourth volume. For discussion of another site suggested by F. H. Russell (*Archaeology*, 1970, 122 ff.) see Scullard in *Polis and Imperium, Stud. in Hon. of E. T. Salmon* (ed. J. A. S. Evans, 1974), 225 ff. (where I have corrected the name of the hill on which Scipio camped from Koudiat el Behaima to Koudiat Sidi Slima).

CHAPTER XI ROME AND GREECE

1. THE HELLENISTIC WORLD.   General works on this period include *CAH*, vii–ix; W. W. Tarn and G. T. Griffith, *Hellenistic Civilization*, edn 3 (1952); M. Cary, *A History of the Greek World from 323 to 146 BC*, edn 2 (1951, repr. 1963); E. Will, *Histoire politique du monde hellénistique*, vol. i, *323–223 av. J.-C.* (1966), vol. ii, *223–30* (1967); M. Rostovtzeff, *Social and Economic History of the Hellenistic World*, 3 vols (1941). On individual states see E. R. Bevan, *The House of Seleucus* (1902); E. R. Bevan, *A History of Egypt under the Ptolemaic Dynasty* (1927); E. V. Hansen, *The Attalids of Pergamum*, edn 2 (1972); P. Fraser, *Ptolemaic Alexandria*, 3 vols (1972); P. Fraser and G. E. Bean, *The Rhodian Peraea* (1952); H. H. Schmitt, *Rom und Rhodos* (1957); F. W. Walbank, *Philip V of Macedon* (1940). A. Aymard, *Les Premiers rapports de Rome et de la confédération Achaienne* (1938), *Les Assemblées de la fédération Achaienne* (1938); R. Flacelière, *Les Aitoliens à Delphes* (1937). See also J. A. O. Larsen, *Greek Federal States* (1968). R. M. Errington, *The Dawn of Empire* (1971) outlines Rome's policy towards the Greek world.

2. THE SYRO-MACEDONIAN PACT.   The attempt of D. Magie (*JRS*, 1939, 32 ff.) to reject this pact as a fabrication of Rhodian propaganda, designed to frighten Rome, which deceived both Rome and Polybius, is not very convincing. It has been revived by R. M. Errington (*Athenaeum*, 1971, 336 ff. and *The Dawn of Empire* (1971), ch. x). In any case the report of the pact, whether it was fact or fiction, will have had the same effect on the Senate and have played the same part in precipitating Roman intervention. The pact is accepted by H. H. Schmitt, *Untersuchungen zur Geschichte Antiochus des Grossen* (1964), ch. iv (this book deals with various aspects of Antiochus' reign, but not primarily with his relations with Rome).

3. CHIOS AND LADE.   On the chronology of events see Walbank, *Polybius*, ii, 497 ff.

4. THE AETOLIAN EMBASSY.   Appian (*Mac.*, 4, 2) places the embassy in 201–200 when the Senate would have welcomed it. This is to be corrected to 202 (rather than rejected as an annalistic invention, as proposed by E. Badian, *Latomus*, 1958, 208 ff.). De Sanctis (*SR*, IV, i, 39) places the embassy before Zama, when the Senate would naturally wish to avoid eastern complications; Holleaux (*CAH*, viii, 152, n. 1) places it after Zama, in which case Philip may

have derived an unwarranted hope from the Senate's attitude. See also Livy, xxxi, 29, 4, on which see J. Briscoe, *Livy*, xxxi–xxxiii (1973), 130; he dates it to 201, but before the Rhodian and Attalid embassies.

5. THE PEOPLE AND WAR.   Livy (xxxi, 6 f.) places the consuls' proposal for the declaration of war at the beginning of the consular year and then recounts a second appeal which resulted in the declaration. Mommsen pointed out that the latter occurred in the summer of 200, not in March. But the assumption that the two appeals were made in quick succession makes it difficult to explain the sudden change in the people's feelings. De Sanctis (*SR*, IV, i, 32 n.) rightly separates the two appeals, placing one in March (as Livy), the other in midsummer (as chronology demands). See A. H. McDonald and F. W. Walbank, *JRS*, 1937, 187 ff.; E. Bickermann, *Rev. Phil.*, 1935, 171 ff. and *Cl. Ph.*, 1945, 139 f.; J. P. V. D. Balsdon *JRS*, 1954, 37 ff. J. W. Rich, *Declaring War in the Roman Republic* (Collection Latomus, vol. 149, 1976), 73 ff. and 107 ff., sticking closer to Livy, argues that only a short interval (a month or so?) intervened between the two meetings and that there was no direct link between the war vote and the embassy to Macedon: the instructions given to the *legati* were to inform the Greeks and Philip that the Senate had passed a *senatus consultum* which set out the terms on which it was ready to remain at peace with Philip. The formal *indictio belli* was therefore not delivered by Lepidus to Philip at Abydus, but was conveyed to a Macedonian post in Illyria after Galba had crossed the Adriatic. This view, like all others (!), involves difficulties. For the question of the state of the calendar in 200 BC see Rich, 75, n. 58.

6. AN EMBASSY TO EGYPT.   Livy (xxxi, 2 and 18) says the embassy went in the summer of 201 to Egypt to report the defeat of Hannibal and to ask the king to remain friendly to Rome if she should be forced to fight Philip. Chronology demands that the embassy started in 200; hence an annalistic error is generally assumed, e.g. by De Sanctis (*SR*, IV, i, 23) and Holleaux (*CAH*, viii, 161, n. 1). The latter remarks: 'It is to be observed that Hannibal's defeat happened a year before'. But it is also to be observed that the peace was only officially concluded in that year (201). May there not be a confused reference in Livy to an earlier embassy sent in 201 by the Senate (on the pretext of announcing Hannibal's defeat) to ascertain the attitude of the Great Powers to one another? If the personnel of the two embassies was the same, confusion would easily arise.

7. ATHENS AND ROME: CEPHISODORUS.   The influence of Athens on Roman policy has been variously assessed. The view of E. Bickermann (*Rev. Phil.*, 1936, 59 ff., 161 ff.; cf. also D. Magie, *Roman Rule in Asia Minor* (1950), 744 ff.) that the Peace of Phoenice was a *koine eirene* which included Athens and that therefore Philip's subsequent attack on Athens involved Rome in a legal obligation to aid Athens since Rome had guaranteed the security of all the signatories, has been rejected by J. A. O. Larsen (*Cl. Phil.*, 1937, 15 ff.) and by McDonald and Walbank (*JRS*, 1937, 180 ff.). The view in the Livian tradition (e.g. Livy, xxxi, i, 10) that Athens appealed directly to Rome for

help *before* the summer of 200 (which De Sanctis attempted to defend against the criticism of Holleaux) may be rejected: see F.W. Walbank, *Philip V*, 311 ff. In any case such an appeal would not have affected the legal aspect of Roman diplomacy, though it might have influenced Roman sentiment. Further light, however, has been thrown upon an Athenian appeal *during* the summer of 200 by the publication of a decree in honour of the Athenian statesman and ambassador, Cephisodorus (see B. D. Meritt, *Hesperia*, 1936, 419 ff. and A. H. McDonald, *JRS* 1937, 198.; cf. Pausanias, i, 36, 5). If Cephisodorus reached Rome just before the second meeting of the Comitia (McDonald, who originally placed the arrival after, now agrees that it was before: contrast *JRS*, 1963, 189 with *JRS*, 1937, 198), his appeal, while not affecting the legal aspect of Rome's procedure, would have afforded the Senate an additional argument with which to persuade the people to declare war; at the same time it would help to explain the impression which the Athenian appeal made on the later annalistic tradition.

8. Socii et amici.   On these see Matthaei, *Cl. Qu.*, 1907, 182 ff.; A. Heuss, 'Die Volkerrechtlichen Grundlagen der römischen Aussenpolitik in republikanischer Zeit', *Klio*, Beiheft 31 (1933); T. Frank, *Roman Imperialism* (1914), 147 ff., 160, n. 19 and *Cl. Phil.*, iv, 122; W. Dahlheim, *Struktur und Entwicklung des röm. Volkerrechts im dr. und zweit. Jahrhund. v. Chr.* (1968), 248 ff. E. Badian (*Foreign Clientelae* (1958), 69), however, thinks that the term *socius et amicus* may be older than the second century, and stresses (68) the growing influence of the concept of *clientela* on the earlier idea of *amicitia* 'until the Romans could no longer imagine the co-existence of genuinely equal states: her *amici* could only be her clients'. Rome was gradually extending her diplomatic categories.

For the view that Pergamum was an ally, not merely an *amicus* of Rome see J. A. O. Larsen, *Cl. Phil.*, 1937, 17. The early history of Rome's relations with Rhodes is uncertain: Polybius (xxx, 5, 6) notes that in 167 BC they had been in political association for nearly 140 years. i.e. since *c.* 306. Holleaux, however, argued that Polybius' text should be emended to '40' and that relations began only at the end of the third century. This view is criticized at length by H. H. Schmitt, *Rom und Rhodos* (1957; on which cf. A. H. McDonald, *JRS*, 1958, 184 ff. and P. M. Fraser, *Cl. Rev.*, 1959, 64 ff.). Even if formal *amicitia* had not existed since 306, some friendly contacts may have been made before *c.* 200, but certainly there was no treaty (*foedus*), while *amicitia*, as Heuss has shown, should be interpreted in a looser way than Holleaux had postulated. The relations of Rome and Rhodes in the second century are also examined by E. S. Gruen, *Cl. Qu.*, 1978, 58 ff.

9. Military imperialism.   This was the view of Wilamowitz and of De Sanctis (*SR*, IV, i, 26) who made Scipio Africanus the prime mover. It has been revived more recently by E. Will (*Hist. pol. du monde hellen.*, ii, 116 ff.), who however makes Sulpicius Galba, not Scipio, the villain. But see T. Frank, *Roman Imperialism*, ch. xiv and *Amer. Hist. Review*, 1912/13, xviii, 233 ff. and De Sanctis, 26, n. 58.

10. PHILHELLENIC POLITICS. See G. Colin, *Rome et la Grèce de 200 à 146 av. J. C.* (1905); T. Frank, *Roman Imperialism*, ch. viii. Criticism by Holleaux, *CAH*, viii, 158 f.; E. Badian, *Titus Quinctius Flamininus* (1970).

11. FEAR OF PHILIP AND/OR ANTIOCHUS. It has often been said, e.g. by Mommsen, that Rome's desire for quiet neighbours was a cause of the war, yet Mommsen himself admits that Philip was not a real danger to Rome. However, others have judged differently: thus R. M. Errington (*The Dawn of Empire* (1971), ch. x and *Athenaeum* 1971, 338 ff.), who rejects the Syro-Macedonian pact, has emphasized alleged activity of Philip against some Illyrian territory and supposes that senatorial distrust or fear of Philip was the basic cause of the war.

The relevance of Illyria is doubtful. At the conference of Nicaea in November 198 Flamininus ordered Philip to 'hand over to the Romans those parts of Illyria of which he had become possessed since the Peace of Epirus', i.e the Peace of Phoenice in 205 (Polybius, xvii, 1, 14; cf. Livy, xxxii, 33, 3). These places probably did not include the territory of the Parthini nor were they within the Roman protectorate (as Briscoe, *Livy, xxxi–xxxiii*, 54 f. argues). Rather, they will have been lands which had no previous connection with Rome (cf. Walbank, *Polybius*, ii, 551). There is no reference to encroachment in Illyria in the Roman ultimatum to Philip in 200, while attempts to find references to such places in the annalistic tradition are not conclusive (e.g. they need not (*pace* Briscoe, loc. cit.) be among the *socii* in Livy, xxx, 26, 2; cf. xxx, 42, 5; xxxi, 1, 9). The importance of Illyria in general has also been stressed by Badian: senators who knew Greece would realize that 'Illyria would only be safe when Macedon had been humbled' (*Foreign Clientelae* (1958), 66). Rome's ultimatum was designed to this end, which could be achieved either peacefully if Philip accepted or by war if Philip rejected it. Without legal justification Rome extended her traditional practice, took her new Greek 'friends' under her protection, and delivered the ultimatum on their behalf, but in order to serve her own purpose which was conditioned by fear and hatred of Philip.

Others prefer to stress fear of Antiochus (in combination with Philip) and accept the attractive theory of Holleaux, expounded in *Rome, la Grèce et les monarchies hellénistiques au iii e siècle avant J.-C.* (*273–205*) (1921) and in *CAH*, viii, 156 ff. (Holleaux's papers are collected in *Études d'épigraphie et d'histoire grecques*, vols i–v (1938–57); see especially vol. iv, *Rome, la Macédoine et l'Orient grecque*). Holleaux argued that the effective cause of the war was the Senate's sudden realization of this joint threat which was revealed when the Pergamene and Rhodian envoys reported the kings' pact at Rome. Philip's action in rebuilding his fleet (on this threat see G. T. Griffith, *Cambr. Hist. J.*, 1935), with which he had gained Caria and the Rhodian Peraea and defeated the Rhodians at Lade, might well seem a direct threat to Rome, now that he was backed by Antiochus, and the possibility of a Syro-Macedonian invasion of Italy might appear foreshadowed. A. Passerini (*Athenaeum*, 1931, 542 ff.), who attempted to refute Holleaux's theory, with less plausibility maintained that the Rhodian embassy emphasized the danger of Philip's supposed intrigues with Carthage. The suddenness with which the Senate changed from an abrupt refusal of the good opportunity to intervene in Greece offered by the Aetolian embassy of 202 to an almost feverish effort to precipitate war two years later suggests the emergence of a critical new factor, and that is best explained as knowledge of the pact and fear of its implication.

The Romans will have had a further grievance against Philip, *if* he had allowed Macedonian troops to support Hannibal in the battle of Zama as recorded by Livy (e.g. xxx, 33, 5; xxxi, 1, 9). These men however do not appear in Livy's description of the battle itself, nor in that by Polybius (e.g. at xv, 11, 1). The tradition is supported by J. P. V. D. Balsdon, *JRS*, 1954, 34 f. and by J. Briscoe, *Livy xxxi–xxxiii* (1973), 55: Balsdon suggests that the *Macedonum legio* were mercenaries who were present in Carthage in 202 but did not take part in the battle. However, the story is likely to have been invented by Roman annalists who wanted to show that Rome's hostile attitude to Philip in 201 was justified on account of his earlier alleged support of Hannibal.

12. CAUSES OF THE SECOND MACEDONIAN WAR. Many suggested causes have been discussed above, but three recent general surveys may be mentioned here: B. Ferro, *Le origini della II guerra macedonica* (1960; on which see A. H. McDonald, *JRS*, 1963, 187 ff.); J. Briscoe, *Commentary on Livy xxxi–xxxiii* (1973), 36 ff. and R. Werner, *ANRW*, I, i, 501 ff. (with some preliminary discussion of imperialism in general; cf. L. Raditsa, ibid., 564 ff.); Briscoe naturally concentrates on the Livian tradition concerning Rome and Macedon in the years 205–200, which was severely attacked by Holleaux but has more recently found a champion in J. P. V. D. Balsdon (*JRS*, 1954, 30 ff.) who argues for its general reliability, but E. Badian (*Foreign Clientelae*, 62 ff.) has not been persuaded in general. Despite some weaknesses in it, Holleaux's thesis is regarded as still the most satisfactory by F. W. Walbank in a valuable survey, 'Polybius and Rome's Eastern Policy', *JRS*, 1963, 1 ff. In general Polybius, as expounded by Walbank, regarded Roman imperialism as the result of 'natural' ambition, sharing the common Greek idea that it is a natural tendency of imperial states to expand. This, combined with his belief in the intrusive activity of Tyche (Fortune, Chance, Providence?) sometimes led him to conclusions which conflicted with his rational analysis of motives and causes; when conflict arises we should follow Polybius' detailed analyses rather than be misled by his superimposition of a general pattern which may be further from the truth. Cf. Walbank, *Polybius* (1972), 164 ff. and 'Political Morality and the Friends of Scipio', *JRS*, 1965, 1 ff.

13. CLASS STRUGGLES IN GREECE. Fustel de Coulanges (*Questions historiques* (1893), 121 ff.) advanced the view that the upper classes in the Greek states supported Rome and that Rome's varying policies in Greece were influenced by the internal class struggles there. This idea has been widely held, though challenged by A. Passerini (*Athenaeum*, 1933, 309 ff.). It is probably true that the Romans favoured the upper classes in general, but only if and when

this did not impinge upon their own interests, which they often conceived as best served by the preservation of a balance of power during the incessant internal quarrels that vexed the Greek states. The 'Greek resistance' to Rome was obviously determined by those who at any given time had political control in their own individual cities or leagues. J. Deiniger, *Der politische Widerstand gegen Rom in Griechenland 217–86 v Chr.* (1971), argues that until Pydna a pro- or anti-Roman policy was decided by internal rival political leaders with little reference to the desires of the people as a whole, whose influence was brought to bear only in the final Achaean revolt (147/6) when members of the upper class supported the lower. Though this view is perhaps too simple (cf. R. M. Errington, *JRS*, 1973, 249 f.; J. Briscoe, *Cl. Rev.*, 1974, 258 ff.), the relevant ancient evidence is usefully collected. Cf. also p. 515 n. 14 below.

14. THE SECOND MACEDONIAN WAR. See Kromayer, *Schlachtfelder*, ii, De Sanctis, *SR*, IV, i, F. W. Walbank, *Philip V* (1940). On Philip's strategy cf. Kromayer, 3 ff., De Sanctis, 44 ff.

15. THE CAMPAIGNS OF 200–198. See the three works cited in previous note, together with N. G. L. Hammond, *JRS*, 1966, 39 ff., for various views of the topography, especially of the Aoüs valley. For the campaign of 198 see also A. M. Eckstein, *Phoenix*, 1976, 119 ff., who limits Flamininus' military and diplomatic skill and thinks that he turned south-east after Aoüs for reasons of supply not of diplomacy.

16. FLAMININUS' TERMS. Cf. T. Frank, *Roman Imperialism* (1914), 161, n. 29. Since the terms were more sweeping than those offered in 200, Flamininus could hardly have made these additions on his own initiative.

17. FLAMININUS. Polybius was fairly critical of Flamininus, and Livy suppresses some of these criticisms. Various assessments of Flamininus' policy and ambitions have been reached: see H. H. Scullard, *Roman Politics, 220–150* BC, edn 2, (1973), index *s.v.* Quinctius; J. P. V. D. Balsdon, *Phoenix*, 1967, 177 ff.; E. Badian, *Titus Quinctius Flamininus: Philhellenism and Realpolitik* (1970, University of Cincinnati); J. Briscoe, *Latomus*, 1972, 22 ff. and *Commentary on Livy xxxi–xxxiii* (1973), 22 ff. For his family and early career, Badian, *JRS*, 1971, 102 ff. Balsdon is more favourably disposed to Flamininus than is Badian, who thinks that on occasion he was ready to sacrifice principle and even Rome's interests to his own personal ambitions (though he emphasizes that Flamininus should be judged by the standards of his own day). Badian's study is an astringent corrective to attempts to 'whitewash' Flamininus; he would even question the extent of Flamininus' personal culture. But however much or little Flamininus shared Greek culture, he certainly showed respect for it and this must have helped his dealings with the Greeks, even though few would now suppose that his policy was based on 'sentimental' philhellenism.

18. CYNOSCEPHALAE. De Sanctis (*SR*, IV, i, 86 n.) roughly follows W. M. Leake (*Travels in Northern Greece*, iv (1835), 457 who places the site between Sulpi and Dulvatan: Kromayer places it some six miles further west. See also

Walbank, *Polybius*, ii, 576 ff. and W. K. Pritchett, *Studies in Ancient Greek Topography*, vol. ii (1969), 133 ff.

19. DANGER FROM THE NORTH.   This threat is minimized by Holleaux, *CAH*, viii, 177.

20. THE AETOLIAN CLAIMS.   When the Aetolians asked for the return of four cities which Philip was willing to concede, Flamininus contended that three of them could not be handed back according to the terms of the Romano-Aetolian treaty of 211 (see p. 499 n. 16 above) which he claimed they had abrogated by making a separate peace in 206: even if the treaty *was* still valid, he asserted that their request contradicted its terms. The issues are uncertain and Flamininus may have been guilty of sharp practice, but in any case his refusal naturally angered the Aetolians, who had played an important part in the battle of Cynoscephalae.

21. PEACE.   Polybius, xviii, 33–9; 44 ff.; Livy, xxxiii, 11–13; Plutarch, *Flam.*, 9. See especially De Sanctis, *SR*, IV, i, 90 ff. Livy, (xxxiii, 30, 6) adds that Philip's armaments were limited and that he was not to engage in foreign wars without Rome's consent. This is probably an annalistic invention to try to justify Rome's interference later: see E. Taübler, *Imperium Romanum*, i (1913), 230.

CHAPTER XII   ROME AND ANTIOCHUS

1. GREEK CITIES IN ASIA MINOR.   On the Greek cities of Asia Minor and on Rome's treatment of them see D. Magie, *Roman Rule in Asia Minor* (1950), especially ch. iv and the Notes in vol. ii where many matters are discussed in detail relevant to the present and following chapters. See also E. Badian, 'Rome, and Antiochus: a study in Cold War' (*Cl. Phil.*, 1959, 81 ff. = *Studies in Greek and Roman History* (1964), 112 ff.). The annalistic tradition (Livy, xxxii, 8; 27) that Attalus appealed to Rome against Antiochus' invasion in 198 has been rejected by Holleaux (*Klio*, 1908, 273 ff.), but is defended by Bickermann (*Hermes*, 1932, 47) and Badian (*Cl. Phil.*, 1959, 82 f.).

2. ROME AND THE AUTONOMY OF GREEK CITIES.   When the Romans based their policy of intervention in Greece upon a proclamation of 'freedom' for the Greek cities, they were using a word with a long and somewhat ambiguous history. Freedom or autonomy had been a catchword of the kings who succeeded Alexander the Great. Although in theory it meant complete sovereignty (and in practice it sometimes did, as at Rhodes), it often in fact involved only a privileged status granted to cities by kings rather than real independence. Theoretically it involved the continuance of the city's constitution, the absence of a garrison and immunity from regular taxation, but in practice it generally fell short of such concessions (cf. e.g. 'those of the autonomous cities which formerly paid tribute to Antiochus,' Polybius, xxi, 46). It was this royal conception of freedom in the main that Rome adopted *vis-à-vis* the cities of the Hellenistic world (cf. A. H. M. Jones, *Anatolian Studies presented to W. H. Buckler*, 103 ff.).

That intervention on the principle of autonomy was justified was not denied by e.g. Philip of Macedon. At a meeting of the Achaean League (200–199) he counter-attacked Roman charges not by refusing to admit the validity of such intervention in principle, but by asserting that the Romans had no right to act upon such a principle in view of their treatment of the Italian Confederacy, especially of Rhegium, Tarentum and Capua. To this charge the Roman envoy put up a spirited reply (see Livy, xxxi, 29–31).

Rome's claim to extend this principle to the Greek cities of Asia Minor (cf. p. 260) was complicated by the fact that so many of these cities had at one time or another been subjected to foreign conquerors (e.g. Persia) and had temporarily been robbed of their freedom: in particular the political relationship of these autonomous cities to the kings of Syria has formed the subject of much discussion. Their status of freedom has sometimes been interpreted as a grant dependent upon the unilateral act of the monarch, and hence revocable and to be renewed at each accession: it was based on the conqueror's right to dispose of 'territory won by the spear' (cf. E. Bickermann, *Institutions des Séleucides*, 106 f., 133 f.; *Hermes*, lxvii, 50 ff.; M. Rostovtzeff, *Soc. and Econ. Hist. of Hellenistic World*, e.g. 153, 525–30, 1343 n. 15, 1347 n. 25). The view of E. Bickermann (*Rev. ét. gr.*, 1934, 346) that Alexander as conqueror of Asia arbitrarily gave autonomy to the Greek cities of Asia Minor has been refuted by W. W. Tarn (*Alexander the Great*, vol. ii (1948), 199 ff.), who shows that Alexander treated them as free allies and restored their original freedom which *de iure* they had never lost (these cities were not parties to the Peace of Antalcidas); he merely removed the obstacle of Persian rule and thus allowed the exercise of free rights which were still there. Those who accept this view will be less ready to follow Bickermann in his belief that Antiochus III laid claim to the possession of the Greek cities by right of conquest since they had formed part of the empire of Lysimachus. Rather, their independence which had been recognized by Alexander was confirmed by Antiochus I when he declared all Greek cities 'free, autonomous and ungarrisoned'. This was the policy of Alexander's successors, pursued in however an opportunist spirit, until it was abandoned by Antiochus III when he started on a career of active aggression (cf. D. Magie, *The Greek Political Experience*, 174 ff., *Roman Rule in Asia Minor*, 825 ff.). But theory and practice often varied, and although 'there certainly was a difference between genuine freedom (independence) and bogus freedom (under royal protection), it depended on the *de facto* situation, and I question whether the kings ever gave it precise legal formulation – it was to their interest to maintain the ambiguity of the term ἐλευθερία' (A. H. M. Jones, *The Greek City*, 315 n. 8).

E. Badian (*Foreign Clientelae*, 69 ff.) has argued that 'freedom for the Greeks' is not a new idea in Roman diplomacy, but a development of her earlier methods (e.g. towards the Illyrian coast), and he shows how the idea developed between 200 and 196 (in 200 Philip was to stop attacking the Greeks, in 198 to withdraw from Greece, then in 196 came the full declaration). But see A. H. McDonald *JRS*, 1959, 149.

3. NEGOTIATIONS, 194–193. See De Sanctis, *SR*, IV, i, 130. A diplomatic manoeuvre by Rome : see Holleaux, *CAH*, viii, 200. Spheres of influence : T. Frank, *Roman Imperialism* (1914), 171.

4. SCIPIO AFRICANUS AND HANNIBAL. The story, given by Livy (xxxv, 14, 5) on the authority of a later Roman annalist, that Scipio was a member of the embassy and met Hannibal at Ephesus, must be dismissed. Scipio was, however, on a mission sent to Carthage in 193 and also travelled in the eastern Mediterranean (he made dedications at Delos and Delphi : Scullard, *Scipio Africanus* (1970), 285 f.), so it is just possible he might have met Hannibal, though not at Ephesus.

5. HANNIBAL'S PLANS. On these and his relations with Antiochus see Kromayer, *Schlachtfelder*, ii, 127, whose views are supported by E. Meyer (*Kl. Schr.*, i, 260 ff.; *Meister d. Politik*, 160 ff.) against the criticism of Lehmann (*Delbrück-Festschrift*, 69 ff.). De Sanctis (*SR*, IV, i, 143 f., 155) rejects Kromayer's belief that Hannibal intended to carry the war into Italy. Groag (*Hannibal als Politiker*, 132 ff.) attempts to defend Hannibal's war plan against Kromayer's criticism, but his attempt is not convincing, especially in its assumption of the weakness of the Italian confederacy.

6. NABIS AND PHILOPOEMEN. It is not certain that the conduct of Nabis was so black and of Achaea so white as our pro-Achaean sources paint it : cf. De Sanctis *SR*, IV, i, 133, 231. In any case the Romans wished to stop the fighting before it spread. On Philopoemen see R. M. Errington, *Philopoemen* (1969).

7. ANTIOCHUS' AIMS. See De Sanctis, *SR*, IV, i, 141 ff.

8. THERMOPYLAE. On the topography see Kromayer, *Schlachtfelder*, ii, 134 ff. and *Atlas*, cols 42, 43 ; G. B. Grundy, *The Great Persian War* (1901), 257 ff. ; W. K. Pritchett, *Studies in Ancient Greek Topography* (1965), i, 71 ff. Traces of the wall survive.

9. LUCIUS SCIPIO. On the political intrigues behind these appointments Livy (xxxvii, 1–2) and Cicero (*Phil.*, xi, 7 ; *Pro Mur.*, 14) give slightly differing accounts. Cf. Scullard, *Roman Politics, 220–150* BC, edn 2, (1973), 284 f. L. Scipio's abilities are not generally rated very highly, but see J. P. V. D. Balsdon, *Historia*, 1972, 224 ff., for a more favourable assessment.

10. THE ROMAN INVASION OF ASIA. In spite of the Polybian tradition to the contrary (Polybius, xxi, 15), Antiochus' decision not to contest the crossing seems to have been wise. Cf. Kromayer, *Schlachtfelder*, ii, 161 ff. The Scipios sent a letter to Prusias, stating Roman policy to kings : Polybius, xxi, 11.

11. MAGNESIA. On the battle see Kromayer, *Schlachtfelder*, ii, 163 ff. and *Atlas*, cols 43–6. The criticism of Delbrück (*Geschichte der Kriegskunst*, i, edn 3, 426 ff.) is far from convincing.

12. THE PEACE OF APAMEA. See Polybius, xxi, 16–17, 24, 45 : Livy, xxxvii, 45. Appian, *Syr.*, 38, includes the surrender of the fleet and elephants in the preliminaries, but Polybius' silence is preferable. Cf. De Sanctis, *SR*, IV, i, 205 ff. On the territorial limits imposed on Antiochus by land and sea, see A. H. McDonald, *JRS*, 1967, 1 ff. (the Taurus frontier to lie along the river Calycadnus in Cilicia Tracheia), and McDonald and Walbank, *JRS*, 1969,

30 ff. (for the naval clauses and types of ships involved). Contrary to the widely accepted view that Scipio's terms were more generous than those finally established by the Senate, E. Badian (*Foreign Clientelae*, 81 ff.) believes (partly because Polybius' account of Scipio's terms is incomplete) that 'the spirit of the Scipios' armistice is the same as that of the Senate's peace treaty'. But would Scipio have approved of the handing over to Eumenes of some Greek cities in the final settlement? We do not know, but the friendly letters that he wrote to some cities (see p. 520 n. 15) and his lack of prejudice against kings (as shown in his letter to Prusias, as well as in his personal relations with Philip) may suggest that he would not have liked the Senate's terms.

CHAPTER XIII ROME AND THE EASTERN MEDITERRANEAN

1. CALLICRATES. New era: Polybius, xxiv, 10. E. Badian, *Foreign Clientelae* (1958, 91) assesses Callicrates more favourably.

2. DEMETRIUS. For this judgement see De Sanctis (*SR*, IV, i, 255) who compares Philip's fortunes with Hanniba.'s. Demetrius was probably used as an unwitting tool by the Senate and Flamininus against the Macedonian royal house: as a future king he would become a pawn of Rome. Flamininus is said to have alleged in a letter to Philip that Demetrius was plotting not only to oust Perseus but also to remove Philip himself: the letter may have been a forgery, as Livy suggests (lx, 23). See Walbank, *Philip V*, 251, Badian, *Foreign Clientelae*, 94.

3. PERSEUS. See P. Meloni, *Perseo* (1953). On the causes of the war see A. Giovannini, *Bulletin de correspondence hellénique*, 1969, 853 ff.; L. Raditsa, *ANRW*, I, i, 576 ff. E. S. Gruen (*Amer. J. Anc. Hist.*, 1976, 29 ff.) has argued that Greek attitudes towards Rome or Macedon were not determined by class membership or social status during the Third Macedonian War.

4. EUMENES. His charges against Perseus included the expulsion of a Thracian chief, now Rome's ally; the harbouring of the murderers of an Illyrian chief; intrigues with Carthage and Byzantium and in Greece, etc. The charges are listed in the accusation of Perseus before the Delphic Amphictiony (Dittenberger, *Sylloge*, 643; translation in Lewis and Reinhold, *Rom. Civ.*, i. 184 f.).

5. Q. MARCIUS PHILIPPUS. See F. W. Walbank, *JRS*, 1941, 86 ff., J. Briscoe, *JRS*, 1964, 66 ff. His diplomatic methods offended some of the more old-fashioned senators. The sources mention four diplomatic contacts between Rome and Macedon after Eumenes' visit. These are discussed by J. W. Rich, *Declaring War in the Roman Republic* (1976), 88 ff., who concludes that only two are authentic, namely Philippus' interview with Perseus at Tempe and the Macedonian embassy to Rome in early 171; he also concludes that at no point did the Romans deliver an ultimatum and discusses the chronological problems involved.

6. THE BATTLE OF PYDNA. This battle presents many difficulties. Polybius'

account (xxix, 15–17) is very fragmentary, while there is a large lacuna in Livy's (xliv, 33–42). See Kromayer, *Schlachtfelder*, II, 294 ff.; criticism by E. Meyer, *Kleine Schriften*, II, 465 ff.; reply by Kromayer, *Schlachtfelder*, iv, 601 ff., and *Atlas*, col. 48 ff.; De Sanctis, IV, i, 322 ff.; W. K. Pritchett, *Studies in Greek Topography*, ii (1969), 145 ff. The date is fixed by an eclipse of the moon on the night of 21 June (cf. De Sanctis, pp. 369–76). This date (rather than the autumn) is confirmed by an inscription, discovered in the Agora at Athens, which contains the earliest known reference to the battle: see *Hesperia*, 1934, 18 ff.; 1936, p. 389 ff., n. 17. Livy (xliv, 37) dated the eclipse to 3 September; hence it has been argued (cf. De Sanctis) that the calendar was at this time some $2\frac{1}{2}$ months out of line with the solar year, i.e that 3 September on the contemporary calendar = 21 June (Julian calendar). This view has been challenged by S. I. Oost, *Cl. Phil.*, 1953, 217 ff., but defended by P. Meloni, *Latomus* (1954), 553 ff.

Kromayer places Perseus' camp eight miles south of Pydna between the Pelikas and Mavroneri. He supposes that the Romans as well as the Macedonians withdrew to their camp at midday before the battle, because otherwise their advance guard by the river would be unnecessary. Yet it may have been necessary to protect their right wing from the possibility of being outflanked. Meyer's view is that the Romans remained in battle array all day and that Perseus succeeded in attacking them suddenly in this position. Even if the first statement is admitted, the second can hardly withstand Kromayer's criticism; the Romans were not taken by surprise when Perseus attacked. More recently Kromayer has changed his ground by suggesting that the Roman army did not advance from its camp into battle line at all in the morning; and it is certainly easier to support this by absence of reference in our sources than it is to find definite reference to a Roman advance.

7. THE SETTLEMENT OF MACEDONIA.   See T. Frank, *Roman Imperialism* (1914), 208 ff.; A. Aymard, *Cl. Ph.* 1950, 97 ff.; J. A. O. Larsen, *Greek Federal States* (1968), 295 ff. E. Badian (*Foreign Clientelae*, 97) notes that the settlement involved 'for the first time the dissociation of *libertas* and *immunitas*': the states were free but paid taxes.

8. THE SETTLEMENT OF EPIRUS.   See S. I. Oost, *Roman Policy in Epirus* (1954), 68 ff.; N. G. L. Hammond, *Epirus* (1967), 629 ff. For the part played by the Epirote traitor Charops see H. H. Scullard, *JRS*, 1945, 55 ff.

9. ROMAN POLICY.   On Roman policy in the east, 168–146 BC, and the factions in the Roman Senate that formulated it see J. Briscoe, *Historia*, 1969, 49 ff. For a general survey of this period see E. Will, *Hist. pol. du monde hellénistique*, ii (1967), 301 ff.

10. PTOLEMY'S TESTAMENT.   See *SEG*, ix, 7, with literature cited there and in *JHS*, 1933, 263 f.

11. DEMETRIUS.   Polybius, Demetrius' friend, helped him to escape and has given a vivid account of the adventure (xxxi, 19 ff.). Perhaps the Senate, or part of it at any rate, turned a blind eye to this escapade; cf. H. Volkmann, *Klio*, 1925, 382 f.

12. JEWISH TREATY.   This treaty, which was granted by the Senate and not

ratified by the Comitia, never became operative, but its existence has been doubted without adequate reason. See 1 *Maccab*. 8; Josephus, *Antiqu.* xii, 10, 6 (414–19). Cf. E. Schürer, *The History of the Jewish People in the Age of Jesus Christ*, vol. 1 (revised by G. Vermes and Fergus Millar, 1973), 171 ff.

13. MACEDONIA AS PROVINCE. M. G. Morgan (*Historia*, 1969, 422 ff.) argues that Macedonia was formally established as a Roman province by Mummius in 146 rather than (as is usually believed) by Metellus Macedonicus.

14. THE ACHAEAN WAR. On its social aspects see A. Fuks, *JHS*, 1970, 78 ff. The lower classes supported the war effort against Rome, but although various measures taken by the League (e.g regarding payment of debts and freeing of slaves) had serious social and economic implications, the war was essentially a national struggle for independence, irrespective in the main of class differences. Cf. W. W. Tarn, *Hellenistic Civilization*, edn 3 (1952), 38; when the League voted to go to war with Rome 'it could do nothing else, unless a small country has no right to fight for its liberties against a big one'. E. S. Gruen (*JHS*, 1976, 46 ff.) has made a further attempt to disentangle the motives which led to the war, which he believes was caused neither by Roman imperialism nor by Greek mob hysteria: rather it 'stemmed from understandable miscalculation on both sides. Rome expected that a combination of intimidating demands and generous proposals would prevent conflict in the Peloponnese. Achaean leaders assumed that coercion of dissident communities in the League could continue – as it had in the past – with impunity. The peculiar circumstances of 146 undermined those expectations. In the end, Rome would not endure a conflagration in Greece when she was about to establish a stable order in Macedon . . . The result was calamity, unplanned and unanticipated' (p. 69).

15. THE SETTLEMENT OF 146. See J. A. O. Larsen, *Econ. Survey of Anc. Rome*, iv, 306 ff.; *Greek Federal States* (1968), 498 ff.; S. Accame, *Il dominio romano in Grecia dalla guerra acaica ad Augusto* (1946).

CHAPTER XIV ROME, ITALY AND THE WESTERN MEDITERRANEAN

1. CISALPINE GAUL. As ancient historians were more interested in Rome's expansion in the east, the dreary wars in the north were ill-recorded by authoritative writers: this afforded an open field for the patriotic imagination of the Roman annalists, and some modern writers have not been slow to seek doublets of events. Thus, e.g., Livy's account of the campaign of 200–199 (xxxi, 10; 21–2; 47–9) is sometimes regarded as merely a doublet of those of 197–196. But while confusion and duplication of many details may have occurred, such radical criticism is scarcely needed: see, e.g., J. Briscoe, *Commentary on Livy, xxxi–xxxiii* (1973), 82 ff. On these northern campaigns see also A. J. Toynbee, *Hannibal's Legacy* (1965), 268 ff. and (for 201–191) A. H. McDonald, *Antichthon*, 1974, 44 ff.

2. NEW ROADS. This Via Flaminia from Arretium to Bononia is to be

distinguished from the old Via Flaminia from Rome to Ariminum (of which the Via Aemilia was a continuation) built by the consul of 223. On the development of Cisalpine Gaul see U. Ewins, *PBSR*, 1952, 54 ff. and for its population and resources see P. Brunt, *Manpower*, ch. xiii.

3. MINUCIUS THERMUS. Livy's account (xxxv, 3, 11, 21; xxxvi, 38) of Thermus' exploits is confused and untrustworthy.

4. LUCA, LUNA. See E. T. Salmon, *Cl. Qu.*, 1933, 30 ff., *JRS*, 1936, 47 ff. and A. J. Toynbee, *Hannibal's Legacy* (1965), ii, 532 ff. It remains uncertain whether or not references in the sources to a colony at Luca should be emended to Luna, and that thus Luca should be eliminated from the list of colonies; Salmon is against retaining it, Toynbee in favour. See now P. Sommella and C. F. Giuliani, *La pianta di Lucca romana* (1974), in favour.

5. CENTURIATION. Traces of the division of land into plots have been found in northern Italy. On this centuriation as revealed by aerial photography see J. Bradford, *Ancient Landscapes* (1957), esp. 157 ff., 261 ff.; P. Fraccaro, *Opuscula* (1957), III, i, ii.

6. MANLIUS. On the topography, see Veith, *Atlas*, cols. 49, 50; De Sanctis, *SR*, IV, i, 431.

7. DALMATIAN CAMPAIGNS. See J. J. Wilkes, *Dalmatia* (1969), 30 ff.

8. THE SPANISH WARS. The account of these wars, which belong to the Great Age of Conquests, partly exceeds the strict chronological limit of this volume (146 BC). The Lusitanian War lasted from 154 to 138, the First Celtiberian from 181 to 179, the Second from 153 to 151 and the Third (or Numantine War) from 143 to 133; Polybius treats the last two as one twenty years' war, 153–133. The sources (mainly Polybius, Livy, Appian and Diodorus: Polybius wrote a monograph on the Numantine War, now lost), are collected in *Fontes Hispaniae Antiquae*, iii (1935), iv (1937), edited by A. Schulten.

9. ROMAN SPAIN. See A. Schulten, *CAH*, viii, 306 ff., C. H. V. Sutherland, *The Romans in Spain* (1939). The ancient sources are collected in *Fontes Hispaniae Antiquae*, ed. A. Schulten, P. Bosch Gimpera and L. Pericot.

10. ROMAN CAMPS. Camps dating from this campaign have been found near Emporiae, Segontia (at Aguilar and Alpanesque) and near Numantia (at Renieblas I).

The survival of many camps, particularly at and around Numantia, throws an interesting light on these wars. Our knowledge of them derives mainly from the work of A. Schulten (see especially his four monumental volumes, *Numantia: die Ergebnisse der Ausgraben*, and more briefly, *Geschichte von Numantia* (1933)). Literary information about Republican camps derives chiefly from Polybius' detailed description (vi, 27 ff.); though the camps of Scipio at Numantia do not quite conform to Polybius' description, that of Nobilior at Renieblas does. Though the Romans did not excel in certain branches of art, the Roman camp, no less than the Roman constitution in the civil sphere, was a work of art, and as early as 280 BC king Pyrrhus could exclaim in wonder, 'The camps of the barbarians are not barbarian', and his remark is now shown to be true.

It may be convenient to list a number of camps which belong to this period:

217 Camp of the Scipios at Almenara, near Saguntum (p. 213).

206 Camp of Scipio at Ilipa (p. 228; cf. H. H. Scullard, *JRS*, 1936, 19 ff.).

c. 195 Camps of Cato's campaigns at Emporiae (?. See A. Schulten, *Arch. Anzeiger*, 1940, 75 ff.), Aguilar, Alpanesque (near Segontia) and Renieblas I and summer camp II.

153 Summer camp of Nobilior at Almazan.

153 Nobilior's camp at Renieblas III (Camps IV and V belong to the war with Sertorius).

152 Marcellus' camp at Numantia on Castillejo I.

141–140 Pompeius' camp at Numantia on Castillejo II.

139 Servilius Caepio's camp near Caceres Castra Servilia (later camps near Caceres date from the Sertorian war).

138 Brutus' camp, the *cava di Viriato*, at Viseu in Portugal.

134 Scipio's seven camps around Numantia.

11. SPAIN 154–133 BC. On these wars see H. Simon, *Roms Kriege in Spanien, 154–133 v. Chr,* (1962); A. E. Astin, *Scipio Aemilianus* (1967), 35 ff., 137 ff.

12. REVOLT AND NOBILIOR. On the site of Segeda see A. Schulten, *Arch. Anzeiger*, 1933, 547. A bronze tablet, referring to a treaty between ten Celtiberian towns, belongs either to this period or later (*c.* 98 BC): see Schulten, *Hermes*, 1915, 237. In order that the consul might start his campaign early, the beginning of the civil year was altered from 15 March to 1 January. Modern Europe thus owes the beginning of its year to the Celtiberian War. On Nobilior's camp see n. 10 above.

13. VIRIATHUS. On the war with Viriathus see A. Schulten, *Neue Jahrbücher*, 1917, 1 ff. and Kromayer, *Atlas*, col. 56. Little was known of details, topographical and strategical, until Schulten's researches revealed the main outline.

14. NUMANTIA. Schulten believes that the town wall was partially destroyed when the inhabitants spread beyond it, so that the attacks of Nobilior in 153 and of Scipio in 134 were against an unwalled town. But the archaeological evidence has been interpreted differently by R. G. Collingwood and M. I. Munro (*JRS*, 1931, 156) who suggest that the town wall was not destroyed.

15. HANNIBAL AS SUFFETE. The date of his office, whether 197, 196 or 195 is uncertain; 196 is the most probable, with 195 as the year of his flight into exile. See E. Groag, *Hannibal als Politiker*, 114, n. 4, Scullard, *Roman Politics*, 284; J. Briscoe, *Comm. Livy, xxi–xxxiii*, 335 at L. xxxiii, 45.

16. MASINISSA. See Polybius' tribute, xxxvi, 16. On Masinissa's achievement cf. P. G. Walsh, *JRS*, 1965, 149 ff.; G. Camps, *Massinissa* (= *Libyca*, viii, 1960).

17. THE FOSSA REGIA. The frontier of Carthage at the beginning of the Third Punic War followed the same course as the boundary between the future province of Africa and Numidia, called the *fossa regia*. The discovery of

boundary stones has shown that Carthage only retained the north-east corner of Tunisia and a narrow coastal strip on the east.

18. CAUSES OF THE THIRD PUNIC WAR.   Commercial jealousy, the view of Mommsen, has been effectively rejected by Kahrstedt (*Gesch. d. Karthager*, iii, 616 ff.), T. Frank (*Roman Imperialism*, 234) and E. Badian (*Roman Imperialism in the late Republic* (1968), 20). After the war the Romans made no attempt to occupy or exploit the commercial facilities of Carthage, while at xxxvi, 9 Polybius is silent about possible trade rivalry. Badian (*Foreign Clientelae*, 125 ff., and esp. 133 ff.) underlines Roman fear of Carthaginian strength (in contrast to Kahrstedt's view of Carthaginian weakness which, it was feared, might tempt Masinissa to attack Carthage and try to dominate North Africa). W. Hoffmann (*Historia*, 1960, 309 ff.) emphasizes the growth of *metus Punicus*. On Roman policy see further F. E. Adcock, *Cambr. Hist. J.*, 1946, 117 ff.; A. E. Astin, *Scipio Aemilianus* (1967), 272 ff; and (on Scipio's policy) H. H. Scullard, *JRS*, 1960, 59 ff.

19. CARTHAGE: TOPOGRAPHY.   See D. B. Harden, *Greece and Rome* (1939), 1 ff.; C. Picard, *Carthage* (1951); B. H. Warmington, *Carthage*, edn 2, (1969), 128 ff. See H. Hurst, *Antiquaries J.*, 1975, 11 ff.; 1976, 117 ff.; 1977, 232 ff.; CEDAC (Centre d'Études . . . arch. de la Conservation de Carthage) Bulletin I (September 1978, Tunis); S. Lancel, *Byrsa*, i (Rome, 1974). The general accuracy of Appian's description (*Lib.*, 96) of the splendid circular naval harbour, with ship-sheds for 220 vessels, has now been confirmed.

CHAPTER XV ROMAN POLICY AND THE GOVERNMENT

1. THE EQUESTRIAN ORDER.   Polybius (vi, 17) gives a description of their activities about 150 BC ('nearly everyone' had an interest in state contracts). See H. Hill, *The Roman Middle Class* (1952); C. Nicolet, *L'Ordre équestre à l'époque republicaine*, i, ii (1966, 1975); (the basic thesis of this book, namely that the *ordo equester* consisted only of *equites equo publico*, has not met with widespread acceptance); P. A. Brunt in *The Crisis of the Roman Republic* (ed. R. Seager, 1969), 83 ff; E. Badian, *Publicans and Sinners* (1972) and briefly *OCD*², s.v. Equites.

2. FREEDMEN.   See in general S. Treggiari, *Roman Freedmen during the Late Republic* (1969) and, for the history of their voting rights, pp. 37 ff.

3. AGRARIAN AND COLONIAL POLICY.   See G. Tibiletti, *Athenaeum*, 1950, 183 ff.; A. J. Toynbee, *Hannibal's Legacy*, (1965), ii, 190 ff.

4. COLONIES.   Latin colonies: Copia (193), Vibo (192), Placentia and Cremona (190), Bononia (189), Aquileia (181), ?Luca (180). Citizen colonies: Volturnum, Liternum, Puteoli, Salernum, Buxentum, Pyrgi, Sipontum, Tempsa, Croton (194), Potentia, Pisaurum, Auximum (184), Mutina, Parma, Saturnia (183), Graviscae (181), Luna (177). The larger size of citizen colonies founded from 183 BC (pp. 293 ff.) perhaps led to the introduction of the duovirate or dual *praetura* (p. 147) and hastened the assimilation of such

colonies to *municipia*: cf. A. N. Sherwin-White, *Rom. Cit.*, edn 2, 81 ff. See also E. T. Salmon, *Roman Colonization* (1969) ch. vi.

5. IUS MIGRANDI. The law that members of Latin colonies founded after 266 must leave a son behind (p. 484 n. 24) might be evaded by manumitting and adopting a slave. Between 187 and 177 the restricted *ius migrandi* was probably applied to *all* Latin colonies.

6. LEGES PORCIAE. See Bloch-Carcopino, *La République romaine*, ii, 145; A. H. McDonald, *JRS*, 1944, 19; A. H. M. Jones, *Criminal Courts of the Roman Republic and Principate* (1972), 22 ff.

7. ALLIED GRIEVANCES. Senatorial interference: Polybius, vi, 13, 3. Sidicinum: C. Gracchus, *apud Aul. Gell.*, x, 3, 2–3.

8. ANTI-EXPANSIONISM. See F. B. Marsh, *The Founding of the Roman Empire* (1927), ch. i.

9. ROMAN POLICY NON-COMMERCIAL. See T. Frank, *Roman Imperialism* (1914), ch. xiv; and *CAH*, viii, 348; also cf. p. 518 n. 13 above. On Italian trade see J. Hatzfeld, *Les trafiquants italiens dans l'Orient hellénique* (1919).

10. PROVINCIAL ADMINISTRATION. The general methods have already been discussed in connection with the formation of the province of Sicily (ch. viii, 1): conditions varied in the different provinces, and it was a great merit of the Roman system to avoid imposing an unnatural uniformity. In general see G. H. Stevenson, *Roman Provincial Administration* (1939); E. Badian, *Publicans and Sinners* (1972).

11. THE TRIBUNATE AND THE LEX AELIA AND FUFIA. On the tribunes' increasing independence of the Senate and magistrates see L. R. Taylor, 'Forerunners of the Gracchi', *JRS*, 1962, 19 ff. On the law see A. E. Astin, *Latomus*, 1964, 421 ff.; A. K. Michels, *The Calendar of the Roman Republic* (1967), 94 ff.

12. LEX VILLIA ANNALIS. See A. E. Astin, *The Lex Annalis before Sulla* (1957).

13. NOBLE EXCLUSIVENESS. '*Consulatum nobilitas inter se per manus tradebat*': Sallust, *Bell. Iug.*, 63, 3. It is instructive to compare the working of aristocracy in England. It is very exceptional to find a commoner in the Cabinet in the eighteenth century, and in the nineteenth 'every Cabinet from Lord Grey's Reform Bill administration to that of Disraeli in 1874 was wholly, or almost wholly, aristocratic. There was this advance from the eighteenth century – that it was not necessary to be a peer in order to be a Cabinet Minister, but birth and connection were almost indispensable to Cabinet rank' (O. F. Christie, *The Transition from Aristocracy, 1832–1867* (1927), 114).

14. POLITICAL FACTIONS. The 'prosopographical' analysis of Roman politics derives mainly from M. Gelzer's work on the nobility (now translated as *The Roman Nobility* (1969) by R. Seager) and the development of some of his ideas by F. Münzer, *Römische Adelsparteien und Adelsfamilien* (1920). For the application of group politics to different periods see F. Cassola, *I gruppi politici romani del iii secolo a.C.* (1962; on this cf. E. S. Starveley, *JRS*, 1963, 182 ff.); A. Lippold, *Consules . . . 264 bis 201 v. Chr.* (1963); H. H. Scullard, *Roman Politics, 220–150* BC, edn 2 (1972); E. Badian, *Foreign Clientelae,*

264–70 BC (1958). Brief general discussions of method are given by A. E. Astin, *Politics and Policies in the Roman Republic* (a lecture, 1968) and T. R. S. Broughton, *Aufstieg NRW*, I, i, 250 ff. On *factio* see R. Seager, *JRS*, 1972, 55 ff. While most historians would now agree that the essential nature of Roman political life was personal, they remain divided about the extent to which groups of friends and clients gathered round an individual and on how durable such groups which were held together by ties of family and *amicitia* (political alliance) may have been. On the ideals of the nobles see D. Earl, *The Moral and Political Tradition of Rome* (1967).

15. SCIPIO AFRICANUS.   The idea that the people wished to make him perpetual consul and dictator is based on late and unreliable evidence (Livy, xxxviii, 56): see H. H. Scullard, *Roman Politics*, edn 2 (1972), 83 ff., 282. Scipio's visit to Delphi in *SEG*, i, 144. Visit to Delos in 193: Holleaux, *Hermes*, 1913, 75; in 189: Dittenberger, *Sylloge*, ii, 617. Decrees of *proxenia* to the Scipios by Aptera in Crete in 189: M. Guarducci, *Inscr. Cret.*, ii, Aptera 5A. Letter to Colophon in 190: M. Holleaux, *Riv. d. Fil.*, 1924, 29 ff. Letter to Heraclea: Dittenberger, *Sylloge*, ii, 618 and De Sanctis *SR*, IV, i, 226 n. and 576 n. On the treaty which terminated the war of Heraclea and Miletus in 180: Dittenberger, *Sylloge*, ii, 633.

16. PHILHELLENISM.   Two camps: R. M. Haywood, *Studies in Scipio Africanus* (1933). The idea of A. H. McDonald (*JRS*, 1938, 155 ff.) that Flamininus supported the old Hellenic ideal of the Greek city-state at the expense of the Hellenistic kingdoms, while Scipio's policy was based more broadly, has not been accepted by all, though it has much to commend it.

17. THE TRIAL OF THE SCIPIOS.   On this vexed question see P. Fraccaro, *I Processi degli Scipioni* (1911) and *Athenaeum*, 1939, 3 ff. (= *Opuscula*, i, 263 ff., 393 ff.); H. H. Scullard, *Roman Politics, 220–150* BC edn 2 (1972), 290 ff. Alternatively to what is said in the text, some maintain that the attack on Africanus occurred in 187 and merely formed an incident in the trial of Lucius; the evidence is inconclusive.

18. CATO.   See D. Kienast, *Cato der Zensor* (1954); F. della Corte, *Cato*, edn 2 (1969); H. H. Scullard, *Roman Politics*, edn 2 (1972), s.v. index; A. E. Astin, *Cato the Censor* (1978).

CHAPTER XVI ECONOMIC AND SOCIAL ORGANIZATION

1. AGRICULTURE.   On agriculture and Roman methods see especially K. D. White, *Roman Farming* (1970); also his *Agricultural Implements of the Roman World* (1967) and *Farm Equipment of the Roman World* (1975). Also W. E. Heitland, *Agricola* (1921).

2. CHANGING AGRARIAN CONDITIONS. See A. J. Toynbee, *Hannibal's Legacy* (1965), ii, chs v–viii; M. Rostovtzeff, *Social and Economic History of the Roman Empire*, ch. i.

3. SICILIAN CORN.   See T. Frank, *Econ. Survey*, i, 158 ff.; H. Last, *CAH*, ix, 4.

4. ARMY REFORMS.   Livy (i, 43, 1; viii, 8, 3) dates the adoption of the long *scutum* in place of the *clipeus* either to Servius Tullius or to *c.* 400 BC, while Sallust (*Catil.*, 51) and the *Ineditum Vaticanum* believe the Romans borrowed the *pilum* and *scutum* during struggles with the Samnites. The looser manipular system may have been introduced at the time of the siege of Veii (an operation for which the older phalanx formation was not suited: see Q. F. Maule and H. R. W. Smith, *Votive Religion at Caere* (1959), 22 ff.), but if so, it did not prove effective at Allia. The manipular formation is described by Livy (viii, 8) under the year 340, but since a riva. Roman tradition (Plutarch, *Camillus* 40) regards Camillus as a military reformer, some (e.g. L. Homo, *CAH*, vii, 568) believe that the reform was designed by Camillus against the Gauls. E. T. Salmon (*Samnium and the Samnites*, 105 ff.) prefers Camillus and the beginning of the fourth century, while F. E. Adcock (*CAH*, vii, 596) argues for the Samnite Wars. On the literary sources for the pre-Marian army see E. Rawson, *PBSR*, 1971, 13 ff. On the earliest use of the cohort see M. J. V. Bell, *Historia*, 1965, 404 ff. and E. Rawson, op. cit. Most books on specialized aspects of the Roman army (e.g. H. M. D. Parker, *The Roman Legions*, edn 2 (1958)) deal only briefly with earlier periods and concentrate on the later Republic and Empire. An excellent picture book, elementary but reliable, *The Roman Army* (1975) by P. Connolly, well illustrates the formation and weapons of the pre-Marian army (and navy). Standard works include Kromayer-Veith, *Heerwesen und Kriegsführung der Griechen und Römer* (1928); P. Couissin, *Les armes romaines* (1926).

5. LEGIONS IN BEING.   The fact that between 200 and 168 BC there were normally eight legions in being (some 42,000 citizens under arms) shows that the standing armies of the Empire were foreshadowed: cf. R. E. Smith, *Service in the Post-Marian Army* (1958), ch. i. On the total number of troops involved see A. Afzelius, *Die römische Eroberung Italiens (340–264 v. Chr.)* (1942) and *Die röm. Kriegsmacht während der Auseinandersetzung mit den hellenistischen Grossmächten* (1944); P. A. Brunt, *Manpower* (1971), ch. xxiii.

6. OSTIA.   On early Ostia see R. Meiggs, *Roman Ostia*, edn 2 (1973), ch. 3.

7. MINING.   If a senatorial decree which closed mining in Italy (Pliny, *Nat. Hist.*, xxxiii, 78) belongs to this period, it did not apparently apply to the iron of Elba. On mining in general see J. F. Healy, *Mining and Metallurgy in the Greek and Roman World* (1978).

8. SHOP-KEEPERS.   The three different signatures on some pottery of *c.* 200 BC found in a deposit of 'throw-outs' from a kiln at Minturnae suggest that the potter was not an individual but a small syndicate or co-operative group: *Amer. J. Arch.*, 1934, 294.

9. ROMAN COINAGE.   On the early coinage see R. Thomsen, *Early Roman Coinage*, 3 vols (1957–61); on Republican coinage in general see E. A. Sydenham, *Roman Republican Coinage* (1952), M. H. Crawford, *Roman Republican Coinage* (1974). Two wider surveys are H. Mattingly, *Roman Coins*, edn 2 (1962) and C. H. V. Sutherland, *Roman Coins* (1974). It is not possible here to enter into problems that have vexed the study of the early coinage, but

there is now wider agreement about the date of its inception and that the *denarius* was introduced in 212/211 BC. On the developments during the Hannibalic War see M. Crawford, *JRS*, 1964, 29 ff.; and for Hannibal's and other coinage in Italy at this time see E. S. G. Robinson, *Num. Chron.*, 1964, 37 ff.

10. WAR BUDGETS. The figures given above for the First Punic War are those of T. Frank (*Econ Survey*, i, (1933), 61 ff.) who equates the cost of the war, some 100 million *denarii*, with 24 million American dollars of 1933. He includes the grain received by the allies, but it is probable that though Rome provided food and equipment for the allies, the cost of this (like that of the allied pay: Livy, xxvii, 9, 2) fell on the allies, who will have made an overall payment to Rome: see Polybius, vi, 39, and Walbank, *Polybius*, i, 722. For the Second Punic War see Frank, op. cit., 76 ff. The figures he gives are only put forward as rough estimates which may give some idea of the relative scale of the various financial operations.

11. PROPERTY. See De Sanctis, *SR*, III, ii, 623 ff. and Frank, *Econ. Survey*, 125 f. Land was worth perhaps 100 *denarii* an acre in 200 BC.

12. PRICES. See T. Frank *Econ. Survey*, i, 188 ff., 208 ff.

13. SLAVERY. On the revolting conditions in the mines see Strabo, iii, 147, and Diodorus, v, 36. In general see W. L. Westermann. *The Slave Systems of Greek and Roman Antiquity* (1955); P. A. Brunt, *JRS*, 1958, 164 ff.; M. I. Finley (ed), *Slavery in Classical Antiquity* (1960); J. Vogt, *Ancient Slavery* (1975).

14. FAMILY LIFE AND SCHOOLING. See J. P. V. D. Balsdon, *Life and Leisure in Ancient Rome* (1969), ch. iii; H. I. Marrou, *History of Education in Antiquity* (1958), 229 ff.; S. F. Bonner, *Education in Ancient Rome* (1977).

15. GREEK INFLUENCES. See G. Colin, *Rome et la Grèce* (1905), still a useful collection of material. He assigns the cause primarily to Rome. At the moment when social inequalities, pride and ambition corrupted the Romans, Greece supplied all manner of evil examples.

16. Cf A. Momigliano, *Alien Wisdom* (1975), 18 f.

17. THE CITY. On the architecture of the early city see A. Boethius and J. B. Ward-Perkins, *Etruscan and Roman Architecture* (1970). On the individual buildings see S. B. Platner and T. Ashby, *Topographical Dictionary of Ancient Rome* (1929) and the splendid complementary work, E. Nash, *Pictorial Dictionary of Ancient Rome*, 2 vols (1961). See also G. Lugli, *Roma antica, Il centro monumentale* (1946) and *Fontes ad Topographiam Veteris Urbis Romanae Pertinentes*, 8 vols (1953–). D. R. Dudley, *Urbs Roma* (1967) is a source book of selected translated texts. Also M. Grant, *The Roman Forum* (1970). F. Coarelli, 'Public Building at Rome from 201 to Sulla', *PBSR*, 1977, 1 ff.

18. FORUM BOARIUM TEMPLES. Hercules Victor: this round temple, near S. Maria in Cosmedin, was destroyed in 1475, when the cult image of gilded bronze was discovered. On the early temples of Fortuna and Mater Matuta see above, p. 000. Either one of the two later well-preserved temples, the pseudoperipteral Ionic, known as Fortuna Virilis, and the round temple known as Vesta or Mater Matuta, may have been dedicated to Portunus, the harbour god.

19. OTHER AVENTINE BUILDINGS. These included temples to Mercury (495; here was held an annual festival of merchants, *mercatores*); Jupiter Libertas (dedicated by Ti. Sempronius in 238; his son placed there a picture of his victory at Beneventum in 214); Flora (240); Consus (built in 272 by L. Papirius Cursor whose portrait, as a triumphator, adorned the walls); Venus Obsequens (295, built from fines imposed on women convicted of adultery). On the Basilica Aemilia see Boethius and Ward-Perkins, *Etr. Rom. Architecture*, 107, E. Nash, *Pict. Dict. Anc. Rem.*, ii, 238 ff.

20. THE PALATINE. Traces survive of the 'Servian' wall, or a contemporary but separate enceinte, in the north-west, and of a separate fort on the west and south sides (the so-called 'wall of Romulus'). Other shrines included a temple of Jupiter Victor (vowed at Sentinum in 295) and an altar erected to Aius Locutus by the Senate in 390 because the Romans had disregarded a warning voice concerning the Gauls. On the temple of Magna Mater see *Arch. Laziale*, i, 1978, 67 ff.

21. VESTA AND THE REGIA. The temple of Vesta contained no statue of the goddess; the foundations of the existing temple, one of the best-known monuments of the Forum, are Augustan. There are no traces of the Atrium Vestae before the second century BC. When the Regia was enlarged in the latter half of the third century it preserved the essential plan of its sixth-century predecessor: see F. E. Brown, *Les Origines de la Rép. Rom, Entretiens Hardt*, xiii (1966), 477 ff. (cf. p. 454 n. 14 above). The Via Sacra ran between the precincts of Vesta and the Regia.

22. THE ARX. Other monuments include: Temple of Concord (216); Columna Rostrata in honour of M. Aemilius Paullus, consul in 255, destroyed in 172. The temple of Veiovis stood between the two summits of the Capitoline. It was discovered in 1939; the existing remains belong to a restoration of 78 BC, but below the podium are traces of the first temple, vowed by L. Furius Purpureo in 194.

23. THE CAMPUS MARTIUS; FORUM HOLITORIUM. Circus Flaminius: recent excavation and new fragments of the Severan marble plan of Rome have shown that its precise site was slightly different from that usually accepted in the past (see Nash, *Pict. Dict. Anc. Rome*, i, 232, with bibliography). Other temples were: Hercules Custos (*c.* 221); Hercules Musarum (187; containing Fasti, and statues brought by Nobilior from Ambracia); Jupiter Stator (beneath S. Maria in Campitelli; built by Metellus *c.* 146). Shrine of Fons, built with booty from Corsica, 231. Four temples were found in 1926–9 in a precinct of Republican date in the Largo Argentina. Their identification is uncertain, but now that the site of the Circus Flaminius has been settled (the temples were 'in campo' not 'in circo') fresh attempts at identification have been made: see *Roma medio repubblicana* (Catalogue of the Mostra of the Capitol, 1973): temple A, late, Juno Curitis (?); B, end of second century, aedes Catuli (?); C, fourth century, Feronia; D, beginning of second century, Lares Permarini (?). For photographs see Nash, *Pict. Dict.*, i, 136 ff. Forum Holitorium: Janus, built by Duilius after Mylae; Spes (First Punic War); Juno (194). A temple of Pietas, vowed by Glabrio at Thermopylae (191)

contained a gilded statue of Glabrio, the first of its kind in Rome. On the Circus Flaminius see T. P. Wiseman, *PBSR*, 1974, 44 ff.

24. QUOTATIONS. See F. de Zulueta, *The Legacy of Rome* (1923), 175; 186.

25. ROMAN LAW. See H. F. Jolowicz, *Historical Introduction to the Study of Roman Law*, edn 3 (1972), to which I am particularly indebted here; W. Kunkel, *Introduction to Roman Legal and Constitutional History* (1966); B. Nicolas, *Introduction to Roman Law* (1962); J. Crook, *Roman Law and Life* (1967); F. Schulz, *Principles of Roman Law* (1936), *History of Roman Legal Science* (1946), *Classical Roman Law* (1951); A. Berger, *Encyclopedic Dictionary of Roman Law* (1951); A. Watson, *Roman Private Law around 200* BC. (1971), rather specialized, and *Rome of the XII Tables: persons and property* (1976).

CHAPTER XVII   LITERATURE AND ART

1. LATIN LANGUAGE AND LITERATURE. On the language see L. R. Palmer, *The Latin Language* (1954); A. Meillet, *Esquisse d'une histoire de la langue Latine*, edn 4 (1930). On literature: J. Wight Duff, *A Literary History of Rome from the Origins to Close of the Golden Age*, edn 3 (1953); T. Frank, *Life and Literature in the Roman Republic* (1930); H. J. Rose, *Handbook of Latin Literature*, edn 2 (1950); W. Beare, *The Roman Stage*, edn 2 (1955).

2. BALLAD POETRY. See A. Momigliano, *JRS*, 1957, 104 ff. (= *Secondo Contrib.*, 69 ff.).

3. SATURNIAN VERSE. The stock line comes from Naevius: '*Dabunt malum Metelli Naevio poetae*'. The question is still unsettled whether Saturnian verse is accentual, semi-quantitative, or quantitative. If accentual, based on the minstrel's beat, the accent probably falls on the first, not on the second syllable (dábunt, málum), so that we must reject the famous example: 'The queen was in her parlour, eating bread and honey'. The verse may then have been affected later by Greek quantitative scansion.

4. ACTORS. It is possible that this social stigma was a later phenomenon, and even then did not apply to all branches of acting alike. There was, however, little to stimulate the acting profession in Rome, so that later dramatists often acted in their own plays. By 200 BC only six days were set apart for dramatic performances. Drama had no religious associations in Rome as in Greece. Atellan farces may perhaps have derived from the Dorian farces of Magna Graecia.

5. LIVIUS ANDRONICUS. Horace (*Ep.*, ii, 1, 62) wrote: '*Ad nostrum tempus Livi scriptoris ab aevo*'. Cf. the lines of Porcius Licinus (second half of the second century BC): 'Poenico bello secundo Musa pinnato gradu/Intulit se bellicosam in Romuli gentem feram'.

6. NAEVIUS. The tradition about his imprisonment has been questioned (e.g. more recently again by H. B. Mattingly, *Historia*, 1960, 414 ff.), but wartime censorship may have muzzled free speech to an unparalleled extent. See T. Frank, *AJPhil.*, 1927, 105 ff. The charge would be made under the restriction

imposed by the Twelve Tables on offensive *carmina*. See A. Momigliano, *JRS*, 1942, 120 ff. *Contaminatio* may mean adapting borrowed scenes (so W. Beare) rather than interweaving two plots.

7. ENNIUS. See *Ennius* (*Entretiens Hardt*, xvii, 1971), especially ch. iv by E. Badian on the tradition about the poet's friends in Rome.

8. ROMAN ART. See R. B. Bandinelli, *Rome, the Centre of Power* (1971); J. M. C. Toynbee, *The Art of the Romans* (1956).

9. ETRUSCAN ART. For a critical assessment cf. S Casson, *CAH*, iv, 442. But see also D. Randall-MacIver, *The Etruscans* (1927); J. D. Beazley, *Etruscan Vase-Painting* (1947); P. J. Riis, *Etruscan Art* (1953) and other works cited above, p. 446 n. 30.

10. GEMS. A specimen was found in 1780 in the sarcophagus and on the skeleton hand of Scipio Barbatus, consul in 298.

11. PAINTINGS. The Esquiline painting (reproduced, e.g. in Bandinelli, op. cit., supra n. 8, p. 111 and *CAH*. Plates, iv, 82) shows in three superimposed bands scenes which include a surrender and another in which two generals (Roman and Italian?) are parleying. One is named Q. Fabius, perhaps Q. Fabius Rullianus, consul of 322 or his son. The painting is to be dated to the first half of the third century: *Roma Medio-Repubblicana* (1973), 200. Another early example is found on the fresco on the façade on the Tomb of the Scipios.

CHAPTER XVIII ROMAN RELIGION

1. ROMAN RELIGION. Four standard works are W. Warde Fowler, *The Religious Experience of the Roman People* (1911), to which this chapter owes much, and *The Roman Festivals* (1889); G. Wissowa, *Religion und Kultus der Römer* (1912); K. Latte, *Römische Religionsgeschichte* (1960). See also C. Bailey, *Phases in the Religion of Ancient Rome* (1932); F. Altheim, *History of Roman Religion* (1938), valuable for the Italian setting of Roman religion, but to be used with caution (so also should G. Radke, *Die Götter Altitaliens* (1965)); J. Bayet, *Histoire politique et psychologique de la religion romaine*, edn 2 (1969); H. J. Rose, *Primitive Culture in Italy (1926)*; G. De Sanctis, *SR*, IV, ii, 1, 121 ff. (1953); H. Wagenvoort, *Roman Dynamism* (1947). Two excellent introductory volumes are H. J. Rose, *Ancient Roman Religion* (1949) and R. M. Ogilvie, *The Romans and their Gods* (1969). For surveys of relatively recent work on Roman religion see A. K. Michels, *Cl. Weekly*, 1955, 25 ff.; H. J. Rose, *JRS*, 1960, 161 ff.; R. Schilling, *Aufstieg NRW* (1972), 1, i, 317 ff.

2. NUMEN. Quotation: Warde Fowler, *Religious Experience of the Roman People*, 8. For discussion of *numen* as equivalent of the idea expressed in the Pacific by *mana* see H. J. Rose, *Ancient Roman Religion* (1949), ch. i, and H. Wagenvoort, *Roman Dynamism* (1947), ch. 3. *Numen* is not identified with a deity until the Augustan age: F. Pfister, Pauly-Wissowa, *s.v.* and S. Weinstock, *JRS*, 1949, 167.

3. LARES.   Some scholars maintain that the Lares were the spirits of the dead and the Lar Familiaris the spirit of the family ancestor; if so, this would be evidence of worship of the dead and ancestor worship. But the dead in Roman practice were honoured at their graves, not in the house. Cf. C. Bailey, *Phases in the Religion of Ancient Rome* (1932), 103 ff. and H. J. Rose, *OCD*, edn 2, *s.v.*

4. DUMÉZIL.   For G. Dumézil's theory that Rome had three gods (Jupiter, Mars, Quirinus) corresponding with three social classes (priests, warriors and herdsman), see above, p. 451 n. 9.

5. THE IGUVINE TABLETS.   See J. W. Poultney, *The Bronze Tablets of Iguvium* (1959). These tablets, the records of a religious brotherhood, throw a wealth of light on early religious belief and practice. For a brief account of the survival of this ritual in the 'Elevation of the Ceri' at modern Gubbio (Iguvium) see R. S. Conway, *Ancient Italy and Modern Religion* (1932). On the survival of other ancient rites in modern Italy see T. Ashby, *Some Italian Scenes and Festivals* (1929).

6. DI INDIGETES.   The view of Wissowa that *di indigetes* meant the old indigenous gods and the *di novensides* the newcomers, has been challenged by F. Altheim (*Hist. Rom. Rel.*, 106 ff.), H. Wagevoort (*Roman Dynamism*, 83 ff.) and others, but little agreement has been reached about the meaning of these words.

7. THE BACCHANALIA.   Livy gives a lively, though highly-coloured, account of the scandal. The so-called *senatus consultum de Baccanalibus* contains the consuls' instructions to the allies: Riccobono, *Fontes*, 240 ff. Cf. M. Gelzer, *Hermes*, 1936 (= *Kleine Schriften,* iii (1964), 256 ff.); A. H. McDonald, *JRS,* 1944, 26 ff.; D. W. L. van Son, *Livius' Behandeling van de Bacchanalia* (1960); A. J. Toynbee, *Hannibal's Legacy,* ii, 387 ff.

8. ORPHISM AND PYTHAGOREANISM.   Cf. R. S. Conway, *Ancient Italy and Modern Religion* ch. ii, 'Orpheus in Italy'; in general, W. K. C. Guthrie, *Orpheus and Greek Religion,* edn 2 (1952). K. von Fritz, *Pythagorean Politics in Southern Italy* (1940).

10. THE SCIPIONIC CIRCLE AND STOICISM.   On the attitude of some members of the so-called 'scipionic circle' to the ancestral religion see E. Rawson, *JRS,* 1973, 161 ff. On Stoicism E. V. Arnold, *Roman Stoicism* (1900); F. H. Sandbach, *The Stoics* (1975).

CHAPTER XIX SOURCES AND AUTHORITIES

1. INSCRIPTIONS, LAWS.   Republican inscriptions are published in *Corpus Inscriptionum Latinarum*, vol. i, edn 2 (1893); A. Degrassi, *Inscriptiones Latinae Liberae Rei Publicae* 2 vols (1957–63); H. Dessau, *Inscriptiones Latinae Selectae* (1892–1916). The number of inscriptions of early Republican times is of course infinitesimal compared with those of the the the late Republic and Empire. Roman laws are published by S. Riccobono, *Fontes Iuris Romani Ante Iustiniani*, i, (1941).

2. FASTI AND CALENDARS. These, respectively, are published in *Inscriptiones Italiae*, XIII, i (1947) and ii (1963). On the *anneles* and their probable content see J. E. Crake, *Cl. Ph.*, 1940, 375 ff.; P. Fraccaro, *JRS*, 1957, 60 ff.; J. P. V. D. Balsdon, *Cl. Qu.*, 1953, 162. E. Rawson, however, has argued (*Cl. Qu.*, 1971, 158 ff.) that later writers did not in fact make much use of the Annales Maximi and that their annual publication did not continue after Mucius Scaevola (*usque ad P. Mucium*: Cicero *de Orat.*, ii, 12, 52).

3. THE GALLIC DESTRUCTION. See Livy, v, 49, 3; 50, 2; vi, l, 10. T. Frank (*Roman Buildings of the Republic* (1924), 53, 78, 33) believed in the survival of the Regia; this is denied by L. G. Roberts, *Mem. Amer. Acad. in Rome*, 1918, 55 ff. The matter is not discussed by F. E. Brown in his report on recent excavations in the Regia (*Entretiens Hardt*, xiii (1967), 47 ff.); he is concerned with the earliest phases and reports destruction by fire *c.* 500 BC or earlier. On traces of devastation by the Gallic raid in the city in general see E. Gjerstad, *Early Rome*, iii (1960), index *s.v.* Gallic invasion. If the Regia *was* sacked and all its records destroyed, then the early *annales* which circulated later must have derived from a priestly reconstruction of the lost earlier material. R. M. Ogilvie's examination of the early books of Livy, however, has led him to the belief (*Livy*, 6, n. 1) that 'a number of *tabulae*, although not a complete set, survived from the period 509–390 (especially 460–390) and contained much more variegated material than is usually assumed'. On the other hand, E. Rawson (*Cl. Qu.*, 1971, 158 ff.) thinks that in fact later writers did not make much use of the Annales Maximi.

4. THE ECLIPSE. Cicero (*de rep.*, i, 1, 25) says that the first observed (not merely computed) eclipse recorded in the Annales Maximi (and by Ennius) was 'about 350 years after Rome was founded'. If 350 may be interpreted as 354, the eclipse of 21 June 400 BC would be indicated. This would take the Tabulae back to *c.* 400, and Cicero seems to suggest that earlier eclipses mentioned in the Annales were based on backward calculations from 400 rather than recorded by contemporary evidence. But even if there was a continuous record only from 400, nevertheless some fifth-century material may have survived, as suggested by R. M. Ogilvie (see n. 3 above) who finds very early material e.g. in Livy on 463 and 431 BC.

K. J. Beloch (*Griechische Geschichte*, IV, ii, 267) would read CCCC (400) for the figure CCC which a scribe had entered into the defective text of Cicero, but this later date is rejected by J. E. Crake, *Cl. Ph.*, 1940, 379 ff. For Beloch on the Fasti Triumphales see *Röm. Gesch.*, 1 f.

5. THE HISTORIANS. The standard collections of the fragments of the lost historians are H. Peter, *Historicorum Romanorum Fragmenta*, edn 2 (1906–14) and F. Jacoby, *Die Fragmente der Griechischer Historiker* (vol. iiic (1958), 845–927 contains the fragments of the Greek historians who dealt with Rome and Italy). Beside the general histories of literature, see valuable surveys of recent work; on the Greek historians by G. T. Griffith and on the Roman historians by A. H. McDonald in *Fifty (and Ten) Years of Classical Scholarship*, edn 2 (1968). 182 ff., 465 ff., and also McDonald on Republican history, *JRS*, 1960, 135 ff.

Timaeus. See Jacoby, *FGrH*, n. 566. Also T. S. Brown, *Timaeus of Tauromenium* (1958) and A. Momigliano, *Terzo Contrib.*, 23 ff. (especially 44 ff. for Timaeus and Rome).

The Annalists. An important survey is provided by E. Badian in *Latin Historians* (ed. T. A. Dorey, 1966), ch. i. On the individual annalists see also articles by A. H. McDonald, *OCD*, edn 2. Cf. M. Gelzer, *Kleine Schriften*, iii (1964), 51 ff.

Fabius Pictor. See A. Momigliano, *Terzo Contributo* (1966), 55 ff. and D. Timpe, *Aufstieg NRW*, I, ii (1974), 928 ff. A Greek inscription from an ancient library in Tauromenium in Sicily has recently been found: see G. Manganaro, *Par. Pass.*, 1974, 389 ff., E. Badian, *Liverpool Classical Monthly*, i, 7, July 1976, 97 f. and Manganaro in A. Alföldi, *Römishche Frühgeschichte* (1976), 83 ff. The inscription summarizes Fabius' work: 'he investigated the arrival of Heracles in Italy and also (the return?) of Lanoios (his ally?) and Aeneas and (?Ascanias). Not(?) much later Romulus and Remus were born, and the foundation of Rome by Romulus, who (?first) ruled.' Thus it is clear that Fabius did not neglect the foundation stories and Rome's earliest period; he probably dealt briefly with the early Republic and then expanded as he reached the third century and his own times. For reference to Alföldi's ideas of Fabius' unreliability, see above, p. 472.

Cato. On his *Origines* see W. A. Schröder, *M. Porcius Cato. Das erste Buch des Origines* (1971); A. E. Astin, *Cato the Censor* (1978), ch. 10. See also G. Calboli, *Cato: Oratio pro Rhodiensibus* (Bologna, 1978).

Licinius Macer, Valerius Antias and Aelius Tubero. See Ogilvie, *Livy*, 7 ff.

Claudius Quadrigarius, See M. Zimmerer, *Der Annalist Q. Claudius Quadrigarius* (1937).

Livy. See especially P. G. Walsh, *Livy* (1961); *Livy*, ed. T. A. Dorey (1971; eight essays); Ogilvie, *Livy*; J. Briscoe, *Commentary on Livy, books xxxi–xxxiii* (1973).

Dio Cassius. See F. Millar, *Cassius Dio* (1964).

Polybius. See F. W. Walbank, *A Historical Commentary on Polybius*, i (1957), ii (1967), iii (1979); *Polybius* (Sather Classical Lectures, 1972) and *JRS*, 1962, 1 ff.; 1963, 1 ff. Cf also K. E. Petzold, *Studien zur Methode des Polybios* (1969); *Polybe, Entretiens Hardt*, vol. xx, 1973; D. Musti, 'Polybios negli studi dell'ultimo ventennio (1950–1970)', *Aufstieg NRW*, I, ii, (1974), 1114 ff.

Diodorus. The passages of Diodorus which refer to early Roman history are conveniently printed in A. B. Drachmann, *Diodors römische Annalen bis 302 a. Chr.* (1912). On Perl's *Kritische Untersuchungen zu Diodors Jahrzählung* (1957) see E. S. Staveley, *Cl. Rev.*, 1959, 158 ff.

Plutarch. See R. H. Barrow, *Plutarch and his Times* (1967), C. P. Jones, *Plutarch and Rome* (1971), D. A. Russell, *Plutarch* (1973).

6. CHRONOLOGY. See E. Bickerman, *Chronology of the Ancient World* (1968); A. E. Samuel, *Greek and Roman Chronology* (1972). On the date of the foundation of Rome see Walbank, *Polybius*, i, 665 ff. On the problems of the dislocation of the calendar in the third and second centuries see A. K.

Michels, *The Calendar of the Roman Republic* (1967); recent discussions include P. Marchetti, *Ant. Class.*, 1973, 473 ff.; P. S. Derow, *Phoenix*, 1973, 345 ff.; M.-T. Raepsaet-Charlier, *Historia*, 1974, 288 ff. Eclipse of 190: Livy, xxxvii, 4, 4; of 168: Livy, xliv, 37, 8 (cf. above, p. 514 n. 6); intercalation of 169: Livy, xliii, 11, 13. Acilius: Censorinus, *De die nat.*, xx, 6; Macrobius, *Sat.* 1, 13, 21.

ADDENDA

The following items appeared too recently to be noted in the appropriate places.

D. and F. R. RIDGWAY, *Italy before the Romans* (London, 1979), a valuable collection of papers by experts.

W. V. HARRIS, *War and Imperialism in Republican Rome 327–70 BC* (Oxford, 1979), argues for a much more aggressive Roman foreign policy than many recent writers.

H. HUMBERT, *Municipium et civitas sine suffragio: L'organisation de la conquête jusqu' à la guerre sociale* (Rome, 1978).

C. R. WHITTAKER, 'Carthaginian Imperialism in the fifth and fourth centuries', in *Imperialism in the Ancient World*, ed. P.D.A. Garnsey and C. D. Whittaker (Cambridge, 1978).

R. RILINGER, *Der Einfluss des Wahlleiters bei dem römischen Konsulwählen von 366 bis 50 v. Chr.* (Munich, 1976). Cf. J. Carter, *JRS*, 1979, 184 ff.

W. DAHLHEIM, *Gewalt und Herrschaft: Das provinziale Herrschafts-system der römischen Republik* (Berlin, 1977). Cf. J. Richardson, *JRS*, 1979, 156 ff.

J. M. FRAYN, *Subsistence Farming in Roman Italy* (London, 1979).

J. POUCET, 'Le Latium protohistorique et archeologique', *L' Ant. Class.*, 1978, 566 ff., a general survey of recent work

M. PALLOTTINO, 'Lo sviluppo socio-istituzionale di Roma arcaica', *Studi Romani*, 1979, 1 ff. This records, *inter alia*, the discovery of a fourth Etruscan inscription in Rome. It is inscribed on a small ivory lion, comes from S. Omobono, and is to be dated *c.* 580–60 BC. It runs *araz silqetenas spurianas*. Thus two names follow the praenomen *araz*, but Spurianas could be a patronymic or a second name.

F. CASTAGNOLI, *Archeologica Laziale*, 1 (1978), 13f., writes about the statues of Minerva, etc., from Lavinium (see above, p. 40).

P. S. DEROW, 'Polybius, Rome and the East', *JRS*, 1979, 1 ff.: Polybius' view was that from *c.* 200 BC Rome sought universal obedience to her wishes and skilfully masked offensive designs as defensive wars.

INDEX